ENCYCLOPEDIA OF FRAUD

JOSEPH T. WELLS, CFE, CPA

ISBN 978-1-889277-37-0

Association of Certified Fraud Examiners
The Gregor Building
716 West Avenue
Austin, Texas 78701 USA
(800) 245-3321
(512) 478-9000
www.ACFE.com

Printed in the United States of America

To Patty and Dianne with love

Preface

In the world of fraud, some things remain the same. Regardless of whether the crime involves a computer or a cash register tape, all frauds have the same basic elements: a material false statement made intentionally for the purpose of deceiving, which is relied upon by a victim to his detriment.

Although the elements of these offenses are similar, the methods used to commit fraud come in an astonishing variety. Over the decades, it has become my life's work to understand the myriad of ways fraud occurs. This search has been a humbling task.

The *Encyclopedia of Fraud* continues the search for answers, but it is not a definitive work. Terminology regarding fraud changes constantly, so this book will be updated on a regular and continuous basis. It is written primarily for practitioners and academics, but others with an interest in fraud may find the material instructional as well.

As any author will tell you, writing is a tremendous learning experience. That has been my prime motivator for this book and for the nine others that preceded it.

You will find the *Encyclopedia of Fraud* is organized as a reference work. The book contains entries about dozens of different fraud schemes organized by both topic and the type of scheme. I have also included biographical entries about notable fraudsters and fraud cases. The appendix includes an extensive list of Internet resources to assist fraud examiners and academics on where and how to find information about fraud prevention and detection.

Writing the *Encyclopedia of Fraud* has involved the efforts of many. I would like to thank Brett-Holloway Reeves for his assistance in researching much of the material in the book and the following employees of the Association of Certified Fraud Examiners for their editorial and production assistance: John D. Gill, J.D., CFE; DeAnn Holzman; Tony Rolston; Andi McNeal, CFE, CPA; Juliana Morehead, J.D., CFE; Suzanne Mahadeo; Cynthia Gomez; and Kassi Underwood.

Finally, I would like to thank the thousands of certified fraud examiners I have met over the years who have contributed to my own education in innumerable ways. Education is the cornerstone of fraud prevention; the more we know the less likely we are to become victims.

Joseph T. Wells, CFE, CPA
Austin, Texas
March 2007

LIST OF ENTRIES

ADELPHIA

A year after the public learned of the $600 million scandal by Enron, one of the country's leaders in cable television media was about to make Enron's financial misrepresentations look like penny change. In March 2002, Adelphia Communications, the cable television conglomerate, admitted to approving $2.3 billion dollars in loans to the Rigas family, the financial backbone of the company. This self-dealing triggered government investigation, which uncovered the misappropriation and theft of tens of billions of dollars.

In addition to the $2.3 billion family loans, the Department of Justice claimed that the defendants: 1) misrepresented the company's financial status as well as the number of its subscribers; 2) caused losses to investors of more than $60 billion; 3) used $252 million to cover family investments; and 4) used fraudulent documents to obtain $420 million in Adelphia stock.

SEC Charges

In July 2002, the SEC filed suit against Adelphia charging the company via its founder, John Rigas, his three sons (Timothy, Michael, and James), and two senior executives, James Brown and Michael Mulcahey, with various counts of fraud, including:

- The fraudulent concealment of billions of dollars in liabilities from its consolidated financial statements by hiding them on the books of off-balance sheet affiliates;
- The falsification of operations statistics and inflated earnings to meet Wall Street expectations; and
- The concealment of self-dealing by the Rigas Family.

In November 2002, in exchange for his testimony against the Rigas men, James Brown was released from prosecution by consenting to an entry of a permanent injunction against him for federal securities law violations. Additionally, Brown has been permanently barred from becoming an officer or director of a public corporation.

Criminal Charges

John Rigas, one of the founders of Adelphia Communications Corporation, was forced to resign from his position as CEO in May 2002 after being indicted for bank, wire, and securities fraud. His sons, Timothy J. Rigas and Michael J. Rigas, as well as his son-in-law, Peter Venetis, and Michael Mulcahey were also charged with participation in these crimes. The executives were accused of looting the corporation by concealing $2.3 billion in liabilities from corporate investors and of using corporation funds as their personal funds. In July of 2004, John Rigas and his son Timothy, a former director of Adelphia and CFO, CAO and treasurer, were convicted of 15 counts of fraud. The jury acquitted Michael Rigas, a former director of the firm, who plead guilty to doctoring financial records in exchange for not being retried on the counts of fraud the jury could not decide on. John Rigas was sentenced to 15 years in prison, while his son Timothy received a 20-year jail sentence. Adelphia Corporation was forced to file for bankruptcy after it had acknowledged that the three Rigases had taken $3.1 billion in loans that were not recorded on the books.

In October 2005 John and Timothy Rigas were charged with income tax evasion that occurred between 1998 and 2005 and was worth an alleged $300 million in taxes that were willfully unreported income in their tax returns.

Acquisition of Adelphia

In April of 2005, Time Warner Inc. and Comcast Corporation announced that they reached agreements to acquire all the assets of Adelphia Communications Corporation for a total of $12.7 billion in cash and 16% of the common stock of Time Warner's cable subsidiary, Time Warner Cable Inc.

Sources:
"Adelphia Execs Arrested for Fraud." *BBC News*, July 24, 2002. news.bbc.co.uk.

"Adelphia Founder, Son Found Guilty." *CBSNews.com*, July 8, 2004. www.cbsnews.com.

"Adelphia Reports Net Loss of Nearly $63M." *Forbes.com*, September 27, 2004. forbes.com.

"Starting Out: For and About Fraud-Fighting Students & New Grads." *Fraud Magazine*, November/December 2006. www.fraud-magazine.com.

"John Rigas Guilty of Conspiracy." *CNNmoney*, July 8, 2004. money.cnn.com.

"Securities and Exchange Commission v. Adelphia Communications Corporation, John J. Rigas, Timothy J. Rigas, Michael J. Rigas, James P. Rigas, James R. Brown, and Michael C. Mulcahey, 02 Civ. 5776 (S.D.N.Y.) (KMW)." U.S. Securities and Exchange Commission, November 14, 2002. sec.gov/litigation/litreleases/lr17837.htm.

"SEC Charges Adelphia and Rigas Family With Massive Financial Fraud." U.S. Securities and Exchange Commission, July 24, 2002. www.sec.gov/news/press/2002-110.htm.

"Time Warner Cable and ComCast to Acquire Assets of Adelphia Communications" Time Warner Cable, April 21, 2005. www.timewarnercable.com/InvestorRelations/PressReleases/TWCPressReleaseDetail.ashx?PRID=492&MarketID=0

Related Entries:

FINANCIAL STATEMENT FRAUD
SECURITIES FRAUD

ANTAR, EDDIE

Eddie Antar came from a family of Syrian Jewish descent that specialized in small retail operations, such as discount stores and gift stores. Antar dropped out of high school to sell TVs and radios in New York's Port Authority during the 1960's. With backing from his father, Sam Antar, Eddie opened his first electronics store in Brooklyn, near the area where all of his family lived.

In 1970 he opened Crazy Eddie's Ultra Linear Sound Corporation. Eventually forty-two Crazy Eddie stores were opened in the New York and Philadelphia area. In 1984 the company went public, opening at $6 a share; in a year the stock had split and was selling at over $21 per share.

Family quarrels caused Antar to resign as company president and CEO in December 1986. The stock price plunged and allowed Viktor Palmieri and Company—a financial firm that specialized in taking over ailing companies, either breaking them up or selling them after a turnaround—to take over Crazy Eddie's. Palmieri auditors discovered that $65 million worth of inventory did not exist. Though Crazy Eddie's had reported a pretax profit of $20.6 million dollars in 1987, in fact the chain had sustained a substantial loss. Palmieri's operatives tried to save the company by divesting itself of 17 of its stores and focusing operations around the remaining 26 stronger stores. However, by June 7, 1989 suppliers of Crazy Eddie's were calling for the store to liquidate itself in order to pay approximately $860,000 in past due debt. In October of that year, the company liquidated its remaining assets to satisfy creditors.

An investigation revealed that the Antar family had been committing fraud since the company began. During the 1970's, family members skimmed receipts to avoid taxes. The bulk of this money was secreted to accounts in Israel, Panama, Switzerland, and elsewhere. While preparing to take the company public in the early 1980's, Eddie Antar had his cousin, Sam E. Antar—who held a CPA license—begin to modify the skimming so that the family took less each year. The strategy made the company books clean by the time public auditors came in, and gave the appearance that Crazy Eddie's was experiencing extraordinary growth.

For two years after the SEC began its investigation in 1987, Sam E. Antar stonewalled authorities along with the rest of the family. But in 1989, abandoned by Eddie, Sam E. became a witness for the prosecution. He revealed that the company's phenomenal status had largely been reached by a series of fraudulent acts. Without the fraud, most analysts would have judged the company average.

As chief financial officer, Sam E. performed whatever fraud was necessary to meet the demands of his boss and childhood hero, Eddie. He testified that the company had:

- Listed smuggled money from foreign banks as sales;
- Made false entries to Accounts Payable;
- Overstated inventory by breaking into and altering auditors' records;
- Taken credit for merchandise as "returned," while also counting the merchandise as inventory;
- Moved inventory from one store to another to boost inventory counts;
- Arranged for vendors to ship merchandise and defer the billing, and claimed discounts and advertising credits with the manufacturers of the merchandise; and
- Sold large lots of merchandise wholesale, then counted the money as retail receipts to boost sales.

Eddie Antar was charged for filing fraudulent financial statements, and for violating insider-trading laws by selling more than $60 million of his private stock while the company's financial condition was deteriorating. Antar skipped his arraignment on February 10, 1990, so a warrant was issued for his arrest. Shortly thereafter he surrendered to authorities but was freed on his own recognizance and subsequently fled the country.

Antar was arrested two years later in Israel, where he had been living under an assumed name and was doing business around the world under various names. In the United States he was convicted on 17 charges, and forced to sign over $52 million. He was sentenced to 12 years in prison, and ordered to repay a total of $121 million to stockholders. Total losses caused by Antar's crimes were estimated at $145.9 million.

However, a Federal Court of Appeals, because of apparently biased statements made by Judge Nicolas Politan during the trial and sentencing, overturned the case. Politan told Antar at sentencing, "It has been my aim from day one to recover this money ..." Antar agreed to plead guilty and received a 7-year prison sentence, followed by 2 years' probation, and a $250,000 fine. Civil actions against Antar exceeded $1 billion. Eddie's brother Mitchell also pled guilty to aiding the fraud as a buyer for the company, and was sentenced to a 20- month prison sentence and forfeited $1.7 million in assets.

Into 2000, the SEC prosecution team (led by Ric Simpson) and the class action filers (led by Howard Sirota) continued to pursue Antar assets. Simpson won a civil judgment against Eddie's father, Sam Antar, for $80 million, representing the amount of stock sold by Sam and his grandchildren, plus interest.

Source:
Wells, J., CFE, CPA. "The Antar Complex: Eddie Antar." *Fraudulent Financial Transactions*, and *Frankensteins of Fraud.* Association of Certified Fraud Examiners, 2000.

Related Entries:

FINANCIAL STATEMENT FRAUD

ANTITRUST

Antitrust refers to acts committed by businesses and their employees that restrain trade or confer an unfair market advantage. The term covers any act that prevents fair and free market competition, including price-fixing, monopolies, and illegal cartels. Annual losses to businesses from antitrust violations are estimated to exceed $250 billion. According to an article by John Berry and Mark Green in *The Nation*, price fixing "inflates prices by some 25% or more above the non-collusive or competitive level."

Common violations of antitrust laws and free-market regulations include:

- Discussing with competitors any matter directly related to competition—for example, sales price, marketing strategies, market shares and sales policies.
- Making overt or implied agreements with a competitor to fix prices, allocate market share, or perform other acts that restrain competition.
- Arbitrarily refusing to conduct business with companies or individuals because they are competitors in other business ventures.
- Requiring a company or individual to purchase goods or services in exchange for purchasing that entity's goods or services.
- Requiring customers to purchase goods or services they do not want in exchange for acquiring goods or services that they do want.
- Engaging in industrial espionage or commercial bribery.
- Making false representations to customers about the quality, features and availability of company products and services.

Illegal Cartels in Various Industries

Illegal cartels have raised prices for gasoline, vitamins, soft drinks, art objects, automobile supplies, carbon fibers, chlorine, compact discs, drugs, food preservatives, frozen foods, graphite electrodes, metal building insulation and installation, newsprint, real estate foreclosure auctions, lysine, scrap metal, tobacco, citric acid, marine transportation and construction, thermal fax paper, yeast, and dynamite.

In a price-fixing case involving vitamins, industry giants F. Hoffmann-La Roche, BASF A.G. and others secretly set prices and production levels, victimizing corporate clients such as General Mills, Kellogg, Coca-Cola, Tyson Foods, and Procter & Gamble. Prosecutors showed that more than $5 billion in commerce was affected. The case was concluded with fines over $1 billion, the highest in history.

Medical and legal associations have been charged with rigging markets and restraining competition. Fee schedules set the minimum price a member of the association charges for any particular service, making it impossible for the client to obtain the service cheaper. The American Medical Association was reprimanded for attempting to limit the number of students accepted to medical school because the aim was to keep the demand for medical services greater than the supply of physicians. The legal profession's ban on advertising was overturned in 1977, when a judge ruled that the prohibition was designed to prevent open competition for clients.

Albert Foer of the American Antitrust Institute charged that the dramatic rise in corporate mergers (up 550% from 1992 to 2000) resulted in airlines monopolizing hub terminals, international cartels setting exorbitant prices, bid rigging, monopolies controlling the global flow of information, and food retailing industries that are unduly concentrated. In a survey by the Ralph Nader organization, Essential Information, 58% of the presidents of the 1,000 largest U.S. corporations said antitrust conspiracies were "a way of life."

Principles of Antitrust Law

In a statement before Congress in 1999, Deputy Assistant Attorney General John Nannes explained, "Antitrust laws prohibit the acquisition of stock or assets if 'the effect of such acquisition may be substantially to lessen competition, or to tend to create a monopoly.'" This enables anticompetitive mergers to be arrested in their incipiency to forestall harm that would otherwise ensue but be difficult to undo after the parties have consummated a merger. Thus, merger enforcement standards are forward-looking and, while the U.S. Department of Justice Antitrust Division often considers historic performance in an industry, the primary focus is to determine the likely competitive effects of a proposed merger in the future.

The DOJ's Antitrust Division shares merger enforcement responsibility with the Federal Trade Commission (FTC), with the exception of certain industries in which the FTC's jurisdiction is limited by statute. The agencies jointly have developed Horizontal Merger Guidelines that describe the inquiry they will follow in analyzing mergers: The unifying theme of the Guidelines is that mergers should not be permitted to create or enhance market power or to facilitate its exercise. Under the Guidelines, market power to a seller is "the ability to profitably maintain prices above competitive levels for a significant period of time."(Merger Guidelines § 0.1.)

The Antitrust Division is likely to challenge a transaction that results in a substantial increase in an already highly concentrated market.

The Supreme Court defines monopoly power as "the power to control prices or exclude competition." More precisely, a firm is a monopolist if it can profitably raise prices substantially above the competitive level. Where evidence indicates that a firm has in fact profitably done so, the existence of monopoly power is clear. Because such direct proof is only rarely available, courts more typically examine market structure in search of circumstantial evidence of monopoly power. Monopoly power may be inferred from a firm's possession of a dominant share of a relevant market that is protected by entry barriers. "Entry barriers" are factors that prevent new rivals from timely responding to an increase in price above the competitive level.

Antitrust Enforcement History

Antitrust issues first surfaced in American life in the 19th century, as men like Jay Gould dominated the railroad business, Carnegie ruled steel, and the Rockefellers built Standard Oil into the industry standard no one could beat. "Trustbusters" like Theodore Roosevelt succeeded in breaking up the largest trusts between 1890 and 1920.

The Sherman Antitrust Act, sponsored by Senator John Sherman of Ohio and passed into federal law in 1890, was not widely used until 1907, when federal charges were first brought against Standard Oil. President Theodore Roosevelt's administration made the first aggressive use of the act in combating major monopolies, and it was under President William Howard Taft that the law was used against Standard Oil and the American Tobacco Company. The Sherman Act proved one of the strongest pieces of regulatory legislation produced by the American Congress.

The Sherman Antitrust Act was rarely used as a weapon against price-fixing before 1938, when Thurman Arnold, one of the great antitrust prosecutors, joined the Justice Department. Over the next five years, 220 of the 330 cases he brought under Section 1 of the Sherman Act included criminal charges.

Antitrust issues in the financial industry were addressed by The Banking Act of 1933, also known as the Glass-Steagall Act. Banks were prohibited from accepting customer deposits and underwriting corporate securities simultaneously. Each bank was given a year to decide whether to become a commercial bank, which could accept customer deposits in checking and savings accounts; or an investment bank, which could engage in the riskier business of corporate underwriting, involving the purchase of new securities from the corporate issuers and their resale to the public. Commercial banks could receive no more than 10% of their income from the securities markets, prompting most to abandon business securities underwriting altogether.

Glass-Steagall was most directly aimed at J. P. Morgan & Company, which wielded immense power by dominating both commercial and investment banking. Morgan became a symbol for the abuses of power that many thought caused the Great Crash. Thus, Congress showed its reform spirit by forcing Morgan to shed one of its two great sources of wealth. Theoretically, if the underwriting market suffered a crisis, the separation would protect commercial banking from the same fate. The legislation was supplemented two decades later by the Bank Holding Company Act of 1956, which restricted banks' involvement in the insurance business.

Antitrust enforcement subsided during the years following World War II, despite a wave of mergers. Samuel Richardson Reid reported that between 1947 and 1968, the 200 largest American corporations increased their share of all manufacturing assets from 42.3% to 60.9%. More than 99% of that increase came from acquiring smaller companies. Setting aside growth from mergers, the corporations only increased their share of manufacturing assets by 0.9%.

In the 1970's and 1980's, Congress increased the potential penalties for executives convicted of antitrust violations. In 1974, violations once considered misdemeanors became felonies, and maximum prison terms rose to three years from one. Maximum fines grew from $50,000 in 1955 to a nearly unlimited amount by 1991. Corporate sentencing guidelines gave the Justice Department the authority to seek financial penalties as high as twice the gain from the crime or twice the amount of the victims' losses. For individual defendants, violations of the Sherman Act carry a potential prison sentence of three years for every count, in addition to nearly limitless fines.

A new corporate leniency program, granting significant incentives for early cooperation, was adopted in August 1993. Under an older policy formulated in 1978, leniency was discretionary and not available after an investigation opened.

The antitrust division of the Justice Department increased its efforts during the 1990's and won a number of high-profile cases. The division won fines from corporations and individuals exceeding $1.7 billion from 1996 to 2000. Of the antitrust indictments filed from 1992 to 1997 that went to trial, there were four convictions and 15 acquittals. When pre-trial settlements are figured in, the division's record is comparable to the Justice Department's 60% victory rate for white-collar defendants.

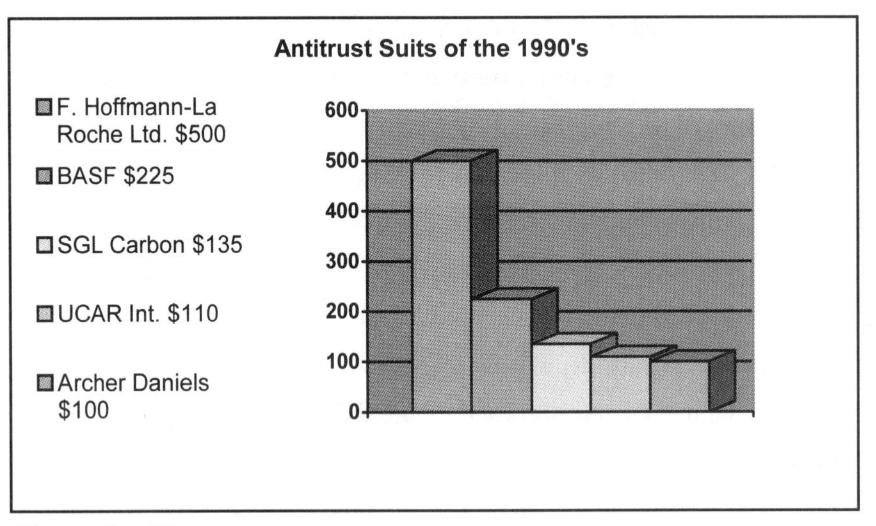

Fines are in millions.

Revisions in 1999 to the Glass-Steagall Act and the Bank Holding Company Act lifted the restrictions on banking and insurance companies commingling assets and operations. For several decades, critics had attempted to change the law, and banking regulators at the Federal Reserve and the Treasury Department's Comptroller of the Currency had interpreted the law in ways that allowed banks to sell insurance through subsidiaries and to trade and underwrite securities, while maintaining their status as commercial banks. Bank holding companies, such as Citicorp, would own securities affiliates as long as they produced no more than 25% of total revenue. The 1999 legislation removed the remaining restrictions and allowed brokerage firms, insurers, and banks all to conduct the full range of financial businesses.

Case Study—Microsoft

The most prominent antitrust case since the original prosecutions under the Sherman Act charged that the Microsoft Corporation used its status as the leader in computer operating systems to cripple its rivals. Specifically, federal prosecutors charged that:

- Microsoft pressured Netscape into dividing up the market for Internet browsers and plotted to drive Netscape out when the company refused to cooperate.
- Microsoft pressured Apple to jettison QuickTime, a piece of software that enables multimedia features, for Windows.
- Microsoft threatened to withhold a license for Windows if IBM heavily promoted its competing office productivity suite.
- Unlike Apple, Sun, IBM and other companies that made operating systems, Microsoft did not offer a browser-less version of Windows and would not let people remove the browser from Windows.

In June 2001, the Washington D.C. appeals court ruled for Microsoft on the claim that it attempted to monopolize the browser market, declaring that it did so on what amounted to a technicality. The court would not say Microsoft's conduct was legal, but that the government failed to introduce sufficient proof to define the browser market.

On the claim that Microsoft illegally tied its browser to its operating system, the court ruled that prosecutors must show that the browser market suffered an anticompetitive effect from Microsoft's actions. Of Microsoft, the court demanded that the company show a pro-competitive justification for commingling its browser and operating system.

The court said the most serious act committed by Microsoft was not to the browser market, but in preventing Netscape and Sun Microsystems's Java from becoming alternative applications platforms widespread enough to challenge Microsoft's monopoly. The court ruled that Microsoft had violated Section 2 of the Sherman Antitrust Act by illegally using its monopoly position in operating systems to force computer makers, software vendors and Internet service providers to agree to a series of anticompetitive license restrictions.

The court threw out a lower court's ruling that Microsoft had attempted to monopolize the market for Internet browser software. Concerning whether the company had tied its Explorer browser to its operating system as a means of squashing competition, the court ruled that Judge Jackson had used the wrong legal standard, directing the case to be reconsidered by a different district court. The appeals court also ruled that Microsoft proffered no justification for integrating Internet Explorer into Windows, excluding the browser from the Add/Remove Programs utility, and for commingling browser and operating system code.

The appeals court suggested that a breakup of Microsoft would be inappropriate; noting that this action was normally reserved for businesses, unlike Microsoft, which has grown through mergers and acquisitions. The court said, "Divestiture is a remedy that is imposed only with great caution, in part because its long-term efficacy is rarely certain. If the court on remand is unconvinced of the causal connection between Microsoft's exclusionary conduct and the company's position in the operating systems market, it may well conclude that divestiture is not an appropriate remedy."

Microsoft's four-year battle with the Federal government came to an end on November 2002 agreeing to an independent panel to monitor the company's practices. The settlement required few changes to its business model.

The agreed upon settlement does not prevent Microsoft from tying software like its Web browser, e-mail client and media player with its operating system — initially an issue that was a cornerstone of the government's case against Microsoft.

It does require the company to provide software developers with the APIs used by Microsoft's middleware to interoperate with its operating systems, allowing developers to create competing products that can utilize the integrated functions Microsoft includes in its own middleware. It also gives computer manufacturers and consumers the freedom to substitute competing middleware software on Microsoft's operating systems.

Case Study — Sotheby's and Christie's

A price-fixing scandal, exposed in 2000, besmirched the reputations of two of the world's oldest and most prestigious auction houses—Sotheby's, founded in 1744, and Christie's, founded in 1766. The collusion between the two auction giants cost clients $100 million and illuminated the shady underside of the $4 billion-a-year auction business.

A. Alfred Taubman, CEO of Sotheby's was convicted of conspiring with his Christie's counterpart, Sir Anthony Tennant, at twelve secret meetings in the mid-1990's to fix the commissions and fees each house would charge. Taubman directed another Sotheby's employee, Diana D. Brooks, to carry out his orders.

Among the government witnesses was the former chief executive of Christie's, Christopher M. Davidge, who exposed the conspiracy in 1999 when he surrendered hundreds of pages of internal records showing how the two businesses agreed to eliminate incentives to clients and raise sellers' rates. Davidge and Christie's obtained amnesty from prosecution.

Diana Brooks pleaded guilty in 2000 and testified against her former boss. Sir Anthony Tennant refused to leave his home in England and stand trial. Christie's obtained immunity to criminal charges, but Sotheby's pleaded guilty to antitrust violations and paid a $45 million criminal fine. Both auction houses together paid 100,000 customers a civil settlement of more than $512 million. Mr. Taubman, to avoid further liability, agreed to foot $156 million of Sotheby's share of $256 million plus another $30 million to settle a stockholder's suit.

On April 22, 2002, A. Alfred Taubman was sentenced to a year and a day in prison and fined $7.5 million. Under a little-used legal provision, he was also ordered to pay for his incarceration, a cost a federal Bureau of Prisons spokesman said was at least $21,601 a year.

On April 29, 2002, Diana D. Brooks, former chief executive of Sotheby's was sentenced to three years probation, including six months of house arrest. Judge George B. Daniels also fined her $350,000 and ordered her to perform 1,000 hours of community service.

Sources:
Berry, J. and Green, M. "White-Collar Crime Is Big Business." *The Nation,* June 8, 1985.

Blumenthal, R., and Vogel, C. "Ex-Chairman of Sotheby's Gets Jail Time." *The New York Times,* April 23, 2002.

Blumenthal, R., and Vogel, C. "Ex-Chief of Sotheby's Gets 3-Year Probation and Fine." *The New York Times,* April 30, 2002.

Coleman, J. "Proposed Microsoft Antitrust Settlement," *Facts on File,* November 2, 2001.

Elhauge, E. "Competition Wins in Court," *The New York Times,* June 30, 2001.

Evans, D. "The Economics of the Microsoft Antitrust Case: A Post-Trial Primer By (National Economic Research Associates) and Richard Schmalensee (MIT Sloan School of Management)." *Based on a presentation to the AEI-Brookings Joint Center on Regulatory Policy,* Washington DC, February 11, 2000.

Geis, G. "The Heavy Electrical Equipment Antitrust Cases." *Corporate and Governmental Deviance.* September 2001.

Geis, G. "White-Collar Crime Is Big Business," *The Nation,* June 8, 1985 Vol. 240.

Labaton, S. "The World Gets Tough on Fixing Prices, " *The New York Times,* June 3, 2001.

Labaton, S. "Appeals Court Voids Order for Breaking Up Microsoft," *The New York Times,* June 29, 2001.

Nannes, J., Deputy Assistant Attorney General. "Antitrust Division Before Subcommittee on Antitrust, Business Rights, and Competition Committee of the Judiciary United States Senate Concerning Agriculture Concentration," Presented on September 28, 2000.

Weissman R. and Mokhiber R. "The Hot 100. Ranking the Worst Corporate Criminals of the 1990's," September 8, 1999.

ASSET MISAPPROPRIATION

Asset misappropriations—using company property or cash without authorization, or stealing cash and property—are the most common occupational frauds. An ACFE survey in 2006 found that nearly 91% of the cases handled by CFEs involved asset misappropriation. There are three major categories of asset misappropriation: cash theft schemes, fraudulent disbursements of cash, and the abuse or theft of inventory and other noncash assets.

Related Entries:

CASH THEFT SCHEMES
CORPORATE CRIME
FRAUDULENT DISBURSEMENTS
INVENTORY FRAUD

ASSET VALUATION, IMPROPER

Improper asset valuation is a form of financial statement fraud that involves either overvaluing or undervaluing assets, depending on the perpetrator's aim. Overstatement boosts net worth, may be used to fraudulently obtain financing, and boosts stock prices. Understating assets may be used for tax evasion or bankruptcy fraud. Asset values are also manipulated in depreciation schedules.

The value of assets is determined by the original cost. Some assets are reported at the lower of cost or market value, but asset values are not increased to reflect current market value. Even so, it is sometimes necessary to use estimates in accounting with the hope that it is near the true value. For example, estimates are used in determining warranty costs, salvage value, and the useful life of a depreciated asset.

Sometimes long-term assets are listed as current assets to satisfy lending institutions, which often require certain ratios between assets and liabilities. The misclassification is of particular consequence when the loan monies come from unsecured or under-secured lines of credit and other short-term borrowings. Sometimes these misclassifications are referred to as "window dressing."

Most improper asset valuations involve the fraudulent overstatement of inventory or receivables. Other improper asset valuations are purchase-versus-pooling accounting methods, misclassification of fixed and other assets, or improper capitalization of inventory or start-up costs. Improper asset valuations usually take the form of one of the following classifications:

- Inventory Valuation
- Accounts Receivable
- Business Combinations
- Fixed Assets

Inventory Valuation

Since inventory must be valued at the acquisition cost (except when the value is determined to be below current market value), obsolete inventory should be written down at its current value, or written off altogether if it has no value. Failing to write down inventory causes assets to be overstated and falsifies the cost of goods sold vis-à-vis revenues. Inventory can also be improperly stated through the manipulation of inventory count, failure to relieve inventory for costs of goods sold and by other methods.

One of the most popular methods of overstating inventory is through fictitious (phantom) inventory. Fictitious inventory schemes usually involve the creation of fake documents such as inventory count sheets, receiving reports and similar items. In some instances, a friendly co-conspirator claims to be holding inventory for the company in question. Finally, it is also common to insert phony count sheets during the inventory observation or change the quantities on the count sheets.

Accounts Receivable

Accounts receivable are subject to manipulation in the same manner as sales and inventory and, in many cases, the schemes are conducted together. The two most common schemes involving accounts receivable are fictitious receivables and failure to write down accounts receivable as bad debts (or failure to establish adequate reserves for the future collectibility problems). Accounts receivable should be held at net realizable value. That is, the amount of the receivable less amounts expected not to be collected.

Fictitious accounts receivable are common among companies with financial problems, as well as with managers who receive a commission based on sales. The typical entry under fictitious accounts receivable is to debit (increase) accounts receivable and credit (increase) sales. These schemes are commonly used at the end of the accounting period to help management meet its earnings estimates.

Business Combinations

Business combinations occur when two or more business entities combine operations. There are two methods for accounting for business combinations: the purchase method and the pooling method.

In general, the purchase method is used when cash or other assets are redistributed as a result of the combination or if liabilities are incurred as a means of financing the purchase. On the other hand, if only voting common stock is issued to effect the business combination, the pooling-of-interest method is generally favored. The use of both methods in the same transaction is usually prohibited. The examiner should consider the nature of the transaction to see if the primary purpose is to overstate assets or income.

Fixed Assets

Bogus fixed assets can be created by a variety of methods and are subject to manipulation through several different schemes. Some of the more common ones are booking fictitious assets, misrepresenting asset valuation, and improperly capitalizing inventory and start-up costs.

Booking Fictitious Assets

Fictitious assets boost the value of the owners' equity account. Because company assets are often physically found in many different locations, this fraud can sometimes be easily overlooked. One of the most common fictitious asset schemes is to simply create fictitious documents. In other instances, the equipment is leased, but recorded as if owned.

Misrepresenting Asset Valuation

Although assets may appreciate in value, this increase in value should not be recognized on company financial statements. Misrepresentation of asset values frequently goes hand in hand with other schemes.

UNDERSTANDING ASSETS

In rare cases (e.g., in companies with government contracts or regulated companies) it is advantageous to understate assets. Additional funding is often based on the need for greater assets, so the understatement simulates that need. Asset understatement can be done directly (overestimating the value) or through accelerated depreciation (reducing the value of an asset too soon).

Assets may also be understated when management is preparing to buy a company from its shareholders—depressing the assets lowers the company's overall value, and thus the purchase price.

Capitalizing Nonasset Cost

The purchase price of an asset may be capitalized over time, provided the asset provides a future and ongoing benefit. However, any interest payments and finance charges incurred in the purchase must be recognized as they are paid. Management commits fraud by improperly capitalizing interest payment and finance charges.

MISCLASSIFYING ASSETS

In order to meet budget requirements, assets are sometimes misclassified into general ledger accounts. The manipulation of entries to accounts in which assets are falsely and incorrectly coded can be beneficial by skewing financial ratios and helping meet borrowing requirements.

Source:
Wells, J., CFE, CPA. *Corporate Fraud Handbook.* Hoboken, NJ: John Wiley & Sons , 2004.

Related Entries:

FINANCIAL STATEMENT FRAUD
OCCUPATIONAL FRAUD AND ABUSE

ATKINS, CHARLES AND WILLIAM HACK

Atkins made a reputation among the rich and famous in the early to mid-1980's for his ingenious manipulations of tax laws to provide so-called "tax straddles." He used a portion of the federal code that allowed for accelerating the amount of credit available for companies that lost money in certain financial transactions. Basically, Atkins continually deferred the tax bill his clients owed. Each year Atkins fabricated new losses that greatly reduced or eliminated the annual amount due. All told, Atkins claimed approximately $1.1 billion in phony losses, producing $350 million in tax deductions for his lucky clientele.

In his defense Atkins claimed that U.S. tax laws did not clearly define improper transactions in the areas Atkins worked—the ambiguities were a matter for lawmakers, not for prosecutors. Additionally, Atkins argued, tax shelters like his and others like it, were practiced across the United States. Atkins and two associates were found guilty in 1987 of conspiracy and fraud. Though prosecutors called his acts one of the largest tax-fraud conspiracies in history, Atkins was sentenced to just two years in prison and two years' community service. One of his associates served four months; the other was given a six-month suspended sentence.

Related Entry:

TAX FRAUD

ATTITUDES TOWARD AND PERCEPTIONS OF FRAUD

USSC Study

A study by the U.S. Sentencing Commission in 1997 compared the sentences for various crimes as recommended by a group of citizens with the legal guidelines used by judges for sentencing the same crimes. Respondents were asked to evaluate crimes by category, including several categories of fraud: minor fraud (bad checks, using a stolen credit card), major fraud (obtaining loans fraudulently, investment crimes, falsifying Medicare claims), embezzlement, antitrust violations, tax fraud, bribery, forgery/counterfeiting, and money laundering. Generally the public recommends higher sentences for fraud crimes than the sentencing guidelines do. Particularly, when addressing "major frauds" such as falsifying Medicare claims and investment crimes, more than half of the respondents asked for punishment higher than the guidelines.

Respondent sentences tended to increase with increases in the amount of money defrauded. However, only three levels make a clear difference in the length of sentence: $200-$4,000, $40,000-$3,000,000, and $17,000,000-$ 80,000,000. In these three ranges, median sentences increase from about two years to about four years to about five years.

SENTENCES FOR FRAUD CRIMES, ACCORDING TO FEDERAL GUIDELINES AND SURVEY RESPONDENTS

TYPE OF FRAUD	Guidelines Sentence	Respondents Sentence
Major Fraud	3.5	6.3
Minor Fraud	1.8	4.4
Extortion	3.8	8.6
Money Laundering	3.8	5.0
Forgery/Counterfeit	2.4	6.3
Bribery	2.1	3.0
Larceny	1.7	4.9
Bank officer causing S&L failure	5.4	6.1
Selling defective helicopter parts to government	3.7	11.2
False mortgage application with intent to pay mortgage	3.0	2.0
Selling worthless stocks and bonds	2.9	7.3
Doctor filing false Medicare claims	2.9	6.9
Company official making use of inside information	2.9	4.3
Using stolen credit cards	1.7	4.2
Writing bad checks	1.6	4.6
Embezzlement: Bank officer stealing bank funds	1.3	4.3
Embezzlement: Bank employee taking bank funds	0.9	4.3
Forgery: Counterfeiting currency	4.7	7.6
Tax: Failure to file tax returns	2.5	4.4
Tax: Under-reporting income on tax	2.5	4.4
Bribery: Local official taking bribe	2.5	2.6
Money Laundering: Coin dealer failing to file required forms	2.4	3.8
Money Laundering: Bank official failing to file proper forms	1.7	4.5
Soliciting funds for nonexistent charity	2.2	4.9
False mortgage application with no intent to pay back mortgage	1.8	3.8
Embezzlement: Postal worker taking postal funds	1.7	5.6

Source: National Sample Survey: Public Opinion on Sentencing Federal Crimes (Berk & Rossi Report) *United States Sentencing Commission*, March 14, 1997.

Cultural Background and Personal Values

Watson Study—Cultural Background

Research by Dr. Douglas Watson found that cultural heritage does not significantly affect people's attitudes toward business-related fraud. A sample of "white-collar" employees of a large multinational corporation located in the Middle East evaluated scenarios describing five frauds—bribery, conflict of interest, embezzlement, management fraud, and industrial espionage. Watson defined culture as those integrated shared meanings, values, and beliefs that reflect attitudes toward life.

Though respondents with different cultural heritages reported dissimilar attitudes toward fraud in general, the respondents from all groups treated each particular fraud with similar disapproval. When discussing broad ethical issues, respondents invoked different terms and principles. When evaluating specific acts, all respondents reached similar conclusions. Only one factor significantly affected a difference in attitude. Younger respondents were more tolerant to fraud than older respondents.

Tulane Study—Stated Values vs. Practice

A study at Tulane University in 1996 tested whether one's stated values affects his/her tendency to commit or approve of fraud. A group of business executives, controllers and students was asked to complete an "in-basket" test in which they had to complete a big pile of paperwork. The executives who finished most quickly and who showed the best financial results were to be promoted. The test offered a number of opportunities to boost profits by failing. Some 47% of the executives, 40% of the controllers, and 76% of the students surveyed were willing to understate write-offs. Respondents also completed a survey ranking such values as "pleasure," "a comfortable life," and "self-respect." Though the self-assessments varied, those values were only weakly and inconsistently related to the person's willingness to commit fraud. Most respondents rated their values highly, though many of them were willing to engage in fraud during the test.

Touche Ross Study/Inder Khera essay—Eastern vs. Western Values

In a comparison of values in Eastern societies and Western societies, Professor Inder Khera acknowledged that corruption and fraud are less prevalent in the West. Khera cites a 1987 survey conducted by Touche Ross (now Deloitte & Touche), in which most American executives ranked the U.S. top in ethical standards, followed by U.K., Canada, Switzerland, and Germany—this despite continuing reports of rising incidences of fraud and corruption in those countries. Khera asserted, "The fact that the West does function much more efficiently on a day to day basis does not necessarily mean that it is no less populated by individuals who do not crave unethically derived privileges. Human nature is not all that different in different spots on this earth. What seems to be different are such things as the degree of power held by people over others, the feedback and control mechanisms to keep abuse of power in check, greater transparency of governments' actions, a greater sense of responsibility and discipline inculcated by the industrial revolution, and other differences."

Source: Witt, R. and Witte, A. "What We Spend and What We Get: Public and Private Provision of Crime Prevention and Criminal Justice," *Fiscal Studies,* March 2001. Vol. 22, No. 1; Pg. 1-40.

Businesspeople in the U.S., U.K., and Europe: Attitudes Toward Fraud

The following material is adapted from an article on businesses and crime by Michael Levi, published in *Urban Studies*, May 2001. Levi recounts the results of a survey of businessmen in America, the United Kingdom, and Europe regarding their perceptions and responses to various crimes, including fraud.

Nearly three-quarters of all respondents felt that a fraud could not have a catastrophic effect. The large 'one big hit' fraud (42%) caused the most anxiety, compared with 35% who were most preoccupied with the cumulative effects low-level employee frauds of the same total value.

Forty percent of respondents believe they have done as much as they cost-effectively could do to prevent and deter fraud; more than half believe they could be doing more. Some respondents used fraud vulnerability reviews when specific frauds were suspected; others used reviews as a continuing internal control.

Half the companies with a turnover over $1 billion provide staff fraud awareness training, compared to an average of 28% for lesser grossing companies. Companies with a higher turnover are also more likely to adopt a fraud hotline. Fifty seven percent of respondents from the U.S. reported staff fraud awareness training, with 47% having a fraud hotline, 62% cover fraud reporting in the staff handbook.

Source: Levi, M. "Business, Cities and Fears about Crime," *Urban Studies*, May 1, 2001. Volume 38, Number 5 & 6, pp 849-868.

Businesspeople in Three Former Soviet Nations: Attitudes toward Fraud

According to analysis by the World Bank, fraud and corruption are tolerated in former Soviet countries, but are viewed as impediments by most participants. A group of researchers traveled to Albania, Georgia and Latvia, surveying household members, enterprise managers, and public officials about the costs and private returns of paying bribes to obtain public services, special privileges, and government jobs. They found respondents generally willing to discuss agency-specific corruption with remarkable candor.

The group published a report in 1998 concluding that systemic corruption in these countries, as elsewhere, reduces public welfare and taxes private sector resources. The portrait that emerges is different in each country. In Georgia, for example, the most common form of corruption is embezzlement of public funds. In Albania and Latvia the most common form is theft of state property. Bribery in procurement is common in all three countries.

Institutional causes of corruption also differ across the three countries, suggesting different priorities for reform. In Albania a weak judiciary is one of the main causes of corruption; while regulatory failures are less important. Regulatory failures are more serious in Georgia and Latvia, both in terms of excessive regulations and the discretion granted to regulators enforcing them.

Several important findings emerge from this survey data. First, most business people said they would be willing to pay higher taxes if corruption were eliminated. In Albania and Latvia bribes account for 7% of revenue in firms that admit to paying them. In Georgia, bribes account for 15% of firms' revenue. Lost fiscal revenues are high in all three countries, especially in Georgia.

Source: Kaufman, D., Parham, S., and Oysterman, R., "World Bank Finds New Ways to Diagnose Corruption Symptoms," *Transition Newsletter*, January 1999.

Survey Reports on Cheating Among High School Students

According to an article published by the Heartland Institute, Donald McCabe, a professor of management at Rutgers University, has conducted a number of surveys of cheating among high school students. In 2001, he conducted a survey of 4,500 high school students and discovered that more than half of them admitted to plagiarizing via the Internet. Seventy-four percent of them admitted to cheating on exams, while 97% admitted to cheating on homework.

In a separate study, McCabe discovered that among 500 middle school and high school students, two-thirds of them did not consider doing work with their classmates cheating. Half of the students did not see anything wrong with their parents doing their homework for them.

When the students were asked why they cheated, many of them replied that academic pressure pushed them to cheat. Many more students responded that society offers little in the way of setting good examples.

When McCabe surveyed faculty, he found that 90% of them were aware of cheating among their students, but 32% said they did nothing to stop it.

Every two years since 1992 The Josephson Institute of Ethics has conducted surveys concerning the ethics of American youth.

In 2004, the Institute surveyed 24,763 high school students and concluded that lying, cheating, and stealing has begun to decrease compared to results in the past, for the first time in the 12 years of surveying. Survey results included the following:

- Students who admitted to cheating on an exam at least once during the past year decreased from 74% in 2002 to 62% in 2004.
- Students who admitted to stealing something from a store during the past year decreased from 38% in 2002 to 27% in 2004.
- Students who said they had lied to their parents about something significant during the past year went down from 93% in 2002 to 82% in 2004.
- Students who said they had lied to their teachers during the past year decreased from 83% in 2002 to 62% in 2004.

It was also discovered that 84% of the students surveyed agreed with the statement, "It's not worth it to lie or cheat because it hurts your character." Nevertheless, 51% of males and 32% of females also agreed that "A person has to lie or cheat sometimes in order to succeed," compared to 43% of respondents who felt that way in 2000. Also, despite the high proportion of students who admitted lying, cheating, and stealing, 74% still said, "When it comes to doing what is right, I am better than most people I know."

While students still continued to lie, cheat and steal, the good news is that the dishonesty in each category actually went down in 2004 for the first time since the survey was conducted in 1992. The downward trend may have something to do with the spread of character education programs and a new level of attentiveness to values and integrity after 9/11 and also in response to corporate frauds at Enron, WorldCom, Arthur Anderson, and others.

Sources:

"Cheating and Succeeding: Record Numbers of Top High School Students Take Ethical Shortcuts: Finds Troubling Trends, Some Good News," Who's Who, November 12, 1998.

Coleman, J. *The Criminal Elite: Understanding the White-Collar Crime*. New York: St. Martin's Press, 1998.

Khera, Inder P. "Business Ethics, East vs. West: Myths and realities," *Journal of Business Ethics*, March 2001.

Marsh, C., "Perceptions of Crime: The 1994 West Virginia Statistical Analysis Center Study of Crime Victimization of West Virginians Age 60 and Over Internal WV SAC report," 1996.

Dr. Watson, D. "Cross-Cultural Interpretations of Fraud: An Attitudinal Study in a Multinational Corporation." October 23-25, 2000. www.megaevents.net/forthcomingevents/doug-watson2.htm.

Heartland Institute: www.heartland.org/Article.cfm?artId=14378

Related Entries:

CAUSES OF FRAUD

COST OF FRAUD

AUDITING FOR FRAUD

Responsibilities for fraud may differ from the type of examination to be performed as well as the type of auditor to perform the examination. The external auditor may take a different view than that of the internal auditor. Still, the fraud examiner may take a view different from that of the internal or external auditor.

SAS 99-Consideration of Fraud in a Financial Statement Audit

In response to the high-profile corporate accounting scandals that occurred during 2001 and 2002, and the resulting public criticism of the accounting and auditing profession, the Auditing Standards Board of the AICPA issued Statement on Auditing Standards (SAS) No. 99, *Consideration of Fraud in a Financial Statement Audit.* This standard, which supersedes SAS No. 82, provides expanded guidance to independent auditors on detecting material fraud.

SAS No. 99 reiterates the responsibility of auditors, as originally promulgated by SAS No. 1:

> *The auditor has a responsibility to plan and perform the audit to obtain reasonable assurance about whether the financial statements are free of material misstatement, whether caused by error or fraud.*

The body of the standard covers ten major areas:

- Description and characteristics of fraud
- The importance of exercising professional skepticism
- Discussion among engagement personnel regarding the risks of material misstatement due to fraud
- Obtaining information needed to identify risks of material misstatement due to fraud
- Identifying risks that may result in a material misstatement due to fraud
- Assessing the identified risks after taking into account an evaluation of the entity's programs and controls
- Responding to the results of the assessment
- Evaluating audit evidence
- Communicating about fraud to management, the audit committee, and others
- Documenting the auditor's consideration of fraud

For purposes of SAS No. 99, fraud is defined as any "intentional act that results in a material misstatement in financial statements that are the subject of an audit." The standard further dissects this concept into two types of misstatements that auditors must consider when conducting a financial statement audit:

- Misstatements arising from fraudulent financial reporting
- Misstatements arising from misappropriation of assets

One of the new requirements under SAS No. 99 is a mandated discussion among audit team members to identify and address the potential for material misstatement due to fraud. This "brainstorming" session should be held during the planning phase of the audit and should include discussions about specific areas where the company's financial statements may be susceptible to material misstatement due to fraud, how management could commit and conceal fraudulent financial reporting, and how assets of the company could be misappropriated.

SAS No. 99 states that, while assessing the company's risk of material misstatement due to fraud, auditors should presume that there is a risk of material fraud related to improper revenue recognition. Additionally, auditors must explicitly address the risk that management could override internal controls to engage in fraudulent activity. To address these risks, the standard requires that auditors perform analytical procedures specifically related to revenue accounts; make direct inquiries of management about fraud; evaluate the design and operation of the company's programs and internal controls related to fraud; and consider any existing fraud risk factors or other information that may be helpful in identifying fraud risks. The appendix to SAS No. 99 contains examples of fraud risk factors that auditors should consider in performing a financial statement audit.

In response to the fraud risk assessments, auditors should adjust the nature, timing, and extent of audit procedures accordingly. This may include incorporating an element of unpredictability into the selection of audit procedures performed from year to year. Further, to assure that the engagement is properly performed and supervised, auditors may need to review the personnel assigned to perform these functions.

If, during an audit, evidence of fraud is discovered, SAS No. 99 directs auditors to report the situation to the appropriate level of management, even if the matter might be inconsequential. If the potential fraud appears to involve senior management, auditors should report it directly to the audit committee.

SAS No. 99 expands the documentation requirements for auditors to include documenting the audit team's "brainstorming" discussion; specific audit procedures performed to identify and assess fraud risks; specific fraud risks identified and the auditors' response to those risks; reasons for not identifying improper revenue recognition as a fraud risk (if applicable); results of procedures performed to address the risk of management override of controls; and the nature of any communications about fraud made to management, the audit committee, or anyone else.

SAS 85 Management Representations

In addition to SAS 99, SAS 85 — Management Representations — provides for specific representations from management to the external auditors on the existence of fraud — management, employee or otherwise. The standard specifically requires that:

> *... The independent auditor obtain written representations from management as a part of an audit of financial statements performed in accordance with generally accepted auditing standards and provides guidance concerning the representations to be obtained.*
>
> *... If a representation made by management is contradicted by other audit evidence, the auditor should investigate the circumstances and consider the reliability of the representation made. Based on the circumstances, the auditor should consider whether his or her reliance on management's representations relating to other aspects of the financial statements is appropriate and justified.*

In Appendix A to SAS 85, there is an illustrative management representation letter which gives the auditor guidance as to items that should be addressed by management.

Appendix B to SAS 85 illustrates additional representations that may be appropriate in certain situations. Listed are conditions and examples for assets, liabilities, equity, and the income statement and in general.

Private Securities Litigation Reform Act

The Private Securities Litigation Reform Act has changed the procedures and proof required in securities fraud cases. The Reform Act also includes responsibilities for independent auditors of public companies. Audits of the financial statements of a public company must include the following:

- Procedures designed to provide reasonable assurance of detecting illegal acts that would have a direct and material effect on the determination of financial statement amounts;
- Procedures designed to identify related party transactions that are material to the financial statements or otherwise require disclosure therein; and
- An evaluation of whether there is substantial doubt about the ability of the issuer to continue as a going concern during the ensuing fiscal year.

Additionally, if in the course of an audit, an auditor "detects or otherwise becomes aware that an illegal act (whether or not perceived to have a material effect on the financial statements of the issuer) has or may have occurred," the auditor must then:

- Determine whether it is likely than an illegal act has occurred, and if so
- Determine and consider the possible effect of the illegal act on the financial statements of the company, including any contingent monetary effects such as fines, penalties, and damages; and
- Inform the appropriate level of management "as soon as practicable," and assure that the audit committee (or the Board of Directors in the absence of an audit committee) is adequately informed of the illegal acts that have been detected unless such acts are "clearly inconsequential."

ISA 240 – The Auditor's Responsibility to Consider Fraud in the Audit of Financial Statements

In February 2004, the International Federation of Accounts' International Auditing and Assurance Standards Board approved a revised version of International Standard on Auditing (ISA) 240. The ISA, "*The Auditor's Responsibility to Consider Fraud in the Audit of Financial Statements*," requires the auditor to focus on areas where there is a risk of material misstatement due to fraud, including management fraud. The revised standard emphasizes the need for the auditor to maintain an attitude of professional skepticism throughout the audit, notwithstanding the auditor's past experience about the honesty and integrity of management and those charged with governance. Some of the most significant provisions of ISA 240 are summarized below. Many of the standard's requirements are similar to those found in SAS No. 99; however, as many countries have adopted ISA 240, auditors should review the entire standard for full details.

ISA 240 requires auditors to:

- *Understand the characteristics of fraud.* Since fraud is a combination of motive, opportunity, and attitude, auditors are required to consider all three of these factors when assessing the risk of fraud. Auditors are also charged with understanding the principle characteristics of fraud.
- *Discuss how fraud can be committed.* Before commencing an engagement, the audit team is required to discuss among themselves the various ways the client *could* commit material fraud, taking into account all relevant factors: the nature of the business, management, internal controls, ethical values, and other information.
- *Obtain information to assess the risk of material fraud.* Auditors are required to interview management and other appropriate personnel within the entity to determine the organization's risk of material misstatements due to fraud. Further, they are to consider unusual or unexpected relationships that are identified when performing or planning analytical procedures, and they are to consider whether fraud risk factors are present. Auditors are also required to make inquiry with respect to fraud risks and countermeasures. Further, the auditor should obtain an understanding of how those charged with governance exercise oversight of management's processes for identifying and responding to the risks of fraud in the entity and the internal control that management has established to mitigate these risks.
- *Identify risks that may result in misstatements due to fraud.* Using the results of the information gathering process, the auditor should determine whether any fraud risks have been identified. Once identified, the auditor will assess the significance, likelihood, and pervasiveness of the risk of fraud.

- *Assess fraud risks in light of the entity's programs and controls.* When considering the identified risks of material misstatements due to fraud, the auditor should evaluate programs and controls designed to address those risks. Factors such as control mechanisms over management overrides and education, prevention, and deterrence programs for employees are to be considered.
- *Respond to the fraud risk assessment.* Once the auditor has assessed the risk of material misstatement due to fraud, he or she will determine how the risk affects the overall audit, the kinds of procedures to perform, and the timing of the audit procedures. Auditors should take particular note of analytical and computer-assisted techniques. Certain procedures to detect potential fraud are required to be performed regardless of the risk assessment.
- *Evaluate audit test results.* The auditor should evaluate the test results looking for such things as discrepancies in accounting records, conflicting or missing evidential matter, or problematic or unusual relationships between the client and the auditor. If the auditor concludes that there is a significant risk of material misstatements due to fraud, the auditor's duty is to communicate this information to appropriate level of management. If the risk of material misstatement is significant, the auditor may elect to withdraw from the engagement.
- *Communicate information about fraud to management and others.* When the auditor has determined that there is evidence that fraud exists or may exist, the auditor will notify the client, even if the suspected fraud is not material to the financial statements as a whole. If the suspected fraud is: (1) material, (2) involves senior management, or (3) involves employees who have a significant role in internal control, the auditor should report the incident to those charged with governance as soon as practicable. In some instances, the auditor may be required to report suspected fraud in response to legal or regulatory requirements.
- *Document the auditor's consideration of fraud.* Finally, the auditor is required to document the auditor's assessment of the risk of material misstatement; the risks that were identified and assessed; the overall responses to the assessed risks; the results of the audit procedures; and the auditor's communications to management about fraud.

Internal Auditor Responsibilities

Internal auditors play a key role in helping organizations prevent and detect fraudulent activity. Because of their proximity to and understanding of the inner workings of the organization, internal auditors are in a unique position to uncover potential unscrupulous acts.

The Institute of Internal Auditors (IIA) has developed the International Standards for the Professional Practice of Internal Auditing. This section contains a description of those IIA Standards that pertain to the internal auditor's responsibilities for preventing and detecting fraud within an organization. More detail on these and all other IIA Standards can be found at the Institute of Internal Auditor's website (www.theiia.org).

Government Audits

Standards for government auditors are taken largely from generally accepted auditing standards as promulgated by the AICPA. However, for audits of government organizations, programs, activities, functions, and funds, Government Auditing Standards, also known as the *Yellow Book,* go beyond the AICPA standards. The Office of Management and Budget included these standards in OMB Circular A-73 as basic audit criteria for federal executive departments and agencies. The Chief Financial Officers Act of 1990 requires that these standards be followed in audits of federal departments and agencies.

The *Yellow Book* also describes the two types of audits conducted by government and non-government audit organizations. The two types described are financial audits (including financial-related audits) and performance audits.

Financial Audits

Generally Accepted Government Auditing Standards (GAGAS) incorporate the AICPA's three generally accepted standards of fieldwork as well as five additional fieldwork standards. Any new AICPA standards relevant to financial statement audits are incorporated into GAGAS unless the General Accounting Office excludes them by formal announcement.

The five additional fieldwork standards are:

1. Auditors should communicate information about the nature, timing, and extent of planned testing and the level of assurance provided by the engagement to the officials of the audited organization, the individuals contracting for or requesting the audit services, and the audit committee.
2. Auditors should consider the results of previous engagements and follow up on known material findings and recommendations that directly relate to the objectives of the current audit.
3. Auditors should design the audit to provide reasonable assurance of detecting material misstatements resulting from violations of provisions of contracts or grant agreements that have a direct and material effect on the determination of financial statements amounts. Auditors should also remain alert to situations that could indicate the existence of abuse that significantly affects the financial statement amounts. If the auditors discover evidence of material misstatements from violations or abuse, they should apply procedures specifically designed to determine whether such violations or abuse have occurred.
4. When auditors identify problems such as internal control deficiencies, fraud, illegal acts, violations of provisions of contracts or grant agreements, or abuse, they should plan audit procedures to develop an explanation of the criteria, condition, effect, and cause of the problem to facilitate developing the auditors' report.
5. Audit documentation should contain sufficient information to enable an experienced auditor, having no previous connection with the audit, to ascertain from the documentation the evidence that supports the auditors' significant conclusions and judgments.

Performance Audits

As it relates to reporting standards for performance audits, GAGAS has adopted standards for report contents. Among other requirements, the report should include:

- Significant audit findings and, where applicable, auditors' conclusions.
- Recommendations to correct problem areas and to improve operations.
- Significant instances of abuse that were found during or in connection with the audit.

- The scope of the work on management controls and any significant weaknesses found during the audit.

For both financial and performance audits, standards require that written reports be submitted to the appropriate officials of the organizations requiring or arranging for audits, including external funding organizations, unless legal restrictions prevent it. Copies of the report should also be sent to other officials who have legal oversight authority or who might be responsible for acting on audit findings and recommendations and to others authorized to receive such reports. Unless restricted by law or regulation, copies should be made available for public inspection.

Related Entries:

COSO
FINANCIAL STATEMENT FRAUD
FORENSIC ACCOUNTING
FRAUD EXAMINATION
ICG COMMUNICATIONS
SARBANES-OXLEY ACT
TREADWAY COMMISSION

AUTO SALES FRAUD

Fraud is committed in the sale of new and used automobiles when the seller omits or conceals derogatory information about the vehicle's condition, status, warranty, or other factors that might otherwise deter a buyer. Common acts include reducing the odometer mileage, selling demonstration or rental cars as new, and disguising functional problems. There are no certain figures for losses, though investigators believe fraud among used cars alone costs $8 billion. The numbers are likely huge, since there are about 200 million registered automobiles in the United States, at an average price of $20,000 per new car.

Auto Sales Fraud Schemes

Typical schemes include:

- Odometer rollbacks
- Advertising unavailable vehicles or unavailable prices
- Boosting sales prices to cover trade-in allowances
- Failing to post the buyer's guide for a used car
- Selling a demonstration or rental car as new
- Concealing defects in safety or materials
- Concealing a car's provenance
- Deceptive leases or financing
- Altering a buyer's personal information to achieve financing
- Unscrupulous lender referrals, including auto loans backed by home equity
- Discrimination on the basis of race, gender, creed, or sexual orientation

Case Study—Salesmen's Confession

Salesmen Bobby G. Lamb and Jay Denham pled guilty in 1990 to charges that they defrauded customers. As part of their plea, the men described their illicit practices.

Writing on a yellow legal pad, the salesmen itemized the cost of the vehicle for the customer, using the advertised near-invoice price as a starting point. During the calculations, the salesmen would inflate tax, license and documentary fees by several hundred dollars. Falsifying finance charges using an illegal method known as "add on" (which increased the total by several thousand dollars) raised the price further. To avoid repercussions, the calculations made on the yellow legal pads were not exactly the same as those on the final contracts.

The salesman's job was to shift the excess money to legitimate line items on the final contract. A favored method accounted for the money as an extended warranty, sometimes called the "Wilson Ford Consumer Protection Plan." The latter included theft insurance, paint sealant, fabric protector, rust inhibitor, and road-noise deadener. Though customers might be charged several thousand dollars for the package, its wholesale value was $275. The protection packages and warranties often were added to contracts even when customers did not indicate that they wanted to buy them.

An upgrade to the dealer's computer system allowed salesmen even more latitude in manipulations. For example, using a start date for interest charges that was 500 to 600 days prior to the first payment boosted finance charges. Lamb said customers usually did not see the discrepancy in the dates because the top of the computer printout reflecting that information was torn off before it was shown to them. Besides the ease of manipulation, the computer provided a prop. "The computer printouts gave veracity to the figures," according to Denham.

Sources:
Greenwald, D., "Con Men Take Car Buyers for a Ride, Mileage Decreased to Increase Value." *The Orange County Register, Evening Edition,* December 30, 1990.

Norrgard, L., and Norrgard, J. *Consumer Fraud.* Santa Barbara: ABC-CLIO, 1998.

Mickadeit, F. "Ex-Salesmen Tell How Staff Allegedly Manipulated Figures; Charges Are That Cost of License, Tax Were Inflated." *The Orange County Register, Evening Edition,* March 30, 1990.

Related Entries:

AUTOMOTIVE REPAIR FRAUD
CONSUMER FRAUD

AUTOMOTIVE REPAIR FRAUD

Automotive repair frauds are committed by businesses and individual mechanics against consumers. Estimates of auto repair fraud vary widely. Paul Blumberg published figures in 1990 estimating that $21 billion of the $65 billion Americans spent each year on repairs went to fraud. This breaks down to $57 million lost per day. An analysis published by Yale in 2001 set fraud losses at $40 billion a year.

Paul Jesilow had women approach randomly chosen garages and ask that their car battery be tested. Though the battery functioned perfectly, almost 11% of the garages said it could not be recharged; 20% recommended a new battery.

A 1989 experiment conducted by Paul Tracy and James Fox sent drivers with damaged vehicles to 91 randomly selected body shops in Massachusetts. Each shop gave estimates on two different cars—one covered by insurance, the other uninsured. The price for repairing the insured car was uniformly higher than the price for the same work on the uninsured car.

Many states have established offices dedicated to anti-fraud efforts in the automotive sales and repair industries. Undercover investigations and class-action lawsuits have resulted in charges of deceptive advertising, bait-and-switch tactics, and fraud at some of the industry's largest companies.

Reader's Digest Experiments in Auto Fraud

A sting in 1941 by the *Reader's Digest* company took a mint-condition car to 347 garages around the nation—63% of the garages said the car needed work. Investigators took a Lincoln Zephyr to repair shops in 48 states, visiting 347 shops in all. Before asking for help, the investigators removed the connecting wire from one of the car's coils.

- 37% of mechanics reattached the wire for free.
- 63% "overcharged, lied, invented unnecessary work, or charged for work not done, for parts not needed, for parts not installed."
- Investigators were provided with 74 different explanations for the car's problem, all spurious.

The magazine ran a version of the same sting in 1987 with equally poor results. A writer took a perfectly maintained three-year-old car to 225 garages in 33 states. Before arriving, he disconnected a spark plug wire.

- 28% of mechanics reattached the wire.
- 75% of garages made the writer wait hours or, in some cases, days for the repair.
- Of mechanics that worked on the car, 44% diagnosed the problem correctly.
- In 56% of garages, mechanics performed unnecessary work, sold unnecessary parts, or charged for repair not done.
- Spurious diagnoses and services rendered included tune-ups, valve adjustments, carburetor repairs, and rebuilt transmissions.
- About 100 unnecessary parts were installed, including catalytic converters, air pumps, engine control modules, distributor caps and rotors, and valve lifters. The parts ranged in price from $2 to $500.

Some Common Automotive Schemes

Most repair frauds involve charging for unnecessary parts and labor. Old parts are cleaned and placed back into the car; the customer is charged for new parts. Alternatively, old parts are sold to the customer as new. Bait-and-switch operations advertise discount prices; the customer is then persuaded that additional services are necessary.

Other tricks include squirting oil on a shock absorber to give it the appearance of being damaged or spraying acid on the electric alternator causing it to smoke alarmingly. In other cases, tires and radiator hoses are punctured with an ice pick or other sharp-pointed instrument when the driver leaves the car unattended at the service station.

Other common automotive schemes are: tune-ups which should have been done for free under warranty; charges incurred for defective parts and/or improper installation; complete brake overhauls when an inexpensive replacement of pads or linings would have sufficed; unnecessary air conditioning servicing, wheel alignments, and ball joint or steering part replacement, etc.

Companies encourage fraud by setting quotas, offering sales bonuses, and sponsoring contests for salespeople who push additional repairs.

Related Entries:

AUTO SALES FRAUD
CON SCHEMES
LEASING FRAUD
CONSUMER FRAUD

AVANT!

Gerry Hsu resigned from Cadence Design Systems in 1994, claiming he would probably leave high-tech altogether. Days later he joined Avant!, Cadence's archrival. The two companies made software products used in microchip production. Hsu's departure seemed to cap a conspiracy begun several years before.

Hsu arrived at Cadence to help fight the threat from Avant! (pronounced "ah VAN tee"), which was then called ArcSystems. Hsu's departure followed up three heists against Cadence, each committed by employees who left Cadence for Avant! In his final weeks at Cadence, Avant! founder Stephen Tzyh-Lih Wuu copied the code for a program called Symbad. Wuu claimed he wrote the 47,000 lines of code himself, though he only had about 19 days to do so. Good code writers average about 100 lines a day.

The second hit came from Mitch Igusa, who e-mailed four files of code to his home PC before he left Cadence in 1994. The following year a Cadence engineer noticed a design flaw in Avant!'s software that worked exactly like a flaw in Cadence's product. The engineer had worked on the Cadence product himself; his flawed code had caused a display screen to look fuzzy during an obscure function of the software. He had caught his mistake during debugging and fixed it, but Avant! must have missed it in their review. Looking further the engineer found his and Avant!'s software contained 4,000 identical lines of code, with the same grammatical mistakes in each.

When Eric Cheng walked out of Cadence, he carried with him a file he'd named "byebye," bearing the code for a Cadence product called V-Size. Avant! never brought out a V-Size rip-off, but they had been planning to until they were derailed by civil and criminal charges.

In July 2001, Judge Conrad Rushing of Superior Court in Santa Clara County, Calif., accepted guilty pleas from six defendants in the Avant! case. Avant! itself, based in Fremont, Calif., will have to pay a $195 million restitution fine to a rival, Cadence Design Systems, for stealing source code for routing software. Those originally charged were Avant!'s four co-founders, Eric Cho, Mike Tsai, Stephen Wuu, and Y.Z. Liao, as well as Eric Cheng, Gerald Hsu, Leigh Huang, and Mitsuru Igusa. Charges against Tsai were dropped. Wuu received the stiffest penalty of two years in prison. Liao, Cho and Cheng were each sentenced to one year. Hsu, Avant!'s chief executive officer, and Huang were placed on probation. Igusa had earlier been sentenced to a year in jail. The executives were also ordered to pay more than $8 million in fines.

Sources:

Burrows, Peter. "A Nest of Software Spies?" *Business Week,* May 19, 1997.

"Avant Reports Strong Earnings Ahead of Mediation With Rival Cadence." *Dow Jones News Service,* January 19, 1999.

Einstein, David. "Avant's CEO, 7 Others Are Indicted by Jury." *San Francisco Chronicle,* December 18, 1998.

Takahashi, Dan. "Did Gerry Hsu Take Rivalries Too Seriously?" *The Wall Street Journal,* April 16, 1997.

Related Entries:

COMPUTER CRIME
INFORMATION CRIME
INTELLECTUAL PROPERTY FRAUD

AVOCATIONAL CRIME

Illegal financial or economic acts committed by people outside their main occupation. It is the opposite of occupational fraud and abuse. Examples of avocational crime include income tax evasion, insurance fraud, loan and credit fraud, customs evasion, and the purchase of stolen goods.

Related Entries:

BANKRUPTCY FRAUD
CREDIT CARD AND DEBIT CARD FRAUD
FINANCIAL INSTITUTION FRAUD
INSURANCE FRAUD
LOAN FRAUD
OCCUPATIONAL FRAUD AND ABUSE
TAX FRAUD

BAIT AND SWITCH

Retail operations advertise low prices or special deals but then steer the consumer to more expensive items. Personnel claim the advertised goods are sold out, temporarily unavailable, or introduce terms of the sale not included in the ad—excuses are provided with the aim of selling the consumer something besides the advertised item. Bait and switch scams are sometimes run by repair services for automobiles, appliances, or homes. An advertised discount deal may be appended with clauses or add-on charges not disclosed in the ad, or the repair personnel are instructed to fabricate extra charges beyond the discounted service.

Related Entries:

CONSUMER FRAUD
FALSE OR DECEPTIVE ADVERTISING

BANCO AMBROSIANO

The collapse of the Banco Ambrosiano in 1982 revealed corruption involving prominent international businessmen and the Vatican. Archbishop Paul Marcinkus, former president of the Vatican Bank, IOR (Istituto per le Opere di Religione) was charged with fraud. The Vatican refused to admit legal responsibility but acknowledged "moral involvement" and paid $241 million to creditors. The Church refused to hand Marcinkus over to the Italian authorities, moving him to a parish in the U.S.

Roberto Calvi, once known as "God's Banker," owned the Banco Ambrosiano. He was found hanging from a rope under Blackfriar's Bridge, London in 1982, his death prompting the collapse of his bank. An investigation later concluded he was murdered. Known in Milan as a financial whiz kid, Calvi had advised Marcinkus about transferring IOR's assets outside of Italy, partly to avoid tax liability. Calvi abused the association with the Vatican Bank, making IOR a de-facto partner in a series of fraudulent banking transactions in the Bahamas and Latin America.

Michele Sindona participated with Calvi and was also chosen by Archbishop Marcinkus to advise on IOR's overseas investments. The Vatican lost millions of dollars when Sindona's U.S. bank, the Franklin National, collapsed in 1974. Convicted on murder charges for having ordered the June 1979 killing of Giorgio Ambrosoli, the liquidator of his Banca Privata Italiana, Sindona died in an Italian jail in March 1986 after drinking a poisoned cup of coffee.

BANKRUPTCY FRAUD

Bankruptcy fraud is committed by making false or misleading representations in the course of petitioning for debt relief. The fraud typically involves the transfer of assets in anticipation of bankruptcy, hiding or undervaluing assets, and intentional bankruptcies known as "bustouts."

According to the American Bankruptcy Institute, the number of bankruptcies has declined from the first quarter of 1999 to the last quarter of 2003.

A survey by Kessler International, an audit and investigations company, polled bankruptcy judges, administrators, trustees, and lawyers in the United States on how much fraud they encountered in bankruptcy cases. About 31% of respondents knew of "flagrant abuses"; 63% stated they knew of some abuse; only 6% said bankruptcy laws were followed and each filing was honest. These results suggest that abuse is common, but Department of Justice statistics show that less than 200 cases of bankruptcy fraud are prosecuted each year.

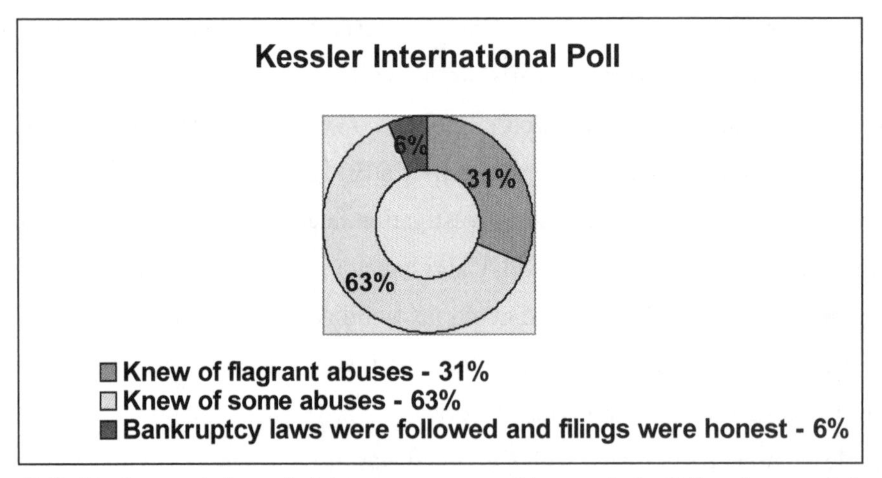

Poll of bankruptcy judges, administrators, trustee, and lawyers in the U.S. on how much fraud they encountered in bankruptcy cases.

All bankruptcies are filed in the local district of the United States Bankruptcy Court. Any charges for misconduct are heard by the Bankruptcy Court, which administers the civil aspects of the case. The appropriate U.S. District Court hears criminal charges related to bankruptcy. If necessary, civil and criminal charges may be reviewed in parallel proceedings.

There are a number of entities involved in a bankruptcy proceeding. The *debtor* is the person, government entity, or corporation filing for relief. The debtor must disclose in the petition all *creditors* who are owed money. Creditors are ranked by whether the debt is secured or unsecured by property and other factors. This ranking determines the order in which creditors are paid, as funds become available.

Counsel may represent both debtors and creditors as a bankruptcy judge hears the case. In complex cases, or cases involving fraud and mismanagement, bankruptcies are administered by the Office of the Trustee, a Department of Justice agency with 21 regional offices responsible for administering bankruptcy cases; appointing trustees, examiners, adjusters, and procedural committees; overseeing and monitoring trustees; reviewing employment and fee applications; and appearing in court on matters of interest to the estate and creditors. Fraud examiners may be called upon by any of the participants.

Historical Background

Laws of the Roman Empire dealt with bankruptcy and the discharge of debt—these statutes set standards for the treatment of debtors, including the grounds for imprisonment and the use of torture. The inability to pay debts was henceforth treated as a heinous crime in Western law until the early 19th century. According to legal scholar R.M. Goode, "Life for the medieval debtor was likely to be nasty, brutish, and short. In 1285 an Act was passed by which debtors were to be imprisoned in irons, and if they were unable to make restitution, they were left to rot, if necessary, for the rest of their lives."

The first comprehensive bankruptcy laws appeared in Europe in the 16th century. As usual, the law focused almost exclusively on the rights of creditors to obtain payment. A person could be declared bankrupt against his or her will (this was in fact the most common method at the time). A debtor had almost no ability to transfer or protect any assets. The "crime" of bankruptcy was punishable by debtor's prison, public floggings and humiliations, indentured servitude, and, in extreme cases, the death penalty.

Laws in post-colonial America were passed in reaction to the harshness of English law, perhaps because so many colonists were sent to America as debtors. The U.S.

Constitution expressly gave Congress the power "to establish uniform laws on the subject of bankruptcies," but it took nearly a hundred years for that to happen.

The economic crisis known as the Panic of 1819, which was provoked by rampant land speculation, caused an unprecedented number of bankruptcies and focused reformers' efforts to pass new laws. After more than 10 years of agitation, debtors' prisons were outlawed by federal statute in 1832. All the states gradually followed suit; Florida was the last to pass a relief law, in 1868, fulfilling Congress's charge to legislate a fair bankruptcy process. An 1867 law extended bankruptcy protection to corporations.

Modern bankruptcy laws have emphasized rehabilitating (or reorganizing) debtors in distress. Most developments have concerned the ranking of creditors for eventual repayment. Recent efforts have focused on preventing debtors from discharging debts so that creditors retain their claims even after the individual files bankruptcy.

Gary Klein, speaking before Congress in 1999, addressed the issue of whether the sharp increase in bankruptcies was due to a rise in bankruptcy frauds. "The reality is that more debtors use the bankruptcy system because more debtors are having serious financial problems," said Klein. "American families increasingly face foreclosure, repossession, utility shut-off, wage garnishment, and extensive collection activity on unsecured credit card debt. In short, more American families are using the bankruptcy system because more American families are having trouble paying their debts."

The rise in bankruptcies, according to Klein, is part of a generalized credit failure that includes foreclosures, repossessions, utility disconnection, credit card defaults and visits to consumer credit counseling agencies. Specifically Klein listed the following as factors causing a rise in bankruptcies: downsizing, economic dislocation, income disruptions, and underemployment; rising debt to income ratios; reliance on two wage earners; rising divorce rates (bankruptcy debtors are disproportionately single parents); uninsured medical debt; aggressive collection action; deregulation of credit, and the general extension of credit.

The Bankruptcy Code (Title 11 United States Code)

The Bankruptcy Code is broken down into eight chapters (1, 3, 5, 7, 9, 11, 12, and 13) under Title 11 of the United States Code. These chapters are "odd" numbered, except for

Chapter 12. In addition, there are two other sources of information dealing with bankruptcy issues which are found in the United States Code. They can be found at Title 18 U.S.C. Chapter 9 (which deals with crimes and criminal procedure) and Title 28 (which deals with the judiciary and judicial procedure).

Chapter 5 — Creditors, Debtors, and the Estate

Part 1 deals with creditors' claims, their priority, and their allowance. This section contains the prioritization of claims and the distribution of estate assets. Part 2 deals with specific duties of the debtor, the exemptions debtors can claim and dischargeability of debts. Part 3 deals with property of the estate, recovery of voidable transfers, and contractual rights of the estate.

Chapter 7 — Liquidation of Debtor's Assets

Part 1 of Chapter 7 deals with officers and the administration of Chapter 7 cases and spells out duties of the trustee. Part 2 deals with the collection, liquidation, and distribution of the estate's assets. Part 3 deals with stockbroker liquidations. Part 4 deals with commodity broker liquidations.

Chapter 11 — Reorganization

Chapter 11 deals with debtors in reorganization. The code allows for debtors to restructure their debt, pay their creditors, and emerge from bankruptcy. Part 1 of the chapter deals with officers and administration. Part 2 deals with the plan of reorganization. Part 3 deals with postconfirmation matters. Part 4 deals with railroad reorganization. The purpose of the Chapter 11 filing is to allow the debtor breathing room from the creditors so that the debtor can reorganize its financial affairs and continue as a going concern. If the court is provided with sufficient probable cause regarding the financial affairs of the debtor, a trustee or examiner can be appointed by the court.

Bankruptcy Abuse Prevention and Consumer Protection Act of 2005

Signed into law by President Bush in April 2005, the Bankruptcy Abuse Prevention and Consumer Protection Act made significant changes to the Bankruptcy Code, primarily in the area of personal bankruptcy filings. Some of the more significant provisions are highlighted below:

Means Test

The trustee or any creditor can bring a motion to dismiss a Chapter 7 filing if the debtor's income is greater than the state median income.

Mandatory Credit Counseling

No individual may be a debtor under Title 11 unless they have, within 180 days prior to filing, received credit counseling from an approved counseling agency.

Mandatory Debtor Education

The court many not grant a Chapter 13 discharge unless the debtor has completed an education course in personal financial management.

Scope of Discharge

Debts owed to a single creditor totaling more than $500 for luxury goods incurred within 90 days of filing and cash advances of $750 within 70 days of filing are presumed non-dischargeable.

Time Between Discharge

A Chapter 7 debtor cannot receive a discharge if a prior discharge was received within 8 years (previously 6) of the new filing.

Homestead Exemption

Debtors may elect state exemptions in the state in which they have lived for the 730 days prior to filing. However, the debtor may only exempt up to $125,000 in a homestead that was acquired within 1,215 days prior to the filing.

Retirement and Education Account Exemptions

Retirement accounts that are exempt from taxes under the Internal Revenue Code are exempt from the debtor's estate. Education savings accounts through education IRAs and 529 plans are also excluded.

Additional Filings

In addition to the list of creditors, schedules of assets and liabilities, income, and expenses, debtors must now provide the documents listed below. Failure to file the documents within 45 days of the original filing date results in an automatic dismissal of the case.

- Certificate of credit counseling,
- Evidence of payment from employers, if any, received 60 days before the filing,
- Statement of monthly net income and any anticipated increase in income of expenses after filing,
- Tax returns or transcripts for the most recent tax year,
- Tax returns filed during the case,
- Photo identification (among other items).

Privacy Provisions

Under the Act, the bankruptcy court is permitted to honor the privacy policies of business debtors. The Act creates a consumer privacy ombudsman to protect personal privacy in bankruptcy proceedings. Measures may be implemented to prevent identity theft and to guide what information is readily accessible to the public. Debtors are permitted to request that courts protect sensitive information before it is placed in public records.

Bankruptcy Schemes

Bankruptcy fraud is accomplished through the schemes discussed below. Often, bankruptcy crimes involve other violations including mail fraud, wire fraud, bank fraud, interstate transportation of stolen goods or property, conspiracy, tax evasion, and money laundering.

Concealed Asset

The most common bankruptcy fraud is the concealment of assets such as cash, consumer property, houses, interests in partnerships and corporations, and lawsuits in which the debtor is a plaintiff. Assets also include books and records of the debtor. Some debtors conceal assets by transferring them to another person or to a corporation sometime prior to filing. If a transfer is discovered by the estate's trustee, the debtor must prove that the transfer was made with no foreknowledge of the bankruptcy. In some instances, assets are disclosed but undervalued.

The "Bustout"

A bustout is a planned bankruptcy of a business. Usually an agent or owner of the business orders large quantities of goods on credit then disposes of those goods, hiding the proceeds. Bustouts are a favorite method of organized crime rings—a business may be formed with the intent of busting out, or a business may be busted out by crime-ring members because the owner cannot pay a debt owed to the ring.

In a credit card bustout, the debtor charges credit cards to the limit and files bankruptcy with no intent to repay. Credit card debts might include purchases for jewelry, luxury items, or other personal properties that are not disclosed in the petition. Credit card debt also might include large cash advances taken prior to filing bankruptcy.

Multiple Filings

Because bankruptcy filings grant automatic stays to debtors (so that creditors may not file suit or take action against the debtor), some debtors intentionally submit faulty petitions (e.g., the document does not contain required statements, or the debtor does not appear for examination). After the initial petition is rejected, the debtor files again, obtaining another stay. False statements on petitions are common, including a denial that the debtor has filed any previous petition.

The most popular ways to perpetrate multiple filing frauds are by filing for bankruptcy in different states, utilizing true personal identifiers, or by using false names and/or Social Security numbers to file in the same or different states. A debtor filing in two or more states usually lists nearly identical assets and liabilities in each filing. The debtor becomes discharged from the debts and in the process makes off with several of the assets left off of a particular petition.

Forged Filings

Bankruptcy petitions sometimes are filed in another (uninvolved) person's name, usually as part of a larger scheme using an assumed identity. It can take years to correct the credit records of the person whose identity has been stolen. Sometimes the debtor's name is obtained from obituary notices.

"Typing Services," "Petition Mills," and "Credit Repair Scams"

Many low-income or debt-ridden individuals are victimized by companies that promise to erase the person's poor credit record or who offer some other bogus financial service. The company may claim to be a "renter's rights" service that settles landlord-tenant disputes. Sometimes the debtor does not know that a bankruptcy petition is being filed. These improper petitions often contain numerous false statements.

Abusive Chapter 7 Bankruptcies

Filing for Chapter 7 is sometimes known as "total bankruptcy" or "last resort bankruptcy." Most or all of the petitioner's debts are discharged in a Chapter 7 filing, as opposed to Chapter 13 which allows some debt protection but requires full or partial payment of most debts. If the petitioner can fund a Chapter 13 plan or has an option other than Chapter 7's last resort, the petition is judged fraudulent (See *In re* Fitzgerald 191 F. 95 and *In re Granada,* 115 B.R. 702).

False Discharges

Not all debts are dischargeable under the law. Child support and alimony are no longer dischargeable. State court actions to establish, modify, or collect child support and alimony are no longer stayed by the bankruptcy automatic stay. Alimony and child support claims are ranked ahead of all general unsecured creditors. Judicial liens for alimony, support, and maintenance are no longer avoidable. Additionally, student loans are no longer dischargeable in bankruptcy unless 7 years old. Federal income taxes *are* dischargeable provided that the debt: is older than 3 years, was filed more than 2 years prior to the bankruptcy, and was assessed more than 120 days before the petition filing date.

The Role of the Trustee

In Chapter 7 cases, Section 704 of the code spells out all duties of the trustee, which include reducing the property of the estate to cash, investigating claims filed by creditors, filing reports, paying creditors, and investigating the financial affairs of the debtor. The code also provides that the trustee "shall ... investigate the financial affairs of the debtor."

Chapter 11 expands the Section 704 duties by allowing trustees to operate the debtor's business. Pursuant to Sections 1106 and 1108, Chapter 11 trustees can take control of the debtor's business, make decisions regarding the operations of the business, hire and fire employees, and attempt to retain or enhance the value of the business until it can be sold or reorganized. Sections 1106(a)(3) and (a)(4) state:

> *A trustee shall ... except to the extent that the court orders otherwise, investigate the acts, conduct, assets, liabilities, and financial condition of the debtor, the operation of the debtor's business and the desirability of the continuance of such business and ... as soon as practicable ... file a statement of any investigation conducted ... including any fact ascertained pertaining to fraud, dishonesty, incompetence, misconduct, mismanagement, or irregularity in the management of the affairs of the debtor, or to a cause of action available to the estate ....*

Investigation by the Trustee

The trustee's power enables him to gather financial information from various sources including the debtor's attorneys and accountants. A trustee steps into the shoes of the debtor, which allows him the opportunity to break the attorney-client privilege. Attorneys might attempt to raise this privilege as a defense to providing information, but they are usually unsuccessful in this regard. Since the trustee is now the client, he must be able to understand what legal actions need to be taken. Therefore, it is imperative that the debtor's attorney cooperates with the trustee. The trustee also should have access to the accountant's work papers, tax returns, and client documents in their possession, which might provide the trustee and creditors with the opportunity to locate and recover hidden assets. Another useful tool at the trustee's disposal is the power to have access to debtor's records that are in the possession of the criminal authorities. Since the trustee steps into the shoes of the debtor, he has the right to inspect and use these records to conduct the business affairs of the debtor.

Case Study

Robert Brennan, who sold penny stocks on television in the 1980's, was convicted in federal court in April 2001 for money laundering and bankruptcy fraud. Brennan was charged with failing to list $4.5 million in assets in a bankruptcy filed in April 1995. Some $525,000 of the assets was in casino chips, which prosecutors charged Brennan had hoarded in anticipation of the bankruptcy; the remaining assets were in municipal bonds. Despite having filed for bankruptcy, Brennan continued to live a lavish life, including around-the-world trips in a private jet, ocean cruises, and second homes in Florida and New York.

Sources:
"Bankruptcy Fraud Rises as Economy Falls, Survey Discloses That Overseers Know of Fraud." *PR Newswire*, September 10, 2001.

Buck, R., J.D., CPA. *"Tax Law Tips."*

Goode, R.M. *"Commercial Law, Chapter 34, Principles of Insolvency Law."* East Rutherford, NJ: Penguin Putnam Inc., 1982.

Hanley, Robert. "Former Penny-Stock Financier is Guilty of Money Laundering and Bankruptcy Fraud." *The New York Times,* April 17, 2001.

"Prepared Testimony by Gary Klein Senior Attorney On Behalf Of the National Consumer Law Center before the Senate Committee on Banking, Housing and Urban Affairs. Bankruptcy Reform: Financial Services Issues." *Federal News Service,* March 25, 1999.

BCCI

BCCI's history and criminality are traceable to the personality of its founder, Agha Hasan Abedi. Abedi rose to prominence working for the Habib family of India, who established a bank in Bombay, India and moved their bank to Pakistan when the nation was formed in 1947. In 1958 Abedi left Habib Bank and assembled investors to form United Bank. Within ten years, United Bank became the second largest bank in Pakistan. Abedi continued the strategies he had learned at Habib: a close knit family structure for management, high salaries and benefits to motivate employees, unusually luxurious offices for the purpose of impressing customers, aggressive expansion, beginning with the Middle East, and a refusal to live within the constraints of governments. Abedi's earliest successes were largely the result of his having recognized the importance in Pakistan of providing payoffs or other under-the-table services to Pakistani officials, especially the leadership of any current governing party. But by the early 1970's, there was an ongoing tension between Abedi's ambition to move beyond Pakistan, and that of the Pakistani government to keep Pakistani institutions generally and Abedi's bank specifically under its control.

Previously, a network of national banks and savings banks mainly conducted international banking. Abedi envisioned a global bank that connected developing and industrialized nations. BCCI would be the first truly international bank. Abedi's relationship with the Sheikh of Abu Dhabi and the Al Nahayan family ultimately made BCCI possible. Abu Dhabi is the largest and wealthiest member of the United Arab Emirates, an oil-rich federation of sheikhdoms with a combined population of fewer than 1.5 million, bordering on Saudi Arabia and Oman, with one of the world's highest standards of living as a result of oil wealth.

Throughout the first critical decade of BCCI's eighteen year existence, as much as 50% of BCCI's overall assets were from Abu Dhabi and the Al Nayhan family, who were earning about $750 million a year in oil revenues in the early 1970's, an amount that rose to nearly $10 billion a year by the end of the decade. Until the formation of a separate affiliate, the Bank of Credit and Commerce Emirates (BCCE), BCCI functioned as the official bank for the Gulf emirates, and handled a substantial portion of Abu Dhabi's oil revenues. Sheikh Zayed received the prestige and benefits of having people all over the world believe it was his bank, without his own funds being at risk Thus, rather than being a major investor in BCCI, in the early years, Abu Dhabi only agreed to place extremely large sums of money as deposits at the bank, which BCCI used in lieu of capital. With

Abedi relying on the Sheikh's resources to finance his rapid expansion, BCCI's finances quickly became so intermingled with the finances of Abu Dhabi that it was difficult even for BCCI insiders to determine where one left off and the other began.

BCCI's Protocol Department

To funnel corruption payments, Abedi established a large protocol department at BCCI. According to Nazir Chinoy, branch manager of BCCI in Pakistan, in 1978 the protocol department's job was "to establish and further the rapport with the sheiks of and ruling families of Dubai and Abu Dhabi." In 1978, the expenses of the protocol department were about 300,000 rupees a month—about $600,000 a year—rising to $2.5 million a year by the early 1980's, and as high as $10 million a year at the height of BCCI's success.

BCCI's aggressive drive for expansion was necessitated by a financial strategy that pursued asset growth, rather than profitability, as the key to success. In short, BCCI had a cash flow problem. And in fact, steadily rising deposits made BCCI's financial obligations even greater, because protecting those assets demanded the company show greater amounts of retained capital.

BCCI's expansion into American banking circles was boosted in 1978, when the company engaged Washington attorney and former U.S. government official Clark Clifford and his law partner, Robert Altman as American counsels. Eventually BCCI took over four U.S. banks, one of which later became First American Bankshares Inc. When questions were raised about First American's solvency, Clifford and Altman assured regulators the bank was not affiliated with BCCI in any fashion that would put First American at risk. In 1991, after federal indictments were issued against BCCI and the relationship between it and First American was revealed, Clifford and Altman resigned their positions on the board of First American. They were indicted in 1992 on federal and New York state charges of bribery. A New York judge dropped the state charges against Clifford, citing his age and deteriorating health. Altman was subsequently acquitted after a four-month trial in New York. Later the two men forfeited $5 million to settle Federal Reserve Board charges that they knew BCCI owned First American and had lied about it to bank inspectors.

Abedi built his organization to provide as little information as possible to his underlings. Officers in one operation knew little about the function of officers in other areas. He bribed and manipulated auditors, dividing his annual audits between Ernst & Whinney and Price Waterhouse, with each firm examining pieces of the business without getting the whole picture. The BCCI umbrella was composed of multiple layers of entities related one a series of holding companies, affiliates, subsidiaries, banks-within-banks, insider dealings and nominee relationships. By fracturing the corporate structure, record keeping, regulatory review, and audits, the company evaded ordinary legal restrictions on the movement of capital and goods. Abedi and his insiders used shell corporations, bank confidentiality and secrecy havens, front men and nominees; back-to-back financial documentation against BCCI controlled entities, kickbacks and bribes, intimidation of witnesses, and retention of well-placed insiders to discourage governmental action.

According to the U.S. government's report on the affair, "Adding to the inherent problem of investigating the largest case of organized crime in history, spanning over some 72 nations, has been the destruction of documents at BCCI and its affiliates by shredding and arson; document backdating and falsification; the removal of most key documents from London to Abu Dhabi in 1990; the refusal of authorities in the United Kingdom and in the Grand Caymans to share information with Congress and other U.S. investigators as a consequence of their interpretation of local bank confidentiality and privacy laws; the inability to question Abedi due to his stroke; the inability to question BCCI's other key officials due to their incarceration and segregation in Abu Dhabi by Abu Dhabi officialdom since July 5, 1991; and BCCI's haphazard method of record-keeping."

Nevertheless investigators found ample evidence for a range of crimes, including fraud by BCCI and BCCI customers involving billions of dollars; money laundering in Europe, Africa, Asia, and the America; BCCI's bribery of officials in most of those locations; its support of terrorism, arms trafficking, and the sale of nuclear technologies; its management of prostitution; its commission and facilitation of income tax evasion, smuggling, and illegal immigration; its illicit purchases of banks and real estate; and a panoply of financial crimes limited only by the imagination of its officers and customers.

As Manhattan prosecutor Robert Morgenthau described in his indictment against BCCI of July 29, 1991, to whose first six counts BCCI's liquidators plead guilty as part of the December, 1991 plea agreement:

> *[BCCI's] scheme was premised on the fact that banks rely on credit. The essence of the scheme was to convince depositors and other banking and financial institutions, by means of false pretenses, representations, and promises that the BCC Group was a safe financial repository and institution for funds, and thereby defendants acted to persuade depositors and banking and other financial institutions to provide the BCC Group banks with deposits and credit.*

The New York District Attorney found that among the major actions taken by BCCI to carry out its fraud were:

- Employing the ruling families of a number of Middle Eastern states as nominees for BCCI, who pretended to be at risk in BCCI but who were in fact guaranteed to be held harmless by BCCI for any actual losses.
- Using bank secrecy havens including Luxembourg and the Cayman Islands to avoid regulation on a consolidated basis by any single regulator of BCCI, and thereby to permit BCCI to transfer assets and liabilities from bank to bank as needed to conceal BCCI's true economic status.
- Paying bribes and kickbacks to agents of other banking and financial institutions, thereby avoiding the scrutiny of regulators.

The Sandstorm Report

An insider's account of BCCI's fraud created by BCCI's own auditors, Price Waterhouse, and provided to the Bank of England dated June 22, 1991, the "Sandstorm Report," was the final evidence that lead to the shutdown of BCCI globally on July 5, 1991. That draft report, based on a review of banking records from several countries and interviews carried out through the spring of 1991, found evidence of "widespread fraud and manipulation," at BCCI, reflecting "the general scale and complexity of the deceptions which have undoubtedly taken place over many years. This information was developed when Price Waterhouse investigated some $600 million of BCCI deposits not recorded in

BCCI's books. Price Waterhouse found significant account manipulation at BCCI beginning as early as 1976.

In 1985, after rumors of BCCI's losses in options trading reached bank regulators, Luxembourg bank regulators asked BCCI to provide an audited review of its central treasury activities. BCCI selected Price Waterhouse Cayman to perform the work, which determined in early 1986 that significant losses had been incurred and not recorded. According to Price Waterhouse, it concluded then that the losses and lack of record keeping were due to "incompetence." However, in the 1991 Sandstorm Report, Price Waterhouse found that "with the benefit of hindsight, it appears more sinister in that it now seems to have been a deliberate way to fictitiously inflate income." In its 1991 review, Price Waterhouse found that among the specific techniques used by BCCI to hide its losses were:

- Misappropriation of deposits without depositor's knowledge to provide funds to adjust non-performing and bogus loan accounts, and Treasury losses.
- Misappropriation of external funds deposited under trust with Sandstorm [BCCI] and Fork [ICIC] to be managed on behalf of a few prominent people who are also shareholders of [BCCI] Holdings.
- The creation of loans with no commercial substance in the names of people without their knowledge.
- Selling certificates of deposit placed with the Central Treasury without informing the depositors, and using the proceeds to fund adjustments.
- Routing funds through [ICIC], LOANS, KIFCO, SDCC and other affiliates and third parties to make adjustments prior to accounting reference dates and audit confirmation dates, which were often reversed at a later date.

In 1991, BCCI's liquidators pled guilty to having engaged in a criminal conspiracy through financial fraud, and thereby constituting a Racketeering Influenced and Corrupt Organization (RICO), whose entire assets, legitimate and illegitimate, were subject to confiscation by the government. Specific crimes admitted to by BCCI's liquidators in the agreement included:

- Seeking deposits of drug proceeds and laundering drug money

- Seeking deposits from persons attempt to evade U.S. income taxes
- Using "straws" and nominees to acquire control of U.S. financial institutions
- Lying to regulators and falsifying regulatory documents
- Creating false bank records and engaging in sham transactions to deceive regulators

Related Entries:

BRIBERY
CORRUPTION, OCCUPATIONAL
CORRUPTION, PUBLIC
FINANCIAL INSTITUTION FRAUD
FINANCIAL STATEMENT FRAUD
MONEY LAUNDERING

BEHAVIORAL THEORY OF FRAUD

The behavioral theory of fraud draws on the work of psychologist B.F. Skinner and others, a school of thought collectively known as Behaviorism. Skinner asserted that human beings act in certain ways because they have been conditioned to do so by their experience. Every act is prompted by a *stimulus*, which produces a *response.* With repetition, the response becomes *conditioned* to appear whenever the stimulus appears. A *conditioned response* is one that has been reinforced by experience; unless there is some interference, the stimulus will prompt the same conditioned response each time it appears. Many aspects of fraud theory, including Dr. Donald Cressey's Fraud Triangle, draw heavily on behaviorist notions.

According to Skinner, neither reprehensible behavior nor responsible behaviors are innate; the behaviors are learned. A man helps his neighbor because he has learned that doing so earns the neighbor's appreciation, and may ultimately benefit himself, either directly—the neighbor returns the favor later—or indirectly, by strengthening the community at large. The act of helping is a learned behavior. The same man steals office supplies from his company because he has learned that stealing is an easy way to obtain the goods, he is not likely to be caught, and, even if he does, the infraction may not be prosecuted. The need for the supplies is the stimulus; stealing them is the conditioned response. The act is reinforced by coworkers who steal, and who declare, "It is not wrong. Everybody does it."

Behavioral theory also applies to the following scenario: A fictional government employee named Beth needed money for an emergency, so she used her government credit card to make personal purchases. When no one detected her action, the employee charged another $4,500 in personal items to the card. The emergency is the stimulus, a situation that demanded a response from the woman. In this case she responded by charging the money to her employer's credit card. As an act of behavior, the event was positively reinforced because the money solved the crisis, there were no adverse effects, and Beth rationalized her decision.

There is now a conditioned response in Beth's mind linking the credit card and ready money. Beth has good evidence that a simple act brought her exactly what she needed. Later she charges $4,500 more to the agency card. Maybe she said to herself, "I will pay back the money eventually, so it is not really stealing," or "No one is being hurt here." That is how many fraudsters rationalize their acts. The rationalizations allay any feelings of guilt and reinforce the urge to steal.

Behaviorists are sometimes accused of disregarding a person's free will and of portraying people as little more than pigeons pecking dots for food. In fact, behaviorists would regard Beth's act of theft as a complex behavior, one finally determined by Beth's free will. Skinner called the process of molding voluntary behaviors *operant conditioning.* Operant behaviors, unlike simple reflexes, occur as a result of an individual's mental state interacting with the environment.

If Beth were to later need money for a house payment, her first thought may well be the agency credit card, since she has already completed two transactions successfully and reinforced her mental tendency to steal with rationalizations. However, Beth may have other options: she can borrow from her parents or friends, she can ask for a salary advance, obtain a forbearance on the past-due payment, or apply for a credit card in her own name.

Behaviorists aim to condition Beth's behavior so that she does not choose theft as a response to her debt. Internal controls are the foundational component of every fraud prevention program—if the agency's procedures and supervision automatically stop personal uses of the credit card, Beth does not have the option. At the least she will have to work harder to overcome the controls, making the choice less attractive. Well-publicized penalties for fraud also have some conditioning effect, but as the rising incidence of fraud shows, punishment alone is not sufficient. Punishment in all of its forms is what Skinner called *negative reinforcement.* A behavior is conditioned by associating it with a negative response: every time a pigeon pecks a green button, he is shocked; every time people are caught embezzling, they lose money and freedom. To be successful, a negative reinforcement must be consistently applied. Take away the punishment or the fear of punishment, and the behavior returns. In this view, many legal sanctions for fraud are applied too inconsistently and sometimes too weakly.

The other way to condition behavior (in Skinner's view the most likely way to succeed) is *positive reinforcement.* Each time the pigeon pecks a red light, he gets food; each time a person asks for help, they receive aid. Thus, any fraud-prevention program ought to include rewards for good behaviors: bonuses and other performance incentives, company benefits, recreational activities, recognition, and incentives for preventing or exposing fraud (for example: a whistleblower program). Like negative reinforcement, positive conditioning requires a sustained application—take away the incentive and the behavior gradually fades. But over the long haul, positive conditioning provides a more effective, lasting effect than punishment. And where punishment or restraint must be more or less constantly applied, positive reinforcement requires only an occasional application. In short, a successful fraud-prevention program, according to behavioral theory, recommends internal controls that place funds beyond people's reach, coupled with positive conditioning that enhances people's strengths.

Sources:
Skinner, B.F. Learning and Cognition.

Staddon, J. "On Responsibility and Punishment." *FEMA, The Atlantic Monthly,* February 1995. Vol. 275; No. 2; Pg. 8.

Related Entries:

ATTITUDES TOWARD AND PERCEPTIONS OF FRAUD
CAUSES OF FRAUD

BENFORD'S LAW

In the April/May 1994 issue of the ACFE's *The White Paper*, Mark J. Nigrini, Ph.D., explained a novel method of detecting fraudulent activity— Benford's Law. The "law" is a mathematical principle that holds that the distribution of the initial digits in natural numbers is not random but rather follows a predictable pattern.

During the 1930's, a physicist named Dr. Frank Benford noticed that the pages of logarithm table books covering the initial digits 1 and 2 were more worn and dirty than the pages for initial digits 7, 8, and 9. Benford speculated that scientists were looking up the logs of numbers starting with the digits 1 and 2 more often because there were more numbers that began with those digits. One might suppose that the first digit in a large number would have an equal chance of being 1 through 9. However, Benford found the following were the actual percentages:

Position in Number		
Digit	1st	2nd
0	-	11.9%
1	30.1%	11.4%
2	17.6%	10.9%
3	12.5%	10.4%
4	9.7%	10.0%
5	7.9%	9.7%
6	6.7%	9.3%
7	5.8%	9.0%
8	5.1%	8.8%
9	4.6%	8.5%

Benford's Law distinguishes between "natural" and "non-natural" numbers. Natural numbers are those numbers that are not ordered in a particular numbering scheme and are *not* generated from a random number system. For example, most accounts payable files will be populated by dollar values that are natural numbers. On the other hand, Social Security numbers and telephone numbers—non-natural numbers—are designed systematically to convey information that restricts the natural nature of the number.

The expected occurrence for the first digit is:

Probability (x is the first digit) = Log10 (x+1) – Log10 (x)

For decades, Benford's discovery lay dormant. Without computers, it was uneconomical and cumbersome to apply it in any practical way. The Law made its debut in fraud examination in 1988, when Dr. Charles Carslaw used it to analyze income reports from a number of businesses. Carslaw checked the frequency of initial digits in the income figures against the expected frequencies according to Benford's Law. He concluded there is substantial evidence that management actively rounds income numbers upward—confirming scientifically what most people had suspected.

In the 1990's, Dr. Nigrini and others showed that Benford's Law could be used to detect tax evasion, economic falsifications, and payroll fraud. In each instance, research confirmed that the numbers used by fraudsters did NOT fit the patterns of natural numbers found in Benford's Law. Continuing efforts have shown it is possible to detect fraudulent numbers (or errors in bookkeeping or accounting) by comparing the frequency of the appearance of initial digits in a list of numbers to those anticipated by Benford.

How to Perform a Benford's Law Analysis

In the late 1990's, David Banks and Stephen Tedrick adapted Microsoft Excel to perform Benford's Law analyses. Banks and Tedrick developed an Excel macro, a program designed to execute a series of commands within a software package such as Excel, which extracted the left-most four digits from numbers in a list and placed them each in a separate column. The technique can be used to analyze tables containing more than 50,000 records. (The Office 2000 version of Excel will run up to 65,536 records.) Below, is Banks' guide to performing a Benford analysis, adapted from its appearance in *The White Paper* (Sep/Oct 1999).

Performing a Benford's Law analysis with Excel is actually a five-step process. First, select a population for analysis. Second, assemble the raw data in a format acceptable to Excel. Third, non-numeric leading characters (such as letters or dollar signs) and decimal points. Fourth, extract leading digits and store for analysis. Fifth, execute the final analysis. While these steps can be executed manually in Excel, the task is shortened through the use of Excel macros. Macros are especially useful for the execution of complex repetitive tasks.

Select a Population

To perform a useful analysis, the data should be natural numbers. Most experts agree that dates are not natural numbers. Attempts to analyze dates normally are frustrating and often futile. Invoice numbers may or may not be natural but it is unlikely that a Benford's Law analysis will generate any useful information. This leaves the fraud examiner or auditor with the dollar amount on invoices or other instruments such as checks, financial reports, and receipts as possible natural numbers suitable for analysis.

NOTE:

There are constraints on dollar amounts. For instance, in one case there was a $500 per transaction limit in the manufacturing plant fund, which restricted the appearance of six through nine as initial digits. When manipulating such amounts, there is a tendency to maximize the amounts, thus leading to an abundance of transactions with dollar amounts slightly under $500, which could skew the data. In any case, the auditor or fraud examiner must select a population of data that *should* be completely natural.

Assemble Raw Data

Fortunately, beginning with Excel's "FILE OPEN" command, the program leads the user through a series of steps that nearly guarantee the successful use of most common data files. Generally, there should be no problems with Microsoft's Excel and Access file types and most Lotus, Comma Delimited Files (files that are used to transmit information between brands of spreadsheets), and text files are also readable by Excel with minor coaxing.

Cleaning Raw Data

Many data files contain non-numeric characters (such as letters or dollar signs) and decimal points and spaces that can impede the analysis. Excel contains functions,

"=CLEAN" and "=TRIM," that can be used to remove these characters. "=CLEAN" removes extraneous characters from the designated cell and "=TRIM" removes leading spaces. Decimal points are eliminated by multiplying each cell by 100 and then using Excel's "FORMAT" command to format the column with "0" decimal places.

While it is possible to perform each of the above functions manually, using a macro will shorten the process. Enter the macros into one sheet of the spreadsheet. On another sheet of the spreadsheet, enter the data to be tested in the "B" column of the spreadsheet. Place the cursor on the topmost cell of the data and execute the command through the "TOOLS," "MACRO," "MACROS," and "RUN" command sequence. The result is a cleaned and sorted data file ready for analysis.

Digital Extraction

This step lies at the heart of the analysis. The object is to separate each left-most digit, placing it in a separate column where it can then be analyzed. This is accomplished using Excel's "=LEFT" function. Because Excel will only apply the "=LEFT" function to non-numeric strings, it is necessary to use functions under the "EDIT" command to convert the numeric string to a non-numeric string; after using the "=LEFT" function, the macro converts the non-numeric string back to a numeric string. Again, this macro should be entered in one sheet of the Excel spreadsheet. The cleaned data should be in the "B" column of another spreadsheet. Place the cursor on the topmost cell of the data and execute the "TOOLS," "MACRO," "MACROS," and "RUN" command sequence. The result will be four columns, each containing leading digits from the target data column.

Execute Final Analysis

The final analysis consists of three steps: data summarization, graphing, and interpretation. While it is possible to use a macro to summarize the data, it is just as easy to sort each of the columns of data produced in the digital extraction using the row numbers to calculate frequencies of appearance. Then produce a line graph using Excel's Chart Wizard (usually found on the standard toolbar). Finally, examine the digital frequencies against those predicted by Benford to reveal any deviations.

NOTE:

Benford's Law cannot be used to extract specific fraudulent transactions, nor can it differentiate between fraudulently manipulated data and legitimate changes. However, fraud examiners and auditors can use Benford's Law as a tool for discovering fraud schemes. For more information, see Nigrini's article in *The White Paper*, (April/May 1994); Banks' article in *The White Paper* (Sep./Oct. 1999); and Nigrini's book, *Digital Analysis Using Benford's Law*, published by Global Audit Publications.

BENNETT, JOHN G., JR.

John G. Bennett Jr. parlayed a knack for fundraising into a Ponzi scheme that netted $354 million. As head of the Foundation for New Era Philanthropy, Bennett collected money from nonprofit organizations such as the American Red Cross, cultural institutions like the Philadelphia Orchestra, evangelical Christian organizations, and colleges and universities. He promised he could double the organizations' money in six months' time, due to an anonymous donor who had agreed to match funds dollar for dollar.

Bennett began building his professional reputation among the burgeoning drug-prevention movement, which was being financed in large part by government grants. He was appointed to a commission by the governor of Pennsylvania, and served several years in state government before leaving to start a private company that promised to help organizations acquire government funds.

Bennett's business career ebbed and flowed throughout the 1970's and 1980's. But he continued to expand his contacts in the world of nonprofit fundraising, specifically within the loose-knit community of evangelical Christian organizations. In 1989, he formed New Era, an organization that conducted fundraising seminars for Christian nonprofits. Bennett also began his Ponzi scheme at this time. Facing hundreds of thousands in overdrafts at his two main banks, and with his businesses ailing, Bennett approached Dr. John Templeton Jr.—a Philadelphia physician and son of the famous investment fund director John Templeton—with an idea. Bennett said that he had talked to "a wealthy individual in our community" who would match donations dollar for dollar if Bennett could find 20 people willing to donate $5,000 each.

Bennett personally drew no salary from New Era, a condition he trumpeted in his banter, but his "consulting business" received as much as $1 million a year. Over time Bennett expanded the donations program until New Era's only function was taking in funds and matching them with funds from the "anonymous donor." In 1989, when first incorporated as a foundation, it took in only $306,000. By 1993, the take rose to $41.2 million; to $160 million in 1994; and $122 million in the first four months of 1995, before federal securities regulators shut down New Era.

Bennett's Ponzi scheme was doomed as all Ponzis are. New Era Philanthropy had virtually no true income; the constant scramble for cash left the company's accounts (mainly securities at Prudential) with a negligible balance, so there wasn't even interest income. There was only the "anonymous donor," or "donors"—Bennett eventually expanded his story to include a committee of *six* anonymous donors, to explain why he could match $50 million deposits. Luckily Bennett was drawing new participants with tens of millions to put into the scheme, but the flow could not have held out much longer. Extrapolating from the $122 million he collected in the first four months of 1995, he might have collected $500 million by year's end, meaning he would have to raise $1 billion in the following year to match the deposits.

Time alone would have caused the Bennett scheme to fail, but the inevitable was assisted by Steve Stecklow's investigative reporting for the *Wall Street Journal*, and by the protestations (both public and private) raised by an accounting professor at a small Michigan university named Albert Meyer. It was Meyer who alerted Stecklow and others that New Era Philanthropy was in all likelihood a Ponzi scheme. Meyer provided accounting services to his university, which invested in New Era's program. The more Meyer looked into New Era's operations, the more John Bennett stonewalled him, and the more Meyer questioned Bennett's operation.

Meyer posed several important questions:

- Why was New Era's audit firm issuing an *audit* report when the public disclosure said the firm had only conducted a *review* of New Era books?
- Why was there a $1.1 million transfer to "non-marketable equity securities" with no other documentation of where the money went and how it would be returned?

- Why was there a transfer in excess of $1 million to an entity called Bennett Group International? Why were not participants' funds (the money each nonprofit deposited into New Era accounts) labeled a liability on the company's balance sheet, since the funds had to be matched and paid at the end of every six months?
- Finally, why did an organization that claimed to have millions at Prudential Securities only draw $33,000 in interest dividends during 1993? (If the account balance averaged $10 million during the year—a modest sum given New Era's scope—dividends would have totaled between $600,000 and $1 million.)

Meyer prompted Stecklow and the Securities and Exchange Commission to investigate New Era. Prudential Securities dealt the final blow by issuing a margin call on Bennett's accounts, which he could not cover.

Bennett proved a recalcitrant defendant. In mid-May 1995, he publicly confessed to his New Era staff that there had never been any anonymous donors. He explained he had concocted the story in hopes that the idea would catch on and he would operate a legitimate foundation. However, Bennett made a videotape, sent to his supporters in October 1995, in which he lamented that some of the anonymous donors had suffered because of his arrest; he addressed the donors directly in the video, despite having denied their existence earlier.

In court, Bennett mounted an insanity defense. He claimed that he had suffered hallucinations that convinced him the donors existed. He described ghostly business meetings in which he would convene the gathering and the donors would "simply appear" around the table. He claimed he had experienced visions since an automobile wreck in the 1970's. Three court psychiatrists conducted extensive tests that showed Bennett was faking. Bennett was convicted and sentenced to 12 years in federal prison, where he continued to issue statements that he had never intended to defraud anyone.

Source:
Wells, J., CFE, CPA. "Loaves and Fishes: John Bennett." *Frankensteins of Fraud.* Austin, TX: Obsidian Publishing Co., 2000.

Related Entries:

PONZI SCHEME
SECURITIES FRAUD

BENNETT, PATRICK, AND GWEN

Patrick and Gwen Bennett of Syracuse, New York (no relation to John G. Bennett, Jr.) have been credited by prosecutors with running the largest Ponzi scheme in history, $1 billion strong. Patrick is the son of Edmund and Kathleen Bennett. The family claims entrée to upstate New York's most elite circles, a standing fostered by their frequent appearances at the Vernon Downs racetrack, in which Patrick and Gwen bought a $4 million stake.

In his role as director of Bennett Funding, Patrick played live-action Monopoly with investors' money. The entire Bennett clan got in on the game. Younger brother Michael bought the Hotel Syracuse, $71 million worth of American Gaming Enterprises, and Harold's Club, a failing hotel in Reno that soon finished failing. Patrick bought the Comfort Suites near the family racetrack. Edmund and Kathleen splurged $600,000 on a yacht and its skipper, while the family trust acquired a 300-acre swatch of the Thousand Islands.

The buying spree was supported by the securities, which Patrick and his wife Gwen sold through Bennett Funding. The securities were supposed to represent a revenue stream from government offices, like the New York Transit Authority, who preferred to lease their office equipment rather than purchase it outright. The Bennett's contracted to fill a $100,000 lease with the NYTA, for example. They would then sell the lease for $88,000 cash. They hoped to make up the difference by placing smart investments, which would return more than the 7 to 12% they had given up to the lease purchasers. As NYTA made its lease payments, Bennett Funding passed the money on to its buyer, so the buyer never risked anything—their $88,000 lease would return them $100,000 in a year's time.

In some cases, the Bennett's actually leased copiers and fax machines to the agencies that used them. Other times they bought leases from a broker and then resold them. Market talk said these lease securities were gold—they were backed, in a manner of speaking, by the American government's appetite for copiers, a hunger that was not likely to recede any time soon. Apparently no one questioned whether the equipment was really being sent. In fact, Bennett Funding began selling phony leases with no contracts backing them, or they sold real leases to as many as seven different investors. Like the infamous mortgage traders of the 80's, the Bennett's were simply pushing paper. (The government lease scam is a popular one. A Millburn, New Jersey outfit named First Interregional Equity was recently convicted of selling equipment leases over and over again. Prosecutors called FIE "the baby Bennett," since the 10-year scam netted just 7,000 investors and about $120 million.)

But while the Bennett family celebrated their clients' naiveté with a feast of self-indulgence and shopping sprees that picked up hotels like they really were plastic game pieces, they were also amassing world-class, real-world debt. By 1995, Bennett Funding was receiving $13 million a month from its lease contracts. But they *owed $30 million a month* to the people who had bought the leases. When the company foundered, the price tag approached $1 billion dollars. Over 12,000 investors lost all their money.

Related Entries:

PONZI SCHEME

SECURITIES FRAUD

BID-RIGGING

See, CORRUPTION, OCCUPATIONAL; CONTRACT AND PROCUREMENT FRAUD

BILLING SCHEMES

Billing schemes are a method of fraudulent disbursement, which is itself a form of asset misappropriation, the most common method of occupational fraud and abuse. Billing schemes are the most popular method of fraudulent disbursement because most of a business's disbursements are made within the purchasing cycle.

There are three principal types of billing schemes: personal purchases made with company funds, false invoicing via shell companies, and false invoicing via vendors. In the simplest version, employees purchase goods or services on behalf of the company and use the goods or services themselves. Keeping the purchase below a limit of internal controls so the purchase is never questioned sometimes hides the abuse.

A shell company scheme is made particularly easy if the perpetrator has unsupervised authority to approve invoices. (*See* SHELL COMPANY) Most shell company schemes involve the purchase of services, rather than goods, because intangible services are harder to verify. In what is known as a "pass-through" scheme, the perpetrator uses his shell company to purchase legitimate merchandise, then resells the merchandise to his employer at an inflated price.

Vendor accounts are also a favorite target of workplace fraudsters. Some employees generate false invoices in the names of legitimate third-party vendors—the vendors may be unaware of the scheme, they may be participants, or they may agree to keep silent. In "pay-and-return schemes," employees intentionally mishandle vendor payments. For instance, a clerk might intentionally pay an invoice twice, then request that the vendor return one of the checks. The clerk intercepts the returned check and converts it to cash, perhaps by depositing it into a shell account.

Billing Scheme Red Flags

TYPE OF SCHEME	FRAUD INDICATORS
Fictitious vendors	Vendors and employees with matching addresses More than one vendor with the same address Vendors with only post office box addresses
Overbilling	Unusual or "one-time" extra charges

Conflict of interest	Vendors with employees who are employee family members An unusually high occurrence rate of complaints Complaints about specific vendors Higher prices and/or substandard quality

Sample Audit Program

The following audit program may be beneficial in detecting red flags association with billing schemes:

- Does the company have a purchasing department? If yes, is it independent of (1) the accounting department, (2) the receiving department, and (3) the shipping department?
- Are purchases made only after the respective department heads sign purchase requisitions?
- Are purchases made by means of purchase orders sent to vendors for all purchases or only for purchases over a predetermined dollar limit?
- Do purchase orders specify a description of items, quantity, price, terms, delivery requirements, and dates?
- Is a list of unfilled purchase orders maintained and reviewed periodically?
- Are purchase order forms prenumbered and is the sequence accounted for periodically?
- Does the client maintain an approved vendors list?
- Are items purchased only after competitive bids are obtained? If so, are competitive bids obtained for all purchases or only for purchases over a predetermined dollar limit?
- Is a log maintained of all receipts?
- Does the receiving department prepare receiving reports for all items received? If yes, are receiving reports (1) prepared for all items, (2) prepared only for items that have purchase orders, or (3) renumbered?

- At the time the items are received, does someone independent of the purchasing department check the merchandise before acceptance for description, quantity, and condition?
- Are copies of receiving reports (1) furnished to the accounting department, (2) furnished to the purchasing department, and (3) filed in the receiving department?
- Are receipts under blanket purchase orders monitored, and are quantities exceeding authorized totals returned to the vendor?
- Are procedures adequate for the proper accounting for partial deliveries of purchase orders?
- Are purchasing and receiving functions separate from invoice processing, accounts payable, and general ledger functions?
- Are vendors' invoices, receiving reports, and purchase orders matched before the related liability is recorded?
- Are invoices checked for prices, extensions, footings, freight charges, allowances, and credit terms?
- Are controls adequate to ensure that all available discounts are taken?
- Are purchases recorded in a purchase register or voucher register before being processed through cash disbursements?
- Does a responsible employee assign the appropriate general ledger account distribution to which the invoices are to be posted?
- Are procedures adequate to ensure that invoices have been processed before payment and to prevent duplicate payment (e.g., a block stamp)?
- Does a responsible official approve invoices for payment?
- Are procedures adequate to ensure that merchandise purchased for direct delivery to customers is promptly billed to the customers and recorded as both a receivable and a payable?
- Are records of goods returned to vendors matched to vendor credit memos?
- Are unmatched receiving reports, purchase orders, and vendors' invoices periodically reviewed and investigated for proper recording?
- Are the accounts payable ledger or voucher register reconciled monthly to the general ledger control accounts?

- Are statements from vendors regularly reviewed and reconciled against recorded liabilities?
- Do adjustments to accounts payable (e.g., writing off of debit balances) require the approval of a designated official?
- Are budgets used? If yes, do responsible officials approve budgets, and are actual expenditures compared with budgeted amounts and variances analyzed and explained?
- If excess inventory purchasing is suspected, then verify that all inventory purchased was received (receiving report) at the proper location. Receiving report or invoice examinations might reveal alternate shipping sites.

Related Entries:

ASSET MISAPPROPRIATION
FRAUDULENT DISBURSEMENTS
OCCUPATIONAL FRAUD AND ABUSE
SHELL COMPANY

BRE-X

In the 1990's, Bre-X announced to the world that it was sitting on a huge gold deposit in Busang, Indonesia. Company reports of the quantities of gold in the deposit helped send the company's stock in the stratosphere. But the story came to a crashing end when it was revealed that gold samples had been faked. The stock crashed, leaving a string of claims of fraud and investor lawsuits against Bre-X, Bresea and their insiders. Bresea is a mineral exploration company based in Calgary, who owned 22% of Bre-X. The claims against Bresea total over U.S. $3 billion.

Investors lost some $6 billion worth of stock value when Bre-X stock became worthless when it was revealed the company's gold mine in Indonesia was a fraud linked to former employees who had tampered with gold samples before they were tested. The chief Bre-X minerals geologist, John Felderhof, who became a multimillionaire by trading shares in a Calgary company behind Canada's biggest gold mining scam was the prosecution's main witness. A documented paper trail from the Indonesia jungle to the Bre-X head office in Calgary established Felderhof's access to crucial information that had not been publicly disclosed.

Both companies sought protection from creditors in May 1997.

As of April 2004, under the terms of the proposed settlement, Bresea would deliver to Deloitte $4.59 million for the settlement of investor actions brought by Bre-X share purchasers pending in the U.S. and Canada (the "Settlement Fund"). After setting aside and holding certain amounts for the payment of legal fees, costs, and disbursements, and creating a reserve for the unlikely event of a future award of court costs in defendants' favor, Deloitte will thereafter distribute the balance of the Settlement Fund to U.S. Bre-X Class Members and to eligible Bre-X share purchasers participating in Canadian investor actions. In addition, Bresea has agreed to pay $1.31 million to Deloitte in consideration for Bresea shares currently held by the Bre-X Trustee.

The Bresea Settlement provides that recoveries obtained from Bre-X/Bresea insiders Jeannette Walsh, the Estate of David G. Walsh, John Felderhof, and Stephen McAnulty in either this Action, class action proceedings pending in Ontario, and certain actions belonging to the Bre-X Trustee will be shared, provided that the Bre-X Trustee obtains an order from the Alberta Bankruptcy Court declaring the injured Bre-X investors are creditors of Bre-X. Recoveries obtained from Bre-X/Bresea insiders Rolando Francisco, Hugh Lyons, John Thorpe, and Paul Kavanagh will not be shared in any event.

Also in the proposed settlement, a pool consisting of shares equal to 10% of the equity of Bresea — now named Sasamat Capital Corp. — would be established for the benefit of U.S. Bresea Class Members. The pool is subject to sharing with certain other claimants against Bresea, including Canadian Bresea share purchasers, class members who opt out of Canadian class action proceedings, U.S. Bre-X class members who opt out of this settlement, and subject to the approval of the Alberta Court (which supervises the Bresea receivership proceeding), persons in the U.S. who purchased Bre-X/Bresea shares after March 26, 1997.

The Bresea Settlement is conditioned on the approval by those courts with jurisdiction over the claims of Bre-X and Bresea share purchasers — the U.S. Court, the Alberta Court, the Ontario Court (which has jurisdiction over Bre-X litigation there), and the

Alberta Bankruptcy Court (which supervises the Bre-X bankruptcy proceeding). The Bresea Settlement is also conditioned on the approval of certain Canadian securities regulators. All approvals, other than final approval by the U.S. Court, have been obtained.

Sources:
Danielson, V. and Whyte, J. *"Bre-X: Gold Today, Gone Tomorrow: Anatomy of the Busang Swindle."* Ontario, Canada: Northern Miner Pr. Ltd., 1997.

Francis, D. *"Bre-X: The Inside Story."* Ontario, Canada: Key Porter Books, 1998.

Goold, D. and Willis, A. *"The Bre-X Fraud."* Ontario, Canada: McClelland & Stewart Inc., 1998.

Walsh, David. "Promoter Caught Up in Gold Mine Scandal." *The New York Times*, June 6, 1998.

Yew, Tom. "Bre-X Defence Says Attack on OSC Valid." *Toronto Star*, November 24, 2001.

Bre-X/Bresea Shareholder Class Action Information Website: brexclass.com/bresea.html

Related Entry:

SECURITIES FRAUD

BRIBERY

Generally, bribery refers to public officials accepting cash, material, or favors in exchange for influence. Cash is the most common offering, though financial instruments, drugs, and sex are also tools of the trade.

Commercial bribery refers to bribes made in the course of business. Particularly in international exchanges, bribery is regarded as an acceptable cost of doing business. In a survey of 34 U.S.-based corporations, company officials admitted to paying $93.7 million in bribes—but the corporations realized $679 billion in sales revenue during the same period. The bribery amounted to a 0.014% transaction fee. The expense can be disguised in financial statements as payments to dummy companies, or to individuals for "consulting or marketing services."

Distinguishing Between Bribery and Acceptable Provisions

Though individual organizations set their own codes of ethics, the distinction between bribes and acceptable provisions can be generally stated. Certain acts or items are allowable, provided that neither party expects a specific act in return. Some items generally allowed include:

- Normal business entertainment items such as meals and beverages.
- Items of minimal value given in connection with sales campaigns and promotions or employee services, safety, or retirement awards.
- Contributions or donations to recognized charitable and nonprofit organizations.
- Items or services with a total value under $100 received within one calendar year.

Case Study—Bribery in the Former Soviet Union

According to an analysis conducted in 1999 by the European Bank for Reconstruction and Development, bribery is often a necessary component of doing business in the nations of the former Soviet Union, particularly the Caucasus nations of Armenia, Azerbaijan, and Georgia.

Georgia extracted the largest amount of bribes as a percentage of annual company revenues at 8.1%. Azerbaijan led the table in terms of paying bribes, with 59.3% of companies operating saying they paid bribes "frequently." The state of Russia fared comparatively well. Of the 3,000 firms in 20 so-called transition countries surveyed by the EBRD, those operating in Russia paid an average 4.1% of their annual revenues on bribes and 29.2% of them said they paid bribes "frequently." (See the chart on the following page.)

COUNTRY	% Bribed "Frequently"	Bribe as % of Annual Revenue
Armenia	40.3	6.8
Azerbaijan	59.3	6.6
Belarus	14.2	3.1
Bulgaria	23.9	3.5
Croatia	17.7	2.1
Czech Republic	26.3	4.5
Estonia	12.9	2.8
Georgia	36.8	8.1
Hungary	31.3	3.5
Kazakstan	23.7	4.7
Kyrgyzstan	26.9	5.5
Lithuania	23.2	4.2
Moldova	33.3	6.1
Poland	32.7	2.5
Romania	50.9	4
Russia	29.2	4.1
Slovakia	34.6	3.7
Slovenia	7.7	3.4
Ukraine	35.3	6.5

In a separate and ongoing project, Daniel Kaufmann, Sanjay Pradhan, and Randi Ryterman have measured corruption on behalf of the World Bank. The group traveled to Albania, Georgia, and Latvia, surveying household members, enterprise managers, and public officials about the costs and private returns of paying bribes to obtain public services, special privileges, and government jobs.

The results were published in 1998. The group found that systemic corruption in these countries, as elsewhere, reduces public welfare and taxes private sector resources. Each country showed particular tendencies. In Georgia, for example, the most common form of corruption is embezzlement of public funds. In Albania and Latvia the most common form is theft of state property. But bribery in procurement is common in all three countries.

Institutional causes of corruption also differ across the three countries, suggesting different priorities for reform. In Albania a weak judiciary is one of the main causes of corruption; regulatory failures are less important. Regulatory failures are more serious in Georgia and Latvia, both in terms of excessive regulations and the discretion granted to regulators enforcing them. In Albania and Latvia bribes account for 7% of revenue in firms that admit to paying them. In Georgia bribes account for 15% of firms' revenue.

Bribery impacts public finances also. A large number of small bribes are paid to officials to avoid paying taxes, customs duties, and other liabilities to the state, reducing fiscal revenues. Other types of bribes (such as unofficial payments to public officials for special privileges, perhaps in exchange for a favorable judicial decision, that do not have direct fiscal implications) may crowd out payment of taxes and other liabilities.

According to a 2001 study conducted by the Economics Institute, the territory of Serbia has a sizable underground economy of bribery and corruption. According to their estimates, at least one million people have been involved in some form of corruption. Their share of the total labor force amounted to 30%. Somewhat more than one half of the participants in this black market performs informal activities every month. If the number of self-employed who performed their activities in the informal sector is added, the total reaches 1.2 million people. In the structure of revenues, the grey economy participates with 18% of total revenues.

Ninety percent of the survey respondents felt compelled to participate in the underground economy as a means of survival and in order to sustain a more normal standard of living.

Tax Revenues Lost As A Result Of Corruption In Albania, Georgia, and Latvia

	Albania	*Georgia*	*Latvia*
Enterprises willing to pay higher taxes if corruption were eliminated	53%	71%	30%
Additional taxes those enterprises would be willing to pay if corruption were eliminated (as percent of total revenue)	11%	22%	15%
Additional taxes all enterprises would be willing to pay if corruption were eliminated (as percent of total revenue)	6%	16%	4%

Source: 1998 World Bank survey of 483 enterprise managers in Latvia (Latvia Facts), 350 managers in Georgia (GORBI), and 356 managers in Albania (ACER).

The group found that corruption disproportionately hurts the poor. In Georgia 14% of households admit to paying bribes; in Latvia the figure is 12%. Although richer households are more likely to pay bribes, the burden of corruption (measured as the fraction of income paid in bribes) is much greater for poorer households. Though the 1998 surveys reported on these three countries in particular, the results may be extrapolated and applied to other countries in the developing world.

Case Study—Bribery in the International Arms Trade

In 1990, an employee of General Electric and an Israeli general were exposed in their ongoing scheme to divert $40 million from U.S. defense contracts with Israel. Herbert Steindler, who worked in GE's marketing department helped arrange a series of disguised payments to accounts controlled by the General Rami Dotan. GE fired Steindler in 1991 and the Israeli government imprisoned General Dotan. Though General Electric officials disavowed knowledge of the scheme, the Defense Department temporarily suspended the corporation's aircraft-engines division's privileges to bid on military contracts. The corporation's status was restored after officials demonstrated it had instituted protocol to prevent fraud in future contracts.

Sources:
Coleman, J. "Caucasus Comes Top In FSU Corporation League." *NEFTE Compass,* November 11, 1999. No. 45, Vol. 8, Pg. 9.

Coleman, J. "The Criminal Elite: Understanding White-Collar Crime." New York: St. Martin's Press, 1998.

Kaufman, D., Pradhan, S., Ryterman, D., "New Frontiers in Diagnosing and Combating Corruption." *The World Bank,* October 1998.

"Pentagon Penalizes GE Over Israel Bribe Scheme." *Chicago Tribune,* June 3 1992.

Related Entries:

CONTRACT AND PROCUREMENT FRAUD
CORRUPTION, OCCUPATIONAL
CORRUPTION, PUBLIC
OCCUPATIONAL FRAUD AND ABUSE

BRINKLEY, JOHN

John Romulus Brinkley became famous and criminal in his life as "The Goat-Gland Surgeon." During the 1920's and 1930's, Brinkley exploited the sexual insecurity of the American male, the rural suspicion of bureaucracy and professionalism, and the sexual organs of the Toggenberg goat to make himself rich and his clients disappointed at best.

Later, in Greenville, South Carolina, he established the "Greenville Electro Medical Doctors," asking, "Are You a Manly Man Full of Vigor?" in newspaper ads. Patients were injected with colored water for $25 a shot. He obtained a mail order M.D. from Eclectic Medical University of Kansas City, and moved to Kansas to practice medicine, its regulations being laxer than in most states. Operating in Milford, Brinkley said a local farmer suggested to him that glands from male goats were useful to stimulate men's energy and sexual potency. Brinkley devised a surgery to implant glands from the local

Toggenberg goat into human subjects. He was inspired in part by Serge Voronoff who was becoming popular by implanting monkey glands in humans.

By 1920, Brinkley's office occupied a 2 1/2-story building and employed three other mail-order doctors to perform the surgeries. A Chicago branch was shut down, but Brinkley moved elsewhere. He was cited for bootlegging that same year, but served no time. Brinkley began promoting the operation in tours of the Midwest and West. In 1922 he won over *Los Angeles Times* owner Harry Chandler, who helped Brinkley establish radio station KFKB 1050, in Milford, Kansas in September 1923, supplementing his mail and newspaper ads. By 1927, over 500 people a day were visiting Milford for consultations at $750 each. The hospital conducted 50 operations per month, grossing at least $37,500 every 30 days.

Brinkley met his critics head-on with admonishments to his listeners, "Do not let your doctor two-dollar you to death...come to Dr. Brinkley...take advantage of our Compound Operation..." He signed up druggists across the U.S. in the National Dr. Brinkley Pharmaceutical Association, providing a number-coded list of standard medicines to be sold at wildly-inflated, fixed rates (six times normal retail was not uncommon). Reading from letters that arrived in the "Medical Question Box," Brinkley recommended treatments by number: "Sunflower State, from Dresden, Kansas. Probably he had kidney stones...My advice to you is to put him on Prescription Number 80 and 50 for men, also 64." Participating druggists collected over $100 a day, at a time when the average laborer earned about $10 a week; each store kicked back $1 per prescription to Dr. Brinkley.

Dr. Morris Fishbein, editor of the *Journal of the American Medical Association*, made Brinkley a chief target of the AMA's war on alternative medicines and quackery. In April 1930, the Kansas Medical Society filed a formal complaint with the Kansas State Board of Medical Registration for gross immorality, addiction to liquor, malpractice, and unprofessional conduct. Addressing the Kansas Medical Society convention in Topeka, Fishbein delivered what is now regarded as a classic anti-quackery warning in which he described "the traits of a typical charlatan as one who is likely to have a pleasing personality; a smooth tongue; able to present his case with eloquence. He will claim educational advantages he does not possess...always he will produce a large number of testimonials from the professional testimonial givers, or from persons who like to see their names in print...(T)he charlatan of the worst type is the renegade physician. That man destroys public confidence in a profession. He destroys, but does not heal."

The Federal Radio Commission commenced hearings on radio abuses, and refused to renew Brinkley's license at KFKB; the following year the station was shut down. The Kansas State Board of Medical Registration hearings demanded Brinkley demonstrate his procedure. After he did so for two attending physicians, the board revoked his medical license.

To win back his medical license, Brinkley announced on September 23, 1930, he was running for Governor of Kansas. His rallies featured warm-ups by preachers and country musicians, a brass band, and a heralded appearance by the "Doctor" himself, who spewed fiery invectives and unattainable promises from the podium—free schoolbooks, free clinics, medical aid, and pensions for the elderly. As a write-in candidate only, Brinkley drew 183,278 votes, ending in third place, just 34,000 votes behind the victorious Democrat Harry Woodring. Brinkley's candidacy had gained such momentum that he won 20,000 write-in votes in three Oklahoma counties. On the Kansas ballot in 1932, he again finished third; he tried again in 1934, but fared poorly in the primaries.

Around this time, Brinkley abandoned the used of goat glands for what he claimed was an easier, more effective operation, cutting or tying off the tube from the prostate, and adding a drop of Mercurochrome. The new procedure was sold in levels—the "Poor Folk's Treatment" at $250, the "Average Man's Treatment" at $750, and the deluxe "Business Man's Treatment," at $1,500. He continued his mail-order consultations for $2 each, and accepted urine samples through the mail.

In January and February 1938, the AMA magazine, *Hygeia*, published a two-part article by Morris Fishbein, "Modern Medical Charlatans," denouncing Brinkley as chief among the offenders. For the second time, Brinkley filed libel charges, aiming to break the record $35 million in libel suits that Fishbein had beaten so far. A Del Rio jury sided with Fishbein.

In mid-1940, the U.S. Government filed against Brinkley for $200,000 in back taxes, and over a dozen malpractice lawsuits came to court that year. Brinkley transferred his assets to his wife and son and declared bankruptcy in January 1941 with over $1 million in liabilities. The U.S. Postal Service filed charges against Brinkley for 20 years of mail fraud, but Brinkley died in May 1941 before the case came to trial.

Source:
Marinacci, M. *Getting America's Goat.* 1997. http://pw1.netcom.com/~mikalm/brinkley.htm

Related Entry:
HEALTH CARE FRAUD

CASH FLOW ANALYSIS

A cash-flow analysis traces funds as they enter and leave a business or individual's bank account. The method is useful for profiling financial activities, recovering funds, defining partnerships, and other financial relationships. The cash-flow analysis is commonly used to profile investment promotions in which fraud is suspected because it shows how investor funds were spent and where they were invested.

To test investment promotions for fraud, the investigator secures a search warrant for a suspect's financial account(s). If records show dispersals into legitimate commercial enterprises and expenses, the operation is clean. If dispersals are made to questionable entities, to shell companies owned by perpetrators, or if large transfers are made to personal use, there may be a Ponzi or a pyramid scheme in progress.

The two main steps of the analysis are as follows.

Step 1. Total the Deposits

From: Individual and Institutional Investors, Promoters and their Backers, and Sales and Fees.

This review determines the amounts (in cash, checks, and securities) placed into the scam by individual and institutional investors, how much promoters and their backers placed as startup funds, and how much the company received in sales and fees as income. Investigators will have to identify the source of some deposits. For example, a check from "Maude Ginland" might have come from an investor, a backer or a co-conspirator. The first step of the analysis yields an aggregate number for how much money flowed into the business. If more than one account was used for investor deposits, the investigator aggregates all deposits into one master account for the cash-flow analysis.

Step 2. Total and Trace Dispersals

To: Operating Expenses, Capital Expenses, Salaries, Other Business Expenses, Dividends, and Investments.

The major work of this step involves verifying the destinations of the deposits. A check to Southern Union Gas obviously counts as Operating Expenses, but suspicious items like "Consulting Fees" may require additional investigative work. Alternately, the analysis may uncover accounts with legitimate-sounding names, such as Southern Union Gas, but with abnormal disbursements, such as 100 checks per month or checks for $10,000 labeled "gas bill." These are probably dummy accounts used to conceal the disbursement of funds or to hide losses.

Related Entries:

FINANCIAL PROFILE
NET WORTH ANALYSIS

CASH THEFT SCHEMES

Cash theft schemes are a form of asset misappropriation, the most common of occupational frauds. Cash theft schemes fall into two categories, *skimming* and *larceny*. The difference in the two types of schemes depends completely on when the cash is stolen. Cash larceny is the theft of money that has already appeared on a victim organization's books, while skimming is the theft of cash that has not yet been recorded in the accounting system. Larceny is a simple filching of the organization's cash. Skimming requires manipulation of the books, which may be a simple or complex act of fraud.

Skimming

Skimming is the theft of cash prior to its entry in an accounting system, which is why skimming is known as an "off-book" fraud. Because the stolen funds are never recorded, skimming schemes means they leave no direct audit trail. Many skimming schemes are perpetrated by employees whose duties include receiving and logging payments made by customers through the mail. Skimming schemes generally fall into one of the following categories: unrecorded sales, understated sales, and theft of checks received through the mail.

Unrecorded Sales

The most basic skimming scheme occurs when an employee sells goods or services to a customer, collects the customer's payment, but makes no record of the sale. The transaction may be disguised so it appears that the sale was conducted legitimately. It is impossible to detect unrecorded sales by comparing the register tape to the cash drawer.

SKIMMING DURING NONBUSINESS HOURS

Another way to skim unrecorded sales is to conduct sales during nonbusiness hours—on weekends or after closing. Skimmers can pocket the proceeds of all sales made during these times because the owners have no idea that their stores are even open for business.

NON-REGISTER SKIMMING

Employees who work at remote locations or without close supervision perpetrate some of the most costly skimming schemes. This can include on-site sales persons who do not deal with registers, independent salesmen who operate off-site, and employees who work at branches or satellite offices.

In the apartment rental industry, for example, apartment managers handle day-to-day operations with little oversight. A common scheme is for an on-site employee to identify the tenants who pay in currency and remove them from the books. This causes a particular apartment to appear as vacant on the records when, in fact, it is occupied. The manager can skim the rental payments from the "vacant" unit, and the revenue will never be missed.

An insurance agent can sell policies to customers and then neglect to file the policies with the carrier. Most customers do not want to file claims on a policy, especially early in the term, for fear that their premiums will rise. Knowing this, the agent keeps all documentation on the policies instead of turning it over to the carrier. The agent is able to skim the customer's payments because the carrier does not know the policy exists. The customer continues to make his payments thinking that he is insured when in fact the policy is a ruse.

Understated Sales and Receivables

Employees and managers with proper clearance can skim money by recording sales at a discounted price, and pocketing the difference. One way employees commit understated sales schemes is by altering receipts or preparing false receipts that misstate the amount of sales.

Theft of Checks

Theft of incoming checks usually occurs because a single employee opens mail and records payments. The theft of checks is not usually complicated, but it is sometimes more difficult to conceal a check theft scheme than other forms of skimming. If the stolen checks were payments on the victim company's receivables, then these payments were expected. As receivables become past due, the victim company will send notices of nonpayment to its customers. A customer is likely to complain when he receives a second bill for a payment he has already made. In addition, the cashed check will serve as evidence that the customer made his payment. Also, a cashed check eventually returns to the person who wrote it and may provide evidence of who cashed it. Endorsements, bank stamps, and so forth may indicate the identity of the thief.

Several ways exist to convert stolen checks to currency. The thief may obtain credentials in a false name or have an accomplice at a financial institution cash the checks under the thief's alias. Or, the thief creates a business account in a name similar to the intended payee's. An employee of the ABC *Company* opens an account for the ABC *Corporation* at a crosstown bank. Because the two names are so similar, the crosstown bank cashes the checks with no questions asked. This method works in the short term, but is dangerous for the thief because eventually the ABC Company and its customers will receive cancelled checks from the crosstown bank and have the account there investigated.

A more direct way for an employee to convert a stolen check is to alter the check so that it is payable to that employee or one of his accomplices. In most cases, it is not possible to change the payee designation without defacing the stolen check. However, if a thief can insert his own name onto the payee designation of a stolen check, it will be easily converted.

Check for Currency Substitutions

For committing fraud, currency is preferable to checks because cash is fungible, i.e., it can be dispersed without leaving a record of the transaction. The paper trail left by check cashing can be avoided by removing currency from the company's receipts and replacing the funds with checks. For example, an employee skims $500 in currency and replaces the funds with an incoming check worth $500. The deposit totals will match the amount of cash on hand and the receipted checks.

While these substitutions make it easier to convert stolen payments, the problem of concealing the theft remains. That the stolen checks are not posted means some customers' accounts are in danger of becoming past due. The most common methods used by employees to deal with this problem are: destroying or altering records of the transaction, lapping, stealing customers' account statements, falsifying accounting entries, and inventory padding. These methods are discussed below.

Destroying or Altering Records of the Transaction

A perpetrator can hide a defalcation by destroying the records of the original transaction. For instance, a salesperson destroys the store's copy of a receipt to hide a skimmed sale. Cash register tapes may also be destroyed to hide an off-book sale.

Lapping

Lapping customer payments is particularly useful to employees who skim receivables. If the customer's account becomes delinquent, the scheme may be discovered. Lapping covers the fraud by crediting the customer's account with money from some other account. It is the fraudster's version of "robbing Peter to pay Paul."

Suppose a company has three customers, A, B, and C. When A's payment is received, the fraudster steals it instead of posting it to A's account. If the payment has not been posted by the time A's next statement is mailed, he will see that the payment was not applied to his account and will almost certainly complain. When B's check arrives, the thief posts this money to A's account. Payments now appear to be up-to-date on A's account, but B's account is behind. When C's payment is received, the perpetrator applies it to B's account. This process continues indefinitely until one of three things happens: (1) someone discovers the scheme, (2) restitution is made to the accounts, or (3) some concealing entry is made to adjust the accounts receivable balances.

While lapping is more commonly used to conceal receivables skimming, it can also be used to disguise the skimming of sales. Employees often steal all or part of one day's receipts and replace them with the receipts from the following day.

Stolen Statements

Another way to conceal the misapplication of a customer's payments is to steal or alter the account statements of that customer. This might be accomplished by changing the customer's address in the billing system. The statements will be sent directly to the thief or to a mail drop. In other cases the address is changed so that the statement is undeliverable, which causes the statements to be returned to the thief's desk. The perpetrator usually alters the statements or produces counterfeit statements to make it appear that the customer's payments have been properly posted. These false statements lead the customer to believe that his account is up-to-date.

False Account Entries

Intercepting the customer's statements will not keep the account from becoming delinquent on the company's books. Besides lapping, another way to prevent delinquency is to make false entries in the victim organization's accounting system.

Debit Accounts

If a payment is made on a receivable, the proper entry is a debit to cash and a credit to the receivable. Instead of debiting cash, the employee might debit an expense account. This transaction still keeps the company's books in balance, but the incoming cash is never recorded. In addition, the customer's receivable account is credited, so it will not become delinquent.

False debits can be made to fictitious accounts, or to existing accounts with special provisions. For example, a thief might record the stolen funds in aging accounts that are about to be written off as uncollectible or to very large accounts where a small debit might go unnoticed.

WRITING OFF ACCOUNT BALANCES

Some employees cover their skimming by posting entries to contra revenue accounts such as "discounts and allowances." If, for instance, an employee intercepts a $1,000 payment, he would create a $1,000 "discount" on the account to compensate for the missing money. Another account that might be used in this type of concealment is the bad debts expense account.

Inventory Padding

The victim organization's inventory, if it has one, will reflect fraudulent actions. Off-book sales of goods will always leave an inventory shortage and a corresponding rise in the cost of goods sold. Concealing the shortage requires falsifying the inventory numbers.

Related Entries:

ASSET MISAPPROPRIATION
OCCUPATIONAL FRAUD AND ABUSE

CAUSES OF FRAUD

In the broadest sense, the causes of fraud are summarized in an axiom known as the Fraud Triangle, developed from the work of Dr. Donald Cressey. The three elements of the Fraud Triangle are: *Pressure or Motive—Opportunity—Rationalization*. Generally, fraud occurs when someone with a financial need (motive) gains improper access to funds (opportunity) and is able to justify the act to themselves and/or others (rationalization). In other words, people commit fraud because they need, or think they need, the money; they believe they will not be caught; and they have justified the act to themselves.

Though this makes virtually everyone a potential fraud offender, the Triangle suggests there are at least three general ways of preventing fraud—by altering the motives of individuals; by limiting the opportunities for secretly gaining funds; and by undermining common rationalizations, through general education or the interrogation of individuals.

Why *Don't* People Commit Fraud?

The Coalition Against Insurance Fraud (CAIF) has studied why people sometimes refrain from committing fraud. Sixty-three percent of respondents answered "moral character." Other deterrents cited were fear of being caught (15%), fear of prosecution (7%), lack of opportunity (3%), and religious beliefs (2%). Though about one-third of the respondents said they had "no tolerance" for fraud, the majority left room for fraudulent acts with proper rationalization. Sixty percent thought people who committed insurance fraud were looking for a fair return on the premiums they paid. Another third thought that people were forced into fraudulent behavior to obtain insurance.

This pattern holds true with other types of fraud. Though most employees admit that fraud against their employer is wrong, many do so anyway and rationalize the act as making up for poor wages or unfair working conditions. Professional cons admit they are committing an unethical act but they absolve themselves by insisting, "You cannot cheat an honest man."

Is the Fraud Offender Deviant?

Scholar James Coleman has written, "In seeing the [criminal] deviant as a wholly different kind of person from ourselves, we bolster our self-esteem and repress the fear that under the right circumstances, we, too, might violate the same taboos. But this system of facile psychological determinism collapses when applied to white-collar criminals. The embezzling accountant or the corporate manager serving in her firm's illegal schemes conforms too closely to the middle-class ideals of American culture to be so easily dismissed."

Coleman cites an experiment in which business students were asked to decide on a course of action for a pharmaceutical company, which had just discovered that a highly profitable drug was dangerous. The scenario was drawn from an actual incident, in which the company's management had refused to withdraw the drug from the market and actively obstructed regulators in the courts and legislature. Seventy-nine percent of the business students made the same decision.

Causes of Fraud, Major Theories

Most theories of crime have some basis in behaviorism. As propounded by B.F. Skinner, behavioral theory holds that behavior is conditioned over time by an individual's interaction with the environment. Any act—criminal or otherwise—can be explained as the product of an individual's desires and the person's understanding of consequences; i.e., a person will perform any act that gratifies desire without inflicting pain or causing deprivation. Fundamentally, behaviorism holds that behavior is (to a great extent) learned, and can thus be modified.

Donald Cressey and the Fraud Triangle

In *Other People's Money: A Study in the Social Psychology of Embezzlement*, Cressey concluded that individuals commit fraud when three factors are present: (1) a financial need that cannot be shared, (2) a perceived opportunity for illicit gains, and (3) a personal rationalization of the act. Cressey reportedly asked offenders why they had not committed violations at other times and received three basic replies: "There was no need for it like there was this time"; "The idea never entered my head"; and "I thought it was dishonest then, but this time it did not seem dishonest at first."

Cressey's ideas have become known as the Fraud Triangle:

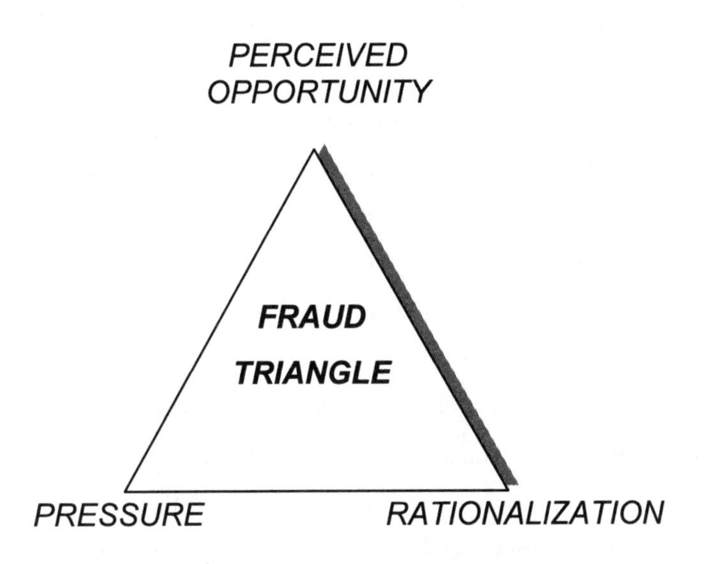

Cressey catalogued six types of "nonshareable" problems that provoke fraud: inability to pay debts, problems resulting from personal failure, business reversals, physical isolation, status gaining, and employer-employee relations. Individuals rationalized their crimes as noncriminal, justified, or as part of an environment over which the offender had no control. The opportunities for fraud are always myriad, though the lack of internal controls over funds is a chief factor. Removing temptation remains the best deterrent of all.

Edwin Sutherland

In *Principles of Criminology* and *White-Collar Crime*, Sutherland developed his theory of differential association. Sutherland studied fraud committed by business executives against shareholders and the general public. Rejecting what he saw as criminology's emphasis on Freudian psychology, Sutherland wrote:

> *General Motors does not have an inferiority complex, United States Steel does not suffer from an unresolved Oedipus problem, and the DuPonts do not desire to return to the womb. The assumption that an offender may have such pathological distortion of the intellect or the emotions seems to me absurd, and if it is absurd regarding the crimes of*

businessmen, it is equally absurd regarding the crimes of persons in the economic lower classes.

Sutherland drew from the work of E.A. Ross, who published *Sin and Society* in 1907. Ross asserted that American capitalism was threatened by "the criminaloid," i.e., businessmen whose greed and moral impairment drove them to put acquiring money above all other considerations, including the welfare and lives of thousands of citizens and the continued health of the capitalist system. The criminaloid prospered because a complacent public allowed him to hide behind a façade of respectability.

Sutherland coined the term *white-collar crime* and first used it publicly in a 1939 speech to the American Sociological Society. He defined the term as "A crime committed by a person of respectability and high social status in the course of his occupation." Though the actions and perpetrators might vary, these crimes all involved "The violation of delegated or implied trust." The cooperative, if clueless, victim was necessary for the predication of the crime.

Sutherland's work focused on business crime. In *White-Collar Crime*, published in 1949, he examined crimes committed by members of 70 of the largest U.S. corporations. All had at least one criminal or civil decision against them, and most of the corporations had committed multiple offenses. Sutherland charged that 97% of the corporations were recidivist offenders.

Sutherland asserted that people interacting in close association learn criminal behavior. Rather than imagine an individual suffering from a pathological mental condition, Sutherland argued that people learned how to be criminals—from pickpockets to corporate embezzlers—by consorting with other criminals.

The criminal learning process includes physical techniques and strategies for committing crime as well as the sharing of motives, drives, rationalizations, and attitudes toward crime. In other words, one not only learns *how* to commit the crime, but *why* to commit the crime. Chief among the rationalizations, Sutherland found, was an acquired sense of legal codes as unfair and/or unfavorable.

The causes of corporate crime were unrelated to the psychology of its perpetrators, Sutherland believed, as evidenced by the fact that criminal corporations may continue committing offenses over time while personnel come and go. However, Sutherland did not consider that management tends to promote people like themselves, so the psychological profile of the typical manager may remain constant through several administrations.

In his theory of *differential association*, Sutherland asserted, "Criminal behavior is learned in association with those who define such behavior favorably and in isolation from those who define it unfavorably. . . a person in an appropriate situation engages in such criminal behavior if, and only if, the weight of the favorable definitions exceeds the weight of the unfavorable definitions." White-collar crimes were driven by peer pressure.

Later scholars and anti-fraud practitioners have criticized Sutherland's work. As summarized by David Friedrichs, observers charge "Sutherland overemphasized an individualistic framework (and social psychological factors) and largely ignored social structural factors (for example, capitalism, profit rates, and business cycles). He failed to make clear-cut distinctions among white-collar crimes, and he did not adequately appreciate the influence of corporations over the legislative and regulatory processes. Still... it is difficult to imagine the study of white-collar crime without Sutherland's contribution."

Albrecht, Howe, and Romney

Dr. Steve Albrecht, Keith Howe, and Marshall Romney, studied frauds in corporate settings in *Deterring Fraud: The Internal Auditor's Perspective.*

They classified nine motivators of fraud.

1. Living beyond means
2. Overwhelming desire for personal gain
3. High personal debt
4. Close association with customers
5. Perception that pay was incommensurate with duties
6. "Wheeler-dealer" attitude
7. Feeling challenged to beat the system
8. Excessive gambling habits

9. Undue family or peer pressure

Perpetrators of large frauds in their study used the proceeds to purchase new homes and expensive automobiles, recreation property, expensive vacations, support extramarital relationships, and make speculative investments. Those committing smaller frauds applied their gains to more pedestrian ends, such as paying the rent or normal monthly bills.

Lack of segregation of responsibilities, placing undeserved trust in key employees, imposing unrealistic goals, and operating on a crisis basis were all pressures or weaknesses associated with large frauds.

Albrecht developed the "Fraud Scale," ranking situational pressures, perceived opportunities, and personal integrity. When situational pressures and perceived opportunities are high and personal integrity is low, occupational fraud is much more likely to occur than when the opposite is true.

Albrecht, Howe, Romney, "Deterring Fraud: The Internal Auditor's Perspective," p6

Albrecht describes situational pressures as "The immediate problems individuals experience within their environments," usually high personal debts or financial losses. Opportunities to commit fraud, Albrecht says, may be created by deficient or missing internal controls—those of the employee or the company. Personal integrity "Refers to the personal code of ethical behavior each person adopts. While this factor appears to be a straightforward determination of whether the person is honest or dishonest, moral development research indicates that the issue is more complex."

Hollinger-Clark

Richard Hollinger and John Clark surveyed 10,000 American workers for the book, *Theft by Employees*, and concluded that employees steal primarily as a result of workplace conditions. External factors such as Cressey's "nonshareable problems" sometimes play a role, but Hollinger and Clark emphasized the structure and behavioral norms of the workplace, declaring that worker dissatisfaction was the single most determinative factor in provoking acts of fraud. A person might need funds to pay off a debt, or the person might feel underpaid and motivated to commit fraud even without an immediate financial need.

Hollinger-Clark concluded that the same kinds of employees who engage in other workplace deviance are also principally the ones who engage in employee theft. They found persuasive evidence that slow or sloppy workmanship, sick-leave abuses, long coffee breaks, alcohol and drug use at work, coming in late and/or leaving early were more likely to be present in the employee-thief.

The researchers found that the single most effective way to prevent theft was to raise the chances, or the employees' perception of the chances, of getting caught: "The stronger the perception that theft would be detected, the less the likelihood that the employee would engage in deviant behavior."

Social control in the workplace, according to Hollinger-Clark, consists of both formal and informal social controls. The former control can be described as the internalization by the employee of the group norms of the organization; the latter, external pressures through both positive and negative sanctions.

These researchers, along with a host of others, have concluded that—as a general proposition—informal social controls provide the best deterrent. "These data clearly indicate that the loss of respect among one's acquaintances was the single most effective variable in predicting future deviant involvement." Furthermore, "in general, the probability of suffering informal sanction is far more important than fear of formal sanctions in deterring deviant activity."

Merton and Schur

Robert Merton determined that social structures provide the chief motivation for misconduct. Capitalist competition, the importance of money in society, and the erosion of norms that encourage legitimate moneymaking behavior all encourage individuals to commit crimes. To Merton, modern industrial societies emphasized the ends (making money) over the means (ethical earning behavior), producing a state of "anomie," or normlessness, in its citizens. Without ethical guidance, a person will use any means necessary to attain money and power.

Edwin Schur also located the impulse for economic crime in social structures. Schur asserted that America hosted so much crime because "American society has what might be termed capitalism with a vengeance—a reverence for the values of individualism, competition, and profit of such intensity as to provide incentives to crime that go well beyond a level that must be considered inevitable in a modern complex society."

The Fraudster Personality Type

There is no clinical evidence to suggest a single personality type of the average fraud perpetrator. For one thing, acts of fraud and white-collar crimes in general vary widely, from embezzlement to market manipulation to junk science to price-fixing. A few studies have suggested two broad labels often apply to fraudsters: "egocentric" and "reckless."

Psychologist Walter Bromberg commented on the personality of a successful banker who was convicted for breach of fiduciary duty and who sought treatment at Bellevue Psychiatric Hospital: [The banker] "impressed the examiners as a realistic, though relatively uncompromising individual, independent rather than stubborn, yet unaware of his rather strong tendency toward recklessness.

On a deeper level, one could sense in him a certain rigidity of character expressed openly in stubbornness, independence, and lack of compromise. Egocentricity and an unconscious feeling of omnipotence shone through his character structure."

John Spencer found that most of the thirty white-collar offenders he examined were "reckless and ambitious," remarkable for "their ambition, their drive, their desire to mix with people of higher social position than their own, and to give their children an expensive private education, and their willingness to take financial risks in the process."

But Spencer cautioned, "It would be a mistake to see the adventurous and ruthless gambler as typical of the white-collar criminal. Such men did not account for more than one-third of the sample." There were plenty of "muddlers and incompetent men" in the group.

A comparison of 350 white-collar offenders in prison with a control group of executives with no criminal or civil record found the convicted executives were more irresponsible, less dependable, and held a stronger disregard for rules than the control group.

Stanton Wheeler examined risk factors to answer the query, "Why do people who are already extremely wealthy individuals risk involvement in white-collar crimes…?" Wheeler asserts that many offenders are "risk seekers" who find their crimes thrilling, who possess "greed as a personality trait: people who want even more, more than they already have." Another personality is driven to defalcation by "fear of falling" from privileged status.

An analysis led by David Weisburd found a similar force at work in its sample of convicted white-collar offenders. Weisburd reported, "The fate of organizational success and failure, or the changing nature of the economy in their line of work, may put them at least temporarily under great financial pressure, where they risk losing the lifestyle they have achieved."

These inconclusive results suggest that white-collar criminals, while generally incautious and driven by ambition, are a varied lot. Some are charismatic, energetic promoters while others are reserved, calculating embezzlers. Coleman suggests, "A particular personality orientation will facilitate criminal activities in one occupational situation and discourage them in another, so that no single set of characteristics is conducive to crime in all situations.

For example, nonconformists might well be more likely to become involved in an occupational crime *directed against* an employer but less likely to go along with an organizational crime *demanded by* the employer" while a strict conformist would tend in the opposite direction."

Social Sanctions Essential to Prevent Cheating

Drs. Ernst Fehr and Simon Gachter published the results of a series of experiments designed to test people's propensity to cheat in social situations, and the effects of economic punishment and social sanctions on known cheaters.

The experiments involved 240 students who were placed in scenarios to determine the "public goods," or altruistic acts, each was willing to commit, how much cheating would take place, and how members of the group responded to cheaters. The students received real money according to how well they fared in the various scenarios. Each was given 20 "monetary units" and played games with rotating groups of three other participants.

The members of each group independently decided how much of their sum to contribute to a community project, then shared in the total proceeds at the end. The more generous each contributor, the better the group did as a whole. But the more each person held back, the greater "profit" each made. For example, A might put in 20 dollars but receive the same dividend at the game's end as B, who put in only eight dollars. In a real-world analogy, A represents an honest citizen contributing a fair share, while B is a scofflaw or fraudster. After each round, students learned the investments made by others in their group. In some cases, the participants were powerless to sanction their fellows. Under these conditions, cooperation quickly broke down and everyone contributed less to the community chest each round.

In other instances, the group was allowed to sanction shirker participants. An indignant group member could donate 1 monetary unit to punishment, forcing the shirker to match the contribution with 3 units. A key factor was that penalizing shirkers cost the cooperative members money as well. The stakes were real because the students only took home as much real money as they managed to acquire in the game.

Still, however costly, punishment was a popular choice:

- 84% of participants chose to punish shirkers at least once.
- 34.3% punished five times or more.
- Almost 10% punished 10 times or more.

Fehr and Gachter concluded they had evidence people will seek to punish a cheat even when the punishment is costly them and offers no material benefit. These factors match the general definition of altruism, i.e., selfless acts for the communal good. The doctors speculated that the threat of such punishment might have been crucial to the development of human societies.

Participants exhibited a high degree of indignation at others' wrongdoing. When asked to describe their feelings toward shirkers on a seven-point scale, from "no big deal" to "very angry," 84% ranked themselves a five or higher. A sense of emotional outrage is very easily evoked, said Dr. Fehr, and sometimes it feels almost good to indulge and stoke it.

"It's a very important force for establishing large-scale cooperation," Dr. Fehr told the *New York Times*. "Every citizen is a little policeman in a sense. There are so many social norms that we follow almost unconsciously, and they are enforced by the moral outrage we expect if we were to violate them."

Dr. David Sloan Wilson, an evolutionary biologist at the State University of New York at Binghamton, said, "People are used to thinking of social control and moralistic aggression as forms of selfishness, and that you must be punishing someone for your own benefit. But if you look at the sort of punishment that promotes altruistic behavior, you see that it is itself a form of altruism."

Sources:
Angier, N., "Altruistic Punishment in Humans." *Nature,* January 22, 2002.

Coleman, J. *"The Criminal Elite: Understanding White-Collar Crime."* New York: St. Martin's Press, 1998.

Gastel, R., Weisburd, et.al. "Crimes of the Middle Classes: Insurance Issues Update." *Insurance Fraud,* October 2000.

Related Entries:

ATTITUDES TOWARD AND PERCEPTIONS OF FRAUD

BEHAVIORAL THEORY OF FRAUD

COST OF FRAUD

ETHICS

WHITE-COLLAR CRIME

CELL PHONE FRAUD, OR CLONING

"Cloning" duplicates a legitimate user's network access codes, allowing the user of the cloned phone to make calls on the legitimate user's account. Though consumers often learn about cellular cloning fraud when they receive their bill, standard industry practice does not charge consumers for cloned calls. Cloning is regarded with particular seriousness by law enforcement because cloned phones are often used by drug traffickers and other smugglers and by the criminal community in general.

Cloning is accomplished by duplicating the electronic serial number of a target phone. The ESN is a unique serial number programmed into the cellular phone by the manufacturer. Generally, in an analog cellular telephone, the ESN and the Mobile Identification Number (MIN) are used to identify a subscriber. One way the ESN is cloned is by capturing the ESN-MIN with a device called an ESN reader. The captured ESN-MIN is then reprogrammed into a computer chip of another cellular telephone. Digital cellular telephones provide more security against cloning because scanners do not as readily pick up digital frequencies.

Besides allowing criminals to communicate with anonymity, cloning cell phones provides criminals with cheap service. Clones can usually be obtained for a few hundred dollars. Some professional cloners guarantee a phone for 30 days and will reclone the phone if the service is terminated before 30 days has elapsed. Regardless of how long the clone phone is active, the typical call volume of an illegal clone phone user is such that the value of the service stolen quickly exceeds the amount paid for the phone.

Intercept devices that capture user information from phones in-use are freely and legally available around the world. Cloners can capture scores of numbers by setting up in a high-use area and set their scanners to intercept cellular account numbers. Another piece of equipment, freely and legally available, allows the cloner to program as many phones as he likes with the intercepted account numbers. A basic clone operation can be established for less than $2,000.

The following are steps recommended by the cellular phone industry for users who want to avoid becoming a clone victim:

- Contact a cellular phone firm to find out what anti-fraud features are available.
- Engage the lock feature on the phone when it is not being used.

- Keep documents containing the phone's ESN in a secured place.
- Verify cellular phone bills thoroughly each month.
- Report a stolen cellular telephone immediately to the cellular telephone carrier.
- Report lost phones if not found within 3 days.

Laws Against Cellular Telephone Fraud

Federal law makes it a crime to knowingly and intentionally use cellular telephones that are altered to allow unauthorized use of such services. (18 U.S. Code 1029) Penalties for violations of this law include up to 15-year imprisonment and/or a fine of not less than $50,000. The Secret Service is authorized by law to investigate cellular phone fraud.

One area of cloning not previously addressed by law was the sale of cloning equipment. According to the FCC, at one time, cloning of cellular phones accounted for a large portion of cell fraud. As a result, the Wireless Telephone Protection Act of 1998 expanded prior law to criminalize the use, possession, manufacture, or sale of cloning hardware or software. Currently, the primary type of cell fraud is subscriber fraud. The cellular industry estimates that carriers lose more than $150 million per year due to subscriber fraud.

What Is Subscriber Fraud?

Subscriber fraud occurs when someone signs up for service with fraudulently-obtained customer information or false identification. Lawbreakers obtain your personal information and use it to set up a cell phone account in your name.

Resolving subscriber fraud could develop into a long and difficult process for victims. It may take time to discover that subscriber fraud has occurred and an even longer time to prove that you did not incur the debts. Call your carrier if you think you have been a victim of subscriber fraud.

The state of California has enacted a number of laws against cell-phone fraud. These laws have been used as models by other states. It is a crime in California to intentionally avoid a telephone charge by the fraudulent use of false, altered, or stolen identification (California Penal Code 502.7). It is against the law to use a telecommunications device with the intent to avoid payment for service. Penalties for use of such a device with the intent to avoid payment or for the possession of such a device with the intent to sell it to another is imprisonment and/or a fine up to $10,000. (California Penal Code 502.8) The California Public Utilities Commission requires cellular telephone service providers to give their subscribers a notice which warns them of problems associated with fraud and provide them with information on ways to protect against fraud. (California Public Utilities Code 2892.3)

Case Study—Call Sell Operation

Michael Stenger recalls a case he worked on in West Palm Beach, Florida: "Working from a preliminary investigation of the local cellular company, our agents arrested a Lebanese national who was conducting a call sell operation. A call sell operation, to give you some background on it, typically provides international calling activity for a variety of customers through the compromise of the telecommunications system. In this case the defendant completed calls for customers in the Middle East by utilizing cellular account numbers that had been stolen with a scanner in New York. On a daily basis, the defendant's conspirators would express mail a new list of stolen account numbers to further this 24-hour-a-day operation. At the time of the arrest, some 26,000 account numbers were seized attributing to losses in the millions of dollars."

Case Study—The DEA and Cloning

Anthony Bocchichio of the Federal Drug Enforcement Agency testified on cellular cloning's role in drug trafficking and also on ways his agency has used cloned phones to apprehend traffickers.

"In Philadelphia in 1996, Harvey Van Huzvan's organization used cloned phones for selling 8 to 12 kilograms grams of cocaine a week on the streets of Philadelphia supplied by the Cali Colombia group. The investigation on the clone phones led to the seizure of ten kilograms of cocaine.

"In the Newark Division, in the Glenn Walker case of 1994, DEA and Secret Service investigators conducted intercepts on cloned cell phones. The telephone company kept the phones in service longer than they usually turn over the turn over time, enabling the investigators the time needed to build the case, which ended with 30 arrests and the seizure of a kilogram and several handguns.

"A Baltimore investigation in 1995 involved kilogram quantities of heroin being brought into New York City by Colombian nationals and distributed in the Baltimore, Maryland area. The Colombians, the middlemen in New York, and the Baltimore distributor used cloned cell phones. The distributor routinely switched phones every two weeks, making it very difficult to identify a new number and maintain the intercepts."

Sources:
Coleman, J. *The Criminal Elite: Understanding White Collar Crime*. New York: St. Martin's Press, 1998.

"Fact Sheet 2: Wireless Communications: Cordless/Cellular Phones." *Utility Consumers' Action Network,* Copyright 1992 – 2001; Revised August 2000.

"Hearing of the Crime Subcommittee of the House Judiciary Committee. Subject: Cellular Telephone, Fraud Witnesses: Michael C. Stenger, Special Agent In Charge, Financial Crimes Division, U.S. Secret Service; Anthony R. Bocchichio, Assistant Administrator, Operational Support Division, Drug Enforcement Administration." Federal News Service, September 11, 1997.
www.fcc.gov/cgb/consumerfacts/cellphonefraud.html

Related Entry:

TELECOMMUNICATIONS FRAUD

CENDANT CORPORATION

The Cendant Corporation was formed in 1997 as a merger of CUC International and HFS. A few months afterward, Cendant shareholders suffered a one-day loss of $14 billion, when it was publicly revealed that the assets and earnings of CUC International had been falsified for 12 years prior to the merger, and that the merger was designed to enable the perpetrators to conceal their fraud in the books of the new corporation.

Walter Forbes was chief executive of CUC International from its inception in 1976 as a seller of memberships in consumer discount buying clubs until its merger with Parsippany, N.J. based HFS Inc., a franchiser of Avis rental cars, Century 21 real estate and Days Inn hotels. E. Kirk Shelton joined CUC as a senior vice president in 1981. According to other company officers who pled guilty, Forbes and Shelton directed revenue from new memberships not yet paid to be recorded immediately, and that a reserve fund to pay for membership cancellations and an account for commissions payable on membership sales be diverted to current earnings.

Over the years, various executives at CUC expanded the strategies for managing the company's earnings reports. They acquired other companies to create merger reserves, a pool of millions of dollars set aside for one-time costs associated with a merger, and used the funds to further pad revenues. This tactic culminated with the HFS merger in late 1997.

When Cendant executives reviewed CUC's books for the first time in 1998, they discovered the discrepancy between actual and reported revenue. In April 1998, Cendant announced it was correcting its 1997 earnings by $115 million (later increased to $500 million). The subsequent loss in stock value was nothing short of a meltdown Cendant settled shareholder class actions in 1999 for $2.85 billion.

In April 1999, Forbes and Shelton pleaded not guilty in federal court in Newark, N.J. In 2000, former CUC Chief Financial Officer Cosmo Corigliano, pleaded guilty to one count of conspiracy to commit mail and wire fraud and make false statements and one count of wire fraud. Anne Pember, 40-year-old former controller, admitted to a single conspiracy count; Casper Sabatino, former vice president of accounting and financial reporting, pleaded guilty to one count of aiding and abetting wire fraud. Corigliano accepted responsibility for his crimes, but added, "My superiors were encouraging me." He said he worked in "a culture that had been developed over many years," and he and his co-defendants' behavior "was ingrained by our superiors."

New charges were filed against Forbes and Shelton in 2001, charging that they misled shareholders in both companies, including the pension fund for New Jersey state workers; they mailed shareholders a statement seeking votes to approve the merger that included falsified earnings. The two are to be tried in 2002 for conspiracy, securities fraud, wire fraud, making a false statement in a Securities and Exchange Commission report, and two counts of mail fraud.

In January 2005, Shelton was convicted of conspiracy, securities, wire and mail fraud in federal court. He was sentenced in August 2005 to serve 10 years in prison. He was also ordered to pay full restitution for contributing to the accounting scandal that cost investors and the company more than $3 billion. Shelton was ordered to pay $3.27 billion to Cendant. Shelton stood trial with former Cendant Chairman Walter Forbes, whose case ended in a mistrial. Forbes was retried in October 2005 and on February 10, 2006 a federal judge declared a mistrial. Prosecutors are trying Forbes for a third time starting the second week of October 2006. Shelton is currently free pending his appeal.

Related Entries:

FINANCIAL STATEMENT FRAUD

SECURITIES FRAUD

CHADWICK, CASSIE

Cassie Chadwick, née Elizabeth Bigley, rose from humble beginnings on a small Canadian farm to become a rich woman in Cleveland, Ohio. Elizabeth Bigley was born in 1855 near Eastwood, Ontario. When she was 19, Bigley ran away to the town of Hamilton, where she convinced local storekeepers she was Lydia Bagley, a recently widowed woman, with connections to British royalty. She was caught after a couple of months, but because of her erratic demeanor was judged not guilty by reason of insanity.

From her first con game in 1876, she lived a life of deception, always one step ahead of bad debts and falsified assets. She married Leroy Chadwick, a widowed Cleveland doctor, in 1897, and used her husband's assets and good name to enrich herself. In her most audacious con, she secured lines of credit from a string of bankers by passing herself off as the illegitimate child of industrial magnate Andrew Carnegie.

In 1880, Bigley went to live with her sister Alice in Cleveland, Ohio. Again she made trouble for herself, this time by mortgaging her sister's furniture without permission and spending the cash. She was married to a man named William Springsteen in 1882, but the marriage was dissolved in 12 days when her new husband discovered his wife had purchased thousands of dollars of household and personal items on his credit.

Fleeing Cleveland, Bigley was next heard from in Erie, Pennsylvania, where she scammed sympathetic residents for cash and support in the person of Maizie Bagley. Soon she returned to Cleveland, acting as a clairvoyant and prostitute under various names, including Lydia Scott, Madame La Rose, Betsy Bagley, Lylie Bagley, and Lylie Clingen. In 1886, she had a child—fathered by a prominent local politician, she claimed.

Soon after the boy's birth, she sent him to live with her parents in Woodstock. She then moved herself to Toledo, Ohio and set up shop as Lydia DeVere, quickly making her quarters one of the most frequented vice spots in a city with more than its fair share of vice.

At the Toledo postal office, Bigley met Joe Lamb, a clerk with five kids and a wife who was charmed by the attentions of a woman he believed came from noble stock and was about to receive a fortune. Bigley borrowed from Lamb until his savings ran out, then convinced him to take out several loans in his own name and turn over the proceeds to her. Eventually she acquired over $40,000 by manipulating Lamb and his bankers, promising them she had a rich patron in Cleveland who would cover all the debts plus interest. When the Lamb affair came out, Bigley was convicted and sentenced to 10 years in the Ohio State Penitentiary, the first woman incarcerated in that institution. She returned to Cleveland in 1895, after a post-incarceration visit to her son and parents in Ontario.

In 1897, Bigley—as Cassie Hoover—married one of her male visitors, Dr. Leroy Chadwick. The Chadwick's was one of Cleveland's oldest, most respected families, and Cassie Chadwick wasted no time using the name and what remained of the family fortune to indulge herself and to fill the mansion on Euclid Avenue with a cornucopia of trinkets, furniture, and a $10,000 pipe organ for her husband. His wife's extravagances strained Chadwick's finances and his patience; in 1901 he left for Europe and did not return until he was called back by his wife's indictment four years later.

Finding herself with no resources through her husband, Chadwick began her greatest con in 1902, passing around letters of credit, stocks, and other documents, which she had forged. She approached bankers around Ohio, offering to pay them two and three times the normal rate of interest in exchange for an advance against the phony stocks and letters of credit. Her greatest draw came from materials she had forged that purported to be statements from Andrew Carnegie, acknowledging Cassie Chadwick as his heir and promising millions to her upon his death.

Many bankers—perhaps 30 or 40 in all—jumped at the chance to charge exorbitant interest, and relishing the day when this apparently naïve and half-deaf woman would come into her fortune. Chadwick's end came about from her dealings with the Citizen's

National Bank of Oberlin. The bank's president, Charles Beckwith, later related, "It was a little matter of speculation. She represented things to me in such a way that I believed the risk was a good one. I had often raised small amounts for her. Sometimes it would be $15,000 or $20,000, and she would pay me when the loans were due. These loans were not from the bank. They came from money that I had secured personally. After this had been going on for a time she gained my confidence and I let her in on the bank's money. It is not strange that she succeeded in getting the money. All of this money was not given to her at one time. At first it was very small amounts that she obtained. These sums kept accumulating, and she kept asking for more money, until I was in so deep that I could not refuse. I had to give her more money in order to keep the loans that I had made from being lost. All the time I was hoping that she would soon be in a position to pay."

By 1904, Chadwick's scheme was unraveling. Herbert Newton, an industrialist and financier from Massachusetts who had been introduced to Chadwick by the pastor of Cleveland's Euclid Avenue Baptist Church, filed suit against Chadwick for $190,000 in November. Soon other bankers joined the legal fray, including Charles Beckwith at the Citizen's National Bank of Oberlin.

Chadwick was arrested in December 1904 after fleeing to New York City. Though Beckwith died in February 1905, Chadwick went on trial for duping him and his bank in March. She was convicted and sentenced to 10 years prison. She died in the Ohio State Penitentiary in October 1907.

Source:
Wells, J., CFE, CPA. "The Trial: Cassie Chadwick." *Frankensteins of Fraud.* Austin, TX: Obsidian Publishing Co., 2000.

CHECK FRAUD

According to the American Bankers Association Deposit Account Fraud Survey Report released in 2004, attempted check fraud reached $5.5 billion in 2003, up from $4.3 billion in 2001. While attempted check fraud continued to rise, actual dollar losses remained relatively stable at $677 million, down slightly from the $698 million that banks lost in 2001. Eighty-eight percent of the $5.5 billion check fraud attempts were caught by banks' prevention systems or measures before any losses were incurred.

Even though the dollar losses decreased, the number of check fraud cases increased 3% to 616,469 cases in 2003. However, average losses per case went down from $1,163 in 2001 to $1,098 in 2003. Counterfeit checks had the highest median loss per case at $3,059 followed by kiting ($2,566) and alterations ($1,452). All types of fraud combined, the median loss per case varied from $530 for community banks to $1,380 for mid-sized banks, to $2,242 for regional banks, and to $1,821 for the largest institutions.

The 2001 ABA survey suggested that small and mid-size financial institutions are being targeted more frequently to commit check fraud. Large banks' share of losses fell from 60% in 1999 to 55% in 2001. Although they continue to have the largest number of attempts, large banks also have the best record in loss avoidance, preventing more than 80% of check fraud attempts.

Losses are not the only expense banks incur from check fraud. The amount of resources that banks devoted to check fraud prevention, detection, investigation and prosecution increased with bank size. One in five money center banks spent more than $20 million each in check fraud-related operating expense (not including actual losses). The median expense per bank ranged from $1 million to $9.9 million for money center banks, $1 million or more for regional banks, $50,000 or more formed-size banks and less than $5,000 for community banks.

Regardless of bank size, the most common type of check fraud in 2003 was forgery, with about one-third of fraud losses attributed to forged signatures (24%) and endorsements (7%). Insufficient funds (NSFs), or bounced checks that customers never pay, ranked second (17%) and counterfeit checks ranked third (15%).

After showing signs of improvement in 2001, new-account fraud reemerged as a serious challenge for banks of all sizes. Compared with the last survey, new account fraud's share of check-related losses rose for community, regional, and super regional/money center banks. The increase was moderate at regional banks. However, 44% of community banks' losses could be attributed to new account fraud in 2003, a substantial increase from 32% in 2001. New account fraud also accounted for a larger share of check fraud cases, regardless of bank size.

For the year 1999, the Federal Reserve estimated that checks represented $75 trillion in annual payments. U.S. consumers and merchants issued and received more than 166 million checks daily or 66 billion annually, equaling over 18 billion at the point of purchase. That annual figure was estimated to have risen to 80 billion checks worldwide for 2000—about 60 billion in the U.S. alone.

According to the U.S. Treasury Department, crimes against financial institutions, including fake checks, counterfeiting, and check kiting grew 25% in 2000 to approximately $2.5 billion. Factoring in the costs of enforcement, restitution, increased labor, and security costs, the impact on the American economy is estimated at $10 billion a year.

The upward trend is expected to continue, as desktop publishing methods and scanner technology makes counterfeiting and passing bad checks easier. Another factor in the rising fraud rate is greater participation in crimes by employees and other insiders. Since 1987, bank frauds committed by insiders have risen dramatically and now account for more than 60% of all financial institution fraud. Most of these frauds involve counterfeit or stolen checks. Banks and other financial institutions absorb about one-tenth of check fraud losses, while customers bear most of the rest.

About 2 million bad checks are accepted in the U.S. every day. Check fraud has been on the increase since the 1980's and continues to do so. Merchants took in more than $13 billion in bad checks in 1996, an 18% increase over the year before. In 1999, check fraud losses were $15 billion, with retailers paying for over 90% of the total loss.

For the period of April 1, 1996 through January 31, 2000, the FBI received 91,322 reports of criminal activity related to check fraud, counterfeit negotiable instruments, and related schemes. These schemes accounted for 48% of the 190,752 reports filed by United States financial institutions (excluding Bank Secrecy Act violations), and equaled approximately $2.89 billion in losses. The FBI says in the United States "today's biggest fraud problem is large-scale check fraud and counterfeiting operations."

In 2001, one in five money center banks spent more than $20 million each in check fraud-related operating expense (not including actual losses). The median expense per bank fell in the range of $5 million to $20 million for money center banks, between $250,000 and $1 million for regional banks, from $10,000 to $50,000 for mid-size banks and less than $5,000 for community banks.

Recently revised UCC regulations add the onus of shared responsibility for check fraud on the business. For example, if a bank offers their customer check stock that contains security features that could have prevented a specific case of fraud, the bank can claim that the customer was negligent and therefore at least partially liable for the fraud loss.

Check Fraud Schemes

According to the National Check Fraud Center, check fraud is usually committed in one of four ways:

- Forgery
- Counterfeiting and Alteration
- Paperhanging
- Check Kiting

Forgery

Businesses often suffer check fraud when an employee issues a check without proper authorization. Criminals sometimes steal a personal check from an individual or business, endorse it, and present it for payment at a retail location or at the bank teller window, probably using bogus personal identification. In payroll check fraud, check procurers obtain legitimate payroll checks and have duplicates printed. The checks may be cashed by members of the procurer's organization or sold to a third-party who arranges for the cashing. To avoid the security employed by financial institutions, the checks are cashed at grocery stores and check-cashing operations with loose controls. The checks are usually written for amounts of $300 or less to avoid suspicion.

Counterfeiting and Alteration

Counterfeiting can either mean wholly fabricating a check—using readily available desktop publishing equipment consisting of a personal computer, scanner, sophisticated software, and high-grade laser printer—or simply duplicating a check with advanced color photocopiers. Alteration primarily refers to using chemicals and solvents such as acetone, brake fluid, and bleach to remove or modify handwriting and information on the check. When performed on specific locations on the check, such as the payee's name or amount, it is called spot alteration. When an attempt to erase information from the entire check is made, it is called check washing, in which acid-based chemicals erase the amount and payee information on a check. The check is allowed to dry, after which a new payee and a greater dollar amount are inscribed.

Paperhanging

People purposefully write checks on closed accounts (their own or others) and may reorder checks on closed accounts (their own or others). So-called paperhangers pass checks at retail stores, where they write the check for over the purchase amount. A variation of this scam is making a fraudulent deposit at a bank and asking for cash back. Women, particularly if accompanied by children, often make successful paperhangers. The term is sometimes used to refer to anyone intentionally passing bad checks. After purchasing an item with a check, the person notifies his bank for a stop payment order. The item may be sold. In a variation, the person stops payment, then returns the item for a full refund.

Check Kiting

Check kiting is opening accounts at two or more institutions and using "the float time" it takes for checks to clear each institution to create fraudulent balances. This fraud has become easier in recent years due to new regulations requiring banks to make funds available sooner, though electronic processing, which makes checks clear faster, has made kiting more difficult in many areas. A check kiting scheme uses two or more bank accounts to support a string of checks. For example, the kiter deposits $100 in Account A and then pays for merchandise worth $500 by check. To cover the loss, the kiter writes a check from a second account, Account B, for $1,000 and deposits the check in Account A. Actually, Account B contains only $500, so the kiter writes a check from Account A. Successful kiters pass checks through multiple accounts, sometimes for a year or longer.

Check Fraud Rings

Since the late 1980's, foreign crime rings have been responsible for the majority of check fraud in the U.S. Most major financial institutions attribute more than 50% of all check fraud to organized crime rings. The perpetrators are often based in Nigeria, Russia, Vietnam, or Mexico. They target areas including San Francisco, Orange County, and Sacramento, California, and the large cities of the Northeast. These rings use digital scanners and offset printing to counterfeit checks. The checks are cashed by members of the ring or sold to third parties.

Most rings specialize in payroll or other institutional checks, written for amounts less than $300. But some groups infiltrate financial institutions, collecting corporate payroll checks, money orders, and master original bank checks, cashing the duplicates for between $2,000 and $5,000.

In recent years, members of Nigerian and Vietnamese rings have infiltrated or obtained accomplices in financial institutions. There they gather personal information on customers, passing the information to counterfeiters who produce falsified identification (drivers' licenses, credit cards, etc.), which is used to open accounts, establish lines of credit, and secure loans. An organized group may include a counterfeiter or printer, a distributor, one or more providers of false identification, and several "smurfs," who open false bank accounts or visit check-cashing establishments to negotiate fraudulent checks.

Because $100 travelers' checks are common, check rings specialize in the production and distribution of this type of check. Criminal rings pass most bogus travelers checks. A ring member makes small purchases using a fake $100 travelers' check and receives the bulk of the amount back in cash. This type of scheme works well in areas that have a lot of tourist business.

Travelers' checks have several distinguishing features. Watermarks and holograms are common, as well as micro-printing and ultraviolet ink. There are basically two methods of counterfeiting travelers' checks: color copying and offset lithography/printing. Color copied checks lack the raised ink texture which the intaglio printing press gives most travelers' checks. The colors and printing of a copied check may be faded, the texture relatively slick and flat.

Counterfeiting Checks

An effective check counterfeiting operation can turn a simple $5,000 investment into a $1,000,000 windfall within a 30-day timeframe. This can be done without high levels of computer expertise or programming. Simple check printing software can be purchased in almost any office supply store along with blank paper stock and magnetic ink cartridges. The overall initial investment consists of a quality computer, color inkjet printer, check format and MICR font software, magnetic ink cartridges, and paper stock. After making the initial investment, the printers only have to concern themselves with purchasing additional ink and paper.

Check Fraud Vulnerabilities

A particular institution may be targeted for check frauds because of its location, inadequate internal controls, or marketing strategies that present opportunities to savvy check fraud artists. Some mutual fund companies, for example, regularly allow customers to open accounts by mail, a form of communication with many security vulnerabilities. A significant number of check fraud complaints from a particular geographic area may indicate the presence of an active, organized group that warrants law enforcement attention.

Investigators assigned to a region or institution should keep regular contact with businesses and regulators. Specific inquiries aim to identify weaknesses, develop controls, and prevent future losses. Analyzing the complaints filed by other victims of check fraud—including retail operations, check cashing establishments, and food stores—may reveal common elements of schemes that might not otherwise seem related.

Leading Indicators of Check Fraud

Other types of criminal activity related to check fraud might serve as leading indicators of organized check fraud operations. These include counterfeit identification documents, theft of identification by pickpockets, credit card fraud, and structured cash transactions. Confidential informants with access to stolen and counterfeit identification documents can help investigators identify check passers and others involved in organized check frauds.

Signs of Counterfeit and Forged Checks

If the printing on the check does not seem uniform in texture and color or slants up or down, the check is not good. Also, the transit number in the top right corner must match the electronically encoded number at the bottom of the check. These numbers normally do not coincide on altered checks. The first three of the electronically encoded numbers indicate the state and district office of the issuer. Again, on forged checks these numbers do not always match properly. The check number itself should be found in the encoded serial number at the bottom. Knowing that many merchants regard checks with low check numbers as suspect, forgers often attempt to add a digit. Here again, they may have difficulty matching the ink used to produce the check.

A simple and effective method of detecting bad checks is to fan a group of checks. Counterfeit checks will sometimes stand out as a slightly different color.

Check 21

The Check Clearing for the 21st Century Act ("Check 21") became effective on October 28, 2004. Check 21 is designed to foster innovation in the payments system and to enhance its efficiency by reducing some of the legal impediments to check truncation. The law facilitates check truncation by creating a new negotiable instrument called a substitute check, which permits banks to truncate original checks, to process check information electronically, and deliver substitute checks to banks that want to continue receiving paper checks. A substitute check is the legal equivalent of the original check and includes all the same information as the original check. The law does not require banks to accept checks in electronic form nor does it require banks to use the new authority granted by the act to create substitute checks.

Check Fraud Prevention Tools

Many employers, public and private, are subverting check fraud by electronically depositing funds directly into employee and vendor accounts, eliminating the need for checks altogether. More direct methods of protecting checks are discussed below.

Special security printing techniques using pastel blue ink or "prismatic lithography," a pattern in colors which are difficult to separate even with special cameras, filters, and film. Another technique uses indicia printing to produce a seemingly random pattern of tiny colored dots on the paper. When viewed with a colored filter, the treated check reveals a word or visual pattern. A "micro-line" on the check appears as a solid line when viewed normally, but a magnifying glass will show the line makes up extremely tiny words or letters. Other security measures include three-dimensional holograms, security seals that are visible only when held up to a light. A heat-sensitive mark inserted into checks is invisible until heat is applied, which causes the word *valid* to appear.

A *biometric fingerprint identifier* requires the check writer to match fingerprints with the account holder's, which are on file. Banks report reductions in check fraud of 40% after the machine was introduced in the mid-1990s.

Financial institutions have been implementing and upgrading electronic databases that verify checks' authenticity and spot chronic abusers. These systems are becoming more comprehensive and are usually updated every few days.

A tool known as *Teller Positive Pay* is designed to stop bad checks at the teller window. Tellers punch in a check's serial number, account number, and amount; customers participating in the program electronically send a list of the checks they have issued. If the check matches one on the list with the right number and amount, it gets cashed or deposited. If it does not, the transaction stops. Otherwise the bank would have to process the check before it was denied. Forgers who buy blank check stock and create forgeries using account numbers can subvert Teller Positive Pay. But odds are that the forger will not be able to randomly pick a check number and guess the exact amount of the legitimate check that is already in the system.

The eBank(TM) Discovery system, developed by ASV Technologies, employs signature verification software. Using "multiple feature set extraction" technology drawn from forensic science, the state and quality of a signature's two-dimensional characteristics are analyzed and verified against samples. The program identifies flourishes, arcs, distances between letters, and up to 100 other features. Rejected signatures, along with the reason for rejection and signature samples, are forwarded to a human for visual verification. ASV Technologies claims its results match those of the most highly trained and accurate signature verifier.

VeriSAND® technology verifies checks by reading encrypted information from a bar code, OCR (Optical Character Recognition) or MICR-line to authenticate the check before it is cleared. MICR stands for "Magnetic Ink Character Recognition." MICR is the string of numbers at the bottom of a check. An acceptable MICR line has to contain the check number, account number, and routing number. The check amount is encoded on the MICR line during processing.

A *fingerprint-reading antifraud tool* has been piloted in Oxford, England. The system allows traders in Templars Square to ask for gel thumbprints from customers using credit cards or checks. The print is stamped on the back of the check or credit card slip and, if the card is later used fraudulently, police have the unique print of the fraudster on the earlier receipt.

FBI Profile of Check Fraud Activity

According to an analysis by FBI investigators in the New York City area, fraudulent check passers use the following common techniques:

- Customer attempts to open an account with a corporate check or other third-party check.
- Customer tries to flatter, hurry, or confuse the teller to draw attention away from the transaction.
- Customer delays endorsing a check or producing identification during peak hours to frustrate the teller and hurry the transaction.
- Customer presents for cash a low-numbered check drawn on a new account.
- Customer offers foreign documentation (birth certificate, passport, visa) or non-photo identification (social security card, credit card) in lieu of photo identification to open an account or cash a check.
- Customer offers altered or damaged identification to open an account or cash a check.
- Customer attempts to cash or convert several small checks into wire transfer, gold, or other tender.

- Customer requests an exception to established rules to force the transaction.

Signs of Check Fraud

General signs of check fraud compiled by the ACFE include:

- Frequent deposits and checks:
  - In the same amounts.
  - In round numbers.
  - With checks written on the same (other) bank.
  - Frequent ATM account balance inquiries.
- Many large deposits made on Thursday or Friday to take advantage of the weekend.
- Large periodic balances in individual accounts with no apparent business.
- Low average balance compared to high level of deposits.
- Many checks made payable to other banks.
- Bank willingness to pay against uncollected funds.
- Deposits not made daily or intact.
- Entity uses receipts, which do not indicate mode of payment.
- One or more personal checks in the cash drawer by the fund custodian.
- Deposit timing lags.
- Irregular check endorsements.
- Amount of deposit does not agree with daily activity report.
- Inappropriate access to signature plate.
- Check numbers, payee name, date, and amount do not agree with entries in the check register.
- Voided checks are not retained.
- Checks are issued to individuals for large, even dollar amounts.
- Supporting documentation for checks is not available or has been prematurely destroyed.
- Cash withdrawal with deposit checks drawn on another bank.

Cashiers and tellers should:

- Be aware of magnetic routing numbers.

- Look for checks with a check number less than 200.
- Be aware of the date that the account was opened.
- Have easy access to the signature card.
- Look for perforated edges on the checks.
- Be aware of what is acceptable identification.
- Recognize forged/altered identification.
- Recognize forged negotiable instruments.
- Be familiar with patterns of behavior related to potential culprits:
  - Overly polite.
  - Nervous.
  - Aggressive and hurried.

Case Study—Banks Liable for Fraudulent Checks

A Massachusetts Appeals Court, reviewing a case of check fraud in 2001, ruled that a bank was responsible for losses in a check fraud scam because bank employees had not practiced basic internal controls. An accountant for a construction company caused checks on his employer's accounts to be cashed for his personal benefit. The accountant, James Maddalena, passed 132 checks in all, including one for over $500,000; total losses were approximately $650,000.

Maddalena slipped the checks, which did not contain proper endorsements from the construction company, into a stack of endorsed checks ready for deposit. Tellers at Mechanics Bank processed the checks without question. Of the 132 checks, 29 were for amounts over $7,500, enough to trigger a manual review, but were not reviewed.

Sources:
Hansen, W. "Combating Check Fraud: A Multifaceted Approach." *The FBI Law Enforcement Bulletin,* May 1, 1999.

Henry, E. "Banking Software Launches New Assault on Check Fraud & Financial Institution Fraud." *Newsquest Regional Press,* May 14, 2001.

National Check Fraud Center - www.ckfraud.org/index.html

Slotter, K. "Check Fraud: A Sophisticated Criminal Enterprise," Federal Bureau of Investigation.

Timmons, H. "Good Times for Bad Paper." *Business Week,* August 13, 2001.

Related Entries:
CREDIT CARD AND DEBIT CARD FRAUD
DEMAND DRAFT FRAUD
FINANCIAL INSTITUTION FRAUD

CHECK KITING

See, CHECK FRAUD

CHECK TAMPERING

Check tampering is a category of fraudulent disbursements, which is itself a form of asset misappropriation, the most common method of committing occupational fraud and abuse. In a check-tampering scheme, the perpetrator gains access to the company checkbook, either through official clearance, by stealing a check, or by forging a check. The perpetrator may write the check in his/her own name, in an accomplice's name, payable to cash, or payable to a vendor (either a phony vendor or one in collusion). Sometimes "ghost employees" are slipped onto a company's payroll.

In some cases, the perpetrator intercepts a check intended for a legitimate payee and forges the payee's endorsement. The check tamper may also alter a legitimate payee's name with ink or through mechanical means—a method that works in the short term, but which is exposed when the check is paid and returned to the company.

Cashing the check usually requires fake identification of some sort. As a way around this obstacle, the perpetrator can write the check in the name of a phony company (ABC, Inc.), which the perpetrator controls—the check is deposited in the ABC account, which the bank holds in the perpetrator's name. The phony account makes cashing the check easier, but anyone who grows suspicious can examine the business's incorporation records, see that the perpetrator controls ABC, Inc., and shut down the scheme.

The Fraudster Reconciling the Bank Statement

If the perpetrator has installed a phony vendor in the company's accounts receivables or placed a ghost employee on the payroll, the scheme may not require any further concealment. But many long-term check tampering frauds require access to the company's bank statement, which normally includes the canceled checks cashed in the preceding period. A person who reconciles the accounts is therefore in a position to hide the existence of any fraudulent checks. He can remove the fraudulent checks or doctor the bank statement or both.

Simply removing the check will leave the statement out of balance. If the perpetrator has total control over the bank account, the balance can be "forced," i.e., the person generates whatever totals are necessary and ignores the details. Some fraudsters physically alter the bank statement to cause it to match the company's book balance.

Detecting Check Tampering

Bank cut-off statements should be requested for 10 to 15 days after the closing date of the balance sheet. These statements may be used to detect cash fraud during periods between monthly bank statements. If employees know that at any time during the month a cut-off statement may be ordered and reviewed independently, cash fraud will be less likely.

Copies of bank reconciliations should be obtained on all checking and savings accounts, certificates of deposit, and other financial instruments. The mathematics and details can be verified, and the statement itself checked for alterations.

Financial institutions will help clients develop controls to prevent check tampering, supplementing the client's internal controls. There are also a number of ways to physically design checks that resist tampering, such as metal strips, holograms, chemical triggers, watermarks, and special inks.

Check-Tampering Red Flags

- Unusual numbers of voided checks may indicate embezzlement, probably to expense accounts. When the expense is paid (from accounts payable), fraudulent checks are marked and entered as void and removed from distribution points. An account-balancing journal entry is then made. The list of voided checks should be verified against physical copies of the checks. Bank statements should be reviewed to ensure that voided checks have not been processed.

- Missing checks may indicate lax control over the physical safekeeping of checks. Stop payments should be issued for all missing checks.
- Checks payable to employees, with the exception of regular payroll checks, should be closely scrutinized. Such an examination may indicate other schemes such as conflicts of interest, fictitious vendors, or duplicate expense reimbursements.
- Altered endorsements or dual endorsements of returned checks may indicate possible tampering.
- Returned checks with obviously forged or questionable signature endorsements should be verified with original payee.
- Altered payees on returned checks should be verified with intended payee.
- Duplicate or counterfeit checks indicate fraud. These checks may be traceable to depositor through bank check coding.
- Questionable deposit dates should be matched to the corresponding customer accounts.
- An examination of all cash advances may reveal that not all advances are properly documented and, therefore, inappropriate payments have been made to employees.
- Customer complaints regarding payments not being applied to their accounts should be investigated.
- A questionable payee or payee address on a check should trigger review of the corresponding check and support documentation.

Businesses are urged to safeguard access to checks and checking accounts. Additionally, the following protocols will help prevent check fraud:

- Assign accounts payable functions to more than one person and make each one responsible for different payment areas. This division of responsibility makes it more difficult for employees to tamper with checks and payments.
- Limit the number of official signers. The fewer check signers you have, the lower your chances are of being defrauded.
- Require more than one signature on large dollar check amounts. In this way, any losses you may incur will be low denominations only.

- Immediately notify the bank of any change to your accounts payable process and personnel. You do not want former employees who may have secreted some checks from your business to retain authorization to sign them after they have left your employ.
- Separate the check writing and account reconcilement functions. Try not to have the same person who balanced the bank statement issue checks. This provides greater safeguards against an employee writing fraudulent checks and covering it up. The reconciler would be able to prevent the crime unless the employees are in collusion.
- Reconcile your account promptly and regularly—quick fraud detection increases the likelihood of recovery. Businesses and personal consumers, who do not balance their accounts monthly and do not find the discrepancies until months have passed, can become liable for losses.
- Use maximum dollar amounts on accounts to limit large denomination losses by authorized or unauthorized persons.
- Set up a separate account of large dollar payments to keep fraud losses at low denomination levels.
- Request detail reports for large dollar items to stay better informed. Increase fraud detection opportunities to find out whether you have a corrupt employee.
- Use a verification system. This type of payment system records pertinent information about each check such as the amount, check number, bank information, and date, then transmits it to the bank to be verified before the check can be paid.

Related Entries:

ASSET MISAPPROPRIATION
FRAUDULENT DISBURSEMENTS
LEONE, LOUIS AND RAYMOND
OCCUPATIONAL FRAUD AND ABUSE

CHIROPRACTIC FRAUD

Chiropractic fraud is a form of health care provider fraud. Typically chiropractors are accused of over-administering diagnostic tests and treatments, billing for patients who have sustained little or no injury, extending treatment beyond a reasonable length of time, billing for chiropractic treatments of non-spinal related ailments (e.g., cancer or diabetes), kickbacks, and abusive patient recruiting practices. Many claims of chiropractic fraud in recent years have involved chiropractors colluding with criminal rings to file false or abusive auto accident insurance claims.

Skeptics say the entire field of chiropractic medicine is a fraud. The treatment is based on the principle of "subluxations," which are partial displacements of a bone in a joint. Chiropractic literally means, "done by hand" (*chiros* = hand; *praktos* practice). Chiropractic critics charge that the treatment is founded on superstition, an extension of so-called "bonesetters" who practiced bone manipulations as part of folk medicine. The World Chiropractic Organization's "Practice Guidelines for Straight Chiropractic" (1993) defines "vertebral subluxation" as "a misalignment of one or more articulations of the spinal column or its immediate weight-bearing articulations, to a degree less than a luxation [dislocation], which by interference causes alteration of nerve function and interference to the transmission of mental impulses, resulting in a lessening of the body's innate ability to express its maximum health potential."

Chiropractor associations distinguish between reasonable practitioners and those who make unfounded claims. These professional groups have successfully demonstrated the treatment's effectiveness for many ailments and injuries. Most insurance policies cover chiropractic treatments subject to conditions, as are all forms of medicine. Scientific controversies notwithstanding, the chiropractic profession has a particular problem with provider fraud. In 1979, chiropractors and other non-medical doctors were allowed for the first time to treat workers' compensation cases.

A study in Oregon almost ten years later found that while chiropractors treated 10% of all cases in 1988, their billings accounted for 37% of total medical costs. The chiropractors' average cost per claim was $703, compared with $284 for a medical doctor. A news investigation in Florida found that most of the fraud claims "accused chiropractors of needlessly ordering costly diagnostic tests or treatments, billing for services they did not render, or illegally paying kickbacks to patients who agreed to undergo treatments."

In 1997, Dennis Jay, executive director of the Coalition Against Insurance Fraud, asserted that figures compiled by his agency showed that chiropractors do commit fraud at a greater rate than other medical providers. Of the cases in the Coalition's "Significant Fraud Database"—which tracks thefts or alleged thefts valued over $100,000—chiropractors represent a "clear majority" of medical provider fraud, according to Jay.

Chiropractic Fraud Schemes

Billing Schemes

- Administering X-rays and other diagnostic tests needlessly.
- Ordering full spine or repeated X-rays.
- Charging for "interpreting" X-rays and other test results, even though a radiologist or neurologist actually performed the function.
- Prescribing treatment before a history and physical are taken.
- Billing for patients who have sustained little or no injury.
- Extending treatment beyond a reasonable length of time.
- Billing for chiropractic treatments of non-spinal related ailments.
- Aiding personal-injury attorneys and insurance-fraud rings with diagnoses and billings.

Patients for Life

Chiropractors may obscure the results of tests and the patient's diagnosis, prolonging treatment as long as possible. Some promote the care of infants, which will continue for the lifetime of the patient. Some critics charge that patients develop a psychological dependency on continued treatment.

Patient Recruiting

Unscrupulous chiropractors are charged with a range of abusive recruiting practices.

- Direct kickbacks to patients.

- Collecting a patient's deductible (from $50 to several thousands) from the settlement of a personal injury lawsuit. Lawyers draft agreements with the chiropractor that certified the patient's disability, thus guaranteeing the chiropractor a portion of the patient's settlement money.
- Payment to "runners" or brokers who recruit patients, many of who have no ailment or injury. In some cases, the chiropractors and brokers split fees and establish suspect "rental" agreements in which the broker pays an inflated fee for leasing the chiropractor's office space during the time it takes to conduct the test.
- Coupons for free meals where the benefits of chiropractic are explained.
- Advertising for free initial care.
- Booths at health fairs, malls, or spas offering free screening.

Treatment for Nonspinal Conditions

Many chiropractors claim they can treat any medical condition, such as cancer, hernias, pneumonia, anemia, and heart conditions.

Other Abusive Practices

- Surrogate testing where the leg of a mother is flexed to diagnose her child's illness.
- Spinal manipulation of newborn babies to get over the trauma of birth.
- Spinal manipulation to treat epilepsy, asthma, bedwetting, and learning disabilities.
- Applied kinesiology, whereby diseases can be diagnosed by testing muscles with the help of particular food or nutrients.
- Analysis of X-rays to identify homicidal tendencies.
- Treatment plan prior to examination.
- Spinal manipulations begun at an early age to prevent colon cancer.
- Iridology or the examination of patients' eyes for markings that will indicate what diseases the patient has.
- A magnetic device over the thymus gland to diagnose nutrient deficiencies.
- Offers of vitamin cures, nutritional remedies, and homeopathic remedies.
- Soliciting family members.
- Advising not to have your children immunized.

- Promising to prevent disease through regular check-ups.
- No out-of-pocket expense.
- Treatment ends when insurance benefits are exhausted, but patients are recontacted when benefits renew for maintenance treatment.

Case Study—Dirty Harry

In 1998, New Jersey authorities arrested a chiropractor known as "Dirty Harry" because of his stained lab coat and brusque demeanor. Harry recruited young immigrants, primarily from the Dominican Republic, to stage car accidents and bring him the business. The sloppy "doctor" was just one of a dozen chiropractors who worked for Steven Verchow and Alexander Kuntzevich, who ran a fraud ring that generated over $52 million in phony claims. Someone like Dirty Harry, who rarely treated a patient for more than 10 minutes, could earn $100,000 a day.

Associate chiropractors received bonuses based on the number of patients they treated, and runners received cash to recruit new people willing to pose as victims. Nearly all of Verchow and Kuntzevich's patients reported that they were riding five people to a car. The driver in one accident was often listed as a passenger in another.

However, despite a two-year investigation and compelling evidence, Verchow and Kuntzevich were given a fine and had their licenses temporarily revoked. New Jersey Attorney General Peter Verniero decided proving a fraud case would be too difficult.

Fraud laws require the prosecution to show that the care was not valid and that the chiropractors intended to commit a deceptive act. But in these cases the chiropractors did examine each patient and could argue that sufficient care had been given. And according to chiropractors, even a minor accident could create a small injury that will cause the musculoskeletal system to try to accommodate for the damage. As a result, distortion will start appearing in the spine. Seemingly minor problems, such as slight lower back pain, headaches, and neck discomfort, could take weeks or months to correct. Therefore, in the New Jersey case, the appropriateness of treatment would have become the central prosecutorial issue, with both sides producing expert testimony to buttress their position.

Case Study – Allan S. Rosenthal

Perhaps the most infamous chiropractic offender, Alan Rosenthal ran his practice on automobile injury referrals from area attorneys. Virtually every insured patient at Rosenthal's clinic all ended up with bills just below $2,000—the threshold under which drivers can file pain-and-suffering lawsuits for soft-tissue injuries under the state's no-fault laws.

Rosenthal ordered unnecessary tests and instituted a policy that insured patients be treated a minimum of 25 times, regardless of condition. Uninsured patients did not receive the tests and were seen less frequently.

Chiropractors in Rosenthal's own clinic helped the FBI and the Internal Revenue Service collect evidence against him. Rosenthal plead guilty to 30 counts of a 36-count indictment and was sentenced to 15 months in prison, surrendered his license, and paid $436,000 in fines and restitution. The Rosenthal case was featured on *60 Minutes* and prompted states to start investigating local practitioners. During 1996, for example, the state of Florida performed "Operation Big Broom" and "Operation False Truth" against crooked chiropractors.

Sources:

Bergal, J., and Schulte, F. "Runners, Lawyers, Chiropractors Mine Auto-Insurance System for Big Money." *Sun-Sentinel,* December 19, 2000.

Brown, C. "Flaws In Florida's Auto-Insurance Law Allow Fraud Artists To Steal $1 Billion a Year." *Oregon Business,* October 1989.

Hennessey, R. "Cracking Down the Chiropractors; Targeting Fraudulent Chiropractors." *Best's Review,* October 1997.

Raso, J., M.S. *"Alternative Healthcare: A Comprehensive Guide."* American Council on Science and Health. New York: Prometheus Books, 1994.

Related Entries:

HEALTH CARE FRAUD

PROVIDER FRAUD

CLONING

See, CELL PHONE FRAUD, OR CLONING

COLUMBIA/HCA

In June 2003, HCA Inc. (formerly known as Columbia/HCA and HCA - The Healthcare Company) agreed to pay the United States $631 million in civil penalties and damages arising from false claims the government alleged it submitted to Medicare and other federal health programs, according to the Justice Department.

This settlement marked the conclusion of the most comprehensive health care fraud investigation ever undertaken by the Justice Department, working with the Departments of Health and Human Services and Defense, the Office of Personnel Management, and the states. The settlement resolves HCA's civil liability for false claims resulting from a variety of allegedly unlawful practices, including cost report fraud and the payment of kickbacks to physicians.

The first criminal convictions of HCA officials occurred in July 1999 when two Florida Columbia executives were found guilty of cost-reporting fraud at the Fawcett Memorial Hospital in Port Charlotte, Florida. Prosecutors discovered at least $3 million in Medicare overbillings. Executives Jay Jarrell and Robert Whiteside were convicted on six counts of Medicare fraud. Executive Michael Neeb was acquitted, and the jury failed to reach a verdict on Carl Lynn Dick, who arranged a plea bargain.

Previously, on December 14, 2000, HCA subsidiaries pled guilty to substantial criminal conduct and paid more than $840 million in criminal fines, civil restitution, and penalties. Combined with the separate administrative settlement with the Centers for Medicare & Medicaid Services (CMS), under which HCA will pay an additional $250 million to resolve overpayment claims arising from certain of its cost reporting practices, the government will have recovered $1.7 billion from HCA, by far the largest recovery ever reached by the government in a health care fraud investigation.

In particular, HCA's Tennessee hospitals were found to have engaged in extensive fraudulent activity, including up-coding patients diagnoses in order to increase hospital's reimbursement; over-billing Medicare, Medicaid and other programs for out-patient laboratory tests; illegally charging Medicare for non-reimbursable marketing and advertising costs that were disguised as costs for educating the community at large about public health issues; illegally charging Medicare for costs incurred in the purchase of home health agencies; improperly billing for home health services; and committing other billing fraud in connection with home health agencies.

The HCA investigation was the largest multi-agency investigation of a health care provider ever undertaken by the government, involving the participation by the department's Criminal and Civil Divisions, more than 30 United States Attorneys' Offices, the FBI, the Office of Inspector General for the Department of Health and Human Services, the Health Care Financing Administration, Defense Criminal Investigative Services, the Department of Defense's TRICARE Program, Office of Personnel Management inspector general, and state Medicaid fraud control units.

Thomas Kubic, Associate Director of the Criminal Division of the FBI called the HCA case, "one of the most complex and one of the most labor-intensive health care fraud investigations that the FBI has been involved in for well over the past eight years. Our agents, working with their counterparts, have reviewed millions of pages of documents. They spent thousands of hours combing through boxes of business records, Medicare cost reports and Medicare audit reports. They interviewed hundreds of witnesses. The investigation required agents to probe all aspects of the health care process, including billing and coding procedures, payments to physicians, corporate acquisitions, and the preparation and submission of Medicare cost reports. As a direct result of this investigation, Medicare auditors have reported an unusually large number of hospitals have voluntarily disclosed overpayments on their previously submitted, and in some cases audited and closed, cost reports."

Sources:
Kirchheimer, B., and Taylor, M. "$745 Million and Far to Go; Columbia's Tentative Settlement With Feds Still Leaves Some Difficult Issues Unresolved." *Modern Healthcare,* May 22, 2000.

"Janet Reno, U.S. Attorney General, Holds News Conference to Announce Settlement With Health Care Company Involving Government Fraud." *Federal News Service,* December 14, 2000.

U.S. Department of Justice Press Release. "Largest Health Care Fraud Case in U.S. History Settled: HCA Investigation Nets Record Total of $1.7 Billion" June 26, 2003.

Related Entries:

HEALTH CARE FRAUD

HOSPITALS, INSURANCE FRAUD BY

MEDICAID/MEDICARE FRAUD

COMPUTER CRIME

Computer crimes are committed against computer systems using computers. These crimes fall in the realm of fraud studies because the perpetrators often employ stealth and disguise. Financial crime committed using a computer is known as computer fraud.

Computer crimes include data alteration, unauthorized access and entry to systems and information (hacking or phreaking), reading e-mail or other communiqués without permission, data destruction and sabotage, Internet fraud, sale of proprietary data, desktop counterfeiting, data extortion, disclosure of confidential data, identity theft, electronic letter bombing, software piracy, PBX fraud, voice mail fraud, cellular telephone fraud, and stolen long-distance calling cards.

Computer Fraud vs. Computer Crime

A line that should be drawn is that between computer fraud and computer crime, terms that are commonly used interchangeably with little distinction made between the two. Some substantial differences exist between them, however, as we shall see.

A general definition of *computer fraud* is:

> *Any defalcation or embezzlement accomplished by tampering with computer programs, data files, operations, equipment, or media, and resulting in losses sustained by the organization whose computer system was manipulated.*

The distinguishing characteristic of computer fraud is that access occurs with the intent to execute a fraudulent scheme. Computer fraud statutes have established two very important principles:

- First, the statutes contain definitions of computer-related terms. These statutes allow the prosecutor to sidestep having to explain to the jury technical "computer speak" and its cumbersome fit with common law terminology.

- Second, the statutes create an offense based on proof of access with a particular intent. Success in carrying away property (money) does not have to be proved. Tracing the flow of proceeds is likely to be difficult without paper records and access might be the only provable event.

Any act of financial impropriety committed or significantly advanced by using a computer or any access gained to confidential information by computer may be prosecuted as computer fraud. The federal computer fraud statute is contained in Title 18, U.S. Code § 1030.

Computer Crime

Computer crime differs from computer fraud in two major ways. Employees who as a part of their normal duties have access to the computers are deemed to have authorized access and thus do not come under the law against access. Manipulation (alteration) or destruction of data (including computer software) is independent of fraudulent or other schemes. Such action does not fit into the normal vandalism crimes because the data is intangible.

Computer-Assisted Crime

It is sometimes said that most computer fraud is not "computer crime" but involves the use of computers instead of other means to break the law. In some cases these traditionally illegal acts can yield more loot by recourse to the high speed of the computer. These are in reality computer-assisted crimes and the existing criminal statutes can be appropriately applied to them. However, where detection and proof problems are exacerbated by the involvement of electronic media, computer fraud laws are invaluable for effective prosecution.

Information Crime

In some cases, the computer is an active weapon. These kinds of cases are termed *information crimes*; the crime would not be possible without computer technology. Examples of information crimes include the theft of computer time, software, and data.

Trends in Computer Crime

According to remarks by Mark Rasch of the Global Integrity Corporation before Congress in 2000, the following trends were discernible in computer crime activity. Distributed attacks had increased during the previous 10 years. "Attackers are using the known and publicized security holes to compromise systems. Most incidents and penetrations seem to be attacks of opportunity. The release of point and click tools (complete programs, scripts, and virus recipes) has made the ability to hack very easy and accessible to everyone."

Online activity increased the vulnerability of corporate information assets. Rasch indicated several major threats online: the disclosure of client related information, overt threats to personnel or facilities, disclosure of stock pricing and stock manipulation, the disclosure of technical information about corporate system and network architecture, disclosure of intellectual property information and/or research and developments secrets, and trademark violations. Intellectual property theft and trademark violations were expected to increase further.

Rasch also expected hacker attacks to increase, particularly in the following areas:

- An increase in attacks from out of the U.S., particularly from Eastern Europe.
- Increase in the use of social engineering to acquire intellectual property, proprietary information, and sensitive information from commercial industries.
- Increase in attacks on online banking, personal, and home systems.
- Increase in coordinated and distributed DOS attacks.
- Lowering of security standards and hiring standards due to a shortage of IT professionals.
- Increase in insider attacks on organizations.
- Increase in number and sophistication of self-mailing viruses, as well as copycat or mutated viruses.

Computer crime is expected to increase globally, particularly in countries with social transitions underway. According to figures issued by the Commercial Crime Bureau, cases of computer crime in Hong Kong increased in 2000 with 380 cases reported compared to 34 the previous year.

Financial Services Companies Are More Vulnerable Than Others

Financial services companies are more prone than most other industries to security breaches of their information system infrastructures, according to analysts at International Data Corporation. In findings published in 2001 researchers at IDC found:

- 96% of financial companies have reported security breaches.
- Viruses on client or server infrastructure were the most common attacks. (Most companies deploy anti-viral tools, but still suffer breaches. Banks were able to repel 56% of virus attacks at inception and another 36% midstream.)
- One in four finance companies reported unauthorized use of information systems, applications, and e-mail. In other industries the average is one in six companies reporting such issues.

Juveniles and Computer Crime

Juveniles have been involved in many of the most prominent computer crimes. Author Joseph De Marco has written that: "Juveniles appear to have an ethical 'deficit' when it comes to computer crimes. In one study, 34% of university undergraduates admitted to illegally pirating copyrighted software, and 16% admitted to gaining illegal access to a computer system to browse or exchange information. Moreover, a recent poll of 47,235 elementary and middle school students conducted by Scholastic, Inc. revealed that 48% of juveniles do not consider hacking to be a crime. This ethical deficit increases the likelihood that even 'good kids' who are ordinarily unlikely to commit crimes such as robbery, burglary, or assault, may not be as disinclined to commit online crimes."

NIPC and RCIS

In response to an expanding number of attacks against key components of the nation's information and economic infrastructure systems, the FBI established the National Infrastructure Protection Center (NIPC) located at FBI headquarters and Regional Computer Intrusion Squads (RCIS) located in selected offices throughout the United States. The NIPC, a joint partnership among federal agencies and private industry, is designed to serve as the government's lead mechanism for preventing and responding to cyber attacks on the nation's infrastructures—including telecommunications, energy, transportation, banking and finance, emergency services, and government operations. The mission of Regional Computer Intrusion Squads is to investigate violations of the Computer Fraud and Abuse Act, including intrusions to public switched networks, major computer network intrusions, privacy violations, industrial espionage, pirated computer software, and other crimes.

Louis Freeh, testifying before Congress as Director of the FBI in 2000, warned that computer crime was on the rise. "In FY 1998 we opened 547 computer intrusion cases, in FY 1999, that had jumped to 1,154. At the same time, because of the opening the National Infrastructure Protection Center in February 1998, and our improving ability to fight cyber crime, we closed more cases. In FY 1998, we closed 399 intrusion cases, and in FY 1999, we closed 912 such cases. However, given the exponential increase in the number of cases opened, cited above, our actual number of pending cases has increased by 39%, from 601 at the end of FY 1998, to 834 at the end of FY 1999. In short, even though we have markedly improved our capabilities to fight cyber intrusions, the problem is growing even faster."

Source:
"Employee Fraud Prevalent In the Workplace: Ernst & Young Study." *Ernst & Young,* January 8, 2001. www1.newswire.ca/releases/January2001/08/c7491.html

Computer Crime Insiders

The greatest threat of computer crime comes from employees inside an organization: operators, media librarians, hardware technicians, and other staff members. Authority may be unduly concentrated, e.g., systems software support entrusted to a single programmer. Information employees may work odd hours or in isolated environments and typically know the vulnerabilities of the computing system.

Sixty percent of all network attacks come from inside the company, making employees the single largest threat to network security, says researcher IDC Technologies. A report from consulting group Ernst & Young found that while 90% of businesspeople surveyed were concerned by the threat of significant fraud by employees, just 10% were confident that adequate controls were in place to prevent it.

Despite new laws addressing specific issues of computer crime, an analysis by Erdwin Pfuhl Jr. found that few defendants are ever charged under the new statutes. Violators are mainly charged using existing laws covering privacy, intellectual property, and wire fraud.

Computer crimes can be especially difficult to prosecute because of the volume of information generated by the act and the investigation. For example, one network intrusion case in 2000 required the analysis of 17.5 Terabytes of data—for comparison, the entire collection of the Library of Congress, which, if digitized, comprises only 10 Terabytes.

According to Datamonitor analysts, approximately 50% of firewall breaches occur when default settings are left unchanged, and 70% of companies do not know when or how often their security policy is revised.

The most prevalent methods of committing computer crime are:

- Altering or falsifying input
- Altering or falsifying output
- Data file manipulation
- Communications systems manipulation
- Operating systems manipulation
- Computer operations manipulation

Sabotage by disgruntled employees is a growing problem. Two of the most common acts of revenge are theft of company property and breaches in the company's computer network, according to an annual survey of Fortune 1000 companies by Pinkerton, Inc. The firm estimates that employee retaliation occurs in only 1% of dismissals, but could be as high as 5% at companies that do not handle layoffs well or that have a hostile corporate culture.

Telecommuting and the spread of Internet devices have made it easier for dismissed workers to wreak havoc outside of the company premises. Wireless networks in offices and factories can penetrate walls and have a range of 300 feet. Security experts suggest cutting off employees' connections to the corporate networks before letting them go.

Even if disgruntled workers cannot access company computers, they can use the Internet to spread false information in chat rooms and send out fake news releases. Blue-collar workers can damage systems by destroying the physical property or by reprogramming computers involved in manufacturing processes.

Intrusion Detection Software

Intrusion Detection Software (IDS) works by looking for patterns that may represent unusual activity and, therefore, an attack. However, users may have difficulty deciding whether to respond to the alerts, which may indicate bad passwords, difficult log-ins, or malicious computer programs. According to security experts, companies and government agencies lack effective computer emergency response plans, and many organizations fail to share information about attacks.

Insider Computer Crime Case Study

Juval Aviv, President and Chief Executive of Interfor Inc., a private investigation firm in New York, had lunch in April with a man he suspected of sabotaging one of his client's computer systems, causing up to $20 million in damage and indefinitely delaying a long-planned public stock offering. Mr. Aviv, whose client was a New Jersey chemical company, told the man, the company's former manager of information-management systems, that all the evidence pointed to him and that he was there to help him make things right. After a few hours and many cups of coffee, the 56-year-old former employee, whose name Mr. Aviv would not disclose to protect the identity of the company, confessed his guilt.

The man was one of 50 people laid off from the company in February. He had known another executive's computer password and had used it after losing his job to tap into the company's computer system from home and delete critical inventory and personnel files. The company veteran, who had been making $186,000 a year, wrote an anonymous note to the president of the company declaring, "I have been loyal to the company in good and bad times for over 30 years. I was expecting a member of top management to come down from his ivory tower to face us with the layoff announcement, rather than sending the kitchen supervisor with guards to escort us off the premises like criminals. You will pay for your senseless behavior."

The New Jersey chemical company committed two classic faux pas in handing out its pink slips, in the view of Mr. Aviv. First, it was unduly harsh toward a high-level executive who was accustomed to being coddled and who was familiar with the ins and outs of its computer network. And second, it failed to maintain a backup filing system to protect its crucial documents against sabotage. The worker was arrested but may avoid jail time because the company wants to avoid publicity, a common occurrence in such incidents.

Security Lapses Caused by Managers and Workers

The following tables show the results of surveys questioning computer security experts and managers at the Federal Computer Security Conferences in Baltimore during 1999.

The 7 Top Management Errors that Lead to Computer Security Vulnerabilities

Number Seven:	Pretend the problem will go away if ignored.
Number Six:	Authorize reactive, short-term fixes so problems re-emerge rapidly.
Number Five:	Fail to realize how much money their information and organizational reputations are worth.
Number Four:	Rely primarily on a firewall.
Number Three:	Fail to deal with the operational aspects of security; make a few fixes and then not allow the follow through necessary to ensure the problems stay fixed.
Number Two:	Fail to understand the relationship of information security to the business problem – they understand physical security but do not see the consequences of poor information security.

Number One:	Assign untrained people to maintain security and provide neither the training nor the time to make it possible to do the job.

The 5 Worst Security Mistakes End Users Make

Number Five:	Using a modem while connected through a local area network.
Number Four:	Not making and testing backups.
Number Three:	Failing to install security patches especially for Microsoft Office, Microsoft Internet Explorer, and Netscape.
Number Two:	Opening unsolicited e-mail attachments without verifying their source and checking their content first, or executing games or screen savers or other programs from entrusted sources.
Number One:	Failing to install an anti-virus, keeping its signature up to date, and applying it to all files.

Source: Sans Institute Resources, May 17, 1999.

Viruses and Worms

Saboteurs often deploy viruses and worms. A computer virus is a program that contains instructions that manipulate any machine the virus enters. Attacks may erase data, crash or destroy hard drives, or display messages. Viruses can copy themselves to other programs and move within networks.

A worm is a self-replicating program that can move autonomously (where a virus is transferred by user actions) from system to system via Internet or other network connections. Worms can find network utilities caches that show network code names, monitor network traffic, and randomly select network identification codes as well as other mischief.

Some of the more common virus carriers are software applications, programs downloaded from electronic bulletin boards, freeware and shareware from the Internet, vendor and supplier transmissions, shared program applications, and demonstration software. Indications that a virus or worm may have infiltrated a system include sudden loss of "free space" on machines, increase in file sizes, time changes in updates, large number of disk accesses or file accesses, unusual messages, unclear maintenance repairs, system fragmentation, changes in memory size or program size, and warnings from virus protection software. Viruses and worms are defeated by protective software, firewalls, and utility monitoring software.

A statement by the U.S. Congress in 2001 blamed the FBI's computer crime unit, the National Infrastructure Protection Center, for not adequately alerting the public of dangerous computer viruses. The agency attributed the lapse to staff shortages and vacancies in key positions.

Logs and History Files

The history files or logs, designed for troubleshooting computer systems, serve as the basis of any audit or investigation. These logs record activity in the following areas:

- Mainframe activity
- Programs executed
- Data files accessed
- Date, time, and duration of access
- User IDs that initiated a particular action
- Error messages
- Equipment malfunctions
- Communications activity
- User ID
- Terminal identifier
- Dial-in port identifier
- Security software activity
- Unsuccessful log-on attempts
- Modifications to the password files and access capability

Electronic Bulletin Boards

An electronic bulletin board is a database of user-posted messages accessible by others over telephone lines. Most bulletin boards have been created for specific purposes, usually for the exchange of messages and information among parties with common interests. Bulletin boards are especially popular among microcomputer users. Using public-domain software, a user can establish tailored menus for anyone dialing into the board. These menus usually contain options on information about the board, bulletins, news summaries, personal mail, conferences, and leaving messages.

Access to bulletin boards generally operates as follows:

- A user dials into the bulletin board.
- The board responds with a message asking for the person's name and password.
- The board then provides a menu showing the options available to the user.
- The user selects an option and starts interacting with the system.
- Typically, the user reads messages, leaves messages, downloads files, uploads files, or joins a conference.
- The user eventually "quits" the session and hangs up from the board.

So-called "pirate" or "elite" boards contain illegal information or have been established to advance an illegal activity. The owners tightly control security on those boards. Users commonly have to contact the owner directly to obtain a password for access to different levels of the system. A degree of trust must therefore be established before the owner will allow access.

Pirate boards have been found with a variety of illegal information on them including the following:

- Stolen credit card account numbers.
- Long distance telephone service codes.
- Telephone numbers to mainframe computers, including passwords, and account numbers.
- Procedures for making illegal drugs.
- Procedures for making car bombs.

- Hacking programs.
- Tips on how to break into computer systems.
- Schematics for electronic boxes (e.g., "black boxes")

Preventing Computer Crime

Passwords can be supplemented with basic security features starting from $10 per desktop. However, large organizations should consider spending more where appropriate.

- Biometrics, such as finger scanners, can protect entry to the system. Prices for such systems have fallen dramatically and they are now available for about $20 each. European spending on biometric products will increase from $80 million in 2000 to $550 million in 2004, $300 million of which will be spent on finger-scanning products, according to IDC Technologies.
- According to a new biometric intelligence report by think tank Allied Business Intelligence (ABI) in 2002, U.S. governmental agencies garnered 15% of the total biometric industry revenue for 2002. Between 2000 and 2007, total biometric revenue is set to grow at a rate of 47%.
- Smartcards can also identify users electronically. As of February 2004, 3.5 million cards have been deployed at a rate of more than 10,000 cards a day from 900 centers worldwide, according to statistics from the Defense Department's Common Access Card (CAC) program.
- Web-filtering tools can also detect employees accessing non-approved Internet content and can be tailored to alert managers to high-risk e-mail or Internet activities.

Case Study — Electronic Bulletin Boards

During the 1980's, The Maricopa County, Arizona Sheriff's Department and the Fremont, California Police Department established their own electronic bulletin boards to combat computer crime. The Maricopa board resulted in over 50 arrests, most commonly for telecommunications fraud. Fremont Police's bulletin board was partially funded by private funds from Visa, Wells Fargo Bank, Western Union, Sprint, MCI, and ITT.

Detectives announced through the board that they had stolen or hacked long-distance telephone service codes and credit account numbers. Over three months, the board logged over 2,500 calls from 130 regular users. In that period, over 300 stolen credit card numbers and long-distance telephone service codes were recovered. Passwords to many government, educational, and corporate computers were also discovered on other boards.

The operation resulted in the apprehension of eight teenagers in the area who were charged with trafficking in stolen credit card accounts, trafficking in stolen long-distance telephone service codes, and possession of stolen property. Within the next week, seven more teenagers in California and other states were arrested on information from this operation. It was established that this group had been illegally accessing between ten and fifteen businesses and institutions in California, bypassing the security of these systems with stolen phone numbers and access codes. One victim company estimated that it intended to spend $10,000 to improve its security and data integrity procedures.

Computer Fraud and Computer Crime Statistics

Computer Security Institute Annual Surveys

Each year the Computer Security Institute (CSI) conducts a survey asking computer security professionals to discuss issues in the field. CSI was established in 1974 in San Francisco and was designed to educate information security professionals and the general public. Results for the 2004 and 2003 surveys are included below. Copies of the surveys are available at www.gocsi.com.

According to a policy statement from CSI's director, Patrice Rapalus, "Each year, the influence and impact of the CSI/FBI Computer Crime and Security Survey grows. It is an invaluable tool for information security practitioners in corporations and government agencies struggling to get the attention of their CEOs, CIOs and CFOs, as well as for law enforcement officials working to make the case for closer cooperation with the private sector to stave off a cyber crime wave. The survey results over the years offer compelling evidence that neither technologies nor policies alone really offer an effective defense for your organization. Intrusions take place despite the presence of firewalls. Theft of trade secrets takes place despite the presence of encryption. Net abuse flourishes despite corporate edicts against it. Organizations that want to survive in the coming years need to develop a comprehensive approach to information security, embracing both the human and technical dimensions. They also need to properly fund, train, staff, and empower those tasked with enterprise-wide information security."

2005 COMPUTER CRIME AND SECURITY SURVEY

The 2005 survey found that there is no shortage of attacks and security breaches in cyber world. The upside of the situation is that the cost and severity of these attacks has taken a downward turn since 1999. The 700 respondents represent several sectors including finance (17%), high-tech (15%), and government (14%). The remaining 54% of the respondents (retail, medical, manufacturing, etc.) come from sectors where security issues are a much greater concern.

The total annual losses reported in the 2005 survey was $130,104,542, down from $141 million reported in 2004 and $201 million in 2003.

Number of Incidents

How many incidents, by % of respondents	1-5	6-10	>10	Don't know
2005	43	19	9	28
2004	47	20	12	22
2003	38	20	16	26
2002	42	20	15	23
2001	33	24	11	31
2000	33	23	13	31
1999	34	22	14	29
How many incidents from the outside, by % of respondents	**1-5**	**6-10**	**>10**	**Don't know**
2005	47	10	8	35
2004	52	9	9	30
2003	46	10	13	31
2002	49	14	9	27
2001	41	14	7	39
2000	39	11	8	42
1999	43	8	9	39
How many incidents from the inside, by % of respondents	**1-5**	**6-10**	**>10**	**Don't know**
2005	46	7	3	44
2004	52	6	8	34
2003	45	11	12	33
2002	42	13	9	35
2001	40	12	7	41
2000	38	16	9	37
1999	37	16	12	35

CSI/FBI 2005 Computer Crime and Security Survey
Source: Computer Security Institute

2005: 453 Respondents

Types of Attacks or Misuse Detected in the Last 12 Months (by percent)

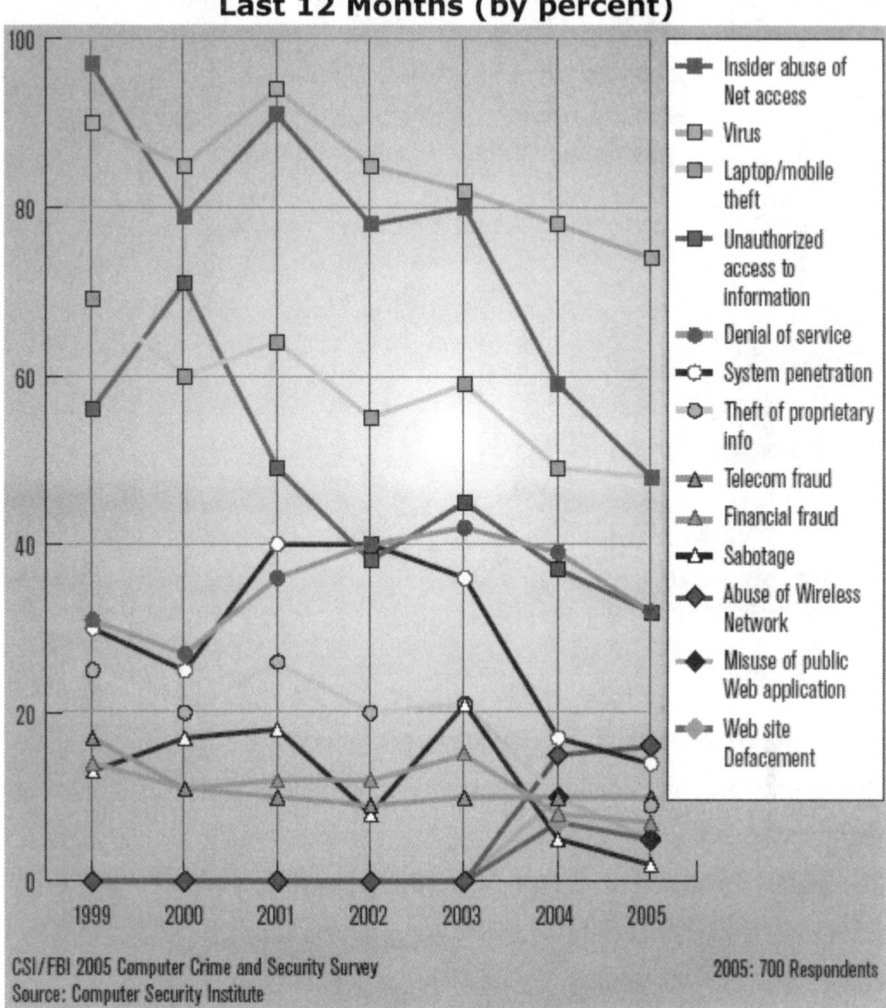

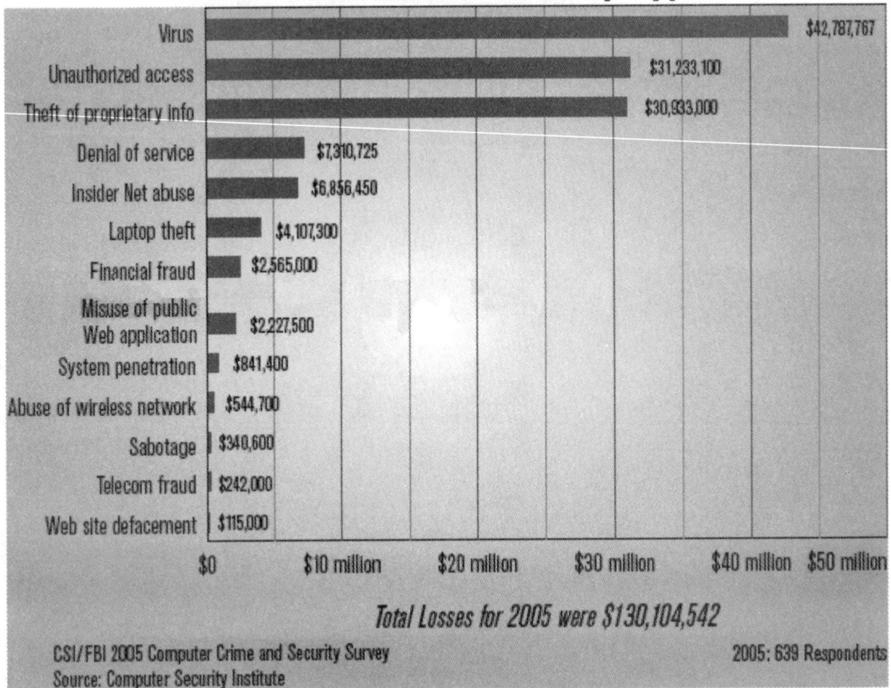

Compared to the 2004 survey, the following trends emerge:

- Cybersecurity breaches continue to decline, as do financial losses resulting from them.
- Virus attacks and denial of service caused the greatest financial loss ($74 million).
- Losses reported for financial fraud were considerably lower, at $2,565,000. This compares to nearly $8 million reported last year.
- 20% of the respondents who said they've suffered serious attacks reported the offense to law enforcement, a drop from 30% in 2003.
- The main reason organizations did not report intrusion to law enforcement was fear of negative publicity that could damage stock value and image. The percentage of respondents identifying this reason as important dropped from 51% to 43% over the last year.

- The percentage of respondents in 2005 that reported security breaches reached an all time low in over a seven-year period. Only 20% of respondents reported computer intrusions to law enforcement and a mere 12% reported to legal counsel.
- The respondents in eight out of 14 sector categories (utility, high-tech, manufacturing, medical, telecommunication, educational, financial and "other") believe that the Sarbanes-Oxley Act is having an impact on organizations' information security. In contrast, last year's survey only showed that five out of the 14 categories felt an impact from the act.

Department of Defense Study

The U.S. Department of Defense (DOD), through its Information Systems Agency (ISA), studied computer systems' vulnerability from 1992 to 1995. The ISA attacked its own systems using software available on the Internet. The results:

- System administrators did not detect the majority of attacks against DOD computers.
- Of the 38,000 attacks perpetrated, 96% of the successful attacks went undetected.
- Of the detected attacks, only 27% were reported.

Conclusions: Approximately 1 in 140 attacks were both detected and reported, representing only 0.7% of the total. The numbers for private businesses, particularly smaller companies lacking sophisticated information technology, are expected to be much higher.

The study characterized attacks as taking three general targets: the confidentiality of a system, the integrity of a system, or the digital information of a system. Such attacks are sometimes called "pure-play" computer crimes because they involve a computer system as the direct target of the attack—i.e., the attacker is not seeking credit card numbers or other information, and he/she is aiming to disrupt or pilfer the computer's operations.

Ernst & Young Survey

Respondents to an Ernst and Young survey of international businesses split over technology's effect on fraud rates:

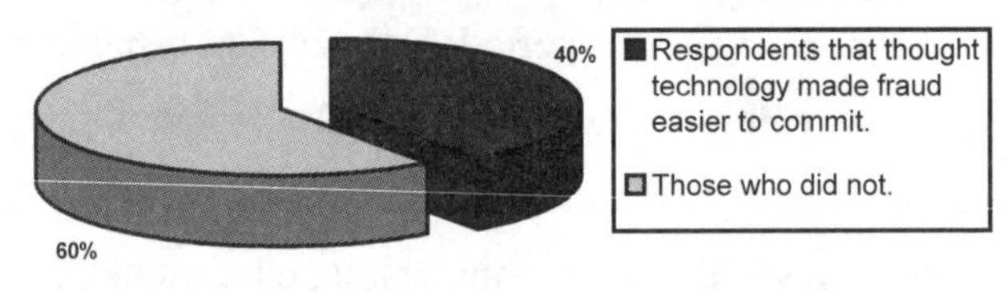

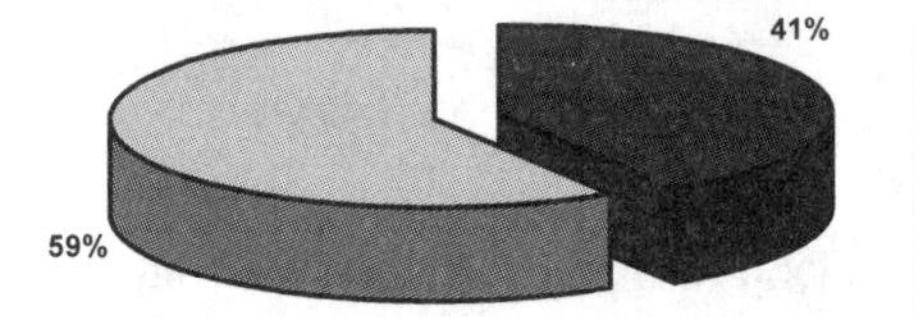

CyberSource Corporation Survey

A survey of 132 Internet companies in 2000 carried out by CyberSource Corporation indicated that 83% of online retailers believed fraud was a problem in their industry, compared with 75% who believed so one year earlier. While 5% of credit card transactions occur online, 50% of all credit card fraud occurs online. Retailers' estimated loss of revenue to online fraud fell from 5% in 1999 to 4%. Sixty-one percent of respondents said they were taking increased measures to prevent fraud.

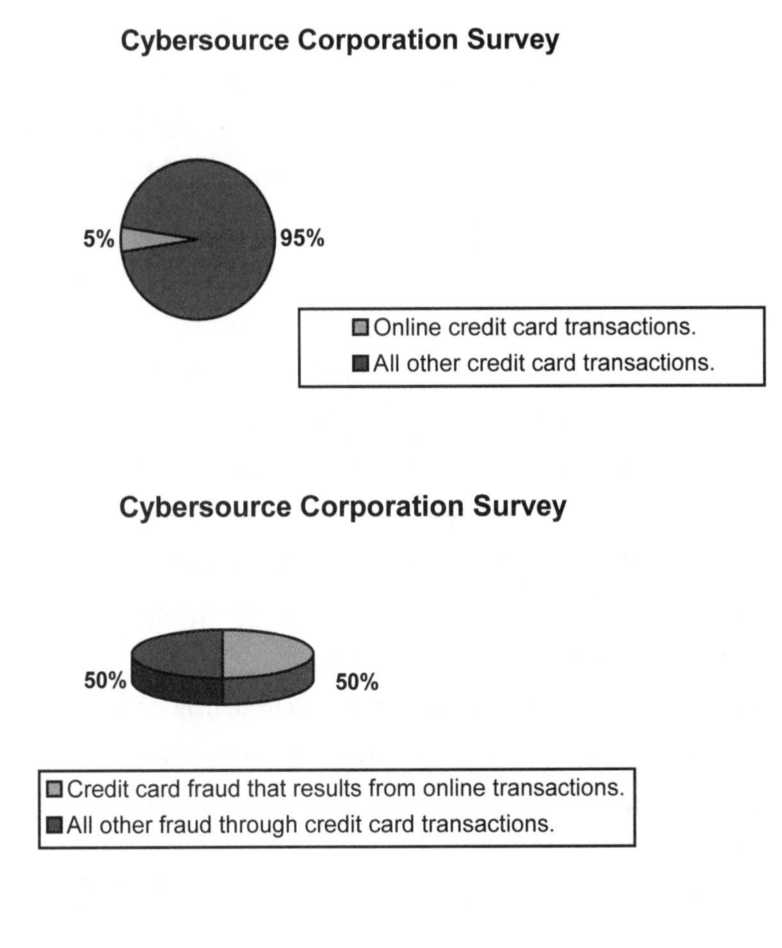

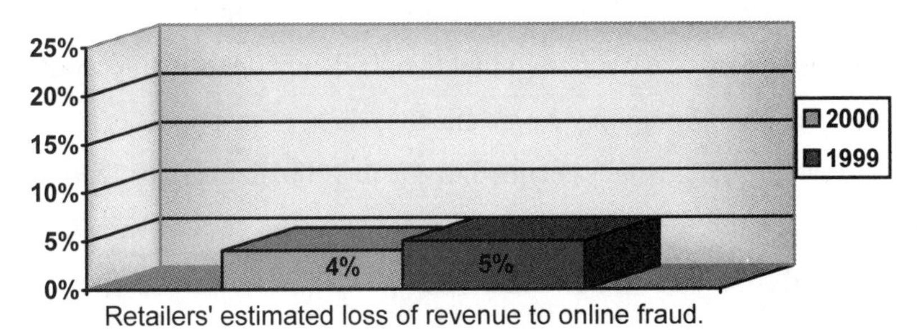

Dollar losses from eCommerce fraud continue to grow. Fraudsters will siphon approximately $3 billion from U.S. eCommerce in 2006, a 7% increase over 2005.

The percent of revenues lost to fraud improved slightly to 1.4%, in 2006, down from 1.6% the year before. This is the third consecutive year to show a decline in the percentage rate of revenue loss, but because eCommerce sales continue to grow 20+% each year, dollar losses to U.S. eCommerce continue to mount.

Approximately 1% of accepted orders ultimately turn out to be fraudulent, but merchants also reject 4% of their incoming orders due to suspicion of fraud — some valid orders are almost certainly being left on the table.

Chargeback statistics may represent only half of the actual impact of fraud.

Though international eCommerce is a major avenue of growth for merchants, orders coming from abroad tend to be far riskier than those from the U.S. or Canada. Merchants say international orders are 2 1/2 times more likely to be fraudulent.

In 2005, survey data showed that all sizes of merchants were reviewing more orders manually. That trend may have peaked. In 2006, merchants said that 23% of their orders were reviewed manually, down from 26% the year before.

Merchants are increasingly automating their fraud management operations. The 2006 survey found merchants were using more fraud detection tools. Also, the number of merchants using automated decision systems had risen 30% over 2005.

Source: www.cybersource.com/fraudreport/ The Eighth Annual CyberSource Fraud Survey was sponsored by CyberSource Corporation and conducted by Mindwave Research.

KPMG Survey

According to the *2003 KPMG Fraud Survey*, reports of fraud were on the rise. Seventy-five percent of organizations surveyed reported that they had experienced at least one category of fraud over the past 12 months. Approximately 12% of respondents in 1999 reported a computer-related fraud, which declined to 8% in 2000, but rose to 18% in 2003. In the 2004, however, the percentage dropped to 15%. Some 36% of KPMG's respondents who reported computer crime were either unaware of how much they had lost or were unwilling to disclose it.

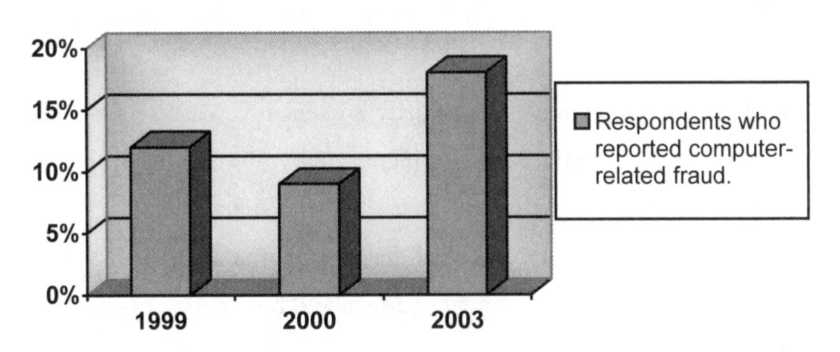

These numbers may be lower than other analyses, perhaps because the survey questioned executives, who are often unaware of their companies' true vulnerability.

An international survey in 2000 found that just 9% of respondents indicated that a security breach had occurred in their organization within the last 12 months. These numbers are lower than other analyses have found, perhaps because the survey questioned executives, who are often unaware of their companies' true vulnerability.

Responses to the 2003 survey show that companies are responding to the threat of fraud with a strong upsurge in anti-fraud measures. The actions taken to combat fraud with the largest increases included seeking legal action and notifying a regulatory or law enforcement agency. Sixty-four percent of respondents to the survey indicated that they had sought legal action or notified a regulatory or law enforcement agency when a fraud was discovered. When respondents to the 2003 survey did indicate a breach had occurred, legal action was not always pursued. The executives gave a variety of reasons for this, including inadequate legal remedies and a lack of evidence. Many companies lacked computer forensic response guidelines, which can significantly increase an organization's response to security breaches and aid in the recovery of misappropriated assets.

Other Computer Statistics

According to the 2005 Global Security Survey conducted by Deloitte, Touche, and Tohmatsu:

- Most respondents admitted the total IT budget spent on information security is 3%, though the percentage they feel would be optimal to protect their organization would be 6%.
- In North America, the incidents of security breaches increased or stayed relatively the same as last year. In Canada, breaches increased by 6% to 50% of respondents, while the US stayed relatively consistent with a 1% increase to 25%.
- The majority of respondents (59%) feel that management still views information security as purely a risk management exercise and not an area essential to the business.

Source: www.deloitte.com/dtt/cda/doc/content/dtt_financialservices_2005GlobalSecuritySurvey_2005-07-21.pdf

In 2001, the University of New Haven, Connecticut conducted a "digital sleuthing" challenge to discover the costs associated with investigating attacks on systems. The University reported that:

- "It took the intruder less than a minute to break into the university's computer via the Internet, and he stayed less than a half an hour. Yet finding out what he did in that time took researchers, on average, more than 34 hours each."
- "Those 34 hours would cost a company about $2,000 if the investigation was handled internally and more than $22,000 if a consultant was called in."
- "The contest also helps illuminate why securing a computer is more cost effective than hiring consultants to come in and do the detective work afterward," said Fred Cohen, director of the online investigations.

Source: CNET, March 22, 2001, news.cnet.com/news/0-1005-200-5217277.html

The Cooperative Association for Internet Data Analysis (CAIDA) found that the "Code Red" worm in 2001 affected more than 359,000 servers in less than 14 hours. CAIDA also determined:

2000	Was the number of new host that were infected at the peak of the infection frenzy.
43%	Total of all infected hosts that were in the United States.
11%	Percentage of virus infection that originated from Korea.
5%	The amount of infected hosts that were in China, and 4% in Taiwan.

Source: CAIDA, July 25, 2001. www.caida.org/analysis/security/code-red/

On November 15, 2000, Datamonitor reported on electronic security issues. Among the findings:

Datamonitor Report on Electronic Security Issues	
\$15B	Worldwide annual damage from e-Security breaches.
50%	Estimate of businesses worldwide that spend 5% or less of their
\$5.9B	IT budget on security.
\$663B	Global business-to-business and business-to-consumer e-commerce revenues.
	Amount in U.S. dollars of generated revenue by 2005, provided companies institute the proper security measures.

Source: "E-Security – Removing the Roadblock to E-Business." Datamonitor, January 18, 2001.

Carnegie Mellon University's Center for Computer Security released the following figures in August 2000:

- 99% of all reported intrusions "result through exploitation of known vulnerabilities or configuration errors, [for which] countermeasures were available." Systems were found to need regular security updates, or patches.
- In a test to see how fast a non-published, unpatched system would be discovered, the San Diego Supercomputer Center placed a default installation, Red Hat Linux 5.2 machine, on the Internet.
- 8 hours after installation, the system was probed for RPC vulnerabilities.

- 21 days after installation, there had been 20 targeted, unsuccessful exploits attempted.
- Approximately 40 days after installation, a vulnerable POP service was compromised, and the intruder installed a sniffer, several backdoors, and wiped out the system logs.

Source: "Overview Incident and Vulnerabilities." *CERT/CC,* August 17, 2000. www.cert.org/present/cert-overview-trends/index.htm

The 2005 E-Crime Watch survey, conducted among security executives and security personnel, revealed the fight against e-crimes may be paying off. CSO Magazine, in conjunction with United States Secret Service and the Carnegie Mellon University Software Engineering Institute's CERT® Coordination Center, showed that 13% of those surveyed (more than double the 2004 finding) report that the total number of e-crimes decreased from the previous year. Other stats include:

- Almost one-third (32%) of respondents experienced fewer than 10 e-crimes (versus the 25% reported in 2004)
- The average number of e-crimes decreased from 136 to 86 per respondent
- Of those who experienced e-crimes, more than half of respondents (55%) report operational losses, 28% state financial loses and 12% declare harm to reputation as a result. Thirty-one percent do not have a formal process or system in place for tracking e-crime attempts, and 39% do not have a formalized plan outlining policies and procedures for reporting and responding to e-crimes, demonstrating room for improvement.

Source: "E-Crime Watch™ Survey" CSO Magazine, May 3, 2005.

Case Study—Cisco Systems Accountants Commit Computer Fraud

The Cisco Systems computing corporation in San Jose employed Geoffrey Osowski and Wilson Tang. According to federal prosecutors, Osowski, a financial analyst, and Tang, an accounting manager, used their positions to obtain 230,550 shares of stock by illegally accessing Sabrina, a Cisco computer system used by administrators to manage stock-option disbursements.

Osowski and Tang twice transferred large blocks of stock into their personal brokerage accounts. In December 2000, they shifted 97,750 shares of Cisco stock, valued at $4 million, into two separate Merrill Lynch accounts. In January 2001, the men liquidated most of the stock. A month later, Osowski spent $52,000 on a new Mercedes 320, $44,000 on a diamond ring, and $20,000 on a Rolex watch. At about the same time, the two deposited 132,800 more shares, worth $2.3 million, into their accounts.

Tang and Osowski were sentenced to three years in prison for illegally breaking into company computers and plundering $8 million in Cisco stock. They were ordered to pay $3 million in restitution, besides the $5 million they had previously forfeited.

Sources:
"Cybersource." *Wall Street Journal,* November 3, 2000.

DeMarco, J. "It's Not Just Fun and 'War Games'—Juveniles and Computer Crime." *USA Bulletin,* May 2001.

Freeh, L. "Subcommittee for the Technology, Terrorism, and Government Information." *Federal Bureau of Investigation: Cybercrime,* March 28, 2000.

Goodman, M. "Making Computer Crime Count." *The FBI Law Enforcement Bulletin,* August 1, 2001.

Lee, H. "2 Ex-Cisco Accountants Sentenced For Fraud; Pair Stole Stock Worth $8 Million." *The San Francisco Chronicle,* November 27, 2001.

Levi, M. " Cities and Fears About Crimes." *Urban Studies,* May 1, 2001.

"Management; Coalface; Threat from Within Poses the Greatest Security Risk." *Computing,* May 10, 2001.

McEwe, T. "Dedicated Computer Crime Units." *U.S. Department of Justice,* June 1989.

"Prepared Testimony of Mark D. Rasch Vice President Global Integrity Corporation Before the House Committee on Government Reform Subcommittee on Government Management, Information and Technology Subject - "Computer Security: Are We Prepared For Cyberwar?" *Federal News Service,* March 9, 2000.

Tahmnincioglu, E. "Management: Vigilance in the Face of Layoff." and "Rage: Employer Miscues Can Breed Retaliation." *The New York Times,* August 1, 2001.

Related Entries:

AVANT!

CORPORATE ESPIONAGE

HACKING

HOAXES

INTERNET FRAUD

COMPUTER FORENSICS

When conducting a computer crime investigation, a primary consideration should be determining whether or not an outside forensic examiner is needed or whether the expertise is available "in-house." This determination will depend, to a large extent, on the complexity of the examination required and whether or not the intended examiner is trained and experienced in forensic recovery techniques, preparing legally sufficient reports, and testifying as a witness. Some organizations have invested in their own, in-house personnel whom they have trained and outfitted with the proper equipment and software tools to conduct the examination and analyze the digital evidence. Others have acquired and retained the services of an outside examiner as a disinterested third-party who will be able to conduct a thorough examination, prepare a proper report, and deliver expert witness testimony if needed in legal proceedings.

A secondary consideration involves determining that in fact a crime has been committed. If it is determined at the beginning of the investigation that a formal referral to a law enforcement or prosecuting agency will be made, then it becomes imperative that the authorities be contacted prior to the onset of the investigation to determine their preference as to whether law enforcement personnel should participate in the examination and analysis procedures or if the law enforcement entity is comfortable with the in-house personnel's level of expertise. In some jurisdictions, an examiner from the law enforcement community may not be available on short notice or available at all.

Digital Evidence

The proper handling of digital evidence is critical; it is easily altered or destroyed if handled improperly. The destruction of digital evidence through improper handling can result in a finding of spoliation of evidence by a judge or can raise questions about the alteration of exculpatory evidence by the defense. If a judge determines that the authenticity of the evidence cannot be satisfactorily made, then they may rule that the evidence is inadmissible.

Examiners should be aware that files on computer can be altered simply through the normal startup process. Most of the Microsoft operating systems, such as Windows XP, change the time and date stamps on a number of files during startup and delete a number of temporary files during the shutdown process. These pieces of information could be critical to the investigation.

Hardware

It is important for the examiner to understand and be able to recognize various pieces of computer hardware so that he will be able to make a decision about whether or not it is necessary to seize a particular computer component. The examiner should be familiar with the various forms that digital evidence can take. Items used for digital storage have become so compact that it is now possible to store vast amounts of data on items that can fit in a pocket or attach to a keychain. There are many such devices, now used primarily in digital cameras, which can hold digital data outside of a camera just as easily as a thumb drive. In most cases these devices are smaller than a matchbook. While these devices were developed for storing images, they are capable of storing anything digitally.

Printer technology is another area where it is necessary to stay current on advancing technologies. Many computer networks today have installed printers with large hard drives designed to do away with the need to have a large print server. The printers themselves may now be the repository of addition evidence that at one time resided on a local machine or on a print server.

Considerations When Conducting the Seizure

Be certain to document the scene with photographs or a diagram, depending on the complexity of the setup, remembering that it may be a year or longer before testimony about what the office looked like on the day of the seizure will be asked for in a legal proceeding. Additionally, it is important to document what is on the screen if the system is on, as well as what processes are currently running. As many people have a habit of writing down or recording their passwords near their computer, examiners should look around for notes that may appear to be passwords. This practice may aide in the discovery of passwords needed to access encrypted data in the event the subject of the investigation is being uncooperative.

Good notes should be taken with regard to the time and date that the system was seized and the personnel involved in the seizure. The status of the system should also be noted. Was it on, off, or on standby? Is there anything unusual attached to the system? Is there any obvious damage? Did any files have to be saved? Make sure to start a chain of custody document and note each person and storage location that each piece of evidence passes through.

Securing the Computer System

When beginning to secure the computer system, it is imperative that two "Golden Rules" be followed. The first Golden Rule has two parts: If the computer is off, don't turn it on, and If the computer is on, don't turn it off. The second part of this rule regards a system that is on and running. Generally, an investigator will not want a desktop machine to go through its normal shutdown routines because Windows is very good about cleaning up after itself. A number of temporary files will be deleted and possibly overwritten during a normal shutdown, some of these files may be important to the investigation. In most cases, the investigator should simply unplug a running machine so that the second part of the first Golden Rule applies and that is, "If the computer is on, then don't turn it off." From the time the investigator takes possession of the system it is imperative not to allow anyone access to the computer, with the exception of a trained forensic examiner.

There are other reasons to conduct the seizure in this way. By preserving the state of the system at the time of seizure one can help to defeat an argument by opposing counsel that exculpatory information was somehow tainted or erased due to mishandling of the system. If one "bit" is changed on the system's data, it will have a completely different hash value; that is to say it is now different from the original, even though the average person may not be able to recognize any difference at all.

The second Golden Rule is, Don't peek through the files. This also applies to floppy disks. When encountering a system that is running, there is a real temptation to click on the "My Computer" icon and look for the evidence of interest and/or copy files out to a floppy disk or CD. This should never be done because each file the investigator touches will have its original time stamps changed; once this is done the original time stamps cannot be recovered. It will be obvious to the forensic examiner that this has occurred.

There are two methods for shutting down a running system, a hard shutdown and a graceful shutdown. Generally, the hard shutdown is preferred. There may be extenuating circumstances that would lead the investigator to perform a graceful shutdown, so it is important to evaluate the best shutdown option based on the type of data being preserved and the possible ramifications of a hard shutdown based on the type of operating system installed. A hard shutdown is basically pulling the power cord from the back of the PC.

Laptop computers present additional considerations. When seizing a laptop, it is important to remove the battery first and then pull the plug. It is essential when seizing a laptop to recover all of the components that belong to the laptop such as floppy drives, CD and DVD ROMs, power supply, etc. Often laptop computers must be imaged with their drives installed and because of the proprietary nature of the laptops themselves, they will function with only their own components. Many times these components can be located in the laptop carrying case.

Once a computer is seized, it is necessary to secure it in such a way that will allow the investigator to testify, if need be, that no unauthorized access to the suspect system occurred.

What Can the Computer Forensic Examiner Locate?

A computer forensic examiner is a trained professional who is capable of analyzing digital media at the hexadecimal level. The hexadecimal level means that every sector and all the bytes in those sectors are available for viewing. This includes the deleted files, both purposefully deleted and those that are deleted through various Windows automated processes. This can also include temporary auto save files, print spool files, deleted e-mails, link files, etc. The hexadecimal level also contains various items found in restore points and registry files that define hardware, such as external drives and websites visited, in addition to the document revisions and files created and maintained by the user.

The increased sophistication level in Windows allows the computer system to store more information about how users use their computers. The forensic examiner will be able to uncover a large amount of data that relates to the use of a computer, what is or has been stored on the computer, and the computer user. Combined with the undertaking by Microsoft to "be all" to the user, they have also incorporated ways to make computer use more secure by offering encryption and other methods to protect data from unwanted access. In the future, these types of innovations will continue to stall the examiner and will sometimes successfully prevent system access. However, these encryption packages are not always foolproof. The Encrypted File System offered by Microsoft has in fact been "cracked" by a number of password cracking software makers. In addition to encryption files, other encryption algorithms exist which are easily installed and can be used to encrypt the entire hard drive. In situations such as this, it becomes necessary for the examiner to be able to identify whether a drive is encrypted before seizing and disconnecting the system.

Handling the Evidence

One of the major differences between investigating computer-related crimes and conventional criminal activities is the volatility of the evidence that resides in the computers themselves. Indeed, the evidence of a computer intrusion might be erased or altered as part of the intrusion itself. It is therefore very important for the organization and/or law enforcement personnel to deal quickly and decisively with evidence of suspected computer-related criminal activities.

Privacy Issues

It should also be noted that personal digital devices are becoming more common in the workplace. Employees often carry PDAs, thumb drives, or MP3 players into the office. Each of these devices is capable of storing large amounts of data and can easily be used to steal a company's intellectual property. Since these devices are often purchased by the employee for personal use, a search warrant may be needed to seize or search these devices because employees may have a "reasonable expectation of privacy" in these types of personal devices. Therefore, it is extremely important to include such devices in the company's search policy. The policy should clearly state that any personal electronic devices, including laptops, cell phones, PDAs, thumb drives, MP3 players, etc., are (just like handbags and briefcases) subject to search if brought onto the company's premises.

COMPUTER FRAUD

See, COMPUTER CRIME

CON SCHEMES

Confidence games involve a range of fraudulent conduct usually committed by professional "con artists" against unsuspecting victims. The victims can be organizations but are usually individuals. Cons usually act alone but sometimes form groups for a particularly complex endeavor. Common hustles target people with visits to their homes or through telephone solicitations.

All frauds require that the perpetrator gain the confidence of the victim, so in that sense all frauds are a con. But for the purposes of this encyclopedia, "con games" are deceptions of limited duration; the perpetrators obtain funds from victims infrequently, perhaps only once or twice the course of the con. The score is quick and may be accomplished on nothing more than a slick presentation. More complex frauds, including some commonly described as "cons" or "scams," are discussed in other entries. (See also TELEMARKETING FRAUD, PYRAMID SCHEME, and CONSUMER FRAUD.)

Common Cons

Directory Advertising Schemes

The essence of directory advertising schemes is the sale of advertising in a non-existent magazine or directory. A fake (in some cases real) directory is shown to the potential victim. The victim contracts and pays for display or classified advertising that is to appear some months in the future. By the time the advertisement is to be posted, the fraudster will have disappeared.

Personal Improvement Frauds

These frauds prey upon the desire of people to improve their education or job skills. In some instances, the fraudster appeals to a one's personal appearance.

Fundraising, Nonprofits, and Religious Schemes

Some groups use terms such as "cancer" or "AIDS" or "Christian" in their titles, use titles similar to legitimate charitable organizations, or impersonate legitimate charitable organizations to raise funds. Some offer prizes or awards in exchange for contributions; potential donors may be led to believe the prize has a greater value than the amount of the contribution.

Home-Based Businesses

Many companies marketing home-based businesses require customers to buy materials for assembly-at-home products. The company promises to purchase the completed products, but either disappears or offers less money than promised. Some home-based business promotions are legitimate, but many are not. Typical frauds include pitches for milk-culture kits, envelope stuffing, and an array of products offered by multilevel marketing organizations.

Home Improvements

A home improvement scam is a common scam that involves phony repair people selling their services door-to-door. The work is usually done shoddily, with substandard materials, or not at all. Sometimes the con quotes a low price for the repair and then intimidates the customer into paying more after the job is done.

Money Manager and Financial Planner

Money managing and financial planning scams involve convincing marks to "invest" in low-risk, high-return opportunities.

Phone Card, Credit Card, and Debit Card Schemes

In phone, credit, and debit card scams, a con artist calls claiming to be with the consumer's long-distance company, credit card company, or financial institution. The consumer is asked to confirm a card number; if successful, the con artist uses the number personally or sells it to a broker.

Conning the Fraud Victim Twice: Scavenger and Revenge Schemes

Victims of con games are contacted by an organization promising to recover the victim's funds. An up-front fee is required to finance the recovery, which never occurs. The promoters target victims by readings news stories and court proceedings, or they may purchase lists of victims from other con artists. The very same group that conned the victim in the first place sometimes runs this scam—new personnel call the victim, offering restitution and revenge.

Sweepstakes, Giveaways, and Prizes

Many of these "free gifts" require the consumer to pay a fee before collecting. This fee actually covers the cost of the merchandise deemed "free." Merchandise may not arrive or may turn out to be much less valuable than represented.

College Scholarship Services

This bogus service usually charges a front-end fee or advanced payment fee for finding a scholarship suitable for an applicant. The information is taken from freely available sources and is often rife with errors. Some promoters "guarantee" scholarship funds, though they have no influence or connection to scholarship-granting organizations.

Advance Fees for Loans, Goods, or Services

In advance fee scams, a customer is "guaranteed" a loan or a credit card regardless of his/her credit rating. In this type of situation a legitimate financial institution rejects the victim. The victim is then told that he/she must pay a processing fee will pay to fix the poor credit rating or obtain "alternative financing." The victim generally does not receive the loan or receives a loan at an exorbitant interest rate.

Advance fee swindles collect funds up-front for the delivery of a product or a service which is never delivered or is delivered with a large balance due. In some schemes, the product is marketed to a large number of customers and then the operation is shut down prior to the delivery stage.

Diploma Mills

For what often is a hefty fee, those who apply can purchase a "diploma." The fraudster usually claims that the fee is for "processing" the application and/or for verifying the experience necessary for the degree to be awarded. The hallmark of the diploma mill is the ease with which the degree is obtained. The degrees, however, are essentially worthless because the school is not accredited.

Correspondence schools also can operate with the same modus operandi as diploma mills. Investigators have at times submitted the scribbling of their infant children to schools that advertise that they will provide art lessons to persons who demonstrate talent; usually the infants' "drawings" are judged to show considerable ability, and the submitter is asked to send a fee to begin receiving the lessons.

Modeling Schools

Modeling schools appeal to the vanity of some people. In the typical scheme, the modeling school representative tells the prospective student that he will prepare a portfolio of portraits to be sent to potential customers who may employ the victim as a model. The victim is then charged an inflated price for the pictures. Con game modeling schools often claim—inaccurately—connections to famous people and maintain that they have been instrumental in starting the careers of successful models. The schools sometimes target parents and grandparents with lures of the money that can be earned by their "exceptionally pretty" infant children or grandchildren.

Equity-Skimming Schemes

In equity-skimming schemes, a conman talks the mark out of the equity in his/her home and tries to persuade the homeowner to borrow against his/her equity.

Block Hustle

Block hustles occur when purveyors of cheap stereo equipment, jewelry, and watches hawk their goods on street corners or traffic lights. The items for sale are generally either "hot" or imitations of brand names.

Pigeon Drop

The pigeon drop is often used on middle-aged or elderly women likely to have savings accounts. This scam is usually committed by two or more actors as follows:

- Actor #1 befriends the victim.
- Actor #2 shows both Actor #1 and the potential victim a "found" package containing a large amount of cash.
- All parties agree to place an ad in a newspaper for the lost package (usually a wallet).
- If the package is not claimed within a certain amount of time, the parties will split the money.
- Actor #1 then insists that the found money be divided equally but only after each person puts up his own money to demonstrate good faith.
- All the money is put in one package and placed with Actor # 3, who poses as an attorney or disinterested party.
- In some cases the mark is given the package to hold, but the package is switched and the actors take all the money.

Bank Examiner Swindle

Bank examiner swindles are usually perpetrated on older women, especially widows with access to life insurance policies. A con man impersonates a bank examiner investigating the woman's bank. The con asks the old lady to withdraw a certain amount of cash from her account, place it in an envelope, and allow him to inspect the bills for counterfeits. Many con men use false IDs and dress up to take on this role.

Jamaican Handkerchief or Envelope Switch

In commencing the Jamaican handkerchief or envelope switch, the criminal puts his money into an envelope with the mark's money and then unobtrusively trades this parcel for another that looks like the same thing but is instead bulked up with worthless paper.

- Two actors working together usually perform the switch.
- Actor #1 approaches a victim looking for the address of a prostitute.
- Actor #1 shows a large sum of money to the victim.
- Actor #2 arrives and tells Actor #1 where he can find the prostitute but cautions Actor #1 on taking all the money as the prostitute might rob him.
- Actor #1 asks the victim to hold the money for him. Actor #1 puts his money into a handkerchief with the victim's money.
- Actor #1 shows the victim how to hide the money under his arm, inside his shirt while switching handkerchiefs.
- Victim takes the handkerchief and the parties split up, however, Actor #1 leaves with victim's money.

The Obituary Hustle

In an obituary hustle, the criminal poses as a delivery person collecting money for a package or other order the deceased supposedly made. The criminal might also pose as someone who is owed money by the deceased or as a business partner of the deceased.

Three-Card Monte

A three-card monte is a card game that involves two people who fleece an unsuspecting onlooker into a rigged game.

Poker Bunco

Poker bunco scam can involve poker, dice, pool, and other games. The con man pretends to be a novice or moderately experienced player, but is an expert. The mark is convinced to wager money on the game and loses.

Missing-Heir Scheme

In a missing-heir scheme, a con man poses as a probate investigator or other genealogist, and charges fees to distribute the inheritance.

Gold Mine Swindle

In a gold mine swindle, a con man claims to own a productive mine but requires money to start operation. The scheme involves selling shares to the mine.

Spanish Prisoner Game

In the Spanish prisoner game, a wealthy individual receives a letter purportedly from a hostage held prisoner in some foreign land stating that the hostage needs money to bribe his captors or pay a ransom. As collateral, a treasure map or other "valuable papers" are often enclosed.

Murphy Game

Also known as "Miss Murphy," "paddy hustle," or "carpet game," the Murphy game is played in places where prostitution occurs. The con artist plays a pimp but never delivers the prostitute.

Badger Game

The badger game is a refined version of the Murphy game, but, in this con, the con woman or prostitute is in on the scam. The con artist robs the mark of his wallet through simple theft or pretense of blackmail.

Goat Pasture Scam

In a goat pasture scam, the con phones pretending to represent an oil and gas service that is sponsoring a lottery on mineral rights. The consumer is told that if he/she invests a certain tax deductible sum, he/she will receive a percentage of the income in royalty payments.

Airport Scam

In an airport scam, an actor approaches a victim in an airport and states that the newspaper stand cannot change his one hundred dollar bill. The con then asks the victim for change and tells the victim that the stand still has his $100 bill. The victim provides the actor with the change, then actor returns to the store to get the one hundred dollar bill back, but never returns to victim.

Auto Repair

Auto repair scams occur when an actor hangs around an auto repair shop and approaches victims who are leaving after receiving estimates. The con claims to do work off duty at a very low cost. Once the negligent car work is completed the victim's car is not returned until the enormous bill for car repair is paid.

Check Kiting

Check kiting occurs when a bank account is opened with good funds and a rapport is developed with the bank. The con man then deposits a series of bad checks. However, before the checks clear, the con withdraws funds from the bank.

Coupon Redemption

In a coupon redemption scam, grocery stores amass large amounts of coupons and redeem them to manufacturers although merchandise is never sold.

Fortune Telling

A fortune telling scam occurs when a con advises a victim that he/she is cursed. The con tells the victim that the curse must be removed by meditating to the spirits, which will require payment. Over a period of time, the victim pays the fortune teller thousands of dollars to remove the curse.

Gypsies

A gypsy scheme occurs when a con states that the victims' money is cursed. In order to remove the curse, the money must be placed into a bag or box that the con provides. The bag or box is switched. The con tells the victim to perform certain rituals over the money and the curse will be removed. The bag or box cannot be opened for a period of time and when it is opened the money is gone.

Inferior Equipment

When actors travel around selling inferior equipment for unjustifiably high prices, inferior equipment fraud occurs. Tools are often sold under this type of scheme.

Land Fraud

Land fraud occurs when an actor induces victims to purchase tracks of land in some type of retirement development that does not exist.

Odometer Fraud

Odometer fraud occurs when a used car salesmen turns back the odometers on used cars. The cars are then sold at higher prices due to deceptively low mileage figures.

Police Impersonation

Police impersonation occurs when a con instructs a victim to take money out of a fraudulent bank and place it into a "good bank." After the money is withdrawn, the con appears to take the money to the police station for safekeeping. The victim never sees the money again.

Ponzi Scheme

A Ponzi scheme is an investment scheme where an actor solicits investors in a business venture, promising extremely high financial returns or dividends in a very short period of time. The actor never invests the money but does pay dividends. The dividends consist of the newest investors' funds. The first investors, pleased to receive dividends, encourage new investors to invest. This scheme falls apart when the actor no longer has sufficient new investors to distribute dividends to the old investors or the actor simply takes all the funds and leaves the area.

Pyramid Scheme

A pyramid scheme is a form of investment fraud in which an individual is offered a distributorship or franchise to market a particular product. The promoter of the pyramid indicates that although marketing of the product will result in profits, larger profits will be earned by the sale of franchises. For example, if a franchise price is $10,000, the seller receives $3,500 for every franchise sold. Each new franchise purchaser is presented with the same proposal so that each franchise owner is attempting to sell franchises. Once the supply of potential investors is exhausted, the pyramid collapses. Many times, there are no products involved in the franchise, just the exchange of money.

Quick Change

Quick change scams occur when a victim is confused by a con's speedy series of short-changed money exchanges.

Shell Game

The shell game occurs when a con manipulates a pea beneath three walnut shells or bottle caps. The con moves the caps around and shows a victim the cap with the pea under it. With the encouragement of another con, the victim places larger and larger bets on which cap contains the pea. The original con ends the game when the take is large enough.

Utilities Impersonators

Utilities impersonators pretend to be utility employees by wearing jumpsuits and nametags. A con approaches a victim with a story about a gas leak or electrical surge to gain entry to the victim's home. The con then takes the victim's personal valuables.

VCR Scam

A VCR scam occurs when an actor purports to sell new VCR's or televisions at an extremely low cost. Victims pay for the VCR or television only to discover that the box has been filled with rocks.

West African Investment Scams

West African investment scams occur when actors target businesses and obtain business' bank account information. Later funds from such accounts are withdrawn.

Related Entries:

CONSUMER FRAUD
CULTURE FARMS
GONDORF, CHARLIE AND FRED
NIGERIAN 419
PONZI SCHEME
WEIL, JOSEPH

CONSUMER FRAUD

Consumer fraud refers to criminal and civil acts committed against consumers by businesses or by individuals practicing business. Among the more common acts are construction fraud, telemarketing fraud, automotive repair fraud, and merchandising fraud.

Shoddy work or fraud by contractors is the biggest complaint by U.S. consumers, according to the nation's 137 Better Business Bureaus. Inquiries and complaints about home improvements and remodeling contractors have risen 60% since 1991 and currently amount to 1.1 million a year, more than double those about poor financial services, bad treatment at retail stores, or faulty auto repairs

Statistics on Consumer Fraud

One reason for the prevalence of consumer fraud is the enormity of the American economy. The average American household had an income of $44,389 in 2004, according to the American Community Survey by the U.S. Census Bureau.

Consumer Sentinel, the complaint database developed and maintained by the Federal Trade Commission, reported that from January to December 2006, there were more than

670,000 consumer complaints. Of the 428,319 fraud related complaints, many were identity theft cases.

Not including identity theft complaints, these are the top consumer fraud complaints for 2005 are as follows:

- Internet auctions (5%)
- Shop-at-home, catalog sales (7%)
- Internet services and computer complaints (6%)
- Foreign money offers (3%)
- Prizes/sweepstakes and lotteries (7%)
- Advance-fee loans and credit protection (2%)

Total reported losses to fraud in 2006 were over $1.1 billion, with a median loss of $500.

NACAA Report

In 2005, the National Association of Consumer Agency Administrators, an association of consumer protection agencies in the U.S. and Canada, reported the previous year's activity, including complaints. Complaints of home improvement and repair fraud increased from the previous year, making it the number one complaint from 2003-2004. The top ten categories of fraud complaints were:

TOP TEN CATEGORIES OF CONSUMER FRAUD

Rank	Fraud Type
1	Home Improvement/Repair
2	Automobile Sales
3	Automobile Repair
4	Credit
5	Telecommunications
6	Debt Collections
7	ID Theft
8	Internet/ISP/E-Commerce
9	Major Purchases
10	Telemarketing/Sales

2005 NACAA Report

The Office of Community Oriented Policing Services

The Office of Community Oriented Policing Services (COPS), a component of the U.S. Department of Justice, reports that it is difficult to accurately determine the amount of fraud against the elderly in the U.S. because there are no national databases that specifically track financial abuse of the elderly. There is also an issue of how each state determines who is considered "elderly."

Regardless, the few existing studies on the matter estimate that 20 – 60% of adult Americans have been victims of fraud. The National Center on Elder Abuse estimated that nearly one third of all elder abuse cases involved financial abuse.

Do the Elderly Fall More Easily?

Analysis by the American Association of Retired Persons contends that elderly people are more vulnerable to fraud than other age groups: "They are less familiar with sources of consumer information and have less knowledge of consumer rights. They tend to be more open to direct appeals from sellers like telemarketers and less wary of misleading sales presentations. One-third of people aged 75 and older were classified in the high-vulnerability category as compared to 7% for younger people." Reviewing materials from an FBI telemarketing investigation, AARP found that over 50% of the victims were over the age of 50.

However, there are indications that telemarketers and other consumer fraud perpetrators target different groups for different scams. Immigrants are targeted for citizenship-related frauds and direct-marketing schemes. Women are more likely to be targeted by home repair or auto repair frauds. An analysis of consumer-fraud victims in 1995 by Richard Titus, et al., found, "No demographic indicator predicts whether a fraud attempt, if received, will be successful. The key factor in victimization by personal fraud appears to be whether one receives an attempt." As the target group for each fraud shifts, the elderly may be targeted more frequently by certain perpetrators. But they are probably not any more likely than people in other age groups to fall for a scam.

Common Consumer Fraud Schemes

Merchandising Schemes

Fraudulent substitution replaces the purchased item with something of lesser value. A bait-and-switch ploy advertises an item at a certain price to draw customers. When the customers arrive the item is not available and the salespeople offer a similar, yet more expensive product.

Direct Debit from Checking Accounts

Debit cards may be stolen or the number obtained at point-of-purchase (particularly with catalog orders, phone orders, and online transactions). If the checking account number is also provided, counterfeit checks may be prepared and drawn against the account. Unlike credit cards, the issuing financial institution does not guarantee debit cards. Consumers are responsible for all losses due to theft or unauthorized use.

Automotive Sales

Common complaints about automobile dealers include deceptive sales techniques, adding on accessories without authorization, and excessive finance charges and fees. Tourists, women, and the elderly are often targets of unscrupulous operators.

Leasing agreements have been used in many automotive frauds. On average, dealer profit on a lease is twice that of a conventional purchase. Dishonest dealers take advantage of consumers by using deceptive lease-vs.-buy comparisons by quoting lower prices or interest rates, then using higher ones in the lease, and quoting higher trade-in allowances than people actually receive.

Salespeople may suggest that the consumer make a down payment on the lease in exchange for better terms. However, a down payment on a lease is nothing but "monthly payments in advance" because down payments do not affect the residual payment or build equity. For example, an advertised "$299 per month" 30-month lease based on $1,800 down is the same as $359 per month with no down payment.

Salespeople, who count on the consumer not to calculate the legitimate price, may inflate the monthly payment. Due to intentional overstatement of the monthly payment by salespeople, some consumers have paid $75 to $100 a month more than they owed under legitimate terms.

Deceptive comparisons are designed to make bad lease deals look better than conventional purchases. Instead of comparing lease payments to 5-year loan payments, salespeople use the higher payments on 4-year or 3-year loans to make the purchase look unattractive. However, a lease is a rental agreement, while a conventional loan plan confers ownership.

Another deceptive comparison is the quoting of inflated loan payments, again, to make purchases look more expensive than leases. Inflated lease payments may also be quoted, with the "extra" money going towards a secret price or APR increase.

The "flip" is a common trick that has been used to overcharge many people on leases. After a buyer agrees to purchase a vehicle at a negotiated or advertised discount from MSRP, the salesperson convinces them to lease the vehicle instead "to lower their monthly payment."

Before cap cost (price) disclosure was required, a dishonest salesperson would simply use a non-disclosure lease to secretly raise the price of the vehicle. These price increases were typically $1,500 to $2,000 (some were $5,000 or more), and victims rarely, if ever, discovered the overcharges.

Debt Consolidation/Credit-Fixing Scams

Debt consolidation agencies act as an intermediary between debtors and creditors. Some agencies are legitimate but many are not. Typically, the agency writes to creditors requesting a workout plan at lower monthly payments spread over a longer period of time. The creditors offer such an arrangement if they feel the debt will thereby be paid or if the workout plans will forestall bankruptcy or default by the creditor. The debtor could make similar arrangements personally; there is no need for the agency to make the request.

Already of dubious distinction, the more unscrupulous debt consolidation agencies collect the money from the debtor but do not forward it to creditors. Considerable time can pass before the debtor finds out that the money was misappropriated. Some firms charge fees to "fix" credit problems. In fact, the firm obtains a copy of the customer's credit report (which the customer can request for free) and then contacts creditors requesting new terms for repayment (which the debtor can also do).

Case Study—Auto Leasing

In 1995, ABC's *PrimeTime Live* found deceptive leasing practices at five out of the ten dealers they visited. That same year, a statewide investigation in Florida resulted in 55 Toyota dealers and their distributors setting up a $4.5 million restitution fund to settle complaints of overcharging on leases. On May 14, 2000, KCBS-TV announced the results of its three-month undercover investigation of 14 new-car dealerships in Southern California. America's largest auto dealers were caught red-handed by hidden cameras—lying, cheating, and overcharging customers on new car leases and purchases.

Case Study—Auto Repair

When undercover investigations in California and New Jersey caught Sears Auto Centers selling unnecessary repairs in 1992, the practice was partially blamed on the company's quotas, sales commissions, and contests that encouraged the sale of additional repairs. Incentives included Caribbean cruises and $10,000 cash prizes for managers. The daily quota for mechanics was $500 per day. Consumer advocates said those practices were responsible for the problems at Sears. The company countered they were only conducting preventive maintenance and that replacing good parts before they fail was "a common practice in the industry." The company later admitted that "mistakes did occur" and agreed to pay $8 million to settle the California charges. Sears also agreed to make restitution to 900,000 customers nationwide and discontinued the use of quotas, commissions, and contests.

Sources:

Berton, L. "Horror Stories from the Remodeling Front." *Wall Street Journal,* December 29, 1995.

Jesilow, P. *"Deterring Automobile Repair Fraud."* PhD. Dissertation, University of California, Irvine, 1982.

Norrgard, L. and Norrgard, J. *Consumer Fraud.* Santa Barbara: ABC-CLIO, 1998.

Related Entries:

AUTO SALES FRAUD
AUTOMOTIVE REPAIR FRAUD
BAIT AND SWITCH
CON SCHEMES
CULTURE FARMS
FALSE OR DECEPTIVE ADVERTISING
GOULDD, BILL
HOME REPAIR FRAUD
HOAXES
IDENTITY FRAUD
INTERNET FRAUD
JESSUP, CHARLES
LEASING FRAUD
NIGERIAN 419
PONZI SCHEME
PREDATORY LENDING
QUACK
TELEMARKETING FRAUD
TURNER, GLENN

CONTRACT AND PROCUREMENT FRAUD

A contract is a mutual agreement, oral or written, between two or more parties which must contain the following elements:

- Competent parties
- Lawful subject matter or objective
- Agreement between the parties to enter into a bargain
- Offer by one party
- Acceptance by the other party
- Legal consideration

Fraud can occur at any point during the contracting process. In general terms, the contracting process can be broken down into five phases:

- Presolicitation
- Solicitation
- Negotiation
- Performance
- Administration

Presolicitation Phase

The activities typically involved during presolicitation are:

- Need recognition
- Notice of intent to contract
- Development of specifications
- Award criteria

The most prominent schemes involved at this phase of contracting or procurement are:

- Determining needs
- Bid specifications

Determining Needs

The typical fraud in the need recognition phase of the contract negotiation is collusion between the buyer and contractor, where the buyer's employee receives a gratuity or kickback for recognizing a "need" for a particular product or service.

Bid Specifications

Bid specifications and statements of work detailing the types and amounts of goods and services to be provided are prepared to assist in the selection process. They are intended to provide both potential bidders and the selecting officials with a firm basis for making and accepting bids.

A well-written contract will contain specifications, standards, and statements of work which clearly detail the rights and entitlements of the contractor. Carelessly written specifications, standards, and statements of work make it easier for a contractor to claim at a later time that he is entitled to more money than the buyer intended to pay.

Sometimes, the buyer's personnel and the contractor deliberately collude to write vague specifications. At other times, there is an agreement to amend the contract to increase the price immediately after the award. One contractor actually developed a "cost enhancement plan," which identified all the changes he would make in order to double the cost of the contract, before it was even signed.

DETECTION

The following is a list of potential red flags for frauds involving specifications:

- Providing the contractor with information or advice on a preferential basis.
- Using statements of work, specification or sole source justifications developed by, or in consultation with, a contractor who will be permitted to bid.
- Permitting consultants who assisted in the preparation of the statements of work, specifications, or design to perform on the contract as subcontractors or consultants.
- Splitting costs into separate categories to avoid review.
- Writing specifications not consistent with past similar procurement.

Solicitation and Negotiation Phase

Fraud schemes involved during this phase typically involve collusion between the buyer and contractor and contractors of competing companies in the bidding process. Schemes in this phase also involve defective pricing.

Bid Submission Schemes

Schemes involving bid submissions can take on many forms. It can involve anyone in the contracting cycle such as a buyer or contracting official, engineer, technical representative, quality or product assurance representative, subcontractor liaison employee—anyone who can *influence* the awarding of a contract.

Examples of bid submission schemes are:

- Premature opening of bids
- Altering bids
- Unjustifiable extension of bid opening dates
- Controlled bid opening
- Falsifying bid logs and documents

DETECTION

To detect bid submission schemes the fraud examiner should be aware of:

- Acceptance of late bid
- Falsification of documents or receipts to get a late bid accepted
- Change in bid after other bidders prices are known
- Change in bid dates
- Receipt of late bids
- Last bid usually receives the bid

Bid-Rigging Schemes

Most bid rigging fraud schemes involve a collusion between contractors of competing companies during the bidding process.

BID ROTATION

Collusive bidding occurs when a group of prospective vendors exchanges information on contract solicitations, taking turns at submitting the "low bid."

BID SUPPRESSION

In a bid suppression scheme, one or more of the competitors agrees with at least one other competitor to refrain from bidding or agrees to withdraw a previously submitted bid so that a contractor's bid will be accepted.

Other forms of this activity involve agreements by competitors to fabricate bid protests or to coerce suppliers and subcontractors not to deal with nonconspirators who submit bids.

A variation of bid suppression occurs when competitors make arrangements to refrain from competing in a designated portion of a market. This might be accomplished based on customer or geographic area. The result of such a division is that competing firms will not bid or will submit only complementary bids (discussed below) when requests for bids are issued in the competitor's unassigned area.

COMPLEMENTARY BIDS

Complementary bidding, also known as "protective" or "shadow" bidding, occurs when competitors submit token bids that are too high to be accepted (if competitive in price, bids on special terms will not be acceptable). Such bids are not intended to secure the buyer's acceptance, but are merely designed to give the appearance of genuine bidding.

PHANTOM BIDS

Several companies have been caught creating dummy companies to submit a variety of bids on a single contract. That way, they give the appearance of vigorous competition while actually bidding against themselves.

DETECTION

To detect these types of fraud, the fraud examiner must be alert for:

- "Unsuccessful" bidders who later become subcontractors

- Wide disparity in bid prices
- Same contractors who bid on all projects with rotating low bidders
- Other qualified vendors who fail to submit bids
- Bid protests from losing, qualified bidders
- Splitting up requirements so contractors can each get a "fair share," and can rotate bids
- A rotational pattern to winning bidders
- A geographical pattern to winning bidders
- Joint venture bids by firms who could have bid individually

Defective Pricing Schemes

Defective pricing occurs during the negotiated contracting process when contractors fail to disclose accurate cost or pricing data in their price proposals, resulting in an increased contract price.

Examples of defective pricing schemes generally involve the submission of inflated labor costs and inflated material/parts costs. Other schemes involve:

- The use of vendors other than the one proposed
- Not disclosing documents on vendor discounts
- Changing make or buy decisions
- Not disclosing residual material inventory
- Inflating costs by channeling work under contract through a dummy company
- Withholding information on batch purchases

DETECTION

To detect defective pricing schemes, the fraud examiner should be alert for the following:

- Failure to update cost or pricing data even though it is known that past activity showed that costs or prices have decreased
- Failure to correct known system deficiencies which can lead to defective pricing
- Repeated denial by the contractor of the existence of historical records
- Delay in the release of data to the buyer to preclude possible price reductions
- Altered supporting data

Contract Performance and Administration Phase

Contract performance activities include change orders; timely review of completed portions prior to sign-off and release of monies; and assessment of deliverables for compliance with the terms of the contract, including quality control. There are two basic schemes perpetrated during the performance phase: product substitution and mischarges (accounting, material, and labor).

Product Substitution

In order to increase profits, the contractor might employ a product substitution scheme, failing to meet the contract specifications in the areas of either quantity or quality of products. Examples of schemes involving product substitutions include:

- Delivery of inferior/substandard material
- Delivery of materials that have not been tested
- Falsification of test results
- Delivery of used, surplus, or reworked parts
- Delivery of counterfeit products
- Submission of false certifications (Certifications are statements that parts or materials are new, domestically manufactured, and meet the contract specifications concerning quality and quantity or that the company is minority-owned.)
- Delivery of commercial equivalents hardware
- Passing off or specially creating samples for inspection
- Surreptitious movement of inspection tags to uninspected goods
- Substitution of look-alike goods

DETECTION

The following is a list of potential red flags for product substitution schemes:

- High percentage of product returns to vendor for noncompliance with specifications
- Product compliance certificate missing
- Compliance certificates signed by low-level employee with no quality assurance responsibilities
- Materials testing done by supplier, using his own personnel and facilities

- Laboratory test reports are identical as to sample descriptions and test results, varying only as to date and lot number tested
- Highest profit product lines have the highest number of material return authorizations or reshipments

In order to detect these types of frauds, the fraud examiner should consider the following audit procedures:

- Conduct both routine and unannounced inspections and testing
- Carefully review the inspection and testing reports
- Request assistance from outside technical personnel to conduct after-the-fact tests
- Interview personnel and others for indications of noncompliance
- Review correspondence and contract files for indications of noncompliance

Mischarges

ACCOUNTING MISCHARGES

Accounting mischarges are defined as knowingly charging unallowable costs to the buyer, concealing or misrepresenting them as allowable costs, or hiding them in accounts (such as office supplies) that are not usually audited closely. Another common variation involves charging types of costs or independent research and development to other cost categories.

MATERIAL MISCHARGES

Material mischarges are usually limited to raw materials which can be used on many different contract products or diverted for personal use. Numerous cases have been discovered where the buyer-owned material, which was used on a similar contract (e.g., commercial), shows up on the accounting records as being used in the manufacturing process for the subject contract (e.g., government).

DETECTION

Material mischarges can be detected by examining material cost transfers. These might include transfers:

- From government contracts to commercial
- Via any type of suspense or holding account
- From ongoing jobs to jobs not scheduled for delivery until far into the future
- From prior lot work orders to current or future work orders
- To inventory write-off accounts
- To scrap accounts
- Of materials ordered and charged in excess of contract requirements
- Of seemingly unrelated materials charged on routing slips
- In which material standards are not updated over periods of time when the contractor recognizes improvements in manufacturing technology or product design
- In which a significant variance exists between proposed versus negotiated vendor prices

LABOR MISCHARGES

Labor costs are perhaps more susceptible to mischarging than are material costs because employee labor can readily be charged to any contract. The only way to ensure that labor costs are charged to the correct account is to actually observe the work of each employee (to determine the contract on which he is working), then determine from the accounting records that the employee's cost is charged to the proper contract.

There are several schemes involving mischarged labor costs. Some of the more prominent mischarges are:

- Transfer of labor costs
- Time and charges do not agree with contractor billing
- Fictitious time cards
- Changes made to individual time cards
- Time card charges by supervisors

DETECTION

Labor mischarges can sometimes be detected by examining the following:

- Distinctive labor-charging patterns on research and development
- Significant increases in charging to overhead accounts (for example, idle time, down time, and nonapplied time)
- Reclassification or reorganization of employees from indirect to direct charges
- Changes in the labor-charging relationships between certain tasks or types of labor
- Decrease in indirect expense pools
- Increased labor hours with no corresponding increases in materials used or units shipped
- Actual hours and dollars consistently at or near budgeted amounts

Related Entries:

BRIBERY
CORRUPTION, OCCUPATIONAL
DEFENSE PROCUREMENT FRAUD

CORPORATE CRIME

Corporate crime refers to crimes committed by corporations. Crimes committed *against* corporations are covered under Occupational Fraud and Abuse. Corporate crime is sometimes called *organizational crime*, following the work of Marshall Clinard. More than 90% of corporations charged with crimes are privately held.

Corporate crime is a broad term, encompassing a range of harmful behaviors, from price-fixing and product liability to discrimination against women and minorities, tax fraud, and fraud against municipal bodies by corporations (overcharging for municipal bonds, for example, or dishonestly obtaining tax breaks). Many acts of corporate crime—child labor, unsafe working conditions, and anti-union violence—were legal until the 20th century. Reform movements have established broad regulatory controls, but enforcement spending has not kept pace with the expanding economy.

Over a two year period, Marshall Clinard and Peter Yeager examined the records of 562 companies (477 of which where on the *Fortune 500* list) and found that 1,533 white-collar crime cases had been filed against them. Some 60% of the firms had at least one case against them. For those companies the average number of violations was 4.4. Clinard and Yeager found that large corporations were far more likely to commit violations than small corporations. The oil, pharmaceutical, and motor vehicle industries had the most violations and were most frequently charged for wrongdoing.

Clinard and Yeager found six main types of corporate illegal behavior:

- *Administrative* violations within the structure or by the activities of a company's business.
- *Environmental* violations of the laws and regulations safeguarding air, water, and land.
- *Financial* violations, including corruption; securities-related violations; financial transaction between companies, vendors, and customers; tax violations; and accounting malpractices.
- *Labor violations*, including discrimination in employment, occupational safety and health hazards, unfair labor practices, and wage and hour violations.
- *Manufacturing violations* involving hazardous substances, improper packaging, and consumer safety.
- *Unfair trade practices* involve abuses of competition such as monopolies, price-fixing, and undisclosed interests.

Costs of Corporate Crime

According to figures compiled by Ralph Estes in 1994, corporate crime cost the U.S. economy about $2.6 trillion. The offenses included discrimination against women and minorities ($165 billion); workplace injuries and accidents ($141.6 billion); deaths from workplace cancer ($274.7 billion); price-fixing monopolies and deceptive advertising ($1.1 trillion); unsafe vehicles ($135.8 billion); cigarette liability ($53.9 billion); other product injuries ($18.4 billion); environmental costs ($307.8 billion); defense contract overcharges ($25.8 billion); income tax fraud ($2.9 billion); violations of federal regulations ($39.1 billion); bribery, extortion, and kickbacks ($14.6 billion); and miscellaneous costs ($82.5 billion). Not included in the data were acts of money laundering, redlining, capital flight, insurance fraud, illegal attempts to destroy unions, and securities fraud.

Besides monetary losses, corporate crime damages land and endangers the health of humans and other animals.

Product Liability

Corporate crime may claim lives as well as cause financial loss and environmental damage. The leading cause of illness and death in America is tobacco, the product of an industry that has spent billions settling and fighting liability suits. Smoking is implicated in an estimated 400,000 American deaths a year, 20% of the total deceased.

The second leading cause of death and illness is the automobile, the product of an industry with its own history of embarrassing and deadly liability issues. Since 1899, when the first automotive fatality was announced, the machine has been involved in over two million deaths. Ralph Nader's crusade against the Ford Motor Company for knowingly selling Pinto models with deadly defects inspired a surge of safety improvements throughout the industry.

More recently, Ford fought a public battle with Firestone, which supplied Ford with tires for many of its vehicles, because problems with Firestone tires caused the Ford Explorer to be prone to rollovers. Though the two companies had been business partners for over 100 years, they ceased their relationship because each company blamed the other for the deaths and injuries that resulted. In Congressional hearings during 2001, Representative Cliff Stearns expressed consternation. "Both companies have conducted tests, performed experiments, and hired experts. Both companies have loaded us with charts, statistics, and diagrams. Unfortunately, when asked the same questions, the companies respond with two different answers. The information presented by both Ford and Firestone is typically contradictory and incompatible. But the one conclusion that cannot be questioned is that there is an increase in consumer confusion."

Pharmaceutical companies have also been exposed for knowingly selling destructive products. Even after its Dalkon Shield was banned in the U.S., A.H. Robbins continued selling the product overseas.

Causes of Fraud and Deviant Behavior in Corporations

The following discussion summarizes research conducted by various academics on the precipitating factors of corporate crime. See the list of sources at the end of this entry for further reading.

Diane Vaughan asserts that the erosion of support for legitimate business procedures motivates price fixing, discriminatory price-cutting, theft of trade secrets, false advertising, and bribery. Perpetrators justify these crimes as the natural act of one organization dominating another in order to obtain resources that provide for upward mobility. Corporate employees regard themselves in a "survival of the fittest" mentality. No ethical precepts are allowed to obviate the struggle not just to survive but also to dominate.

Competition within a company among its constituent divisions has a similar effect, spurring members to achieve goals without observing ethical norms. Vaughan notes that the interests and needs of departments sometimes conflict with the interests of the larger organization. Lower-level managers tend to act in the interests of their departments. Vaughan hypothesizes that the complexity of internal processes and structures of a business, regardless of its size, create the opportunity for deviant behavior.

Vaughan writes that organizational growth naturally leads to a progressive loss of control over departments. Executives rely on subordinates to carry out policy. When the distance between executives and subordinates reaches a sufficient measure, "authority leakage" results; the structure has become too unwieldy for an executive to enforce rules. "The organization," Vaughan writes, "can diversify beyond the capability of those at the top to master it."

The tiered structure of most organizations obscures personal responsibility. Author John E. Conklin writes, "The delegation of responsibility and unwritten orders keep those at the top of the corporate structure remote from the consequences of their decisions and orders, much as the heads of organized crime families remain 'untouchable' by law." According to Conklin, executives at the higher levels of the corporation can absolve themselves of responsibility for crimes by stating that the illegal means used by their employees was done without their knowledge, much the same way heads of organized crime families remain "untouchable" by the law by keeping themselves remote from the illegal activity.

Many large corporations with intricate hierarchical structures share the problem of a split between what the upper levels believe is going on below and the actual procedures being carried out. Clinard and Yeager say that the chief executive officer of a corporation is often isolated and messages transmitted down the line tend to become distorted.

Dr. John Braithwaite views white-collar crime as a product of corporate subcultures in which fractured social bonds and internal competition prevent individuals from aligning their goals. Corporate members turn to crime as a result of "blocked opportunities" that discourage ethical means. Because white-collar crime can exist only in secrecy, deviant subcultures develop (conspiracy among executives, for example). Lines of communication are splintered or non-existent, and people operate within isolated spheres of responsibility.

Clinard and Yeager found that all levels of the corporation often agree to perpetuate the lack of full information, for the key to any successful conspiracy to violate the law generally lies in the fact that the higher-ups do not inquire about what is going on and those at the lower levels do not tell them. Often in corporations, no single individual at the highest levels may make a decision alone to market a faulty product or take shortcuts on product testing, Clinard and Yeager say. Instead, decisions are made in small steps at each level, possibly without any awareness of the illegal and potentially dangerous result.

Sociologist Edward Gross suggests that all organizations are inherently criminogenic though not necessarily criminal. The criminologist Oliver Williamson concurs, noting that managers tend to maximize their department's interests to the detriment of the organization.

Organizations can also be criminogenic because they are self-reinforcing. Diane Vaughan cites several practices that contribute to a criminogenic atmosphere.

- The organization tends to recruit and attract similar individuals.
- Rewards are given out to those who display characteristics of the "company man."
- Long-term loyalty is encouraged through company retirement and benefits.
- Loyalty is encouraged through social interaction such as company parties and social functions.

- Frequent transfers and long working hours encourage isolation from other groups.
- Specialized job skills can discourage personnel from seeking employment elsewhere.

Vaughan writes that organizational processes create "an internal moral and intellectual world" that causes individuals to identify with organizational goals.

Gil Geis found that quite often individuals are trained in illegal behavior as part of the occupational role. Schrager and Short say criminal behavior stems mainly from the roles an employee is expected to fill, rather than individual pathology. Luthans and Hodgetts said that after performing a study with the American Management Society, 3,000 executives questioned "felt under pressure to compromise personal standards to meet company goals," but that they felt "that business ethics should still be a concern."

Christopher Stone found that the success of law enforcement "ultimately depends upon its consistency with and reinforcement of the organization's rules for advancement and reward, its customs, conventions and morals." He maintains that if the law is too much at odds with the corporation's culture employees will tend to cover up their tracks rather than to change their behavior.

Clinard and Yeager believed that in rationalizing their behavior, corporate personnel and management obey laws selectively, according to situational needs, and influenced by factors such as social class and occupation. Many executives justify their behavior as standard practice in the business world, whatever the norms of society at large. Silk and Vogel found that people defend a corporation's acts to function beyond government authority; in the rashest version of this mindset, "all legal measures proposed constitute government interference with the free enterprise system."

Silk and Vogel found corporations also argue that "regulation is faulty because most government regulations are incomprehensible and too complex." Conklin found that antitrust laws are seen as inconsistent, hypocritical, poorly defined, and rarely enforced. Therefore, most regulations must be written in detail to cover as many contingencies as possible.

According to Clinard and Yeager, corporations often try to protect their executives from liability by agreeing to pay fines, court costs, and attorney's fees with corporate funds; bonuses or raises or liability insurance might offer protection to officers or directors. Generally, executive compensation and tenure remain untouched. There is much difficulty in criminal prosecution of executives because corporate violations are usually far more complex than conventional crimes. Also, the complexity of the legal proof required allows businessmen to test the limits of the law.

Silk and Vogel outlined the justifications used by businesses to rationalize conduct:

- Government regulations are unjustified because the additional costs of regulations and bureaucratic procedures cut heavily into profits.
- Regulation is unnecessary because the matters being regulated are unimportant.
- Although some corporate violations involve millions of dollars, the damage is so diffused among a large number of consumers that individually there is little loss.
- Violations are caused by economic necessity; violators aim to protect the value of stock to ensure an adequate return for stockholders, and to protect the job security of employees by ensuring the financial stability of the corporation.

McCaghy asserts that profit pressure is "the single most compelling factor behind deviance by industry, whether it be price fixing, the destruction of competition or the misrepresentation of a product." In Clinard and Yeager's opinion, certain industries such as the drug and chemical businesses face severe competition and a demand for continual development of new products. These pressures encourage corporate members to falsify test data, to force products to market too quickly before adequate testing ensures safety and performance, or to engage in dishonest sales techniques.

Controlling Corporate Crime

Clinard and Yeager assert that corporations are made criminal by "corporate cultures" or ethical climates that foster ethical disregard. Efforts to control corporate crime follow three approaches: voluntary change by the corporation, legal intervention by the state, or consumer action.

Voluntary changes would involve the development of ethics programs and organizational reforms. The criteria for bringing legal action, whether civil or criminal, includes: the degree of loss to the public, the duration of the violation, the level of complicity by high corporate managers, the frequency of the violation, evidence of intent to violate, evidence of extortion, the degree of notoriety threatened by the media, precedent in law, a history of serious violations by the corporation, deterrence potential, and the degree of cooperation demonstrated by the corporation. Consumer pressure is exerted through lobbying, selective buying, boycotts, and the establishment of large consumer cooperatives. Unfortunately consumers are often unaware of violations or harmful conditions, and sustained public demonstrations are rare.

Government controls might involve federal corporate chartering, deconcentration and divesture, increased enforcement activities, stiffer penalties, negative publicity, and the nationalization of corporations. Government action is likely to be civil or regulatory. A study by Irwin Ross tracked 1,043 companies from the *Fortune* list. Five kinds of offenses were included in his study: bribe-taking or bribe-giving by high-level executives, criminal fraud, illegal campaign contributions, tax evasion, and antitrust violations. One hundred and seventeen of the corporations, or 11%, were violators.

Enforcement strategy comes down to two alternatives: compliance and deterrence. *Compliance* systems provide economic incentives for voluntary compliance to the laws and administer guidelines to avoid violations. The IRS and the SEC emphasize compliance because their constituencies are too large for constant patrol. *Deterrence* penalizes offenders in order to deter future violations. Deterrence systems try to control the immediate behavior of individuals, not the long-term behaviors targeted by compliance systems.

Figures from the U.S. Sentencing Commission reveal that convicted corporations almost never have compliance programs. From 1991 to 1997, only one of the sentenced corporations had a formal compliance program, and that company's plan had been mandated by law.

U.S. Sentencing Commission Report for 2002

The U.S. Sentencing Commission figures for 2002 reported that the number of organizations sentenced for corporate crime was 252; this is a 5.9% increase from 2001 and a 17.1% decrease from 2000. As of 2001, fraud remained the most frequent offense committed by an organization, accounting for 102 of the 252 cases reported (40.5%). Other significant offense categories included—environmental pollution (17.9%), antitrust

(9.1%), money laundering (7.5%), and food, drugs, agricultural and consumer products (7.5%).

The USSC data shows that fines were given more frequently and in greater numbers over time. For the 252 cases overall, restitution was ordered in 112 cases and a fine was imposed in 166 cases. The average organizational fine imposed in 2001 was $2,815,154, an increase from $1,475,312 in 1997. The average restitution ordered in 2001 was $6,292,650, which is a substantial increase from the 1997 amount of $873,416.

In addition to restitution and monetary penalties, offenders sentenced under the organization guidelines were subject to other sanctions. Of the 252 cases sentenced, 74.2% received one month or more of probation. Of the 251 cases with court-ordered compliance program information available, 38 (15.1%) were ordered to make some sort of "ethics"-related or "compliance"-related improvement.

Record Corporate Fines

A record number of corporations were prosecuted in the 1990's, and various courts levied record fines. Figures compiled in 1999 by the *Multinational Monitor* ranked the top 100 corporate criminal fines for U.S. corporations during the decade. The amounts ranged from $500 million for antitrust violations to $150,000 for a securities fraud.

In 2004, outside the health care arena, defense procurement fraud accounted for $112 million in settlement and judgment awards with another $41.9 million recovered from PriceWaterhouseCoopers, L.L.P., for alleged false claims for travel expenses in connection with its contracts with numerous federal agencies, and $30.5 million from Harvard University and its agents in connection with a United States Agency for International Development agreement to advise Russia in its transition to a market economy.

Among the Department's largest recoveries in fiscal year 2005 were:

HealthSouth Corporation	$327 million — settle allegations of overbilling fraud against Medicare
Gambro Health care	$310 million — false claims for Medicare and Medicaid

GlaxoSmithKline	$140 million — settle allegations of fraudulent drug pricing
Advance PSC	$138.5 million — kickbacks

Source: www.usdoj.gov/opa/pr/2005/November/05_civ_595.html

A trend toward substantial criminal penalties continues, but the typical corporate criminal prosecution usually involves relatively small fines against privately-held corporations where high-level management personally participated in the offense.

Organizational Sentencing Guidelines and Their Impact

In 1991, the United States Sentencing Commission submitted a report to Congress, which became the basis for the Organizational Sentencing Guidelines passed into law that year. Among other provisions, the guidelines provided for the substantial reduction of fines for corporations that have vigorous fraud prevention programs. The guidelines set maximum possible fines of $290 million per offense and possible corporate suspensions of business for up to five years. The OSG outlines seven critical and indispensable steps for corporations to demonstrate they are actively combating wrongdoing by employees and executives. The organization should:

- Enact policies defining standards and procedures.
- Assign specific high-level personnel who have ultimate responsibility to ensure compliance.
- Use due care not to delegate significant discretionary authority to persons whom the organization knew or should have known had a propensity to engage in illegal activities.
- Communicate standards and procedures to all agents and employees and require participation in training programs.
- Take reasonable steps to achieve compliance, e.g., by use of monitoring and auditing systems and by having and publicizing a reporting system where employees can report criminal conduct without fear of retribution (hotline or ombudsman program).
- Consistently enforce standards through appropriate discipline ranging from dismissal to reprimand.

- After detection of an offense, take all reasonable steps to appropriately respond to the offense and to prevent further similar offenses, including modifying its program and appropriately discipline the individual(s) responsible for the offense and those who failed to detect it.

Fine amounts must be at least equal to the dollar value of the fraud. For a corporation found guilty of perpetrating a $10 million fraud, the base fine is $10 million. The guidelines set a schedule to determine extra punitive fines based on the seriousness of the offense and the culpability of the organization. In serious cases of widespread criminality in the organization, the guidelines provide for the divestiture of all assets of that corporation and its abolition.

The United States Sentencing Commission recently promulgated modifications to the existing provisions of the Chapter Eight Sentencing Guidelines dealing with effective compliance and ethics programs for business organizations that became effective November 1, 2004. These new provisions narrowly tailor the criteria for compliance and ethics programs, thereby providing organizations with guidance in establishing and maintaining effective programs for detecting and preventing internal illegal activities, as well as mitigating sentencing culpability.

Dean Reeves, a Certified Fraud Examiner, analyzed the impact of the guidelines for the ACFE in 2000.

- *Number of Sentences.* From the inauguration of the guidelines in November 1991 through September 1993, only 26 organizations were sentenced nationwide. In 1995, more than 100 organizations were sentenced under the guidelines, and in 1996 more than 150 organizations were sentenced. In 1999 (the most recent figures available), 255 organizations were sentenced under the guidelines, an increase of 15.9% from 1998 and a ten-fold increase from 1991 through 1993. Two hundred of the 255 organizations sentenced in 1999 received fines, and 91.4% of the 255 organizations plead guilty with 8.2% being convicted after trial (one case pleaded *nolo contendere*). The trend of prosecutions has clearly risen over the past nine years.
- *Crimes Targeted.* Fraud is the number one crime for which companies are sentenced under the guidelines. In 1995, 38.9% of companies fined under the guidelines were

found guilty of fraudulent activities; in 1997, 41%; and in 1999, 33.7%. Environmental prosecutions have consistently remained the second most prevalent prosecution type with 20.4% of all violations in 1995 and 23.5% in 1999.

- *Financial Impact on Organizations.* Between 1991 and 1993, fines ranged from $3,000 to $400,000. In 1995, the mean fine was just under $250,000 and the median fine approximately $30,000. By 1999, the mean fine for an organization sentenced under the guidelines with total fine and restitution imposed was more than $5.5 million with a median fine of $100,000. In 1999, 75% of the organizations sentenced under the guidelines were able to pay the fine imposed while 25% had to have the fine reduced because they couldn't pay the full penalties. Nearly one-third of the companies sentenced in 1995 and 1996 either went out of business or filed for bankruptcy.
- *Compliance Programs.* According to a study involving 333 corporations of various sizes representing various industries, 44% of the respondents stated the guidelines triggered the enhancement of their compliance procedures while 20% said the guidelines were directly responsible for the implementation of a compliance program within their organization. A separate study of large companies concluded that 38% of organizations significantly improved their compliance environment after the enactment of the guidelines.

Sources:

Clinard, Marshall. *Corporate Corruption: The Abuse of Power.* New York: Praeger, 1990.

Clinard, Marshall and Peter Yeager. *Corporate Crime.* New York: The Free Press, 1980.

Benson, M., et. al, "District Attorneys and Corporate Crime: Surveying the Prosecutorial Gatekeepers." *Criminology,* 26:505-518, 1998.

Geis, Gilbert, and Robert Meier, eds. White Collar Crime: Offenses in Business, Politics, and the Professions. New York: The Free Press, 1972.

Gross, Edward, "Organizational Structure and Organizational Crime" reprinted in Gilbert Geis and Ezra Stotland (Eds.), *White Collar Crime: Theory and Research.* Beverly Hills: Sage, 1980, pp. 53-76.

Hughes, T., and Savage, J, Jr., "Corporate Criminal Liability Goes Mainstream; Organizational Sentencing Data '91-'97: Preview of Coming Attractions?" *Business Crimes Bulletin,* June 1999.

McCaghy, Charles H. Deviant Behavior, Crime, Conflict and Interest Groups. New York: Macmillan, 1976.

Mokhiber, R., and Weissman, R. "Corporate Predators: The Hunt for Mega-Profits and the Attack on Democracy." Monroe, ME: Common Courage Press, 1999.

Murphy, K. "Honesty in the Workplace." *Pacific Grove:* Brooks/Cole Publishing, 1993.

Reeves, D. "Have Organizational Sentencing Guidelines Produced Results?" *The White Paper,* January/February 2001.

Ross, Irwin. *Shady Business.* New York: Twentieth Century Fund, 1992.

Silk, Leonard and David Vogel. Ethics and Profits: The Crisis of Confidence in American Business. Simon & Schuster, 1976.

Stone, C. "Where the Law Ends: The Social Control of Corporate Behavior." New York: Harper & Row, 1975.

Utton, M.A. *Market Dominance and Antitrust Policy.* Brookfield: E. Elgar, 1995.

Vaughan, Diane. "Transaction Systems and Unlawful Organizational Behavior." *Social Problems*, 29:373-380.

Vaughan, Diane. Controlling Unlawful Organizational Behavior: Social Structure and Corporate Misconduct. Chicago: University of Chicago Press, 1983.

Vaughan, Diane. The Challenger Launch Decision: Risky Technology, Culture, and Deviance at NASA. Chicago: University of Chicago Press, 1996.

Winslow, G. "Capital Crimes: The Political Economy of Crime in America." *Monthly Review,* November 1, 2000.

Related Entries:

ANTITRUST

CAUSES OF FRAUD

ENTERPRISE CRIME

MANAGED EARNINGS

SECURITIES FRAUD

CORPORATE ESPIONAGE

Corporate Espionage refers to the unlawful gathering of information about a company, theft of trade secrets and intellectual property, and other acts of spying and sabotage committed against businesses. The term contrasts with "competitive intelligence," which is the gathering of information on companies using legal means. Accessing publicly available records and analyzing the data is competitive intelligence, a thriving profession in the last few decades. A majority of Fortune 500 companies now have a full-time staff devoted to gathering intelligence information about competitors. However, posing as a vendor to obtain a company's internal communications is corporate espionage which is a crime.

According to Steven Fink, author of *Sticky Fingers: Managing the Global Risk of Economic Espionage*, corporate espionage is a $250 billion a year growth industry. According to a survey conducted by the American Society for Industrial Security (ASIS), proprietary information and intellectual property loss in American business from $53 to $59 billion in 2001. The White House Office of Science and Technology states that foreign companies and governments spying on U.S. businesses cost approximately $100 billion a year in lost sales. ABC News estimates that corporate espionage caused over six million job losses during the 1990's.

Corporate spies target Research and Development, Marketing, Manufacturing and Production, Human Resources, and Technology personnel. Every form of information in the company—digital, paper, and audiovisual recordings—may be targeted.

Companies that are involved in spying sometimes dodge legal culpability by hiring operatives off the books. These people are known as "kites." According to a self-avowed corporate spy, "A kite is somebody who is essentially expendable, somebody who is flown out there, and if it hits the fan, the controller can cut the string, deny knowledge, and let the kite fly off on its own."

To guard against espionage or to repel attacks, some companies hire consultants who specialize in Safeguarding Proprietary Information (SPI); others maintain a security management staff.

Social Engineering

The term social engineering refers to manipulating people using trickery, persuasion, threats, or cajolery. The term was first used to describe manipulations by computer criminals, but may be applied to any act of deception that yields information.

False-flag recruiting plays on the target's social or political convictions, suggesting the person's help will further the person's "cause." Romantic or sexual seduction also waves a false flag, arousing the target's desire to divulge information. In its simplest form, the flag is a prize, such as a gift certificate or employee bonus. The target is offered fake prizes and gift certificates or sweepstakes prizes, which can be claimed by logging onto a website the spy has set up. Access to the site requires the person to enter an employee user ID and password; the site may also ask the person to divulge other personal or company information.

In *recruiting by justification*, the spy convinces a recruit that an otherwise improper act is acceptable because of circumstances. Employees who feel bitter or victimized make good justification targets. Entrapment recruiting plays on a target's weakness—excessive gambling, drug or alcohol abuse, bizarre sexual proclivities, past criminal convictions, or excessive spending habits—to force the person into participating.

The spy may assume one of several roles. As a *neophyte*, the spy feigns ignorance or inexperience. In the guise of *asking for help*, the spy convinces personnel to divulge key information, such as passwords, phone numbers, entry codes, recent hiring and firings, and so on. The *power broker* claims to be a high-ranking company official, influential client, or other authority figure that can convince or compel the target to open up. For computer-related acts, the spy pretends to be the *systems administrator,* asking for passwords, common practices, physical locations, and other details.

Some common ruses used in social engineering are described below:

- Employees answer *bogus employment ads*, expecting a "technical interview" concerning their current duties. The spy uses the interview pretext to probe the target's knowledge. In a variation, the spy poses as a headhunter, calling to offer the employee a new position. The "headhunter" asks for a résumé and information about projects on which the employee is currently working. An in-depth interview by someone posing as the headhunter's "client" firm can provide additional details. A spy may also answer employment ads posted by the target company, turning the interview into an interrogation.
- In *market research scams*, the spy pretends to conduct market research, using a phony questionnaire to obtain information. The spy frequently offers the employee a bogus reward of some kind in return for responding to the questionnaire. These calls tend to aim at lower level workers who have operational knowledge of the business, but who are not likely to be as defensive as higher-level managers.

- *Personal surveys* ask employees personal information, such as the names, nicknames, ages, birth dates, names and birthdays of spouses or children, pets, favorite hobbies, favorite song, favorite movie and dozens of other personal preferences and attributes. This information can be used to impersonate the employee, to track a company's hiring practice, or put into a computer cracking system as a way of acquiring people's passwords (since most people choose a password that has some personal significance).
- A spy might send out *"Request for Proposals"* (RFP) to a company, asking for certain operational and financial data pertinent to an upcoming project. Typically, the spy poses as a manufacturer or wholesaler who wishes to purchase a large amount of goods from the company. This ruse helps assess the target company's ability to manufacture a certain product. The return address on the RFP is a mail drop, which insulates the spy from detection. The deadline set forth in the phony bid requirements helps ensure that the spy gets the information in a timely manner. Sales people and purchasing personnel make good targets for this scam.

In social engineering, the spy poses as someone who needs the target's help. *In reverse social engineering*, the spy offers help to the target. The scam can be perpetrated by telephone, e-mail, or regular mail. In a typical scheme, the spy poses as a representative of some software company. He sends a message to the target indicating that a software product that the target owns has a possible defect. The target is instructed to call the software company (the spy) with his user ID and password in order to receive the fix. When the target calls, the spy obtains his access codes.

Physical Contact and Surveillance

Spies can obtain information directly by entering company property or obtaining company property. Break-ins are rare; instead the spy poses as an employee or contract laborer. The spy may actually hire on (becoming a "sleeper" or "mole"), or pretend to be working at the company. Stealing or counterfeiting employee badges is a common infiltration method. Once inside the spy can steal a range of materials and engage in social engineering. Obtaining company materials is possible through other physical means, such as sorting through a company's trash.

Corporate spies use a number of surveillance techniques, including photography, secret audio recordings, wiretapping, and video surveillance. Using a detector known as a Van Eck receiver, spies can capture keyboard entries made on a target's computer. When computer pixels form an image on a computer screen, high voltage pulses emanate into the surrounding environment. These computer emanations form a detectable and decodable pattern.

The Van Eck unit consists of a directional antenna, logic circuits, and two adjustable oscillators (one for the vertical and one for the horizontal). With proper adjustments, a van parked across the street, equipped with a Van Eck receiver, can decode the emanations from a keyboard operator inside a neighboring building. Devices like CPU's, tape drives, disk drives, and communications devices all generate electromagnetic radiation, which Van Eck receivers can detect.

To prevent competitors from monitoring computer emanations, organizations can shield their computer equipment and transmission lines, a process known as *Tempesting*. While this process is used extensively in the military and by certain defense contractors, the costs involved prevents many private sector businesses from employing *Tempest* procedures.

Computer Infiltration

Spies can use a number of techniques to gain entry to company computers. A computer attack may involve social or reverse-social engineering, obtaining physical materials, and electronic infiltration.

Sources:
Berger, James T. "Corporate Security Avoiding Economic Espionage." *Plants Sites & Park*, September 2003.

Calhoun, J. "Clean the Air with TSCM." *Security Management,* September 1992.

Flanagan, W. and Toddi G. "The Perils of Voice Mail (Information Theft)." *Forbes,* January 17, 1994.

Hansen, M. "Counterespionage Techniques That Work." *Security Management,* September 1992.

Himelstein, L. "Computers, The Snitch in the System." *Business Week,* April 17, 1995.

Mokhiber, R. "Go Spy a Kite. Focus on the Corporation." *San Francisco Bay Guardian,* March 6, 2001.

Murray, K. "HR Takes Steps to Protect Trade Secrets." *Personnel Journal,* June 1994.

Tanzer, M. "Foiling the New Corporate Spy." *Security Management*, September 1992.

Related Entries:

AVANT!
COMPUTER CRIME
INFORMATION CRIME
LOPEZ, JOSE IGNACIO DE ARRIORTUA

CORRUPTION, OCCUPATIONAL

Occupational Corruption is one of the three categories of occupational fraud and abuse, along with Financial Statement Fraud and Misappropriation of Assets. Employee corruption manifests itself as bribery or through conflicts of interest. Bribery schemes generally fall into two broad categories: *kickbacks* and *bid-rigging schemes*.

Kickbacks

Kickbacks are undisclosed payments by outsiders to a company's employees. Kickbacks are classified as corruption schemes rather than asset misappropriations because they involve collusion between employees and vendors. Sometimes an employee-fraudster receives a cash kickback simply for directing business to a vendor; there is no effect on the victim company's books. A customer may bribe an employee to obtain an unauthorized discount—the customer saves $10 per unit, and pays the employee $1 per unit.

Most commonly a kickback scheme attacks a company's purchasing function—the employee helps the vendor submit invoices that are either overpriced or completely fictitious. The employee receives a cash payment for the service. Nebulous account titles such as "consulting fees" are sometimes used for kickbacks.

When proper controls are in place, the fraudster may have to create a purchase order corresponding to the vendor's fraudulent invoice, either by forging a supervisor's signature, obtaining the signature under false pretenses, or by altering computerized materials. In less sophisticated schemes, a corrupt employee might simply take a fraudulent invoice from a vendor and slip it into a stack of prepared invoices.

People inside a company may also make kickbacks to outsiders. Inspectors are paid to accept substandard materials and grant other special considerations. A department head may be obtaining great sales results by giving customers kickbacks for large purchases.

Bid-Rigging

In bid-rigging, a bribe or some other favor is exchanged to influence the awarding of contracts. Employees involved in bid-rigging schemes, like those in kickback schemes, tend to have a good measure of influence or access to the competitive bidding process. Potential targets for accepting bribes include buyers, contracting officials, engineers and technical representatives, quality or product assurance representatives, subcontractor liaison employees, or anyone else with authority over the awarding of contracts.

A company becomes the beneficiary of bid-rigging when it bribes someone in order to obtain business. The company may be the victim, by losing business to corrupt competitors, for one. Companies also fall victim by paying higher prices when employees rig the company's own bidding—the employee awards a service contract to the most expensive supplier. In this case, the employee receives a kickback for rigging the bid. The flip side of bribery schemes is economic extortion, requiring kickbacks from vendors in exchange for business.

Detection of Kickbacks and Bid-Rigging

General Purchasing

The following practices may indicate that single (sole) source vendors are being favored, or competitive bidding policies are not being followed:

- Materials are not being ordered at the optimal reorder point.
- Orders are consistently made from the same vendor.
- Established bidding policies are not being followed.
- The costs of materials are out of line.

Bid-Rigging

Restrictions in an organization's solicitation documents that tend to restrict competition are a red flag. Examples of restrictive conditions include:

- Specifications and statements of work, which are tailored to fit the products or capabilities of a single contractor.
- "Pre-qualification" procedures that restrict competition.
- Unnecessary sole source or noncompetitive procurement justifications:
  - Containing false statement
  - Signed by unauthorized officials
  - Bypassing necessary review procedures
- A buyer who provides information or advice to a contractor on a preferential basis.
- New vendors that are added to the "qualified" list for no apparent reason.
- Statements of work, specifications, or sole source justifications that are developed by, or in consultation with, a contractor who will be permitted to bid.
- Consultants who assisted in the preparation of the statements of work, specifications, or design and are later permitted to work on the contract as subcontractors or consultants.
- Projects that are split into smaller contracts to avoid review.
- Information that is released by firms participating in the design and engineering to contractors competing for the prime contract.
- Requirements that are split up so contractors can each get a "fair share" and can rotate bids.
- Specifications that are not consistent with similar procurements in the past.

The following suspicious activity in the bid solicitation phase may indicate fraud:

- The time for submitting bids is limited so that only those with advance information have adequate time to prepare bids or proposals.
- One contractor receives confidential information that is not revealed to his competitors.
- The conducting of a bidders' conference, which permits improper communications between contractors who are then in a position to rig bids.

- The failure to ensure that a sufficient number of potential competitors are aware of the solicitation by:
  - Using obscure publications to publish bid solicitations.
  - Publishing bid solicitations during holiday periods.
  - Bid solicitations which are vague about the time, place, or other requirements for submitting acceptable bids.
  - Inadequate internal controls over the number and destination of bid packages sent to interested bidders.
  - Improper communication between purchasers and contractors at trade or professional meetings.
  - Improper social contact with purchasers and contractor representatives.
  - A purchasing agent who has a financial interest in the business of a contractor.
  - A purchaser who discusses possible employment with a contractor.
  - The purchaser assisting a contractor in the preparation of his bid.
  - A contractor being referred to a specific subcontractor, expert, or source of supply by an employee of the purchasing organization.
  - The failure to amend a solicitation to include necessary changes or clarifications in the bid, such as telling one contractor of changes that can be made after the bid.
  - The falsification of documents or receipts so that a late bid is accepted.
  - Any indication of collusion between bidders.
  - The falsification of a contractor's qualifications, work history, facilities, equipment, or personnel.

Bid Submission or Contract Acceptance

Red flags in the submission and post-submission phase of the bidding process include the following:

- Procurement that has been restricted to exclude or hamper any qualified contractor.
- The improper acceptance of a late bid.
- A bidder who always bids last on contracts and consistently wins them.
- The falsification of documents or receipts to get a late bid accepted.

- Bids that are changed after other bidders' prices are known. This is sometimes done by mistakes deliberately "planted" in a bid.
- A low bidder who withdraws to become a subcontractor of a higher bidder who gets the contract.
- Collusion between bidders.
- Bidders who reveal their prices to one another.
- Bids tend to be awarded in a geographic pattern or in a noticeable rotation.
- Bids for a particular type of work are always awarded to a particular company.
- False certifications by a contractor.
- The falsification of information concerning contractor qualifications, financial capability, facilities, ownership of equipment and supplies, qualifications of personnel, and successful performance of previous jobs, etc.

Methods of Proving Corrupt Payments

There are three basic ways to prove illegal payments: through auditing, by obtaining a cooperative witness, or by monitoring ongoing transactions. On-book schemes are best approached from the point of payment; off-book schemes are most easily identified at the suspected point of receipt, through the use of an inside witness or surveillance.

The *business profile* begins the examination process. It identifies prospective witnesses and targets, as well as relevant documents and transactions, and should provide leads as to whether an on-book or off-book scheme is being used.

Conflicts of Interest

A conflict of interest occurs when an employee, manager, or executive has an undisclosed economic or personal interest in a transaction that adversely affects that person's employer. In bribery schemes, fraudsters are paid to exercise their influence on behalf of a third-party. Conflict cases instead involve self-dealing by an employee, or the employee's influence on someone else's behalf. The employee may consistently award contracts to a company he secretly owns, or one owned by a co-conspirator. Or, the employee argues against the purchase of a building because he wants to buy the building himself.

Other ways that conflict of interest affects businesses include: underbilling to employee-owned companies, reducing the receivables owed by employee-owned companies, delayed billing, and running a competitive business that takes away clients from one's employer.

Detection of Conflict of Interest

Conflict schemes are among the most difficult to uncover. Many conflict schemes use false billing, overbilling, or some other attack on the purchasing account. (*See* ASSET MISAPPROPRIATION for more information on these schemes.) Some of the more common methods for investigating conflict include tips and complaints, comparisons of vendor addresses with employee addresses, review of vendor ownership files, review of exit interviews and comparisons of vendor addresses to addresses of subsequent employers, and interviews with purchasing personnel.

Identifying and tracing off-book payments usually is more difficult than locating on-book schemes. Success generally depends upon identifying the source of the funds or accounts (from which payments can be traced out), using an inside witness, and focusing on the point of receipt. The source of off-book funds might be unrecorded sales, which will show up as an unbalance in the ratio of costs to sales.

Sources:
Husted, B. "Wealth, Culture, and Corruption." *Journal of International Business Studies,* June 22, 1999.

Wells, J., CFE, CPA. *Corporate Fraud Handbook.* Hoboken, NJ: John Wiley & Sons, 2004.

Related Entries:

BRIBERY

CONTRACT AND PROCUREMENT FRAUD

LOCKHEED AIRCRAFT CORPORATION

OCCUPATIONAL FRAUD AND ABUSE

CORRUPTION, PUBLIC

Corruption in the public sector includes any act in which a public official or employee performs favors in exchange for money, goods and services, influence, sex, or other reward. White-collar crime scholar James Coleman has estimated that nearly 42% of the criminal indictments against congresspersons since 1940 "have involved some kind of bribery."

Factors of Corruption

Economists cite the level of economic development as an important contributor to corruption. Some researchers have suggested that corruption occurs because the government has a monopoly over particular resources.

Economic and institutional differences often limit the ability of individuals to resist a corrupt system. Factors which empower individuals and lessen the influence of corruption include: (a) secular increases in wages, education, and urbanization; (b) growth of mass media; (c) advances in transportation and communications technology; (d) improvements in managerial and accounting skills; (e) growth of capitalist classes, urban middle classes, and an urban labor force; and (f) upward pressures on government expenditure.

Another factor is what researchers call "power distance," which is the extent to which the less powerful members of institutions and organizations within a country expect and accept that power is distributed unequally. In high power-distance countries the masses of people are subordinate to a paternalistic class. Decisions are made on the basis of favors and loyalty. These cultures also tend to be chauvinistic in terms of gender, and favor planned economies over a market-driven model.

In 1977, the U.S. Congress passed the Foreign Corrupt Practices Act (FCPA), which provides for heavy fines and jail terms for American individuals and companies who know or have reason to know of violations of the Act. The International Chamber of Commerce (1996) has also issued strict rules of conduct with regard to bribery and extortion.

Case Study—Abscam

During a covert investigation by the FBI called Abscam in the late 1970's, eight U.S. officials agreed to use their influence in exchange for cash and other favors. Agents posed as emissaries representing the fictitious Sheik Kambir Abdul Rahman and his company, Abdul Enterprises. It was for Sheik Abdul that the operation got its name—Abscam was short for "Abdul-scam"—but after the investigation became public many Arab-Americans regarded the term as an offense.

The first news of Abscam came in February 1980, when the *Philadelphia Inquirer* and other newspapers published reports about a secret two-year FBI sting operation. In 1978 the FBI, via a fictitious company named "Olympic Construction Corp.," rented a house in Washington D.C. from Lee Lescaze, a reporter for the *Washington Post.* Lescaze had no knowledge of the investigation; he was simply renting the property for profit. He later wrote, "The FBI pays its rent on time."

The house was part of an elaborate front that included a yacht in Florida and hotel rooms in Pennsylvania and New Jersey. These properties were used for meetings between various public officials and a mysterious Arab sheik named Abdul who sought:

- To purchase asylum in the U.S.
- To involve the officials in an investment scheme.
- Help in smuggling money into the U.S.

FBI agents posing as associates of Abdul approached various public officials on the sheik's behalf. Representative Richard Kelly of Florida was captured on videotape stuffing $25,000 into his pockets. After finishing he turned to one of the agents and asked, "Does it show?" Kelly was convicted but an appeals judge decided the case was tainted by entrapment and overturned the conviction. A higher court reinstated the conviction.

Besides Kelly, the investigation also brought convictions against Angelo Errichetti, mayor of Camden, New Jersey; Representative Frank Thompson of New Jersey; Senator Harrison Williams of New Jersey; and six attorneys: Raymond Lederer, Michael Myers, Louis Johanson, and Howard Criden of Pennsylvania, John Murphy of New York, and Frank Thompson of New Jersey.

Sources:
Carelli, R. "High Court Affirms Abscam Convictions." *Associated Press,* May 31, 1983.

Coleman, J. "The Criminal Elite: Understanding White-Collar Crime." New York: St. Martin's Press, 1998.

Related Entries:

BCCI

BRIBERY

CONTRACT AND PROCUREMENT FRAUD

CORRUPTION, OCCUPATIONAL

OCCUPATIONAL FRAUD AND ABUSE

COSO

The National Commission on Fraudulent Financial Reporting (commonly known as the Treadway Commission) was established in 1987 with the purpose of defining the responsibility of the auditor in preventing and detecting fraud. The commission was formed by the major professional auditing organizations—the American Institute of CPAs, the Institute of Internal Auditors, and the National Association of Accountants. The Treadway Commission made several major recommendations that, in combination with other measures, are designed to reduce the probability of fraud in financial reports:

- A mandatory independent audit committee made up of outside directors
- A *written charter* which sets forth the duties and responsibilities of the audit committee.
- The audit committee should have *adequate resources and authority* to carry out its responsibilities.
- The audit committee should be informed, vigilant, and effective.

COSO Recommendations

The Committee of Sponsoring Organizations (COSO) was formed to support the implementation of the Treadway Commission. In 1992, the committee issued *Internal Control—Integrated Framework*. This report was a collaborative effort of the American

Accounting Association, the American Institute of CPAs, the Financial Executives Institute, the Institute of Internal Auditors, and the Institute of Management Accountants. The report is meant to apply to all entities, public and private, regardless of size.

The COSO report complements Treadway's recommendation to the SEC that public companies' management reports include an *acknowledgment for responsibility* for internal controls and an assessment of effectiveness in meeting those responsibilities. The report provided the following definition:

- Internal Control is a broadly defined process … designed to provide reasonable assurance regarding the achievement of objectives in the following categories:
  - Reliability of financial reporting
  - Effectiveness and efficiency of operations
  - Compliance with applicable laws and regulations

COSO also identified five interrelated components of internal control. The effectiveness of internal controls can be determined from an assessment of whether these five components are in place and functioning effectively. The five components are control environment, risk assessment, control activities, information and communication, and monitoring.

Control Environment

The control environment sets the moral tone of an organization, influencing the control consciousness of the organization and providing a foundation for all other control components. This component takes into account whether managers and employees within the organization exhibit integrity in their activities.

COSO envisions that upper management will be responsible for the control environment of organizations. Employees look to management for guidance in most business affairs, and organizational ethics are no different. It is important for upper management to operate in an ethical manner, and it is equally important for employees to view management in a positive light. Managers must set an appropriate moral tone for the operations of an organization.

In addition to merely setting a good example, however, COSO suggests that upper management take direct control of an organization's efforts at internal controls. This idea should be regularly reinforced within the organization. There are several actions that management can take to establish the proper control environment for an organization.

These include:

- *The establishment of a code of ethics for the organization.* The code should be disseminated to all employees and every new employee should be required to read and sign it. The code should also be disseminated to contractors who do work on behalf of the organization. Under certain circumstances, companies may face liability due to the actions of independent contractors. It is therefore very important to explain the organization's standards to any outside party with whom the organization conducts business.
- *Careful screening of job applicants.* One of the easiest ways to establish a strong moral tone for an organization is to hire morally sound employees. Too often, the hiring process is conducted in a slipshod manner. Organizations should conduct thorough background checks on all new employees, especially managers. In addition, it is important to conduct thorough interviews with applicants to ensure that they have adequate skills to perform the duties that will be required of them.
- *Proper assignment of authority and responsibility.* In addition to hiring qualified, ethical employees, it is important to put these people in situations where they are able to thrive without resorting to unethical conduct. Organizations should provide employees with well-defined job descriptions and performance goals. Performance goals should be routinely reviewed to ensure that they do not set unrealistic standards. Training should be provided on a consistent basis to ensure that employees maintain the skills to perform effectively. Regular training on ethics will also help employees identify potential trouble spots and avoid getting caught in compromising situations. Finally, management should quickly determine where deficiencies in an employee's conduct exist and work with the employee to fix the problem.
- *Effective disciplinary measures.* No control environment will be effective unless there is consistent discipline for ethical violations. Consistent discipline requires a

well-defined set of sanctions for violations, and strict adherence to the prescribed disciplinary measures. If one employee is punished for an act and another employee is not punished for a similar act, the moral force of the company's ethics policy will be diminished. The levels of discipline must be sufficient to deter violations. It may also be advisable to reward ethical conduct. This will reinforce the importance of organizational ethics in the eyes of employees.

Risk Assessment

Risk assessment involves an entity's identification and assessment of the risks involved in achieving organizational objectives. This component involves tailoring ethics policies or compliance programs to the nature of the organization's business. According to COSO, risk assessment is a three-step process:

- *Set objectives for the organization*. Management should establish mission statements or similar expressions of organizational objectives. These statements must take into account the nature of the organization's business, the industry in which the organization operates, and the political and economic environment in which it operates, as well as the organization's resources and goals. In stating its goals, the organization should establish measurable criteria so that progress can be measured. Goals should not be so lofty that they cannot be reached considering the organization's resources and environment. In setting objectives, input from all levels of management should be sought. Once an appropriate statement of objectives is established, it should be communicated to all employees.
- *Analyze potential risks of violations*. COSO divides risks into two categories: external risks and internal risks. External risks include things like increased competition, changes in technology, shifting economic conditions, and new legislation. Internal risks are factors such as personnel changes, availability of funds for organizational projects, new operating systems, and the development of new products.
- *Develop a strategy to manage risks*. Organizations should identify and be prepared to react to any external or internal risk. This means developing controls which are

tailored to the inherent risks of the organization's business and establishing set policies for dealing with violations.

Control Activities

Control activities are the policies and procedures that enforce management's directives. Management should set forth policy and procedure guidelines in a manual that is issued to employees. A person or persons should be designated to keep statements of policies updated and to make sure they are properly disseminated. All control activities should be closely monitored by management, and changes should be made where control failures are identified. Consistent with the risk analysis component, when a control failure is identified the risk of additional failures should be considered in redesigning controls.

Information and Communication

This component relates to the exchange of information in a way that allows employees to carry out their responsibilities. Organizations should work to identify pertinent information and see that it is delivered to those who need it most. A proper information system will accomplish the following:

- *Assimilate important financial, operational, and compliance information.* This information should be drawn from both internal and external sources, meaning management may have to go outside the organizational structure to identify pertinent information. There should be a means of screening incoming information so that pertinent information is maintained but unnecessary information is not allowed to clog channels of communication. Examples of pertinent information include facts on organizational performance, market conditions, competitor programs, economic changes, and legislative or regulatory changes.
- *Pass on pertinent information to those who need it.* Management should provide timely information to employees to help them carry out their duties more effectively. Important facts should be communicated in readily usable form. It is also important to communicate the importance of observing controls. Management should help employees understand their own roles in the internal control system and make it clear that internal controls have a high priority.

- *Provide for upstream communication.* Communication in an organization should flow in all directions. Employees should be provided with clear channels for reporting suspected control violations. Provisions should be made for employees to make anonymous reports in order to avoid fears of retaliation which can have a chilling effect on upstream communication. A similar reporting mechanism for customers and other external parties should be in place. Serious efforts should be made to follow up on these communications.

Monitoring

Monitoring is the process that assesses the quality of a control environment over time. This component should include regular evaluations of the entire control system. It also requires the ongoing monitoring of day-to-day activities by managers and employees. This may involve reviewing the accuracy of financial information, or verifying inventories, supplies, equipment and other organization assets. Finally, organizations should conduct independent evaluations of their internal control systems. An effective monitoring system should provide for the free flow of upstream communication as discussed under the information and communication component.

In addition, in 1987, the Treadway Commission recommended that management of publicly held companies include with their management reports an acknowledgement of responsibility for internal controls and an assessment of its effectiveness in meeting those controls. It formed the Committee on Sponsoring Organizations (COSO) to actualize Treadway's recommendations.

COSO issued *Internal Control – Integrated Framework,* with a later issued addendum, which defined internal control as "a process…designed to provide reasonable assurance regarding the achievement of objectives in the following categories:

- Reliability of financial reporting,
- Effectiveness and efficiency of operations, and
- Compliance with applicable laws and regulations."

COSO also identified, for management, five interrelated components of internal control:

- Monitoring is the process that assesses the control environment over time.

- People other than management also are responsible for the detection and deterrence of fraudulent financial reporting, including external auditors, internal auditors, and Certified Fraud Examiners.
- Control environment sets the tone of an organization, influences the control consciousness of the organization, and provides a foundation for all other control components.
- Risk assessment is an entity's identification and assessment of risks relevant to achieving control objectives.
- Control activities are an entity's control policies and procedures.
- Information and communication is the exchange of information in a way that allows employees to carry out their responsibilities.

Related Entries:

AUDITING FOR FRAUD
INTERNAL CONTROLS

COST OF FRAUD

The true cost of fraud is impossible to determine precisely. This is due in part to the fact that many frauds are not discovered, and many that are discovered, are not reported. However, based on the experiences of fraud examiners and other anti-fraud professionals, it is possible to estimate the losses due to fraud.

In 1996, the Association of Certified Fraud Examiners released its first "Report to the Nation on Occupational Fraud and Abuse." The first of its kind, it estimated that $400 billion a year was lost to fraud.

The Association of Certified Fraud Examiners again surveyed its members about their experiences in 2002 and 2004. In 2006, the Association again released the results of its survey of members in the "2006 ACFE Report to the Nation on Occupational Fraud and Abuse." The most important findings of the Report are summarized below:

- The study covered 1134 occupational fraud cases.

- Certified Fraud Examiners estimate that 5% of revenues will be lost in 2006 as a result of occupational fraud and abuse. Applied to the U.S. Gross Domestic Product, this translates to losses of approximately $652 billion in total losses.
- The median loss for all cases in the study was $159,000. Nearly one-quarter of the cases caused at least $1 million in losses and nine cases caused losses of $1 billion or more.
- All occupational frauds fall into one of three categories: asset misappropriations, corruption, or fraudulent statements.
  - Over 91% of occupational frauds involve asset misappropriations. Cash is the targeted asset over 87% of the time.
  - Corruptions schemes account for nearly 31% of all occupational frauds and they cause over $538,000 in losses, on average.
  - Fraudulent statements were the least commonly reported frauds (10.6%) but they had the highest median loss at $2,000,000.
- The most common method for detecting occupational fraud is by a tip from an employee, customer, vendor, or anonymous source. The second most common method is by accident.
- Organizations with fraud hotlines cut their fraud losses by approximately 50% per scheme. Internal audits, external audits, and background checks also significantly reduce fraud losses.
- The typical perpetrator is a first-time offender. Only 7.7% of occupational fraudsters in this study were known to have prior convictions for fraud-related offenses.
- Small businesses are the most vulnerable to occupational fraud and abuse. The average scheme in a small business causes $190,000 in losses.

The full *2006 Report to the Nation* can be downloaded at no charge from the ACFE website: www.ACFE.com.

COUNTERFEIT ART

Experts distinguish between three types of counterfeit in the art world. There are deliberate fakes, prepared by forgers to pass as a legitimate item of an artist or period; deliberate fakes prepared to pass as a heretofore-undiscovered item; and there are legitimate items whose provenance has been falsified. Provenances are the written histories of artworks that detail their creation, transfers of ownership, and exhibitions.

Art forgery has been on the rise in the past 50 years, driven by waves of first-time buyers with little expertise and by increasing competition among museums. Forgers often learn what works or types of work that neophyte collectors and museums desire and then fill the need. In the late 1980's, a rising international demand for art spawned a boom in forgeries and an underworld of rogue artists, art dealers, galleries, and financiers.

Some critics charge that museums are complicit in circulating forgeries. To avoid offending patrons and financiers, museums will sometimes accept a gift of dubious provenance, hiding it in storage or selling it to another dealer. Curators and administrators plead that they have no obligation to report their suspicions about an object's provenance before offering it for sale—beyond alerting the former owner, the institution is not required to disclose the conclusions of its research.

Museum personnel acknowledge the problem of counterfeits, but argue that the public overestimates the phenomenon. De Montebello, director of the Metropolitan Museum of Art, has said, "Most fakes around the world have been uncovered through the examination by the institutions themselves." He calls forgeries "the lurid subset" of an otherwise respectable art world.

Scientists seem to agree. In an article on the radiocarbon dating of art objects, A.J.T. Hull commented, "It is rare that a museum is surprised with our results. We have not as yet seen a valuable painting that came from someone's attic or was left by their grandfather to be a genuine article."

Counterfeit Paintings and Drawings

Besides technical skills in the discipline, forgers must collect the proper materials to counterfeit a painting. One convicted forger possessed rare typewriters, manufactured between 1920 and 1950, and writing paper from the period. He also owned a collection of stamps bearing the names of well-known art experts frequently asked to verify a painting's provenance.

Renaissance works, perhaps the most popular target of counterfeiters, must be prepared with paints, fixers, and brushes that match those used in the period. Canvases and paper for drawings are often stolen from reference works in libraries and private collections. Other materials in the counterfeiter's toolbox include poster paints, quick-drying household emulsion for texture, acrylics, and KY jelly to make the paint flow.

A counterfeit may be detected by close observation. The paper on which a drawing is executed may seem too smooth, over-washed, and unnaturally aged. The ink in some works appears "tired," as though the fading had been accelerated; the iron-gall ink used by Renaissance artists tends to darken, not lighten, with age. Artists work with great speed and fluidity, while forgeries often show evidence of a halting, jaunty, or "spidery" style. Even the best forgers can never fully capture the nuances that define an artist's "handwriting."

Turning a picture upside down is a good way to test its authenticity. This is because our brains automatically correct subtle mistakes. Upside down, the lines and shapes are clearer and mistakes, such as poorly proportioned figures and exaggerated shading, become apparent.

Forgeries can sometimes be revealed by precise observation of the work. Cutting a pigment sample from the work and studying its cross-sections shows how each layer of pigment was applied. However, the destructive nature of this analysis means that most owners refuse to allow sampling. A less destructive but laborious test counts the threads of a canvas and gauges their thickness in order to identify the bolt of cloth from which the canvas was taken. Dendrochronology, the dating of wood objects by examining their rings, can be used to estimate the age of a wooden panel. A tree-ring pattern can also identify the very piece of lumber from which a panel was taken.

Counterfeit Sculptures and Figures

Thousands of fake antiquities— from Assyrian bronzes to 4,000-year-old Sumerian figurines in lapis lazuli—reside in the world's leading museums, according to experts. A study led by Oscar White Muscarella of the Metropolitan Museum concluded that 40% of ancient materials on display are fake, half the antiquities brought to Sotheby's auction are turned away as fake, and that 25,000 forgeries of ancient art enter the market every year.

Some ''ancient'' Greek sculptures in bronze are simulated by melting down inferior pieces from the time period and using the materials to fashion a figure. Marble sculptures from the 18th and 19th centuries are often faked as well. The figures are prepared from a mixture of marble dust and resin, which is poured into molds like cake mix. A sparkling crystalline surface completes the authentic look. Black and gray striations simulate marble and are aged with dust that enters cracks. Forgers sometimes use a marble simulation similar to hotel bathrooms where baths and basins look like marble but are made of acrylic, resin, and dolomite powder.

Because stone ages in a peculiar way, some fakes are exposed by observation and touch. A forged piece is smooth and bright, while the naturally weathered surface of a genuine becomes dotted with crystals resembling sugar.

Counterfeit Prints

A demand for low-and mid-priced works, especially "multiple" pieces such as lithographs, has prompted galleries to open in shopping malls and hotel lobbies. Not all are run by shysters, but most lack the expertise to spot prints of questionable origin. Popular targets for counterfeiters include prints by Salvador Dali, Marc Chagall and Joan Miro, which are sold as "original, hand-signed, limited-edition" prints, fetching between $1,000 and $8,000 apiece. Experts call the forgeries "high-quality posters," worth less than $100, containing forged or facsimile signatures. Many dealers use high-pressure sales techniques and phone promotions to move the counterfeits.

Forgers can photograph a print and use laser scanners to transfer it to a lithograph or silkscreen process, producing a print almost indistinguishable from the original. The methods of choice for most forgers are photomechanical lithography and photomechanical serigraphy, techniques for transforming a photograph of an original work of art into a lithograph or a silk-screen print. Counterfeiters apply the image to high-quality rag paper, for a product that many experts cannot distinguish from original "hand pulled" prints.

Counterfeit Photographs

All photographic prints, by definition, are mechanical reproductions of the original image imprinted on film. But a photograph's value soars enormously if the photographer actually made the print in the darkroom, attending to its tones and shading. Experts refer to a "league table" of vintage print values: those made by the photographer within five years of the shoot, those made by the photographer later, and prints made by a family member.

Ironically, the first prints made by a photographer may not be the best ones in terms of quality. The photographer may have used inferior equipment or materials, or may not have possessed printmaking skills equal to photographic abilities. Still the "vintage" distinctions make the difference in a form that accounts for $200 million of the art business.

In the late 1990's, a scandal arose when prints supposedly created by the photographer Man Ray were discovered to be artificially aged reprints. Soon afterward some 300 to 500 prints of Lewis Hine photos were branded fakes, having sold for as much as $50,000 each. Valerie Baas, Senior Paper Conservator at the Detroit Institute of Arts, tested the Hine prints under a fluoroscope, a black-light machine that makes wood-pulp paper glow. Before World War II, most photographic paper was made from higher quality rag-pulp that does not glow under a fluoroscope; shortages during the war forced manufacturers to turn to wood pulp. Many of the Hine prints showed fluorescence and thus could not have been prepared in the 1940's as dealers claimed.

Antiques

Antique furniture and collectibles are faked as often as so-called high art. Originals of early American furniture, for example, fetch several thousand to a million dollars, making a forger's time worthwhile even if the counterfeit takes six months to assemble.

Furniture counterfeiters usually choose something not instantly recognizable and popular. The stool is one of the most commonly faked items. Tables are sought after and very easy to fake—all that is required is a set of old legs and a flat top. Dining room tables accommodating 10 or 12 are popular today, but were not made very often in early America, so tables are reconstructed with larger tops or rebuilt on old bases.

In ceramics, one-of-a-kind items are rare because china manufacturers made pieces for mass replication. Generally speaking, pieces are evaluated against the historical record of the period and details of their decoration, design, and coloration. The history of materials, techniques, technology, and maker's marks all help. Knowing how items were made and used and how they reflect wear is crucial.

Chinese antiques are favorite targets of counterfeiters. Some experts believe up to 90% of the Chinese antiques for sale in Hong Kong are fakes. High-tech factories, staffed with government-paid workers, mix broken pieces of old china and clay from aged pits to produce instant antiques that can fool experts' eyes and modern dating techniques.

Forensics

Art experts evaluate works by observation, by historical analysis, and by testing the work scientifically. A magnifying glass can reveal cracks, imperfections, and other details. An array of non-destructive tests can make observation more accurate and verify physical composition. Using microscopes, radiography, chemical analysis, and dating techniques, experts evaluate the integrity, age, and authenticity of objects, from antique sculptures to modern paintings.

X-rays reveal details of a painting's construction, such as an underdrawing or a false start, repairs, alterations to sculptures (like adding a plaster nose), touchups to a canvas, or a signature. Because lighter elements allow more rays to pass than heavier ones and because the X-ray image shows all the levels of a painting on one plane, X-radiographs may provide inconclusive evidence.

Spectroanalysis determines the chemical composition of physical elements. A work that contains materials not available during the artist's lifetime is an outright forgery or has been altered in some way.

Accelerator mass spectrometry (AMS) measures the radioisotopes in an object directly. Though AMS is a destructive test, only a small piece of the material—a few square millimeters of wood, canvas, silk, or other element—is necessary. The technique is similar to the carbon dating used to measure geological formations, but AMS is thousands of times more sensitive than traditional large-scale testing.

Autoradiography reveals the chemical composition of pigment by bombarding a sample with low-energy neutrons. Because different elements emit radiation differently, scientists identify the pigment's constituents by the way each element glows.

Infrared reflectography shines a band of light invisible to the eye onto a painting's surface. The painting is then filmed with a video camera specially fitted to capture and detect the carbon in the underdrawing. Unlike X-rays and autoradiography, which show all of an image's layers on a single plane, infrared reflectography reveals one shallow field at a time.

Thermoluminescence can determine the time elapsed since a piece of pottery was last fired. By measuring the amount of light emitted from a ceramic object when it is heated, scientists can infer how much radiation the piece has been exposed to and extrapolate its age. The less light, the more recently the piece was baked.

Digital image analysis divides a painting into hundreds of tiny zones to detect the effects of aging, fading, and preservation. The technique is sometimes used with other tests such as X-rays and infrared imaging. Curators not only detect forgeries using digital analysis, but also use the technique to research how artworks decay.

However scientific these techniques are, interpreting their results is often subjective and controversial. Most questions of authenticity in art are decided through a combination of scientific testing and learned observation.

Sources:
Alberge, D. "Is It Real or Fake? Only the Experts Know." *The Gazette (Montreal),* June 5, 1999.

Bradley, J. "Chinese Antiques Rife With Forgeries, Art Consultant Says." *The Denver Post*, October 9, 1997.

Brookes, S. "A Changing Landscape Art Forgery Turns to Low-Profile Artists and Works." *Chicago Tribune*, July 15, 1990.

Coman, J. "The Most Sophisticated and Prolific Forger In History." *Sunday Telegraph* (London), October 1, 2000.

"Forged Art a Lucrative Business." *The Jakarta Post*, March 18, 2001.

Jull, A. "Accelerator Radiocarbon Dating of Art, Textiles, and Artifacts." Nuclear News, June 1998.

Katz, R. "A Near-Perfect Counterfeit: Stolen or Faked Art" *Colonial Homes*, November 1997.

Landesman, P. " A Crisis of Fakes." *The New York Times Magazine*, March 18, 2001.

McGill, D. "Fake Art Prints: Big Business Getting Bigger." *The New York Times*, July 22, 1987.

Schwartz, G. "Truth In Labeling; Evaluating Authentic Versus Fake Rembrandt Paintings; Includes Related Article on Technology Used to Date and Authenticate Paintings." *Art in America,* December 1995.

Watson, P. "Fake Antiquities Litter Top Museums." *Sunday Times* (London), December 10, 2000.

Wigmore, B. "Masters or Fakes?" *The Times* (London), June 8, 2000.

Woodward, R. "On Artificial Rarity and Fakery." *The New York Times*, April 23, 2000.

COUNTERFEIT CURRENCY

Counterfeiting is the unauthorized duplication of a negotiable instrument with the intent to defraud. A negotiable instrument includes cash or any item that can be exchanged for cash, including checks of all sorts, money orders, and warrants. (For information about the counterfeiting of checks and documents, please see the following entries: CHECK FRAUD and COUNTERFEIT DOCUMENTS.)

The U.S. Secret Service estimates that one-tenth of 1% of the American currency outstanding (about $500 billion) is counterfeit. Vigorous enforcement efforts are not motivated by direct losses, but are mounted in order to maintain economic confidence. About 75% of all known counterfeit currency is seized before it reaches the public.

In fiscal year 2003, the U.S. Secret Service and international authorities seized $63 million in counterfeit notes before they ever made it into circulation. Another $38 million in counterfeit U.S. currency that had been passed into circulation was detected and removed worldwide. In these cases, innocent victims who received the bogus bills suffered a financial loss.

Counterfeiting U.S. Bills in Foreign Nations

Amazingly, according to Secret Service figures in 2005, it is estimated that some three-quarters of a trillion of genuine U.S. currency is currently in worldwide circulation, and the majority of this is circulated overseas. The Secret Service estimates that approximately $37 million in counterfeit U.S. dollars were passed successfully in the United States in 2003. This would represent about a 14% reduction from the amount of counterfeit U.S. currency passed in the previous fiscal year.

Russia is the largest user of U.S. currency; each week the Federal Reserve ships at least half a billion dollars in new hundreds to Russian banks. As South American and Caribbean countries—including Ecuador, Guatemala, and El Salvador—adopt the dollar as their national currency, counterfeiters have flocked to these locales.

Secret Service statistics also show that approximately $63 million in counterfeit U.S. currency was seized last year by the Secret Service and other authorities worldwide. Of this amount, approximately $10.7 million was seized in the United States. The remaining notes were seized overseas, with over $31 million seized in Colombia alone.

Although Colombia is the single largest producer of counterfeit U.S. currency, cooperation between U.S. and Colombian authorities has yielded numerous successes, including a 37-percent reduction in Colombian-produced counterfeit currency passed in the United States, from approximately $15.3 million passed in 2002 to approximately $9.6 million 2003.

The economic and social conditions that fostered significant counterfeiting of U.S. currency in Colombia are not restricted to South America. More recently, the breakup of the Soviet Union triggered the growth of organized crime networks throughout the former Soviet Bloc countries in Eastern Europe. Bulgaria has experienced a significant growth in organized crime activities, with groups becoming involved in narcotics trafficking, smuggling, illegal arms distribution, money laundering, and the production and distribution of counterfeit U.S. currency.

Foreign arrests for counterfeiting have been on the rise—from 421 in 1998, to 593 in 1999. U.S. Secret Service made more than 3,640 arrests in the United States for currency counterfeiting activities. The conviction rate for counterfeiting prosecutions is about 99%. About 42% of the counterfeit notes detected being passed in the U.S. in fiscal year 2003 originated outside the U.S, whereas about 50% originated outside of the U.S. in 2002. Counterfeiters are turning increasingly to digital methods, as advances in technology make digital counterfeiting easier and cheaper.

While serious note counterfeiting was once exclusively practiced by organized criminal groups using traditional printing methods that require a high degree of skill, today increasingly deceptive counterfeit notes are produced using basic home computer systems.

In 1995, less than 1% of counterfeit notes detected in the U.S. were digitally produced. In 2002, the Secret Service made 555 seizures of digital equipment, such as personal computers, involved in currency counterfeiting. In 2003, more than 42% of all counterfeit currency passed domestically was printed outside of the U.S. using traditional offset printing techniques. Virtually every note that was produced overseas and passed in the U.S. was produced by offset printing. In contrast, 46% of the counterfeit currency passed domestically in 2003 was produced within the U.S. by individuals using digital technology such as home computers and color copiers. Countries with the greatest counterfeit activity include Columbia, China, and South Africa. Colombia is the single largest producer of counterfeit U.S. currency in the world, accounting for approximately 26%, or $10 million, of the $37 million in counterfeit dollars passed in the United States last year.

Hong Kong as a Counterfeiting Center

Hong Kong once headed the list of countries hosting counterfeit operations. As described by John Simpson of the Treasury Department, "The need for a full-time presence in Hong Kong became evident during the period June 1992 through August 1993. . . During that period, the agents participated in the arrests of over 100 individuals involved in counterfeiting U.S. currency and multiple 'access device fraud,' commonly referred to as credit card fraud. Cooperative efforts with Hong Kong authorities during that period resulted in the seizure of over $10 million in counterfeit U.S. currency. . . [Agents] discovered in fiscal year 1993 almost 6,000 counterfeit U.S. notes that had originated in Hong Kong. Statistics for fiscal year 1994 were similar. This placed Hong Kong among the top ten foreign sources of counterfeit U.S. financial instruments." From 1994 to 1997 more than $7.5 million in counterfeit U.S. currency was seized in Hong Kong. Simpson reported, "Fictitious U.S. financial instruments, including items such as bonds and high dollar-value Federal Reserve instruments were being produced in the region." However, the Treasury Department removed Hong Kong from its watch list in 2000 and hailed the cooperative enforcement efforts of local and international police for curbing the practice.

Counterfeiters' Techniques

Advances in reprographic technology mean large quantities of counterfeit currency or other obligations can be produced quickly and efficiently. With little knowledge or specialized training a criminal can counterfeit currency or other financial instruments, utilizing equipment that ranges from inexpensive color copiers, scanners, computers, and inkjet printers, to small offset duplicators and large commercial presses. Currency counterfeiting by traditional offset-printing operations is more prevalent abroad, while digital counterfeiting is more prevalent in the U.S. The Treasury Department estimates that counterfeiters printed more than 100 times the amount of computer-generated cash in 2000 than they did in 1995. Of the 651 counterfeit-currency printing operations suppressed in the United States during fiscal year 2001, 608, or 93.4%, used digital processes, a phenomenal increase from the 29 digital operations (or 18.9% of the total) suppressed in 1995.

Individual operations using computers tend to make less currency than their analog counterparts, but there are many more computerized operations at work.

Computer forgeries are believed to account for 47% of all bogus currency, up from 0.5% in 1995. Offset presses created $29.8 million counterfeit dollars in 1995; copy machines created $2.4 million, and computerized printers created $175,000. In 2000, offset presses created $20.2 million, computer operations created $18.5 million, and copying machines produced about $1 million.

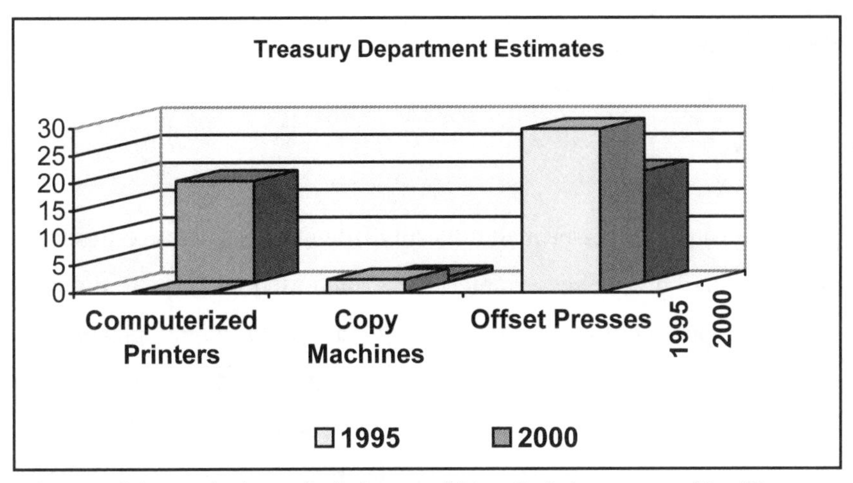

Estimates of changes in the method of counterfeiting. Scale increments of 5 million.

Common counterfeiting techniques include using black and white, monochromatic, or color photocopiers; cutting and taping or gluing numerals from high denomination notes to the corners of a note of lower denomination, also known as making "raised notes"; using computers, scanners, and laser or ink jet printers to digitize and print notes; bleaching good notes and reprinting higher denominations on the genuine paper; and using photomechanical or "offset" methods to make a printing plate from a photographic negative of a genuine note.

Inkjet Counterfeiting

Inkjet printers allow the counterfeiter to produce notes on an as-needed basis, without maintaining a large inventory. Ink Jet copiers/printers spray tiny droplets of ink from the printer head through a small gap of air onto the paper to form the image. With traditional offset printing methods, the cost of printing and handling required large runs and warehousing of bills. Cases involving computer-generated notes rarely involve seized currency in excess of $2,000. The low seizure amount means the typical defendant faces less than a year imprisonment. If the amount of seized counterfeit currency is less than $5,000 and a defendant accepts responsibility, the person may be eligible for probation. In 1995, $174,924 (.5%) of all counterfeit currency passed in the United States was inkjet produced, compared to $6,121,292 (19%) in 1997—an 805% increase. For the first five months of fiscal year 1998, some $7,224,712 (43%) of counterfeit currency passed in the United States was inkjet produced.

Using Change Machines

Though photocopied and inkjet-printed bills are difficult to pass in face-to-face transactions or through businesses, counterfeiters often use these bills to drain change machines. Crude copies, cut to size—some with oven lines or other signs of processing clearly visible—are fed into change machines at laundromats, car washes, and other locations. The coins can be converted to bills at financial institutions or at larger supermarkets that often house change-counting machines.

Anti-Counterfeiting Efforts

Since 1999, the Secret Service has published information about counterfeit U.S. currency on the World Wide Web. The Counterfeit Note Search Site allows the Secret Service to track known instances of counterfeiting by distinguishing characteristics, regional circulation, and other factors. The database contains over 21,630 different counterfeit circulars with over 20,000 variations. Manual comparisons are supplemented by a computerized system that classifies counterfeit notes using pixels present in the Treasury seal.

Anti-counterfeiting efforts are conducted by the Secret Service, the Department of the Treasury, the Federal Reserve System, the Bureau of Engraving and Printing, and the foreign law enforcement community. Private companies associated with inkjet and other color printers, color copiers, digital output cameras, imaging software, and Internet software participate as well.

The U.S. Department of the Treasury showcased its anti-counterfeiting design with a 100-dollar bill introduced in the late 1990's. Hundred-dollar bills make up some two-thirds of U.S. currency. In the new design, Ben Franklin's portrait was made larger and set off-center, making it easier to read the details on the portrait and leaving room for a large portrait watermark that is difficult to counterfeit and easy to verify. The new bill used advanced color-shifting ink that changes appearance when the bill is tilted. A security thread embedded in the paper was enhanced and placed in a different spot for each denomination. The new 20-dollar bill was introduced in 2003. A new 50-dollar note will be introduced in late 2004.

The Cost of Counterfeited Currency

In a 1996 address to Congress, Secret Service spokesperson Jack Blum explained that, while counterfeiters are not economically significant, they rob the U.S. government. "A new $100 bill costs the Bureau of Printing and Engraving between four and six cents to produce. The difference between the cost of production and face value of the bill is called seigniorage. The net profit to the government is somewhere between ninety four and ninety six cents a bill. . . The foreign counterfeit problem is irrelevant to the control of the money supply. . . The amount of paper money in circulation in the United States and the world is irrelevant to domestic inflation. Currency is a tiny fraction of the U.S. dollar denominated money in use in the world economy in a given day. . . [The major] dollar wire-transfer systems handle between one and two trillion dollars each business day. Even if the foreign counterfeiters worked around the clock their output would be an economically insignificant blip. . . What the counterfeiters are doing is stealing the profit on the manufacture and sale of paper money."

Recognizing Counterfeit U.S. Currency

Security measures are integrated into bills and can be used to distinguish between legitimate and counterfeit currency. Simply rubbing a note will not suffice since legitimate bills will also give up ink.

Major characteristics include:

- Security threads imbedded into the note will glow when held beneath a light; the denomination of the note is signified by the pattern of the glowing thread.
- Security threads are color-coded: red for $100's, yellow for $50's, green for $20's, orange for $10's, and blue for $5's.
- For $100 notes, the Ben Franklin watermark on the right hand side of the bill's face is visible beneath a light. In other denominations, the appropriate presidential portrait (e.g., Lincoln on the $5 bill) is used as the watermark.

- The denomination numeral in the lower right corner on the note's face shifts color from green to black as the viewing angle shifts.
- Recent bills (post 1997 for $100's, post 2000 for other denominations) contain a larger portrait than earlier versions, and the portrait is offset to the left.
- The term "United States of America" is microprinted on Franklin's coat.

Comparing Counterfeits with Genuine U.S. Currency

COUNTERFEIT	GENUINE
Portrait is lifeless; background is too dark; portrait merges into background; hairlines are indistinct	Portrait is sharp, distinct from the screened background
Saw-tooth points on the colored seal are uneven, blunt, broken off	Saw-tooth points are even, clear, sharp
The fine lines on the border are smudged, indistinct	Border lines are clear, distinct, unbroken
Serial numbers are wrong color, improperly spaced or aligned; the same serial number may be used on multiple bills	Serial numbers are evenly spaced and aligned; each bill bears a different number
No watermarks made in the portrait's image; other type of watermark may be present	Newer denominations contain a watermark identical to the bill's portrait; older bills have no watermark
Paper lacks red and blue fibers; red and blue marks may be printed or drawn onto the bill	Red and blue fibers are embedded in the paper
No security threads; a printed line may mimic the thread, but will not show the denomination or glow beneath light	Security thread, when held beneath light, shows the denomination of the bill and glow a particular color according to denomination
Printing of "United States of America" on front of bill is flat, cannot be felt with fingertips	The intaglio printing is raised, perceptible to fingertips

Sources:
Atlas, R. "Report Says Money Launderers Exploit Banks." *The New York Times*, February 5, 2001.

Ball, A. "In PC Era, Counterfeiting Is the Sport of Amateurs." *The Austin American-Statesman*, July 6, 2001.

Blanco, J. *Business Fraud*. Huntington: Humanomics, 2001.

"Counterfeit U.S. Currency: Issues and U.S. Deterrence Efforts." Letter Report, 02/26/96, GAO/GGD-96-11.

"Prepared Testimony of Jack A. Blum." Federal News Service, February 27, 1996.

Rohter, L. "Ecuador's Use of Dollars Brings Dollars' Problems." *The New York Times*, February 5, 2001.

"The Use and Counterfeiting of U.S Currency Abroad." Federal News Service, March 30, 2000.

U.S. State Department: usembassy.state.gov/mumbai/wwwhwashnews379.html

COUNTERFEIT DOCUMENTS

Any document can be counterfeited. Among the most common targets are passports, birth certificates, drivers' licenses and identity cards, divorce proceedings, and estate settlements. Sports memorabilia and documents related to celebrities are also prone to forgery.

Most counterfeit documents are prepared by one of several photo-reproduction processes such as the photo-offset printing process (lithography) and flexography, which uses rubberized printing "plates." These processes begin with the photographic reproduction of a model genuine document. The photographic negatives are then carefully retouched to remove the filled-in text, serial numbers, etc. which appeared on the genuine document. Printing plates are then made from the retouched negatives, and counterfeit copies are printed from the plates.

Technology allows people with no commercial printing experience to use sophisticated computerized scanners, computer graphics software, multicolor computer printers, and full-color photocopy machines to produce high quality counterfeit documents.

Questioned Documents

Professional document examiners refer to the materials they examine as "questioned documents." A questioned document is any signature, handwriting, typewriting, or other mark whose source or authenticity is in dispute or doubtful. Letters, checks, driver licenses, contracts, wills, voter registrations, passports, petitions, threatening letters, suicide notes, and lottery tickets are the most common questioned documents, although marks on doors, walls, windows, or boards may also be included.

Among the more common terms used in discussions of questioned documents are:

- *Questioned Document Examiners* (QDE). A document examiner analyzes any questioned document and is capable of more than just questions of authorship, limited only by their access to laboratory equipment.
- *Historical Dating*. This is work involving the verification of age and worth of a document or object, sometimes done by a document examiner, and can get as complicated as Carbon-14 dating.
- *Fraud Investigators*. A fraud investigator does work that often overlaps with that of the document examiner and focuses on the money trail and criminal intent.
- *Paper & Ink Specialists*. These are public or private experts who date, type, source, and/or catalogue various types of paper, watermarks, ink, printing/copy/fax machines, computer cartridges, etc., using chemical methods.
- *Forgery Specialists*. These are public or private experts who analyze altered, obliterated, changed, or doctored documents and photos using infrared lighting, expensive spectrography equipment, or digital enhancement techniques.
- *Handwriting Analysts*. Also called graphologists or graphoanalysts, these are usually psychology experts who assess personality traits from handwriting samples. Forensic stylistics refers to the same purpose but by looking at semantics, spelling, word choice, syntax, and phraseology.
- *Typewriting Analysts*. These are experts on the origin, make, and model used in typewritten material.
- *Computer Crime Investigators*. This is an emerging group that relates to QDE through some common investigative and testimonial procedures.

Source: faculty.ncwc.edu/toconnor/425/425lect05.htm

Detecting Counterfeit Documents

Many counterfeits can be detected by making a side-by-side comparison with a corresponding genuine document. Subtle differences in ink colors and brilliance, different types of paper substrate, the use of different typestyles and type sizes (fonts), and evidence of retouching can distinguish a fake from the real thing. Retouching will be most evident in areas where the text, serial numbers, etc., especially if printed in black ink, are superimposed on a background design.

The type of paper used and its treatment should be the same in all pages of a genuine document. "Trash marks" and other signs of debris are good identification marks: in a stack of photocopies, for example, a spot that appears on every page except one suggests the page was not copied at the same time as the others.

In some instances, the printing device or method may not have been available at the time the document was supposedly prepared. Many counterfeits have been exposed by showing, for example, that a signature in ballpoint pen is dated before the ballpoint appeared in 1948. Some types of paper were also available only in certain places and times.

Comparing genuine documents with suspected counterfeits, forensic document examiners use tools and techniques to spot differentiations between printing processes, ink formulations, and paper substrates. Portions of filled-in text and serial numbers that were removed in the retouching process may be reconstructed. Fading ink that disappears gradually over time can be restored by chemical treatment. Evidence also can be found on the equipment used to create false documents. A tape reader used by the IRS can decrypt imprints made on typewriter and correction ribbons.

Common Forms of Alteration

An original document is *altered* by taking away or adding something. The forger may add or remove digits, add or remove letters, or change the wording of a document. Negotiable instruments like checks are prime targets. So are legal documents such as wills, which confer a monetary award on the forger. Alterations are also used in embezzlement schemes to disguise improper transactions.

Substitution is a form of alteration in which entire pages of a document are replaced with bogus pages that favor the forger. *Interlineations* are additions inserted between lines of text. Interlineations are usually handwritten. All parties customarily initial all interlineations which indicates approval, though initials may also be forged. Improper interlineations are usually discredited by identifying the handwriting of the forger, or by demonstrating that the purported author's handwriting differs significantly from the interlineations.

Signature Stamps

Many organizations allow key personnel to use signature stamps, which affix a facsimile of a person's signature to a document via a rubber stamp and ink. The key to securing these stamps is to limit access to the materials. Some simple rules:

- Use only one stamp at a time. Keep this item in a secure place and limit access to one or two persons.
- Note the date each stamp is purchased and when it is retired. Obtain samples of the stamp immediately and lock these in a secure space.
- Lock old stamps in a safe place. They may help authenticate or disprove questioned signatures in the future.

Document Classifications

A *questioned document* is disputed on some grounds. Certain aspects or the entire document may be challenged.

A *known document* serves as a control sample for analysis. This includes authentic signature samples, writing samples, authenticated negotiable instruments, or other item. These documents are drawn from previous transactions; they are not prepared specifically for testing.

An *exemplar* or *standard* is a sample—of handwriting or a signature, for example—obtained specifically for testing.

Handwriting Analysis

The principles of handwriting analysis used by questioned document examiners were first iterated by Albert Osborn in *Questioned Documents* (1910).

- The most identifying characteristics are those that are most divergent from the regular system or national average.
- Repeated characteristics, which are inconspicuous, should be sought first and given the most weight.
- Regular or national system similarities alone are not sufficient to base judgments on.
- It is the combination of particulars, common and uncommon, that identifies handwriting.
- It is impossible to discover how all strange and peculiar characteristics came to be developed.
- People do wholly unaccountable things in their speech, gestures, and writing.
- An individual characteristic may be the survival of an error overlooked by a teacher.
- Many characteristics are outgrowths or copies of a design admired by the writer at an earlier time.

Osborn founded the American Society of Questioned Document Examiners (ASQDE) in 1942. His books *Questioned Documents* and *The Problem of Proof* provided the basis for the discipline.

Handwriting analysis by document examiners is not to be confused with the pseudoscience of *graphology*, whose practitioners claim to divine a person's psychology by identifying certain handwriting traits. These claims are spurious. Handwriting analysis cannot reveal age, gender, or whether the person is right-or left-handed. Certain characteristics, such as the person's health at the time, or whether or not the person was inebriated at the time of writing, can be inferred.

The main function of a handwriting analysis is to determine if the person in question performed the handwriting or not. This is best done by comparing the questioned writing to known samples or standards of the person's writing.

There are two types of standards: collected and requested. *Collected* standards are those already in existence that the attorney or investigator collects. They may be bank records, letters, or legal forms. *Requested* standards are those that the subject is requested to give to facilitate the document examination. The best standards are those that most closely emulate the timeframe, circumstances, materials and content of the questioned document. Therefore, investigators should examine collected standards executed near the questioned document. This is especially critical in cases involving illness, death, accident, mental imbalance, substance abuse, or anything likely to cause a dramatic change in the subject's behavior.

Sample Libraries and Document Databases

A library maintained by the Internal Revenue Service contains nearly 8,000 ink samples on paper from around the world. Each sample includes a breakdown of the different dyes that comprise an ink.

The U.S. Secret Service operates a counterfeit documents database used to make forensic connections between known and questioned counterfeit documents. Agencies worldwide can track the source and proliferation of counterfeit documents such as driver licenses, credit cards, and checks. Besides forensic information about the counterfeit document, the database contains investigative information regarding the use, passing, or seizure of the document. Most of the documents are counterfeit financial instruments, such as travelers' checks and credit cards.

The American Society of Questioned Document Examiners provides standards and references for a range of document issues. Many resources are available online at www.asqde.com. In addition to the Society's own resources, the site provides information on materials available elsewhere.

Case Study—Kynge Leare

In 1795, a Mr. Ireland claimed to possess a new version of "Kynge Leare" written in the handwriting of William Shakespeare himself. But one year later, Edward Malone published an examination of the document refuting Ireland's claims. Malone had discovered that the questioned manuscript contained pages with twenty different watermarks. Malone argued that Shakespeare was already famous and affluent at the time his play *King Lear* was written and would have gone to a papermaker and secured as much paper of one type as he needed. At the most, he might mix two batches together, but not 20.

On the other hand, a forger in the 18th century trying to duplicate an Elizabethan play 200 years earlier would have to rely on scraps of old paper taken from the flyleaves and blank pages of old manuscripts. Indeed, in 1805 Ireland wrote his confession and denounced the work.

Case Study—Howard and Melvin

The multimillionaire tycoon and infamous recluse Howard Hughes died in 1976, leaving an estate estimated to be between $2 and $3 billion, and no will. One Hughes attorney stated that Hughes had asked him twice about the legalities of a proper holographic will, that is, one written completely by hand.

Shortly after this information was published, a Howard Hughes' alleged holographic will was found on a desk in the office building of the Church of Jesus Christ of Latter Day Saints (the Mormon Church). An accompanying note said that the document had been found near the home of Joseph Smith (founder of the Mormon Church) and that it should be delivered to the President of the Mormon Church. A questioned document examiner gave the preliminary opinion that the will may have been written by Howard Hughes, and the Mormon Church filed the will in a Las Vegas county court where the Hughes estate was located.

One provision of "The Mormon Will" was that a 1/16th share of the estate ($156,000,000) would go to 32-year-old Melvin Dummar of Gabbs, NV. Dummar and his wife owned and operated a small gas station in Willard, UT and he sang country music in local bars. Dummar claimed that he had no knowledge of the will, but told reporters that years before he had picked up a bum in the desert who claimed to be Howard Hughes. Dummar said he gave the man a ride into Las Vegas and dropped him off behind the Sands Hotel after giving him the spare change in his pocket.

From April through December of 1976, Melvin Dummar spoke publicly and gave private interviews, always maintaining that he knew nothing about the will. Meanwhile, a team of forensic examiners were testing the will and Dummar's story. The will had been found inside an envelope that contained a fingerprint matching Melvin Dummar's print.

In the library of Webster State College, where Dummar was a part-time student, examiners found a book on Clifford Irving's attempts to forge Hughes's handwriting in a bogus autobiography. The book, *Hoax* contained many examples of Hughes's writing and anecdotal information about his handwriting and habits. The book also contained a fingerprint that matched Mr. Dummar's print.

Experts concluded that the writing on the envelope and the slip of paper inside were probably the disguised writing of Melvin Dummar. When Mr. Dummar was confronted with the fingerprinting and handwriting evidence, he denied all allegations of his involvement in forgery of the document and insisted that Hughes corporate executives were faking the evidence in a conspiracy against him.

After waffling through various changes in his story, Dummar settled on one version—a mysterious man drove into his service station and gave him the will along with several pages of instructions. Dummar admitted that in following these instructions (which he had since burned) he had placed the will in the envelope, written the note on the slip of paper, and delivered the package to the Mormon Church offices.

In the end, four document examiners concluded that the will was forged. A definite conclusion was possible because there were three full pages of questioned material and a large body of Howard Hughes' contemporaneous, verified writings to use as standards. Because of deteriorating health, Hughes's handwriting habits had changed during a two-year period just before the alleged will was written, and these changes were not identifiable in the questioned will.

After a seven-month trial, a Las Vegas court ruled the will a forgery. Dummar received nothing from the Hughes estate, but the notoriety of his claim brought him money from a movie sympathetic to his claim (*Melvin and Howard*) and from singing engagements. He wrote a song, "Thank You, Howard." The Andrews & Kurth law firm of Houston, representing the Hughes estate, claimed to have spent $3 million discrediting Dummar and his three sheets of paper.

Sources:
Abram, L. "Billions of Loose Ends, Authors Track battle for Hughes' Fortune." *Houston Chronicle,* December 07, 1997.

Ambrose, E. "On the Lookout for Tax Cheats; IRS Crime Lab Sleuths Use Variety of Means to Sniff Out Fraud." *Weekly Edition,* April 14, 1997.

Gaudreau, M.O., Purdy, D.C., and Harris, J.S. "Where Document Imaging and Scientific Image Analysis Meet: Document Forensics." *Advanced Imaging,* March 1996.

Kruger, D. "Every Touch Leaves a Trace, Says Lawyer/Forensic Document Examiner." *The Lawyers Weekly,* August 18, 2000.

Maloney, R. "A Signature Business; Buying and Selling Historical Items; Statistical Data Included." *Maclean's (Toronto Edition),* November 15, 1999.

Nicol, J. "Passports For Sale: Sophisticated Forgeries Are Fueling a Tidal Wave of Global Migration." *Macleans' (Toronto Edition),* April 3, 2000.

Wake, B. "Making Silent Witnesses Talk: Experts Gather to Share Secrets of Crime Documents." *The Ottawa Citizen,* August 25, 2000.

Related Entry:

HITLER DIARIES

COUNTERFEIT DRUGS

In the pharmaceutical industry, the term "counterfeit drug" refers to a compound prepared by someone other than the authorized manufacturer, but circulated under the manufacturer's labeling. There are also drugs made or distributed by unauthorized sources with the supervision or tacit approval of the authorized manufacturer. These drugs may not technically fit the legal definition of "counterfeit drug" but withholding the identity of the true manufacturer is a violation of Food and Drug Administration (FDA) laws.

The World Health Organization (WHO) estimates that 10% of the world's supply of branded medicines is counterfeit, with the level rising to 50% in some developing countries. The pharmaceutical industry provides another illustration. It can take ten years and $125 to $160 million to bring a pharmaceutical product to market. A chemist can easily copy (counterfeit) a drug in days with a few thousand dollars of equipment, especially since safety and efficacy are of no concern.

Counterfeit drugs pose a number of potential public health issues. WHO has found that the majority of counterfeit drugs contain a less potent active ingredient than claimed, ingredients other than those listed, or no active ingredient at all, making the compounds less effective and possibly toxic. Even when the product contains the proper amount of the active ingredient, it can pose hazards. The effectiveness of drugs depends on factors that include measures in quality control, distribution, and inventory control.

Besides finished drug products, drugs imported in bulk, also known as Active Pharmaceutical Ingredients (API's), are also targeted by counterfeiters. The U.S. FDA uses a database, available electronically to all field inspectors, that contains information or "fingerprints" on 330 API's.

Fighting counterfeiters is particularly difficult because of the international reach of the drug trade. Customs inspectors in the U.S. maintain contact with their counterparts at the World Health Organization, the World Customs Organization, Interpol, and FDA counterparts in such countries as the United Kingdom, Germany, Spain, and Australia. Additionally, the FCC participates in the International Laboratory Forum on Counterfeit Medicines.

U.S. Customs officials say their seizure of counterfeit and other prescription drugs has risen sharply in recent years. The service seized 9,725 parcels of prescription drugs in 1999, compared with 2,145 the year before. Most of the seizures were drugs purchased by Americans from websites operating in foreign countries, though some lots were hijacked commercial shipments intended for resale through legitimate channels. Customs conducted a survey of imported drug products entering the U.S. through the Carson City, California mail facility. Over a five-week period, with FDA inspectors present for 40 hours per week, and a much higher staffing level than is normally possible, an estimated 16,500 international packages could have been set aside as a baseline sample for FDA inspection. Of the 16,500, only 1,908 packages were inspected. Of the 1,908 packages examined by the FDA, 721 parcels originating in 19 countries were detained and the addressees notified that the products appeared to be unapproved for use in the U.S., misbranded and/or a drug requiring a doctor's prescription.

Source: www.fda.gov/ola/2002/drugimportation0709.html

Case Study—Drug Smugglers

In 2001, the Food and Drug Administration found counterfeit versions of three injectable drugs in wide circulation. The counterfeit drugs were: Serostim, a growth hormone used by AIDS patients; Nutropin, a growth hormone prescribed more generally; and

Neupogen, a cancer drug. In each case, the counterfeit drug looked nearly identical to the real product. For Serostim, even the lot number, which is used to trace drugs, was a real number. The only difference between the real and the counterfeit was in the expiration date, which had been changed from August 2001 to August 2002. Some of the counterfeit vials were found to contain cheap, generic versions of the drugs, while others had been filled with clear liquid that contained no active ingredient. At least one vial of Nutropin contained human insulin.

All three drugs are expensive. For example, a 12-week course of Serostim costs $21,000. These drugs are particularly desired because they are believed to help users lose weight, build muscle and smooth wrinkles. The FDA found websites promoting the drugs for these uses and some that offered to sell the drugs without prescription.

Serono, which manufactures Serostim, was alerted to the counterfeiting when patients began complaining that they had suffered a slight swelling or a skin rash after being injected. Counterfeit versions of Serostim were found in at least seven states. At least some of the counterfeit Serostim was found in pharmacies. FDA officials said the drugs were bought and resold by small distributors operating in a gray market that is expanding. According to the distributors and government officials, a small Florida distributor sold some counterfeit Serostim to Dutchess Business Services Inc., a small distributor in Las Vegas, which then sold it to Quality King Distributors Inc., a distributor in Ronkonkoma, N.Y. Quality King officials said they then sold it to other distributors. Counterfeit drugs are attractive to smugglers because they are small and in demand. Individuals often divert prescription drugs into the gray market or small businesses who claim they are buying the medicines for nursing homes or other institutions that are offered price discounts.

In another example of trafficking in counterfeit drugs, Moshe Milstein operated a drug wholesaling business out of his Brooklyn home from 1991 to 1993, repackaging drugs from overseas to look like brand-name drugs from the U.S. Milstein sold the drugs to other wholesalers and to pharmacies and doctors in the New York area. Milstein's company, Gem Distributors, carried counterfeits of Pergonal and Metrodin, which are fertility drugs, and Eldepryl, a drug for Parkinson's disease. Laboratory tests showed that some of Milstein's stock contained bacteria and endotoxins, the powerful poisons produced by bacteria. In 2000, Milstein was convicted of five felonies, including distribution of misbranded drugs.

In 1997, Medical Sales Inc. of San Diego County, CA, bought drugs made by an Indian manufacturer and repackaged them under the name "American Pharmaceutical." The company planned to sell the drugs, which included antibiotics, painkillers, and diet drugs, to pharmacies in Tijuana, Mexico, where they would be sold to American tourists. Medical Sales president Christopher Kirkman was arrested before he was observed actually selling any drugs. He was convicted of a misdemeanor charge of selling misbranded drugs in 1999 and given six months' probation.

Sources:
Henney, J. M.D. "Capitol Hill Hearing Testimony on Counterfeit Drugs." *Federal Document Clearing House Congressional Testimony,* October 3, 2000.

Maher, P. "Capitol Hill Hearing Testimony on Counterfeit Drugs." October 3, 2000.

Petersen, M. "Three Fake Drugs Are Found in Pharmacies." *The New York Times*, June 5, 2001.

COUNTERFEIT FINANCIAL INSTRUMENTS

It is estimated that "desktop publishing" crimes cause financial institutions, businesses, and individuals to lose some $12 billion a year. "Desktop publishing" crime is the computerized counterfeiting of financial instruments, including counterfeit commercial checks, traveler's checks, money orders, securities, and negotiable instruments. Criminal rings may offer a "one-stop shopping" service, using a single computer or several computers in one location to produce phony documents of every kind—not just spurious checks and securities, but the identification and supporting documentation necessary to convert the documents into cash (the latter are known as "breeder documents").

The most popular counterfeiting of financial instruments in recent years is the circulating of documents claiming to originate in the more arcane areas of international finance. The documents are often called "prime bank instruments," claiming to be from the world's most prominent, or prime, banks. Prime bank scams first came to widespread attention in 1993; after a downturn in reports, the scam gained prominence again in the late 1990's. In fact, neither prime-bank instruments, nor the markets in which they allegedly trade, exist. International organizations and law enforcement agencies have issued warning circulars and bulletins about prime bank instrument schemes, but have not been able to deter their proliferation.

The documents are circulated under various names, including bank debenture programs, bank guarantees, bank secured trading programs, blocked fund certificates, discounted standby letters of credit, high-yield/no-risk debentures, International Chamber of Commerce letters of credit, London Short Form Letters of Credit, medium-term notes or MTNs, roll programs, seasoned instruments, and other terms. "Prime," "secured," and "letters of credit" are commonly employed terms.

"Standby letters of credit" are sold under the following pretense: they were issued at 85 cents to the dollar to be redeemed at face value after one year and a day with an interest rate in excess of 18% and far higher than that on offer from other bank-guaranteed investments. Banks rarely issue standby letters of credit. For example, banks will accommodate an important customer undertaking a major project by issuing a letter guaranteeing payments to subcontractors if the customer defaults. But banking sources say that less than 1% of these letters are ever called on. One reason for this is that the letter can be transferred only once: from the customer to the subcontractor.

The International Chamber of Commerce warns, "By adapting and twisting the terminology that is commonly used in international banking transactions, the fraudsters have avoided potential challenges from people who are not closely involved in international banking. Many persons, except those who have extensive knowledge of international banking, find these documents confusing and intimidating and some may even feel embarrassed to challenge the legality of the documents presented."

These scams all promise huge rates of return (100 to 200%) at little or no risk. They purport to draw their money from a highly secretive market in instruments produced by world banks. Supposedly the investor is aiding the cash flow of these institutions by purchasing small portions of the large amounts of debt being held. The trading process is sometimes described as the dividing of large instruments into smaller denominations: a "cutting house" buys the lot, then sells the new debentures, "fresh cut," to investors lucky enough to be admitted into the trading circle. The sold denominations are called "seasoned debentures."

Prime bank instrument schemes are often run as Ponzi schemes. Others are advance-fee frauds, targeting individuals and companies who need loans. These potential borrowers are advised that a "prime bank" will fund their loans, provided that they paid a large up-front fee to secure the funding. These schemes are conducted at so-called wholesale and retail levels. At the wholesale level, wealthy individuals and corporations are sold huge quantities of bond-like investments. At the retail level, smaller investors are convinced that a selling agent, who has prominent large corporations waiting to purchase the instruments, requires some working capital to make the sale, after which the loan will be repaid many times over.

Financial Documents Database

The U.S. Secret Service operates a counterfeit financial documents database, housing over 90,000 documents, used to make forensic connections between known and questioned counterfeit documents. Besides forensic information about the counterfeit document, the database contains investigative information regarding the use, passing, or seizure of the document. Most of the documents are travelers' checks, bank checks, and credit cards. The database allows investigators to link documents with no apparent connection, matching counterfeit food coupons to travelers' checks to postage stamps, for example.

Case Study—Prime Bank Instruments

The Securities Commission of Canada busted an Internet-based investment club in 2001 as part of an investigation of prime bank instrument fraud. The Tri-West Investment Club and its backers were convicted of committing fraud and selling securities without being registered.

- The panel issued a statement outlining the characteristics of prime-bank schemes and other similar schemes.
- The program guarantees unrealistically high rates of return within a short period of time.
- The program claims to be risk free.

- Investors are told that they are among the privileged few whose money will be pooled to invest in secret programs reserved for top financiers.
- Investors are asked to sign secrecy or confidentiality agreements.
- Some part of the program is transacted through a country regarded as a secrecy haven which, it is claimed, enables investors to avoid paying taxes on their returns.
- Investors are given financial incentives for bringing in new investors.
- The money from one group of investors is used to show a profit to a subsequent group. Eventually, the promoters pocket the proceeds and disappear, leaving the pyramid to collapse.
- Investors are solicited through the Internet.

The victims of these schemes may be individuals, but institutions are a favored target. In 2000, the Salvation Army, Britain's largest charity, announced it had paid more than $6 million for "standby letters of credit" issued by the "Islamic Pan American Bank," which never existed. CMI Insurance, a large England-based corporation, also admitted it had paid $20 million to Hanover Bank Limited of Antigua to buy "prime bank instruments."

Sources:
Baines, D. "Investment Club Termed 'Quintessential' Fraud." *Business,* October 25, 2001.

Boccagna, D. "Inside the World of Investment Fraud, Scams, and Deceptive Practices." Miami: IESC Press, 1998.

"Herbert A. Biern, Deputy Associate Director, Division of Banking, Supervision and Regulation. U.S. Senate, July 17, 1996; Prime Bank Financial Instrument Fraud." *Federal Reserve Bulletin,* September 1996.

Manuel, G. "Latest Fraud Scam Hooks Even the Smart." *South China Morning Post,* March 28, 1994.

Wells, J., CFE, CPA, et al. *Fraud Examiners Manual.* The Association of Certified Fraud Examiners, 2002.

Related Entry:
FINANCIAL INSTITUTION FRAUD

COUNTERFEIT GOVERNMENT SECURITIES

Some of the most commonly counterfeited financial instruments are government-issued securities. Besides copying existing securities, some counterfeiters create phony securities that never existed. Some of the more common types include "limited edition" Treasury securities, one-year "fresh cut" Treasury bills, "U.S. dollar bonds," the "U.S. Dollar Bond," and "federal notes." Many of these notes are touted as rare, underground securities not available to the general public. The instruments are sold to individual investors, pension funds, and retirement accounts, or sometimes used to underwrite loans. Many of the instruments are phony and others with legitimate origins have been declared worthless by their issuing agencies.

The "U.S. dollar bonds," for example, were supposedly issued in the Far East during the 1930's or early 1940's by the Central Intelligence Agency (which did not exist at the time) to help Chiang Kai-shek's attempt to overthrow China's Communist government. Phony bonds often refer to fictitious agencies, such as the Ministry of Finance of the United States, or the Washington Bank of America. The so-called "fresh cut" T-bills and "federal notes" are spurious also—though thousands have been sold under the pretense that the notes were shipped by the U.S. to the Philippines during World War II and were left unredeemed.

So-called historical bonds are also favored counterfeiting targets. These bonds were once valid obligations of American entities but are now collected and traded by memorabilia buffs since they are worthless as securities. Fraudsters have been successful, particularly with railroad bonds from the 19th century, in passing these notes off as redeemable securities.

The circulation of financial "warrants" by anti-government groups is a peculiar offshoot of securities counterfeiting. Generally, these groups argue that "real money" is gold and silver, and the notes they circulate are as legitimate as notes from the Federal Reserve.

Financial crime investigations have become more dynamic and international in scope. In response, the Secret Service created a worldwide counterfeit financial documents database that is used to make forensic connections between known and questioned counterfeit documents. This database is used to determine common origins through link analysis conducted by research specialists. Police agencies all over the world are now able to track the source and proliferation of counterfeit documents such as driver licenses, credit cards, and checks.

Catalog of Phony Government Securities

- Gold Ore Certificate
- Georgian Imex Bank Certificate
- U.S. Dollar Bond
- Indonesian Promissory Note
- Japanese Yen Bond
- Philippine Victory Note
- German War Bond
- Comptroller Warrant
- Republic of Texas Warrant
- Freemen Warrant
- Posse Comitatus
- We The People
- W.D. McCall
- LA. Pethahia
- Mount Calvary Baptist
- Central Dominion Trust Bank

Sources:
Connor, J. "Fraudsters Use Varied Bag of Tricks in Pushing Bogus Treasury Securities." *Wall Street Journal,* February 8, 2001

"Prepared Statement Of Brian L. Stafford Director, U. S. Secret Service Department Of The Treasury U. S. Secret Service." *Federal News Service,* March 30, 2000.

"Prepared Statement of Eljay B. Bowron Director U.S. Secret Service Sources." *Federal News Service,* February 26, 1997.

Related Entry:

COUNTERFEIT CURRENCY

COUNTERFEIT IDENTIFICATION AND FAKE IDS

Counterfeiters exploit every type of personal identification. The popularization of the Internet made "fake IDs" more widely available and affordable than ever. Phony IDs are sometimes called "breeder documents" because they can be used to obtain other documents, to open bank and stock accounts, and to perform a host of financial transactions. Often IDs are only one of a counterfeit ring's several offerings—everything from phony checks to currency, a kind of "one-stop shopping" approach.

According to a study by the Senate Committee of Government Affairs, one website operator sold 1,000 false IDs a month, yielding $600,000 in annual sales. Many Internet sites offer phony identification documents, some of extremely high quality that includes security features such as holograms. Promoters tout the ability of the fraudulent IDs to pass as authentic, though most sites carry a nominal disclaimer that the materials are for "novelty" purposes only.

Some websites offer do-it-yourself services, providing templates and other tools that make it easy to create false documents from sources such as a driver's license or a diploma. With $50 worth of art supplies, one can easily design authentic-looking identification documents.

Birth Certificates

Birth certificates are widely accepted as proof of identity, and can be used to obtain other documents. They are the counterfeiter's breeder document of choice, mainly because birth certificates are not very secure documents. Certified copies of birth certificates are available through local vital records offices, which number over 7,000. Over 80% of requests for birth certificates are made and processed through the mail with the name and return address as the only indication of the requestor's identity. There are over 1,000 different authorized forms of certified birth certificates in the United States.

Counterfeiters can obtain new digitally produced identity documents or models directly through the Internet. Once a counterfeit birth certificate is obtained, an individual can easily apply for a genuine driver license and a genuine social security card, establishing legitimacy for the false identity.

Fake IDs for Immigrants

Phony Social Security cards, ID cards, resident alien cards, and birth certificates are used by illegal immigrants traveling into the U.S. and other nations. Fraud in this area includes creation of false documents, as well as using valid documents by someone other than the original bearer.

Home computers, scanners, and printers make the fraudulent immigration documents easy and profitable to create. For less than $2,000, a counterfeiter can set up operation and recoup the investment within 48 hours.

The Immigration and Naturalization Service endows the latest generation of "green cards," which are actually white, with several anti-fraud items, including holographic images of the Statue of Liberty, an outline of the United States, the letters *USA*, and the INS seal. The back contains a laser-etched stripe that stores machine-readable information about the cardholder. Many of the documents bought "on the street" tend to be of low quality. The price of fraudulent documents can range from less than $100 for a Social Security card and "green card" to thousands of dollars for a U.S. passport.

Microtaggant Particles

Originally developed by the 3M Corporation, Microtaggant® is a microscopic identification particle currently used as part of a new anti-counterfeit technology. The Microtaggant contains a unique numeric code sequence for each customer or application that is certified and registered in a central database, never to be used again for any other purpose. Thus, the code becomes a unique "fingerprint" for that particular item.

Microtaggant Particles have previously been used by Swiss manufacturers of explosives in the source identification of bomb remnants. The particles can also be used to foil forgers. Microtaggant particles are laminated on an identification card, allowing each card to be individually encoded with one of more than 37 million possible combinations. Only Microtrace Inc. (Minneapolis), which holds the license to the technology, can assign the code. The technology costs around five cents per document.

The Microtaggant Particles, about one-tenth of a millimeter in size with about 30 to 40 particles used per inch, come in 10 colors and can be stacked in up to five layers. Each color is assigned a numeric code, such as 0 for black, 2 for red, and 3 for orange. Combinations of colors are arranged in the laminate with specific numeric sequences assigned to each user. Because there are more than 37 million possible sequences, it is almost impossible for counterfeiters to duplicate the particle sequence contained on a card or document.

The substance has been used in labels, adhesives, and put into fibers and inside video recorders and other electronic equipment to determine if the devices are bootlegged. Particles are used to control unauthorized production of products by controlling the supply of authenticated components, and to identify manufacturing facilities in case of defects in finished products. Particles can also be applied with a clear spray to the exterior of packaging to identify distributors in product diversion cases.

Sources:
"An Explosive Identifier." *FEMA, Federal News Service,* September 1999.

"Capitol Hill Hearing Testimony, K. Lee Blalack, Chief Counsel and Staff Director Senate Governmental Affairs False Identification and the Internet." *Federal News Service,* May 19, 2000.

"Friday Special White House Briefing Re: International Crime Assessment Report Briefer: Richard Clarke, National Coordinator for Security, Infrastructure Protection, and Counterterrorism." *Federal News Service,* December 15, 2000.

"Prepared Statement of Eljay B. Bowron Director U.S. Secret Service." *Federal News Service,* February 26, 1997.

Rodriguez, R. "Fortune in Frauds: Fake Papers Cottage Industry." *Fort Worth Star-Telegram,* May 20, 2001.

Related Entry:
COUNTERFEIT DOCUMENTS

COUNTERFEIT PRODUCTS

Organized crime syndicates in the United States and China dominate product counterfeiting. Legitimate businesses lose $200 - $250 billion in revenue each year, according to the U.S. Chamber of Commerce. Counterfeiting damages their reputations and their employees lose jobs due to the decline in sales of legitimate goods. By some estimates, product counterfeiting results in the loss of 750,000 American jobs every year. Counterfeiting affects almost every American industry.

In 1982, U.S. losses to product counterfeiting were estimated at $5.5 billion. In 2000, the International Anti-Counterfeiting Coalition (IACC) set those losses at $200 billion a year, more than a 3,000% increase. The IACC is a non-profit trade association of corporations, business trade associations, and professional firms from a wide range of industries.

American organized crime rings have joined their efforts with those of Chinese organized crime syndicates known as triads. Based in Hong Kong, triads use their global drug distribution networks as a means of channeling counterfeit goods and the proceeds from their sale. Counterfeit product distribution networks in the U.S. include major warehouses and sub-distribution sites along both coasts.

Counterfeit Product Codes

Product codes are a kind of serial number used by companies to track products, issue recalls, and other transmissions. They are typically stamped in ink or embossed on the bottom of packaging and are not to be confused with the UPC code, which identifies only the manufacturer and the product. Unscrupulous distributors alter or remove coding in order to divert products to unauthorized retailers.

Unauthorized distributors deface or remove product coding before distributing the goods to retailers to prevent manufacturers from identifying the source of diverted or stolen products. Fake codes and counterfeit labels are often affixed to the packaging to disguise the fact that such goods are stolen, outdated, or intended for a foreign market. Infant formula has been a target of many product code counterfeiters. One phony formula operation handled 70,000 cases of product per month and posted sales of $44 million in a 15-month period.

Examples of Product Counterfeiting

Some examples of how product counterfeiting affects American industry:

- The U.S. auto industry loses more than $12 billion a year to counterfeit parts such as brake pads and oil filters. Industry sources suggest some 200,000 jobs are lost to counterfeiting in the auto industry alone. Counterfeit brake pads are sometimes made from wood chips, compressed cardboard, and other substandard materials, with a lifespan of 200 miles. Counterfeit auto products have been responsible for deaths and injuries.

- The manufacture and sale of mislabeled and counterfeit airplane parts became a scandal in the mid-1990s. In 1995, the FAA said that 26 million parts were installed on airplanes every year; if 2% of those parts were counterfeit, as estimated by an internal FAA audit, more than half a million bad parts are installed every year. An investigation by *Business Week* magazine found that from 1973 to 1993, bogus parts played a role in at least 166 U.S.-based aircraft accidents or mishaps. Four of those were accidents involving commercial carriers that resulted in six deaths.
- Many counterfeiting operations involve substandard parts such as combustion liners, which are used in air jets to confine the heat of the combustion process to a particular region of the engine. Counterfeiters falsify the FAA certification required for each part; the yellow tags are sold on the black market for about $100. Substandard parts are prepared, or repaired, at machinist shops which can copy a highly engineered $30 bolt for about $3. Old parts are sold illegally in what is known as "strip-and-dip" operations. Scrap compressor blades can be bought for $1 a piece, then smoothed, coated, and tagged with a phony yellow tag, selling for up to $1,200.
- Counterfeit-labeled foods and other consumer products pose a health risk. Consumers cannot depend on the constituent material, preservatives used, or expiration dates. Counterfeits often contain unacceptable levels of mold, bacteria, and insect parts. A copy version of a popular infant formula caused allergic reactions in some children because of undisclosed materials used to make the copy. A counterfeited shampoo contained bacteria harmful to users with weakened immune systems.
- As reported in a February 2003 article in the Xinhua General News Service, a survey conducted by the Nigerian Institute of Pharmaceutical Research revealed that 80% of drugs in the major pharmacy stores in Lagos, Nigeria were fake or counterfeit.
- Logo-based marketing in the fashion world has created a market for demand for branded goods. The Anti-Counterfeiting Group estimates up to 11% of clothing and footwear sold are fakes. Some 52% of shoppers admit they would buy fake goods. The counterfeit capital of Europe is Leicester, England. In 1999, over 500,000 fake brand labels, from Tommy Hilfiger to Kickers, were seized from Leicester factories.
- Counterfeiters can ship a low-quality quartz watch that resembles a high-priced designer watch from Hong Kong to the United States for as little as $3. A counterfeit

trade name and logo can be attached to the watch for fifty cents. The end product sells on the street for at least $30, ten times its original cost.

- Counterfeit bolts and fasteners have caused bridge joints to fail and military equipment to break down.
- A 1999 survey of office-supply manufacturers named counterfeiting as the industry's chief criminal threat. Intellectual property violations worldwide were set at over $1 billion retail per year.
- Sales of pirated motion pictures account for 8% of movie revenues. For some films, pirate copies are available before the theatrical release. Most pirate films are distributed in foreign countries. In a common technique, a counterfeiter videotapes the movie in an American theater using a video camera. The copies—of varying quality—are sold to distributors and theaters overseas.
- Counterfeit videotapes are copied or distributed illegally. Crime rings establish distribution networks that supply stores with tens of thousands of unauthorized products.
- Millions in phony Pokemon cards were seized in 2000. Some ways of identifying counterfeits: the phonies are not standard height and weight, the paper is thin and gauzy, there is no line of legal text on the cards and packaging, the legal text appears blurry, and the cards are stamped "Made in China."

Preventing Product Counterfeiting

Microtaggant Particles

Originally developed by the 3M Corporation, Microtaggant® is a microscopic identification particle currently used as part of a new anti-counterfeit technology. The Microtaggant contains a unique numeric code sequence in multiple colored layer format. Each Microtaggant is assigned a unique code sequence for each customer or application that is certified and registered in a central database, never to be used again for any other purpose. Thus, the code becomes a unique "fingerprint" for that particular item.

Microtaggant particles are embedded into an item's material, allowing the item to be individually encoded with one of more than 37 million possible combinations. Only

Microtrace Inc. (Minneapolis), which holds the license to the technology, can assign the code. The technology costs around five cents per document.

The Microtaggant Particles, about one-tenth of a millimeter in size with about 30 to 40 particles used per inch, come in 10 colors and can be stacked in up to five layers. Each color is assigned a numeric code, such as 0 for black, 2 for red, and 3 for orange. Combinations of colors are arranged in the laminate, with specific numeric sequences assigned to each user. Because there are more than 37 million possible sequences, it is almost impossible for counterfeiters to duplicate the particle sequence contained on a card or document.

The substance has been used in labels, adhesives, various fibers, electronic equipment, coin and stamp collections, artworks, roofing, tires, trees, automotive replacement parts and sealants. Indeed, particles are used to control unauthorized production of products by controlling the supply of authenticated components, and to identify manufacturing facilities in case of defects in finished products. Particles also can be applied with a clear spray to the exterior of packaging to identify distributors in product diversion cases.

Radio Frequency Identification (RFID)

A silicon chip is implanted into consumer goods, recording the origin and ownership of the product. RFID technology.

- Confirms that goods are stolen.
- Provides proof of ownership and certificate of genuineness.
- Provides an audit trail showing where the goods have been and who handled them.
- Makes selling stolen items more difficult.

Sources:

"Capitol Hill Hearing Testimony, S. Lawrence Kocot Senior Vice President Government Affairs and General Counsel House Judiciary Courts and Intellectual Property Ban Tampering with Product Identification Codes." *Federal News Service*, October 21, 1999.

"Faking it: From the Street Trader to the Fashion Stylist, 10 Percent of the Clothing We Wear is Fake." *The Observer,* November 19, 2000.

"Hi-tech Scheme to Chip Away At Business Crime." May 6, 2001.

"John Bliss President, the International Anticounterfeiting Coalition, Inc. Senate Judiciary Cracking Down on Trademark Counterfeiting." *Federal News Service,* October 10, 1995.

"John S. Bliss President, International Anticounterfeiting Coalition Courts and Intellectual Property Subcommittee." *Federal News Service,* December 7, 1995.

"Mardi K. Mountford Executive Director International Formula Council House Judiciary Ban Tampering with Product Identification Codes." *Federal News Service,* October 21, 1999.

Stern, W. "Warning!" *Business Week,* June 10, 1996.

"William R. Duffy President and C.E.O. International Intellectual Property Protection Inc., Senate Small Business Office Supply Scams." *Federal News Service,* March 28, 2000.

COUNTERFEIT SOFTWARE

Counterfeit software refers to software copied and distributed illegally, software encoded to simulate another application's appearance and function, and access codes and other "keys" that defeat manufacturer encryption methods. Committing these acts is sometimes called "software piracy."

The worldwide package software market in 2000 was estimated at $135 billion. The U.S. market accounts for approximately 47% of this figure. Other noteworthy markets include Western Europe with 34% of the worldwide market share in 1998, and Japan with 7.6% of total revenues. The U.S. software industry estimates that it loses $12 billion a year to counterfeiters. American computer and video game publishers put yearly losses at $3 billion. Some 38% of software used worldwide is said to be "pirated" in some form or another. In countries such as China, Vietnam, Russia, and Indonesia, more than 90% of business software is either counterfeited or bootlegged. The U.S. piracy rate is estimated at 25%. A study in 1998 found that software counterfeiting cost the U.S. economy 109,000 jobs, $4.5 billion in wages, and $991 million in tax revenues.

Organized crime is heavily involved in the manufacture and distribution of counterfeit software, according to federal enforcement agencies and the software industry. Profits from counterfeiting often fund other high profile criminal activities. Chinese organized crime syndicates, commonly known as triads, have used counterfeiting U.S. goods as a source of funds and to launder drug money. In a celebrated raid in Los Angeles, law enforcement officials seized counterfeit software and collaterals valued at over $10.5 million. Software, manuals, and hologram labels were found, along with four pounds of plastic explosives, two pounds of TNT, shotguns, handguns, and silencers.

"Look-Alikes," "Compilations," and "Bootlegs"

Counterfeit software is often distributed via "look-alike" CDs that mimic the packaging of legitimate products and via "compilation" CDs or "bootlegs," which are generically packaged discs containing illegally copied versions of software made by various companies. Look-alike CD-ROMs bear reproductions of the manufacturer's logo and other labeling and are often distributed with packaging, manuals, security features (e.g., holograms), and other documentation.

The computer software industry as a whole is losing between $12 - $16 billion per year because of rampant piracy and counterfeiting. This amounts to more than 40% of all software industry revenues. In some countries, more than 90% of computer software is illegitimate.

A compilation CD usually contains the most popular business software applications of the day. They are sold at swap meets, flea markets, outdoor fairs, mail order houses, and Internet auction and software websites. Although compilation CDs do not exactly replicate the packaging and logos of genuine software, unsophisticated consumers are often led to believe that compilation CDs are legitimate promotional products. A "bootleg" is the term for a single software program distributed without packaging.

Counterfeiters manufacture software using a range of technology. Some use the sophisticated, expensive equipment employed by legitimate manufacturers, while others use inexpensive CD recorders available to any consumer. A single CD-ROM replication facility can produce more than a million discs every day, at a per-unit cost of less than two dollars. In the United States, most CD-ROM replication occurs at fully dedicated "pirate" replication facilities, using equipment purchased by counterfeiting rings. However, some counterfeit CD-ROMs have been traced to "legitimate" replicating plants, which have contracted with counterfeiters to produce counterfeit CD-ROMs.

Counterfeiting software is extremely profitable because the counterfeiter bears none of the publisher's research and development costs, marketing, or support costs. This not only slashes overhead, it allows the counterfeiter to sell the software at a cost cheaper than the manufacturer's cost-per-unit. At the most, counterfeiters invest in packaging and circulate advertisements; the bulk of the selling price is profit.

Compilations and bootleg software are especially lucrative and easy to make because there is no attempt to mimic legitimate packaging and support materials. A compilation can be replicated using a CD recorder, which, when connected to a personal computer, employs a laser to transfer, or "burn," installed software programs or files onto a blank disc. Professional replication technology can produce 14,000 to 15,000 CD-ROMs per month.

A counterfeit copy of Windows 2000 costs about $10 to produce but sells for between $60 and $80. Microsoft sells legitimate copies for $120 to $130 retail. A modestly sized counterfeiting ring can clear $1 million a month.

Source: "Facts on Fakes." International Anticounterfeiting Coalition, 2003.

Counterfeit Software and the Internet

Until the late 1990's, most counterfeiting occurred through the unauthorized copying, installation, or physical distribution of floppy disks and CDs. The Internet's adoption into popular culture permitted electronic sales and the transmission of illegal software to the world's 150 million Web connections. In a 2000 survey, there were nearly one million webpages that offered, linked to, or otherwise referenced "warez," a slang term for counterfeit software; 281,900 webpages referenced "appz," a similar term.

The Internet is used to: (1) transmit and download digitized copies of pirated software; (2) advertise and market pirated software to be delivered on physical media through the mails or other traditional means; and (3) offer and transmit codes or other technologies that are used to circumvent copy-protection security features.

Internet auction sites serve as digital marketplaces that allow counterfeiters to reach average consumers. Typically the seller claims the software is a genuine product obtained through wholesale channels. According to the Business Software Alliance, in 1999 a member company test-purchased almost 300 of its own products from Internet auction sites. Forensic analysis of the copies confirmed that 63% were outright counterfeits, and all additional 34% were sold in violation of the company's licensing agreement. Some 97% of the software purchased in the investigation was illegal. Research by the Adobe Corporation found that 70% to 90% of the software offered on auction sites is illegitimate.

The Internet is widely used to distribute information for circumventing software protection devices. Serial numbers, access codes, and software program "patches" that bypass or circumvent encryption or other technical protections are shared, sometimes freely and sometimes for profit. This sort of information is generally referred to as "crackz"(or "cracks") and "keygens." In 2000, a study found more than 368,000 webpages offering some type of unauthorized information or code.

Other methods used to distribute counterfeits include bulletin boards, e-mail, newsgroups, chat rooms, file transfer protocol software, and linked websites.

The Business Software Alliance Study

The Business Software Alliance conducted its Second Annual BSA and IDC Global Software Piracy Study and released its results in 2004. They noted that piracy had decreased one point to 35% from the previous year. Though it was only a one point decrease between 2003 and 2004, piracy has dropped tremendously since 1994 when there was a 49% rate of personal computer software piracy around the world. Much of the decrease in piracy since 1994 has been due to intensified education efforts, new technologies used by software makers to protect their products from unauthorized use and better antipiracy laws, according to the BSA.

The BSA study looks at piracy rates of business software applications in 85 countries. The results confirm that software piracy continues to be a major challenge. Although piracy rates decreased in 37 countries, they increased in 34. In more than half the countries studied, piracy was above 60%. In 24 countries, the piracy rate exceeded 75%. Just over a third of the countries studied had a piracy rate under 50%. In 2004, the world spent more than $59 billion (U.S. dollars) for commercial packaged PC software. Yet, software worth over $90 billion was actually installed. For every two dollars' worth of software purchased legitimately, one dollar's worth was obtained illegally.

Worldwide dollar losses due to piracy rose from $10.97 billion in 2001 to $13.08 billion in 2002, a 19% increase attributed to generally higher software prices, which offset the lower piracy rates and smaller software shipments, according to the group.

US/Canada

North America has the lowest piracy rate in the world, and of which continues to drop. From 2003 to 2004, the North American piracy rate dropped one point, bringing it down to 22%.

Latin America

Between 2003 and 2004, piracy rates in the Latin American region increased 3 points from 63% to 66%. Guatemala had a 1 point increase, from 77% in 2003 to 78% in 2004. Ecuador increased 2 points, from 68% in 2003 to 70% in 2004. El Salvador increased its piracy rate 1 point, from 79% in 2003 to 80% in 2004. Brazil and Mexico, the two largest countries in the region, increased 3 points between 2003 and 2004, from 61% to 64% and 2 points from 63% to 65% respectively.

European Union

From 2003 to 2004, the piracy rate of the European Union fell 2 points, from 37% to 35%. Ireland improved the most in the last ten years, moving from 74% in 1994 to 41% in 2003 (a decrease of 33 points) and then to 39% in 2004. Spain followed with a 30 point improvement, dropping from 77% in 1994, to 44% in 2003 and stood at 43% in 2004. The piracy rate in Slovenia improved, reducing its piracy rate from 52% to 51% between 2003 and 2004. Hungary increased by 2 points from 44% in 2003 to 42% in 2004.

Middle East/Africa

The Middle East/Africa region increased in computer piracy by 2 points in the last year, from 56% in 2003 to 58% in 2004. In 1994, this region had an 84% piracy rate. Leading the region is Egypt with the biggest drop of 4 points, with 69% piracy in 2003 to 65% in 2004. Israel had the least amount of piracy, and dropped from 35% in 2003 to 33% in 2004. In the Middle East, all countries made improvements or stayed the same. South Africa had the second lowest level of piracy with 37% in 2004 (a one point increase from the previous year).

Asia/Pacific

The piracy rate in the Asia/Pacific region stayed the same over the last year. China (92% in 2004), Malaysia (63% in 2004) and South Korea (48% in 2004) had the largest drops (2 points) in computer piracy. New Zealand had the lowest piracy rate which has stayed the same over the last year at 23%. Japan had the second lowest piracy rate at 28% in 2004, a one point improvement from 2003.

Hong Kong

In 1999, according to the Business Software Alliance, Hong Kong, a city of almost 7 million people, pirated $110 million of software, thanks to first-world levels of computer usage and piracy levels closer to that of the developing world. For the first time, new laws mandate the possibility of jail and fines for anyone using illegal software in a business, though the law does not cover home use. Employees, managers, and information technology staff all risk a $50,000 fine per copy and four years in prison.

In February 1999, Hong Kong was removed from the U.S. government's list of piracy hotspots, known as the "Special List," where it had been even before the advent of CD-ROM technology created the explosion in software piracy. The decision was justified, U.S. sources said, because of successful law enforcement and cooperation among international agencies.

Signs of Counterfeit Software

- Prices far below standard
- Certificate of authenticity missing
- End-user license agreement missing
- Product registration card missing
- No backup disks, manuals, or other materials for software installed on a new computer system
- Backup disks with handwritten labels, without shrink wrapping, or of inferior quality
- Photocopied manuals without shrink-wrapping, or of inferior quality

- Printing on the front cover of the user's guide: "For distribution with a new P.C. only"

Sources:
Blumenthal, B. "L.A Area Key to Software Piracy." *Sacramento Bee*, July 11, 1999.

BSA Global Software Piracy Study: global.bsa.org/globalstudy/?CFID=156423&CFTOKEN=82516764

Gren, M. "Anti-Piracy Legislation Boosts Software Sales in Hong Kong." *The Wall Street Journal*, April 18, 2001.

James, G. "Organized Crime and the Software Biz; Industry Trend or Event." *MC Technology Marketing Intelligence*, January 1, 2000.

"Testimony Internet Music and Software Privacy: Jack Krumholtz, Director of Federal Government Affairs and Associate General Counsel, Microsoft Corporation." *Federal News Service*, July 19, 2000.

CREDIT CARD AND DEBIT CARD FRAUD

Credit card and debit card fraud is the misuse of a card—without authorization or for unapproved purchases—or the counterfeiting of cards. The Electronic Fund Transfer Act (EFTA) covers these crimes. Bankcard fraud losses to Visa and MasterCard alone increased from $110 million in 1980, to $700 million in 1995, and rose to $1 billion by 2000, and by 2005 reached $1.14 billion in losses.

Unsurprisingly, credit card fraud has increased as the number of cards in circulation has grown. In 1970, only the most credit-worthy 15% of Americans had a credit card; by 1983, 43% did; in 1998, 68% did, approaching 140 million cardholders. As many as one in every four students between 18 and 25 has at least four credit cards.

Though credit card fraud on the Internet is a relatively minor problem (see below), the medium has also aided fraudsters. Instructions for committing card fraud are available on the Web, websites, newsgroups, and bulletin boards are used by criminals for networking. Software such as Creditmaster is also available, which automates the counterfeiting process.

In Britain, credit card fraud is one of the fastest growing crimes. The Association for Payment Clearing Services said it cost banks 300 million pounds in 2000 and although banks bear these costs, they are inevitably eventually passed on to customers. Between

1999 and 2000 there were 14,191 offenses of fraud and forgery reported in the Thames Valley area, making up 7% of all recorded crime.

Chargebacks a Red Flag for Fraud

A little less than 1% of all credit card transactions are written off as losses due to fraud. When chargeback rates reach 2.5%, most companies investigate. After the fourth month of excessive chargebacks, credit card companies can fine banks that process the transactions at the rate of at least $25 per chargeback, plus a $5,000 administrative fee. Visa and MasterCard can also terminate credit card processing rights for banks and merchants with excessive chargeback rates.

Online Credit Card Fraud

Online credit card fraud originating in the U.S. costs as much as $24 million per day in bogus charges, totaling nearly $9 billion in 2000. European credit card fraud hit $544 million in 2000, up 50%, with much of the rise occurring in Internet transactions. A ring of credit card fraudsters targeted Scotland during 1999 and 2000; consumer victims lost an average of 1,500 pounds per incident.

According to Cybersource Corporation's 7th Annual Online Fraud Report, an estimated $2.8 billion was lost to eCommerce Fraud in 2005. Medium and large merchants (online sales greater than $5 million) were the hardest hit, and the risk from international orders was found to be two to three times higher than the overall fraud rate.

However, the chargeback rate for Internet sales is slightly lower than the rate for all credit card sales, according to major credit card companies.

Debit Cards

The theft or counterfeiting of a debit card can cause more harm to the cardholder than the loss of a credit card because the cardholder is responsible for all purchases on most debit cards made before the loss is reported. Cardholders are only liable for the first $50 of charges to a stolen credit card but are fully liable for most debit card purchases. However, a few issuers have voluntarily instituted the $50 limit for all cardholders.

The American Bankers Association Deposit Account Fraud Survey Report released in 2004 stated that banks lost a total of 145.3 million in 522,327 cases of debit card fraud with signature-based transactions comprising nearly three-fourths of losses. Signature-based debit card losses totaled $102.2 million in 452,958 cases. Personal Identification Number (PIN) based debit card losses totaled $43.1 million in 69,369 cases. All sizes combined, the median value of losses per fraud case was $294 for signature debit cards and $371 for PIN debit cards.

Debit card fraud is not as widespread as credit card fraud. In 1996, MasterCard reported two cards in 10,000 were fraudulent. MasterCard reported 19 million of its debit cards in circulation in the U.S. for the year 2000; at the 1996 rate, this would mean that 3,800 cards were subject to fraud. Visa reported 119 million of its debit cards in circulation, conducting $305 billion in transactions a year. The company states that one-tenth of 1% of transaction volume is lost to fraud.

In Canada, debit card fraud has reached epidemic levels. According to police in Ottawa, debit card fraud, particularly at ATMs, is hitting $150 million a year. The problem seems to stem from ATMs that have been tampered with by con artists. Fraudsters make alterations to the machines so that information on the magnetic strip of the victim's card is copied and transferred to another card. The victim's PIN is also retrieved from the machine via a camera strategically placed out of the view of the victim to capture keypad strokes.

Debit card losses at ATM machines are a minor issue. Justice Department statistics put the average ATM loss at roughly $200. Debit cards allow merchants, or fraudsters, to charge a customer's checking accounts without written authorization. People may unwittingly give information over the phone that provides access to their accounts.

Basic Offenses

- Unauthorized use of a card. This happens particularly among family members.
- Fraudulently obtaining a card by providing false information or using stolen information.
- Selling a card to thieves and not reporting it stolen. Since consumer liabilities are limited to $50, the company absorbs all losses.

- Phony Payments. Credit card companies are required to credit a customer's account as soon as payment is received—in the case of checks; this means that the credit is issued before the check clears the bank. Fraudsters make a payment on a credit card account using a worthless check, which may take several days to be returned to the company. But the credit is issued immediately, so the card may be used immediately. Credit card thieves may use this technique with stolen cards or consumers can use the technique, sometimes as part of a check kiting scheme.
- Skimming. Using a device known as a wedge, which stores up to 200 numbers, skimmers capture credit card information from retail customers. Skimming works best in restaurants and other situations in which the employee leaves the cardholder's presence to process the transaction. Skimmers may make counterfeit cards with the numbers or sell numbers to counterfeiters.

Organized Crime Rings

Professional criminals target credit cards in both sophisticated and simple ways.

- Stealing credit card and bank information from a victim's person, residence, automobile, mailbox, trash, and elsewhere. The information is used to generate false identification documents, such as driver's licenses and Social Security cards, which in turn can be used to obtain credit cards or pass a stolen card.
- Credit "Doctors" sell stolen credit card account numbers via newspaper ads to people unable to get credit cards.
- Shave and Paste. Any number of alpha or numeric characters is sliced from the card surface and other characters are attached to the card surface, utilizing fast drying epoxy-type glues. This might be done to put an entirely different but valid account number on the card or to change the name.
- De-Emboss/Re-Emboss. The card is exposed to heat, usually from a household iron, a candle, or hot water in the microwave. Plastic cards, comprised primarily of polyvinylchloride, become more elastic when heated, and the embossed alpha/numeric characters are removed. An embosser puts new numbers and names on the cards.

- "White Plastic" cards are nothing but a piece of plastic the size and shape of a credit card with account numbers and names embossed on the card. A corrupt merchant or a merchant's employee agrees to accept the card for purchases.
- Counterfeit cards are produced in great numbers in Taiwan, China, and Hong Kong, where professionals specialize in reproducing the holograms and magnetic-strip security devices that appear on many cards. Desktop computers, embossers, tipping foil, and laminators are common tools in the reproduction process. Some phony holograms are decals attached to the surface of the card, rather than fixed into the plastic and some do not change colors when viewed from various angles. Lax merchant procedures often allow counterfeits to pass.
- Telephone/Mail-order fraud scams call offering the victim a prize, provided the person has a credit card number along with other personal identification. Some crooks pretend to be a representative from the person's credit card company—the victim is told his or her card may have been used illegally and is asked to recite the number for "verification." The crook can sell the numbers or use them to buy mail-order items from catalogs and the Internet.
- The Creditmaster software program, downloadable from the Internet, allows the user to produce valid credit card numbers. Counterfeiters can then put these numbers to use in phony cards.
- *Probing* is a strategy that uses software to run stolen numbers through various financial institutions. Numbers that clear are often sold en masse to counterfeiters.
- In a credit card bustout, the debtor intentionally charges credit cards to the limit and files bankruptcy with no intent to repay. Credit card debts might include purchases for jewelry, luxury items, or other personal property, which are not disclosed on the schedules. Credit card debt might also include large cash advances taken prior to filing bankruptcy. Organized crime sometimes forces businesses and individuals to commit a credit card bustout in order to repay a debt.

Merchant Scams

Collusion occurs between the sales people and the credit card fraudster to process valid credit card numbers on white plastic cards. They might also make several imprints on sales tickets and fill them in later on.

Laxness Aids Fraud

Companies have instituted a number of technological safeguards over the years. But credit card frauds often succeed due to laxness—on the part of cardholders who do not report thefts for several months and from merchants who do not follow procedure. A study by *Money* magazine found that 95% of store clerks and cashiers did not check credit card signatures.

Anti-Fraud Measures, General

- Signature panels usually contain images of the issuer's logo. Blank or damaged signature panels are red flags of forged credit cards. Signatures on the panel and the sales receipt should always be compared for consistency.
- The customer, who provides personal information such as mother's maiden name and birth date, must activate new cards.
- Computer edits are programmed into some cards that track usage patterns, and alert security if there are dramatic divergences from the usual pattern. If a card is usually used five times per month, and it is suddenly used 25 times in one day, the system will prohibit authorization of further purchases.
- Merchants must verify four key authorization components of each card submitted—signature, expiration date, authorization number, and card imprint. If any component is missing from the transaction record and the transaction turns out to be fraudulent, the merchant takes the loss, not the credit card company.

Anti-Fraud Measures, Visa and MasterCard

- The first four digits of the Visa account number (the bank identification number—BIN) must be preprinted above the embossed number. If these numbers do not match exactly, the card has been altered or is counterfeit.

- Visa's embossed account numbers begin with a 4 and contain either 13 or 16 digits. A unique embossed **V** appears in **CV or BV** Visa Classic or Business cards.
- The embossed characters should be in alignment and of the same size, height, and style.
- If there are "ghost images" of the numbers behind the embossing on either the front or back of the card, it has been re-embossed. If the card has been re-embossed the hologram might be damaged.
- Check the valid dates for evidence of tampering. Employees should not accept an expired card.
- The hologram is distinct and three-dimensional.
- MasterCard's embossed account numbers begin with a 5 and contain 16 digits.
- A repetitive color design of either the Visa or MasterCard name should appear on all signature panels.
- Microprinting appears around the Visa logo.
- A large "MC" is visible under ultraviolet light for MasterCard and a large dove is visible under ultraviolet light for Visa.
- Numbers printed on the signature panel slant to the left and match the number on the front of the card.

Anti-Fraud Measures, American Express

- Ultraviolet inks are used so that when a genuine card is examined with a black light, the letters AMEX, as well as phosphorescence in the portrait of the Centurion, are visible.
- The card member account number is 15 digits beginning with "37"; the prefix "34" is also reserved for use by American Express, with limited use beginning in 1988.
- A duplicate account number on the reverse of the card ensures the card number has not been altered.

Internet/Telephone Orders

Online credit card fraud costs as much as $24 million per day in bogus charges, totaling nearly $9 billion in 2000. With these transactions, vendors never have the opportunity to see the customer's credit card.

Internet merchants bear the costs of online fraud because signed credit card slips do not accompany their sales. In such "card-not-present" transactions, if a charge is disputed by the rightful owner of a card, sellers must cover the cost of the item, an occurrence called a "chargeback." The merchant with a disputed sale is also charged fees ranging from $20 to $30 to cover the bank's costs in processing the dispute. Chargebacks can account for up to 30% of some Web merchants' overall sales.

The only fail-safe, self-protective measure open to online merchants is to postpone delivery until the transaction has cleared the customer's account. In this "next-day-delivery society," however, this may be detrimental to business for some vendors. There are a couple of other options open to merchants:

- Beware of orders with different "bill to" and "ship to" addresses unless the item is intended as a gift.
- Setting up free e-mail accounts with companies like *Hotmail* or *Yahoo* is very simple and allows the user anonymity. Orders received from free e-mail accounts should be treated with extra scrutiny.

Financial Institutions

Banks and other financial institutions have policies to prevent credit card fraud.

- New account screening—personnel are educated to thoroughly check applicants' information, comparing ID information, addresses, and credit reports for accuracy.
- PIN activation—bank customers are often required to provide personal identification numbers in order to activate their cards over the phone. Callers who are not able to provide the PIN number may have manufactured or stolen the card in question.
- Caller ID—most people calling to activate their card will do so from home. If the number on Caller ID does not match any of the telephone numbers listed in the customer's account information, bank personnel should ask some identifying questions.

- CVV2/CVC2— The CVV2/CVC2 is a three-digit security code that is printed on the backs of cards. It is designed to validate that a genuine card is being used during a transaction. When a point-of-sale (POS) terminal reads a card's magnetic stripe, Visa's Card Verification Value (CVV) or MasterCard's Card Validation Code (CVC) can be verified during the authorization. Merchants using CVV2/CVC2 can expect to reduce their chargebacks by as much as 26%. Most companies' cards, both credit and debit, were required to contain CVC2 by 2001. The number appears in reverse italic at the top of the signature panel at the end.

Mail order, telephone order, and other card-not-present transactions have higher fraud rates than face-to-face transactions. When the card is not present, the CVV or CVC cannot be validated. To help reduce fraud in the card-not-present environment, acquirers, merchants, and issuers can use the CVV2 or CVC2 program.

Holograms and Smart Cards

Holograms have been used since the early 1980's, though a counterfeiting industry has kept pace with advances in technology. In 1994, Visa and MasterCard suffered losses estimated at over $700 million caused by one Chinese hologram-producing syndicate alone. Smart Cards contain a microprocessor memory chip instead of holograms. This allows cardholders more purchasing options as well as increased security. However, implementation of the Smart Card system is extremely expensive and unlikely to become common soon.

Case Study—Credit Card Numbers Over the Phone

The following material was posted on the Internet by a confessed credit card fraudster, adapted here from Bartholomew Henderson's *www.fraudabc.com*. The author illustrates how to obtain credit card numbers by phone. Here he impersonates an employee of the credit card company, pretending to answer a request from the store.

"This is how I've obtained just about every one of my Visa and MasterCard's. All you have to do is all up a store… that uses a credit card…. Here's a typical conversation if you called a convenience store."

"Clerk:" *May I help you?*

"Caller:" *This is Bill from Visa. I was just returning your call.*

"Clerk:" *Huh?*

"Caller:" *I just received a page regarding a problem with your Visa credit card machine. Were you having problems there?*

"Clerk:" *Nobody here paged you. Who is this again?*

"Caller:" *This is Bill with Visa. When there's some kind of error on your validation system the machine will page us with the problem. Did you just have a credit card transaction?*

"Clerk:" *About 15 minutes ago.*

"Caller:" *That's probably the one. Could you dig up the receipt and tell me the exact time the transaction occurred?*

"Clerk:" *Hold on.... Here it is. I made the sale at 7:45 p.m. for some beer and chips.*

"Caller:" *What was the amount of the sale?*

"Clerk:" *13.94*

"Caller:" *And the account number?*

"Clerk:" *It's 4053-xxxx-xxxx-xxxx.*

"Caller:" *And the expiration date?*

Once the caller gets a first number, he might suggest the number is not the one he was looking for. He would prompt the employee, "That is not the one. How about the previous transaction? What's the info on that one?" He claims to have called the same store and the same employee more than once, explaining that the inquiry is routine.

"Clerk:" *I don't think it's a good idea to give out that information without talking to my manager.*

Even if the person balks at this point, the perpetrator has acquired plenty of useful information.

Sources:
American Bankers Association: www.aba.com/Press+Room/111302checkfraud.htm

"Capitol Hill Hearing Testimony, Irene Katen Vice President MasterCard International Incorporated House: Banking Financial Institutions and Consumer Credit Debit Cards." *Federal News Service,* September 24, 1997.

"Capitol Hill Hearing Testimony, Russell W. Schrader Senior Counsel and Vice President VISA U.S.A. Inc.: House Banking Financial Institutions and Consumer Credit Debit Cards." *Federal News Service,* September 24, 1997.

"Debit card fraud an 'epidemic'." CBC.CA News, January 9, 2003.

Lorek, L. "Foreign Flim Flam." *Interactive Week*, February 25, 2001.

Wessel, D. "A Law's Muddled Course." *Wall Street Journal*, February 22, 2001.

Related Entry:

MERCHANT PROCESSING FRAUD

CREDIT SUISSE FIRST BOSTON FRAUD

An investment banking branch of Credit Suisse Group, Credit Suisse First Boston (CSFB), is a worldwide company that offers financial services. CSFB has been accused of false allocation of IPOs, or Initial Public Offerings, by creating false and misrepresented analyst reports to boost stock sales of their investment banking partners. CSFB was considered the top underwriter for technology IPOs. Frank Quattrone, star tech banker, helped the company underwrite $6.08 billion in IPOs. The company earned $700 million just in fees for its role in turning technology companies into public entities.

After regulators reviewed more than 100,000 subpoenaed emails, they alleged that Credit Suisse First Boston manipulated the research reports for its investment banking clients. CSFB was alleged to have also conducted illegal underwriting schemes that harshly impacted their smaller investors.

According to the Law Offices of James Sokolove: "Investigators allege that Credit Suisse First Boston underwriters helped create a frenzy as to which favored customers would be given access to the high tech IPOs. This deceptive hype inflated the after-market price paid by individual investors. Then, just as small investors were rushing in to buy the new stocks, insiders and favored customers were selling so that the small investors suffered huge losses when the stocks collapsed. It is also alleged that certain underwriters gained profits from the IPO boom not only through the bloated fees they charged for their services in making the companies IPOs, but also by conducting kickback schemes with their favored customers."

In late 2002, Pomerantz Haudek Block Grossman & Gross LLP on behalf of investors who purchased common stock of Agilent Technology, Inc. between the period of December 13, 1999 and September 9, 2002, filed a class action lawsuit against CSFB and Elliott Rogers (a managing director and senior analyst in the Global Technology Group of CSFB). CSFB was charged with violations of Sections 10(b) and 20(a) of the Securities Exchange Act of 1934 for issuing false and misleading analyst reports on Agilent in order to sustain and enhance its investment banking relationship with Agilent. Another lawsuit was filed by the same law firm on behalf of investors who purchased the common stock of NewPower Holdings, Inc. between October 5, 2000 and December 5, 2001. Again, CSFB was accused of misrepresenting analyst reports in order to make the stocks seem lucrative to investors.

The most recent news is that Frank Quattrone was granted a new trial after a federal appeals court in March 2006 overturned his conviction. The jury instructions in Quattrone's trial were said to be erroneous by the 2nd U.S. Circuit Court of Appeals. Quattrone was convicted in May 2004 on federal charges of obstruction of justice, after his first trial ended in a hung jury.

CRESSEY AWARD

The Cressey Award is the highest honor bestowed by the Association of Certified Fraud Examiners, recognizing a significant lifetime achievement contributing to our understanding and deterrence of fraud. The Cressey Award was established in 1991. It is named in honor of Dr. Donald Cressey, whose scholarship provided the foundation of fraud studies, and who encouraged the development of the Association of Certified Fraud Examiners.

CULTURE FARMS

Perhaps the most phenomenally successful work-at-home scam ever, Culture Farms first hit South Africa, then spread to the American heartland. A group of South African nationals based their operation in Lawrence, Kansas after fleeing their homeland under charges for running a similar scam there.

Investors were recruited as "growers." They were to act as the ground troops in a huge venture that would revolutionize the cosmetics industry. Growers bought starter kits for $1,500 to $2,000 each, which contained an urn, a strainer, and a large envelope of flaky chips, white in color, swirled with blue streaks. The chips floated in an urn full of milk until the liquid evaporated. What resulted was a large sheet of foul-smelling dried milk, which the grower broke into pieces, placed inside the starter-kit envelope, and mailed back to Culture Farms.

Culture Farms forwarded the kits to a cosmetics factory in California that used the fecund materials in a new product called "Cleopatra's Secret." In massive revival-tinged meetings, growers were pumped up for the harvest ahead—when the health and beauty line would take hold, delivering a bounty of retail sales and immeasurable gains in Cleopatra stock.

When securities regulators for the state of Kansas investigated complaints, they found Culture Farms was a filthy sham. The starter kits returned by growers were mailed to a front office in a California industrial park. Workers at the California office ground up the kits, envelopes and all, and mailed them to new growers as . . . starter kits. The tiny blue jars of "Cleopatra's Secret" face cream used to whoop up enthusiasts were filled with generic product and pasted with a logo that promoters paid a couple hundred bucks for.

Culture Farms lasted just six months before regulators locked the gates. But in that short time, promoters had managed to rake in $100 million.

Related Entries:

CON SCHEMES
CONSUMER FRAUD

DAIWA BANK

From 1984 to 1995, Toshihide Iguchi lost more than $1 billion trading government bonds for Daiwa Bank in New York City. Senior management at the bank was convicted for failing to detect and prevent the fraud, and for conspiring to cover up the crimes once they were revealed.

Iguchi was born in Kobe, Japan, leaving soon after graduating from high school in 1969 to attend Southwest Missouri State University. He graduated with a degree in 1975. Later he worked for Daiwa in New York City in the government-bond trading department. He became a trader in 1984 and later supervised the trading of U.S. government bonds for the Tokyo-based financial institution. Soon after he began trading, Iguchi lost an estimated $200,000 trading bonds and began his 11-year scheme. When he lost money trading bonds, he sold bonds from Daiwa's corporate accounts or customer accounts, forging documents to authorize the transactions, using the funds to cover his losses. Over time, he increased his efforts to recoup his losses, trading as much as $500 million worth of bonds in a single day. Iguchi eventually made 30,000 unauthorized transactions to cover losses of $1.1 billion.

In late 1993, Daiwa New York split its bond-trading and record-keeping functions, but Iguchi continued his scheme for two more years. He was suspected of having confederates who aided his scheme, but they were never exposed.

Iguchi reported his crimes to Daiwa New York's president, Akira Fujita in July 1995. But bank officials did not file a criminal report until Sept. 18, despite the fact that regulations require banks to give immediate notification of criminal behavior. Iguchi was not fired until Sept. 26, 1995. Iguchi later revealed that soon after Daiwa executives learned of his confession, they met at the Park Lane Hotel in Manhattan to discuss covering up the infraction. Iguchi was told to say nothing while the bank planned the cover-up. Daiwa Bank pled guilty in 1997 to conspiring to help hide Iguchi's losses. The company paid $340 million in fines and closed its U.S. offices.

In December, a U.S. District Court sentenced Iguchi, who pleaded guilty to fraud, to four years in prison. He also was ordered to pay a $2 million fine and $70,000 in restitution. Iguchi claimed a lack of risk control and lax supervision by Japanese and U.S. financial authorities allowed him to carry on his scheme for so long. A Japanese court agreed. In 2000, a group of senior Daiwa executives were ordered to pay more than $750 million to the bank for the Iguchi losses. This was the largest award ever made to shareholders by a Japanese court. The judicial order said the executives failed to supervise staff and detect the fraud, besides their roles in the cover-up.

Source:
Greenwald, J. "Blown Billion." *Time,* October 9, 1995.

Related Entry:
FINANCIAL INSTITUTION FRAUD

DE ANGELIS, TINO

Known to history as "The Salad-Oil King," Tino De Angelis was an unscrupulous New Jersey-located businessman who committed frauds from the 1950's through the 1990's. De Angelis combined his underworld connections with astounding persuasive abilities to make and lose several fortunes. In the early 1950's, he began a meatpacking business that was plagued with regulatory and legal complaints. He was cited by the Justice Department for selling uninspected meat and shorting weights. Two banks in New York closed his accounts for check kiting. Eventually De Angelis filed for bankruptcy.

He would make his fortune and reputation in the salad-oil business. The Allied Crude Vegetable Oil Refining Corporation was founded in 1955, taking over an abandoned tank farm in Bayonne, New Jersey. The company's main business was shipping oil for the U.S. government's Food for Peace program, though De Angelis's motivations were more pecuniary than humanitarian. In fact, his shipments frequently prompted complaints for short weights, leaking barrels, and low-quality oil.

De Angelis struck gold by participating in a financial practice known as "warehouse collateral." Because oil traders often held large reserves waiting to be shipped, financial institutions agreed to loan companies' money against their reserves—these were intended as bridge loans to help companies maintain cash flow until they could ship the goods and receive payment. The reserves were inspected by "field warehousing" companies that certified the materials on hand and assigned a value to it—the oil trader, De Angelis, for example, used the certification to obtain loans.

Unfortunately, the system was subject to easy manipulation. De Angelis's field warehousing certifier was American Express Field Warehousing Corporation, which hired three of De Angelis's own personnel to conduct the inspections and issue the collateral certificates.

Using these insiders and several tricks to fool outsiders, De Angelis borrowed millions against non-existent reserves. Each year the amounts grew exponentially:

1957	$10 million
1958	$40 million
1959	$75 million
1962	$225 million
October 1963	$440 million
November 1963	$1 billion

The Bayonne tank farm had a maximum capacity of 500 million pounds of oil—a figure De Angelis exceeded in mid-1962 without attracting notice. By November 1963, his outstanding notes represented 2 billon pounds of oil, equivalent to the entire world's commercial output that year.

De Angelis brought about his own downfall with a typical act of hubris. He began speculating in oil futures with his borrowed funds, and even as the market turned against him, he continued borrowing more and losing more in the market.

When the various financial institutions began to call in their loans, De Angelis disappeared, along with about $875 million in cash. The tanks at Bayonne were mostly empty or contained sludge. Inspectors found a clever network designed to fool anyone outside the organization. As described by Andreas Shroeder, "All the tanks were interconnected, linked by hundreds of underground pipes that crisscrossed the tank farm… A small amount of oil was all it had ever taken to keep up appearances… As the inspectors walked from tank to tank, in-line pumps transferred the oil from tanks already inspected into tanks awaiting inspection. This could be done quickly because it did not involve much pumping; most tanks were fitted with false bottoms or narrow cylinders attached to the inside rim of their inspection portholes."

Regulators eventually found some 70 million pounds of the 2 billion pounds of oil De Angelis claimed to have on hand. After selling off the remains at huge discounts, the government discovered that front companies secretly controlled by De Angelis, who was determined to get back into the business, had purchased a portion of the material.

In May 1965, De Angelis was sentenced to 20 years in prison, and served seven. He was arrested again in 1978 for fraud involving pork commodities, and served three years in prison. He was arrested again in 1993, at age 78, for defrauding Maple Leaf Meats of Canada of almost a million dollars. He was sentenced to 21 months in prison.

Related Entries:

FINANCIAL INSTITUTION FRAUD

LOAN FRAUD

DEBIT CARDS

See, CREDIT CARD AND DEBIT CARD FRAUD

DEFENSE PROCUREMENT FRAUD

Fraud in the procurement of goods and services is a form of government fraud. The Department of Defense has played host to a spate of frauds. The General Accounting Office reported in 1982 that the chance of cost overruns on military contracts was 91%, and estimated the cost of fraud and waste in military disbursements at $15 billion a year. The Department of Justice reported in November 2000 that it had recovered $100 million in funds from organizations convicted of defense procurement fraud. Procurement involves huge amounts of money. From 1981 to 1995, procurement of military equipment and services by the U.S. Department of Defense (DOD) consumed 26% of total defense outlays and 1.43% of the Gross National Product.

Among the most common acts are bribery and kickbacks, billing schemes, purchasing schemes, selling substandard materials with phony certifications, and price-fixing. Well-publicized scandals have highlighted the absurdity of some DOD disbursements, such as the $600 toilet seat and the $1,100 plastic cap for a stool leg. The FBI conducted a special investigation, known as Operation Illwind, into defense procurement frauds during the early 1990's. At least 20 companies were convicted, along with 46 individual defendants.

Top Contracting Firms Are Bulletproof

Research by academics Jonathan Karpoff, D. Scott Lee, and Valaria Vendrzyk examined the market and legal penalties imposed on firms suspected or accused of procurement fraud. The group found that firms investigated for procurement fraud suffered economically and statistically significant market value losses, roughly 1.5% in the days immediately following the announcement of offenses.

However, losses varied significantly among firms. Firms ranked among the Top 100 military suppliers that presumably exercise influence within the DOD were much less likely to suffer significant downturns than firms outside that ranking. These results hold even after controlling for firm size, fraud characteristics, the firm's recidivism, and the percentage of the firm's revenue obtained from government contracts.

Unranked firms also had a more difficult time recovering from the negative effects of exposure. These firms' stock remained depressed for longer periods than that of the Top 100. Stock analysts and investors were anticipating—correctly—that unranked firms would probably not continue to fill government contracts or would likely see a reduction in their government-derived revenues.

The Top 100 contractors, by contrast, saw their stock affected in a minor and temporary fashion. These contractors usually continued to fill government contracts and to derive a significant portion of their revenues from government sources.

Defense Industry Initiative

The Defense Industry Initiative (DII) is an outgrowth of the work of the 1986 President's Blue Ribbon Commission on Defense Management (also known as the Packard Commission). The Commission observed that public confidence in the defense industry had been eroded by reported instances of fraud or waste. The primary tool chosen to combat this trend was greater emphasis on corporate self-governance.

The principles of the DII specifically obligate each signatory to adopt a written code of conduct, to conduct employee orientation and training with respect to the code, to provide employees with a mechanism (such as a hotline or help line) to surface concerns about corporate compliance with procurement laws and regulations, to adopt procedures for voluntary disclosure of violations of federal procurement laws, to participate in best practice forums, and to make information public which shows the commitment to do all of these things.

Defense Procurement Fraud Schemes

According to whistleblowers.com, there are five general ways in which companies defraud the government in defense procurement.

Cross-Charging

One of the most common types of defense procurement fraud, cross-charging refers to companies that bill for goods or services covered by one contract as if the goods or services were provided under a more lucrative contract.

For example, a company has a "fixed-price" contract in which it receives a fixed price for a certain number of weapons regardless of production costs. The company may also have a "cost-plus" contract in which the government covers the company's production cost and provides a percentage of those costs as a profit. So the company charges time it spends working on the fixed-price contract to the cost-plus contract. This may be accomplished by instructing employees to write on their time cards that they worked on the cost-plus contract when they actually worked on the fixed-price contract.

Product Substitution

Defense contractors violate contract provisions requiring them to build products using a certain grade or quality of parts. Often contracts also require that the parts must be purchased from American companies. Criminal companies are tempted to substitute cheaper and/or foreign-made parts.

Improper Cost Allocation

Improper cost allocation is related to cross charging. If a company has both government contracts and private commercial contracts (as most large aircraft companies do), it is supposed to allocate costs fairly among the jobs. Accounting for direct costs, such as time a worker spends actually building an engine or other part for the aircraft, is a simple matter. The full cost of building the item is charged to the government.

Costs not directly tied to a particular project, such as supervisors' time, are more complex to allocate. All or some of the costs properly associated with the private contract may be shifted to the government, which often pays on a cost-plus basis. This cost shifting allows companies to provide lower prices to their commercial customers at the government's expense.

Failure to Comply With Contract Specifications

The Defense Department requires its contractors to build systems in accordance with detailed product specifications. These specifications dictate not only the type of materials to be used for the contract, but also items such as quality assurance steps. The costs are covered as part of the contractor's payment.

But a company experiencing budget overruns, particularly on a fixed-price contract, or missing delivery deadlines may be tempted to cut corners by omitting required testing, quality procedures, or other steps in the production process.

Violations of the Truth-in-Negotiations Act (TINA)

Highly specialized weapons systems often must be purchased from a single company, known as a "sole-source supplier." To ensure the government pays a fair price, TINA requires the contractor to truthfully disclose all relevant information about its costs to the government in sole-source contract negotiations. Companies sometimes conceal relevant information, alter information, or deliberately inflate their projected costs to get a higher price.

Sources:
Coleman, J. *The Criminal Elite: Understanding White-Collar Crime*. New York: St. Martin's Press, 1998.

"Defense Contractor Fraud." www.whistleblowers.com

Karpoff, J., and Lee, D. "False Claims Act Recoveries Reach Record Level in 2000." *U.S. Department of Justice Defense Procurement Fraud, Penalties, and Contractor Influence,* November 15, 2000.

Valaria, V. *The Journal of Political Economy*, November 16, 1998.

Related Entry:

CONTRACT AND PROCUREMENT FRAUD

DEMAND DRAFT FRAUD

This is a relatively new form of fraud that has arisen as companies become more vigilant to regular check fraud tactics. Demand drafts are sometimes referred to as "remotely-created checks" which telemarketers use in order to process consumer checking account payments over the phone. These payment devices do not require a signature, which makes them different than writing a regular check. The demand draft, instead of having a line for a consumer's signature, will include a message that says something to the extent of: "signature not required; your depositor has authorized this payment to payee." Over 70 percent of the demand drafts a single bank encounters is estimated to be fraudulent.

Banks that have automated check processing centers are susceptible to this type of fraud because the signature lines are rarely ever verified. The Federal Reserve is considering a proposal that would hold financial institutions that cash fraudulent demand drafts accountable. The bank would have 60 days to return bad checks or demand drafts if the proposal goes through.

Qchex.com is a company that allows anyone with a checking account number and routing code to send a payment to a merchant on the Internet. This company does not verify whether the person sending the payment is the actual holder of the account, nor does it even require the account holder's name. The company has been criticized for adding to the potential of defrauding consumers whose account numbers have been taken by fraudsters.

Source:

Schaeffer, Mary. "Demand Draft Fraud - The Fraudster's New Vehicle." www.cpa2biz.com. October 5, 2006.

Related Entries:

CHECK FRAUD

CREDIT CARD AND DEBIT CARD FRAUD

FINANCIAL INSTITUTION FRAUD

DISCLOSURES, IMPROPER

Making improper disclosures in a financial statement is one of the five methods of financial statement fraud. False or misleading disclosures may be found in narrative notes, supporting schedules, lawsuit notifications, and other information describing the company's condition.

Management has an obligation to disclose all significant information through a viable medium. If not disclosed in the financial statements themselves, disclosure should appear in the footnotes or management's discussion and analysis. Improper disclosures usually include one of the following inadequacies: liability omissions, significant events, management fraud, related-party transactions, and accounting changes.

Liability Omissions

Typical omissions include the failure to disclose loan obligations or contingent liabilities. Contingent liabilities are obligations a firm may be required to honor in certain cases. A pending lawsuit is a representative example of a contingent liability. The company's potential liability, if material, must be disclosed.

Significant Events

Examples of significant events might include new products or technology having an impact on sales. Also, obsolescence of merchandise or manufacturing methods should be disclosed. Lawsuits whose outcome is unknown and any other significant event that, if not disclosed, would mislead the reader when considering the available information should also be disclosed.

Management Fraud

Management has an obligation to disclose when officers, executives, and others in positions of trust are charged with fraud. According to *Roeder v. Alpha Industries, Inc., 814 F.2d 22,* (1 Cir. 1987), this obligation only applies if the persons are legally charged with the crime; unindicted offenses need not be disclosed.

Related-Party Transactions

Related-party transactions occur when a company official has an undisclosed financial interest in a transaction that causes economic harm to the company. Common directors of two companies which do business with each other, any corporate general partner and the partnerships with which it does business, and any controlling shareholder of the corporation with which the person does business are all illustrations of related parties. Family relationships can also be considered related parties. Related-party transactions are sometimes referred to as "self-dealing."

Accounting Changes

It is important that any major changes to a company's accounting policies and procedures be disclosed in its financial statements. The importance lies in the user's comparison from one period to the next. For example, a company may follow a stated policy of recognizing revenues only when payment is received, but then switches to a policy of recognizing the revenue earlier, as soon as a contract is completed. Recognizing the revenue sooner makes it appear that the company's quarterly revenues are growing, when they continue at the same pace.

Accounting Principles Board (APB) Opinion No. 20 describes three accounting changes. Changes in estimates such as depreciation of useful life estimates, bad debt expense, certain amortization estimates, warranty liability, and earned revenue estimates must be disclosed. Changes in accounting principle such as depreciation methods, construction reporting, capitalization methods, and changes in certain tax methods are very important to the statement user. Thirdly, changes in the accounting entity occur and should be reported when the composition of the company changes from the prior period. Examples of this include mergers and acquisitions, and selling of company subsidiaries. For these types of changes, financial statements should be retroactively restated.

Related Entries:

FINANCIAL STATEMENT FRAUD
OCCUPATIONAL FRAUD AND ABUSE

DOCUMENTS: HANDLING AND EXAMINING

Properly handling and examining documents is especially crucial to fraud investigations because much or all of the evidence may be in document form. If the document is being examined to discover facts about its origin and conveyance, it is called a questioned document.

More than 95% of all FBI Laboratory document examinations concern signatures, handwriting, hand printing, or documents created by a typewriter or word processor. Issues concerning photocopies and the date of a document's preparation frequently arise.

Forensic Examinations

The forensic examination of documents is used in the following tasks:

- Detection of forged signatures.
- Identification of the writers of signatures, handwriting, and hand printing.
- Detecting altered documents.
- Detecting and restoring erasures and eradications.
- Determining when a document was or was not prepared.
- Detecting counterfeited documents and examining printed documents.
- Detecting and restoring faint indented writings.
- Comparisons of paper and inks.
- Determining whether two sheets of paper came from the same tablet or pad of paper.
- Examinations of paper folds and sequence of folds.
- Comparisons of torn or cut paper edges.
- Restoration of charred and partially burned documents.
- Identifying the machine that made a photocopy and whether two copies were made on the same machine.
- Examinations of facsimile (fax) copies.
- Identifying the source of, or alterations to, notary seals, wax seals, and cachets.
- Detecting the opening and resealing of sealed documents and examining adhesives.
- Detecting inserted text in typewritten, printed, or handwritten documents.
- Determining the sequence of handwritten text, signatures, and typewriting.
- Identifying rubber stamp impressions.

- Identifying mechanical check-writer and numbering device impressions.

Handling Documents as Physical Evidence

The most fundamental principle in handling documents or any physical evidence is to preserve the item's chain of custody. A thorough record of the document's condition on acceptance, its care, and its custodian must be maintained for the document to be accepted as evidence. The basic custodial memorandum should state:

- What items were received?
- When they were received?
- From whom they were received?
- Where they are maintained?
- Who maintains custodianship?
- The general condition of the items received.
- Any distinguishing marks or characteristics.

Documentary evidence should be stored in a sealed, initialed, and dated container to avoid damage or contamination. Plastic envelopes and covers can stick to paper and destroy features of the document.

Working copies should be used whenever possible, and the original document preserved. Other than initialing a non-critical area, an examiner should never write or mark a document. The document should not be folded, stapled, paper clipped, crumpled, or have anything else done which would affect or change it from its original condition. If stored in an envelope, examiners must be careful not to write on the envelope and cause indentations on the original document inside.

Because fingerprints may be obtained from paper, gloves should be used to handle documents. Tweezers may leave indentations, which might obscure text or alter the distinctive indentations sometimes left by photocopy and fax machines.

Charred or Partially Burned Documents

For proper preservation and storage, experts use special polyester film sheets and envelopes for storing and transporting fire-damaged documents. Laypersons can best preserve such evidence using a sturdy crush-proof container lined with layers of cotton. Sliding a sheet of paper or thin cardboard underneath lifts the burned document; it is then set gently into the cotton lined box, and the lifting paper is removed. The container should be sealed, initialed, dated, its contents labeled, and the word "Fragile" should be written on the container.

Identifying Phony Documents

Forensic document examiners apply scientific methods and use a variety of technical instruments to evaluate documents. Instruments used include low-power magnifying glasses, microscopes, ultraviolet and infrared lighting, optical filters, micro and macro photography, computerized image enhancement systems and others. Various chemical analyses are also conducted.

Handwriting and typewriting characteristics are examined and compared with a comparison standard (e.g., a verified sample of a person's handwriting, or a sample of typing from a certain machine.) Changes and modifications are catalogued.

Although each document question is unique, some general factors often indicate fraud.

- *Signature forgeries* often contain irregularities in written letters and/or differences in size from a genuine signature. A side-by-side comparison with a genuine signature might reveal the differences. However, advanced age, poor health, temporary injury, and the use of drugs and alcohol can result in similar characteristics.
- *Substituted pages* in multiple-page documents such as contracts, wills, etc. can often be spotted by holding each page in front of a bright light. Differences in the whiteness, density, thickness, opacity, and paper fiber patterns of the substituted sheets are observable.
- *Ink differences, alterations, erasures, and obliterations* are also revealed by holding the paper in front of a bright light or holding a light over the writings at different angles and observing differences in the color and reflectivity of the inks or disturbances to the paper surface.
- *Counterfeited printed documents* such as checks, stock and bond certificates, business forms and stationery, birth certificates, drivers' licenses, and other identification documents, etc., may be identified by side-by-side comparisons with

corresponding genuine documents. Examiners should be alert for the use of incorrect forms, outdated forms, or form revisions of document types. For forensic examinations it will be necessary to obtain and furnish genuine comparison samples of the printed documents to the document examiner.

- *Suspicious indented writings* might be revealed by reducing the light in the room and holding a bright beam of light (a narrow beam flashlight or small high-intensity lamp will do the job) low and parallel to the page surface.

Anachronisms in Documentary Materials

Exposure of fraudulent historical documents often relies upon the combined skills of investigators, historical experts, scientific laboratories, and forensic document examiners. The materials used to produce documents–paper, ink, printing, adhesives and seals, bindings, and covers–may reveal forgery because those materials were not available at the document's purported date of preparation.

Expert examinations of contemporary documentary materials include:

- Ink analysis and comparison with a library of ink standards maintained by the U.S. Secret Service Laboratory in Washington, D.C. to determine the kind of ink and when it was first manufactured.
- Examination of typewriting and comparisons with collections of typewriter reference standards maintained by forensic laboratories to determine the kind of typewriter that was used and when the typewriter was first manufactured.
- Examination of paper, especially watermarked paper, and searches of reference materials to determine who manufactured the paper and when it was first produced.
- Examination of photocopies and fax copies and comparisons with reference standards to determine what kind of machine was used and when those machines were first produced.
- Comparison of questioned photocopies with photocopies known to have been produced on a particular machine on a particular date can prove or disprove the date of the questioned copy.

Issues with Ink

- Ink chemists collect standards from manufacturers and establish ink libraries. A library maintained by the Internal Revenue Service—the largest in the world—contains nearly 8,000 samples. Each sample includes a breakdown of the different dyes that comprise the ink.
- The physical decay of ink can also be a clue. Old ink is less soluble than new ink. In addition, electrically charged atoms or "ions" in ink will migrate into paper over time. Normally these patterns are hidden, but chemical treatment can bring them to light. Makers of ink and paper are starting to lace products with special clues as to when they were manufactured.
- Thin-layer chromatography, neutron activation analysis, X-ray fluorescence, and radiocarbon dating are used to test documents.
- Accelerator mass spectrometry (AMS) measures the radioisotopes in an object directly. Though AMS is a destructive test, only a small piece of the document is necessary. The technique is similar to the carbon dating used to measure geological formations, but AMS is thousands of times more sensitive than traditional large-scale testing. AMS has been used to date, among other items, the Shroud of Turin and the Dead Sea Scrolls.

Paper

The type of paper used can determine a document's validity. For example, the paper of a purported historical document might not have been available at the time. Paper was made from rags until esparto grass was introduced in 1861. Wood pulp paper was not commercially available until 1880 and not widely used for legal materials until after World War II. Synthetic and glass fibers in a paper mean it was manufactured sometime after 1950. In some cases, a type of paper was available but not widely used.

Simple techniques often suffice in the dating of paper. If documents glow under an ultraviolet light, there is a good chance they contain optical brightener—chemicals not introduced by paper manufacturers until the 1950's. Other chemicals that reveal age are the resins, starches, and binders that help hold paper together.

Watermarks provide aging clues because they sometimes change from year to year. Samples can be obtained from manufacturers and used as standards in examinations. Manufacturers often use design techniques to identify papers—for example, placing a tiny line under certain letters in the watermark and moving the line from year to year.

Handwriting Analysis

Analyzing the characteristics of a person's penmanship as part of a forensic document examination is a practice of scientific observation. It is not to be confused with so-called graphoanalysis, which claims that handwriting traits reveal psychological characteristics of the writer. Graphoanalysts are often self-taught or educated through short courses; their conclusions have not been corroborated by independent investigation. A forensic examination of handwriting catalogs the physical characteristics and leaves psychoanalysis to other experts.

Each handwriting sample belongs to a "class" of other writings with similar characteristics. The most common class is based on the copybooks, which most schools use to teach handwriting to children. Each copybook style uses particular techniques for producing letters and numbers. A person's mature handwriting is usually a combination of a copybook style and individual distinctions acquired over time.

Class features may also include distinctions based on region, age, or gender. A writer's native language may affect handwriting, even if the person is writing in a second language. Persons taught in a Cyrillic (Russian) alphabet style will be influenced by those letter styles when writing in English or any other language. Certain professions, such as drafting, architecture, and engineering teach letter and numeral techniques that influence general handwriting characteristics. Samples can also be classed according to the type of document under examination—an authorizing signature on a legal document may differ significantly from the same person's usual handwriting.

Forgeries, Distortions, and Disguise

A forgery is defined as any writing prepared with the intent to deceive or defraud. Most forgeries are signatures. Forgery can be done by simulation, tracing, or freehand preparation. Distortions are unintentional changes to a person's writings beyond the range of natural variation. Distortion can be caused by: (1) temporary impairment due to illness, injury, substance abuse, extreme physical weakness, etc.; (2) an unusual writing environment, irregular or unusual writing surface, unfamiliar writing materials, etc.; or (3) advanced age.

Disguise is the conscious effort by a person to conceal handwriting characteristics. Usually the person is attempting to produce a piece of legally pertinent writing but does not want to be recognized as the preparer. In cases of auto-forgery, the forger signs his own name, but alters the writing because he intends to deny authorship. Auto-forgery occurs in falsely reported traveler's check theft cases, in cases involving disputed home mortgage and other loan documents, and credit card frauds, among others.

The success of an attempt to disguise writings depends upon the writer's skill and knowledge of writings. Most attempts at disguise involve one or more of the following: change in slant, change in size, change in shapes of capital (upper-case) letters, changes in the shapes and sizes of loops in letters which contain them, use of bizarre letter designs, or block (squared) hand printing. In rare cases, the opposite, non-writing hand is used.

Typewriters and Computer Printers

Typewriting prepared on traditional type bar/segment-shift typewriters, both manual and electric, can often be positively identified by experts from mechanical defects unique to each machine. Typewritten texts prepared on later model typewriters equipped with interchangeable daisy wheel, ball, or basket type elements are difficult, if not impossible to identify. Computerized dot matrix, ink jet, thermal transfer, or laser (electrostatic) printers are rarely identifiable. Usually, the only expert determinations concerning these typewriters and printers are that the same typeface design and size (font), letter spacing, and print process were used.

Old-style fabric typewriter ribbons are seldom helpful in document examinations because the ribbons circulate and new typing is struck over previous efforts. However most modern manual and electric typewriters are equipped with single-use ribbons, and may reveal the text of the document by the impressions on the ribbon.

Counterfeit Printed Documents

Most documents that have monetary value, such as currency, bank checks, traveler's checks, money orders, bearer bonds, postage stamps, gift certificates, lottery tickets, etc. have all been counterfeited. Other documents often counterfeited include identity documents such as passports, birth certificates, drivers' licenses, and government and commercial employee identity cards. Others include commercial product labels, business stationery and forms, business logos, motor vehicle titles and registration forms, and safety inspection stickers.

Most counterfeit documents are prepared using photo-offset printing (lithography) and flexography, which uses rubberized printing "plates." These processes begin with the photographic reproduction of a model genuine document. The photographic negatives are then carefully retouched to remove the filled in text, serial numbers, etc. that appeared on the genuine document. Printing plates are then made from the retouched negatives and counterfeit copies are printed from the plates. Computerized scanners, graphics software, multicolor computer printers, and full-color photocopy machines are also used to produce high-quality counterfeit documents.

Many counterfeits can be detected by making a side-by-side comparison with a corresponding genuine document. Subtle differences in ink colors and brilliance, different types of paper substrate, the use of different typestyles and type sizes (fonts), and evidence of retouching indicate a fake. Retouching will be most evident in areas where the text, serial numbers, etc., especially if printed in black ink, are superimposed on a background design.

Comparing genuine documents with suspected counterfeits, forensic document examiners can also make expert differentiations between printing processes, ink formulations, and paper substrates. Portions of the filled-in text or serial numbers, which appeared on the model genuine document, may be perceptible because they were not fully removed in retouching.

Photocopies

The machine used to make copies can be identified by observing the minute markings, indentations, and other features such as "trash marks" (specks, spots, streaks, edge markings, etc.) transferred to the paper during copying. Permanent trash marks are uniquely identifiable markings usually caused by deep scratches and imperfections in the copier's glass surface or document cover, in the printing element surface, or other permanent machine parts which are not readily replaced or changed during servicing of the machine. These marks can be reproduced on copies for years until the machine is repaired or the part replaced.

Dirt, smudges, or small bits of foreign matter on or in machine surfaces that appear between cleanings usually cause transient trash marks. Two or more documents that share the same transient trash marks were probably produced around the same time.

Fingerprints

Latent (non-visible) prints are left on surfaces by the body oils, salts, and amino acids clinging to or exuded by friction ridges in the skin on fingers, palms of the hands, and soles of the feet, or may be retained by oils and other materials on the surface itself. Patent (visible) prints are deposited on surfaces by hands, fingers, and bare feet through the transfer of materials such as blood, paint, soot, and soil.

Latent prints absorbed onto paper can survive for decades and be lifted through chemical development, such as iodine fuming, brushing or spraying silver nitrate solutions, and ninhydrin spray. Traditional methods of lifting prints, including fingerprint powder, can destroy older prints. Chemical methods must be used sparingly with documents because the chemicals may permanently discolor paper or other materials.

The Federal Bureau of Investigation's Identification Division and other law enforcement agencies throughout the world maintain the fingerprints of millions of persons. Anyone who was ever arrested, served in military services, applied for employment at various levels of government, or voluntarily had themselves printed for personal identification has fingerprints on file at some agency or another. Many of these fingerprint databases have been computerized and are linked by networks.

Electronic Signatures

Computerized business and communications have brought about a need for electronic signatures. These are similar to the signature stamps used by many officials, but with a unique set of security issues.

To be considered valid, an electronic signature ought to contain:

- The printed name of the signer.
- The date and time the signature was executed.
- The activity (such as review, approval, responsibility, and authorship) associated with the signature.
- Electronic and handwritten signatures executed to electronic records must be linked to their respective records so that signatures cannot be excised, copied, or otherwise transferred to falsify an electronic record by ordinary means.

Biometric Identification

Biometrics is the method of verifying an individual's identity based on measurement of physical features or repeatable actions that are unique to that individual. Biometric devices use one or more biometric parameters to identify the individual. These devices include palm-print readers, fingerprint readers, iris scanners, and retinal-pattern scanners. The devices are connected to a computing system that requires authentication and are typically placed next to a desktop computer.

Most of these devices are easily adapted to a variety of situations. For instance, iris scanners are already being used by Japanese banks to authenticate users of automatic teller machines. When biometric devices are used for electronic signatures, the computing system may integrate the biometric information with cryptographic technology that binds signatures with time and date stamps to documents. Some biometric-based electronic signature systems use dynamic signature verification with a parameter code recorded on magnetic-strip cards. These biometric devices are highly effective, but are also expensive.

In April 2004, Britain started a pilot program to introduce compulsory ID cards containing biometric details including fingerprints, facial dimensions and an eye scan, as well as basic personal details. By the end of 2005 patrons were only being asked to carry the cards with them on a "voluntary" basis.

Sources:
www.washtimes.com/world/20040424-105833-7535r.htm

www.telegraph.co.uk/news/main.jhtml?xml=/news/2004/04/27/ncard127.xml

Forensic Document Experts

Qualified and court certified expert forensic document examiners usually belong to one of the following organizations: American Board of Forensic Document Examiners, American Academy of Forensic Sciences Questioned Document Section, or the American Society of Questioned Document Examiners.

Sources:
Broad, W. "Forgeries Face New Arsenal of Anti-HOA X Techniques." *The New York Times,* May 10, 1983.

Harris, M. and Myers, R. *Fakes and Frauds.* Delaware: Oak Knoll Press, 1996.

Jull, A. "Radiation Dating: Accelerator Radiocarbon Dating of Art, Textiles, and Artifacts." *Nuclear News,* June 1998.

"Today's Chemist at Work." *American Chemical Society,* November 1997.

Related Entry:

COUNTERFEIT DOCUMENTS

DYNEGY, INC.

Dynegy, Inc. is a large operator of natural gas liquid power plants based out of Houston, Texas. In April of 2001, a midlevel tax expert at Dynegy, James Olis, along with his boss, Gene Foster and a colleague named Helen Sharkey committed financial statement fraud to the tune of $300 million. They used an accounting gimmick called a special purpose entity to falsely increase Dynegy's operating cash flow. Dynegy also overstated its energy-trading activities from "round-trip" or "wash" trades (which are simultaneous, pre-arranged buy-sell trades of energy with the same counter-party, over the same term, and at the same price and volume, which results in neither profit nor loss to either transacting party).

In June 2003, federal prosecutors indicted Foster, Olis, and Sharkey for conspiracy, securities fraud, mail fraud, and three counts of wire fraud. Foster and Sharkey pleaded guilty to a single count of conspiracy and received sentences of 15 months and one month. Olis, on the other hand, was the only one who risked attempting to defend himself by maintaining his innocence on trial. In November of 2005, he was convicted for his role in "Project Alpha," which was a scheme intended to inflate Dynegy's cash flow by $300 million while cutting its taxes by $79 million. Olis was found guilty on the six counts he was charged for and received a staggering 24 year prison sentence. The prosecution team had heavily charged Olis in order to pressure him to plead guilty. In September of 2006, after already serving two years in prison, Olis' sentence was reduced to six years instead of the original 24.

ENRON

As of early 2007, the Enron saga continues. A federal judge approved three more banks to pay $6.6 billion to settle civil claims. With interest, the litigation's settlement total so far has reached $7.3 billion, against Wall Street firms that were accused of helping the energy trader inflate profits and hide losses before it spiraled into bankruptcy proceedings in December 2001. Between founder Kenneth Lay's death from a heart attack in July 2006 and former CEO Jeff Skilling's citation for public intoxication in September 2006, this case is constantly unfolding.

The U.S. Congress has been in the midst of hearings trying to determine whether the management of Enron committed fraud and/or violated SEC rules. Arthur Andersen LLP, Enron's audit firm, was in the middle of a criminal trial in Houston for obstruction of justice. This conviction was overthrown in late May of 2005 because of errors in the jury instructions.

Very few financial frauds have generated as much interest and media coverage as has Enron. The public perception is that Enron's top management used a variety of questionable accounting practices to falsely inflate Enron's bottom line and to fool the investing public (and employees) into buying Enron stock. The fringe benefit of these questionable practices was to line the personal pockets of some of Enron's management and their friends.

Again, since the story is still unfolding, it is difficult to provide a definitive and completely accurate account of what happened at Enron. The following summary of the Enron scandal is based on news reports, testimony before Congress, and the report prepared by University of Texas Law School Dean William Powers, Jr. (the Powers Report) at the request of the Enron board of directors.

Enron began in 1985 when two Houston-based natural gas companies merged, but it soon expanded its business by becoming a futures trader in natural gas. In the mid-nineties, Enron was focused on growth, but many of its investments were risky and required large amounts of capital upfront. In order to keep the cash coming in, Enron had to look good to banks and investors. Management engaged in several methods of "creative accounting" to keep its profits looking healthy. One of the most creative was the formation of various Special Purpose Entities (SPEs).

As Enron began pouring more money into other avenues of business, such as fiber optics, it was generating enormous losses. Rather than report these losses on their financial statements, Enron's management chose to conceal these losses (and its debt) by the use of SPEs.

SPEs are perfectly legal. The use of SPEs is intended to contain financial risk for companies entering into specific ventures removed from their main base of operations. Enron, however, used SPEs to expand its operations while keeping billions of dollars in related debt off the balance sheet. The loans were listed as a liability of the SPE, not Enron, even though Enron was compelled to guarantee the loans since the SPEs had no assets of their own.

Under accounting rules, only 3% of an SPE must be owned by an outside entity. Therefore, Enron could own as much as 97% of the SPE without having to classify the entity as a subsidiary. Apparently, however, Enron failed to follow this rule.

For example, then CFO Andrew Fastow created a partnership called Chewco Investments LLP in 1997. Chewco was created to buy out Enron's partner in another venture called JEDI, which was legally kept off the books. However, Enron could not find enough outside investors to purchase the required 3% to be classified as a SPE. But rather than classifying Chewco as a subsidiary, Enron ignored the 3% rule and used Chewco to overstate Enron's profits by $405 million and understate a debt of $2.6 billion.

How much the board of directors knew is the subject of dispute. Although the Chewco proposal was approved by the board, Fastow allegedly left out several key details such as the fact that there was virtually no outside equity in Chewco, and he also failed to disclose that Chewco was affiliated with Enron. Neither did he inform the board that one of his protégés, Michael Kopper, would manage the partnership.

Chewco was such a success that in 1999, Fastow constructed two more SPE partnerships called LJM Cayman (also called LJM1) and LJM2. They were soon followed by four more partnerships known as the Raptors.

Although the partnerships benefited Enron by keeping its debts off its books, it also appears that Enron executives personally profited from partnership deals. According to Congressional reports, Fastow structured several partnership deals so that he was both buyer and seller. Fastow sometimes negotiated the terms (on behalf of the partnerships) with Enron employees who worked for him. These employees were enriched by tens of millions of dollars at Enron's expense.

There is still much that is unknown about how the partnerships worked. In several cases, Enron transferred money to partnerships as part of transactions that made no economic sense, at least for Enron. For example, in September 1999, Enron sold an interest in a Brazilian power plant to LJM1. After the sale, the plant began experiencing a variety of mechanical problems. Two years later, Enron bought back LJM1's interest for $14.4 million — $3.1 million more than the partnership paid for it. Although the sale generated a 27% profit for LJM1's investors, there was evidence that the plant was in poor condition and worth much less than it was previously.

LJM1's investors, however, were certainly not in poor condition. It is reported that Ben Glisan, then a senior executive, and Kristina Mordaunt, a lawyer who worked for Fastow, each invested $5,800 in an LJM1 deal. When Enron bought out their interests two months later, Glisan and Mordaunt each made $1 million. Fastow's $25,000 investment reportedly earned him $4.5 million.

In the spring and summer of 2000, Fastow created the four Raptor partnerships to provide "hedges," or insurance, against the potential decline in value of Enron's investments. As part of a series of complex transactions, Enron spent $164 million to purchase hedges against the value of its stock. This enabled Enron to tell the public that its stock was a good buy, while privately it was betting that the value would decline. The partnerships lacked the cash or other assets to provide much protection in the event the stock price did decline. In other words, the value of the hedges Enron purchased was much lower than what it paid for them. The partnerships did, however, benefit Enron because it used the Raptor partnerships to avoid reporting almost $1 billion in losses.

And, of course, the partnerships generated huge profits for its private investors. Fastow's LJM2 partnership controlled the Raptor partnerships. Fastow reported to LJM2's investors in October of 2000 that the Raptor deals had created a rate of return ranging from 125% to 2,500%.

Unfortunately for investors and employees, this house of cards tumbled in October 2001 when Enron announced its first quarterly loss in more than four years. In its quarterly report, Enron announced a $638 million loss and a $1.2 billion reduction in equity partly related to the partnerships run by Fastow. This announcement caught the attention of the Securities and Exchange Commission, which announced that it was launching a formal inquiry into Enron's financial situation.

In November, Enron announced a restatement of its financial statements from 1997 to reflect consolidation of SPEs that it had neglected in previous years. The effect was almost $600 million in losses and an additional $630 million in debt that had not been previously disclosed. By the end of the month, Enron's stock was trading at $0.26 a share, and on December 2, 2001, Enron filed for bankruptcy.

Ken Lay resigned on January 23, 2002 from his post as the chief executive officer and chairman of Enron Corporation. Lay was indicted on July 7, 2004 by a grand jury in Houston, Texas on counts of securities fraud, wire fraud, and making false and misleading statements. He was convicted on all counts on May 25, 2006. Before he could pay for his crimes, Lay died on July 5, 2006 in Aspen, Colorado of a massive heart attack. As a result of Lay's death prior to exhausting his appeals, his conviction is abated, and Lay is legally considered never to have been indicted or convicted of criminal charges. Civil suits are expected to continue against Lay's estate. However, claimants may not seek punitive damages against a deceased defendant, only compensatory damages. He would have been sentenced on September 11, 2006. In October 2006, a federal judge cleared Ken Lay's criminal record. Lay's death vacated his conviction of 10 counts of fraud, conspiracy, and lying to banks. Lay's attorneys pointed to a U.S. Court of Appeals ruling that a defendant's death pending appeal extinguishes the entire case. The government planned on seeking $43.5 million from Ken Lay's estate for the fraudulent gains he received. They may now only pursue the case in civil court, competing against any other litigants going after Lay's estate.

Jeffrey Skilling, former CEO of Enron, was convicted of federal felony charges relating to the company's financial collapse. His trial took 56 days and ended with a jury verdict on May 25, 2006. Skilling was found guilty of 19 out of 28 counts against him, including one count of conspiracy, one count of insider trading (although he was acquitted of the other nine counts of this particular charge), five counts of making false statements to auditors, and twelve counts of securities fraud. Each conviction carries a maximum sentence of five to 10 years. In October 2006, Skilling was sentenced to 24 years and four months in prison. This is the harshest sentence in a corporate crime case to date.

Andrew S. Fastow was the CFO of Enron until the U.S. Securities and Exchange Commission opened an investigation into his conduct in 2001. On October 31, 2002, Fastow was indicted by a federal grand jury in Houston, Texas on 98 counts including fraud, money laundering, and conspiracy. On January 14, 2004, he pled guilty to two counts of wire and securities fraud, and agreed to serve a 10-year prison sentence. He also agreed to cooperate with federal authorities in the prosecutions of other former Enron executives. On September 26, 2006, Fastow's received a reduced sentence of six years for cooperating with prosecutors.

On May 6, 2004, his wife Lea Fastow, a former Enron assistant treasurer, pled guilty to a misdemeanor tax charge and was sentenced to one year in a federal prison in Houston, Texas, and an additional year of supervised release. Lea was released to a halfway house on July 11, 2005.

Related Entry:

FINANCIAL STATEMENT FRAUD

SARBANES-OXLEY ACT

ENTERPRISE CRIME

Enterprise crimes are illegal acts performed cooperatively between organized crime and legitimate businesses. Examples include organized crime involvement in various labor unions—most prominently the United Auto Workers, and the Teamsters' unions. Organized crime figures have infiltrated many, if not most, forms of business, including gambling enterprises, garbage collection, and securities trading.

Case Study—The Mob Moves to Wall Street

A series of enforcement actions in the late 1990's uncovered significant activity in the trading of securities being conducted by, or influenced by, organized crime figures. From 1995 to 2000, members of the Bonanno, Colombo, Gambino, Genovese, and Luchese families were arrested for stock market crimes.

The families infiltrated or controlled several brokerage firms through bribes and intimidation. They conspired with companies issuing securities and used boiler-room tactics to "pump and dump" the stock of dubious or wholly fictitious companies, often selling stock directly to investors in what is known as a "private placement." Besides the financial violations, defendants were charged with making threats, extortion, physical intimidation, and solicitation to commit murder. The charges were levied across the U.S., including Alabama, California, Connecticut, Florida, Georgia, Illinois, Maryland, New York, New Jersey, Pennsylvania, Texas, Utah, and Virginia.

In mid-2000, federal authorities announced the culmination of Operation Uptick, a 10-month investigation that resulted in the largest securities fraud crackdown in history. Some 120 people were arrested, including organized crime members, stockbrokers, company executives, and a retired New York City police detective. The alleged scams, preying mainly on elderly investors, cost about $50 million and involved racketeering, extortion, money laundering, illegal kickbacks, securities fraud, and witness tampering.

According to a description by the U.S. Attorney:

- The Bonanno crime family took control of DMN Capital.

- The Bonanno and Colombo families worked together to infiltrate five brokerage firms and recruit corrupt stockbrokers. DMN Capital purchased small, inexpensive stocks that were not widely traded.
- The brokers touted those stocks to the investing public, sometimes using boiler room tactics or falsely touting some as Internet companies.
- After the stock's value increased, DMN Capital would sell its stakes and divide the profits among the stockbrokers and Bonanno and Colombo families.

Related Entry:

ORGANIZED CRIME AND FRAUD

EQUITY FUNDING

The Equity Funding Corporation began in March 1960 as a partnership among five businessmen in Southern California: Gordon McCormick, reputedly the leading seller in the United States for the Keystone mutual fund; Ray Platt, an insurance salesman; Eugene Cuthbertson, a civil engineer looking for an easier way to make a living; Stanley Goldblum, also an insurance salesman, though he preferred management to sales; and Milken Riordan, who worked for Keystone Funding in Boston, where Gordon McCormick's bid idea and big sales were gaining attention.

McCormick and a few others in the mutual fund business found a way to convince customers to move the cash value of their life insurance into a mutual fund. The customer then borrowed against the mutual fund account to continue paying life insurance premiums on a new policy. The loan to pay the premiums cost 6% interest annually. But the life insurance paid 3% annually, so the real cost of the loan was halved, to 3%. With mutual funds averaging a 9% annual return, the profits more than covered the policy cost. In the equity-funding model, as the practice came to be known, the life-insurance money boosted profits in the mutual fund, and the mutual fund profits covered the costs of the insurance premium. A dip in mutual fund might upset the balance, but salesmen obscured or ignored this possibility.

The company incorporated in 1961, but was forced to suspend business for 18 months when the Securities and Exchange Commission ruled that packaging mutual funds and life-insurance policies constituted a security in its own right. Public shares in the Equity Funding Corporation were first offered in October 1963. Two years later, only Milken Riordan and Stanley Goldblum remained of the original founders. Goldblum and Riordan ran Equity Funding together from 1963 to 1968.

From Equity Funding's first year as a public entity, Goldblum and Riordan were committing fraud. In 1964's financial statements, they recorded profits they *expected* to make on an upcoming insurance deal as cash in hand. They made up for the eventual shortcoming by recording more policies than they actually sold. They planned to cover this second fraud in later years through increased sales and by merging other businesses into the corporate umbrella.

Any of a few simple comparisons might have revealed their scam. Early on, Equity sold virtually all of its insurance policies on behalf of Penn Life. Equity's annual report in May 1967 claimed the company sold $225 million worth of policies. But Penn Life issued a report on *its* operations a month later, stating the company had underwritten $60 million worth of policies for Equity Funding. Some of the discrepancy came from a handful of smaller agencies Equity did business with, but not $165 million worth.

Upon Riordan's death in 1969, Goldblum immediately assumed control of the company and moved its headquarters to Century City. Following Riordan's death, Goldblum's chief assistants were Fred Levin and Sam Lowell. Fred Levin came from Presidential Life of Chicago in 1968—where he had served as general counsel—when Presidential was acquired by Equity Funding. At Equity Funding he ran the life insurance subsidiary. Sam Lowell had been an auditor for Haskins & Sells, the company that had audited Equity's books until a few years prior. As Stanley Goldblum's executive vice-president in charge of finance, Lowell oversaw enormous domestic and international funding operations. He was later called "the financial architect of the corporation."

Soon after Lowell's arrival, Goldblum recruited him into helping perpetrate and cover up the ongoing fraud. He created shell companies, which were paid commissions and other fees, which were used to cover loans and operating costs. Goldblum also enlisted Lowell's help when Equity acquired a big sales organization called IPC. The merger agreement included millions in guaranteed sales, to be generated by the IPC *Plan*, an investment program in which clients agreed to specific cash layouts over a period of 5 to

10 years. At best, the *Plan* represented what a client hoped to be doing, not a firm commitment. Despite this, Stanley had Lowell record the entire value of the IPC *Plan* as income for the year 1969.

As cover, Lowell rigged a sale of the $14-million commission rights to the *Compana de Estudios y Asuntos*, a shell corporation chartered in Panama. *Estudios* was held by another shell, in Lichtenstein, named *Etablissement Grandson*. The head of *Grandson* was listed as Heinrich Wangerhof, presumably an alias. In fact Equity Funding chartered the Grandson shell.

In 1968, Goldblum and Fred Levin set up a life insurance subsidiary called Equity Funding Life Corporation of America (EFLCA). During the reorganization, it was discovered that a group of mid-level executives were defrauding some of Equity Funding's partner companies. The scam hinged on a common industry practice called *reinsuring*. Equity Funding sells a policy to a customer, then immediately *resells* the same policy to another company. The second company pays cash, equal to two years' premiums, for the rights to collect the customer's monthly payments. For a 10-year policy, for example, Equity received two years worth of monthly premiums up front; the reinsurer received eight years of steady cash flow. In the scam, an executive would create a phony policy and slip it into the batch marked for reinsuring. The executive collected a big commission (about $1,100) on the sale from Equity Funding. Then, sometime in the second year of the policy, the executive killed off his phony customer and collected the death benefits check at a mail drop.

According to Equity Funding lore, Levin did not fire the executives who were caught running the scam. Instead, around 100 other executives began creating bogus files and fobbing them off on reinsures—this time on behalf of Equity Funding, as a way of boosting the company's net worth, cash flow, and thus its stock price. The perpetrators called their work *Y* policies: you took a Xeroxed original (an X), and you made a *Y policy.* A co-conspirator said later, "It took a long time and you had to be careful about date stamps and other details. But I had fun being the doctor and giving the guy's blood pressure and all that." Eventually the forgery was committed on a grander scale: a group of young women were hired to work in a small office building, preparing the phony policies according to a formula.

Keeping the records straight on this massive illusion required constant attention and lots of computer work. With guidance from Fred Levin and others, Bill Gootnick, in charge of Equity's computing center, wrote software to track the phony policies with a hidden "Department 99" code. Since the computer automatically rejected duplicate names and policy numbers, Gootnick adjusted the software to allow for the *Y* policies, which repeated entire blocks of information from legitimate policies. Gootnick also altered the computer's *Print* function to have the machine list the policies by a three-digit prefix instead of the full five-digit policy number. An auditor looking at a scroll of computer paper who saw two policies both numbered 10234 might become suspicious. But since Gootnick's printouts only displayed each policy's three opening numbers, the auditor saw a range of policies beginning 102. In late 1971, under orders from Goldblum, Levin arranged for the Equity Funding print shop to counterfeit $100 million in corporate bonds, in the names of the country's largest companies, including Dow Chemical, Firestone Tire & Rubber, Woolworth, and Southwestern Bell.

The Equity Funding scam unraveled in March 1973, when a disgruntled former employee tipped New York stock analyst Ray Dirks to the goings-on. Former accountant Frank Majerus confirmed to Dirks that he'd "adjusted" the Income and Accounts Receivable lines under Levin's guidance. Both men spoke of the "*Y* Business," the phony policies, which were also called by other names, including: "Stanley Goldblum's Friends," "the Employees' Franchise," and "the Telephone Directory."

Subsequent investigations by the SEC revealed that Goldblum and his co-conspirators had created 64,000 phony insurance policies, $25 million in counterfeit bonds, and claimed $100 million in unconfirmable assets. In 1972, Fortune ranked Equity Funding as the fastest-growing financial conglomerate in America. In fact the company had been operating at a loss for at least eight years.

Stanley Goldblum was convicted of fraud in 1976, and served four years of an eight-year sentence. In 1990, he was charged with insurance fraud as controller in a company called Primedex, which ran a chain of medical clinics—charges included invoicing for services not performed, giving and receiving illegal kickbacks, and forging medical reports. In February 1999, the 72-year-old Goldblum was charged with faking the collateral on a $150,000 loan.

Fred Levin changed his name to Fred Evans after he left prison, two years into a four-year sentence. As Fred Evans he worked at an L.A. plastics firm, until he was indicted in 1984 for embezzling $250,000 from the firm's pension fund.

Related Entry:

INSURANCE FRAUD

ETHICS

Ethics is a branch of philosophy that has developed since ancient times as a way to describe and evaluate how people interact with one another, and how they ought to interact. The Greek word *ethos* refers to how other people regard a person's character. Someone has strong ethical standing if others respect him; a person is unethical, and socially unfit, if most honest people disapprove of his behavior.

Most of the 500 largest corporations in the U.S. have a written code of ethics. Among U.S. companies in general about 80% have a written code. The London Business School and Arthur Andersen found that among the 350 largest companies in Britain, 78% had a code of conduct.

Dr. Wesley Cragg, professor of business ethics at York University and President of Transparency International Canada, noted, "a principal function of ethics is to facilitate cooperation." The focus of any ethical system, then, seeks the best way for people to cooperate and coexist.

Decisions about how to behave—to take a few dollars from the register, to invest company funds for personal gain—are made by individuals. But the evaluation of those acts occurs socially. Even one's most private feelings about individual acts are influenced by perceptions of others' approval or disapproval.

Ethical Training

Ethical philosophers are divided on how and when a person's ethics is formed. One point of view holds that a person's ethics is shaped from late childhood through adolescence. Therefore businesses, which normally hire adults, are contracting with people who already have most of their ethical understanding in place.

An opposing theory holds that a person's values or ethics are not formed until early adulthood and remain malleable. So long as individuals have the capacity to reflect and make value judgments, they can modify their personal ethics and change their behavior. Business ethics programs are based on the latter theory, aiming to mold employees' behavior over time.

Ethics and Morality

Ethics and morality are obviously related but the two terms indicate different approaches to judging behavior. Morality is concerned with general issues of right and wrong. Ethics is concerned with specific acts as measured by specified criteria.

Determining whether an act is ethical or not, one would consult one's professional code of conduct or laws pertaining to one's position. To determine if the same act were moral or immoral, the person would consult generally accepted moral premises, religious teachings, or philosophical works.

Ethics and Money

In its basic physical characteristics, money is molded metal, or a paper rectangle printed with ink, or a plastic rectangle with a magnetic stripe. The materials gain value by the power of symbolism—the paper and ink does not contain a dollar's value; the imprint represents the value. Published exchange rates are the record of a currency's agreed-upon value at any given moment.

But even allowing for the symbolic nature of money, it is still, on its own, worthless. Money only gains value by being exchanged. A trunk full of Confederate scrip is worthless not because it is paper and ink, but because nobody will exchange it for anything.

The dollar's value is measured by its exchange rates. Money's exchange value carries special weight in any discussion of ethics because ethics is also about exchange. Codes and law books record our prescriptions for behavior. But these publications are only guides; ethical values are manifested in the exchanges between people.

Financial professionals have always appreciated the social nature of money. A mattress full of dollar bills is money lying dormant, while a savings account would at least produce interest, because the bank circulates the funds—through loans and investments. The same principle applies to ethics. Mary Worth cannot be declared a "good" or "bad" person by simple interrogation or observation. Mary's values will be discerned by noting how she works and interacts with others and how her actions affect others.

Recognizing that both the monetary value of our currency and the ethical value of our actions are determined by exchange rates, each should be treated as social issues. Every economic exchange ought to be regarded as a social act. The act is judged ethical or unethical according to its impact on the community in which it occurs.

Corporate Ethics

A 1992 U.S. study by the Institute of Chartered Financial Analysts of 5,000 people in the financial services industry showed that only 11% of financial services managers who witnessed unethical behavior reported their concerns.

"Companies obsessed with maximizing profits," says analyst John Dobson, "miss the ethical mark and occasionally miss their financial goals by adopting a brute mentality that seeks to win at any cost. In the current business climate, which emphasizes profits and market advantage over ethical principles, ethics function primarily as a constraint on behavior. If ethical principles come up, they are seen in a negative light; these are all the things we are not supposed to do."

However, "throughout the 2000-year history of moral philosophy," Dobson writes, "ethics has generally been viewed as a behavioral motivation, not as a constraint." Dobson suggests that businesses should adopt a more positive approach, treating ethics as an initiative or an incentive, not as a regulatory burden, fine, binding judgment, or some other form of punishment. Ethical principles are not seen as a constraint but as the means to an end; these are the things we do to maintain an honorable, productive, and profitable company.

Many ethicists suggest that businesses with strong, well-enforced ethical codes are more profitable in the long run than businesses that sacrifice principles for short-term profits. The more ethical business commands better employee loyalty, customer relations, and public standing than its unethical counterparts.

In 1999, researchers Roman, Hayibor, and Agle examined data from 52 reports on corporate ethics and profit. The authors concluded that 33 studies showed a positive link between corporate ethics and profit. Five studies suggested that ethical principles exerted a negative economic effect. Fourteen of the studies showed no effect or were inconclusive.

KPMG's 2000 integrity survey found that four out of five employees who felt that managers would uphold ethical standards said they would recommend their company to potential recruits. Of those who did not believe their managers supported ethical standards, only one in five would recommend the firm to others. Four out of five employees who felt management would uphold ethical standards believed their customers would recommend the company to others, while only half of the employees who doubted their managers' ethical standards thought their customers would recommend the company.

Other research suggests that ethics programs are most successful when they emphasize values instead of compliance with laws and regulations. A 1999 report by Weaver and Trevino showed that when employees construed companies' ethics programs as being oriented towards "values" rather than "compliance," they displayed a greater commitment to the organization, were more willing to deliver bad news, and were more willing to seek advice.

2005 National Business Ethics Survey

The 2005 National Business Ethics Survey (*NBES*) asked employees across the United States to share their views on ethics and compliance within their organizations.

The *NBES* 2005 is the fourth survey over an 11-year period. The participants consisted of 10,053 employees across for-profit, nonprofit, and governmental sectors. They were asked questions that focused on a number of key areas including: ethics practices of executives, supervisors, and co-workers; prevalence of formal ethics programs; pressures to compromise ethics standards; misconduct at work and the influences on reporting it; frequency with which certain ethical values are practiced; and accountability for ethics violations.

The key findings are summarized below.

- 81% of employees in 2005 said that top management in their organizations keeps promises and commitments, as compared with 84% in 2003.
- Observed misconduct is a key indicator of ethics-related problems in the workplace. The level of observed misconduct has increased from 22% in 2003, to 52% in 2005.
- In both 2003 and 2005, 10% of employees felt pressure to compromise its company's ethics standards.
- Only 55% of employees in 2005 said that they reported misconduct observed in the workplace. This was a 10% decrease from 2003.
- Reporting of misconduct by employees had increased steadily in the surveys conducted in 1994 (48%), 2000 (57%) and 2003 (65%). In 2005, however, reporting of misconduct dropped to 55%.
- Employees indicate that values such as honesty and respect are practiced more frequently in their organizations in 2003.
- Nearly a third of respondents say their coworkers condone questionable ethics practices by showing respect for those who achieve success using them.
- Employees in transitioning organizations (undergoing mergers, acquisitions or restructurings) observe misconduct and feel pressure at rates that are nearly double those in more stable organizations.
- One in three employees is exposed to situations inviting misconduct, regardless of age or length of tenure in an organization.
- In past NBES surveys, younger employees under age 30 with little tenure (less than three years) were the least likely to report ethical misconduct than any other group. This was due to their fear of retaliation from management and coworkers. They also felt that managers would consider them "trouble makers" if they reported unethical conduct. In 2003 middle managers and senior managers were most likely to report misconduct. However, in 2005, there was no significant statistical relationship between age/tenure and reporting.
- Despite an overall increase in reporting of misconduct, nearly half of all non-management employees (44%) still do not report the misconduct they observe. The top two reasons given for not reporting misconduct are: (1) a belief that no corrective action will be taken and (2) fear that the report will not be kept confidential.

- Nearly half of all employees (48%) received positive feedback for reporting misconduct. Nearly one in four employees (22%) experienced retaliation from their colleagues or supervisors for reporting misconduct. A small portion of employees (8%) received *both* positive feedback and retaliation.
- Over eight in 10 employees (83%) were dissatisfied with the response to their report of misconduct because they did not believe that action taken by the organization was severe enough.
- In many areas, views of ethics remain "rosier at the top." For example, senior and middle managers have less fear of reporting misconduct and are more satisfied with the response of their organizations. They also feel that honesty and respect are practiced more frequently than do lower level employees.
- The presence of ethics program elements is associated with increased reporting of misconduct by employees. Specifically, 78% of employees are most likely to report in organizations with all four program elements in place (employer talks about importance of ethics, informs employees, keeps promises, and models ethical behavior). Employee reporting declines steadily in organizations with fewer program elements such as: written standards plus (67%), written standards only (52%), or none (39%).
- Ethics programs are associated with higher perceptions that employees are held accountable for ethics violations.
- In larger organizations (over 500 employees), ethics programs are associated with lower pressures on employees to compromise company standards of business conduct.
- When employees feel that their supervisors and coworkers act ethically, the relationships to observed misconduct, pressure, and related outcomes is similar to that for top management.
- Smaller organizations (less than 500 employees) are less likely to have key elements of ethics programs in place than larger ones. For example, 41% of employees in smaller organizations say ethics training is provided, as compared with 67% in larger organizations. Similarly, 77% of employees in larger organizations say that

mechanisms to report misconduct anonymously are available, versus 47% in smaller organizations.

- Employee perceptions of ethics in smaller and larger organizations converged in 2003. This finding contrasts with the 2000 survey findings, which showed employees in smaller organizations generally holding more positive views of ethics. The convergence is due primarily to more positive ethics trends in larger organizations between 2000 and 2003.
- According to the National Business Ethics study, these are the common types of ethical violations observed by employees (as well as their corresponding percentages) in the workplace in 2005:
- Abusive or intimidating behavior of superiors toward employees (21%)
- Lying to employees, customers, vendors, or the public (19%)
- A situation that places employee interests over organizational interests (18%)
- Violations of safety regulations (16%)
- Misreporting actual time or hours worked (16%)
- E-mail and Internet abuse (13%)
- Discrimination on the basis of race, color, gender, age, or similar categories (12%)
- Stealing, theft, or related fraud (11%)
- Sexual harassment (9%)
- Provision of goods or services that fail to meet specifications (8%)
- Misuse of confidential information (7%)
- Falsification or misrepresentation of financial records or reports (5%)
- Price fixing (3%)
- Giving or accepting bribes, kickbacks, or inappropriate gifts (3%)

The NBES points out that every organization needs to be able to answer this question: How much misconduct is considered acceptable/inevitable within the company? This question will help prepare upper management on the appropriate ways in which they deal with employee behavior and omissions.

Ethics Programs

A written ethics policy, communicated prominently to employees, vendors, and others, is the basis of any successful ethics program.

There are four factors that generally affect the ethical decisions of employees:

1. The law and other government regulations.
2. Industry and organizational ethical codes.
3. Social pressures.
4. Tension between personal standards and organizational needs.

Federal law requires companies to institute fraud prevention and deterrence programs or face increased liability if a fraud is discovered within the company. The Treadway Report, on which the legislation was based, said the key to any program was demonstrating "due diligence" in deterrence and prevention efforts. Due diligence is defined by the following characteristics:

- The organization must have established compliance standards and procedures to be followed by its employees and other agents.
- Specific individuals must be assigned to supervise compliance.
- The organization must avoid placing discretionary authority on those with a known propensity for illegal activities.
- The organization must communicate its policies aggressively, through required training or other media, such as printed or videotaped materials made widely available.
- The organization must monitor compliance through methods such as auditing systems and violation reporting systems.
- Policies must be enforced consistently by treating offenses with disciplinary actions appropriate to the offense.
- Once an offense has been detected, the organization must have taken reasonable steps to respond appropriately and to prevent future offenses through actions such as modification of existing practices.

Ethics Program Development

Identifying key organizational characteristics and issues is a start to development of an ethics program. These items include:

- Understanding why good people can commit unethical acts.
- Defining current as well as desired organizational values.
- Determining if organizational values have been properly communicated.
- Producing written ethics policies, procedures, or structures.
- Ascertaining how board members, stockholders, management, employees, and any other pertinent members of the organization define success.
- Determining if ethics is a leadership issue in the organization.

A 1999 study by the Conference Board demonstrated that the reasons behind ethics codes are markedly different in different cultures. Codes dominated by considerations of bottom-line success turn out to be far more popular in the U.S. than elsewhere. The study showed that 64% of all U.S. codes are dominated by self-interested or "instrumental" motives, while 60% of European codes were dominated by "values" concerns.

Twelve Key Components of Ethics Programs

The following 12 components are recommended for any ethics program:

1. Focus on ethical leadership.
2. Vision statement.
3. Values statement.
4. Code of ethics.
5. Designated ethics official.
6. Ethics task force or committee.
7. Ethics communication strategy.
8. Ethics training.
9. Ethics help and fraud report telephone line.
10. Ethical behavior rewards and sanctions.
11. Comprehensive system to monitor and track ethics data.

12. Periodic evaluation of ethics efforts and data.

The Ethics Officer

The Ethics Resource Center, an independent organization formed in 1992 to help individuals and institutions improve their ethical practices, defines an ethics officer as "someone who provides leadership and company-wide strategies to effectively integrate the corporation's ethics and compliance program and its values with all aspects of the company's operations, stakeholders, and the communities in which it operates."

The U.S. government's Defense Industry Initiative on Business Ethics and Conduct gave rise to the ethics officer position in the early 1980's, after a series of scandals concerning how the defense industry handled its contracts with the federal government.

The Ethics Officer Association (EOA), founded in 1992, is the professional association for managers of ethics, compliance, and business conduct programs. Current EOA membership includes members of over 720 firms in manufacturing and service industries.

Sources:
Chordas, L. "Code of Ethics; Brief Article." *Best's Review,* March 1, 2001.

Henderson, B. *fraudabc.com.* San Jose: iUniversity Press, 2001.

Khera, I. "Business Ethics, East vs. West: Myths and Realities." *Journal of Business Ethics,* March 2001.

"Survey—Mastering Management: Adding Corporate Ethics to the Bottom Line." *Financial Times (London),* November 13, 2000.

Related Entries:

ATTITUDES TOWARD AND PERCEPTIONS OF FRAUD
BEHAVIORAL THEORY OF FRAUD
CAUSES OF FRAUD
COSO
TONE AT THE TOP

EXPENSE REIMBURSEMENT SCHEMES

Expense reimbursement schemes are the most common forms of occupational fraud and abuse. The four most common types of expense schemes are mischaracterized expenses, overstated expenses, fictitious expenses, and multiple reimbursements.

Mischaracterized Expenses

Because companies only cover certain expenses, employees may disguise an illegitimate expense as one that is reimbursable. Examples of mischaracterized expenses include claiming personal travel as a business trip and listing dinner with a friend as "business development." A common element to mischaracterized expense schemes is the failure to submit detailed expense reports.

Overstated Expenses

Some employees overstate the cost of actual business expenses. If the company does not require documentation, the person can simply lie; but if necessary, the person may alter receipts and other documents to support the bogus claim. Another method of overstatement involves the "overpurchasing" of business expenses. For example, an employee buys an airline ticket at a discount price with his own money. Later, the employee buys another, more expensive, ticket and charges the ticket to his expense account. Once the expense report is filed, the employee returns the second ticket for a refund, and uses the first (less expensive) ticket for the travel.

Some overstatement schemes are perpetrated by workers who process expense reports—the person conspires with other employees or simply overstates the reimbursement and pockets the difference. Supervisors may encourage employees to overstate expenses as a way of supplementing their salary.

Fictitious Expenses

In a fictitious expense scheme, the employee invents a purchase and files for reimbursement, creating bogus support documents if necessary. Personal computers can create realistic-looking counterfeit receipts. Other counterfeiting strategies include changing calculator tapes, cutting and pasting of old receipts, and engaging professional printers. Blank receipts may be obtained from vendors or from other employees.

Multiple Reimbursements

Multiple reimbursements, the submission of a single expense several times, is the least common expense scheme because most companies track the documentation used to support reimbursements. This strategy works only in companies with extremely lax controls.

Detection of Expense Schemes

A historical comparison of expense accounts compares the balance expended in the current period with earlier periods. Provided the situational factors are similar, the comparison may reveal abuse. Comparing budgeted expenses with actual payments may also reveal inordinate spikes in disbursements.

The best expense scheme detection method is a detailed review of employee expense reimbursements, using a calendar and a copy of the employee's schedule. The examiner should be familiar with the travel and entertainment policies of the company. Detailed expense reports should require the following information:

- Receipts or other support documentation.
- Explanation of the expense including specific business purpose.
- Time period expense occurred.
- Place of expenditure.
- Amount.

Case Study $60,000 Worth of Wine

Barclays Capital fired five investment bankers in 2002 for charging $60,000 worth of wine to the company. At a London dinner, the executives consumed several top-shelf bottles, including a 1947 Chateau Petrus, costing about $18,000 and a bottle of 1945 Chateau Petrus for $17,000. The executives paid the bill themselves, and then later tried to report some of the expenditure as a client expense.

The party spent so lavishly on drinks that the restaurant management included the meal for free. Besides the bottles mentioned, the executives also consumed a Chateau Petrus, 1946; a 1984 Le Montrachet; two Kronenberg beers; six glasses of Champagne;

one bottle of juice; 10 bottles of water; a pack of cigarettes; and a 100-year-old bottle of Chateau d'Yquem dessert wine.

Source: Kapner, S. "Five Bankers Fired." *The New York Times,* February 26, 2002.

Related Entries:

FRAUDULENT DISBURSEMENTS

OCCUPATIONAL FRAUD AND ABUSE

EXPORT DIVERSION

Export diversion is committed by acquiring goods from a manufacturer under certain market provisions and then violating those provisions by selling the goods in an unapproved market. It is a form of corporate crime committed by one business against another.

Export diversion is often part of a money-laundering scheme. It is also a fundraising tool used by terrorist organizations. Generally the act involves goods which are sold to countries in the developing world at a price lower than the U.S. market price. The goods are then resold to conspirators in the U.S. or other developed markets.

Export Diversion Illustrated

A U.S. based Big Business sells its Big-Stuff for $10 in the U.S. The same Big-Stuff is sold in developing countries at $5 a piece. Theoretically the company has "stripped" the normal distribution, advertising, and promotional costs from the cost of goods sold, allowing the cheaper price.

In an export diversion scheme, a company in Mozambique—Mozambique Incorporated—purchases Big-Stuff from the U.S. at a discount. But the contract states that the Big-Stuff can only be sold in Mozambique. At Mozambique's request, the goods are shipped to Rotterdam, where accomplices put the Big-Stuff in new containers. The Big-Stuff is then shipped back to the U.S. as "U.S. Goods Returned." This allows Mozambique to avoid customs duties. After clearing customs, the Big-Stuff is received by an importer conspiring with Mozambique Incorporated. The importer sells the Big-

Stuff to a wholesaler—who may or may not be a co-conspirator—at U.S. prices, perhaps $8.25 for a $10 item.

There are at least two red flags in these transactions that should trigger examination:

- The money for the original transaction may originate in a region known for money laundering and liberal banking regulations, such as Panama, Hong Kong, Colombia, or Pakistan, and is then routed through banks in the Caribbean or Switzerland.
- The goods are shipped to someplace other than the buyer's location. In the example, the goods were shipped to Rotterdam. Tracking by Big Business should have demanded confirmation of the goods being received by Mozambique.

Avoiding Export Diversion

There are a number of sources available from the U.S. government and private organizations to help prevent and deter export diversion. These include:

- Bureau of Export Administration's Denied Persons List: www.bxa.doc.gov/DPL/Default.shtm
- U.S. Treasury Office of Foreign Assets: www.treas.gov/ofac.
- Trade Compass: www.tradecompass.com

Source:
"Terrorist Links to Commercial Fraud in the U.S." *The White-Collar Crime Fighter,* December 2001.

FALSE OR DECEPTIVE ADVERTISING

The Federal Trade Commission (FTC) defines deceptive advertising as "a representation, omission, act, or practice that is likely to mislead consumers acting reasonably under the circumstances." Exaggeration ("we are as good as it gets") and figurative language ("packed by the Green Giant") are acceptable; courts have regarded these and other sales techniques as separate from the factual claims attached to the product. To be judged deceptive, the claim must be factual in nature and material to the purchasing process. From the Commission's standpoint, a materially deceptive advertisement presents something as fact which is likely to affect consumers' "choice of, or conduct regarding, a product."

Common sense dictates most decisions about false advertising. The FTC considers the "net impression" conveyed to consumers: "the entire mosaic, rather than each tile separately." The wording of an ad may be literally truthful, but the net impression may still be misleading. Accurate information in the text may not remedy a misleading impression created by a headline because reasonable consumers may glance only at the headline. Written disclosures in fine print or legalistic disclaimers too complex for consumers may be insufficient to correct a misleading impression. An ad may be deceptive by omission if it fails to disclose qualifying information necessary to prevent consumers from being misled. Qualifying disclosures must be legible and understandable.

Viral or Underground Marketing

Because media saturation has made it harder to reach people between the ages of 12 and 34, some advertisers have begun practicing viral, or underground, marketing. Companies recruit attractive people from the target demographic group to promote the product. These stealth agents may be paid to smoke a particular cigarette, make conversation about the cigarette's taste in public, and leave cigarette packs in bars. In 1999, Ford Motor Company loaned its new Focus model to 120 "key influencers" in five major markets. Alcohol companies sometimes pay operatives to order and promote particular brands at trendy bars.

Consumer advocates say that viral marketing is deceptive. Jeff Chester of the Center for Media Education has called the operatives "commercial kamikazes… They're not disclosing that they have received financial remuneration to promote and target products, and that is inherently deceptive."

Case Study—A Sampler of Deceptive Advertising

Some notable cases of deceptive advertising include:

- Rise shaving cream—A television commercial showed a man shaving with "ordinary" product that quickly lost its body, and then again with Rise, which remained "moist and creamy." In fact the "ordinary" product was treated with an aerosol mixture that caused it to dry out and shrink.

- Campbell's Chunky Soup—a bowl of soup was filled with marbles and the chunks of meat forced to the top, making the soup appear "chunkier" than it was.
- Anacin—the pain reliever's claims that it was stronger than aspirin, was activated within 22 seconds, and relieved nervous tension, stress, and depression were found wanting by the FTC.
- Beech-Nut Apple Juice for Children—the Beech-Nut Corporation sold an apple juice product aimed at children, labeled "100 percent juice" and "no sugar added," that contained little or no juice. The mixture contained beet sugar, cane sugar, corn syrup, and caramel coloring dissolved in water.

Case Study—The Federal Trade Commission and Phone Advertising

A policy statement by the FTC and the Federal Communications Commission offered a number of examples of deception in the advertising of long-distance service.

- The headline of a direct mail ad for a dial-around service reads, "All day. All night. All calls. 10 cents a minute." In fact, the rate is applicable only for state-to-state calls after 7:00 p.m. and on weekends. Even an otherwise prominent disclosure to that effect will likely not be sufficient considering that the disclosure directly contradicts the express, and false, representations in the headline.
- An advertisement says that long-distance calls cost 10 cents a minute. In fact, that rate is only available if customers pay a $5.95 monthly fee. Because the imposition of the monthly fee would significantly increase the consumer's per-minute charge, the advertiser's failure to clearly and conspicuously disclose the monthly fee in the advertisement would likely be deceptive.
- A company advertises "all calls up to 20 minutes for only $1.00," but charges 10 cents for each additional minute. Consumers are likely to be misled by the affirmative claim in the absence of a disclosure about the significantly higher rate after 20 minutes. Because many consumers will make calls that last longer than 20 minutes, the cost of each minute beyond the first 20 minutes' duration of a call is information that likely would be material to consumers considering whether to use the service. Thus, the advertiser's failure to clearly and conspicuously disclose in the

ad the per-minute rate for calls longer than the initial calling period would likely be deceptive.

- In an advertisement in a daily newspaper, an advertiser conveys the message that its rates are the lowest, using a chart that compares its per-minute rate to the rates offered by two competitors. The stated rates of one of the competitors are three months old, and the stated rate of the other is eight months old. By representing the competitors' rates, the advertiser is implying that those rates are reasonably current. If the information upon which the ad is based is outdated and the rates have changed materially, the ad would likely be deceptive. However, if the advertiser verified the competitor's rate in January—for an ad running in February—and clearly and conspicuously discloses that the competitor's rate was being used in January, the disclosure is likely to be sufficient to avoid deception.

Source:
"Federal Communications Commission. Joint FCC/FTC Policy Statement: For the Advertising of Dial-Around and Other Long-Distance Services to Consumers." *Federal News Service,* March 1, 2000.

Related Entry:
CONSUMER FRAUD

FICTITIOUS REVENUES

A form of financial statement fraud, fictitious or fabricated revenues involve the recording of goods or services sales that did not occur. Fictitious sales most often involve fake or phantom customers, but can also involve legitimate customers. For example, a fictitious invoice can be prepared for a legitimate customer although the goods are not delivered or the services not rendered. Often, at the beginning of the next accounting period, the sale is reversed, concealing the fraud. Another method is to utilize legitimate customers and artificially inflate or alter invoices reflecting higher amounts or quantities than actually sold.

An example of a sample entry from this type of case is detailed below. A fictional entry is made to record a purchase of fixed assets. This entry debits fixed assets for the amount of the alleged purchase and the credit is to cash for the payment:

Date	Description	Ref.	Debit	Credit
10/01/06	Fixed Assets	104	350,000	
	Cash	101		350,000

A fictitious sales entry is then made for the same amount as the false purchase, debiting accounts receivable, and crediting the sales account. To cover the fictitious sale, the cash outflow that supposedly covered the purchase of assets is returned as payment on the receivable account:

Date	Description	Ref.	Debit	Credit
10/01/06	Accounts Rec	120	350,000	
	Sales	400		350,000
10/15/06	Cash	101	350,000	
	Accounts Rec	120		350,000

The result of the completely fabricated sequence of events is an increase in both company assets and yearly revenue.

Conditional Sales and Consignment Sales

Conditional sales are contingent on certain terms that must be met before the sale can properly be recorded. Perhaps a company's contract requires that its software must be installed, customized, and automated before the customer pays. If the company records the sale as soon as the customer takes possession (before the conditions are met), the revenue has been fraudulently recognized.

A consignment sale is not a completed sale with respect to the revenue recognition by the seller until such time as the ultimate end-user (purchaser) accepts the product. Perhaps a company offers trial versions of a product, which customers can accept or reject—but records the trial version as a completed sale.

Misrecording Discounts and Returns

There are two basic schemes that increase revenues indirectly: failing to record discounts on sales, and failing to record returns as a reduction of gross sales. Returns and allowances can be misclassified as expenses rather than reductions to gross sales. At the very least this is a mismatching of the sales revenue and the returned merchandise.

Related Entries:

FINANCIAL STATEMENT FRAUD

OCCUPATIONAL FRAUD AND ABUSE

FINANCIAL INSTITUTION FRAUD (BANK FRAUD)

Financial institution fraud is committed against financial institutions by insiders, consumers, businesses, and other institutions.

Fraud is more likely to occur in new accounts than established ones. Accounts are opened with false identifications. New business accounts are opened using checks stolen from a legitimate business, or an individual opens a personal account with checks in other people's names.

In the 1980's and early 1990's, most of the fraud reported by financial institutions (approximately 60%) was committed by insiders. Since then, external fraud schemes have replaced insider abuse as the dominant problem confronting financial institutions, with 60% or more fraudulent acts committed by outsiders.

The FBI continues to work to protect our nation's financial system. Through Fiscal Year 2005, cases pursued by the FBI resulted in 497 indictments and 317 convictions of corporate criminals. Numerous cases are pending plea agreements and trials. From July 1, 2002 through March 31, 2005, accomplishments regarding Corporate Fraud cases were as follows: $2.2 billion in Restitutions, $34.6 million in Recoveries, $79.1 million in Fines, and $27.9 million in Seizures. As Corporate Fraud statistical accomplishments were not provided before July 1, 2002, the following statistical accomplishments are reflective of this time frame through Second Quarter, Fiscal Year 2005.

Select corporate fraud investigations conducted by the FBI throughout Fiscal Year 2004 include Enron, HealthSouth, Cendant Corporation, Credit Suisse First Boston, Computer Associates International, WorldCom, Imclone, Royal Ahold, Peregrine Systems, and America On-Line. The above-highlighted ten investigations have resulted in 120 indictments and 79 convictions.

Since 1996, the FBI received 268,536 Suspicious Activity Reports (SARs) for criminal activity related to the crimes previously listed. These fraudulent activities accounted for 47% of the 569,294 SARs filed by U.S. financial institutions (excluding Bank Secrecy Act violations), and equaled approximately $8 billion in losses.

Financial Institution Schemes

- *Check fraud* and *credit card* fraud are usually committed by outsiders. The checks and credit cards are counterfeited or obtained improperly. Checks can be used for kiting. Because institutions are responsible for all but the first $50 of losses due to theft, consumers may sell their cards to organized crime rings and wait a period before reporting the theft.
- *Embezzlement* is defined as the fraudulent appropriation of money or property by a person to whom it has been lawfully entrusted (or to whom lawful possession was given). Embezzlement involves a breach of trust, although it is not necessary to show a fiduciary relationship between the parties, which can be committed by:
  - False accounting entries to the general ledger, crediting one's own accounts, or covering up thefts from customer accounts.
  - Unauthorized withdrawals from customer accounts.
  - Cash stolen/counterfeit items for outside accomplices.
  - Disbursement of bank funds from expense accounts to pay personal bills.
  - Theft of physical materials such as office equipment, building materials, and furnishings by an employee.
  - Transferring funds from dormant accounts into one's own accounts.
  - Disbursals from bank cash to self or accomplices.
  - Stealing, selling, or using collateral or repossessed property for one's self or accomplices.
- *Misapplication* often accompanies embezzlement, but is a separate and distinct offense. Misapplication is the wrongful taking or conversion of another's property for the benefit of someone else.
- *Loan fraud schemes* often involve real estate lending and collusion between insiders and outsiders. Loan fraud represents the highest risk area for financial institutions,

because the dollar amounts are usually large. Insiders make loans to nonexistent borrowers, sometimes using an accomplice who kicks back part of the funds; applications contain false information; collateral is falsified, its value exaggerated, or pledged for more than debt; loan limits are exceeded; insiders create agreements in which they buy and sell each other's loans as a way of concealing bad loans from regulators; loans are made contingent on a third-party making large deposits offered to the bank; and other acts.

- *Leasing fraud schemes* are perpetrated by leasing companies, which receive underwriting from banks on phony leases. Perpetrators use fake IDs, stolen IDs, and sometimes pay accomplices for IDs that allow them to process the leases and collect funds from the institution.
- Banks and other institutions are sometimes victimized by *advance fee fraud*, which works much like advance-fee scams do against consumers. Bank officers, desperate for cash, agree to pay an up-front finder's fee to a person claiming to have access to the money. The money may not ever appear, or the funds may be from illicit sources. Signs of advance fee fraud include the use of highly restrictive nondisclosure agreements and middlemen who facilitate transactions without participating.
- *Loan brokering*, a variation of the advanced fee scheme, applies to either packages of individual residential (consumer) loans or single commercial loans. In some cases the purchaser participates in the loan but does not purchase the entire loan. The fraud schemes associated with brokered or participated loans generally involve selling phony loans (packages) or selling participations in loans that have not been properly underwritten.
- Most *letter-of-credit* frauds arise from foreign trade and contracting. Perpetrators convince banks to lend them funds based on forged or fraudulently obtained letters of credit. These frauds are sometimes called "prime bank instrument" frauds, because perpetrators represent their vouchers as issued by the world's most prominent, or "prime" banks. (*See* COUNTERFEIT FINANCIAL INSTRUMENTS.)
- Insiders sell *account information* to organized rings or use the information themselves. Account information resides in many forms, such as 24-hour customer operators, online systems, printed documents, credit card information, and so on.

- *Automatic Teller Machine schemes* include the theft of cards, PIN numbers, and account codes, and employee manipulation of ATM records, counterfeiting cards, and machines.

Sources:
Association of Certified Fraud Examiners. *Financial Institution Fraud*, 2000.

Federal Bureau of Investigation: www.fbi.gov/pressrel/pressrel04/fif2003.htm

Related Entries:

BCCI
CHECK FRAUD
CREDIT CARD AND DEBIT CARD FRAUD
DAIWA BANK
DEMAND DRAFT FRAUD
DE ANGELIS, TINO
LEASING FRAUD
LEESON, NICK
LOAN FRAUD
MERCHANT PROCESSING FRAUD
MORTGAGE FRAUD
WIRE TRANSFER FRAUD

FINANCIAL PROFILE

Most fraud investigations require a detailed understanding of an individual or organizational suspect's finances. This information is assembled into a report known as a financial profile. The four components of a financial profile are assets, liabilities, sources of funds, and expenditures.

Assets

Typical assets include residences, real estate, bank accounts, stocks and bonds, automobiles, cash, jewelry, clothing, collectibles, pensions, furnishings, and boats or other recreational craft.

Liabilities

Typical liabilities include mortgages, secured and unsecured loans, lines of credit, credit cards and credit accounts, accounts payable, taxes and other bills, alimony, and child support. It is particularly important when examining liabilities to note the initiation date of each liability and details of payments made against the debts.

Sources of Funds

Typical sources of funds include salary, gifts, rental income, dividends, interest, sale of assets, insurance proceeds, commissions and fees, awards, inheritances, disability payments, and government payments.

Expenditures

Typical expenditures include rent and mortgage, health costs, interest payments, credit cards, car loans, travel, clothing, utilities, food, insurance, and travel.

Source: *Financial Investigations*. IRS Publication, 1714.

Related Entries:

CASH FLOW ANALYSIS
NET WORTH ANALYSIS

FINANCIAL STATEMENT FRAUD

Intentionally publishing false information in any portion of a financial statement is fraud. Typically, management commits these frauds in order to enhance the economic appearance of the company. Usually they are accounting frauds, performed by either overstating revenues or understating liabilities. Concealing lawsuits and liability issues are also acts of financial statement fraud.

Members of management may benefit directly from the fraud by selling stock, receiving performance bonuses, or by using the false report to conceal other illegal acts. Management benefits indirectly from financial statement fraud when the tactic is used to obtain financing on a company's behalf, or to inflate the selling price of a company.

Regulating public companies, the SEC brings as many as 100 enforcement actions involving financial statement fraud each year, representing about 20% to 25% of its caseload. The commission itself must first approve a formal investigation; then staffers use legal subpoena power to compel employees, ex-employees, and customers to speak.

Committing Financial Statement Fraud

Financial statements for most businesses are made fraudulent in two ways:

- *Overstating assets or revenue*: recording assets that don't exist; valuing assets above market value; recording revenues from bogus sources; inflating revenues from legitimate sources.
- *Understating liabilities and expenses*: omitting costs or obligations entirely; understating costs or obligations; forestalling the recognition of expenses through improper accounting.

The situation is reversed for companies that service government contracts. This is because the contracts often allow funds to be dispersed if a company can demonstrate the need for more equipment or revenues, or that costs are greater than anticipated. For government business, financial statement fraud is committed by understating assets and revenues, or overstating liabilities and expenses.

Five Financial Statement Schemes

The five classifications of financial statement schemes are:

ASSET VALUATION, IMPROPER; DISCLOSURES, IMPROPER; FICTITIOUS REVENUES; LIABILITIES AND EXPENSES, CONCEALED;

AND REVENUE RECOGNITION, IMPROPER. These are each covered in separate entries.

Tax Returns and Financial Statement Fraud

Federal and state tax returns are good sources of additional and comparative information on the operations of the business. A complete review and comparison to the financial statement may provide information unknown to the lender or disclose unexplained discrepancies. Again, the lack of properly prepared or timely filed tax returns may be a method of stalling or not providing the required information. Most perpetrators of fraud are reluctant to continue the deception and falsify a tax return. Year-after-year extensions and filing of the tax returns on the last possible date could be ploys to cover up financial statement and tax return differences.

Corporate Tax Return Areas for Review

Form 1120, *U.S. Corporation Income Tax Return*, requires a breakdown of income into dividends, interest, rents, royalties, capital gains, and sale of business assets. Page 2, Schedule E, shows the compensation of officers, percentage of time devoted to the business, and stock ownership.

Answers to questions on Page 3, Schedule K, may reveal stock ownership or other corporate affiliations, dividend payments, foreign stock or bank account ownership, foreign owners, and information about NOL (net operating loss). Schedule L, balance sheets, on Page 4 is the book version over two years. Comparison to the financial statements could show unknown changes or differences, provide more detail on types of assets or liabilities, and reveal officer loans.

Schedule M-1, *Reconciliation of Income (Loss) per Books with Income per Return,* will detail income or expense differences. Finally, Schedule M-2, *Analysis of Unappropriated Retained Earnings per Books*, reveals distributions of cash, stock, or properties.

Financial Statement Fraud on the Increase

During the years 1997 to 2002, Internet and computer-related startups helped drive the Dow Jones above 10,000 for the first time. More and more publicly traded companies were forced to restate their earnings and charged with some form of financial statement fraud.

The COSO Study on Financial Statement Fraud

In 1999, the Committee of Sponsoring Organizations for the Treadway Commission (COSO) published a follow-up study to its 1987 report. The new report, entitled *Fraudulent Financial Reporting: 1987-1997, An Analysis of U.S. Public Companies*, examined a random sample of 204 financial statement fraud cases that were the subject of SEC enforcement.

- The most common methods used to misstate financial statement fraud were improper revenue recognition, overstatement of assets, and the understatement of expenses, in that order. With respect to revenue frauds, recording fictitious revenues was the most common and recording revenues prematurely was the second most common. With respect to overstating assets, overstating existing assets was most common, recording fictitious assets or assets not owned was second most common, and capitalizing items that should have been expensed was third most common.
- The assets most often misstated were accounts receivable, inventory, property, equipment, loans/notes receivable, cash, investments, patents, and natural resources, in that order.
- The mean cumulative financial statement misstatement was $25 million while the median cumulative misstatement was $4.1 million; however, the mean was disproportionally increased by several very large frauds.
- The chief executive officer (CEO) was the person most often named as the perpetrator (72% of cases). Other positions, in descending order, were chief financial officer (CFO), controller, chief operating officer, other vice presidents, members of the board of directors, and lower level personnel. In 29% of the cases, the external auditor was also named in the enforcement action.

- Most companies either had no audit committee or a committee that met less than twice per year.
- The boards of directors were generally insiders or "gray" directors (outsiders with special ties to the company or management) with significant equity ownership and apparently little experience. In nearly 40% of the companies, the proxy provided evidence of family relationships among the officers and/or directors. The founder was on the board or the original CEO/President was still in place in nearly half of the companies. In nearly 20%, there was evidence of officers holding incompatible job functions such as CEO and CFO.
- Pressures of financial strain or distress may have been an incentive for some companies to commit fraud. The lowest quartile of companies indicate that they were in a net loss position, and the median company had a net income of only $175,000 in the year preceding the first year of the fraud period. Some companies were experiencing downward trends in net income in the preceding periods, while others were experiencing upward trends. This means that some companies may have committed fraud to reverse a downward spiral or to preserve an upward trend for others.
- The majority of companies were relatively small. The typical size ranged well below $100 million in total assets. Seventy-eight percent were not listed on the New York or American Stock Exchanges.
- Most frauds were not isolated to a single period. Most overlapped at least two fiscal periods. The average fraud period extended over 23.7 months. Only 14% of the sample companies engaged in fraud fewer than 12 months.

The report also gives some excellent advice to auditors on what they can do to prevent such frauds. Among the recommendations are the following:

- The relatively small size of the companies suggests that they may be unwilling or unable to implement cost-effective internal controls. Auditors need to challenge management to ensure that a baseline of internal control is present.

- Given that some companies experienced financial strain in the periods preceding the fraud, auditors need to monitor an organization's going-concern status, especially with new clients.
- Because frauds so often run over many reporting periods, auditors need to consider interim reviews of quarterly financial statements as well as the possible benefits of continuous auditing strategies.
- Auditors need to consider and test internal controls related to transaction cutoff and asset valuation. They should design testing procedures to reduce audit risks to an acceptable level. Procedures affecting transaction cut-off, transaction terms, and account valuation for end-of-period accounts and transactions may be particularly pertinent.
- Companies with weak boards and audit committees present an audit challenge. Auditors should assess the substance and quality of client boards and be alert for boards dominated by insiders or others with strong ties to the company or its management.

Fraudulent Financial Statement Red Flags

In a survey of large accounting firm auditors, respondents said management's attitudes were more important warning signs of fraud than situational factors.

Auditors' Ranking	Fraud Warning Signs
1.	Managers have lied to the auditors or have been overly evasive in response to audit inquiries.
2.	The auditor's experience with management indicates a degree of dishonesty.
3.	Management places undue emphasis on meeting earnings projections or other quantitative targets.
4.	Management has engaged in frequent disputes with auditors, particularly about aggressive application of accounting principles that increase earnings.
5.	The client has engaged in opinion shopping.
6.	Management's attitude toward financial reporting

	is unduly aggressive.
7.	The client has a weak control environment.
8.	A substantial portion of management compensation depends on meeting quantified targets.
9.	Management displays significant disrespect for regulatory bodies.
10.	Management's operating and financial decisions are dominated by a single person or a few persons acting in concert.
11.	Client managers display a hostile attitude toward the auditors.
12.	Management displays a propensity to take undue risks.
13.5	There are frequent and significant transactions that are difficult to audit.
13.5	Key managers are considered highly unreasonable.
15.	The client's organization is decentralized without adequate monitoring.
16.	Management and/or key accounting personnel turnover is high.
17.	Client personnel display significant resentment of authority.
18.	Management places undue pressure on the auditors, particularly through the fee structure or the imposition of unreasonable deadlines.
19.	The client's profitability is inadequate or inconsistent relative to its industry.
20.	The client is confronted with adverse legal circumstances.
21.	Management exhibits undue concern with the need to maintain or improve the image/reputation of the entity.
22.	There are adverse conditions in the client's industry or external environment.
23.	Accounting personnel exhibit inexperience or laxity in performing their duties.
24.	The client entered into one or a few specific transactions that have a material effect on the financial statements.

25.	Client management is inexperienced.
26.5	The client is in a period of rapid growth.
26.5	This is a new client with no prior audit history or insufficient information from the predecessor auditor.
28.	The client is subject to significant contractual commitments.
29.	The client's operating results are highly sensitive to economic factors (inflation, interest rates, unemployment, etc.).
30.	The client recently entered into a significant number of acquisition transactions.

Heiman-Hoffman, Morgan, and Patton, "The Warning Signs of Fraudulent Financial Reporting," *The Journal of Accountancy*, October 1996.

Auditors and Fraudulent Financial Reporting

A study by Bryan Church et al., asked 127 internal auditors from 38 companies to examine a set of accounts that contained an unexpected fluctuation in operating income. The analysis found that auditors were more likely to test for fraud when income *surpassed* expectations than they were when income fell short. Other factors that auditors considered red flags when combined with excessive income were strict debt covenants and earnings-based compensation plans for management; these factors were seen as providing motive for the inflation of figures.

Using Fuzzy Numbers to Assess the Risk of Financial Statement Fraud

Fraud examiners, auditors, and other analysts assess the risk of financial statement fraud by noting red flags and pursuing those indicators. Red flag indicators are usually measured in absolute terms; for example, queries are designed to be answered as either yes or no. Researchers Deshmukh and Romine have criticized this approach, arguing that many factors, such as "weak internal controls," cannot be measured in absolute terms. The state of controls may vary from weak to moderate to excellent.

Traditional efforts compare the frequency of red flags in known fraud cases and known fraud-free cases to establish the risk-assessment scale. Deshmukh and Romine advocate using a technique known as "fuzzy numbers" to assess the risk of financial statement fraud and other management frauds. Fuzzy number theory allows for measuring risks along a continuum. For example, traditional methods set "strong internal controls" as those that theoretically capture 90% of irregularities, so everything above 90% is "strong" and everything below is "weak." Fuzzy number theory measures a range of possible values.

As summarized by Henderson, fuzzy number analysis first establishes a level of possibility, confidence, or expectation in at least three points—the maximum, the minimum, and the most likely frequency of occurrence. Examiners collect data on the target organization and input the data into a fuzzy-number spreadsheet for analysis. Software designed for fuzzy numbers, such as FuziCalc for Windows, is commercially available.

Preventing Financial Statement Fraud

According to Cressey's Fraud Triangle, people commit fraud when they are under financial or social pressure, have an opportunity to gain funds undetected, and can rationalize their actions. Any attempt to prevent financial statement fraud should focus on these three factors.

1. Reduce the Situational Pressures that Encourage Statement Fraud

Avoid setting unachievable financial goals.
Eliminate external pressures that might tempt accounting personnel to prepare fraudulent financial statements.
Remove operational obstacles blocking effective financial performance such as working capital restraints, excess production volume, or inventory restraints.
Establish clear and uniform accounting procedures with no exception clauses.

2. Reduce the Opportunity to Commit

Maintain accurate and complete internal accounting records.
Carefully monitor the business transactions and interpersonal

relationships of suppliers, buyers, purchasing agents, sales representatives, and others who interface in the transactions between financial units.
Establish a physical security system to secure company assets, including finished goods, cash, capital equipment, tools, and other valuable items.
Divide important functions between employees, separating total control of one area.
Maintain accurate personnel records including background checks on new employees.
Encourage strong supervisory and leadership relationships within groups to ensure enforcement of accounting procedures.

3. Reduce Rationalization of Fraud—Strengthen Employee Personal Integrity

Managers must promote honesty by example. Dishonest acts by management, even if they are directed at targets outside the organization, create a dishonest environment that can be used to rationalize other illicit business activities by employees or externals.
Honest and dishonest behavior should be defined in company policies. Organizational accounting policies should address any questionable or controversial areas in accounting procedures.
Consequences for violating rules and provisions for punishment of violators should be written and prominently communicated.

Sources:

Church, B., et al. "Detection of Fraudulent Financial Reporting." *Auditing: A Journal of Practice and Theory,* March 2001.

Heiman-Hoffman, Morgan, and Patton, "The Warning Signs of Fraudulent Financial Reporting," *The Journal of Accountancy*, October 1996.

Henderson, B. *fraudabc.com.* San Jose: iUniversity Press, 2001.

Related Entries:

ADELPHIA

ANTAR, EDDIE
ASSET VALUATION, IMPROPER
AUDITING FOR FRAUD
BCCI
CENDANT CORPORATION
COSO
DISCLOSURES, IMPROPER
DYNEGY, INC.
ENRON
FICTITIOUS REVENUES
FINANCIAL STATEMENT FRAUD, ANALYSIS OF STATEMENTS
FINANCIAL STATEMENTS
KREUGER, IVAR
LIABILITIES AND EXPENSES, CONCEALED
MINKOW, BARRY
OCCUPATIONAL FRAUD AND ABUSE
PARMALAT
SARBANES-OXLEY ACT
TRIPPET, ROBERT
WORLDCOM

FINANCIAL STATEMENT FRAUD, ANALYSIS OF STATEMENTS

Percentage Analysis

There are traditionally two methods of percentage analysis of financial statements. *Vertical analysis* is a technique for analyzing the relationships between the items on an income statement, balance sheet, or statement of cash flows by expressing components as percentages. This method is often referred to as "common sizing" financial statements. In the vertical analysis of an income statement, net sales is assigned 100%; for a balance sheet, total assets is assigned 100% on the asset side; and total liabilities and equity is expressed as 100%. All other items in each of the sections are expressed as a percentage of these numbers.

Horizontal analysis is a technique for analyzing the percentage change in individual financial statement items from one year to the next. The first period in the analysis is considered the base, and the changes to subsequent periods are computed as a percentage of the base period. Like vertical analysis, this technique will not work for small, immaterial frauds.

The following is an example of financial statements that are analyzed by both horizontal and vertical analysis:

BALANCE SHEET	Vertical Analysis				Horizontal Analysis	
	Year One		Year Two		Change	%Change
Assets						
Current Assets						
Cash	45,000	14%	15,000	4%	(30,000)	-67%
Accts Receivable	150,000	45%	200,000	47%	50,000	33%
Inventory	75,000	23%	150,000	35%	75,000	100%
Fixed Assets (net)	60,000	18%	60,000	14%	-	0%
Total	330,000	100%	425,000	100%	95,000	29%
Acc'ts Payable	95,000	29%	215,000	51%	120,000	126%
Long-term Debt	60,000	18%	60,000	14%	-	0%
Stockholder's Equity					-	
Common Stock	25,000	8%	25,000	6%	-	0%
Paid-in Capital	75,000	23%	75,000	18%	-	0%
Retained Earnings	75,000	23%	50,000	12%	(25,000)	-33%
Total	330,000	100%	425,000	100%	95,000	29%

INCOME STATEMENT	Vertical Analysis				Horizontal Analysis	
	Year One		Year Two		Change	%Change
Net Sales	250,000	100%	450,000	100%	200,000	80%
Cost of Goods Sold	125,000	50%	300,000	67%	175,000	140%
Gross Margin	125,000	50%	150,000	33%	25,000	20%
Operating Expenses						
Selling Expenses	50,000	20%	75,000	17%	25,000	50%
Administrative Expenses	60,000	24%	100,000	22%	40,000	67%
Net Income	15,000	6%	(25,000)	-6%	(40,000)	-267%

Additional Information		
Average Net Receivables	155,000	210,000
Average Inventory	65,000	130,000
Average Assets	330,000	425,000

Vertical Analysis Discussion

Vertical analysis is the expression of the relationship or percentage of component part items to a specific base item. In the above example, vertical analysis of the income statement includes total sales as the base amount, and all other items are then analyzed as a percentage of that total. Vertical analysis emphasizes the relationship of statement items within each accounting period. These relationships can be used with historical averages to determine statement anomalies.

In the above example, we can observe that accounts payable is 29% of total liabilities. Historically we may find that this account averages slightly over 25%. In year two, accounts payable total rose to 51%. Although the change in the account total may be explainable through a correlation with a rise in sales, this significant rise might be a starting point in a fraud examination. Source documents should be examined to determine the rise in this percentage. With this type of examination, fraudulent activity may be detected. The same type of change can be seen as selling expenses decline as a part of sales in year two from 20% to 17%. Again, this change may be explainable with higher volume sales or another bona fide explanation. But close examination may possibly point a fraud examiner to uncover fictitious sales, since there was not a corresponding increase in selling expenses.

Horizontal Analysis Discussion

Horizontal statement analysis uses percentage comparison from one accounting period to the next. The percentage change is calculated by dividing the amount of increase or decrease for each item by the base period amount. The resulting percentages are then studied in detail. It is important to consider the amount of change as well as the percentage in horizontal comparisons. A 5% change in an account with a very large dollar amount may actually be much more of a change than a 50% change in an account with much less activity.

In the above example, it is very obvious that the 80% increase in sales has a much greater corresponding increase in cost of goods sold, which rose 140%. These accounts are often used to hide fraudulent expenses, withdrawals, or other illegal transactions.

Financial Ratios

Ratio analysis is a means of measuring the relationship between two different financial statement amounts. The relationship and comparison are the keys to the analysis. Many professionals, including bankers, investors, and business owners, as well as major investment firms use this method. Ratio analysis allows for internal evaluations using financial statement data. Traditionally, financial statement ratios are used in comparisons to an entity's industry average. They can be very useful in detecting red flags for a fraud examination.

As the financial ratios present a significant change from one year to the next, or over a period of years, it becomes obvious that there may a problem. As in all other analysis, specific changes are often explained by changes in the business operations. As a change in specific ratios is detected, the appropriate source accounts should be researched and examined in detail to determine if fraud has occurred. For instance, a significant decrease in a company's current ratio may point to an increase in current liabilities or a reduction in assets, both of which could be used to cover fraud.

In the analysis of financial statements, each reader of the statements will determine which portions are most important. Like the statement analysis discussed previously, the analysis of ratios is limited by its inability to detect fraud on a smaller, immaterial scale. Some of the types of financial ratio comparisons are shown below.

Many of the possible ratios are used in industry-specific situations, but the nine comparisons mentioned below are ratios that may lead to discovery of fraud. The following calculations are based on the example financial statements presented earlier:

Current Ratio

$$\frac{\text{Current Assets}}{\text{Current Liabilities}}$$

The current ratio—current assets divided by current liabilities—is probably the most-used ratio in financial statement analysis. In a strong company, current assets should exceed current liabilities several times over. The ratio measures a company's ability to meet its financial obligations from its liquid assets.

The current ratio, current assets to current liabilities, is probably the most-used ratio in financial statement analysis. This comparison measures a company's ability to meet present obligations from its liquid assets. The number of times that current assets exceed current liabilities has long been a quick measure of financial strength.

In detecting fraud, this ratio can be a prime indicator of manipulation of accounts involved. Embezzlement will cause the ratio to decrease. Liability concealment will cause a more favorable ratio.

In the case example, the drastic change in the current ratio from year one (2.84) to year two (1.70) should cause an examiner to look at these accounts in more detail. For instance, a check-tampering scheme will usually result in a decrease in current assets, cash, which will in turn decrease the ratio.

Quick Ratio

$$\frac{\text{Cash+Securities+Receivables}}{\text{Current Liabilities}}$$

The quick ratio, often referred to as the acid test ratio, compares assets that can be immediately liquidated. This calculation divides the total of cash, securities, and receivables by current liabilities. This ratio is a measure of a company's ability to meet sudden cash requirements. In turbulent economic times, it is used more prevalently, giving the analyst a worst-case look at the company's working capital situation.

An examiner will analyze this ratio for fraud indicators. In year one of the example, the company balance sheet reflects a quick ratio of 2.05. This ratio drops in year two to 1.00. In this situation, a closer review of accounts receivable shows they are increasing at an unusual rate which could indicate fictitious accounts receivable have been added to inflate sales. Of more concern perhaps is the increase in accounts payable which might require, at a minimum, a closer review to determine why.

Receivable Turnover

$$\frac{\text{Net Sales on Account}}{\text{Average Net Receivables}}$$

Receivable turnover is defined as net sales on account divided by average net receivables. It measures the number of times accounts receivable is turned over during the accounting period. In other words, it measures the time between on-account sales and collection of funds.

This ratio is one that uses both income statement and balance sheet accounts in its analysis. If the fraud is caused from fictitious sales, this bogus income will never be collected. As a result, the turnover of receivables will decrease, as in the example.

Collection Ratio

$$\frac{365}{\text{Receivable Turnover}}$$

Accounts receivable aging is measured by the collection ratio. It divides 365 days by the receivable turnover ratio to arrive at the average number of days to collect receivables. In general, the lower the collection ratio, the faster receivables are collected. A fraud examiner may use this ratio as a first step in detecting fictitious receivables or larceny and skimming schemes. Normally, this ratio will stay fairly consistent from year to year, but changes in billing policies or collection efforts may cause a fluctuation. The example shows a favorable reduction in the collection ratio from 226.3 in year one to 170.33 in year two. This means that the company is collecting its receivables more quickly in year two than in year one.

Inventory Turnover

$$\frac{\text{Cost of Goods Sold}}{\text{Average Inventory}}$$

The relationship between a company's cost of goods sold and average inventory is shown through the inventory turnover ratio. This ratio measures the number of times inventory is sold during the period. This ratio is a good determinant of purchasing, production, and sales efficiency. In general, a higher inventory turnover ratio is considered more favorable. For example, if cost of goods sold has increased due to theft of inventory (ending inventory has declined, but not through sales), then this ratio will be abnormally high. In the case example, inventory turnover increases in year two, signaling the possibility that an embezzlement is buried in the inventory account. An examiner should look at the changes in the components of the ratio to determine a direction in which to discover possible fraud

Average Number of Days Inventory is in Stock

$$\frac{365}{\text{Inventory Turnover}}$$

The average number of days inventory is in stock ratio is a restatement of the inventory turnover ratio expressed in days. This rate is important for several reasons. An increase in the number of days inventory stays in stock causes additional expenses, including storage costs, risk of inventory obsolescence, and market price reductions, as well as interest and other expenses incurred due to tying up funds in inventory stock. Inconsistency or significant variance in this ratio is a red flag for fraud investigators. Examiners may use this ratio to examine inventory accounts for possible larceny schemes. Purchasing and receiving inventory schemes can affect the ratio. As well, understating the cost of goods sold will result in an increase in the ratio. Significant changes in the inventory turnover ratio are good indicators of possible fraudulent inventory activity.

Debt to Equity Ratio

$$\frac{\text{Total Liabilities}}{\text{Total Equity}}$$

The debt to equity ratio is computed by dividing total liabilities by total equity. This ratio is one that is heavily considered by lending institutions. It provides a clear picture of the relative risk assumed by the creditors and owners. The higher the ratio, the more difficult it will be for the owners to raise capital by increasing long-term debt. Debt to equity requirements are often included as borrowing covenants in corporate lending agreements. The example displays a year one ratio of 0.89. This is very favorable. However, Year 2 shows a ratio of 1.84; this means that debt is greatly increasing. In this case, the increase in the ratio corresponds with the rise in accounts payable. Sudden changes in this ratio may signal an examiner to look for fraud.

Profit Margin

$$\frac{\text{Net Income}}{\text{Net Sales}}$$

Profit margin ratio is defined by net income divided by net sales. This ratio is often referred to as the efficiency ratio, in that it reveals profits earned per dollar of sales. This percentage of net income to sales relates not only the effects of gross margin changes, but also charges to sales and administrative expenses. As fraud is committed, artificially net income will be overstated, and the profit margin ratio will be abnormally high. False expense and fraudulent disbursements will cause an increase in expenses and a decrease inflated sales will not have a corresponding increase to cost of goods sold, in the profit margin ratio. Over time, this ratio should be fairly consistent.

Asset Turnover

$$\frac{\text{Net Sales}}{\text{Average Assets}}$$

Net sales divided by average operating assets is the calculation used to determine the asset turnover ratio. This ratio is used to determine the efficiency with which asset resources are utilized. The case example displays a greater use of assets in year two than in year one.

By performing an analysis of the financial statements, the examiner may be directed toward the direct evidence to resolve an allegation of fraud. After performing a financial statement analysis, the examiner can select statistical samples in the target account and eventually examine the source documents. If an irregularity of overstatement is suspected, the examiner should begin the examination with the financial statements. If, however, an irregularity of understatement is suspected, an examination with a review of the source documents should be conducted. This rule of thumb is of particular effectiveness in the area of omission of liabilities, such as litigation, contingent liabilities, leases, and some product warranties.

Related Entries:

AUDITING FOR FRAUD
FINANCIAL STATEMENT FRAUD
FINANCIAL STATEMENTS

FINANCIAL STATEMENTS

Financial statements are accounting reports that describe the assets, liabilities, and operating results of an entity. According to SAS No. 62, promulgated by the Auditing Standards Board, financial statements include presentations of financial data and accompanying notes prepared in conformity with either generally accepted accounting principles or some other comprehensive basis of accounting.

The Balance Sheet and the Income Statement

The most common financial statements are the balance sheet and the income statement. The *balance sheet* of a company is an extension of the accounting equation. The balance sheet lists all assets on one side of the page and all liabilities and owners' equity on the other side. The *income statement* is another major corporate financial statement. While a balance sheet shows total assets, liabilities, and owners' equities at a specific point in time (usually the last day of a fiscal year), an income statement details how much profit or loss a company sustains during a period.

Two types of accounts are reported on the income statement—*revenues,* received from the sale of goods or services, and *expenses,* incurred as the cost of doing business. A sporting goods store collects revenues from the sale of jet skis, and incurs expenses such as purchasing costs (inventory), labor, and utilities.

The format for an income statement is:

$$\boxed{\text{Revenue} - \text{Expenses}} = \boxed{\text{Net Income}}$$

The income statement's accounts are reduced to a zero balance (closed) at the end of each fiscal period. The net income or loss is added to the balance sheet as retained earnings.

At the end of each period revenues and expenses are closed or brought to a zero balance, and the difference, net income (loss), is added to retained earnings on the balance sheet. The following diagram shows how the income statement links to the balance sheet through the retained earnings account. When net income is a positive number, retained earnings increase; when net income is a negative number, earnings are reduced.

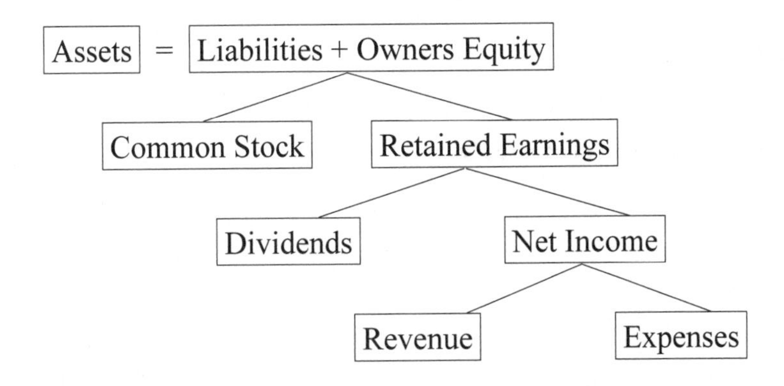

Types of Financial Statements

The following list contains financial statements as promulgated by the AICPA Auditing Standards Board in its Statement on Auditing Standards No. 62:

- Balance sheet.
- Statement of income or statement of operations.
- Statement of retained earnings.
- Statement of cash flows.
- Statement of changes in owners' equity.
- Statement of assets and liabilities that does not include owners' equity accounts.
- Statement of revenue and expenses.
- Summary of operations.
- Statement of operations by product lines.
- Statement of cash receipts and disbursements.

Financial statements typically include other financial data presentations, such as:

- Prospective financial information (forecasts).
- Proxy statements.
- Interim financial information (for example, quarterly financial statements).
- Current value financial presentations.
- Personal financial statements (current or present value).
- Bankruptcy financial statements.
- Registration statement disclosures (Securities Act of 1933).

Related Entries:

AUDITING FOR FRAUD
FINANCIAL STATEMENT FRAUD

FISK, JAMES, JR.

Jim Fisk, a con man in the mid-1800s, conned his way into the elite, becoming one of the most colorful of so-called robber barons. Fisk was born in 1835 in Pownal, Vermont. He literally ran away with the circus at 14, and married a circus performer named Lucy Moore the following year. The couple stayed with the show for eight years before he rejoined his father to run the family peddling business. Fisk made his first fortune as a war profiteer—at the start of the Civil War he obtained a contract to supply the Union with blankets, though he did not have the inventory as he claimed. But with the government guarantee in hand, he was able to buy blankets at cut-rate prices from mills whose business was hurt by the war, then sell them to the War Department for a handsome profit. After the war he dealt in cotton, buying at depressed prices from desperate Southern farmers.

Fisk joined in a stock scam with two other infamous members of the robber-baron set, Jay Gould, and Daniel Drew, who owned the Erie Railroad. As the titular heads of the Erie, Fisk and Gould put out word that the railroad's stock was about to be purchased by a secret group of businessmen. In reality the men were trying to convince Commodore Cornelius Vanderbilt that he ought to corner the market on Erie stock and sell out when the investment group was ready to buy. Vanderbilt took the bait, but for every 100 shares he acquired Fisk and Gould had 500 more printed up. Erie stock rose from $20 million to $50 million. In the scandal that followed Fisk openly admitted his role. Gould meanwhile arranged for the New York legislature to legitimize all the existing Erie stock. Fisk and his co-conspirators returned $4.5 million to Vanderbilt, and split the remaining $3 million in profit.

Also with Gould, Fisk perpetrated a market fraud in 1869 that left many broke and some dead. By bribing sources in the Grant administration, Fisk and Gould learned that the federal reserves would not be releasing gold in the market for some time. Using purchasing agents hired in secret, Fisk and Gould bought approximately $15 million in gold. When the price, which had started at 133, rose to 165, the two made about $10 million profit each. A market panic followed the sell-off, bankrupting thousands of investors, causing nervous breakdowns, and prompting some to commit suicide.

Source: Goldsmith, Barbara. *Other Powers.* New York: Knopf, 1998.

FORENSIC ACCOUNTING

Forensic accounting is the use of professional accounting skills in matters involving potential or actual civil or criminal litigation, including, but not limited to, generally acceptable accounting and audit principles; the determination of lost profits, income, assets, or damages; evaluation of internal controls; fraud; and any other matter involving accounting expertise in the legal system.

The word "forensic" is defined by *Black's Law Dictionary* as "used in or suitable to courts of law or public debate." Therefore, "forensic accounting" is actually litigation support involving accounting.

Accordingly, most fraud examinations are forensic accounting but not all forensic accounting is fraud examination. For example, the valuation of a property in a minority shareholder derivative suit would be included under forensic accounting but may not necessarily involve fraud.

Fraud examinations will generally fall under the category of forensic accounting because the majority of examinations, investigations, and reports involving fraud are all done with "an eye toward litigation." In other words, fraud examiners are taught to conduct their examination with the assumption that the case may end in litigation.

Related Entries:

AUDITING FOR FRAUD
FRAUD EXAMINATION

FORGERY

Forgery is committed by imitating a document or object with the intent to deceive. Besides monetary gains, forgers might be motivated by status or personal reasons such as revenge.

The forgery of legitimate documents—through handwriting or printing—is classified by the forger's method and aim. *Simple forgeries* are those in which the forger makes no attempt to reproduce someone else's handwriting or printing. *Simulated forgeries* are copied from a legitimate sample such as a letter, check, or other document. Trace forgeries are made by shining a light behind a legitimate document and tracing the lettering onto a new document. Cut-and-paste forgeries are obtained using photocopiers or computer scanners.

Forge-Proofing a Signature

Persons can make their signatures difficult to forge with a few simple practices.

- Never write abbreviated signatures. Use all the characters and all given names.
- Personalize signatures with flourishes and special features.
- Write rapidly.
- Use a ballpoint or fountain pen, never fiber-tip.

Case Study—Mark William Hofmann and the White Salamander Letter

Mark William Hofmann became known as one of the world's most notorious forgers when he was exposed in the 1980's. Hofmann specialized in Mormon holographs and currency, though he did forge other Americana, successfully passing items to the Federal Bureau of Investigation, the Library of Congress, the American Antiquarian Society, and the Church of Jesus Christ of Latter-day Saints. He has been begrudgingly praised as perhaps the greatest forger ever apprehended.

In the early 1980's, apparently motivated by his secret rejection of the Mormon Church which occurred sometime during his teenage years, Hofmann began forging documents related to church history. The documents were supposed to be in the handwriting of Joseph Smith, Mormon founder. Mormon elders were elated and purchased every document Hofmann produced, including:

- The Anthon Transcript, purchased April 1980: Apparently written in 1828 in Smith's own hand, it contained characters believed copied from the golden plates of the Book of Mormon, the church's major scripture.
- The Joseph Smith III Blessing, purchased March 1981: The document, dated 1844, appears to be Smith's blessing to his son to carry on church work. A lynch mob killed Smith later that year.
- The Joseph Stowell Letter purchased May 1985: Dated 1823, it was believed to be the earliest example of Smith's actual handwriting.

The early forgeries corroborated accepted Church history and teachings. But Hofmann also began producing documents that contradicted the Church. Most infamous among these was the "White Salamander Letter," which he sold in 1984 for $40,000 to Steven F. Christensen, a Mormon bishop. Christensen later donated the letter to his church. According to the letter, supposedly written by Smith's associate, Martin Harris, the Mormon leader confronted a talking "white salamander" – something never mentioned in official church accounts—in his quest for the golden tablets that Mormons believe Smith used to found the sect. The White Salamander Letter provoked a controversy both within and outside the Church, as news spread of the revisionist history and the Church's alleged attempts to conceal the documents it had purchased from Hofmann.

In October 1985, Hofmann offered Christensen the so-called McLellin collection, named for an early excommunicated apostle of Smith's. Hofmann had convinced Christensen and others that he could obtain the collection from underground sources and had already borrowed almost $200,000 against the purchase. As Christensen moved the deal along and scheduled an authentication hearing, Hofmann panicked that he would not be able to provide the materials in time.

To avoid exposure, Hofmann decided to kill Christensen and Gary Sheets, Christensen's former boss at a local financial services company that had recently failed and left both men facing bankruptcy. On October 15, 1985, the morning of the scheduled authentication hearings, Hofmann planted a homemade bomb in Sheets' home; it exploded that morning, killing Sheets' wife, Kathleen. A similar bomb outside Christensen's office door killed him that same day.

Church authorities were alarmed, but undeterred in their pursuit of the potentially damaging McLellin collection. They rescheduled the authentication for the next day. Before the meeting, Hofmann was critically injured by an exploding pipe bomb in his own car. He had apparently planned to kill someone else in the Mormon circle, but accidentally exploded the bomb himself.

As part of the investigation, questioned documents examiners were able to detect Hofmann's method for chemically aging ink that was then applied to old paper. Hofmann agreed to plead guilty to two counts of second-degree murder and to discuss his crimes in exchange for a reduced sentence on the Sheets homicide, and to allow concurrent sentences. He was sentenced to serve one five-years-to-life sentence in the Utah State Penitentiary. He attempted to commit suicide using drugs twice, but was unsuccessful.

Sources:
Goodman, W. "How Mormon's Fraud Led to Death." *The New York Times,* November 12, 1998.

Nelson, B. "The Forgeries that Shook the Mormon Church." *The Washington Post,* October 9, 1988.

Sillitoe, Linda. "Mark William Hofmann." *Utah History Encyclopedia.*

Sillitoe, L, and Roberts, A. *Salamander: The Story of the Mormon Forgery Murders.* Salt Lake City, UT: Signature Books, 1998.

Turley, R., *Victims: The LDS Church and the Mark Hofmann Case.* Chicago, IL: University of Illinois Press, 1992.

Related Entries:

COUNTERFEIT CURRENCY
COUNTERFEIT DOCUMENTS
COUNTERFEIT FINANCIAL INSTRUMENTS
COUNTERFEIT GOVERNMENT SECURITIES
COUNTERFEIT IDENTIFICATION AND FAKE IDS
DOCUMENTS: HANDLING AND EXAMINING
HITLER DIARIES

FORTUNA ALLIANCE

One of the Federal Trade Commission's most prominent Internet prosecutions, the Fortuna Alliance, has also been one of the most recalcitrant offenders. Fortuna Alliance ran a website promising visitors that, for an opening payment of $250, they could receive profits of over $5,000 per month. Individuals could operate "business centers" for as much as $1,750 a month each, and many people chose to operate several centers at once. Supposedly a portion of Fortuna's proceeds would benefit impoverished children, and the rest would make participants rich.

The Alliance billed itself as a discounting service: the benefits of membership in this "socially conscious company that regularly donates a portion of its proceeds to charity" included long distance service discounts, travel discounts, and savings on over 275,000 products.

As participants sponsored others into the Alliance, the sponsors took a cut of the recruits' monthly fees. Not only did participants become alarmed when their downlines did not produce as they had planned, they also complained about Fortuna's merchandise. The company was supposed to be selling useful, everyday stuff, but the catalog advertised $19 t-shirts and $20 pens emblazoned with the Fortuna logo, plus an assortment of vitamins, gee-gaws, and magic devices guaranteed to double users' gas mileage.

The Commission filed suit against Fortuna as a pyramid scheme and secured a permanent injunction. Investigators uncovered several offshore accounts, which the defendants were ordered to repatriate. But when the court ordered Fortuna to reimburse its victims $2 million, the owners balked. Two separate contempt-of-court motions were waved off. FTC agents obtained an injunction to remove Fortuna's website from the Internet, but two hours after its removal an Alliance hacker had reposted the material elsewhere.

A 1997 webpage claimed the Alliance had been exonerated of all charges and accused the FTC of harassment. The page remains available, as are several pro-Fortuna commentaries. *See* www.ultranet.com/~success1/fa.html. However, by 1998, the FTC had successfully recovered $5.5 million of the estimated $15 million gathered by the Alliance. A contempt of court citation for $2.2 million remained unpaid.

FRANCHISE FRAUD

Fraud in franchising may occur at each stage of the franchise relationship, creating disclosure, relationship, and termination issues. Franchised businesses accounted for about one-third of all retail sales in the United States during the last years of the 1990's, and were predicted to make 50% of all retail sales in the new century. Franchises are also attractive to entrepreneurs because they have a higher survival rate than ordinary start-ups. While more than half of all independent small businesses go under within the first five years, only one-tenth of franchises fail in that period.

Disclosure Issues

"Disclosure issues" arise when the franchiser fails to communicate material information or discloses false information to induce the franchisee to purchase a franchise that he would not have otherwise purchased. Two prime examples of potentially misleading information are earnings claims and success rates.

Earnings Claims

If one assumes that a prospective franchisee relies upon earnings claims published by the franchiser as a key factor in his decision to buy the franchise, but those earnings claims can be materially misleading, or even blatantly false. This is a prime example of disclosure fraud in connection with the franchiser's inducement of potential franchisees to buy the franchise.

Disclosure fraud has historically been the primary target of franchiser regulations. The FTC reported that from 1989 to 1992, 100% of its franchise enforcement cases were based on allegations that the franchiser had provided fraudulent or misleading earnings claims. But, surprisingly, the FTC does not require franchisers to disclose earnings. The FTC rule provides for the disclosure of earnings claims regarding actual or potential sales. Income, costs, or profits of either existing or prospective franchisees is optional. But if a franchiser elects to make earnings claims, it must have a "reasonable" basis for those claims.

Without published earnings claims, the prospective franchisee is vulnerable to non-written, boastful earnings claims made by franchise salespeople who make their living selling franchises, instead of selling the underlying goods or services. Those non-written claims may turn out to be false, but the franchiser may try to protect itself by including in the written franchise agreement a "no reliance" or "integration" clause that states in effect:

> *Franchisee acknowledges that this Agreement is the entire agreement of the parties, and that in entering into this Agreement, he or she is not relying upon any statements or representations that may have been made on or before the date of this Agreement, which are not expressly made a part of this Agreement.*

Clauses similar to this one have often been used to defeat claims of fraud submitted by franchisees that were induced to sign a contract based upon the franchiser's verbal representations.

Success Rates

Another important disclosure issue is a franchiser's claim that a certain percentage, usually a high number, of its stores has been successful. The franchise salesperson may not have told the franchisee that a number of stores were sold many times and in each sale the old franchisee sold the store back to the franchiser who resold it to a new franchisee. Two main issues are in question:

- Would that additional information be material to the prospective franchisee?
- Would failure to disclose that information amount to fraud?

The FTC rule does not require franchisers to disclose re-sales or turnovers from one franchisee to the next.

Relationship Issues

Once the franchising relationship is established, the franchiser and franchisee stand in a business relationship that typically involves the transaction of funds at several levels under a series of contracts:

- The payment of royalties under the franchise or license agreement for the right to use the franchiser's trademark, trade name, and business system.
- The payment of rent under a lease or sub-lease of real property and/or equipment.
- Contributions to an advertising fund.

All of these financial transactions may be subject to claims for breach of contract, fraud, or breach of a fiduciary duty. Of course, to determine the exact claims, the franchisee must consult the exact language in the franchise agreement.

Numerous issues also may arise in the course of the franchise relationship, each of which reflects an inherent tension between the interests of franchiser and franchisee:

- *Training and support.* Has the franchiser provided the level of training and technical support that was promised?
- *Control.* What degree of control is the franchiser entitled to exercise over the franchisee's products, suppliers, and pricing? To what extent may the franchiser derive profit from the franchisee's supplier relationships?
- *New products.* To what extent does the franchiser have a duty to introduce new products to keep ahead of the competition? Once the decision to introduce new products is made, is the franchiser held to any "standard of care" to ensure that the product is successful?
- *Expansion or contraction of the system.* Does the franchiser's natural desire to expand the franchise system conflict with a franchisee's desire to maximize profits at his location? Conversely, what duties, if any, does a franchiser owe to franchisees in a particular market if the franchiser plans to withdraw from that market?
- *Encroachment.* To what extent does the franchiser have a duty to refrain from opening new outlets "too close" to existing units? How close is "too close" if the license agreement is silent?
- *Expansion by the franchisee.* To what extent is an individual franchisee's desire to expand in conflict with what is best for the system as a whole?
- *Reinvestment.* May a franchiser require a franchisee to reinvest a portion of his revenue back into the business? Does it depend on whether the franchisee owns or leases the real estate?

Termination Issues

The end of a franchise relationship may also provide grounds for litigation:

- *Renewal.* Does a franchiser have a duty to renew a franchisee beyond the initial term of his license agreement?
- *Early termination.* Under what circumstances may a franchiser terminate a franchise before the expiration of his contractual term?
- *Sale of a franchise.* Under what circumstances may a franchiser veto a franchisee's proposed sale of his franchise to a third-party?
- *Post-termination restrictions on competition.* To what extent may the franchiser restrict the franchisee's right to compete after termination? Even if a franchisee is allowed to compete after the franchise relationship is ended, the franchiser may sometimes validly demand that the franchisee leave his business telephone number to the franchiser as it departs the system.

Statistics for Comparison

General figures from the International Franchise Association's study "The Profile of Franchising, Volume III," published in 1999, provide a basis for evaluating some franchise offers.

- The areas of fast food (18% of all franchises) and retail (11%) made up the largest sectors of franchising.
- About 70% of franchisers charged a fee of $30,000 or less, though the lodging industry generally charged higher fees.
- 88% of franchisers charged fees of $40,000 or less.
- 34% of lodging franchisers charged fees over $40,000, 21% charge more than $50,000.
- 36% of travel industry franchise fees were less than $10,000.

Franchise Regulation

In 1978, the U.S. Federal Trade Commission (FTC) began regulating franchises by enacting the "Disclosure Requirements and Prohibitions Concerning Franchising and Business Opportunity Ventures" ("FTC Rule") (16 C.F.R. Part 436). The FTC is charged with addressing the disclosures made by franchisers to potential franchisees, but not ongoing issues in the relationship between franchisers and franchisees, or other issues in the termination of franchise relationships.

As stated by the FTC, "the Rule is designed to enable potential franchisees to protect themselves before investing by providing them with information essential to an assessment of the potential risks and benefits, to meaningful comparisons with other investments, and to further investigation of the franchise opportunity."

Under Federal Trade Commission (FTC) rules, as well as the statutory and/or common law of nearly all states, there are three prerequisites to apply the rule to a business format or product franchise:

- *Trademark.* The franchiser offers the right to distribute goods or services that bear the franchiser's trademark, service mark, trade name, advertising, or other commercial symbol.
- *Significant control or assistance.* The franchiser exercises significant control over, and/or offers substantial assistance to the franchisee in the operation of the franchised business.
- *Required payment.* The franchisee is required to pay the franchiser. These payments usually include initial franchise fees and ongoing royalties that are calculated as a percentage of sales, net of sales tax. Another typical fee is a transfer fee that is applicable on the sale of a franchise.

Revisions to the FTC Rule

The following changes to the FTC Rule became effective December 1, 2000.

- A clear statement that the Rule is inapplicable to franchises operated outside the United States.
- Addition of procedures for electronic publishing of offering circulars on the Internet.
- Abandonment of the obligation to provide an offering circular at the "first face-to-face meeting" to discuss sale of a franchise.
- Simplification of the waiting period between disclosure and conclusion of a franchise agreement to 14 calendar days.

- Adoption of the Uniform Franchise Offering Circular (UFOC) format, with numerous enhancements and variations, including new disclosure requirements that must include information about franchiser-initiated litigation, post-termination "gag clauses" (clauses which prevent current or former franchisees from discussing their experiences with potential franchisees), and names and addresses of trademark-specific franchisee associations that request to be included in the UFOC.
- The FTC alone has jurisdiction to enforce the rule. However, any misrepresentations in a UFOC certainly could be used to support claims for fraud under state statutory and/or common law. The FTC rule preempts inconsistent state laws. As a practical matter, it creates a minimum disclosure standard which many states have equaled or enhanced by statute.

State Laws

Sixteen states have enacted franchise disclosure laws that create a cause of action for failure to register a franchise with the designated state agency and/or failure to provide the franchiser's UFOC to the prospective franchisee in a timely manner. These statutes provide damages or rescission as the remedies available to the successful franchisee. Issuing states include California, Hawaii, Illinois, Indiana, Iowa, Maryland, Michigan, Minnesota, New York, North Dakota, Oregon, Rhode Island, South Dakota, Virginia, Washington, and Wisconsin. Eighteen jurisdictions go beyond disclosure and legislate in the area of relationship issues.

Other Remedies

The failure of the FTC to outlaw fraud in franchising specifically beyond the disclosure phase does not leave a defrauded franchisee without remedies. However, *common law fraud* can be used to prosecute franchise fraud. To prove common law fraud, one must show:

- Proof of a knowing or reckless misrepresentation or omission of a material fact;
- Reliance on the material misrepresentation or omission; and
- Injury was caused by the material misrepresentation or omission.

- It is important to note that well-written franchise agreements can defeat common law fraud claims.

The *Racketeer Influenced and Corrupt Organizations Act (*RICO), 18 U.S.C. Sec. 1961 *et seq.*, may also be used to prosecute franchising fraud. RICO is the most powerful anti-fraud statute available to civil litigants because it provides for automatic trebling (tripling) of damages plus attorneys' fees and costs. Class-action plaintiffs have established RICO claims based on the ongoing system-wide fraud that occurred in the use of advertising funds.

Franchise Facts

- There are an estimated 1,500 franchise companies operating in the U.S. doing business through more than 320,000 retail units.
- 75 industries use franchising to distribute goods and services to consumers.
- Average initial investment level for nearly 8 out of 10 franchises, excluding real estate, is less than $250,000.
- Average royalty fees range from 3% to 6% of monthly gross sales.
- Most franchise companies have fewer than 100 units.
- Average length of franchise contract is 10 years.

Source: www.franchise.org/resourcectr/faq/franchisfacts.asp

Franchise Fraud Schemes

In 1997, the editors of *Success* magazine compiled a list of "The Seven Most Devious Franchise Scams." These include:

- "The Chain of Pain." Franchisers misrepresent their failure rate by selling unsuccessful stores to a string of different owners over the years. The stores are never closed so the company's disclosure documents continue to report a favorable survival rate.
- "The Turn." The franchiser sells an under-performing store with inflated claims, and then offers to buy the property back at a sizable discount when the business fails. The franchiser may sell the same store to a string of new buyers. The company's Uniform

Franchise Offering Circular (UFOC), the disclosure document that all franchisers must provide to prospective franchises, is required to divulge the company's prior litigation, civil suits, and settlements, as well as any felonies committed by its executives. Franchise associations also keep records on repeat offenders.

- "The Real-Estate Shuffle." The franchiser claims to have advanced demographic information to determine store locations. This may be an attempt to steer business to a real-estate partner, who often has undesirable property for sale.
- "The Claim Game." Franchisers make exorbitant earnings claims. In response to FTC action against these frauds, perpetrators often include fine print in contracts disavowing any claim of future earnings.
- "Gauge-o-Matic." Franchiser requires buyer to purchase raw materials or equipment from a particular supplier who is charging inflated prices and may be providing kickbacks to the franchiser. Legitimate franchisers may require franchisees to use certain suppliers, and receiving referral monies is legal. To prove fraud, the claimant must show that the franchiser did not make an effort to demand the best price from vendors.
- "I've Got a Secret." Franchiser claims to offer a unique recipe, secret process, or a proprietary right that does not exist.
- "Toy Story." Franchisers selling toy distributorships claim the franchisees need only display racks and a license from the parent company. But the contract entails expensive set-up costs, offers retail prices instead of wholesale, and the franchiser then sends outdated merchandise.

Franchising Organizations

General information and certain franchising records can be obtained through the following:

- American Association of Franchisees and Dealers, 1420 Kettner Blvd., Suite 415, San Diego, CA 92101; 619-235 2556.
- Federal Trade Commission, Sixth St. and Pennsylvania Ave. NW, Washington, DC 20580; 202-326 2180.

- International Franchise Association, 1350 New York Ave. NW, Suite 900, Washington, DC 20005-4709; 202-628-8000; www.franchise.org.

Case Study—Oily Chips and Flavored Water

In the largest franchise fraud case ever prosecuted by the New York State Attorney General, prosecutors obtained judgments totaling more than $1 million against a family selling franchises in four states that distributed inferior snacks and drinks.

Michael J. Glass operated Westcool Snacks and Beverages and Maricopa Products with his wife Adriane and his sons, Joshua and Peter, who were in their 30's during the mid-1990's when the fraud took place The franchisers charged up to $50,000 each to people who believed they could earn $780,000 a year from the businesses.

All told the Glass family received almost $1 million from victims in New York City, on Long Island, and in Westchester County, as well as in 19 counties in New Jersey, and in Ohio, Connecticut, and Washington, D.C. All of the investors lost money and two declared bankruptcy.

According to testimony, Glass provided oily potato chips and a line of flavored water. Retail stores often refused the merchandise because chip bags leaked oil and bottle labels peeled off to reveal different beverage labels. Five years after the operations were shut down, victims had recovered about 10% of their investments.

Sources:
Maull, S. "New York Attorney General Settles Franchise Fraud Case for $1 Million." *The Associated Press State and Local Wire,* July 2, 2000.

Purvin, R. *The Franchise Fraud: How to Protect Yourself Before and After You Invest*. New York: John Wiley & Sons, 1994.

Stapinski, H. "How to Lose Your Nest Egg with the Stroke of a Pen: The Seven Most Devious Franchise Scams; the Franchise Gold 100." *Success,* November 1997.

Related Entries:

CONSUMER FRAUD

FRAUD EXAMINATION

Fraud examination is a methodology for resolving fraud allegations, which involves obtaining and analyzing evidence, taking statements, writing reports, testifying to findings, and detecting and preventing fraud. The term examination indicates the testing of a body of material regarding a theory or supposition.

Fraud Examiners

Fraud examiners are employed in a wide array of fields and positions. They are law officers, paralegals, attorneys, private detectives, accountants, auditors, loss prevention officers, ethics officers, competitive intelligence providers, academics, writers and producers, to name a handful. Examiners need not have an accounting background or legal experience. Anyone who deals with fraud in some professional manner can become a Certified Fraud Examiner. (See below.)

The CFE designation has been acknowledged as a meaningful credential by various public media, including *Money* magazine, the *Wall Street Journal*, the *New York Times*, and others. *U.S. News and World Report* rated the field of fraud examination/forensic accounting one of the fastest growing in 1997, 1999, and again in 2002.

CFE Salaries

Because CFEs work in a variety of industries and fields, determining an average salary range is difficult. However, the ACFE does conduct salary surveys periodically. For information about the latest salary estimates, please see ACFE's 2006 Compensation Guide: www.ACFE.com

Duties of Certified Fraud Examiners

A Certified Fraud Examiner may be responsible for the initial detection of fraud or, more likely, become involved when the act is detected or suspected. Examiners commonly supervise or direct the fraud examination or investigation. When conducting examinations, the examiner obtains and interprets evidence to conclude the inquiry. However, the ACFE Code of Ethics requires that examiners express no opinion regarding the guilt or innocence of any person or party.

The responsibilities of the Certified Fraud Examiner are to:

- Help resolve allegations of fraud, from inception to disposition. The disposition of a case might be a settlement or some other form of agreement, rather than trial and conviction or acquittal.
- Obtain and review evidence. This includes all documents and relevant physical materials.
- Take statements. Interviewing witnesses and suspects assists the evaluation process.
- Write reports of fraud examinations. Without declaring the guilt or innocence of any given suspect, the examiner summarizes the investigation and details its conclusions.
- Testify to findings. Examiners may be called to explain how various frauds are perpetrated, how each investigation proceeds, and to support the investigative conclusions.
- Assist in fraud prevention. Besides investigating and detecting fraud, the examiner may help establish controls and practices that prevent fraud from occurring.

Axioms of Fraud Examination

Fraud Is Hidden

A key element of fraud crimes is concealment. Where a bank robber uses threat or force, a bank embezzler steals money through stealth. Fraud can be concealed in so many ways that almost anyone—even a trained examiner—can be defrauded. Therefore, fraud examiners cannot be sure that fraud does or does not exist within a specific environment. For any given allegation, the fraud examiner evaluates the evidence and renders judgments about that evidence.

Fraud Requires Reverse Proof

To prove that a fraud has occurred, the examiner must attempt to prove fraud has not occurred. Inversely, when attempting to prove fraud has not occurred, the examiner must also attempt to prove it has. The law demands that proof of fraud must preclude any explanation other than guilt.

Fraud Examiners Do Not Decide Guilt or Innocence

The examiner postulates a theory and tests that theory. Any discussion of guilt or innocence is only a part of that theory. Legal judgments are solely the purview of the courts and juries. The examiner must not express opinions on the legal guilt or innocence of any person or party.

Establishing Proof in a Fraud Examination

According to author Herbert Edelhertz, "One of the characteristics that most distinguishes the investigation of white-collar crime from that of common crimes is the necessity for the investigator to establish the intent and underlying motives of the subject." Listing every variation of offense is not reasonable; successfully demonstrating that a fraud has occurred, however, will require the following proofs.

- *Intent*—the accused committed the act knowing it was wrong. A common defense to fraud charges is that the accused did not realize the act was wrong. The examiner must show that the act was not the result of a mistake or ignorance.
- *Misrepresentation*—the accused misrepresented key aspects of the transaction to the victim. An investment promoter might claim he is investing funds in government contracts when he is using the money to buy hotels or is simply running a Ponzi scheme with no investment activity whatsoever.
  - Concealing an act counts as misrepresentation. An embezzler who keeps two sets of books is misrepresenting his actions as legitimate. An investment promoter who does not fully inform clients of the risks involved is misrepresenting by concealment.
  - Misrepresentation is generally demonstrated by showing that a representation was made and that representation was made false by the accused's intentional omission or commission.
- *Reliance*—by the victim on the accused's misrepresentation. Perhaps a promoter claimed he drove a Lexus when he drove a Volkswagen. That is a lie in personal terms, but in legal terms the issue is whether the misrepresentation was *material*, i.e., did the lie cause the victim to hand over some money? In the case of employee thefts,

the company is the victim, having entrusted the care of assets to the employee—the company relied on the employee's fiduciary duty.

- *Loss*—because the victim relied on the intentional misrepresentation of the accused, financial losses resulted.

Fraud Examination Compared to Auditing

Though many fraud examiners work as auditors, the two fields are not the same. Fraud examination is a forensic procedure where auditing is a method for monitoring activities and assets in an ongoing fashion. Below is a summary that contrasts fraud examiners, internal auditors, and external auditors.

	Fraud Examiners	External Auditors	Internal Auditors
Employer	Accounting firms, companies, organizations, and governmental units	Accounting firms	Companies, organizations, and governmental units
National Organization	Association of Certified Fraud Examiners (ACFE)	American Institute of Certified Public Accountants (AICPA)	Institute of Internal Auditors (IIA)
Certifying Designation	Certified Fraud Examiner (CFE)	Certified Public Accountant (CPA)	Certified Internal Auditor (CIA)
Primary Responsibility	To third parties and/or management	To third parties	To board of directors
Scope of Examination	All activities of an organization	Primarily financial statements	All activities of an organization

THE FRAUD TRIANGLE

See, ATTITUDES TOWARD AND PERCEPTIONS OF FRAUD

CAUSES OF FRAUD

FRAUDULENT DISBURSEMENTS

Fraudulent disbursements are a form of asset misappropriation, the most common of all forms of occupational frauds. Where cash theft schemes take money as it comes *into* a company, fraudulent disbursements take money coming *out* of a company. Common acts include forging company checks, submitting false invoices, and doctoring timecards.

Employees and managers commit fraudulent disbursements using one of several methods: BILLING SCHEMES, CHECK TAMPERING, EXPENSE REIMBURSEMENT SCHEMES, PAYROLL SCHEMES, AND REGISTER DISBURSEMENTS. Billing schemes are the most popular because most of a business's disbursements are made in the purchasing cycle.

Related Entries:

ASSET MISAPPROPRIATION
BILLING SCHEMES
CHECK TAMPERING
EXPENSE REIMBURSEMENT SCHEMES
OCCUPATIONAL FRAUD AND ABUSE
PAYROLL SCHEMES
REGISTER DISBURSEMENTS

GARVEY, MARCUS

Marcus Mosiah Garvey was born in St. Ann's Bay, Jamaica, in 1887. He became a printer's apprentice at 14 and a master printer at 18. Beginning with his involvement in union organizing, Garvey eventually became a well-known activist and political journalist in his native country.

He moved to America and settled in Harlem in 1916. There he began giving speeches on the street and to groups, exhorting them "to work for the general uplift of the Negro Peoples of the world." He formalized his mission by founding the Universal Negro Improvement Association and its house publication the *Negro World*, which was circulated throughout the Western Hemisphere, and eventually to Africa and Europe, despite national and regional bans from various authorities. Garvey struck a dandyish public pose, appearing in elaborate costumes, often military-style uniforms with feathered hats; stores sold Marcus Garvey cigars; he sometimes sponsored parades in which he rode sitting in the back of a limousine.

He became famous championing the so-called Back-to-Africa movement, urging American blacks to return to their "homeland." A bewildered Garvey began to ask unanswerable questions. "Where is the black man's government?" he wrote in an essay. "Where is his king and kingdom? Where is his president, his country and his ambassador, his army, his navy, his men of big affairs?"

Garvey started a steamship company, the Black Star Line, that he said would provide affordable but comfortable passage for blacks making the trip. Beginning in 1919, he financed the project by selling stock to black investors, urging, "Let us guide our own destiny" and "Have you bought your shares in the Black Star Line? If not, please do so today. The SS Frederick Douglass is afloat and has made a successful trip to Central America and the West Indies." A new ship, the Phillis Wheatley, would sail by the end of 1920. However, Garvey only raised $750,000, and the ships he bought were old and in poor repair. In January 1921, Garvey sought to stave off disaster by selling stock to investors in Central America and the West Indies.

Garvey's activist message alarmed conservative white Americans. His opposition portrayed him as a madman who was trying to rouse the black population into a murderous uprising. The American Protective League, a private group that tracked suspected radicals reported Garvey's activities to the federal government's Bureau of Investigation, forerunner of the FBI, where the case was assigned to a young J. Edgar Hoover.

Cultivating a network of spies, Hoover targeted Garvey with fraud charges. Because Black Star was in financial collapse, the indictment charged, Garvey was raising money illegally. Garvey's flamboyant, luxurious lifestyle was being supported by unsuspecting investors. In fact, the money Garvey was raising might have saved the shipping line, but the indictment ended the operation forever. It was true that Garvey had diverted cash raised for the Black Star to other enterprises, such as a restaurant owned by the UNIA and to the *Negro World*, but these were acts of a naïve, improvisational businessman, not the cunning stratagems of a master criminal, as the government's charges maintained.

On Jan. 12, 1922, federal agents arrested Garvey, and charged him with mail fraud. He was indicted in February, and trial began in 1923, more than a year after his arrest. Garvey was convicted, sentenced to five years in prison and fined $1,000. He appealed and remained free, continuing his programs until March 1925. That year, when the Supreme Court refused to review his case, he was sent to the Atlanta Federal Penitentiary.

After repeated legal maneuvers and petitions from Garvey's followers, President Calvin Coolidge commuted his sentence on Nov. 18, 1927. He was released and, two weeks later, deported to Jamaica. Despite major efforts to revive the UNIA in his homeland, Garvey's movement never regained its former momentum. In 1935, he moved to London, where he died in 1940. The Jamaican 50-cent coin bears Marcus Garvey's likeness. After his death in 1940, Jamaica proclaimed him the country's "First National Hero."

Sources:
Cronon, D. *Black Moses: The Story of Marcus Garvey and the Universal Negro Improvement Association.* Madison, WI: University of Wisconsin Press, 1969.

DuCille, M. "Black Moses, Red Scare; The Clash of Marcus Garvey and J. Edgar Hoover." Sunlight Gospel Association, February 12, 1997.

Lawler, M. *Marcus Garvey, Part of the Black Americans of Achievement Series.* Broomall, PA: Chelsea House Publishers, 1988.

GEE, CHARLIE AND DOROTHY (CHANG HOR-GEE)

Charlie Gee was a banker who embezzled millions from the Bank of America. Gee was a shoe seller who moved from China to San Francisco in 1901, later establishing a store in Oakland in 1906. He made a fortune brokering deposits from the Chinese community to the French-American Bank. His eldest daughter, Dorothy, joined the business and helped her father found the China Specie Bank in Hong Kong.

The China Specie Bank failed in 1923, all but bankrupting the Gee family. Mr. Gee began embezzling from the French-American Bank to cover the losses. When the bank was bought by Bank of America in 1927, Gee managed to conceal his acts. Dorothy Gee was promoted to manager at Bank of America in 1929, and discovered her father's defalcations soon after. Instead of exposing Charlie Gee, Dorothy began committing her own embezzlements to cover the trail. Over 50 years she stole an estimated $300,000.

Whatever her faults, Dorothy Gee ran her bank with great talent. The Chinatown branch became one of the most profitable and respected in the city. Ms. Gee was a well-known figure, somewhat infamous because of her profligate lifestyle, which involved luxury purchases, gambling, and drinking Scotch. It was rumored that the Gee family secretly ran a smuggling operation, bringing Chinese immigrants to America. Others said the Gees spent most of their money at casinos.

Dorothy Gee redesigned the local Bank of America's physical plant in 1962, the new structure modeled on a Chinese pagoda.

When Dorothy retired in 1963, she confessed to her and her father's (who had died in 1956) crimes. She expressed remorse, but said she felt trapped when she learned what her father had done. "We talked all night," she said, describing Charlie's revelations in 1929. "The question for me was whether I would betray my father. But I couldn't go down and betray him. And once I made that decision I just stuck with him for more than 30 years." Dorothy Gee was sentenced to five years, later reduced to 16 months.

GLOBAL CROSSING

In the late nineties, Global Crossing, Ltd. emerged as a colossal figure in the telecommunication industry with fiber-optic cables as its golden ticket. Yet within four years, the multi-billion dollar giant abruptly collapsed into bankruptcy. By October 2002, Gary Winnick, Global Crossing's founder and chairman, was explaining the hasty chain of events to a Congressional investigative committee.

The crux of the issue surrounding Global Crossing is the allegation that corporate insiders knowingly sold more than $1.5 billion of artificially inflated company stock. In addition to an ongoing investigation by the Securities and Exchange Commission, numerous civil actions have been filed against the company. The investigation and complaints have consistently focused on the issuance of false and misleading statements, insider trading, and fraudulent accounting practices.

In April 2005, Global Crossing settled with the SEC after the three year investigation. A cease-and-desist order was issued by the SEC against Global Crossing and three former executives: CEO Thomas Case, accounting officer Joseph Perrone, and CFO Dan Cohrs. There was no monetary penalty was assessed against the company. Unlike most executive officers connected to corporate fraud, the Justice Department has cleared Winnick of all criminal charges in December 2004.

Winnick resigned from the company following the development of a reorganization plan for the company in early 2003. Since this time, Winnick, former company attorneys, and Global Crossing, Ltd. have settled over $300 million in lawsuits brought by investors and former employees. Since the company's reorganization, several large investors have contributed millions to Global Crossing hoping to revive the former fiber-optic giant.

Sources:
Antczak, John. "Justice Department Won't File Charges in Global Crossing Probe." *Information Week*, December 26, 2002. www.informationweek.com.

Feeley, Jef. "Global Crossing to Pay $325 Mln to Settle Lawsuits (Update2)." Bloomberg.com, March 19, 2004. quote.bloomberg.com.

Nuzum, Christine. "UPDATE: Global Crossing: Very Confident Will Gain $300M Financing." *CNNmoney*, October 11, 2004. money.cnn.com.

O'Brien, Timothy L. "A New Legal Chapter for a 90's Flameout." *The New York Times*, August 15, 2004.

Wieland, Ken. "What now for Global Crossing? Global – Global News Analysis." *Telecommunications International*, January 2004.

Related Entry:
SECURITIES FRAUD

GONDORF, CHARLIE AND FRED

The Gondorf brothers developed and ran legendary cons in the 1890's and early 1900's. Their exploits were celebrated in the film *The Sting.* Among the most infamous "games" the Gondorf's ran was a kind of masquerade poker. The brothers recruited a rich man, or someone middle-class with some cash and feeling rich, and offered to introduce the mark to a high-stakes, high-society poker game. Cohorts, dressed as well-known figures from business and society, were waiting for the arrival and proceeded to cheat him of his available funds.

Another game was *the wire*, the type of con portrayed in the climax of *The Sting*. In this elaborate ruse, a phony betting parlor, complete with tellers, betters and loiterers, and a radio system carrying the broadcast of an actual horse race. The brothers convinced the mark that they had inside information on the race, ostentatiously placing large bets at the phony counter. When the Gondorf's horse lost, they protested alongside the mark to anyone who would listen. Later the Gondorf's split the mark's money with their gang and moved on.

Charlie Gondorf was sentenced to Sing Sing prison in 1914 for his part in staging a version of the wire in England. A mark was convinced to bet $10,000 in what was constructed to resemble an underground betting parlor. The mark won $135,000 and was celebrating when Gondorf accomplices dressed as policemen staged a raid. When the jilted bettor went to the real police, Charlie was arrested and later convicted. Fred Gondorf served time in Sing Sing after he was caught in an American-based fraud. Both brothers served their time and died in obscurity.

Sources:
Duchene. P. "Real to Reel: When Art Imitates Life, Facts Often Get Lost in the Translation, Says the Authors of a Book on Popular Movies Inspired By True Stories." *The Oregonian,* January 20, 2000.

Related Entry:

CON SCHEMES

GOULDD, BILL

Most Multi-Level Marketing schemes are still hawked the old-fashioned way, by word of mouth. Like pure cash operations, they are a prime example of affinity fraud, which is a fancy way of saying they hit you where you live. People usually first hear the pitch from a friend or coworker. Maybe it is someone they know casually from their health club. The pyramid schemer uses some prior relationship to draw the mark into the game.

Religious organizations are especially fertile ground for recruiters, since they involve a large group of people with familiar ties and a patina of respectability. But MLMers do not just comb churches for their prey; they create their own quasi-religious hold on new marks. Equinox International, pushing nutritional supplements and water filters, provides an outrageous example.

Equinox's founder, Bill Gouldd, held huge conventions, whipping 7,000 or more recruits into frenzy with shouts like "For God said ye go forth and multiply." Gouldd, a baby-faced huckster who never stopped beaming, intentionally added an extra "d" to his name because his spiritual adviser told him he was destined to make millions of d-d-dollars.

Equinox "seminars" rolled on for 12 hours a day or more, spanning a long weekend. Participants danced nonstop, emitting random whoo-hoos, sharing spontaneous hugs, sometimes breaking into fits of uncontrollable laughter and tears. When ABC's John Stossell covered a Gouldd gathering, he was astounded to find, "On Sunday, it went all night. People didn't leave until seven the next morning."

Gouldd charged $5,000 for a "manager" package whose inspirational urgings would magically produce riches once one started hawking the package themselves. Seminars cost $2,000 a piece, plus travel expenses, and Equinoxers needed lots of rejuvenation. One woman, approached by a reporter at an Equinox gathering, gushed, "I'm so excited to be here! God, I really needed this. I bought into manager at $5,000, and nothing's happening! So I really needed this. It's been since January!" Some members, encouraged to "fake it till you make it," slept in their leased BMWs outside Equinox conventions.

Gouldd's life story changed with the seasons. One night he was a homeless guy who staggered into inspiration, or a corporate do-gooder squeezed by wicked colleagues into going it alone, or a victim of childhood disease who survived to become healthy and rich.

In fact Gouldd served 20 years in multi-level marketing scams, putting half-a-dozen shaky enterprises under his belt, staying a step ahead of criminal charges, and paying a $75,000 civil penalty for his role in National Safety Associates, which sold water filters (and distributorships). As head of Equinox, he was savior and prophet to thousands. Gouldd settled a suit with 14 states in 1996, agreeing not to misrepresent Equinox's earning potential and to make sure members complied with the law.

Many of Gouldd's converts found that the Equinox doctrine worked better in theory than practice. One woman said she had not only ruined her own life, "I misled people because I believed, and then I dragged Sandy [a friend] in. I destroyed this woman's life." When Equinox believers grew shaky, they were told, "If your husband, your mother, your friends, your family are in the way of your success, get rid of 'em. You don't need them. You'll have new friends in Equinox."

Gouldd provided his followers with easy lessons on how to respond to challengers: "There are two kinds of friends: true friends and false friends. True friends support Equinox. False friends don't believe in Equinox." Another favorite was the parable of the apples. "They told us there'd be ripe apples who are ready—who see it. They told us there'd be green apples that weren't ripe yet—who needed help to see it. And they told us there'd be rotten apples... who'd never see it."

Sources:
Fenn, D. "Fast-Sinking Star." *Inc. 500,* October 17, 2000.

Guidera, J. "FTC Charges Nevada Marketing Scheme Operator with Fraud." *Dow Jones Newswire,* August 9, 1999.

Halper, E. "A Road Map to Riches or Ruin? Some Companies Are Busy Marketing a Network of Lies, and Many People Are Buying." *The Philadelphia Inquirer,* May 29, 2000.

Mills, A. "Shaking the Money Tree." *Metro,* October 3-9, 1996.

Related Entries:

CONSUMER FRAUD
PONZI SCHEME

GOVERNMENT AUDITING STANDARDS

See, AUDITING FOR FRAUD

GOVERNMENT FRAUD

Government fraud refers to acts of defalcation committed against government agencies and government-sponsored projects, and also to acts committed by government officials or employees in the course of their work. Common types of government fraud include making false claims and statements to a governmental body, beneficiary fraud, and procurement fraud.

False Claims and Statements

Making a false claim or statement of any sort to a governmental body is considered fraud and prosecutable under several federal statutes. False statements can be oral, written, sworn or unsworn, or signed or unsigned. To be prosecuted for fraud, the person must make a materially false statement that influences the outcome of a governmental body's action, and the statement must be made knowingly with the intent of influencing the action. The false statement need not lead to a favorable agency action. Rather, the government needs only show that officials relied on the statement and the statement is capable of influencing a decision.

The U.S. government suffers particularly from false claims made by care providers and others in the medical industry. Approximately 10% of funds distributed by Medicare/Medicaid are lost to fraud.

Beneficiary frauds are a subset of false claims fraud, which tends to be perpetrated by individuals, such as the taxpayer who claims an unearned tax credit or the Social Security applicant who fakes a disability. Some of the programs most vulnerable to beneficiary fraud include Social Security, Medicare/Medicaid, Farm Aid programs, and Health and Human Services.

Examples of False Claims and Statements

- Falsified qualifications or credentials.
- Falsified certifications or assurances.
- Falsified records or invoices.
- Duplicate claims.

Red Flags of False Claims and Statements

- Failure to produce documents in a timely manner.
- Failure to respond to inquiries in a timely manner.
- Unfulfilled reporting requirements (untimely reports and incomplete reports).

- Inadequate information management system.
- Altered or missing documents.
- Photocopied or duplicate documents.
- Inadequate supporting documentation for reports and summary data.

Procurement Fraud

Procurement fraud refers to acts committed in government purchasing. This fraud may be committed by insiders who manipulate the system to profit themselves or others; outsiders who manipulate or deceive government personnel; or by a conspiracy of insiders and outsiders.

Because procurement fraud is such a problem for the government, the Department of Defense has been involved in the fight against it for years. In fact, the Department of Defense created a Defense Procurement Fraud Unit to handle the heavy caseload.

Government Fraud Auditing Standards

Standards for audits of government organizations, programs, activities, functions, and government assistance received by contractors, nonprofit organizations, and other non-government organizations have been developed by the Comptroller General of the United States, General Accounting Office (GAO). These standards are taken from generally accepted accounting principles. However, the *Government Auditing Standards (2006 Revision)*, also known as the *Yellow Book*, goes beyond the AICPA standards. Generally accepted government auditing standards (GAGAS) are to be followed by auditors and audit organizations when required by law, regulation, agreement, contract, or policy.

Related Entry:

AUDITING FOR FRAUD

CONTRACT AND PROCUREMENT FRAUD

GROCERY COUPON FRAUD

Grocery coupon fraud involves the illegal redemption of merchant coupons for cash. It is committed by retail business owners and individuals. Organized criminal rings commit many coupon frauds. Because clearinghouses that redeem coupons only accept materials from approved vendors, grocery stores and convenience stores are often used to front these operations.

In a typical case, ringleaders acquire coupons en masse by stealing them from manufacturers' facilities, print shops, or newsstands. The materials are stored in a "cutting house," where workers, mainly women, children, and college students, clip individual coupons and sort them.

Workers are instructed to handle the paper aggressively so that it attains a wrinkled or disheveled appearance, mimicking a coupon handled through a retail register. The clipped coupons are shipped in bulk to industry clearinghouses where they are verified and redeemed for cash.

Grocery Coupon Fraud Red Flags

Coupon fraud can be detected by monitoring the account activity of approved vendors.

Red flags include:

- A sudden increase in redemptions.
- Redemptions in excessive amounts, e.g., a convenience store redeeming coupons beyond the norm for a store its size.
- Unruffled coupons—perpetrators do not always attend to the cosmetic factors, instead submitting stacks of coupons in pristine condition.
- Redemptions on items not available in the vendor's geographic location—some brands are only distributed regionally; submissions from stores located outside the region are suspect.

Case Study—1993 WTC Bombing Financed With Coupon Fraud

The 1993 bombing of the World Trade Center was financed in part by an organized coupon-fraud ring. Mahmud Abouhalima, one of four suspects sentenced to life in prison for his involvement in the 1993 bombing, conspired with Ibrahim Abu-Musa and Radwan Ayoub, to establish and maintain the operation.

Source:
"Terrorist Links to Commercial Fraud in the U.S." *The White-Collar Crime Fighter,* December 2001.

HACKING

The term *hacker* originated in the 1950's and 1960's at the Massachusetts Institute of Technology. The term applied to members of the Technical Model Railroad Club who shared an enthusiasm for computing. After these members ("hackers") committed a series of well-publicized computer crimes, the term came to refer to anyone who attempts unauthorized access to computer systems.

The first hackers began networking extensively in the 1970's, using mainframe computers, personal and homemade computers, and phone lines. Hacking remote networks over the telephone system became known as "phone phreaking." Computer enthusiasts distinguish between hackers—who manipulate code legally—and *phreakers* or *crackers*, who use their skills to commit illegal and unethical acts. Proper hacker ethics precludes damaging computer systems or corrupting data.

Hackers in the early 1980s formed loose-knit but highly functional groups, most of whom never spoke in person. The groups chose strange science fiction-like names, such as the Cult of the Dead Cow (cDc), l0pht (one of the oldest and most respected hacking networks), newhackcity, the Masters of Downloading, and milw0rm.

Electronic hacker gathering places on the Internet include the X.25 networks, private computer systems, and other networks. Users exchange information about systems recently compromised, and guides to how the compromise occurred. These electronic gathering places usually include searchable databases, making information available for others. If the information is not immediately available, an attacker interested in a specific target can query others for guidance.

Hacker bulletin boards generally provide system documentation that includes system level accounts and default passwords, known system vulnerabilities, and a variety of other information that facilitates an attack. Bulletin boards also have a variety of tools to facilitate an attack. The tools, such as SATAN, provide a user-friendly method for even the most inept hackers to take advantage of known vulnerabilities. These tools provide various services: some search for vulnerabilities in systems while others attempt to obtain a user's password.

Hacker Techniques

Hacker techniques and the terms that describe them are constantly evolving. Following are some common strategies and tools used to infiltrate computer systems.

War-Dialers

War-dialers are programs configured to call a series of telephone numbers to determine if any of the numbers are connected to a computer. These programs can also be configured to dial a range of numbers to discover valid long-distance calling card numbers. A war-dialer can dial hundreds of numbers in random patterns to avoid detection. The war dialer can recognize when a computer answers because of the unique tone of the answering modem. When the war-dialer finds a valid long-distance calling card number or the number of a computer, the program saves this information in a separate file.

Denial of Service Attacks

Denial of service attacks are accomplished when hackers remotely commandeer large numbers of personal computers connected to the Internet and use them to send huge streams of data packets to a target computer, usually a corporate mainframe or website. The attack ties up the target's system resources with millions or even billions of messages, keeping legitimate users from gaining access to the site. The owners of the hostage computers usually do not know their machines are being used. Denial of service attacks are a growing Internet security threat, especially since many users have high-speed network connections that encourage them to keep their computers almost continuously online.

During three weeks of observation in February 2001, researchers at the University of California at San Diego recorded nearly 13,000 attacks against 5,000 websites. At any one time, there were about 40 brief attacks under way, most lasting less than an hour.

However, about 2% of the attacks spanned a period of days or weeks. The researchers suspect they only catalogued about half of the actual attacks that occurred during the period.

Trojan Horse

A Trojan horse is a set of covert instructions in a program that causes the computer to perform unauthorized functions but usually still allows the program to perform its intended purpose. This is the most common method used in computer-based frauds and sabotage.

Trap Doors

When developing large programs, programmers insert instructions for additional code and intermediate output capabilities. The design of computer operating systems attempts to prevent this from happening. Therefore, programmers insert instructions that allow them to circumvent these controls; the instruction sets are known as trap doors.

Salami Techniques

Salami techniques involve the theft of small amounts of assets
from a large number of sources without noticeably reducing the whole. In a banking system, the amount of interest to be credited to an account is rounded off. Instead of rounding off the number, that fraction of it is credited to a special account owned by the hacker.

Logic Bomb

A logic bomb is a computer program executed at a specific time period or when a specific event occurs. For example, a programmer can write a program to instruct the computer to delete all personnel and payroll files if his name were ever removed from the file.

Data Diddling

Data diddling is the changing of data before or during entry into the computer system. Examples include forging or counterfeiting documents used for data entry and exchanging valid disks and tapes with modified replacements.

Scavenging

Scavenging is the obtaining of information left around a computer system, in the computer room trashcans, etc.

Dumpster Diving

Dumpster diving refers to gleaning sensitive information from an organization's trash receptacles and dumpsters.

Data Leakage

Data leakage is the removing of information by smuggling it out as part of a printed document, encoding the information to look like something different, and removing it from the facility.

Piggybacking/Impersonation

Using another person's identification or physically following someone closely to gain access into an area is referred to as piggybacking or impersonation. Examples include following someone in through a door with a badge reader, electronically using another's user identification and password to gain computer access, and tapping into the terminal link of a user to cause the computer to believe that both terminals are the same person.

Simulation and Modeling

Simulation and modeling are computer manipulation techniques that use the computer as a tool or instrument to plan or control a criminal act.

Wire Tapping

Wire tapping into a computer's communications links to be able to read the information being transmitted between computers is another technique used by hackers.

E-Mail

E-mail can be used to forward viruses or to overload a system. Using email through such systems as the Internet endows senders with identity protection, whereby the original sender of the message can be disguised or obscured.

Hacker Detection Measures

- Almost all communication systems maintain a log file that records all successful and unsuccessful system access attempts. These also allow for the printing of reports containing sign-on and sign-off activity. These reports should be printed out regularly and reviewed by the data security officer. Where possible, special reports should be printed on the number of unsuccessful access attempts. These attempts at logging onto the system should be followed up by data security to determine their cause.
- The data security department should have sufficient resources and staff to administer passwords, maintain the security software, review system activity reports, and follow up on all potential security violations.
- Consultants and/or internal or external auditors should perform periodic reviews of telecommunications security, if they have the necessary experience and qualifications.

Hacker Prevention

- Unless necessary, all computers connected to the Internet should have their file-sharing capability disabled. This protects data from outsiders and keeps the machine from being remotely commandeered.
- Requiring complex alphanumeric passwords and changing them often makes hackers' jobs more difficult and often impossible.
- Firewalls are computer-run filters that control access to internal operations and data.

- Intrusion detection systems back up firewalls by monitoring network activities for irregularities and invader-like behaviors.
- Training all computer users in hacker methods.

Famous Crackers

Cap'n Crunch

Real name: John Draper. Draper taught others in the 1970's after he learned that the Bell Telephone System required a tone of 2600 Hz to authorize a phone call. Draper got his nickname because he found that a toy whistle from a box of Captain Crunch cereal produced the 2600 Hz tone. The term 2600 remains a prominent term in hacker parlance, including its use as the title for hackers' most popular journal *2600.*

Robert Morris

Known to hackers as rtm, Morris became famous when he released an Internet worm in 1988. A graduate student at Cornell at the time, Morris claimed he had accidentally sent out the rogue code, afflicting thousands of computers, primarily at universities, NASA, the military, and other federal government agencies. In one of Morris's early attempts at hacking, he used his account with Bell Labs to attain super-user status, commanding entire systems. Morris drew three years' probation and was fined $10,000.

Kevin Mitnick

Known as Condor, Mitnik was the first hacker featured on an FBI Most Wanted poster. Mitnik became a fugitive in the 1990's when he was charged with attacking the Netcom system and stealing 20,000 credit card numbers. Mitnick claimed he did not use the cards for financial gain. He was also charged with stealing computer code from high-tech companies and causing nearly $300 million in damage.

Legion of Doom

A cracker alliance in the 1980's hacked into and reproduced Bell Telephone's 911 networks. They were also known for breaking into phone company computers, seizing phone lines, and eavesdropping on phone conversations. Two Legion members were convicted of conspiracy and another was convicted of possession of illegal access devices and intent to defraud. Franklin Darden, 24, and Adam Grant, 22, both received 14-month prison sentences, and Robert Riggs, 22, received 21 months. In addition, the men were forced to pay $223,000 in restitution.

Kevin Poulsen

Also known as Dark Dante. After he was caught hacking the US Department of Defense's Arpanet (the predecessor of the Internet) and other networks as a teenager, Poulsen became a security expert with a government contractor. But he continued to break into Pacific Bell computing systems. Besides hacking, he gained information by burgling phone company offices for information. He was charged with computer crimes, espionage (a charge later dropped), and telephone fraud in 1990, but taunted prosecutors with his hacking prowess and evaded arrest for 17 months. On the lam, Poulsen and his two friends seized control of the phone lines of a Los Angeles radio station, ensuring that they'd be the "lucky" 102nd callers. Between them, they won new Porsches, $20,000, and two Hawaiian vacations in a listener contest. When Poulsen was featured on *Unsolved Mysteries*, a reality television crime-solving show, the program's 800 number went dead as Poulsen's picture came on the screen. He was caught in 1991 shortly after the episode aired and was held without bail for five years, then charged with money laundering and wire fraud, while more serious charges were dropped. His eventual release came with the stipulation that he not touch a computer for three more years.

Masters of Deception

An alliance of crackers that attacked the networks of blue-chip corporations (including AT&T, Bank of America, and TRW) hacked into the National Security Agency, using primitive computing machines such as the Commodore 64. Five members of MOD, all under age 22 and of various ethnicities, were tried for computer intrusions and stealing confidential information from credit reports. Convicted in 1992, Phiber Optik (Mark Abene) was sentenced to one year in jail. Acid Phreak (Eli Ladopoulos) and Scorpion (Paul Stira) were given six-month sentences, community service, and probation. Corrupt (John Lee) was sent to prison for a year. Outlaw (Julio Fernandez) cooperated with investigators to avoid jail. Phiber Optik was named by *New York* magazine as one of the city's 100 smartest people.

Vladimir Levin

Levin graduated from St. Petersburg Tekhnologichesky University and went on to lead a cracker alliance. Levin was arrested in London in 1995 and charged with bank fraud and wire fraud for masterminding a break-in of Citibank computers that stole $10 million.

Related Entry:

COMPUTER CRIME

HARPER, ROBERT N.

Robert Harper sold a derivative of coal tar and acetanilide as headache remedy. According to *Stedman's Medical Dictionary,* acetanilide is a poison causing a variety of symptoms, including weakness, faintness, pallor or cyanosis of the face, weak and rapid pulse, and slow and shallow respiration. The drug also causes death in some instances.

A pharmacist by training, Harper was a respected member of society in Washington D.C. in the 1880's. He began selling acetanilide in 1888. He called his product Cuforhedake Brane-Fude—though Brane-Fude means "brain food" in German, Cuforhedake was a Harper coinage that played on the many cognates between the German and English languages. Harper convinced his public that Cuforhedake was an ancient and extremely potent "cure-for-a-headache," selling two million bottles by 1908.

Perhaps because of Harper's social status, authorities treated him laxly. When the Pure Food and Drugs Act was passed in 1906, Harper sought guidance on how to label Cuforhedake, but was told the agency would issue no firm guidelines. Harper listed the ingredients of his concoction as sixteen grains of acetanilide, in a solution of 30% alcohol. Basically Brane-Fude was a strong shot of alcohol with an extra rush provided by the acetanilide. It was known among those who sold patent medicines as a "repeater," because of the repeat business caused by the highly addictive substance. Nevertheless, the government ignored Harper's business, even as *Collier's* magazine published a series of exposés against the patent medicine industry, including 22 deaths caused by acetanilide poisoning. Physicians discussed various case studies and published reports about the drug's deleterious effects, but for several years the government remained quiet on acetanilide sales. Harper's was not the only acetanilide product on the market. A rash of imitators sold cures under the names Orangeine, Koehler's Powders, and Royal Pain Powders.

Harper was indicted in January 1908, charged with fraudulent misrepresentation of a product. The judge instructed the jury to consider whether Harper's remedy could be considered "brain food" by an average citizen. Though he was found guilty, Harper again escaped any significant punishment for his acts. Despite a phone call from President Theodore Roosevelt, asking the prosecutor to "make an example of this man," Harper was charged a fine of $500 on one count, and $200 on a second count.

Sources:
Adams, S. (2000). The Great American Fraud [Electronic Version]. *Colliers.* Retrieved from www.mtn.org/quack/ephemera/dec02-01.htm

Dr. Harris, E. "iMirgraine by Troost: Substance Abuse or Withdrawal." Originally printed in *"Campane,"* the NAPA newsletter, by Harold Segal. 1994. Retrieved from imigraine.net/other/substance.html.

HEALTH CARE FRAUD

The cost of fraud in the American health care industry is estimated at around $100 billion a year, with approximately 10% of the $1-trillion-plus spent each year on health care. Loss estimates range from 3% to as much as 14%. In 2003, health care fraud was estimated to total $85 billion, or 5% of U.S. health care spending. For Medicare, $1 out of every $7 was lost on fraud and abuse, according to the Blue Cross and Blue Shield Association and the U.S. Government Accountability Office.

Besides government insurance programs, there are over 1,500 private insurance companies processing over four billion medical claims every year. These organizations also estimate annual fraud losses at about 10% of all claim dollars. Americans pay up to $1 billion in inflated drug prices caused in part by fraud and loopholes in insurance programs.

Successful Enforcement Efforts

In 2002, the Federal government gained more than $1.8 billion in judgments, settlements, and administrative impositions in health care fraud cases and proceedings. As a result of these activities, and prior year judgments, settlements, and administrative impositions, the Federal government collected over $1.6 billion. Such recovery allowed a $1.4 billion reimbursement to Medicare and $59 million reimbursement to Medicaid.

According to an analysis by *New Directions for Policy,* released in 2001, the U.S. government recovered more than $8 for every dollar spent on anti-fraud efforts using the False Claims Act.

Perpetrators and Methods

Health care fraud is usually committed against private and public insurance companies (Medicare/Medicaid) by providers, subscribers, non-subscribers masquerading as subscribers, insured groups, claims processors, insurance company employees, brokers, and agents. Providers commit most of the acts because they have greater access to the claims system than others.

The Health Insurance Association of America reports that health care professionals commit 72% of these frauds; laboratories and hospitals, 18%; and consumers, 10%.

The most common methods are:

- Billing for services not rendered.
- "Upcoding" a procedure to one reimbursed more lucratively.
- Making a fraudulent diagnosis or applying fraudulent dates to a diagnosis.

Kickbacks are also common in health care fraud. Providers waive deductibles and co-payments for patients; and/or offer free transportation, free goods and services, and cash to patients. Some services pay from $50 to $500 to "cappers" or "runners" who bring in new patients—many of the "patients" are indigent or homeless people who may receive treatment or simply allow their identification to be used for filing false claims. Providers also offer kickbacks in return for insurance and vendor contracts.

The health care industry is especially susceptible to electronic data interchange (EDI) fraud. EDI is used by providers to file claims directly and is widely used for Medicare claims. According to the Health Insurance Association of America, at least a quarter of health insurers' claims are processed electronically.

Who Commits Health Insurance Fraud?

Insurance Fraud Cases By Type of Perpetrator	
Doctors, dentists, chiropractors, and other professionals	72%
Laboratories, medical equipment suppliers, billing agencies, pharmacies, and more	10%
Consumers	10%
Hospitals, outpatient or ambulatory care clinics, and psychiatric hospitals	8%

Source: Health Insurance Association of America

Organized Crime and Health Care Fraud

In late 1999, the Government Accounting Office (GAO) released a study of the Medicare, Medicaid, and private health insurance sectors, which confirmed that organized crime is heavily involved in health care fraud. The GAO examined seven cases of health care fraud.

In those cases alone, about 160 health related groups—medical clinics, physician groups, labs, or medical suppliers—had submitted fraudulent claims. The perpetrators were not health care workers; they were career criminals with records for securities fraud, forgery, and auto theft. Offenders were extremely mobile, moving from New Jersey to California, for example, before authorities in the first state could arrest them. The criminals illegally obtained beneficiary names and medical provider numbers, which they used to file false claims.

Revenue Recovery Firms

Revenue recovery firms employ billing consultants who review bills issued by hospitals, nursing homes, and other facilities (months or even years after treatment) looking for charges that were missed.

Sometimes these firms pad medical bills by adding on fictitious charges. The more charges added onto the bill, the more the recovery firm collects as its share of the institution's reimbursement. Billing consultants are pressured to meet monthly quotas and may be paid bonuses for adding extra charges.

Some facilities aid recovery firms or ignore fraudulent practices in exchange for kickbacks. Common methods of committing fraud in this area are discussed below.

- Consultants change the codes used by facilities. By changing codes, for example, an ordinary five-cent bandage can be billed as a $5 surgical dressing.
- Extra charges are added onto hospital bills by assuming that hospitals used certain items but did not record them. For instance, if video equipment is sometimes, but not always, used in a surgical procedure, the auditor adds the equipment to the bill without verifying its use.
- Recovery firms bill for the removal and handling of donated organs as if the surgery was part of a life-saving treatment.
- Firms charge for additional hours of anesthesia by increasing the time billed to include time spent in a recovery room, or the time the patient waited for the operating room.
- Recovery firms sometimes handle accounts written-off as bad debts. These accounts may be assigned prematurely to a recovery firm before reasonable efforts have been made to collect. Usually this scheme involves collusion between staff and the firm, with the employee receiving a kickback for premature assignments.

Case Study—Police Blotter of Health Care Frauds

The following cases were cited by Gerald Stern, acting as Special Counsel for the U.S. Congress, as part of his investigation into health care fraud. Speaking in 1994, Stern discussed these successful prosecutions as evidence of increased government enforcement.

- In 1992, National Health Laboratories, Inc. (NHL) and its president and CEO pleaded guilty in San Diego to submitting false claims to the United States. The corporation paid a $1 million criminal fine, and its President paid a $500,000 criminal fine and served three months in prison. The corporation also paid $100 million in a civil settlement involving Medicare and CHAMPUS, and $10.4 million to 33 state Medicaid Fraud Control Units.

- In 1994, McKesson Corporation paid $765,000 to settle claims that it overcharged the Oregon Medicaid program for the cost of drugs dispensed to State Medicaid recipients. The United States charged that McKesson had submitted several hundred thousand claims for payment to Medicaid for prescription drugs in which they falsely represented that the brand name drug—which was more expensive than the generic drug—was medically necessary.
- Group Health Association, Inc. (GHA), a Health Maintenance Organization, agreed to pay $12,629,123 to resolve claims by the United States that GHA overcharged federal agencies and employees for health care benefits from 1990 through 1993, based on misleading disclosures of rates paid to other large groups of employees.
- An attorney was convicted in Philadelphia in March 1994 of 107 counts of mail fraud and 17 counts of money laundering in connection with his operation of three unlicensed insurance companies, which falsely claimed that Blue Cross funded the policies. His companies took in $34 million in health insurance premiums and left victims with $5.6 million in unpaid claims. He faces between 97 and 121 months in prison.

Sources:
Gastel, R. "Insurance Issues Update." *Insurance Information Institute,* October 2000.

The Department of Health and Human Services and the Department of Justice Health Care Fraud and Abuse Control Program Annual Report For FY 2002.

Related Entries:

BRINKLEY, JOHN
CHIROPRACTIC FRAUD
COLUMBIA/HCA
COUNTERFEIT DRUGS
HEALTH INSURANCE FRAUD BY CLAIMANTS
HOME HEALTH FRAUD
HOSPITALS, INSURANCE FRAUD BY
HOXSEY, HARRY

INSURANCE COMPANIES, FRAUD BY
LABORATORY FRAUD,
MANAGED CARE FRAUD
MEDICAID/MEDICARE FRAUD
NURSING HOME FRAUD
PHARMACY FRAUD
PROVIDER FRAUD
PSYCHIATRISTS AND PSYCHIATRIC FACILITIES, FRAUD BY
QUACK
SUPPLIER FRAUD,
WORKERS' COMPENSATION FRAUD

HEALTH INSURANCE FRAUD BY CLAIMANTS

The Health Insurance Association of America says the most common health-insurance frauds committed by customers are falsifying claims, falsifying records of employment and eligibility, and pharmacy fraud.

Common acts include:

- Sharing an ID card with someone not entitled to use it.
- Enrolling ineligible people for coverage.
- Altering amounts charged on claim forms or prescription receipts.
- Fabricating claims.
- Submitting claims in the names of dead people.
- Concealing pre-existing conditions or history.
- Filing for multiple surgeries and multiple office visits.
- Filing false claims in foreign countries, often in collusion with foreign providers.
- "Doctor/ER shopping," visiting several doctors or health care facilities to obtain drugs.
- Bribing adjusters to collude in fraud.
- Continuing to file claims on a family policy following a divorce.

Recognizing Health Care Fraud by Claimants

The following traits often indicate a fraudulent claim perpetrated by the claimant:

- Misspelled medical/dental terminology.
- Unusual charges for a given service.
- Similar handwriting by the claimant and the provider of service.
- The claimant requests substantial payments to be made to him/her rather than the provider.
- Typed, not printed, billheads.
- Bills with irregular columns.
- Unassigned bills that are normally assigned, such as large hospital or surgical bills.
- Typed or handwritten hospital bills.
- Drug receipts from the same pharmacy but on different colored paper.
- Erasures or alterations.
- Lack of any provider's signature on a claim form.
- Absence of the provider's medical degree, i.e., "Dr. John Doe" instead of "John Doe, M.D."
- An illegible provider signature on the bill submitted or the signature does not match the one on file.
- Surgeries that do not have other related services such as hospital charges.
- Physician's specialty does not agree with diagnosis.
- Services billed do not agree with diagnosis.
- Impossible or unlikely services.
- Photocopied bills.
- Pressure by a claimant to pay a claim quickly.
- Individuals who hand deliver their claim insist on picking up their claim check.
- A threat of legal action if a claim is not paid quickly.
- Anonymous telephone calls regarding the status of a pending claim.
- Identical claims for same patient in different months or different years.
- Dates of service just prior to termination of enrollment or just after enrollment.
- Services billed that do not appear to agree with the medical records.
- Billing for services or equipment that are clearly unsuitable for the patient's needs.

- Foreign claims listing charges in U.S. dollars when that is not the country's currency.
- Foreign claims giving documentation in English when English is not the primary language spoken.
- Multiple foreign claims for the same subscriber.
- Multiple foreign claims from the same physician or hospital.

Testing for Fraudulent Claims

The following steps can pinpoint health care fraud in claims:

- Review and evaluation of all elements of the claim file.
- Determining if the medical language appears to be proper by comparing sample of bona fide claims.
- Submission of a letter to the attending physician to determine if the charges are correct.
- Obtaining information from law enforcement regarding the legitimacy of the claim.
- Checking the style of the date. In many foreign countries, dates are listed with the day first, and then the month and year, e.g., 07/01/96 would be 7 January 1996. If the U.S. style of dating is used (month/day/year) in a foreign claim, it may indicate a fraudulent claim.

Additional Reference Sources:
Health Insurance Association of America

National Health-Care Anti-Fraud Association

Wells, J., CFE, CPA, et al. *"Fraud Examiners Manual."* Association of Certified Fraud Examiners, 2002.

Related Entry:

HEALTH CARE FRAUD

HEALTHSOUTH CORP. FRAUD

HealthSouth Corp. is considered one of the largest providers of healthcare services in the US. Between the period of 1996 and 2000, the company was found to have falsified financial records in order to show a progressive quarter-to-quarter growth per year. On

March 19, 2003, the SEC Complaint for Injunctive and Other Relief exposed this case. The company's employees manipulated records, inaccurately accounted for receivables and bad debt, and altered reserve accounts in order to make the company's stock price fluctuate according to estimates on Wall Street.

Red Flags

Auditors in this case should have noticed the red flags. Specifically:

- Having seen that HealthSouth met Wall Street earnings' estimates each quarter, auditors should have questioned *how* exactly the company managed to consistently pull this off.
- Auditors should have been alert to the fact that the company experienced slowing revenue growth directly after stints of above average returns. This fluctuation in revenue is a key motivator for financial statement fraud and skeptical auditors should have confronted management about this.
- The provision for doubtful accounts varied more than other factors should have supported. Auditors should have paid more attention to the fact that the numbers reported varied from the "expected accounted balances" estimates that were prepared before the audit.
- The asset turnover ratio declined, despite the claim that acquisitions would improve efficiency.

Convictions

In June 2005, former (and fired) CEO Richard Scrushy was acquitted of all 36 federal counts of conspiracy, false reporting, fraud, and money laundering. He was the first CEO to be charged under the Sarbanes-Oxley corporate reporting law. He blamed 15 former HealthSouth executives, who all plead guilty, for the $2.7 billion earning overstatement fraud at HealthSouth, the rehabilitation and medical services chain. Scrushy sued HealthSouth for $70 million on the grounds of being wrongly fired from the company. He was subsequently convicted of civil charges in a separate government bribery scheme that occurred during his time at HealthSouth.

Of those executives that Scrushy blamed, Hannibal "Sonny" Crumpler, was convicted in November 2005 for conspiracy charges as well as for lying to auditors. He received an eight year prison sentence, much to the dismay of the government who requested that he serve 15 years. In December 2005, Bill Owens, a former one-time CFO, was given a five year prison sentence for his role in the HealthSouth fraud. In September 2006, after being tried three times, Michael Martin, another one of HealthSouth's five former CFOs who plead guilty in this case, was sentenced to three years in prison with the possibility of being released to a half-way house after 30 months. Martin's first two trials ended in relatively light sentences (probation and then seven days in jail) for pleading guilty and testifying against former CEO, Richard Scrushy. Martin was given the three year prison sentence when he was retried after the 11th Circuit Court of Appeals found that his first two sentences were insufficient.

Settlement

In September 2006, a finalized $445 million settlement agreement between HealthSouth and investors was announced. HealthSouth will pay $215 million in cash, stocks and warrants to investors, while insurance companies will pay the $230 million balance.

Sources:

lawprofessors.typepad.com/whitecollarcrime_blog/healthsouth/index.html

msnbc.msn.com/id/15029181/

Related Entries:

FINANCIAL STATEMENT FRAUD

SECURITIES FRAUD

HEBBORN, ERIC

Eric Hebborn was born in 1934, attended the Royal Academy School, and later became a scholar at the British School in Rome where he won the prize for engraving in 1959. At the Royal Academy he worked as an apprentice restorer and there he learned to fake watermarks, wormholes, fox marks, collectors' stamps, and various techniques for aging paper and ink.

Hebborn was an infamous art forger who passed off his drawings as works of the Masters for more than 40 years, his productions passing the most intense scrutiny of the world's greatest experts. Hebborn claimed he created over 1,000 fake drawings, though only about 250 have so far been pinpointed.

According to his own account, he began forging to seek revenge against the art-dealing establishment, which he regarded as "vulgar, avaricious creatures with good backgrounds, smart accents, fine educations, and infinite pretensions, who control the art trade from the top and for whom a work of art is as good or bad as the amount it fetches." He claimed "the real criminals are those who give wrong information about works of art. They fall into two categories—the expert and the dealer… The more competent the expert, the more pleasure I derive from being able to lead him astray."

Supposedly Hebborn had bought several drawings in a junk shop for £12 and sold them to Colnaghi's, a prominent art house in London for £25. He later saw the same drawings displayed at Colnaghi's on sale for thousands of pounds. Hebborn said he began planning a way to ensnare all the major dealers.

Between the late 1950's and 1996, Hebborn forged more than 1,000 drawings and paintings in a broad range of styles. He specialized in European artists from the 15th to the 20th centuries. Besides the actual paint strokes, he faked the Masters' materials: He made ink from historically accurate ingredients; he bought Renaissance-era books and manuscripts and tore out the pages to use as his sketchpad. He reproduced tiny abrasions and nicks in the paper and canvas.

His specialty was to fake the drawings a Master might have used as the first steps to a painting. These drawings are sometimes even more valuable than the paintings they were prepared for. For example, Hebborn studied the painting "The Crowning with Thorns," by the Flemish-born Anthony van Dyck and then faked a series of "preparatory studies" in which the painter had supposedly sketched certain pieces of the larger composition.

Many of Hebborn's early fakes gained authority from the endorsement of Sir Anthony Blunt, an art historian and director of the Courtauld Institute. In 1964, Blunt was exposed as a Soviet spy, the elusive "fourth man" in the Cambridge espionage ring, regarded as the biggest case of political treason in the history of England. Blunt claimed he knew the

Hebborns were fakes, though Hebborn always maintained he had duped Blunt, who was a friend and lover, along with the rest of the art establishment.

Hebborn was exposed in the late 1970's when curators at the National Gallery noticed that drawings by two Italian artists, both purchased from Hebborn, were drawn on paper from the same source. Hebborn gloated about his exploits in two publications, *Drawn to Trouble: Confessions of a Master Forger* (1991) and *The Art Forger's Handbook* (1997).

Hebborn was beaten in a public park in Rome in January 1996, sustaining serious injuries and a broken skull. He died a few days later.

Sources:

Golomstock, I. "The Forger and the Spy; Eric Hebborn and Anthony Blunt." *Commentary,* May 1, 1999.

Landesman, P. "From the Crisis of Fakes." *The Scotsman,* March 18, 2001.

Related Entry:

COUNTERFEIT ART

HIDDEN ASSETS

Perpetrators often hide the assets of crimes such as embezzlement, bankruptcy fraud, tax fraud, or drug smuggling. Following is a discussion of the various methods of hiding assets.

Methods of Hiding Assets, General

Transfer to Family Members or Parties under Their Control

The most common means of hiding assets, particularly real estate and business interests, is to transfer the asset(s) into the hands of another party that will allow the target to maintain control. Assets can be transferred to a spouse or another member of the spouse's family. Husbands sometimes transfer assets into a wife's maiden name.

Such transfers can be identified through a search of voter registration, marriage records, and probate records in the spouse's maiden name. Transfers to family members can be detected by comparing the target's previous financial statement with the newest one. Those assets appearing on the oldest statement but not appearing on the most recent statement should be examined closely to determine the nature of the transaction, the purchaser's identity, and the consideration for the sale.

Children's or Family Trust

The defendant in a financial case might seek to protect assets by transferring them to a children's or family trust from a personal estate. These assets would then be protected from judgment or bankruptcy proceedings in a court of law. If the transfer was made to defeat creditors, however, the court can set it aside.

Home Mortgage Pay-Down

Subjects prepay a significant portion of their home mortgage. Assets can be sheltered in a homestead exemption (in Texas, Florida, and other states) that will survive bankruptcy or other claims against them.

Insurance Policies

Under the terms of a whole life or universal life insurance policy, the borrower may make additional payments that accrue at a high interest rate and enhance the overall value of the insurance policy.

Substantial monies can be deposited into an existing insurance policy using the face value of the policy to disguise equity accumulated through prepayments. The person's financial statement may reveal the existence and details of these insurance policies.

Prepaid Credit Cards

Many credit accounts permit the cardholder to prepay their accounts. This allows people to hide cash from creditors. Prepayment of credit card accounts can also be found in Cash Management Accounts (CMA's) offered by stock brokerage firms.

Savings Bond Purchases

Drug dealers, tax evaders, and people filing, or about to file bankruptcy often use savings bonds to conceal their ready cash. Perpetrators may purchase bonds in their individual names, the name of a spouse (a maiden name), or in their children's names.

Cashier's Checks and Traveler's Checks

Cashier's checks and traveler's checks allow users to hide their financial dealings and reduce the amount of cash they carry. Through the purchase of cashier's checks or traveler's checks in denominations of less than $10,000 the criminal can carry negotiable financial instruments that can be exchanged almost any place in the world.

Divorce Cases and Hidden Assets

Divorce proceedings often provide an opportunity to hide assets. Some of the common methods particular to these cases include:

- A spouse may persuade an employer to delay delivery of a bonus, stock option, retirement benefit, or pay raise until after a divorce is final.
- Payments to nonexistent employees, with the checks becoming void after the date of divorce.
- Monies are paid from a business account to someone with close personal ties, such as a father, brother, or uncle, for services never actually performed.
- Custodial accounts appear in the name of a child, under the child's Social Security number.
- Signing of formal business contracts is delayed.
- Cash is converted to traveler's checks.
- Antiques, artwork, hobby equipment, gun collections, or tools are physically hidden.
- Other cases include skimming cash from a business owned, "debt repayment" to a friend for an alleged outstanding obligation, or expenses paid to a new girl or boyfriend for items such as gifts, travel, rent, or tuition for college or other educational classes.

Locating Hidden Assets

The following sources may reveal hidden assets:

Public Records

Many documents useful in tracing illicit transactions, particularly real estate and personal property filings, are public record.

Computer Databases

Information on individuals and businesses can be obtained through commercial databases and online services. The text of newspapers such as *The New York Times* or *The Washington Post* may be searched for articles on the foreign bank or the foreign country involved. The texts of these and other large newspapers are available through online services such as LEXIS-NEXIS or through CD-ROM disks.

Locating Assets through Subpoenas

Criminal and certain civil fraud examiners have subpoena power allowing them to obtain nonpublic records, including bank account and loan records, records from accountants and tax preparers (including income tax returns and related documents), mortgage company records, telephone toll records, credit card statements, credit reporting company records, hotel and travel records, telex records, overnight package envelopes, and passports.

Locating Assets with a Check

If the subject engages in a mail order or retail business, a simple way to get information about the subject's bank accounts is to purchase an item via check. The canceled check provides the name and possibly the account number of the subject's bank. If the subject does not engage in mail-order sales, sending the subject a small "refund" check will accomplish the aim.

Locating Assets Offshore

Perpetrators may shift assets offshore to tax havens and secrecy jurisdictions. Historically, some of the most popular offshore jurisdictions have been Switzerland, Cayman Islands, Netherlands Antilles, and Panama.

Strategies for locating offshore assets include:

- Reviewing domestic bank account records for wire transfers or other transactions involving offshore bank accounts.

- Determining whether the subject personally traveled overseas. Overseas travel can often be traced from U.S. Customs records available through FinCEN.
- Attempt to locate the subject's travel agency.
- Attempt to identify the means employed to move cash offshore by multiple cashier's checks, overnight mail envelopes, or other methods.

Transferring Assets to the U.S.

For transfers back to the United States, a perpetrator may use a foreign attorney or bank officer as a trustee or front to purchase assets in the United States, or appoint the trustee as manager of a United States business.

Subjects might also obtain access to their assets offshore by using foreign credit cards. Many international institutions now offer MasterCard or Visa accounts. All account records are maintained in the foreign country. Sophisticated subjects might obtain foreign passports (in a fictitious name, if requested). Some countries offer such passports to people who deposit $25,000 in the state-run financial institution.

Locating Information on Foreign Banks and Businesses

Dun & Bradstreet publishes several guides with information about businesses in Latin America, Europe, and other regions of the world. The U.S. Department of Commerce employs international experts who can locate business information on any country in the world.

In *Competitor Intelligence*, Leonard Fuld suggests the following resources as starting points:

- Securities brokers with expertise in dealing with foreign businesses.
- The International Trade Commission.
- International trade shows.
- Foreign consulates.
- Foreign chambers of commerce.
- Foreign magazines and directories.

Fuld provides a list of consulates, chambers of commerce, magazines, and directories in his book. He suggests consulting *Euromoney 500*, which contains profiles of the world's top 500 banks, and *The Europa Year Book*, which provides basic data on banks around the world.

Case Study—Waste Company Owner Hides Assets

William Douglas Lomow owned a waste-hauling company, Orinda-Moraga Disposal, serving 11,000 customers until the company folded in 1996. Lomow was convicted and sentenced to six years in federal prison for stealing $3 million in assets diverted from the company during 1994 and 1995. Lomow's partner, Robert Sliepka, served 15 months for income tax fraud for assisting.

Lomow bought the franchise from a local family in 1991 and operated more or less without incident until 1995, when the franchise was up for renewal. At that time Lomow demanded a 28% rate increase to stave off bankruptcy and refused to bid on renewing the contract. He continued to appear before city councils served by the franchise, offering to haul trash for less than the district charged.

Even after the conviction, Lomow would not cooperate with court officers seeking to recover the assets. Investigators searched from 1997 to 2000 before announcing their success. The search led across the western United States and Canada, covering multiple businesses and scores of bank accounts.

The case was brought to light by forensic auditors who were hired by the regional Sanitary District to investigate suspicious circumstances in the operation of the company. According to the trustee, "Auditors noticed there were all these regular payments in the same amount to title companies in Idaho and Oregon, and to me that meant they were buying land on sales contracts, so it was a matter of following leads and asking questions. That eventually led to the equipment Lomow had hidden all over the western U.S. and Canada."

Sources:
Wells, J., CFE, CPA, et al. *"Fraud Examiners Manual."* Association of Certified Fraud Examiners, 2002.

Wiley, W. "Officials Unearth Assets Hidden by California Hauler." *Waste News,* December 11, 2000.

Related Entries:

CASH FLOW ANALYSIS

FINANCIAL PROFILE

MONEY LAUNDERING

NET WORTH ANALYSIS

HITLER DIARIES

In early 1983, a West German weekly magazine, *Stern*, announced it had acquired 62 volumes of Adolph Hitler's secret diaries, kept during the years 1932 to 1945. The contents were sold for serialization to magazines and newspapers in England, France, Italy, and elsewhere. Throughout the world, the diaries became a major news event.

The diaries' pages were bound in black imitation leather. They were brought to *Stern* by a correspondent, Gerd Heidemann, who got them from an undisclosed source and sold them for 10 million marks to *Stern*. Supposedly the diaries had been first recovered in April 1945—a plane crashed and Hitler loyalists hid the books in a nearby barn, where they sat until Heidemann's associates recovered them.

Many historians hailed the diaries as an amazing discovery. Hugh Trevor-Roper argued that the materials had to be authentic because there was so much material and contents that displayed an internal coherence. Handwriting experts found that the handwriting matched other samples of Hitler's script. However, a number of critics challenged the documents' authenticity after *Stern* published excerpts and allowed only certain people to examine the materials. West Germany's Interior Minister Friedrich Zimmermann declared, "The Federal Archive is convinced that documents they were given did not come from Hitler's hand, but were produced in the postwar period."

Luis-Ferdinand Wener, who had supervised chemical analysis on the paper, cover, bindings, labels, and glue used in three of the seven volumes, said flatly that the diaries were "obvious fakes." Federal Archives President Hans Booms believed the materials were mostly plagiarized from *Hitler's Speeches and Proclamations* 1932-45, written in 1962 by a former Nazi Federal Archivist, Max Domarus. The *Stern* diaries contained some of the same errors that historians had discovered in the Domarus book after its publication.

German scientists conducted a chemical analysis, which found, among other things, that the books' binding contained polyester threads, which were not produced until after World War II. The glue also contained postwar chemicals. The ink was composed of postwar chemicals and had only recently been applied to the paper. The same typewriter had been used to type the labels on all the volumes.

As evidence mounted that the diaries were faked, German authorities convinced Heidemann to reveal his source. Known as "Dr. Fisher" to *Stern* editors, the purveyor of the diaries was Konrad Kujau. An investigation revealed that Kujau had become rich by forging *Mein Kampf* manuscripts and paintings supposedly done by Hitler himself.

Kujau confessed that he had forged almost over 150 Hitler paintings and sketches that were published in *Adolf Hitler: The Unknown Artist*, collected by Billy Price and published in 1983. Kujau and Heidemann were each later sentenced to four and a half years in prison. Following the scandal, Kujau began selling his acknowledged forgeries and copies and continued to do so until he died in September, 2000.

Source: Magnuson, E. "Hitler's Forged Diaries." *Time Magazine*, May 16, 1983.

Related Entries:

COUNTERFEIT DOCUMENTS
FORGERY

HOAXES

A hoax is an act of mass deception in which material gains credibility by repetition and the endorsement of respected public figures. Sometimes the endorsers are participating in the hoax; more often, they are deceived. As the information in a hoax circulates, it is often exaggerated beyond the source. Hoaxes may be stories with little direct consequence, following the 1808 definition of the term from the Oxford English Dictionary: "Contriving wonderful stories for the public." Or, they may have destructive effects, like those caused by the Piltdown Man hoax, discussed below.

Hoaxes and Urban Myths

The term hoax is sometimes used synonymously with "urban myth." Urban myths cover everything from stories about slashers stalking teen lovers to the "Neiman Marcus Cookies" recipe, in which a recipe from the retailer, supposedly selling for $225, is shared free of charge. However, Alex Boese, compiler of the Internet's "Museum of Hoaxes," argues that urban myths are not hoaxes. A true hoax is deliberately launched by a specific individual or group, where the urban myth is more or less "authorless," as myths and folktales are.

Scientific Hoaxes

Scientific hoaxes are more serious than most hoaxes because they alter collective knowledge, can be expensive to disprove, and may be used to gain research funds on faulty premises.

One of the most infamous and successful scientific hoaxes was known as the Piltdown Man. An amateur anthropologist named Charles Dawson claimed in 1912 that he had discovered ancient human bones in gravel pits near Piltdown, England. Dawson convinced Arthur Smith of the British Museum that the bones, which Dawson had planted himself, dated to 500 million years B.C., during the Lower Pleistocene period. Other finds in the area included animal bones, a crude hammer-like tool, and two more humanoid skulls. The British Museum exhibited the Piltdown findings and the discovery was featured in articles and textbooks.

But in 1953, an inquiry by the British Museum discovered the materials were faked. The Piltdown Man skull was approximately 50,000 years old, but the jawbone was no more than 30 to 40 years old. The jaw had been painted with potassium dichromate to simulate aging. Someone, apparently Dawson, had taken the jawbone and teeth of a modern ape, probably an orangutan, and used it to construct the Piltdown Man. Subsequent investigation found that Dawson had passed off other creations as authentic finds.

Computer Hoaxes

Many virus warnings and files shared over the Internet and e-mail are hoaxes. Usually the hoax is a text file that describes the devastation being perpetrated by a new virus. Sometimes hoax files are executable files that send a message to the computer owner that the virus is attacking or destroying files, even though the program is harmless.

Nevertheless, even though hoaxes do not harm machines, they can be time-consuming for system administrators and others who must investigate them, clear material from large systems, and reassure others that the material was bogus.

How to Recognize a Computer Hoax

Hoaxes almost always come with a directive to circulate the material—"send this to everyone you know," for example. This is a red flag, because a real warning message from a credible source would caution against forwarding materials that might be infected.

Hoaxbusters, a website supported by the U.S. Department of Energy, suggests that there are two known factors that make a successful hoax:

- Technical sounding language that does not stand to reason.
- Credibility by association.

For example, the Good Times hoax contained a message that read,

> "*...If the program is not stopped, the computer's processor will be placed in an nth-complexity infinite binary loop which can severely damage the processor...*"

However, there is no such thing as an "nth-complexity infinite binary loop" and processors are designed to run loops for weeks at a time without damage.

The following sites contain archives and regular updates concerning computer hoaxes.
hoaxbusters.ciac.org/
www.symantec.com/avcenter/hoax.html
www.datafellows.fi/virus-info/hoax/

Source: Boese, D. www.museumofhoaxes.com/

HOME HEALTH FRAUD

A form of health care fraud, home health fraud refers to acts committed by agencies specializing in caring for patients in the patients' residence. Common acts include charging for unnecessary care or care not provided.

From fiscal years 1990 to 1997, the provision of home health agency services was one of the fastest growing expenditures in Medicare. During this period, expenditures rose from $3.3 billion to $18 billion. Home health was impacted by Medicare payment reductions imposed by the Balanced Budget Act of 1997, and by the year 2000, more than 3,000 agencies closed or merged. The introduction of the Medicare Home Health Prospective Payment System (PPS) in October 2000 stabilized the industry, and it is now expected to grow at an annual rate of 5% to 10% due to demographic trends, relative cost advantages, and efficiencies under the PPS. The sector's stock price performance has mirrored this trend. Since 2002, the home health agency (HHA) sector has outperformed the S&P 500.

Profitability within the HHA industry varies and profit margins are difficult to gauge. The median operating margin for publicly traded HHAs has been positive since 1999 and reached 2.3% in 2002. Significant variability exists among the publicly traded HHAs and there have been many bankruptcies in the sector. Analysts note that smaller HHAs have shifted patient mix to favor Medicare patients as Medicare payments under the PPS offer the highest margins. Because many HHAs do not have a proven track record of success and are subject to regulatory reimbursement risk, both equity and debt investors perceive the sector as risky, which ultimately leads to limited access to capital.

The fraud rate has grown with the industry. A study of Medicare claims showed that $4 billion out of the $18 billion paid to home-health providers in 1996 was suspect. Less than 4% of agencies receive on-site audits by Medicare contractors and the beneficiaries are not required to make a co-payment, making it less likely that a beneficiary will complain about the extent of service.

1997 Reforms to Home Health in Medicare/Medicaid

In late 1997, the Medicare program accepted no new home health agencies for 6 months because of rampant abuse. The General Accounting Office found high levels of fraudulent billings in numerous studies of home health care. In a July 1997 report, results of the Operation Restore Trust Audit of Medicare Home Health Services in California, Illinois, New York, and Texas, analysts evaluated a sample of 3,745 services in 250 home health claims in four states. An estimated 40% of the services did not meet Medicare reimbursement requirements.

Significant levels of inappropriate billings were noted in the June 1997 report. A review of 80 of the most expensive claims in one state revealed that 43% of the claims should have been partially or totally denied. For example, 83 home health agencies in one state have been reviewed under this project since 1995. About $33 million was identified in inappropriate Medicare payments.

As part of the 1997 reform to Medicare and Medicaid programs, Congress required home health agencies to obtain surety bonds; the funds were to cover any fraud complaints later proved against the agency. The bond measure was based on a state law in Florida, where it helped save $200 million over a two-year period.

Demographic Profile of Home Health Patients

About 4 million beneficiaries of Medicare/Medicaid receive care at home. Compared to the Medicare population as a whole home health patients:

- Are more likely to be female.
- Are more likely to live alone.
- Tend to be poor; 43% have incomes below $10,000.
- Are more likely to have two or more daily living impairments and rate their health status as poor.

Significant departures from this profile in an agency's patient records may indicate fraud.

Requirements and Provisions for Government-Sponsored Home Health Care

To receive home health care, a beneficiary must be recommended to the program by a physician who has established a plan of care. The beneficiary must be confined to the home and require intermittent skilled nursing care, physical therapy, speech language pathology services, or have a continuing need for occupational therapy.

Medicare pays for the following home health services:

- Skilled nursing care on a part-time or intermittent basis.
- Physical and occupational therapy.
- Speech language pathology services.
- Medical social services.
- Home health aide services for personal care related to the treatment of the beneficiary's illness or injury on a part-time or intermittent basis.

Home Health Fraud Schemes

The most common fraud schemes in the home health area are:

- Cost reporting fraud.
- Billing for services not rendered.
- Upcoding visits to a higher reimbursement code, such as a skilled nursing visit.
- Billing for services rendered to persons not "home bound."
- Altering medical records to justify continuing visits.
- Recording visits that are never made.
- Forging physicians' signatures on plans of care.

Procedures associated with venipuncture, or the drawing of blood, are particularly rife with fraud. Before regulatory provisions were revised in 1997, a condition involving a blood draw allowed for virtually unlimited home health visits, even when the beneficiary did not require skilled medical care. Under the later guidelines, only individuals needing other skilled therapy or nursing services in addition to venipuncture can receive blood draws paid for by Medicare.

Numerous examples of abuse continue to be associated with venipuncture. Investigators have discovered beneficiaries submitting to blood draws who had been prescribed a blood-thinning drug, but needed no other skilled treatment. As part of adjusting a patient's drug dose, physicians ordered skilled nursing visits to patients' homes to draw blood for laboratory testing. In a case described by Nancy-Ann Min Deparle of the U.S. Health Care Financing Administration, a patient whose condition did not require skilled treatment was visited 1 to 2 times weekly by a skilled nurse. Additionally, a home health aide attended the residence 12 hours a day, 7 days a week to assist in showering, meal preparation, shopping, laundry, housekeeping, safety supervision, and transport.

Related Entry:

HEALTH CARE FRAUD
MEDICAID/MEDICARE FRAUD

HOME REPAIR FRAUD

No firm numbers are available on the total cost and frequency of home repair fraud, but studies show this to be a major economic and social issue. In 2005, the National Association of Consumer Agency Administrations reported that the number one complaint they received from consumers dealt with home improvement and repair fraud. Americans spend an estimated $133.9 billion on contracted home improvement projects and do-it-yourself repairs. If 10% of that went to fraud, the U.S. figure alone would exceed $13 billion. Many states have acknowledged an epidemic of construction fraud. In Denver, Colorado during 1999, home repair fraud accounted for 20% of the cases handled by consumer services. Statewide, construction cases made up 8% of the attorney general's caseload, and some 20% of consumer losses prosecuted by the state, about $3 million.

Groundbreaking Illinois Law

A law regulating the home repair business in Illinois, ratified in 2000, has become a model for reformers. Key points of the law include:

- Prior to initiating home repair or remodeling work for over $1,000, a person engaged in the business of home repair or remodeling must furnish customers a written contract or work order that states the total cost, including parts and materials listed with reasonable particularity and any charge for an estimate.
- The contract must state the business name and address of the person engaged in the business. If the person uses a post office box or other service, the contract must state

the residence address of the person engaged in the business or home repair or remodeling.

- Persons selling home repair and improvement services must provide their customers with notice of any change to their business name or address that comes about prior to the agreed dates for beginning or completing the work.

Home Repair Schemes

Some typical schemes include:

- The quick repair made with materials left over from another job. The perpetrator approaches a homeowner with an offer to repair the driveway or roof with materials left over from another job in the neighborhood. Many of these fraudulent workers appear after heavy rains, winds, snow, or other disasters that wreck lawns, roads, and driveways. The person may use inferior materials, make faulty repairs, or not do the job at all.
- A home improvement loan, financed through a lender the contractor knows. Once the job is underway, the contractor and the lender pressure the homeowner to sign a series of blank or vaguely written contracts. The homeowner has unwittingly signed a contract for a home equity loan with alarmingly high interest rates and payments. The contractor may not complete the job satisfactorily or even finish it at all.
- Homeowners may be tricked into signing papers that allow fraudulent contractors to obtain mortgages or assign liens against their property. In these instances, homeowners—especially older homeowners—could face foreclosure if they cannot make the high mortgage payments.

Home Repair Fraud Red Flags

- Door-to-door salespersons with no local connections that offer to do home repair work for substantially less than the market price.
- Solicitations for repair work from a company that lists only a telephone number or a post-office box number to contact, particularly if it is an out-of-state company.
- Contractors who fail to provide customers references when requested.

- Persons offering to inspect your home for free. Do not admit anyone into your home unless he or she can present authentic identification establishing his or her business status. When in doubt, do not hesitate to call the worker's employer to verify his identity.
- Contractors demanding cash payment for a job or who ask you to make a check payable to a person other than the owner or company name.
- Offers from a contractor to drive you to the bank to withdraw funds to pay for the work.

Avoiding Home Repair Fraud

- Homeowners should get all estimates in writing.
- Consumers should not allow themselves to be induced into signing a contract by high-pressure sales tactics.
- Consumers should never sign a contract with blank spaces or one they do not fully understand. If they are taking out a loan to finance the work, they should not sign the contract before their lender approves the loan.
- Remember, consumers have 3 business days from the time they sign the contract to cancel the contract if the sale is made at their home. The contractor cannot deprive them of this right by initiating work, selling the contract to a lender, or any other tactic.
- If the contractor does business under a name other than the contractor's real name, the business must either be incorporated or registered under the Assumed Business Name Act. Check with the Secretary of State to see if the business is incorporated or with the county clerk to see if the business has registered under the Assumed Business Name Act.
- Homeowners should check with local and county units of government to determine if permits or inspections are required.
- Determine whether the contractor will guarantee his work and products.
- Determine whether the contractor has the proper insurance.
- Do not sign a certificate of completion or make final payment until the work is done to satisfaction.

- Remember, homeowners should know who provides supplies and labor for any work performed on their home. Suppliers and subcontractors have a right to file a lien against the homeowner's property if the general contractor fails to pay them. For homeowners to protect their property, they need to request lien waivers from the general contractor.
- Any home repair contract should include the following information:
  - Contractor's full name, address, and telephone number.
  - A description of the work to be performed.
  - Starting and estimated completion dates.
  - Total cost of work to be performed.
  - Schedule and method of payment, including down payment, subsequent payments, and final payment.
  - A provision stating the grounds for termination of the contract by either party. However, the homeowner must pay the contractor for work completed. If the contractor fails to commence or complete work within the contracted time period, the homeowner may cancel and may be entitled to a refund of any down payment or other payments made towards the work, upon written demand by certified mail.
  - Homeowners should obtain a copy of the signed contract and keep it in a safe place for reference as needed.

Sources:
Illinois Public Act 91-0230 Entitled the Home Repair and Home Remodeling Act Was Passed By the State Legislature and Took Effect on January 1, 2000.

Kerven, A." Growth's Unscrupulous Elements." *ColoradoBiz,* March 1, 1999.

"Preventing Home Repair Fraud." *Catalyst. Changing Our Communities Through Crime Prevention,* October 1999. www.ncpc.org/catalyst/9910d.htm

Related Entry:

CONSUMER FRAUD

HOSPITALS, INSURANCE FRAUD BY

Hospitals are one type of organization that commits provider fraud. Common schemes in which hospitals are primarily involved include filing false cost reports, DRG Creep, billing for experimental procedures, improper relationships with physicians, and prematurely writing-off debts.

False Cost Reports

Cost reports sometimes include non-covered items disguised as covered items. By miscoding procedures or simply faking them, hospitals bill insurance companies for:

- Expenses for tax penalties, late charges, and promotional advertising.
- Costs incurred from a related-party transaction with a mark-up over the costs incurred by the related party.
- Expenses that are reimbursed under other programs (i.e., billable medical supplies and therapies).
- Excessive expenses such as hotel, food, travel expenses for recreational events such as golf outings, parties, and exotic trips.
- Luxury items (i.e., lavish furnishings, corporate planes, swimming pools, and spas).

DRG Creep

Diagnostic Related Groupings (DRG) is a standard method that insurers use to set payments for procedures. The system categorizes patients according to primary and secondary diagnosis, age, and complications, and then assigns a reimbursement figure. DRG creep occurs when a hospitalization is coded as a more complex admission than that which occurred. When it becomes a pattern and intent is established, it becomes fraud.

Another type of DRG fraud involves billing for the code and for the services that were already covered by the DRG payment—billing for an MRI, for example, when the test is already reimbursed as part of the DRG.

Billing for Experimental Procedures

Hospital staff and doctors file insurance claims for procedures and tests still in the research phase of development, i.e., the Food and Drug Administration has not yet approved them. Effectively, the insurance company pays for the manufacturer's research. Some doctors involved own stock in the manufacturing companies.

Improper Relationships with Physicians

Certain relationships between hospitals and physicians result in fraud to the insurer. For instance, a hospital provides no or token reimbursement to pathologists for Medicare Part A services in return for the opportunity to perform and bill Part B services at that hospital.

The following transactions are generally regarded as suspect:

- Payment of any sort of incentive by the hospital each time a physician refers a patient to the hospital.
- Provision of free or significantly discounted billing, nursing, or other staff services.
- Free training for a physician's office staff in areas such as management techniques, CPT coding, and laboratory techniques.
- Guarantees that provide that if the physician's income fails to reach a predetermined level, the hospital will supplement the remainder up to a certain amount.
- Low-interest or interest-free loans, or loans which may be forgiven if a physician refers patients to the hospital.
- Payment of the cost of a physician's travel and expenses for conferences.
- Payment for a physician's continuing education courses.
- Coverage on the hospital's group health insurance plan at an inappropriate or very low cost.
- Payment for services (which may include consultation at the hospital), which require few, if any, substantive duties by the physician, or payment for services in excess of the fair market value of services rendered.

Write-Off of Patient Accounts

Patient accounts or other receivables may be written-off as bad debts prematurely. Any funds recovered later go to the employee. The employee can collect the receivable and divert the funds to himself, because companies typically do not keep track of old, written-off accounts receivable. (*See also* REVENUE RECOVERY FIRMS under the entry on "Health Care Fraud.")

Credit Balances

Institutions treating patients covered by more than one payer may collect more than due for the services by billing different companies for the same procedures. This fraud is most likely to occur in cases involving accident insurance or workers compensation. The institution may also collect the deductible and co-payment from the patient.

Theft of Pharmaceuticals and Supplies

Hospitals may bill for narcotic drugs, admission kits, and supplies such as canes or sunglasses after cataract surgery, and then sell these items. Stolen pharmaceuticals and supplies are commonly sold on the street or through improper channels.

Related Entry:

COLUMBIA/HCA
HEALTH CARE FRAUD

HOXSEY, HARRY

From 1924 through the 1960's, Harry Hoxsey touted an herbal treatment, which he claimed would cure cancer, perhaps not for all patients, but for as many as 80%. He opened his first clinic in 1936 in Taylorsville, Illinois. Thousands came from far and wide to receive the "Hoxsley treatment." Several federal government agencies and private organizations, most significantly the American Medical Association, charged that Hoxsey was a quack. But even today Hoxsey's treatment enjoys a salutary reputation among practitioners of herbal medicines and homeopathic treatments.

Born in 1901, Hoxsey was a coal miner who claimed he inherited the recipe for his cancer treatment, along with other herbal remedies, from his great-grandfather, who had been a horse farmer in Illinois around 1840. As the Hoxsey family told it, the great grandfather's prize stallion developed a malignant tumor and was literally put out to pasture. Instead of dying, the horse grew healthier each week, a result, the elder Hoxsey guessed because it was eating several unusual plants that were not part of its normal diet. Gathering the plants together, Hoxsey created a potion, which he used in his layman's practice of veterinary medicine. Harry Hoxsey was supposedly given the secret recipe as the old man lay dying in 1924. He opened his first clinic soon afterward.

The AMA contended that the main ingredient in Hoxsey's cure was arsenic, and that it was not in fact a cure at all. The FDA charged that Hoxsey had not cured anyone; at best he had offered hope to the hopeless, at worst he had hastened people's deaths by convincing them to avoid treatments recommended by their physicians. Rebutting Hoxsey's contention that his records showed his patients reached remission at rates three or four times the medical norm, the FDA charged that Hoxsey's successes fell into one of three categories: they had never really had cancer; they had received traditional treatments of surgery or radiation previous to their admittance at Hoxsey's clinic; or the persons still had cancer and were dying from it despite superficial indications to the contrary. Hoxsey was harassed throughout the 1940s, but he was never formally charged with any crime. Meanwhile he attracted the support of the homeopathic community, and also won endorsements from politicians and ministers.

Hoxsey established a clinic in Dallas, Texas in the 1940's and became a licensed naturopath. Not only did his practice thrive, but also he pursued and won charges of libel against Morris Fishbein and *Journal of American Medicine* because of their unsupported accusations. The federal government did request an injunction against Hoxsey, forcing him to shut down until conclusive scientific experiments could be conducted on the treatment, or at least to cease distributing the product across state lines. A judge ruled in Hoxsey's favor.

In 1950, the FDA won an injunction against Hoxsey, but the victory was limited. To comply Hoxsey had to package his products with an explanation of the controversy surrounding his treatment and theories. In 1956, the FDA circulated posters in nearly 50,000 postal offices announcing "Public Beware!" The posters warned that Hoxsey was administering worthless products to gullible patients, and that the Hoxsey treatment was "imminently dangerous to rely on. . . in neglect of competent and rational judgment."

Responding to the federal campaign, Texas authorities acted in 1957 to revoke the licenses of physicians working in Hoxsey's clinic, and imposed a permanent injunction against the practice. Some of Hoxsey's personnel moved the operation to Tijuana, Mexico, where a version continues to this day.

Hoxsey was never charged with a crime, though he is still regarded as a fraud or quack in many circles. Homeopaths consider him a noble advocate of their cause. The Hoxsey treatment has never been formally tested by government or unaffiliated private agencies. However, the U.S. Congress has conducted hearings to consider testing Hoxsey's materials and their current uses.

In a twist of fate, Hoxsey discovered in 1967 that he had prostate cancer. When several administrations of his treatment failed to restore him, Hoxsey agreed to have surgery, a practice he had spent his life denouncing. He lived for seven years after the surgery, but was a shut-in. He died in 1974, with no obituary or public acknowledgment of his passing. Writer and filmmaker Kenneth Ausubel compiled a documentary film and book, both entitled *When Healing Becomes a Crime: The Amazing Story of the Hoxsey Cancer Clinics and the Return of Alternative Therapies*, published by Healing Arts Press with a foreword by cancer surgeon Bernie Siegel.

Source: "Harry Hoxsey: Healer Before His Time. An Interview with Kenny Ausubel." *Conscious Choice,* September 2001.

Related Entry:

HEALTH CARE FRAUD

ICG COMMUNICATIONS

ICG Communications was a popular telecommunications consortium with access to political and financial power around the world. CEO J. Shelby Bryan brought in almost $2 billion in capital into the company from 1996 to 2000. Telecom billionaire John Malone and Texas investment guru Thomas Hicks invested and raised almost $1 billion more. The company was transformed from a satellite communications firm that linked cruise liners and Navy ships to shore into the biggest competitive local exchange carrier in the country.

But the company's overextending attracted skeptics' attention, which determined that insiders had been committing fraud. Sales agents falsified order documents; employees and executives padded expense accounts, charged the company for presidential campaign fund-raising activities, and indulged in a wide range of personal luxuries at company expense; equipment was stolen; and millions of dollars in improper commissions and kickbacks were paid. The former security officials and auditors who revealed these practices said they existed at all levels of ICG.

Interactive Week magazine revealed:

- Company directors ignored or sought to suppress internal audits that exposed fraud, theft, corruption and kickbacks by employees, including senior management officials, a former auditor said.
- CEO Bryan was often reimbursed more than $45,000 per month for expenses that included personal shopping trips and the rental of a yacht on which Bryan hosted a political event. One of Bryan's private companies, Austin Resources, was also reimbursed by ICG for his personal expenses, internal audits show.
- Company executives entrusted network security to people with falsified resumes and at least one convicted thief, a former security official said.
- Millions of dollars in improper commissions were paid to dozens of sales agents and their supervisors, according to internal records.
- Line counts were inflated and auditors were unable to determine how many were actually in use in order to properly bill customers, according to former employees and documents. One audit showed 60% of the dial tone accounts and 54% of the access accounts were delinquent in February 1999, totaling $27 million.
- Hundreds of thousands of data and voice lines recorded as sold never generated revenue because of faulty record-keeping, said security officials who think outsiders "tapped" the network to illegally gain free access.
- Lax inventory controls left ICG unable to track or account for millions of dollars in servers, ports, routers, switching and fiber-optic equipment, satellite dishes, and high-speed data line equipment, internal investigators said.

- An accounting policy change initiated by ICG in 1996 allowed the company to book revenue based on sales, rather than installations. While accepted procedure at some companies, in ICG's case it led investors and lenders to believe that the company was growing far more rapidly than it was.
- Hundreds of millions of dollars worth of sophisticated equipment was stored under tarps in contract warehouses where poor security allowed people to check out equipment without proper authorization.
- Security at data centers, internal reports show, was routinely violated. Employees at one California facility were allowed to "tailgate" each other, entering on a single pass, according to an internal report from July 2000. That practice made it impossible to determine who might have stolen expensive transmission equipment.
- Millions of dollars in unnecessary equipment was installed but not used, according to internal memoranda. One report said the company was using "less than 10% of its available [network] capacity."

Source: Luzadder, D. *Interactive Week,* June 4, 2001.

Related Entry:
AUDITING FOR FRAUD

IDENTITY FRAUD

Identity fraud is the illegal use of another's identification or property. The FBI rates identity theft as the fastest growing white-collar crime in the United States; between 500,000 and 700,000 Americans are victimized each year. While identity fraud can be committed in furtherance of many types of crime, a number of recent federal prosecutions have combined identity fraud and Internet fraud into one cause of action.

In August 2004, Congress passed the Identity Theft Penalty Enhancement Act (commonly referred to as *Aggravated Identity Theft*) (18 U.S.C. § 1028A). This new Act provides that where one "knowingly transfers, possesses, or uses, without lawful authority, a means of identification of another" during and in relation to any felony violation of/or relating to fraud, embezzlement, false statements, and the like, an additional term of imprisonment of 2 years will be imposed on the individual.

Identity fraud may be committed digitally via computer access or by direct physical means, such as a stealing a purse or wallet, pilfering garbage, or stealing files from businesses and employers. Credit information is a fairly new and very rich source of personal identification for identity thieves. Extensive credit card mail solicitation gives rise to identity theft because many individuals discard the solicitations without cutting them up.

Social security numbers are naturally major targets of identity thieves. The Social Security Administration (SSA) reported that social security identification abuses tripled from 1998 to 1999. Furthermore, four out of five calls to the SSA hotline in 1999 involved identity theft.

Credit and Insurance are Targets

Credit fraud has been identified as the most common form of identity theft, accounting for at least 90% incidents. It is estimated that over 10 million Americans have been inflicted with some form of credit fraud since 2000. Most acts of identity theft are "account takeovers," whereby a thief gains access to an existing, legitimate account, and then steals money out of the account.

Another way an identity thief profits is by targeting insurance companies. Personal information can be used to purchase life insurance in the name of a dying patient, or a separate false identity as a beneficiary. Such information is often obtained by bribing lab personnel to distribute personal records to the thief. Viatical agencies also commit fraud by insuring terminally ill people with the personal records of healthy individuals.

In addition, health insurance can be abused by stealing a doctor's identity and submitting phony bills to Medicare or private insurers. UnitedHealthcare uncovered 1,000 phantom billings in South Florida between January and March of 1998.

Federal Trade Commission's Identity Theft Clearinghouse

The Federal Trade Commission operates an identity theft hotline at 1-877-ID THEFT (438-4338). This hotline is commonly referred to as the FTC's Identity Theft

Clearinghouse. The Clearinghouse is a database that continuously logs and monitors consumer complaints regarding actual and potential identity theft occurrences. The following graphs show facts reported by victims of identity theft:

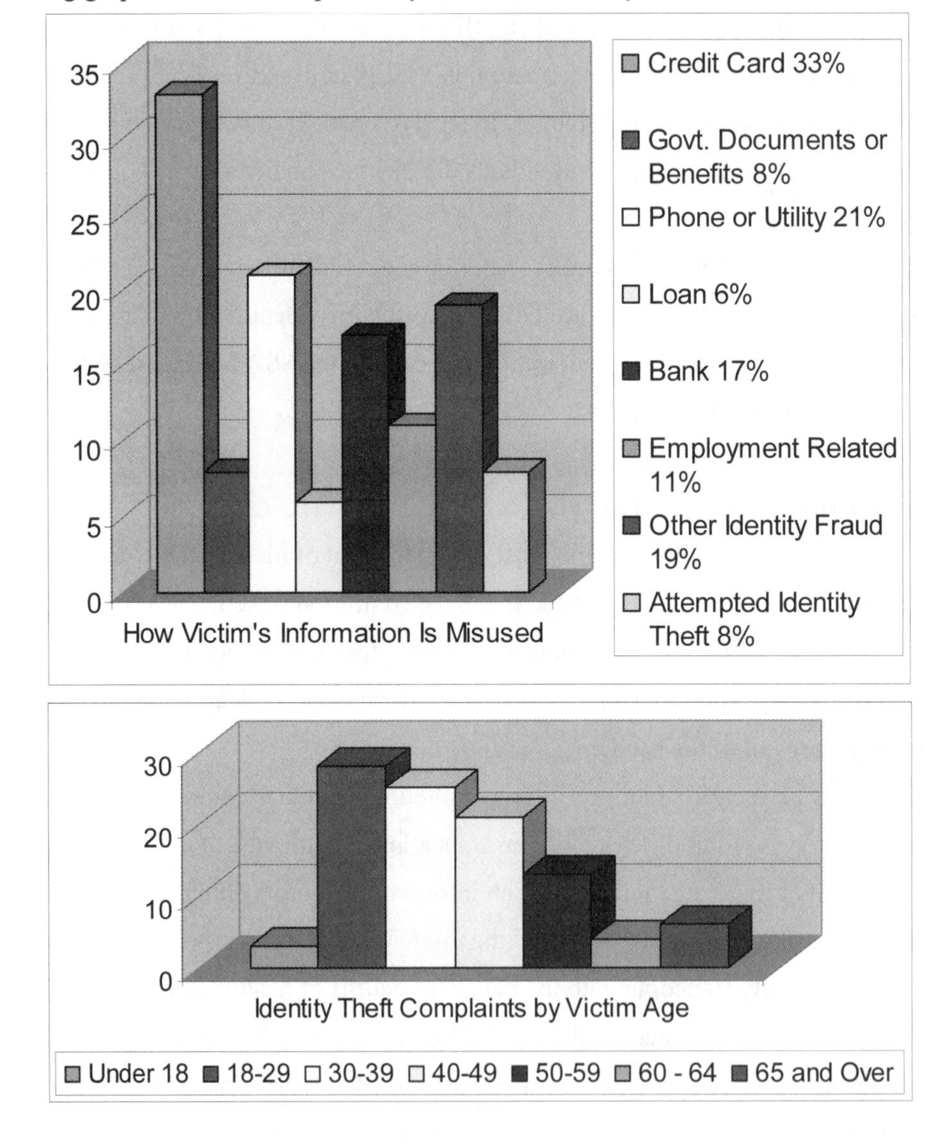

In the last graph:

- About 55% of victims calling the identity theft hotline report their age. Of these, 40% fall between 30 and 44 years of age. Approximately 27% are between age 45 and 64, and another 22% are between age 19 and 29. About 8% of those reporting their ages are 65 and over and over 3% are age 18 and under.

- 29% of respondents complained about a bank credit card issuer, 25% reported complaints about a bank creditor, and 22% reported complaints about a depository institution. The majority of consumer complaints associated with bank credit card issuers, bank creditors, and depository institutions fall into three categories: (1) the institution refused to correct information or close the disputed account, (2) customer service personnel were not helpful, and (3) the institution's security procedures were inadequate.
- Two-thirds of states have laws against identity fraud. Some insurance companies offer policies to protect against identity fraud; premiums range between $57 and $195 yearly for $30,000 worth of coverage. Self-help kits for victims are available via the Internet.

Source: Identity Theft Clearinghouse. Based on 214,905 victims reporting.

Victim Reports

The Privacy Rights Clearinghouse estimated that, on average, it takes 14 months for people to discover their identity has been misappropriated. Moreover it is estimated that victims spend about 600 hours in repairing the damage caused by identity theft.

Consumer Fraud Report

The Consumer Sentinel collects information about consumer fraud and identity theft from the Federal Trade Commission (FTC) and other organizations. The following statistics can be found in the FTC's 2004 Consumer Fraud and ID Theft Report:

- The FTC received more than half a million (635,173) consumer complaints during calendar year 2004, up from 542,378 in 2003. These include 327,285 complaints about fraud and 215,093 identity theft reports;
- 39% of all complaints received by the FTC related to ID theft, down from 42% in 2003;
- All fraud victims reported losses of $$547,854,781 with a median loss of $259;

- Victims of Internet related fraud reported losses of $265,337,866 in 2004, with the median loss of $214, up from a median loss of $195 in 2003; and
- The major metropolitan areas with the highest per capita rates of consumer fraud reported are: the Washington, DC area; San Jose, Sunnyvale, and Santa Clara, CA; and Las Vegas, and Paradise, NV (note: higher reporting of fraud does not necessarily indicate a higher overall incidence).

Identity Theft Resource Center

The following figures are drawn from the Identity Theft Resource Center (ITRC). The ITRC is an organization that helps individuals prevent and recover from identity theft. Two studies in July 2003 (Gartner Research and Harris Interactive), indicated that approximately 7 million people were victims of identity theft that year, totaling 19,178 per day, 799 per hour, 13.3 per minute.

The new ITRC study, *Identity Theft: The Aftermath 2004*, revealed the following:

- Victims in 2004 spent an average of 330 hours recovering from this crime, often over a period of years. The total reported hours ranged from 3 hours to 5,340 hours. This directly correlates to lost productivity.
- Victims reported lost wages ranging from $1,820 to $14,340. They reported expenses ranging from $851 to $1,378 for such items as phone calls, copies, affidavits, travel, notary fees, court documents, attorney fees and certified mail. The average medical expenses incurred to restore their physical or emotional health were $810 in the 2003 sample and $614 in the 2004 sample.
- Per victim estimation, losses increased in 2004 over 2003 by about $7,500 ($49,254 and $41,717 respectively). Forty percent of both sample groups reported business costs that exceeded $15,000 in their identity theft cases.
- In both years, 26 to 32% responded that they had spent a period of 4 to 6 months dealing with the identify fraud case. However, a higher number of respondents in 2003 (23%) as compared to those in 2004 (11%) responded that they had been dealing with their case for a period of seven months to a year.

- While victims are finding out about the crime more quickly, it is taking far longer than ever before to clear their records and recover from the situation. Overall, 22% reported the theft affecting their lives for 1 month to a year, 23% reported effects of 1-3 years, and 32% reported effects of 4 years or more.
- According to the 2003 ITRC study, the business community loses between $40,000 - $92,000 per name in fraudulent charges, based on reported fraud losses seen by surveyed victims. While this conflicts with other findings by other groups, there was a wide range of responses by the ITRC study respondents. The answer is that we may never know the true financial impact of this crime due to misclassification of identity theft crime definitions by the business community and by victims.

Financial Institutions and Anti-Theft Measures

The Gramm-Leach-Bliley Act directs the Federal Deposit Insurance Corporation (FDIC) and other agencies to ensure that financial institutions have policies in place to prevent the unauthorized disclosure of customer financial information. In addition, the FDIC requires financial institutions to have means to detect and deter fraudulent access to such information. Banks must take various steps to safeguard customer information. These include: (1) establishing procedures to verify the identity of individuals applying for financial products, (2) establishing procedures to prevent fraudulent activities related to customer information, and (3) maintaining a customer information security program.

Verification Procedures

Verification procedures for new accounts should include steps to ensure the accuracy of information.

Typical procedures include:

- Using independent sources to confirm information submitted by a customer;
- Calling a customer to confirm that the customer has opened a credit card or checking account; using an independently verified telephone number;
- Verifying information through an employer identified on an application form; and

- Verifying that the zip code and telephone area code provided on an application are from the same geographical area.

Fraud Prevention

To prevent fraudulent address changes, banks should also verify customer information before executing an address change and send a confirmation of the address change to both the new address and the address of record. If a bank receives a request for a new credit card or new checks along with a change of address notification, it should verify the request with the customer.

When opening a new account, a bank should check to ensure that the information provided on an application has not previously been associated with fraudulent activity. For example, if a bank uses a consumer report to process a new account application and the report is issued with a fraud alert, the bank's system for credit approval should flag the application and ensure that the individual is contacted before it is processed. In addition, fraud alerts should be shared across the bank's various lines of business.

Information Security

On February 1, 2001, the federal banking agencies issued guidelines on the security of customer information ("Interagency Guidelines for the Safeguarding of Customer Information by Financial Institutions," *66 Fed. Reg. 8616*). The guidelines require financial institutions to implement a comprehensive information security program that includes appropriate administrative, technical, and physical safeguards for customer information. To prevent pretext callers from using pieces of personal information to impersonate account holders, the guidelines require banks to establish written policies and procedures to control access to customer information.

Other measures that may reduce the incidence of pretext calling include limiting the circumstances under which customer information may be disclosed by telephone. For example, a bank may not permit employees to release information over the telephone unless the requesting individual provides a proper authorization code (other than a commonly used identifier). Banks can also use Caller ID or a request for a call back number as tools to verify the authenticity of a request. Banks should train employees to recognize pretext calling and test the effectiveness of controls. Independent staff or third parties can conduct unscheduled pretext phone calls to various departments.

Case Studies—Prosecutions for Identity Theft

In *United States v. Christian*, No. 00-03-SLR (D. Del. filed Aug. 3, 2000), two defendants obtained the names and Social Security numbers of 325 high-ranking United States military officers from a public website, then used those names and identities to apply for instant credit at a leading computer company and to obtain credit cards through two banks. They fenced the items they bought under the victims' names, and accepted orders from others for additional merchandise. The two defendants, after pleading guilty to conspiracy to commit bank fraud were sentenced to thirty-three and forty-one month's imprisonment and restitution of more than $100,000 each.

In *United States v. Wahl*, No. CR00-285P (W.D. Wash., 2000), the defendant obtained the date of birth and Social Security number of the victim (who shared the defendant's first and last name and middle initial). He then used the victim's identifying information to apply online for credit cards with three companies and to apply online for a $15,000 automobile loan. He actually used the proceeds of the automobile loan to invest in his own business. The defendant, after pleading guilty to identity theft, was sentenced to seven months of imprisonment and almost $27,000 in restitution.

Sources:
"Federal Trade Commission 2004 Consumer Fraud and ID Theft Report." Consumer Sentinel. www.consumer.gov/sentinel/trends.htm

"Facts and Statistics on Identity Theft" *Identity Theft Resource Center.* www.idtheftcenter.org/index.shtml

"Guidance on Identity Theft and Pretext Calling." *Federal Deposit Insurance Corporation,* May 2001.

Lee, J. "Fight Back When Someone Steals Your Name." *The New York Times*, April 8, 2001.

Stimpson, H. "Identity Theft: Nothing Personal; Crooks Targeting Auto Insurers in Growing Scam Wave." *The Coalition Against Insurance Fraud.*

"Testimony of Identity Theft Protection by Betsy Broder of the Federal Trade Commission." *Federal News Service,* September 13, 2000.

Related Entry:

CONSUMER FRAUD

INFORMATION CRIME

Examples of information crimes include the theft of computer time, software, and data. Crackers who use some of the computer's processing power to commit computer break-ins or to help process large amounts of information and conduct large calculations can commandeer computers that have an open Internet connection.

Stolen software code is a major type of intellectual property violation. Pirate versions of major software packages are sold around the world. Data may be sold as trade secrets to companies engaged in corporate espionage. Personal information is also stolen by employees in government and private business and sold to crime rings engaged in credit card fraud, counterfeiting, and identity theft.

Case Study—Police Officer Sells Data

Karol Chouinard was a detective in West Valley who illegally obtained data from a Los Angeles Police Department computer and sold the information to a private investigator. She was charged with unlawfully using a department computer for personal gain and unlawfully disclosing Department of Motor Vehicle records. Chouinard used the Police Department's Network Communications System to access DMV records throughout most of 1991. She sold the records to the Searchlight private investigative agency that specialized in locating people.

A search of Searchlight's offices found about 100 Teletypes of Police Department computer printouts that contained personal information from DMV records, some of which contained Chouinard's name. Authorities also recovered Chouinard's Police Department business card and 26 canceled checks in which agency owner Diane Castellano had paid Chouinard $1,405.

Chouinard's activity was discovered during an unrelated investigation by the San Carlos Police Department into the firm's alleged unauthorized use of Pacific Bell computer databanks. Authorities speculated that the two women might have met when Castellano was working as an investigator for an Encino law firm while Chouinard was at the West Valley station.

Source:

Meyer, J. "Ex-Officer is Charged with Stealing Information." *Los Angeles Times,* March 26, 1993.

Related Entries:

AVANT!
COMPUTER CRIME
CORPORATE ESPIONAGE
COUNTERFEIT SOFTWARE
HACKING
IDENTITY FRAUD
INTELLECTUAL PROPERTY FRAUD
LOPEZ, JOSE IGNACIO DE ARRIORTUA

INSIDER TRADING

Insider trading is a form of securities fraud in which individuals with access to privileged, non-public information about securities trade based on that information. These individuals are also prohibited from passing privileged information to others who use the information to perform trades.

As author Nancy Reichman describes, "The material, non-public information that has been the traditional focus of SEC enforcement includes information about company's operations, assets, and liabilities that, when made public, may affect the price of a publicly traded stock." Reichman points out, "Prohibitions to abstain from trading are not statutorily defined. They are grounded, instead, in more sweeping securities fraud regulations such as Securities and Exchange Commission Rule 10b-5, which prohibits individuals from engaging in any act, practice, or course of business that would operate as a fraud or deceit on any person in connection with the purchase or sale of a securities product."

SEC Rule 14e-3, adopted in 1980, prohibits anyone with information about a takeover from trading in the target company's stock. Even if the person did not acquire the information directly, if the person "knows or has reason to know" that the tip came from an insider, the person cannot trade on the information.

Legal Basis and Background of Insider Trading Laws

SEC regulations are based on the assumption that insider trading violates the fiduciary relationship of insiders to their companies and to the markets in general. Simply possessing material, or non-public information is not illegal. There are certain instances in which someone possessing such information can make legal trades, for example, if the person declares the information as part of the trade.

The fundamentals of insider trading were established in the U.S. Supreme Court's decision involving executives of the Texas Gulf Sulphur Company. The executives purchased stock in their own company before making public their discovery of a rich pool of mineral deposits. The Supreme Court ruled against the executives in 1969.

Types of Insider Trading Violators

Reichman identifies three types of insider trading violators:

- Those with direct access to information who use the information to trade in their own accounts. This includes corporate officers, journalists, and other service providers.
- Those who have a relationship with insiders, such as family members, lovers, or psychiatrists.
- Those who broker information on the black market. These include individuals and organizations. Many of the people convicted of insider violations in the 1980's were among this group.

Insider Trading Scandals of the 1980's

Reichman concludes that the rash of insider cases in the 1980's "developed out of a changing securities market. New information technologies brought new product possibilities and added new dimensions to investment decisions. Markets became connected as never before. The outlets for exchanging inside information unlawfully increased as the capacity to move and hide information and money became easier."

Insider Trading Scandals in the New Millennium

Securities violations and insider trading scandals found their way back onto the front pages of every newspaper and magazine across the U.S. in the 2000s with high profile cases including Samuel Waksal of ImClone Systems, Inc. in 2002 and Martha Stewart in 2003.

In 2000, the U.S. Securities Exchange Commission reported 40 insider trading cases making up a total of 8% of its total securities violations cases for the year. In 2001, the number of cases increased to 57 increasing the percentage to 12%. In 2003 and 2004, the percentage decreased to 7%. But in 2005, it slightly increased to 8%.

Sources:
Tonry, M. and Reiss, A. "*Beyond the Law. Crime in Complex Organizations.*" Chicago: University of Chicago Press, 1993.

U.S. Securities Exchange Commission Annual Reports: www.sec.gov/about/annrep.shtml

Related Entry:
SECURITIES FRAUD

INSURANCE COMPANIES, FRAUD BY

Fraud is committed by insurance agencies against consumers, government agencies, health care and other service providers, and against other insurance companies.

Frauds committed by health insurance companies include submission of false documentation and improper billing, mishandling claims, failure to pay legitimate claims, charging unapproved rates, requesting rate increases based on fraudulent data, using illegal or deceptive tactics to sell insurance, failure to give "fee breaks," and patient screening. Because premium rates for group policies are determined in part by the number of people with known health problems, dishonest insurance brokers separate a group's members into healthy people and sick people. The unhealthy people are covered by an insurer of last resort, who is given favorable tax status in exchange for issuing coverage to anyone, while the healthy members are covered by a cheaper, more generous plan.

Agents commit fraud in a number of ways. The agent sells the customer a certain policy and collects the premium, but places the customer in a cheaper policy with less coverage. The agent pockets the difference.

ERISA Fraud

The Employee Retirement Income Security Act regulates all trust accounts held by an employer for the purpose of paying benefits such as retirement annuities or health and life policies. Under the Act, if an insurance company believes that a plan administrator is engaging in violations of the Act, it is required to report the matter to the U.S. Department of Labor. As an example, a corporation may use funds collected from employees through payroll deduction to finance daily operations of the company.

Related Entry:

HEALTH CARE FRAUD

INSURANCE FRAUD

Insurance fraud is any deliberate deception perpetrated against an insurance company, or by an insurance company or its agents, for the purpose of financial gain.

Industry analysts refer to two types, "soft fraud" and "hard fraud." Soft fraud occurs when legitimate claims are exaggerated or when legitimate policies are modified improperly. Hard fraud is a deliberate attempt to invent a claim or counterfeit policies. Sophisticated conspirators, often medical personnel, lawyers, and other professionals allied with members of organized crime, often perpetrate hard frauds.

Insurance Industry Statistics

The industry loses an estimated $120 billion a year to fraud, mostly in the health care industry. All forms of insurance—health, life, property, and other—are susceptible to fraud. Service providers, particularly in health care, submit most fraudulent claims. Customers and insured groups also commit these acts. An insurance organization's employees may fabricate claims or alter subscriber accounts for their own gain. Insurance agents may submit falsified data on applications, collude with clients on fraudulent claims, fabricate claims, and give or receive kickbacks.

According to the 2003 Accenture Study, approximately 25% Americans believe exaggerating insurance claims is permissible, and about 10% approve of "padding" claims for treatments not provided, or items not lost or destroyed. Although the percentages appear high, this justification of insurance fraud by the American populus has been decreasing since 1997.

According to the Accenture Study, the most common justifications of insurance fraud include:

- The belief that one can get away with insurance fraud (56%);
- The belief that insureds pay too much for insurance (32%); and
- To compensate one's self for payment of deductibles (24%).
- Furthermore, almost all of the respondents (95%) responded that it is important for insurance companies to investigate any potentially fraudulent claims. The foremost reason given was to control premium expenses (63%).
- More than half (56%) of respondents agree that as the economy gets better, people are less likely to commit insurance fraud.
- About half (49%) of respondents said that they believe people are discouraged from committing fraud as a result of the increase in conviction rates, severe punishments and media coverage of high-profile corporate scandals.

Source: www.insurancefraud.org/stats_set.html

Signs of Fraudulent Filers

A person filing a fraudulent claim usually exhibits one or more of the following behaviors:

- Threatens legal action to force a quick settlement.
- Eagerly accepts blame and/or demands a quick settlement.
- Demonstrates unusual familiarity with insurance, medical, or repair terminology.
- Lists post office box or hotel as an address.
- Demands that transactions are performed in person rather than by phone, computer, or mail.
- Has no permanent address or does not reside in the region where the claim is being filed.

Common Insurance Fraud Scams

The National Insurance Crime Bureau (NICB) reported that the most common insurance fraud scams in 2000 were:

- *Bodily Injury Frauds* which are often associated with staged or deliberately caused auto accidents, and which involve fabricating physical injuries, often in cooperation with dishonest doctors and lawyers who are part of the conspiracy. Commercial vehicles such as taxis, rental cars, and commercial trucks are often special targets of fraud rings.
- *Auto Repair Fraud* in which a claimant, in cooperation with an unscrupulous repair shop, gets a vehicle repaired for less than the insurance appraisal and pockets the difference.
- *Homeowners Claim Fraud* includes arson for profit, fabricating claims for phony burglaries, falls by visitors, and the padding of legitimate claims for theft or damage to the home. For example, a claim is filed for a bogus theft from a home or car of expensive items such as laptop computers, golf clubs, and jewelry. Sometimes the value of items stolen in an actual theft is inflated in the claim.
- *Workers Compensation Fraud* involves faking injuries or exaggerating the extent of a minor injury to collect wage loss benefits from an employer's workers compensation policy. These "injured" employees are often seen working on a second job or performing activities beyond what their claimed injury would permit.

Insurance Fraud Schemes since Hurricane Katrina

The hurricanes of 2005, especially Hurricane Katrina which affected Louisiana and Mississippi, are expected to cause in an influx of insurance fraud. In addition to insurance fraud schemes whereby homeowners and renters make claims for expensive items that were never purchased (such as televisions and stereos), or inflate claims for items that were actually destroyed, home arsons have risen. Numerous house fires erupted in New Orleans and in other affected communities after Hurricane Katrina. Some of these fires may have been the result of arson committed by flood victims who did not have any protective flood coverage.

According to the National Insurance Crime Bureau (NICB), there were 206,000 vehicles in its flooded motor vehicle and boat database by March 2006, which was set up by catastrophes teams to combat title fraud in the hurricane-affected states. The NICB warned that flooded vehicles may be cleaned up, moved and sold in other areas of the country by unscrupulous operators. Although the vehicles were totaled by insurance companies and identified with the word "salvage" on their titles (meaning that they are not fit for any use except for scrap or parts), they could end up on the market in states where it is relatively easy to apply for a new title. In August of 2006, the NICB said that flooded cars from New Orleans had shown up in salvage lots and for sale in over 20 states.

Costs of Insurance Fraud

According to the Insurance Information Institute (III), the total cost of all kinds of insurance fraud (including life and health insurance) is estimated to be between $85 billion and $120 billion a year. III estimates that property/casualty insurance fraud cost insurers about $30 billion in 2004, up from $29 billion in 2003. III estimates that 10% of every claim dollar goes to combat fraud; the Insurance Research Council (IRC) puts the figures at 17 to 20%, or $6.3 billion per year. The National Insurance Crime Bureau states that insurance fraud adds $200 to $300 to total insurance premiums for the average household.

At the end of 2004, the Coalition Against Insurance Fraud said that auto insurance fraud amounted to $14 billion in false claims a year. The Insurance Research Council found that one-third of all bodily injury claims for auto accidents contained some amount of fraud. Most of the 33 out of 100 bodily injury claims identified as fraudulent included "padding" or "build-up," which are considered an exaggeration of injuries based on actual accidents. The CAIF reported in 2003 that $54 billion was lost to health insurance fraud.

Anti-Fraud Efforts Save Money

In the mid-1990's insurers said that for every dollar they invested in anti-fraud efforts, including special investigative units, they were getting up to $27 back. By the end of

1999, according to the director of the Coalition Against Insurance Fraud (CAIF), these returns have been harder to achieve as the more apparent fraud schemes have been uncovered and more effort is necessary to ferret out the sophisticated fraud that remains. The CAIF is an independent, nonprofit organization of consumers, government agencies, and insurers that compiles information on all forms of insurance fraud and lobbies legislatures.

The costs of insurance fraud are enormous, but anti-fraud efforts have dented those costs. Private companies who have stepped up their anti-fraud efforts and have reported savings as a result, reducing fraud losses by several percent, suffered most of those losses.

For a while, health care insurance fraud was on a decline. In 1997, the nation's health care bill was $53.9 billion, down from $58.4 billion in 1996. Auto claims fraud fell from $14.3 billion to $13.9 billion, and fraud in business and commercial lines fell from $10.6 billion to $9.8 billion. Property/casualty insurers, who lead the other sectors in combating fraud, reported saving $5 billion a year as a result of their efforts to fight fraud. However, in 2003, health care insurance fraud totaled $85 billion, according to Blue Cross, Blue Shield of Association and the U.S. Government Accountability Office. This accounted for 5% of the total US health care spending for that year.

The consolidation of claims databases provided by the Insurance Services Office (ISO) and its subsidiary, the American Insurance Services Group, has built a comprehensive database of bodily injury and property loss claims. The National Insurance Crime Bureau (NICB) runs a vehicle database on the same system. Using such data, fraud examiners can easily detect abnormal claim patterns and fraud rings using query strategies and search tools.

State Insurance Fraud Units Prove Successful

A study of 43 state fraud bureaus conducted by the Coalition Against Insurance Fraud (CAIF) found that they opened a record 33,000 cases in 2002 compared with 27,000 in 2000. Cases brought to prosecution in 2002 rose 14% from 2001. Florida led the states with 771 cases. Criminal convictions rose by a third in 2002, compared with 2001, totaling over 2,500, a new record. Florida, New York, New Jersey and Pennsylvania led the states in the largest gains in convictions. These gains do not include California. In 14 states, however, convictions were flat or down.

In New York, the State Insurance Fraud Bureau made a record 811 arrests in 2003, a new record and 15% higher than in 2002. Some of the bureau's achievements were attributed to the affirmation of Regulation 68 related to no-fault auto insurance fraud. The Insurance Information Institute says that average personal injury protection costs (first-party medical benefits under no-fault) fell from $8,518 in June 2002 to $7,514 in June 2003. Insurers in the state continue to press for additional reform.

Source: www.iii.org/media/hottopics/insurance/fraud/

Fraud against Britain's National Insurance Fund

Fraud and errors caused losses of £400 million in benefits paid from the National Insurance Fund in 1999/2000, according to government figures. Estimates produced by the Department of Social Security found that most of the losses could be attributed to:

- Errors by officials in assessing Incapacity Benefit amounting to £252 million, or 3.6% of expenditure.
- Losses from the fraudulent encashment of order books and girocheques, adding up to much as £59 million.
- Losses from Jobseeker's Allowance due to errors by officials, customers, and fraud amounting to £54 million, or 12% of expenditure.
- Losses of retirement pensions and widows' benefit from errors by officials amounting to £32 million.

According to one Social Security official, there are 82 million National Insurance numbers active in the United Kingdom, far more than the population, which numbered about 60 million in 2001.

Most People Would Commit Insurance Fraud

Insurance fraud in England costs an estimated £650 million a year. A survey of English citizens issued by household insurer Royal & Sun Alliance, released in 2001, found the following:

- 76% thought that home insurance fraud was common practice among those making household insurance claims.
- Seven out of ten believe people would exaggerate a claim if they could get away with it.
- Just under half believe that people inflate the value of their claims by at least a third.
- The top five items people cite when making inflated claims are: carpets, jewelry, Tag Heuer and Rolex watches, computers, and three-piece suits.
- Some 60% of the 2,017 people questioned said they did not believe insurance was fairly priced, compared to 47% the year before.
- One-third saw an inflated claim as being a return on the years of paying insurance premiums.

Sources:
"Benefits Fraud and Errors Hit Pounds 400M." *Birmingham Post,* May 4, 2001.

Gastel, R. "Insurance Issue Update." *Insurance Information Institute,* October 2000.

Jackson, P. and Wilkes-Barre, P. "Insurance Scams Cost First Billions, Families Thousands Each Year." *The Time Leader,* May 7, 2001.

McGann, M. "Believe Home Insurance Fraud is Rife." *Press Association Newsfile,* May 21, 2001.

A Statistical Study of State Insurance Fraud Bureaus, A Quantitative Analysis — 1995 to 2000. *Coalition Against Insurance Fraud.* www.insurancefraud.org

Related Entries:

AUTOMOTIVE REPAIR FRAUD
EQUITY FUNDING
HEALTH CARE FRAUD
HOME REPAIR FRAUD
INSURANCE COMPANIES, FRAUD BY
INSURANCE FRAUD BY COMPANY AGENTS AND EMPLOYEES
INSURANCE FRAUD—AUTO POLICIES
INSURANCE FRAUD—LIFE INSURANCE
INSURANCE FRAUD—PROPERTY AND CASUALTY
PERSONAL INJURY FRAUD
RENTAL CAR FRAUD

SOCIAL SECURITY FRAUD
VIATICAL INSURANCE FRAUD
WORKERS' COMPENSATION FRAUD

INSURANCE FRAUD BY COMPANY AGENTS AND EMPLOYEES

Company agents and employees commit insurance fraud against companies by filing false policies, false claims, or by misdirecting payments on legitimate claims to personal accounts. Agents and others commit fraud against customers by concealing the true costs of policies and transactions, and misleading customers about the nature and provisions of their policies.

Employee Fraud Against the Company

Employees of insurers, especially claims examiners and customer service representatives, use their access to claims and subscriber files to commit a range of frauds. Employees fabricate claims, provide false application data, and change subscriber addresses to intercept subscriber payments. Claims are fabricated using the employee's contract number, another insured's or a relative's contract number, or by altering the claims adjustment system to disburse payments for items such as canceled contracts or deceased insured.

Cash, Loan, and Dividend Checks

Without the knowledge of the insured or contract holder, a company's employee requests cash, a loan, or a dividend check, and deposits the check into either his bank account or a fictitious account. The employee, in order to minimize his chances of being detected, might change the company policyholder's address of record to either his address or a fictitious address. Once the check is issued, the address is changed back to the previous address.

Settlement Checks

Company employees can misdirect settlement checks such as matured endowment, paid up, etc., to the branch office, to their homes, or to a fictitious address. The employee can easily create a check defalcation by changing the address of record prior to the settlement check issue date. Periodically the parent corporation may assign an orphan contract holder—a policyholder who has not been assigned to a servicing agent or whose whereabouts is unknown—to an agency. Employees can file claims in the orphan's name and direct settlement to a mail drop or a co-conspirator's address.

Fictitious Payees and Death Claims

An agent or clerk can change the beneficiary of record to a fictitious person and obtain payments in the assumed name. Fictitious death certificates are used to obtain life insurance payoffs.

Agent Fraud Against the Company

Agents and policy brokers commit fraud against the company by participating in bribery, claims fraud schemes, or kickback schemes.

In a common claims scheme, agents establish bogus companies to sell health insurance to individuals at group rates, costing the company thousands in lost premiums. Some agents simply sell a phony policy and disappear with commissions. Agents write a policy knowing the client has pre-existing conditions that would prevent acceptance for coverage. A broker may add ineligible family members, girlfriends, or associates to a group policy by representing them as employees. The agent is compensated with a kickback.

Agents can also write a fictitious application and, after the contestable period (two years), submit a phony death claim. The agent, by investing a couple of thousand dollars, could receive $50,000 or more in misappropriated claims. A company is particularly vulnerable to this scheme if the perpetrator has knowledge of the underwriting procedures, such as the limits under which insurance can be written without a medical exam and what items are submitted on a death claim.

The most prevalent insurance fraud by agents is embezzlement. Agents may falsify request for loans against existing policies and direct the proceeds to personal accounts. This act can impact customers too, whose accounts are debited for the loan and who may be pursued for repayment.

Agents can move policyholders into new policies or to new companies in order to generate extra commissions. Both customers and insurance companies may pay the cost in the form of commissions. However, in some cases, companies themselves encourage agents to prod customers into products produced by the company, its subsidiaries, or partners.

Agent Fraud Against the Customer

Many acts of agent fraud impact both the customer and the company. Agents target customers by selling bogus policies with no financial backing, or misrepresent the nature and details of coverage.

A widespread form of agent fraud is known as churning, or twisting, in which agents convince customers to cash in their existing life insurance policies for new ones. Consumers are told that inflation has undercut the value of their death benefit. There may be some truth to the assertion, but the agent conceals or de-emphasizes the fact that changing policies may consume all or most of the policyholder's accumulated cash value in the existing policy.

The agent, on the other hand, receives a commission ranging from 55% to over 100% on the new premiums during the first years the policy is in force. Much of the commissions are paid for by the cash value of the consumer's former policy. Consumers switching from an older policy to a new one may face huge surrender charges if they need to cash in the policy to pay for a family emergency. Surrender charges can be so high on relatively new policies that they absorb all or most of the policy's cash value.

Inflation can impact a life insurance policy's value, but the best advice, according to industry analysts, is for customers to retain existing policies with a cash value, and add to coverage by purchasing simple term insurance. Unscrupulous agents do not disclose that information because the commission on term insurance is small compared to that on whole life policies, particularly in the first year or two of the new policy when companies use most of the consumer's premiums to pay agents.

Case Study—Loeb's Empire Blue Cross Fraud

In a scheme that came to be known as the Empire Blue Cross Fraud, more than 7,000 people from California to New York were taken in, including ministers and terminally ill patients. The scheme's chief promoter was William Loeb, a New York union organizer with a long criminal record for perjury and other offenses. In 1988, he formed a fake labor union—the New York Labor Union, Consolidated Local 867—to sell what he claimed was affordable major medical insurance underwritten by a New York carrier, Empire Blue Cross.

Loeb targeted people who were already sick and found it difficult to obtain coverage. Loeb also convinced consumers to trade in more expensive policies for the cheaper ones offered through his union. For example, Louise Jones of San Francisco had never met Nicholas Chinnici, but the Huntington Beach agent was referred to her when the agency she had been dealing with closed. When Chinnici first proposed the coverage, Jones was wary because of a huge $800-a-month reduction in the premium over their previous policy. But she and her husband found it hard to obtain any coverage, especially an affordable policy.

Loeb had persuaded Empire Blue Cross to back the policies he offered through his bogus union, gambling that the carrier would not conduct a thorough background check on him or the union. He also bribed a company official with cash and prostitutes.

In the spring of 1990, Florida insurance regulators halted sales of the policies, declaring that the union could not do business there because Empire Blue Cross was not an authorized carrier in the state. Empire Blue Cross was not authorized to operate in California either, but the state's insurance regulators were slow to take action. Critics say the lapse cost California victims millions of dollars in additional losses. A widely distributed industry newsletter also warned brokers in 1989 that the insurance was a scam, but brokers ignored it.

A review of Loeb's operation by Empire auditors in the summer of 1990 discovered that the union owed more than $5 million in claims. Empire withdrew from the relationship with Loeb. Loeb announced his union would self-insure, but most claims and complaints went unanswered. As Loeb bounced between carriers—shady companies without proper authorization who would soon dissolve the relationship once customers started to complain—agents collected additional commissions as customers were switched over.

Late in 1990, federal labor officials shut down Loeb's union. Three years later, he went to federal prison, convicted of bribery and fraud. Other top promoters were also imprisoned, including two from the Bay Area, J. Paul Stoddard and Jon Berg. The two agents, who peddled the insurance to many clients, were sentenced to three years in federal prison in 1997 for mail fraud.

Loeb's victims were left with $24 million in unpaid medical bills. Many joined a 1993 class action suit, charging racketeering and fraud. The suit claimed the policies should never have been sold in California in the first place, because the carriers were not licensed to operate there. Most of the agents later settled the case for $8 million, with their liability insurance paying the bulk of the money.

The California Department of Insurance took no action against the agents promoting the policies. In one case a federal jury ordered brokers to pay $2 million in damages for civil fraud in a spin-off of the class action suit, but state regulators took no action.

Case Study—Insurance Companies Involved in Agent Fraud

By the year 2000, Prudential Life Insurance had paid over $1 billion to settle charges it "abused" 650,000 customers by tricking them into expensive policy conversions and disguising the risks involved. The company set aside another billion and a half for future settlements.

The abuses occurred over a 12-year period, from 1983 to 1995. Prudential was fined $65 million by state insurance regulators and $20 million by the National Association of Securities Dealers (NASD). NASD represented a task force of insurance regulators from thirty states that conducted an eighteen-month investigation into churning practices committed by Prudential salespeople, often with the knowledge and overt approval of officials up to at least regional vice presidents. Certain salespeople were promoted to managerial positions because of their churning successes.

According to investigators, as many as 10 million customers were misled into using the cash value of their old insurance policies to pay the premiums on new, more expensive policies. They were not warned that the upgrading could be costly and deplete their equity.

Arthur Ryan, Prudential's chairman from late 1994, admitted that the charges were accurate and fired several salespeople and managers and a senior vice president. Some of these disgruntled employees agreed to cooperate with the government, revealing the details of their jobs and the roles of their superiors. Investigators obtained sworn statements from employees claiming that Prudential officials had ordered them to destroy any documents that might reveal illicit marketing practices.

Prudential was only the most prominent of companies caught up in abuse by agents. Metropolitan Life announced in 2000 it would spend nearly $2 billion to settle complaints about its deceptive sales practices. The company's troubles began in March of 1993, when a former Metropolitan Life sales representative told a Pittsburgh television station and the Pennsylvania Insurance Commissioner's office that regional insurance agents were churning policies. MetLife agreed to perform a thorough review of its life insurance sales, and later made restitution to approximately 29,000 Pennsylvania policyholders who might have been victimized by churning. Apparently churning is a problem industry-wide. From 1995 to 2000, John Hancock, State Farm, and Nationwide all settled similar charges.

Sources:
"Deceptive Practices in the Sale of Life Insurance." *Congressional Hearing Transcripts,* September 29, 1994.

Dietz, D., and Lynch, A. "Insurance Nightmare; Rogue Agents Leave Policyholders with Pain and Hardship." *The San Francisco Chronicle,* September 30, 1998.

Robert Hunter, Commissioner Texas Department of Insurance. *Federal News Service,* September 29, 1994.

Related Entry:

INSURANCE FRAUD

INSURANCE FRAUD—AUTO POLICIES

Industry records show that auto policies are a prime vehicle for fraud. In a survey of American insurers, fraud accounted for 10% of losses in the auto liability sector. In all other sectors, about 5% losses were due to fraud. Staged auto accidents have become one of the nation's top insurance scams. In 1995, in California alone there were 14,112 reports of insurance claims stemming from suspicious accidents, three times the rate reported four years earlier.

Law enforcement officials have discovered pockets of organized activity in virtually every major city and in dozens of smaller towns. According to the National Insurance Council Board, the average American household pays an additional $200 in premiums each year to make up for the fraud.

Though no firm numbers exist, observers have used enforcement results to extrapolate the economic effects of accident rings. In the 1920's, accident rings were thought to take in millions; in the 1940's, tens of millions; by the 1970's, with more cars than ever on the road and the requirement by law that drivers carry insurance, the numbers reached into the hundreds of millions.

In 1992, the National Insurance Crime Bureau estimated that all personal injury frauds together cost more than $10 billion a year. Of this amount, staged auto accidents are thought to account for about 10% of the total, or $1 billion annually.

Statistical Roundup

The Coalition Against Insurance Fraud offers the following statistics about auto insurance fraud. The year of reporting and original source is cited.
More than one of every three bodily-injury claims from car crashes involves fraud. *Insurance Research Council (1996)*
17-20 cents of every dollar paid for bodily injury claims from auto policies involves fraud or claim buildup. *Insurance Research Council (1996)*
Fraud adds $5.2-$6.3 billion to the auto premiums that policyholders pay each year. *Insurance Research Council (1996)*
Claims for bodily injuries under the Personal Injury Protection portion of New York's no-fault auto coverage rose 79% between 1999 and 2000, compared to 25% in all no-fault states. *Insurance Research Council (2001)*
Insurers increased auto premiums up to 25% for New York City in 2001. *Insurance Information Institute (2001)*
The average personal injury claim is $7,950 in New York State — 47% higher than

the national average. *Insurance Information Institute (2001)*

Massachusetts Study Finds Prosecution is Difficult

An analysis of auto insurance claims by the state insurance board of Massachusetts in 1993 found that, while fraud and abuse were widespread, actually prosecuting cases was not very likely, and achieving a conviction was even less likely. Among the findings:

48%	Claims had some sign of fraud or abuse.
9%	Had some perception of fraud.
1%	Claims were referable for criminal investigation.
0.67%	Were acceptable for criminal investigation.
0.33%	Were referable for prosecution.
0.17%	Were prosecuted successfully.

Staged-Accident Rings

Organized rings have been staging auto accidents since the automobile was invented, and have grown with the machine's prominence in American life. In 1925, the *Saturday Evening Post* ran a series of articles about such rings. Leaders would buy "battered old wrecks posing as automotive vehicles" to use in staging accidents. The favored method was to have a pedestrian accomplice jump in front of the vehicle and claim damages. Sometimes the accomplice did not have to fake the injury if he did not move quickly enough.

By the 1960's and 1970's, staged-accident rings had become so common and successful that the state of California—which was overwhelmingly the favored locale for staging accidents—launched a special enforcement effort against them. According to Ken Dornstein's book on the subject, "In addition to the usual runner and solicitors working for attorneys, they discovered rings of 30 to 40 people who were engaged in several different types of 'accidents through prearrangement.'" Some rings crashed cars intentionally in traffic, one complicit car into another; and others worked strictly paper accidents where damage was created to support a made-up collision.

The basic organization of staged accidents remains the same today. Cappers, or recruiters, arrange for the vehicles and passengers, who are often immigrants. The accidents may be staged between two complicit vehicles, or by a capper's auto targeting an innocent victim. In the latter instance, culprits usually target new and luxury cars because they are more likely to have extensive insurance coverage. They prefer women driving alone or with children, because these victims are more likely to become overexcited, fearful, and easily manipulable after an accident.

Once a capper has all the elements in place, the deal is then sold to a law firm, whose office managers arrange for the clients to be seen at a particular medical clinic.

What has changed is the economy of accident rings. Cappers in the 1970's received from $200 to $250 per person. In the late 1990's they might demand several thousand dollars per rider, who are also known as "cows."

The states of California, Florida, Texas, and Arizona in particular have experienced epidemics of auto accident fraud, most likely because these states have more registered automobiles than other states, combined with poor public transportation; there is a concentration of professionals handling low-level claims; and they host large immigrant populations, who are usually recruited to act as victims.

Organized rings and "cappers" actively solicit others in the community to participate in the creation of accidents that only exist on paper. No innocent parties are involved in this type of staged accident.

Auto Insurance and Medical Claims

U.S. insurers lose about $5.4 billion a year to fraudulent medical claims filed in relation to auto accidents. The Coalition Against Insurance Fraud estimates these frauds add $35 a year in premiums for every policy in force.

No-fault auto insurers are especially vulnerable to fraud because they have to settle claims quickly and because auto insurance claims are the only area in health care that has not come under managed care controls. No authorization is required for treatment, and insurers are required to pay the "usual and customary" prices for treatments.

Medical Brokers

So-called medical brokers, usually in collusion with a provider, turn the requirements to their advantage by excessive billing and by billing for procedures that would be disallowed under other types of insurance. Brokers negotiate reasonable rates with providers, and then charge the insurance company a much higher "usual and customary" price for the test or treatment.

Brokering medical services is legal, as long as the broker discloses to all parties that a third-party provides the treatment. Unscrupulous brokers cross the line by pretending they provide treatments themselves, by offering kickbacks to providers willing to cooperate, and by inducing providers to provide unnecessary tests or treatments. To support the illusion that they provide treatment, brokerage companies may contract with diagnostic centers to lease blocks of time on their scanners.

Most states that provide for no-fault auto insurance have instituted guidelines for tests and treatments.

Auto Insurance Schemes

- The "sideswipe" occurs in a dual left turn lane of a busy intersection. The driver in the inside lane drifts into the outer lane intentionally forcing a collision.
- In the "swoop and squat," fraud engineers, known as "cappers," pay people desperate for cash—usually immigrants—$100 each to ride in cars that become struck in staged accidents. The drivers of these cars usually stop without warning in front of another vehicle, often a well-insured commercial truck. After the accident, the capper files personal injury claims against the other vehicle's insurer. The "swoop and squat" occurs when the vehicle one is following is suddenly passed by another vehicle that "swoops" in front of it. This causes the vehicle in front to stop abruptly, or "squat." As a result, the driver is unable to avoid colliding with the rear end of the vehicle. This is no "accident." The drivers of both the swoop and squat planned the collision. The swoop car will never be seen again and the driver of the squat car plans to submit vehicle damage and personal injury claims to the victim's insurance company.

- The "drive down" occurs when an innocent driver tries to merge into traffic or pull out of a parking space. The perpetrator waves the driver to proceed, then intentionally smashes into the driver's car.
- The "hit and run": a suspect driver uses a damaged vehicle, drives it to a public location, and claims to be the victim of a hit and run. The police are often called to verify the damage.
- The "nightclub": A scam driver waits outside a bar or nightclub for someone who appears inebriated to head home. He causes a crash with the impaired driver, who may settle out of pocket rather than call the police and risk a driving-while-intoxicated charge.

Airbag Fraud

Insurance industry statistics show that approximately 50,000 airbags are stolen annually, resulting in an annual loss of more than $50 million to vehicle owners and their insurers. As driver and passenger safety continues to be a prominent design and engineering factor for vehicle manufacturers, more airbag-equipped vehicles (including front-and side-impact bags) are on the road.

Airbags are sold illicitly to traffickers in stolen vehicle parts. A new airbag, which retails for approximately $1,000 from a car dealer, costs between $50 and $200 on the black market. Because of their portability, airbags can be easily removed and installed as "new" by unscrupulous collision repair shops. These dishonest operators will then charge the vehicle owner or their insurer the full price for the replacement, thus committing insurance fraud.

Airbag Schemes

Two common schemes committed by unscrupulous repair facilities are "The Switch," and "The Pullout."

- The Switch. Prior to an insurance repair estimate, an unscrupulous collision repair facility removes a non-deployed airbag and switches it with a deployed airbag. After the estimate, the original non-deployed airbag is reinstalled. The insurer is then billed for a new airbag, resulting in a 100% profit for the unscrupulous repair facility.

- The Pullout. A dishonest repair facility cuts open the non-deployed airbag's cover and pulls out the airbag to make it appear as if it deployed. After the insurance estimate is completed, the non-deployed airbag is then replaced with an airbag purchased on the black market. Like the Switch scheme, the insurer pays the bill for this fraudulent act.

Case Study: Staged Accident Ring

Over 60 people, including two police officers, were arrested as participants in a staged-accident ring that bilked insurers under New York state's no-fault insurance law. Quentin Hawkins headed the ring, recruiting drivers and passengers to stage minor collisions and then to seek care from certain medical clinics, where co-conspirators created medical records for nonexistent injuries. One police officer helped stage a collision; another wrote reports for collisions that never occurred. Hawkins's ring was accused of collecting more than $1 million in medical insurance payments for fake injuries.

Phone surveillance tapes revealed Hawkins boasting on his cellular phone that he had been in the auto insurance fraud business for 21 years. Hawkins coached his assistants to speak in code: Staged accidents were called "movies;" phony victims were "pineapples;" cooperative medical clinics were "fruit stands." After staging accidents, Hawkins spoke of "delivering pineapples to the fruit stand." Federal agents understood the references because Hawkins, in various conversations on his wiretapped phone, explained the details of his code.

Sources:
Bergal, J., and Schulte, F. "Money Drives Auto Accident Schemes; Some Chiropractors, Clinics Play Key Roles." *Sun Sentinel,* December 17, 2000.

Bergal, J., and Schulte, F. "Industry Taps Variety of Players; Entrepreneurs are Everywhere." *Sun Sentinel,* December 19, 2000.

Chivers, C. "Two Police Officer Are Indicted With 65 Others in Insurance Case." *The New York Times,* August 16, 2001.

Domstein, K. *Accidentally on Purpose: The Making of a Personal Injury Underworld in America.* New York: St. Martin's Griffin, 1998.

Gastel, R. "Insurance Information Institute (III) Insurance Issues Update." *Insurance Fraud,* October 2000.

Insurance Fraud Roundtable. *Coalition Against Insurance Fraud,* October 7, 1993. www.insurancefraud.org

Panko, R. "Getting a Jump on Crime." *Best's Review,* October 1, 1999.

Treaster, J. "Scanning for Dollars by Middlemen." *The New York Times,* March 22, 2001.

"Testimony by William J. Mahon, Executive Director of the National Health Care Anti-Fraud Association." *Federal News Service,* June 15, 1995.

Related Entries:

HEALTH CARE FRAUD

INSURANCE FRAUD

RENTAL CAR FRAUD

INSURANCE FRAUD—LIFE INSURANCE

Life and disability insurance frauds are committed by insurance companies and their agents against consumers, by viatical dealers against their clients and insurance companies, and by consumers against insurance companies. According to the Insurance Information Institute, life insurance fraud totaled $11.8 billion in 2000, more than double the $5 billion total in 1998.

Agents and companies sell phony policies or mislead customers about the nature and details of policies. Most commonly these companies encourage their agents to engage in churning, discussed below.

A specialized form of life insurance fraud is known as viatical fraud, which involves selling a terminally ill person's life insurance policy to speculators for lump sum cash payment. Viaticals may disguise an ill person's health status or submit healthy patients' records in place of an ill person's.

Customers commit life insurance fraud by providing false information on a policy, insuring nonexistent individuals, buying a policy using a stolen identity, and by faking deaths. Some customers actually do kill others to collect benefits, but that is murder, not fraud. Personal information can be used to purchase life insurance in the name of a dying patient and name an accomplice, or separate false identity, as beneficiary. These records are often obtained by bribing lab personnel.

Churning and Twisting

A widespread form of agent fraud is known as churning, or twisting, in which agents convince customers to cash in their existing life insurance policies for new ones. Consumers are told that inflation has undercut the value of their death benefit. There may be some truth to the assertion, but the agent conceals or de-emphasizes the fact that changing policies may consume all or most of the policyholder's accumulated cash value in the existing policy.

The agent on the other hand receives a commission ranging from 55% to over 100% on the new premiums during the first years the policy is in force. Much of the commissions are paid for by the cash value of the consumer's former policy. Consumers switching from an older policy to a new one may face huge surrender charges if they need to cash in the policy to pay for some family emergency. Surrender charges can be so high on relatively new policies that they take all or most of the policy's cash value.

Inflation can impact a life insurance policy's value, but the best advice, according to industry analysts, is for customers to retain existing policies with a cash value, and add to coverage by purchasing simple term insurance. Unscrupulous agents do not disclose that information because the commission on term insurance is small compared to those on whole life policies, particularly in the first year or two of the new policy, when companies use most of the consumer's premiums to pay agents.

Sources:
Insurance Information Institute. www.insurancefraud.org

Lynch, A., and Dietz, D. "Insurance Nightmare: Rogue Agents Leave Policyholders with Pain and Hardship." *The San Francisco Chronicle,* September 30, 1998.

Related Entries:

INSURANCE FRAUD
VIATICAL INSURANCE FRAUD

INSURANCE FRAUD—PROPERTY AND CASUALTY

Fraud involving property and casualty insurance is committed by consumers against insurance companies. Consumers provide false information in policies, disguise one item for another, and fake accidents.

Fraud in the property/casualty insurance industry in 2004 cost about $30 billion, according to the Insurance Information Institute. Fraud bureaus in the 43 states in which they are set up reported a record number of new investigations and significant increases in referrals, or tips about suspected fraud, and cases brought to prosecution. Despite these gains and in recognition of the prevalence of fraud many states are actively lobbying for new and stronger antifraud laws.

Anti-fraud efforts are increasing in this area. Anti-fraud spending by insurers rose from $200 million in 1992 to $650 million in 1996. Virtually all insurers maintain an anti-fraud program and most employ special-investigation units. Half of insurers conduct public information programs designed to deter fraud.

Case Study—Couple Used Trade Center Bombing

Following the September 11th terrorist attacks on the World Trade Center, Charles Gavett filed a claim with his property insurer that his wife Cynthia had died in the buildings' collapse while in New York City on business. He was collecting the family's $200,000 mortgage insurance policy to pay the mortgage on their $270,000 home. The couple resided in a small town in Georgia, but Cynthia had supposedly been attending a meeting in the WTC on September 11, 2001.

Investigators working for Minnesota Mutual simply interviewed officials in Pike County, Georgia, who reported that Cynthia Gavett was alive and well, and had made no attempt to conceal that fact from them.

Charles Gavett produced an appointment book that placed his wife in the WTC, plus an affidavit from his 14-year-old daughter saying she had not seen her mother since she left for New York City. Gavett also wrote a survivors' group, requesting ashes from the WTC, and filed for relief from the Red Cross.

Investigators acting with local officials discovered Mrs. Gavett and arrested her and her husband for fraud in December 2001. Though the Gavetts were the first on record for the WTC tragedy, insurance industry sources report that others have attempted this same fraud.

Source: Insurance Information Institute. www.insurancefraud.org/

Related Entry:
INSURANCE FRAUD

INTELLECTUAL PROPERTY FRAUD

The U.S. Treasury's annual "301" list of intellectual property offenders for 2000, examined intellectual property protection in over 70 countries. The analysis identified 59 trading partners that deny adequate and effective protection of intellectual property or deny fair and equitable market access to United States artists and industries that rely upon intellectual property protection.

FBI sources believe that more companies than ever before are engaged in economic espionage–unlawful practices engaged in by private companies and sometimes by foreign governments aimed at stealing assets such as formulas, blueprints, or marketing strategies. The FBI estimates that a significant number of countries are targeting U.S. firms, with high-tech companies as the most frequent targets.

One common copyright infringement violation is the posting of copyrighted material on the Web. The Copyright Infringement Act, the Computer Fraud and Abuse Act, and the Economic Espionage Act of 1996 are some of the laws that protect intellectual property rights in the media including the Internet.

The transmission of confidential data and trade secrets by employees is a violation of nondisclosure agreements designed to protect companies' intellectual property. Any intellectual work and product used for a business purpose or software that contains novel or unique elements, procedures, or compilations should be classified as intellectual property or a trade secret and should be protected by nondisclosure agreements and policies.

In developing nations, countries that fail to protect intellectual property often lose their best talent. The loss of jobs and tax revenues encourages an environment of corruption and an increase in crimes financed by intellectual property theft.

Some figures on intellectual property losses:

- Federal authorities estimate that copyright infringement cost the United States $12 billion in 2000.
- The U.S. music industry estimates its losses to copyright infringement at $210 million a year.
- Manufacturers of office machines lose $1 billion a year, according to a 1999 Survey of Original Equipment Manufacturers.

U.S. Attorney Statistics on Intellectual Property Cases

The following figures cover cases handled by the U.S. Attorney's office from 2001 to 2003.

Referrals and Cases	FY 01	FY 02	FY 03
Number of Investigative Matters Received by U.S. Attorneys:	191	169	229
Number of Defendants:	283	289	333
Number of Cases Filed:	84	78	100
Number of Defendants:	121	149	165
Number of Cases Resolved/Terminated:	81	82	65
Number of Defendants:	106	135	119

Source: www.usdoj.gov/ag/annualreports/ar2003/appendices.htm#cc

WTO Agreement

The World Trade Organization (WTO) Agreement on Trade-Related Aspects of Intellectual Property Rights (TRIPS agreement) requires all WTO members to provide certain minimum standards of protection for patents, copyrights, trademarks, trade secrets, and other forms of intellectual property. The agreement also requires countries to provide effective enforcement of these rights. In addition, the TRIPS agreement is the first broadly subscribed to multilateral intellectual property agreement that is enforceable between governments, allowing them to resolve disputes through the WTO's dispute settlement mechanism.

Trade Secrets

Trade secrets refer to unique intellectual property that is used by an entity, but is not covered by patent. The recipe for Kentucky Fried Chicken, for example, is a trade secret.

Patent applications require a full description of the intellectual property and only remain valid for 20 years from the time of application, whereas a trade secret can be maintained in perpetuity. While patents, copyrights, and trademarks are addressed in international trade agreements, trade secrets are not.

Patents are considered legally binding and any infringement is punishable; trade secrets must first be authenticated before a court will consider an infringement charge. Usually courts consider how many people were privy to the secret, the security precautions maintained, the competitive advantage conferred by the secret, and how difficult and expensive it would be for an outsider to obtain the secret.

Sources:
"2000 Special 301 Report." *Office of the U.S. Trade Representative,* September 20, 2000. www.ustr.gov/html/special.html

Chartrand, S. "Patents." *The New York Times,* February 5, 2001.

"Richard Clarke, National Coordinator for Security: Infrastructure Protection and Counterterrorism." *Federal News Service,* December 15, 2000.

Siau, K., Fui-Hoon Nah, F., and Teng, L. "Acceptable Internet Use Policy." *Association of Computing Machinery,* January 1, 2002.

"William R. Duffy, President and C.E.O. of International Intellectual Property Protection Inc. Senate: Small Business Office Supply Scams." *Federal News Service,* March 28, 2000.

Related Entries:

AVANT!

COMPUTER CRIME

CORPORATE ESPIONAGE
HACKING
INFORMATION CRIME
LOPEZ, JOSE IGNACIO DE ARRIORTUA

INTERNAL AUDITING

See, AUDITING FOR FRAUD

INTERNAL CONTROLS

The Committee on Sponsoring Organizations (COSO) was appointed by the Treadway Commission in 1987 to oversee a reform of internal controls in American corporations. The Commission recommended that management of publicly held companies include with management reports an acknowledgement of responsibility for internal controls and an assessment of its effectiveness in meeting those controls.

COSO issued *Internal Control – Integrated Framework*, which provided the following definition: Internal Control is a process designed to provide reasonable assurance regarding the achievement of objectives in the following categories:

- Reliability of financial reporting.
- Effectiveness and efficiency of operations.
- Compliance with applicable laws and regulations.

COSO also identified five components of internal control:

- Control Environment sets the tone of an organization, influencing the control consciousness of the organization, and providing a foundation for all other control components.
- Risk Assessment is an entity's identification and assessment of risks relevant to achieving control objectives.
- Control Activities are an entity's control policies and procedures.
- Information and Communication is the exchange of information in a way that allows employees to carry out their responsibilities.

- Monitoring is the process that assesses the control environment over time.

Principles of Internal Controls

The University of California School of Business offers this list as the key general principles of a successful internal controls program.

- Separation of Duties: Duties are divided so that no one person has complete control over a key function or activity.
- Authorization and Approval: Proposed transactions are authorized when they are consistent with policy and funds are available.
- Custodial and Security Arrangements: Responsibility for custody of assets is separated from the related record keeping.
- Review and Reconciliation: Records are examined and reconciled to determine that transactions were properly processed and approved.
- Physical Controls: Equipment, inventories, cash, and other assets are secured physically, counted periodically, and compared with amounts shown on control records.
- Training and Supervision: Well-trained and supervised employees help ensure that control processes function properly.
- Documentation: Well-documented policies and procedures promote employee understanding of job duties and help ensure continuity during employee absences or turnover.
- Cost/Benefit: Costs associated with control processes should not exceed expected benefits.

Source:
"Internal Control Guidelines." *The University of California, Santa Barbara.*
www.audit.ucsb.edu/icguideline.html

Related Entries:

AUDITING FOR FRAUD

COSO

SARBANES-OXLEY ACT

INTERNET FRAUD

The U.S. government defines Internet fraud as any scheme in which one or more components of the Internet—such as websites, chat rooms, or e-mail—play a significant role in offering nonexistent goods or services to customers, communicating false or fraudulent representations about the schemes to consumers, or unlawfully transmitting a person's funds or access passwords into someone else's control.

Consumer Sentinel

In 1997, there were fewer than 1,000 Internet fraud complaints to the Federal Trade Commission's Consumer Sentinel database. By 2003, there were 516,740 complaints. These include 301,835 complaints about fraud and 214,905 identity theft reports. The Consumer Sentinel receives Internet fraud complaints from the FTC's Consumer Response Center, which processes both telephone and mail inquiries and complaints from 64 public and private law enforcement partners.

Between 1994 and 2000, the Commission brought 170 Internet-related cases against 573 defendants, ordering more than $180 million in redress. In 2001, there were 55,727 Internet-related complaints. That number increased to 166,617 in 2003. After analyzing all of the complaints collected in 2003, the Consumer Sentinel published its "Top 10 Dot Cons" list, with identity theft leading the pack:

- *Identity Theft*. Consumers' identification or property is used illegally.
- *Internet Auction Fraud*. Consumers receive nothing or an item less valuable than promised.
- *Shop-at-Home and Catalog Sales*. These schemes include problems such as, undisclosed costs, failure to deliver on time, non-delivery and refusal to honor a guarantee, with purchases made via the Internet (not including auction sales), telephone, or mail.
- *Internet services and computer complaints*. Some of these complaints include, trial offers from ISPs; difficulty canceling an ISP account; undisclosed website charges and problems with computer software and equipment purchases.
- *Prizes/Sweepstakes and Lotteries*. Cons in this category include promotions for "free" prizes for a fee, foreign lotteries and sweepstakes offered through the phone, fax, e-mail or mail.

- *Foreign Money Offers*. Letters or e-mails offer the "opportunity" to share in a percentage of millions that a self-proclaimed government official is trying to transfer illegally out of a foreign country in return for money, bank account numbers, or other identifying information from the victim.
- *Advance-fee Loans and Credit Protection/Repair Offers*. Some of these schemes include the promise of a loan that requires you to pay a fee upfront, worthless credit card loss protection and insurance programs, or the promise that accurate negative information can be removed from your credit file for a fee.
- *Telephone Services*. Cons involving telephone services include charges for calls to "toll-free" numbers, unauthorized charges for calls not made, and unauthorized switching of phone service providers.
- *Business Opps and Work-at-Home Plans*. This category includes, medical billing scams, misleading franchise and Internet-based business opportunities, and wealth building plans that don't make good on their promises.

Online Credit Card Losses

In the last decade the national media has stressed the dangers of entering credit card numbers to companies on the Internet. Because the Internet is the most impersonal form of communication to date, it is understandable that many businesses and individuals have apprehensions concerning Internet commerce. The feeling that a criminal might be "lurking in the shadows" of the Internet scares many potential customers from making initial transactions. There are some precautions to be made before purchasing online items, but conducting business transactions on the Internet is ultimately as safe as making an order from a company via the telephone.

In 2001, total annual online sales were $61.8 billion. This number rocketed to $114 billion in 2003, representing 5.4% of all retail sales. Total online sales are expected to grow 27% to $144 billion in 2004, representing 6.6% of total retail value. More than $700 million in online sales were lost to fraud in 2001. This number increased to $2.4 billion by 2003. The lack of face-to-face or voice interaction on the Internet makes fraudsters more daring by providing them with anonymity, which makes the detection and prevention of online frauds more difficult. Lists of stolen credit card numbers are also being posted on the Internet or sold in newsgroups and can be used by a variety of individuals to purchase goods online without the authorization of the credit card's owner.

National Consumer League Report

For the first time, wire transfers are No. 1 on the National Consumer League's (NCL) list of Internet frauds reported in 2005. It replaces web auctions since NCL began tracking Internet fraud in 1997. Payment by wire was most common in connection with fake checks, lotteries and lottery clubs, advance fee loans, prizes and sweepstakes, and Nigerian money offers.

Based on information that consumers provided in 2004 to NCL's National Fraud Information Center/Internet Fraud Watch program, the average loss to telemarketing fraud rose from $1,974 in 2004 to $2,892 in 2005, and Internet fraud losses more than doubled, from an average of $895 in 2004 to $1,917. The number of scams reported rose by 39% for telemarketing fraud and 12% for Internet fraud.

Among the Top 10 Internet Scams, the most expensive was Nigerian money offers, with an average loss of nearly $7,000. These scams originate from con artists, typically in other countries, who promise to share their fortunes if consumers agree to pay to transfer the funds to their own bank accounts for safekeeping. Even more alarming was the increase in victims. Forty-two people acknowledged losing money to these scams, compared to 18 in 2004.

Methods of Solicitation

Websites are the most common way that consumers are solicited for fraudulent Internet offers, but a rising number of initial contacts have been made by con artists in newsgroups:

2000 Solicitation Methods		2001 Solicitation Methods	
Websites	82%	Websites	78%
E-Mail	12%	E-Mail	18%
Newsgroups	4%	Newsgroups	2%

The amount of money consumers are losing to Internet fraud is increasing, Losses overall are $4,371,724, up from $3,387,530 in 2000. The average loss per person rose from $427 in 2000 to $803 in 2004. There are significant differences in the per person average for each category.

Top Scams	Average Loss Per Person
Online Auctions	$478
General Merchandise Sales	$845
Nigerian Money Offers	$6,542
Internet Access Services	$568
Information Adult Services	$234
Computer Equipment/Soft.	$1,102
Work-At-Home	$120

Internet Fraud Complaint Center

The Internet Crime Complaint Center (formerly the Internet Fraud Complaint Center) is a partnership between the FBI and the National White-Collar Crime Center, which began operating in May 2000. Victims report complaints to the Center and are linked to the appropriate authorities. Complaints logged by the Center during 2005 totaled more than 231,000, an increase of 11.6% over 2004. The IC3 processed more than 228,400 complaints that could lead to Internet crime investigations by law enforcement and regulatory agencies nationwide.

The total dollar loss from all referred cases of fraud in 2005 was $183.12 million with a median dollar loss of $424.00 per complaint. This is up from $68 million in total reported losses in 2004.

Victim profiles drawn from IC3 data show that:

- The typical victim reporting to the IFCC (64%) was male, between 30 and 50 years of age.
- Males tend to lose more than females.

- Of those who reported a dollar loss, the highest median losses were found among Nigerian letter fraud ($5,000), check fraud ($3,800), and other confidence fraud ($2,025) complainants.

Business Losses to Internet Fraud

Businesses, as well as individuals, are victims of Internet fraud. The Computer Security Institute (CSI) with the participation of the San Francisco Federal Bureau of Investigation's (FBI) Computer Intrusion Squad today released its 2006 report citing that virus attacks are the leading cause of financial losses. The top four categories—virus attacks, unauthorized access to networks, lost/stolen laptops or mobile hardware and theft of proprietary information or intellectual property—according to the 2006 Computer Crime and Security Survey, account for more than 74 percent of financial loss. The complete 2006 CSI/FBI Computer Crime and Security Survey is available for download on the CSI Website at GoCSI.com.

Fake Business Websites

The identities of company websites are often hijacked by Internet fraudsters. Companies in the financial industries are favorite targets, because the phony site can be used to promote stock scams. In 2000, phony sites emulating Bloomberg, the financial publisher, and the clearing bank Euroclear, were used to manipulate a U.S. penny stock.

Hoax websites are surging in popularity, posing risks to customers' cash and corporate credibility. Some search engines are fooled by these ploys and direct customers towards the sham sites.

Companies are investing in staff and consultants to scour the Web for hoax pages. In some cases, websites are not copied to add authority to false information, but to use a company's proprietary information or marketing presence for the perpetrators' own business. Security firms market services that regularly scan the Internet for stolen information and logos, identifying graphics and text taken from corporate websites.

Many copied sites imitate e-business companies in order to trick consumers into entering their credit card numbers.

KPMG Survey on Fraud in E-Commerce

In 2001, the accounting and consulting firm of KPMG surveyed the world's largest companies in 12 countries on the topics of electronic fraud and security-related issues. Participants included 14,000 CEO's, CIO's, and other senior executives of the largest public companies in Australia, India, Belgium, Italy, Canada, South Africa, Denmark, Switzerland, Germany, the United Kingdom, Hong Kong, and the United States.

Results include:

- 62% conduct e-commerce in their business, which may include business-to-business, business-to-consumer, consumer-to-business, and/or Webpage exposure.
- Respondents indicated overwhelmingly that security of credit card numbers and personal information were by far the most important concerns to their customers.
- Less than 35% of respondents reported having security audits performed on their e-commerce systems.
- Only 12% of respondents reported that their website bears a seal identifying that their e-commerce system had passed a security audit.
- 50% of businesses identified hackers and the poor implementation of security policies as the greatest threats to their e-commerce systems.
- 79% of respondents stated that the highest probability of a breach occurring to their e-commerce system would be through the Internet or other external access. Most analysts believe, however, that a company is at greater risk of being the victim of an internal security breach.
- 50% of respondents stated that their organization has incident response procedures to deal with security breaches of their e-commerce system.
- Of those respondents who have incident response procedures, 43% include computer forensic response guidelines. This number represents 22% of the total respondents.
- Survey respondents from the majority of the participating countries stated that the security of their e-commerce system could be most improved by regular system penetration testing (authorized hacking), the use of software specifically designed for security issues in an e-commerce environment, and the increased use of encryption technology.

- No significant disparities were found among the reporting regions. The authors of the report conclude that national and geographic boundaries are insignificant in e-commerce.
- 88% of respondents feel that the public perceives the traditional, or established "bricks and mortar" business as being more secure than e-commerce based "click and mortar" companies.

How Merchants Fight Fraud

The Merchant Risk Council, formerly known as The Worldwide E-Commerce Fraud Prevention Network, reported in 2001 that nearly half of its members—merchants conducting business via the Internet—who responded to an internal survey, felt that online fraud was a significant problem. However, 70% agreed that fraud prevention tools could reduce incidence rates and losses. As a result of extra spending on fraud prevention tools, a study conducted in 2003 revealed that online fraud incidence rates and losses had decreased.

Merchants taking the survey represent large, medium, and small online sites. In 2003, merchants spent about 17% of their revenues on fraud prevention, up from 13% in 2002. Also in 2003, the average number of merchants reporting a decrease in chargeback rates had increased from 48% in 2002 to 64% in 2003. Although improvements were noted in all merchant groups, the most notable improvement occurred among the small merchants (those with less than $100,000 in online revenue).

The one area all merchants are still having difficulties with is in international fraud. Thirty-eight percent of the respondents in 2003 considered international fraud to be "out of control" or "a big problem").

In an effort to help curb online fraud, merchants are moving ahead with the use of Verified by Visa and MasterCard SecureCode. In 2002, an average of 31% had implemented or would be implementing one of these programs during the upcoming year. This average has now risen to 45% of companies surveyed in 2003. Sixteen percent of merchants have never heard of Verified by Visa, including over 20% of the medium merchants and the large merchants that have between $1 million and $5 million in online revenue.

Positive Outlook

Fraud on the Internet is likely to subside in the coming years. Traditionally, "fraud operators are always among the first to appreciate the potential of a new technology to exploit and deceive consumers," according to Hugh Stevenson, associate director of the Federal Trade Commission's Bureau of Consumer Protection. When long-distance telemarketing and pay-per-call technology were introduced, fraudsters immediately began devising ways to attack the services. But as technology develops, anti-fraud methods catch up to abusers.

Anti-fraud software is becoming more prevalent and powerful. Consumers and businesses are aware of the dangers and behave more cautiously. And the Internet may not grow as quickly as predicted. The Gartner Group, a technology firm that monitors business transactions on the Internet, had predicted in January 2000 that by the year 2004, the Internet would host $7.3 trillion a year in transactions. In March 2001, the company revised its estimates to less than $6 trillion a year. Nevertheless that figure represents a six-fold increase over the $1 trillion a year in transactions for 2001.

In 2000, the European Union announced a three-year "Action Plan" of enforcement, education, and prevention, meant to reduce "the growing problem of fraud and counterfeiting on (credit) cards and other non-cash means of payment widely used for cross-border transactions."

Responding to the surge in Internet fraud, Bruce J. Gebhardt of the FBI's Northern California office, based in San Francisco, announced in 2001 an ongoing initiative between the FBI and the private sector known as "InfraGard" to gather information on fraud in e-commerce and prosecute violations.

Internet Abuse by Employees

Besides using the Internet to commit outright defalcations, many employees abuse their companies via the medium.

- Newsgroup postings take up bandwidth and waste office time.
- It is estimated that one in five white-collar male workers access pornography at work.
- Workers of both genders access news, information, and financial sites.

- Hacking involves the act of exploiting weaknesses in website security to access proprietary data such as confidential information or passwords. Some users hack for the thrill, others gather information to use certain online services for free.
- Non-work related downloading and uploading of materials is another issue. At its height—before being suspended by a federal judge—Napster, the controversial former site that permitted users to download and upload songs, took up over 80% of the bandwidth at some workplaces.
- Other Internet activities conducted at work include paying personal bills, playing games, stock trading, auctioning of personal items, gambling, and chatting.
- In a recent survey by Websense, 57% of 300 respondents acknowledged having accessed non-work related sites approximately an hour each week. Thirty percent admitted to watching sports online during work at least once a month. Approximately 27% confessed they accessed stock trading sites at work.
- Game playing on office computers costs businesses an estimated $50 billion a year in lost productivity, and middle managers are the biggest perpetrators.
- Using external ISP's to access the Internet at work to avoid detection is another form of Internet abuse. Despite the use of external ISP's, employees are still misusing the company's communication lines and resources.
- Employees may utilize these resources to work on an external assignment for additional income. These culprits include programmers, system analysts, and those equipped with advanced skills like Java, C++, and XML. Moonlighting is not only lucrative; it provides the allure of an entrepreneurial life.
- Nearly two-thirds of U.S. firms have disciplined employees for Internet abuses.

Monitoring Software—A Solution or a Privacy Issue

Monitoring software is increasingly used to combat Internet abuses. According to International Data Corporation (IDC), about 40% of companies used monitoring software in 1999, an increase of 23% compared to the number in late 1998.

Among those who deployed monitoring software, 58% of employers do so to control recreational use; 47% do so to reduce bandwidth abuse; 47% do so to eliminate downloads of pirated software; and 33% monitor to reduce sluggish Internet connections due to non-work related use.

Case Study—Faked Web Bank

An Internet scam involving fake banking documents worth approximately $3.9 billion was shut down in 2000 by the International Chamber of Commerce (ICC). Fake European banking guarantees on at least 29 different websites convinced people to invest in various investment scams. Internet domain names used to facilitate the Web scam incorporated the names and appearance of such major financial institutions as Euroclear Bank, Eurobonds, and Bloomberg. The digital promotions and counterfeiting cost scam artists hundreds of thousands of dollars to produce, but netted huge profits.

Internet Schemes

Modem Hijacking

While users are online, their computer modems are secretly disconnected from their ISP and reconnected to the Internet, only this time through an expensive international line. Victims have usually downloaded a special "viewer" program from a website offering free computer images. Once activated, the downloaded material begins the hijacking disconnection and reconnection process. Long distance charges continue to mount until victims shut down their computers, even if their Internet connection has already been terminated.

Get Rich Quick

Entering the phrase get rich quick in an Internet search results in sites with names like *$50,000 First Ten Months, Secrets of the Millionaires*, and *It's Your Turn to Get Rich.* These types of sites hawk everything from home businesses to investment opportunities.

Pyramid Schemes

The tried and true pyramid has found a new high-tech home on the Internet. As in most pyramid schemes, the initial participants of the scheme are rewarded handsomely, while the participants that join the scheme later are bilked out of their investment money.

Off-Shore Trusts

The set up of off-shore trusts caters to the desire to avoid taxes. For a fee, the company purports to be able to create an offshore trust to which taxpayers can transfer their assets. Since the trust is not within the U.S., the logic goes, the assets are not subject to taxation.

Naturally, the logic is faulty and for several reasons. First, if the taxpayer derives use from the funds in the trust, according to law those funds are considered taxable income, and the person may be prosecuted for tax evasion. Additionally, some operators simply take consumers' money and disappear. Some convince consumers to place their assets in a trust, naming the operator as beneficiary; once validated, the consumer no longer controls his own assets.

Chain Letters

E-mail allows the fraudster to compose one letter and send thousands of copies to potential victims. The letter sent to unsuspecting targets generally forewarns of the grave dangers that await the target should he or she not reply to the letter. The letter may ask for a small cash donation in exchange for the target's piece of mind that no bad tidings will be spread, providing examples of some of the unfortunates who did not heed the letter.

Investment and Securities Fraud

A fraudulent website may claim to have insider information about the value of a given stock, suggesting that something unexpected will soon happen to that company. When the unknowing stock investor takes the advice of the supposedly knowledgeable investment advisor, the "advisor" manipulates the stock price to his advantage.

Some sites promote stocks without disclosing that they have been paid to do so by the issuing company. In some situations, promoters are not affiliated with the issuing company, but they drive up the price of a stock then cash out their own holdings.

Spamming

Spamming involves sending mass e-mails to electronic lists and posting ads on discussion and chat groups. These postings are often disguised to look like tips from individual citizens who are supposedly engaged in a lawful enterprise, when in fact they are part of an Internet boiler room. The FCC and many service providers have taken steps to shut down spammers.

Credit Card Fraud

Online credit card fraud rates are much higher than when cards are used for off-line transactions. The GartnerGroup surveyed 166 retailers, half of whom sell on the Internet, to find that online credit- card fraud equaled 1.13% of transactions, more than 18 times higher than the fraud rate on all credit card transactions, which is as low as 0.06%.

Online retailers pay as much as 89 cents per credit card transaction to maintain security, including verification networks and scoring services that rate the risk of each purchase and reject those below a threshold. Scoring services mainly track each cardholder's historical shopping patterns, noting deviations from the norm.

Temporary card numbers, generated for each sale then disposed of by the issuer's system, are being developed to prevent fraud. ActiveMedia predicts that newer transaction systems will account for 10% of online sales volume this year.

Internet merchants bear the costs of online looting because signed credit card slips do not accompany their sales. In such "card-not-present" transactions, if a charge is disputed by the rightful owner of a card, sellers must cover the cost of the item, an occurrence called a "chargeback." The merchant with a disputed sale is also charged fees ranging from $20 to $30 to cover the bank's costs in processing the dispute. Chargebacks can account for up to 30% of some Web merchants' overall sales.

The most popular items in Internet fraud are electronic devices: cameras, DVD players, radios, stereo equipment, and VCR's. Most goods cost from $100 to $200, though some thieves target high-ticket items such as desktop and laptop computers. Credit card numbers are obtained by hacking into websites, from discarded credit card receipts, and from clerks, waiters, and others who regularly handle credit cards.

Anti-Fraud Techniques on the Internet

Encryption

Confidential information can be encrypted using software that scrambles communications utilizing one of several mathematical formulae. The only way to unscramble an encrypted message is to provide the unique answer "key," thus unlocking the message. Encryption is the best method to block access.

Customer Validation

Customer validation safeguards may include a customer code or password. Some businesses participate in validation systems that assure customers the company is legitimate.

Internal Network Security

Sensitive information is stored on internal systems, with access limited to a few key personnel.

Firewalls

Firewalls are advanced software programs which effectively "lock up" access to an Internet sight or e-mail transmission. Firewalls govern the interface between a computer network and the Internet, surveying transmissions and stopping any transmission that violates protocol. Intruders can defeat firewalls, but they are effective against most intrusions.

Registration

Internet consultants recommend that companies register not just domain names and company trademarks, but misspellings of the name as well.

Sources:
Atanasov, M. "The Truth about Internet Fraud; Industry Trend or Event?" *Ziff Davis Smart Business for the New Economy,* April 1, 2001.

"E-Merchants Recognize Online Fraud As a Serious Problem, But Majority Believes Fraud Prevention Tools Can Keep It In Check." *Worldwide E-Commerce Fraud Prevention Network,* April 5, 2001. www.merchantfraudsquad.com/pages/release_040501.html

Eisenhauer, C. "Electronic Commerce Work Group, Final Report." *Intergovernmental Information Technology and Telecommunications Plan,* December 15, 2000. www.state.ia.us/government/iitt/workelec.htm

Enos, L., and Micek, J. "U.S. Agency Says E-Commerce is Fertile Ground for Fraud." *E-Commerce Times,* April 6, 2001.

Gad, I. "Electronic Price Tag Manipulation." *The White-Collar Crime Fighter,* May 2001

Hawkins, R. "Finance Fraud Spreads on Internet." *Sunday Business (London),* May 6, 2001.

Keng. S., Fui-Hoon Nah, F., and Teng, L. "Acceptable Internet Use Policy." *Communications of the ACM,* January 1, 2002.

"Law Enforcers Target 'Top 10' Online Scams." *Federal Trade Commission,* October 31, 2000. www.ftc.gov

Lorek, L. "Foreign Flimflam." *Interactive Week,* February 25, 2001.

Luening, E. "Net Fraud Costs Consumers $117 Million." *CNET News,* May 23, 2001.

Mahoney, M. "Europeans Crack Down on $3.9B Internet Banking Scam." *E-Commerce Times,* April 12, 2001.

Maloy, T. "Watch Out For Investment Schemes." *United Press International,* April 23, 2001.
National Consumer League's Internet Fraud Watch. www.fraud.org

Tedeschi, B. "E-Commerce Report. Revised Forecasts." *The New York Times,* March 26, 2001.

Related Entries:

COMPUTER CRIME
CON SCHEMES
HACKING

INVENTORY FRAUD

Inventory fraud is a form of asset misappropriation, the most common of occupational frauds. There are two ways a person can misappropriate inventory and other noncash assets. The asset can be misused (or "borrowed") or it can be stolen. Assets that are misused but not stolen typically include company vehicles, company supplies, computers, and other office equipment. Losses from asset theft can run into the millions of dollars. Most inventory losses fall into one of four categories: larceny schemes, asset requisition and transfer schemes, purchasing schemes, and shipping and receiving schemes.

Inventory Fraud Schemes

Larceny

Larceny is a simple theft of physical property. Employees remove the item themselves or have an accomplice pretend to buy the item. In a related scheme, the accomplice returns goods that the employee has stolen, converting the stolen inventory into cash with the return refund.

Asset Requisitions and Transfers

Asset requisitions and transfers allow the employee to move merchandise without raising suspicion. An employee requisitions materials for a project, then makes off with the materials. In some cases the employee simply overstates the amount of supplies or equipment it will take to complete his work and pilfers the excess. In more ambitious schemes the employee might invent a completely fictitious project.

Purchasing Schemes

Dishonest employees with proper access can obtain goods by charging the company's purchasing accounts. This type of scheme is also discussed as false billing in the entry, BILLING SCHEMES. The item may be used in actual work and then stolen, or may be purchased for the fraudster's use alone.

Shipping Schemes

Shipping schemes target goods as they are received or distributed. A receiving clerk can reduce the count of incoming goods (e.g., from 1,000 to 900) and steal the units not accounted for. The bill for the goods, with the proper count, is sent to accounts payable, but the inventory count is recorded short. Portions of goods may also be marked as "substandard," which the employee then keeps rather than returning. Alternatively, a falsified packing slip causes inventory to be delivered to the perpetrator or an accomplice.

To conceal shipping thefts, employees may create false shipping documents and false sales documents. The fake receivables may eventually be written off as uncollectible, or the perpetrator may alter financial statements in order to cover the loss. Delinquent receivables may be hidden in accounts such as discounts and allowances, bad debt expense, or lost and stolen assets.

For inventory thefts generally, the key concealment issue is shrinkage, the unaccounted-for reduction in the company's inventory. In a "forced reconciliation" the perpetrator simply changes the inventory numbers to match the actual items on hand. During a physical inventory count, the count can be altered to match the actual number of items. However, the forced adjustments do not have a sales transaction to account for the numbers. To fix this, a perpetrator can debit accounts receivable and credit the sales account so that it appears that the missing goods have been sold, but payment has not yet been received.

Detection of Inventory Thefts

Statistical sampling allows an examiner to predict the occurrence rate of various phenomena, and compare current figures to the statistical norm. Unexplained entries in the perpetual records should be verified. A comparative review of shipping records against physical counts and financial statements may reveal inventory theft.

A review of financial statement ratios is sometimes revealing. If the cost of goods sold increases by a disproportionate amount relative to sales, and no changes occur in the purchase prices, quantities purchased, or quality of products purchased, one of two things has occurred: (1) ending inventory has been depleted by theft, or (2) someone has been embezzling money through a false billing scheme.

A computerized trend analysis isolates certain factors for inspection. For example, in a lumberyard operation, the examiner may view all purchases of four-by-four cedar fence posts. Investigators should examine all the source documents that are represented by the listing. The following table lists trend analysis factors and the schemes suggested by each factor.

Searches and Sorts	What to Look For
Purchases by vendor	The same vendor is receiving favorable treatment
Inventory levels by types and dates	Inventory is being purchased at its reorder point or if excess inventory is being ordered
Inventory shipped by address	The vendor's address matches either an employee address or the address of another vendor
Cost per item	Discounts are properly credited to purchases
Direct labor by item	There are excess labor hours being added to a particular job or item
Direct materials by item	Materials are properly charged to the job (too much or the wrong materials)
Overhead per inventory item	Overhead is being properly applied, and applied only once
Disposals then reorders	Usable inventory is being prematurely designated as scrap
Shortages by inventory item	There is inventory theft or the reorder system is not functioning
Returns and Allowances	There is an unusually high incidence of returns and allowances
Sales Allowances	Sales allowances are not properly credited to promotional allowances
Buyer	The buyer is not acting within scope of authority

Inventory Audit Questions

The following questions will also be helpful in establishing inventory control:

- Do adequate, detailed, written inventory instructions and procedures exist?
- Do inventory procedures give appropriate consideration to the location and arrangement of inventories?
- Do inventory procedures give appropriate consideration to identification and description of inventories?
- Is the method of determining inventory quantities specified (e.g., weight, count)?
- Is the method used for recording items counted adequate (e.g. count sheets, prenumbered tags)? Are inventory tags used? If yes: (1) Are they prenumbered? (2)

Is accounting for inventory tags adequate and does it include control with respect to tags used, unused, and voided?

- Are adequate procedures in place to identify inventory counted, ensure that all items have been counted, and prevent double counting?
- Are obsolete, slow-moving, or damaged inventories properly identified and segregated?
- Is the inventory reasonably identifiable for proper classification in the accounting records (e.g., description, stage of completion)?
- Are inventory counts subject to (1) complete recounts by persons independent of the ones involved in the initial counts, (2) recounts only of merchandise having substantial value, or (3) spot checks by supervisory personnel?
- Do employees whose functions are independent of the physical custody of inventories and record-keeping functions perform counts?
- Do proper accounting controls and procedures exist for the exclusion from inventory of merchandise on-hand, which is not property of the client (e.g., customers' merchandise, consignments in)?
- Do proper accounting controls and procedures exist for the inclusion in inventory of merchandise not on-hand, but the property of the client (e.g., merchandise in warehouses, out on repair, consignments out)?
- Will identical inventory items in various areas be accumulated to allow a tie in total counts to a summary listing subsequent to the observation?
- Is the movement of inventory adequately controlled (e.g., shipping and receiving activities suspended) during the physical count to ensure a proper cut-off?
- Are significant differences between physical counts and detailed inventory records investigated before the accounting and inventory records are adjusted to match the physical counts?
- Will inventory at remote locations be counted?
- Will special counting procedures or volume conversions be necessary (e.g., items weighed on scale)?
- How will work-in-process inventory be identified?
- How will the stage of completion of work-in-process inventory be identified?

- Are there any other matters that should be noted for the inventory count?

Related Entries:

ASSET MISAPPROPRIATION

OCCUPATIONAL FRAUD AND ABUSE

JESSUP, CHARLES

Charles Jessup was the son of a preacher named Walter Jessup, who was a founding member of the Assemblies of God denomination, the most popular expression of Pentecostalism. In the early 20th century, Pentecostals were, and remain, a loosely affiliated movement among charismatic churches that practiced faith healing and speaking in unknown tongues. Charles began preaching at the age of 16, when his father prevailed upon a pastor in Memphis to give the boy some pulpit time.

Jessup's ministry had an advantage over his father's because he could broadcast his sermons—and his appeals for funds—over the radio, particularly using stations located along the Mexico-America border, which were not subject to FCC regulation. Shameless exploiters often used these airwaves to sell live animals, cures for sexual impotence and a host of diseases, and solace for the lonely and bemused. Jessup began broadcasting from XERF 1570 in Del Rio, Texas in 1942.

Jessup, who called himself Reverend despite his lack of credentials, sold "prayer insurance" on his broadcasts—listeners who sent in a contribution had their names mentioned in a prayer on their behalf, live on the air. Jessup also offered "personal prayer records," a recording in which Jessup supposedly prayed specifically on the contributor's behalf. In fact, the prayer records were prepared by having Jessup record a generalized prayer in one session, then record people's names and ailments later so that a technician could splice the material together, giving the illusion that the preacher interceded for each and every donor. He promoted expeditions to the Holy Land, including arrangements for fasting and praying at different stages of the trip. Jessup also promoted the Faith Hospital, collecting donations for its establishment and operation, though the hospital was nothing more than rented rooms in an old hotel in Gulfport, Mississippi employing a single nurse. Jessup's accounting was conducted by women in his office, who opened envelopes and scribbled names and amounts into notebooks. The business was conducted almost completely in cash, making it difficult to verify or challenge Jessup's declarations about the financial activities of the Fellowship Revival Association.

Jessup thrived for decades, supported mainly by his legions of female listeners, who did find some sort of solace through the sound of his voice and his teachings. Jessup was arrested in 1964, just one of many caught in a large investigation of radio abuses that began in 1961, occasioned by charges that American citizens were being preyed upon, even if the radio stations broadcasting the fraudulent advertisements were technically located in a foreign country. Jessup was charged by the Medical Fraud Unit of the Bureau of Alcohol, Tobacco and Firearms in 1962. However, Jessup's trial was not set until January 22, 1968. In the interim he continued to conduct his various ministries.

As the date for Jessup's trial approached in 1967, Jessup agreed to plead no contest to the mail fraud charges and the other charges were dropped. In their brief, prosecutors had shown that Jessup promised to pray for listeners' needs individually, though he was sending out doctored versions of generic recordings. Furthermore, while he regularly pleaded for monies to stay on the air, Jessup had paid for airtime several years into the future. Since he used the mail to exchange money and goods, he was charged with mail fraud as well. Jessup's cash-only accounting system was a mess, but prosecutors noted that "currency was seldom deposited" into any verifiable Jessup accounts; instead, Jessup kept the money and directed its distribution himself. He also misrepresented the nature and progress of the Faith Hospital.

Jessup was sentenced to a year in federal prison, five years' probation, and a $2,000 fine. He was forced to sell the 14-room house and estate he owned in Mississippi. After his release he lived in a modest home with his fourth wife, and served as a caretaker for a local realtor. He died in 1993 of natural causes.

Related Entry:

CONSUMER FRAUD

KICKBACKS

See, CORRUPTION, OCCUPATIONAL

KREUGER, IVAR

Ivar Kreuger was born in Stockholm, Sweden. He came from a family of industrialists who owned textile operations, a papermaking plant, and a facility for making safety matches. His grandfather, Peter Edvard, helped usher Sweden into the modern era, and the family was widely respected in Sweden and elsewhere. At the height of his career in the 1920's Ivar Kreuger controlled an estimated 80% of the world's business in matches. He became known as the Swedish Match King.

The week the American stock market crashed in 1929, Kreuger was featured on the cover of *Time* magazine as one who did not believe there was anything seriously wrong economically. Articles in the *Saturday Evening Post* and the *Literary Digest* extolled his leadership. Kreuger met with President Hoover to advise him on handling the crisis. But after Kreuger shot himself in a Paris apartment in 1932, it was discovered that much of his financial empire was faked.

Kreuger left Stockholm for New York City in 1900, shortly after earning his degree in civil engineering. He sold real estate briefly, then obtained a surveyor's permit and joined crews along the East Coast. Returning to New York in the fall of 1901 as an employee of the Fuller Construction Company, Kreuger helped build a number of New York City's noted landmarks, including the Plaza Hotel, R. H. Macy & Co., and the Met Life Tower. For the next seven years Kreuger worked construction projects around the world: Germany, South Africa, India, and finally back to the U.S. by way of Canada.

In 1909, Kreuger borrowed 10,000 kroner (about $25,000) from his father and set up Kreuger & Toll, in partners with fellow engineer Paul Toll. The company constructed buildings using a new technique involving reinforced concrete. Besides its "contracting and building operations," the company's prospectus suggested the undertaking might "in connection with its affairs acquire shares in other concerns in investments." However, Kreuger & Toll promised to "not carry on a regular trading business in securities." Two years later, in early 1914, the company began trading securities on the Stockholm Exchange without revising its corporate status.

Around this time Kreuger also entered the match business. Since 1844, when a chemist named Gustaf Erik Pasch created the safety match, Sweden had been synonymous with matchmaking. The Jönköping Trust, a popular name for the nation's largest matchmaking conglomerate, produced most Swedish matches. During World War

I, Kreuger obtained loans and arranged deals to consolidate those factories outside the Jönköping trust—eleven different plants altogether, including the two run by the Kreuger family—into the gigantic United Match Factories.

Over the next few years, particularly after destabilized business operations, Kreuger's United Match Factories absorbed the Jönköping Trust. After 1920, Kreuger controlled virtually all of Sweden's match factories, materials suppliers, paper mills, printing mills, machine-making facilities, and 100,000 acres of prime Swedish woodland. His personal worth was estimated at over $5 million. By the end of the decade, Kreuger owned 250 match factories providing 80% of the world's supply. Meanwhile he expanded into other industries: paper-and-pulp, telephone service in 17 countries, several newspapers, and a much-touted gold mine.

Fraud became a vital part of Kreuger's empire. For example, in 1925, Kreuger formed a company called Garanta, which he claimed would handle a large contract to produce matches in Poland. No such contract existed. But Kreuger sold 450,000 shares of the project on the New York Stock Exchange. International Match Company (IMCO) another Kreuger-controlled company, would pass the first $17 million from the stock sale to Garanta in October 1925. IMCO also promised to send $8 million more to its Polish subsidiary the following July. In fact Kreuger arranged to embezzle the funds for his own use.

The Swedish Match Company, Kreuger and Toll's flagship concern, owed IMCO about $50 million. Kreuger arranged his books to show Swedish Match paying the IMCO subsidiary's debt to the Garanta subsidiary. But Swedish Match did not send the money either. Kreuger drew up the paperwork for the transaction—lowering the debt on Swedish Match's books, clearing IMCO's obligation to Garanta, and crediting Garanta's account with the payment—then he used the cash for himself. He took the cash; he reduced Swedish Match's debt to its subsidiary by half; and IMCO carried the Garanta financing as an asset, recording (though not collecting) interest at 24% a year. Garanta was just a shell company—no one but Kreuger ever saw the account books. He dictated figures for the general ledger to his assistants, who wrote down whatever numbers Kreuger gave them. In other manipulations, he sold properties from one of his companies to another, sometimes "selling" the property several times over, each time increasing the profit to his selling company and the net assets of his acquiring company.

Kreuger expanded his international business connections by loaning money to governments hard hit by World War I. In 1922, he loaned France $75 million, stabilizing the dangerously volatile franc, and in return won the unlimited rights to ship luxury matches (instead of cheap wartime knockoffs) into the French market. In late October 1929, while most people were hoarding cash, Kreuger announced he was loaning Germany $200 million. But the demand on Kreuger's own cash forced him into his crudest act ever in 1930, when he counterfeited a batch of Italian bonds with a face value of about $142 million. As *Fortune* later reported, "About 425 million kroner of assets shown on Kreuger & Toll's 1930 balance sheet were created by fictitious gains. . . and more than half the company's net profit for that year was the product of bookkeeping, not match selling. Some of the subsidiaries were real, some were a set of books, some were a name; but name, books, or reality, the entries spun back and forth, the debit and credit items tangled from roof to wall."

In summer 1931, Kreuger proposed a merger between his Ericsson Telephone Company in Sweden and the American-owned International Telephone and Telegraph. During the deal, Edwin Chinlund, leading the ITT merger team, grew suspicious of Kreuger's bookkeeping. About $6 million of Ericsson's assets, Chinlund discovered, were listed as "cash in hand and in banks" on the English-language contract describing the merger. But a translator revealed that the Swedish version read "cash, bankings and *on deposit*." Meaning that the $6 million was *on deposit* at Kreuger & Toll—the funds had been shifted from Ericsson into the parent company, and "replaced" with some of the counterfeited Italian bonds.

When the deal collapsed, Kreuger left New York for Paris. There he shot himself in the heart with a 9-millimeter revolver while lying in his bed. He left a simple statement by the bedside: "I'm too tired to continue."

Source: Wells, J., CFE, CPA. "Keeper of the Flame." *Frankensteins of Fraud,* Austin, TX: Obsidian Publishing Co., 2000.

Related Entry:

FINANCIAL STATEMENT FRAUD

LABORATORY FRAUD, HEALTH CARE

Laboratories submit fraudulent insurance claims, either directly or through a doctor's office or treatment facility, which is a form of provider fraud. During the 1980's and 1990's, organized crime perpetrated laboratory frauds on a large scale.

Rolling Labs

A rolling lab is a mobile laboratory that solicits insured individuals to participate in health screening tests at no cost to the insured. These labs are usually located in semi-trailers parked at health clubs, spas, shopping centers, or on vacant property. Patients are offered a free physical exam, which is ultimately billed to the patient's insurance as multiple treatments (perhaps 8–10) usually totaling $8,000–$10,000. Additional claims are billed later, even though no further testing is done. The lab moves to another location prior to the patient receiving the test results to avoid detection.

The favored method is to open a small office and conduct telephone solicitations. Mobile labs are often parked outside a large shopping center. Some labs rent office space in a doctor's office for one day and test all of that doctor's patients. Health spas sometimes allow labs to use their facilities.

Bundled Testing

Clinical labs encourage physicians to order tests unnecessarily by including a range of blood tests with any order. The physician pays nothing or only a nominal fee for the extra tests. The lab staff later unbundles the extraneous tests and bills the patient's insurance. Medicare/Medicaid has lost about $500 million to bundling abuses, and private payers have also lost millions.

Related Entry:

HEALTH CARE FRAUD

LAPPING

See, CASH THEFT SCHEMES

LARCENY

See, CASH THEFT SCHEMES
INVENTORY FRAUD

LAW, JOHN

John Law was born in Edinburgh, Scotland in 1671. In his youth, he displayed a penchant for mathematics, but preferred to spend his time gambling and womanizing. He fled Scotland in the late 1690's after being charged with murder. He spent the next 25 years on the Continent, continuing his reputation as a scoundrel, but also gaining some infamy as an economic thinker, who believed no country would prosper in the 18th century without instituting a paper currency.

In 1715, he moved to France, where he and his friend, the Duc d'Orleans, set about revolutionizing the country's economy with a series of currency reforms. He had been arguing for such reforms since 1705, when he published a pamphlet on money and trade, and introduced the term *circulation* into economic parlance. The time was ripe: Louis XIV had just died; the heir to the throne was not yet seven years old; and the Duke had been named Regent, in effect directing the French crown.

Law argued that currency was a medium for exchanging goods, not a repository of intrinsic value. As money was passed from one transaction to another, it tended to increase an economy's gross national product. Thus, he designed a system that emphasized exchange. He created a "land bank," essentially a national bank, La Banque Générale, that based its assets on the gross national product. He substituted paper currency for gold, and provided general acceptance and trading of various notes, including bonds, credit notes, and company shares.

Law also founded the Mississippi Company, named and originally chartered to harvest the riches of France's holdings in the New World. The Mississippi Company grew into a giant national conglomerate that controlled the French holdings in Mississippi, East

India, and China; it also controlled the tobacco monopoly, the tax farms, the national bank, the government's national debt, and the currency mint.

The intertwining of so many private and public interests laid the foundation for an economic disaster. As described by Edward Chancellor, "The Mississippi shares rose in value, [so] more money was printed, producing an inflationary spiral which pushed the share price from under 500 livres … to over 20,000" in a few months' time. Rents, and the cost of living generally, rose by 200% to 400%. Chancellor explains, "Law's great error was his confusion of shares with money. Since rising share prices led to the printing of more money, which in turn was ploughed back into shares, there was no potential limit to the ensuing asset inflation."

Mississippi Company shares sometimes rose 10% or 20% within an hour. Brokers operated out of stalls in the marketplace, or with nothing more than a table in an alley. One man swore he bought 1,000 francs worth of shares at one end of a street and sold them for 1,100 francs at the other end. Inflation drove the cost of living, and Law's currency reform, through the roof. A space that once rented for the equivalent of $200 a year was fetching $4,000 a year.

All the ruling countries of Europe, including France, Spain, and England, caught bubble mania. Bubble companies were funded for everything from the importation of Swedish iron to "the trading of hair." A citizen could buy shares in a venture "for furnishing funerals to any part of Great Britain" or in one "for buying and fitting out ships to suppress pirates." As many schemes as people could think of, they sold shares for.

Charles McKay, who chronicled Law and other early schemers in his *Extraordinary Popular Delusions*, stated, "Persons of distinction, of both sexes, were deeply engaged in all these bubbles; those of the male sex going to taverns and coffee-houses to meet their brokers, and the ladies resorting for the same purpose to the shops of milliners and haberdashers." So many people were making so much money a new word was coined to describe them: *millionaires*.

Law's friend Duke tried to stem the tide by taking control of the land bank, but this drove speculations even higher. "Under Law's sole direction," writes economist Marietta Morgan, "the bank had kept issues to 60 million livres, but this amount was drastically expanded to the level of 2,600 million livres, 1,500 million of which were created between 1 February and 1 April 1720."

John Law has gone down in history as a con man *par excellence*, but when the bubble popped, Law suffered with everyone else. Virtually all of his own assets were tied up in the Mississippi Company. Law probably intended the venture to be part of his general reform, expecting to get rich on the increasing gross national product, not on investment mania. McKay recounts, "His all, with the exception of one diamond, worth about five or six thousand pounds sterling, was invested in the French soil; and when he left that country, he left it almost a beggar." In October 1720, Law fled for his life.

For a while he hoped to return after a suitable time of exile, but the death of the Regent in 1723 took away Law's main protector. He supposedly drifted through Rome to Copenhagen and eventually back to Scotland, where he had been pardoned for a murder he had committed in his youth. He spent about four years in England, and then left for Venice, where he died in 1729.

It now appears that Law never set out to con anyone. But he held on against all hope that the mania would subside and return the economy to healthier levels of circulation. Unfortunately maniacs, by definition, do not exercise cautious reasoning.

Source:
McKay, C. *Extraordinary Popular Delusions and the Madness of Crowds*. New York, NY: Random House Publishing, 1995.

LEASING FRAUD

Leasing fraud is a form of financial institution fraud. Individual lessees may file false information, and fake or inflated collateral values. Individuals may also purchase leases fraudulently through brokers who assist them in obtaining leases they would not otherwise qualify for. Leasing brokers may also create phony lessees and steal the leased items. Lax internal controls, overworked personnel, and poor or nonexistent audits are among the factors allowing leasing fraud to occur.

Fraudulent Brokers

In a typical legitimate leasing arrangement, a leasing company originates leases on behalf of a bank. The company warrants that each lease is valid and that the lessee accepted delivery of the equipment. After funding, the company assigns the leases to the bank; lessees then remit payments directly to the bank. The leasing company agrees to repurchase any lease that does not conform to its representations. The owner of the leasing company may personally guarantee all leases.

Leasing brokers defraud their underwriters in several ways. People are paid for their credit histories, financial statements, and signatures on lease documents, allowing others without requisite credit history to obtain equipment. The leasing company may send funds to the purported lessees for making monthly payments or may have co-conspirators maintain the accounts. In certain cases, signatures of individuals with requisite credit histories—and their personal identification materials—are forged.

Red Flags of Leasing Fraud

Red flags associated with this type of fraud:

- Lease originations that grow at an uncharacteristic rate.
- Financial documentation missing requisite Uniform Commercial Code filings.
- Insurance certificates that list the lease company owner as agent.
- The leasing company owner's spouse signs equipment appraisals.
- The leasing company owner mails payments intended for conspiring lessees to the bank.
- A customer mails the coupon book to the bank, saying he or she does not have a lease with the bank.
- A correspondent bank learns of fraud allegations from a customer and relates the concerns to the bank.
- A finance company informs the bank that it is having difficulty confirming that certain lessees have leased equipment.

Preventing Leasing Fraud

The following steps will help prevent leasing fraud:

- Implement adequate written policies and operational guidelines.
- Obtain background checks and references on the leasing company, principal officers, and guarantor.
- Assess the financial capacity of the leasing company and guarantor.
- Implement ongoing internal audit or independent review of lease operations, including the testing of underwriting, periodic inspection of collateral, and direct verification of lease obligations.

Source:
Hodson K., and Hodson, M. "Leasing & ISO's: Two Wallops from Fraud; Independent Sales Organization, and How Banks Can Prevent Fraud." *The RMA Journal,* July 1, 2001.

Related Entry:
FINANCIAL INSTITUTION FRAUD

LEAVENWORTH PRISON FRAUD

A 300-page report in 1977 detailed how convicts at Leavenworth Prison were programming computers to defraud the IRS. The convicts had been hired by the Department of Agriculture to write computer programs that would handle the disbursal of government payments to the farming industry. The perpetrators were able to file bogus tax returns and claim refunds by forging W-2 forms and other records. Besides the prisoners, several former employees of the IRS were charged with aiding the crime.

The false claims were kept relatively low so that the computer would not mark the file for inspection. An IRS investigator estimated the average refund fell between $600 and $1,000. The report from the Senate Government Operations Committee did not specify total losses, but placed the cost in the "millions of dollars."

LEBED, JONATHAN

The youngest person ever charged with an investment crime, Jonathan Lebed was only 15 when he was arrested for illegal stock touting in September 2000. The SEC alleged that Jonathan G. Lebed, beginning at the age of 14, used the Internet to manipulate small-company stocks, reaping gains of $272,826. Without admitting or denying the findings, Lebed agreed to abide by securities laws and turn over profits and interest totaling $285,000.

Lebed ran a "pump and dump scheme." According to the SEC filing, on 11 separate occasions Lebed purchased a block of a thinly traded microcap stock, and then within hours sent "numerous false and/or misleading unsolicited e-mail messages touting the stock he just purchased." He then sold his shares at a profit.

Lebed said he had been investing in the stock market since he was 12, and had learned about the market by reading books, watching CNBC and CNN, and visiting investing websites. His parents, Constance and Gregory Lebed, said they knew their son was trading and encouraged him. Lebed started trading "well-known" stocks with his savings of several thousand dollars through a custodial account opened by his parents, later moving to stocks with low capitalizations of $3 million to $20 million and low trading volume.

He became a regular on Internet investment message boards on such sites as Yahoo!. Beginning in early 1998, he was regularly writing on Silicon Investor, another financial website. While many people choose to talk about stocks on these sites using a pseudonym, Lebed registered on Silicon Investor under his real name as a resident of Greenwich, Conn., and, when asked for occupation or title, he called himself "The Great One."

The SEC zeroed in on the youth's transactions between August 23, 1999 and February 4, 2000 when Lebed was trading in OTC bulletin board stocks. He would buy a large share, between 17% to 46% of a day's volume of a thinly traded stock, then post hundreds of messages on message boards under assumed names, touting the stock.

His profits on each trade ranged from a few hundred dollars to $74,000, the SEC said. He was charged because he used fictitious names and because he made baseless predictions about stock-price increases and relayed other false information about company prospects. The SEC said that personally benefiting from such a scheme is illegal.

Source:
Lewis, M. "Teenager Trader Runs Afoul in Stock-Fraud Case, by Michael Schroeder, Ruth Simon, and Aaron Elstein." *Wall Street Journal,* September 21, 2000.

Related Entry:
SECURITIES FRAUD

LEESON, NICK

Barings Bank collapsed in 1995 when it could not meet the enormous trading obligations established on the bank's behalf by Nick Leeson. At receivership, the bank held futures positions on Japanese equities and interest rates of $27 billion, $7 billion on the Nikkei 225 equity contract, and $20 billion on Japanese government bond (JGB) and Euroyen contracts. Leeson sold 70,892 Nikkei put and call options with a nominal value of $6.68 billion. At the time the bank held a reported capital of about $615 million.

Nick Leeson's official assignment was arbitrage trading in three futures markets:

- Futures on the Nikkei 225 stock index (Nikkei futures) traded on SIMEX (Singapore International Monetary Exchange) and on the Osaka Securities Exchange (OSE).
- 10-year Japanese Government Bond Futures (JGB Futures) traded on the SIMEX and on the Tokyo Stock Exchange (TSE.)
- 3-month Euroyen Futures traded on SIMEX and on the Tokyo International Financial Futures Exchange (TIFFEE).

However, Leeson engaged in unauthorized activities almost as soon as he started trading in Singapore in 1992. He took proprietary positions on SIMEX on both futures and options contracts. His mandate from London allowed him to take positions only if they were part of "switching" and to execute client orders. He was never allowed to sell options. Leeson lost money from his unauthorized trades almost from day one. Yet he was perceived in London as one who single-handedly contributed to half of Barings Singapore's 1993 profits and half of the entire firm's 1994 profits. But in that year alone, Leeson lost Barings $296 million, while his bosses thought he had earned them $46 million, for which they paid him a bonus approaching $1 million.

Leeson bet against the Nikkei average; as the Japanese stock market fell, Leeson's increased his position. His official trading strategy was to take advantage of temporary price differences between the SIMEX and OSE Nikkei 225 contracts. This arbitrage practice, called "switching," required Leeson to buy the cheaper contract and to sell simultaneously the more expensive one, reversing the trade when the price difference had narrowed or disappeared. There was little market risk because positions are always matched.

Instead, Leeson established massive, unauthorized speculative positions in all SIMEX contracts. He managed to conceal these positions from SIMEX and Barings' headquarters by using an account, which was established to take care of errors during the hectic trading sessions at SIMEX. From July 1992, this "88888-account" increasingly became Leeson's place to hide his unauthorized positions.

The largest part of Barings' losses came from a massive long position in Nikkei futures. In July 1992, Leeson started to use the 88888-account to hide unhedged positions outside his formal Nikkei futures trading limits for the first time. Until October 1993, these losses were always recovered. However, from October 1993, losses increased gradually, with acceleration in the final two months leading up to the collapse of Barings in 1995.

The total monthly trading volume that went through account 88888 increased from 2,051 in July 1992 to a peak of 96,121 in September 1994. In January 1995, the total was 90,000 contracts. However, when the Nikkei dropped 1,000 points on Monday, January 23, 1995, Leeson incurred losses on his two-day old long futures position and faced unlimited damage from selling put options. So he tried to single-handedly reverse the negative sentiment that had swamped the Japanese stock market. Large falls in Japanese equities also made the market more volatile, which impacted Leeson's short option position—a seller of options wants volatility to decline so that the value of the options decreases. With volatility on the rise, Leeson's short options would have incurred losses even if the Tokyo stock market had not plunged.

Leeson was able to deceive Barings by using a tactic known as the *cross trade*. A cross trade is a transaction executed on the floor of an exchange by just one member who is both buyer and seller. If a member has matching buy and sell orders from two different customer accounts for the same contract and at the same price, he is allowed to cross the transaction (execute the deal) by matching both his client accounts. However he can only do this after he has declared the bid and offer price in the pit and no other member has taken it up. A cross-trade must be executed at market price.

Leeson entered into a significant volume of cross transactions between his secret accounts. After executing these cross trades, Leeson would instruct the settlements staff to break down the total number of contracts into several different trades, and to change the trade prices thereon to cause profits to be credited to his "switching" accounts, while the losses were hidden in the secret account "88888." The cross trades appeared genuine and within the rules of the Exchange. Alternatively, Leeson would enter into cross trades of smaller size in which he would arrange for the price to be amended, again enabling profit to be credited to the "switching" account and losses to be charged to account "88888."

A report by the British government found, "In each instance, the entries in the Contac system reflected a number of spurious contract amounts at prices different to those transacted on the floor, reconciling to the total lot size originally traded. This had the effect of giving the impression from a review of the reported trades in account '92000' that these had taken place at different times during the day. This was necessary to deceive Barings Securities Japan into believing the reported profitability in account '92000' was a result of authorized arbitrage activity. In addition to crossing trades on SIMEX between account '88888' and the switching accounts, Leeson also entered fictitious trades between these accounts, which were never crossed on the floor of the Exchange. The effect of these was again to credit the 'switching' accounts with profits whilst charging account '88888' with losses."

Through Leeson's manipulations, Barings was counter party to many of its own trades. Leeson bought from one account and sold to the other. Barings was thus not arbitraging between SIMEX and the Japanese exchanges but taking open (and very substantial) positions, which were buried in account "88888." Details of this account were never transmitted to the treasury or risk control offices in London, an omission that ultimately had catastrophic consequences for Barings' shareholders and bondholders.

Related Entries:

FINANCIAL INSTITUTION FRAUD
SECURITIES FRAUD

LEGAL ELEMENTS OF FRAUD

Early references in England's common law—on which the American system is based—define fraud as cheating or deceit. A common-law cheat induced someone to part with property or personal rights by deploying false pretenses, false tokens, or intentionally false representations. Common-law cheating or fraud was considered a misdemeanor crime (as distinguished from larceny which was a felony of the times) and grounds for civil action.

This dual status is retained in modern American courts. Tax evasion, for example, can be treated as a criminal and civil fraud. Many acts of fraud prompt both criminal and civil actions—prosecutors may file a criminal complaint on behalf of the public, while a group of shareholders file a civil action for recovery of losses.

In many states fraud is now known as larceny by trick or false pretenses. Larceny refers to what is more widely called theft or stealing—a physical act that wrongfully deprives someone of assets. Fraud refers to taking assets through guile or deception, by false representation, false pretenses, or by concealment of crucial information. The deception may be designed to cause others to act, or for concealing one's own actions. If the taking is by stealth or force, the act is larceny; if by deception or manipulation, the act is fraud.

Embezzlement is a particular kind of fraud, distinguished from larceny not by the act of deception, but by a breaching of one's fiduciary responsibility. An embezzler is someone who has been given legal custody of assets for a period of time, or for a specific purpose, and has either stolen those assets or used them for personal gain. Embezzlement violates fiduciary responsibility because the act exceeds the originally authorized custody agreement.

Fraud, in practice, embraces all the multifarious means which human ingenuity can devise for one person to get an advantage over another, either by false suggestion or suppression of the truth. According to Black's Law Dictionary, the act includes surprise, trick, cunning, and a range of unfair ways by which people are cheated.

Legal Elements of Fraud

Generally stated, the legal elements required to prove criminal fraud are:

- A material false statement,
- Made with knowledge of its falsity,
- Which is relied upon by the victim,
- Who suffers damages as a result.

Civil Fraud Actions

In *Southern Development Co. v. Silva*, 125 U.S. 247, 8 S.Ct. 881, 31 L.Ed. (1887), the U.S. Supreme Court defined the legal elements of a civil fraud as follows:

- The defendant has made a representation in regard to a material fact;
- The representation was false;
- The defendant knew the representation was false;
- The representation was intended to provoke an action;
- By the plaintiff, who suffered damage as a result; and
- In acting, the plaintiff reasonably assumed the representation was true.
- Statements or representations, which express an opinion or judgment, honestly entertained, are excluded from this definition. An investment adviser who causes big losses with a bad recommendation has not committed fraud if he reasonably believed his strategy would succeed. If plaintiffs can demonstrate that the adviser knew or ought to have known better, the tout was a fraud. Statements made during commercial exchanges have special protection. Only deliberate misrepresentations with clearly demonstrated damages are actionable as fraud.

Burden of Proof and Parallel Proceedings

The burden of proof in a criminal case is always beyond a reasonable doubt. In civil cases the burden of proof calls for a preponderance of the evidence. Practically, this makes proving civil cases easier—any room for doubt nullifies a criminal charge, but a civil charge can be won even if some elements of the case are not proven directly.

Criminal cases are punished by outcomes such as imprisonment, fines, order of restitution, probation, and community service. Civil cases, if successful, result in an award of damages or, in some instances, the entry of an order or injunction that compels the losing party to take remedial action or to avoid future illegal acts.

Criminal and civil actions for fraud may proceed simultaneously even though such "parallel proceedings" present a dilemma for the defendant. For example, a defendant lawfully may assert his Fifth Amendment right against self-incrimination to avoid answering questions or producing certain documents in the criminal investigation. But he may not do so in the corresponding civil case without suffering the possibility of sanctions that can include the dismissal of affirmative defenses or the striking of testimony. If a defendant takes the stand in a civil case and testifies on his own behalf, he cannot later invoke the Fifth Amendment and refuse to answer questions concerning the same subject matter on cross-examination. If the witness does, the judge may strike the testimony from the record.

Generally, courts have not been sympathetic to the defendant's dilemma, and have allowed civil discovery to proceed even though criminal charges are pending. In some instances, the court or the parties by agreement may seal the civil record. In rare cases the court may order that the civil case be stayed pending resolution of the criminal case. Normally, however, the court will allow the cases to proceed simultaneously despite the substantial prejudice to the defendant. In parallel civil and criminal cases in which the government is a party, the criminal process, including the use of grand jury subpoenas, may not be used to obtain evidence solely for a civil case.

Criminal and civil actions for fraud may be brought in federal or state court. Federal courts have jurisdiction over federal criminal or civil statutes and certain common-law claims that usually involve parties who are residents of different states and controversies where $75,000 or more is at issue. State courts have jurisdiction over state statutes and most common-law civil claims.

Intent and Materiality

There are two fundamental factors in proving a fraud charge—intent and materiality. The accused must have intended and worked deliberately to deceive the victim. For instance, in an embezzlement case, in which Hunter Pascal is accused of embezzlement, plaintiffs must demonstrate that Pascal meant to siphon off the money—the loss was not a case of misapplication or mismanagement. This might be demonstrated by showing the different ways the defendant circumvented financial controls in order to get hold of the funds.

Any misrepresentations must also have had material consequences on the outcome. This means showing that statements by the defendant were not only false, but helped the fraud succeed and directly contributed to damages. It may not be material, for example, if Hunter Pascal tells auditors he has three kids when he doesn't have any. But when Pascal alters financial records and pockets cash receipts, the act is material because it enabled the fraud. If Pascal destroys records to conceal his embezzlement, the act is also material because it allows the fraud to continue.

In civil trials, plaintiffs have to show they actually suffered damages as a result of a fraudulent act, while criminal prosecutions have no such burden. Practically, this means that prosecutors can charge defendants with attempting to defraud. For civil actions, the person must have caused someone to lose funds.

Fraud claims have to meet tougher requirements under the Federal Rules of Civil Procedure than some other civil actions. Rule 9(b) says the plaintiff's grievance must be stated with "particularity." This means including details about what misrepresentations were made, to whom, how they were false, why the plaintiff relied on them, and the requested claim for damages. A plaintiff in a traditional negligence case can file a claim by simply making the accusation (e.g., the defendant's inattentive driving caused an accident) without including any details or supporting evidence.

The 9(b) requirement can cause a catch-22 for fraud plaintiffs. The officers of Lapis Bank may be convinced that they are the victims of a kickback fraud. But they don't have the documentation necessary to levy the charge. They need access to the discovery system in order to get their hands on specific documents that are possessed by the defendant accused of perpetrating the fraud. Some judges ease the 9(b) requirement in civil actions, allowing a complaint to be brought pending the results of discovery. There may have to be some hearing after the original filing, and some agreement to amend the complaint after discovery has produced the information necessary to state the claim with the required particularity.

Civil and Criminal Actions

Civil actions can be filed by individual or group plaintiffs in state or federal courts. Prosecutors on behalf of public safety file criminal actions. The difference between criminal and civil fraud is basically a matter of who files the suit, an injured party or the government. Most fraud suits are fashioned as misrepresentation claims and are filed in state courts. Federal courts hear cases involving parties from different states with more than $50,000 in controversy, and actions covered by federal statutes, such as the Civil RICO provisions. A federal trial is preferable for larger cases, since procedural rules allow for witnesses and documents located in different states to be named in the complaint. Otherwise, building a case can become a nightmare of navigating jurisdictional bureaucracies.

Most criminal prosecutions will take place on the local or state levels, using laws declared within the jurisdiction. In order to apply the criminal fraud statutes in the U.S. Code to a case, there must be some basis for federal jurisdiction. Crimes committed during interstate commerce, or through the use of the mail, are typical examples. Federal law is often used to prosecute crimes that result in extreme economic losses or other damages, primarily because the superior resources of federal law enforcement agencies and their nationwide jurisdiction makes proving the charge more attainable.

The following are some of the more common civil and criminal actions for fraud:

Misrepresentation of Material Facts

Misrepresentation cases can be prosecuted criminally or civilly under a variety of statutes, such as false statements, false claims, mail and wire fraud, or they might be the basis for common law claims. The key issue is demonstrating that the defendant deliberately made false statements to induce the intended victim to part with money or property.

The elements of this charge generally include:

- A material false statement
- The defendant's knowledge of its falsity
- Reliance on the false statement by the victim
- Damages incurred

In most instances, only false representations of "presently existing facts" may be prosecuted. Opinions, or speculative statements about future events, even if made with the intent to mislead, cannot serve as the basis for a misrepresentation case. A used car salesman, for example, who assures the naive customer that the 20-year-old car that was towed to the lot will give him "years of driving pleasure" probably, cannot be prosecuted for fraud. The salesman would claim he was only speculating. The salesman could be prosecuted, however, if he told the customer the car had been driven only 15,000 miles when he knew the engine had logged 150,000 miles.

Although a misrepresentation fraud case may not be based on negligent or accidental misrepresentations, in some instances a civil action may be filed for negligent misrepresentation. The defendant must have suffered a loss as a result of the carelessness or negligence of another party upon which the defendant was entitled to rely. For example, a person selling stock in private company who makes unreasonable or false statements about the stock's value or the accuracy of the company's financial statements may be prosecuted for misrepresentation if the buyer loses money on the stock.

Concealment of Material Facts

Legal actions for fraud may also be predicated on the withholding or concealment of material facts, but only if the defendant had a duty in the circumstances to disclose. The essential elements of fraud based on failure to disclose material facts are:

- The defendant's knowledge
- Of a material fact
- That the defendant had a duty to disclose
- And failed to do so
- With the intent to mislead or deceive the other party.

The duty to disclose usually depends on the relationship between the parties. Those people who occupy a special relationship of trust, such as the officers or directors of a corporation, an attorney, accountant, trustee, stockbroker, or other agent, may be found to have a duty to fully and completely disclose material facts to the parties who rely upon them. Statutes might expand the duty to disclose to areas in which traditionally there was no such duty, such as to the sellers of personal or real property, or the purchasers or sellers of securities.

Proof that the concealed fact was material probably is the most important element in a concealment case; there can be no liability if the withheld information would not have affected the other party. In addition to fraudulent concealment, a defendant might also be liable for negligent failure to discover and disclose material facts. An accountant, for example, might be liable for failure to discover or report material facts in a financial statement or audit.

The penalties for concealment of material facts—like those for negligent misrepresentation—are usually less severe than for fraudulent misrepresentation. There is no criminal liability in concealment cases.

Bribery

Bribery includes official bribery, which refers to the corruption of a public official, and commercial bribery, which refers to the corruption of a private individual to gain a commercial or business advantage.

The elements of official bribery generally include:

- Giving or receiving
- A thing of value
- To influence
- An official act.

The thing of value is not limited to cash or money. Courts have held that such things as lavish gifts and entertainment, payment of travel and lodging expenses, payment of credit card bills, certain loans, promises of future employment, and interests in businesses, can be bribes if they were given or received with the intent to influence or be influenced. Some state laws distinguish between felonies or misdemeanors according to the amount of illegal payment.

Proving a bribery charge requires a demonstration that the person receiving the bribe favored the bribe-payer in some improper or unusual way—by providing preferential treatment, bending or breaking the rules, taking extraordinary steps to assist the bribe-payer, or allowing the bribe-payer to defraud the agency or company.

It is not necessary to demonstrate that the bribe-taker's action violated specific laws or regulations. The defendant may have performed a legal act; the defendant may argue that he or she would have performed the act without a bribe. Nevertheless, if the thing of value was proffered and accepted as part of a *quid pro quo* (one thing in exchange for another), both parties have violated laws against bribery.

Illegal Gratuity

An illegal gratuity is a lesser-included offense of official bribery. The elements of an illegal gratuity are:

- Giving or receiving
- A thing of value
- In exchange for or as a result of
- An official act.

An illegal gratuity charge does not require proof of intent to influence. The statute prohibits a public official from accepting any payment of money or other thing of value other than his lawful compensation. In practice, the statute is applied when relatively small payments, such as gifts or entertainment, are used to attempt to influence a public official.

Commercial Bribery

Commercial bribery may be prosecuted either as a criminal act or by civil action. About half of U.S. states have criminal statutes that prohibit commercial bribery. If a state does not have a commercial bribery statute, such schemes can be prosecuted under criminal fraud statutes since the payment of a commercial bribe defrauds the business owner of the right to an employee's unbiased and loyal services.

There is no federal statute prohibiting commercial bribery. However, such offenses may be prosecuted at the federal level as mail or wire fraud, RICO, or other violations.

The elements of commercial bribery typically include:

- Giving or receiving
- A thing of value
- To influence
- A business decision
- Without the knowledge or consent of the principal.

The principal's knowledge pertains to the charge because a private business owner, as chief executive, is not defrauded if he or she allows employees to accept gifts, favors or other payments from vendors or other business contacts.

Businesses injured by commercial bribery schemes may sue for treble damages and attorney's fees under the Civil RICO statute (Title 18, U.S. Code, Section 1964) and the Clayton Act (Title 15, U.S. Code, Section 13(c)), and for compensatory and punitive damages for common law fraud, conflict of interest, and breach of fiduciary duty. Civil actions may be brought even if commercial bribery is not a crime in a particular jurisdiction.

Extortion

Extortion is committed by using actual force, the threat of force, or some other form of intimidation to obtain assets. A demand for a bribe or kickback also constitutes extortion.

In most states and the federal system, extortion is not a defense to bribery. That is, a person who makes a bribe payment upon demand of the recipient still is culpable for bribery. In New York, however, extortion may be a defense in certain circumstances.

Conflict of Interest

The U.S. federal code, state laws and regulations, and common law in all jurisdictions prohibit conduct by public officials and others with fiduciary duty, which involves a conflict of interest. A conflict arises when one's personal interest or the interest of others with influence over the decision maker is at odds with the decision maker's fiduciary duty. Examples include employees directing business to friendly vendors who charge above-market prices, and managers who own shares in companies that do business with their principal employer.

Conflicts may be prosecuted civilly or criminally. Criminal statutes vary widely and include prohibitions on public officers from accepting employment with government contractors or lobbying government agencies during specified time periods.

Elements of a typical civil claim for conflict of interest include:

- An agent taking an interest in a transaction
- That is actually or potentially adverse to the principal
- Without full and timely disclosure to and approval by the principal.

An agent includes any person who, under the law, owes a duty of loyalty to another, including officers, directors, and employees of a corporation, public officials, trustees, brokers, independent contractors, attorneys, and accountants. People who do not occupy positions of trust with another party, such as arms-length commercial parties, do not owe a duty of loyalty to each other and therefore are not subject to conflict of interest restrictions.

The defendant in a civil conflict-of-interest case must repay any losses that the conflict caused and must disgorge any profits he earned as a result of the conflict even if there was no actual loss to the principal. The violating party also might be required to forfeit all compensation received during the period of illicit conduct. The victim of a conflict of interest may void any contracts entered into on its behalf that were the result of or influenced by the conflict.

Embezzlement

Embezzlement is the wrongful appropriation of money or property by a person to whom it has been lawfully entrusted. Embezzlement implicitly involves a breach of trust, although it is not necessary to show a fiduciary relationship between the parties.

The elements of embezzlement typically include:

- The defendant took or converted

- Without the knowledge or consent of the owner
- Money or property of another
- That was properly entrusted to the defendant.

Larceny

Larceny is defined as the wrongful taking of money or property of another with the intent to convert or to deprive the owner of its possession and use. Larceny obtains by force, where fraud obtains by misrepresentation or concealment. Embezzlement occurs after the perpetrator obtains permission from the owner to handle assets. In a larceny, the defendant never has lawful possession of the property.

The elements of larceny typically include:

- Taking or carrying away
- Money or property of another
- Without the consent of the owner
- With the intent to permanently deprive the owner of its use or possession.

Theft of Trade Secrets

Theft or misappropriation of trade secrets may be prosecuted under a variety of federal and state statutes and the common law. Trade secrets include not only secret formulas and processes, but more mundane proprietary information, such as customer and price lists, sales figures, business plans, or any other confidential information that has a value to the business and would be potentially harmful if disclosed.

The elements of a typical theft of trade secret claim are:

- A party possessed information of value to the business
- The information was treated confidentially
- The defendant took or used the information by breach of an agreement, confidential relationship, or other improper means.

It is critical that the information was treated confidentially, although absolute secrecy is not required. The secrecy is sufficient if the information was "substantially" undisclosed. Limited disclosure to people with a need to know or pursuant to confidentiality agreements will not void the secret. Methods of demonstrating that information was intended to be kept confidential include a written policy describing the information as proprietary or secret; strict limitations on distribution of the information; and physically securing the information to prevent unauthorized access and use.

The owners of the information also should enforce restrictive agreements and act promptly to remedy any inadvertent disclosures. Failure to do so might be construed as a waiver of confidentiality and make it impossible to prevent future use or disclosures.

The most typical defense in trade secret cases is that the defendant developed the information independently. If the aggrieved party demonstrates that the information came to the defendant as the result of or during a confidential relationship, the burden of proof shifts to the defendant to demonstrate independent discovery. The defendant also might defend a misappropriation claim by showing that the information was not in fact a secret, that the third-party's use was authorized, or that the trade secret or proprietary information had been abandoned by the owner.

Breach of Fiduciary Duty

People in a position of trust or fiduciary relationship, such as officers, directors, high-level employees of a corporation or business, and agents and brokers, owe certain duties imposed by law to their principals or employers. The primary fiduciary duties are loyalty and care.

DUTY OF LOYALTY

The duty of loyalty requires that the employee/agent act solely in the best interest of the employer/principal, free of any self-dealing, conflicts of interest, or other abuse of the principal for personal advantage. Thus, corporate directors, officers, and employees are barred from using corporate property or assets for their personal pursuits, or taking corporate opportunities for themselves. More traditional fraudulent conduct, such as embezzlements, thefts, acceptance of kickbacks, and conflicts of interest also violate the duty of loyalty, and may be prosecuted as such in addition to or instead of the underlying offense.

A breach of duty of loyalty is easier to prove than fraud. The plaintiff does not need to prove criminal or fraudulent intent or the other elements of fraud. To prevail, the plaintiff must show only that the defendant occupied a position of trust or fiduciary relationship as described above and that the defendant breached that duty to benefit personally.

A breach of fiduciary duty claim is a civil action. The plaintiff may receive damages for lost profits and recover profits that the disloyal employee earned—in some instances, even the salary paid to the employee or agent during the period of disloyalty. The plaintiff may recover profits earned by the disloyal agent even if the principal did not suffer an actual loss. The plaintiff may also void any contracts entered into on its behalf that were the result of or were influenced by employee or agent disloyalty.

DUTY OF CARE

A corporate officer, director, or high-level employee, as well as other people in a fiduciary relationship, must conduct business affairs prudently with the skill and attention normally exercised by people in similar positions. Fiduciaries who act carelessly or recklessly are responsible for any resulting loss to the corporate shareholders or other principals. Damages may be recovered in a civil action for negligence, mismanagement, or waste of corporate assets.

People in a fiduciary relationship, however, are not guarantors against all business reverses or errors in judgment. The Business Judgment Rule protects corporate officers and directors from liability for judgments that were made in good faith (e.g., free of self-dealings or conflicts) and that appeared to be prudent based on the then-known circumstances.

Corporate officers breach their duty of loyalty if they accept kickbacks, engage in a conflict of interest, or otherwise are disloyal. Corporate officers who carelessly fail to prevent such conduct, fail to enforce controls, or fail to pursue recovery of losses might breach their duty of care. Corporate defendants in such cases might raise the Business Judgment Rule in defense by showing that they had no reasonable grounds to suspect improper conduct or that the cost of prevention or recovery was too high compared to the anticipated returns.

Selected Federal Fraud Laws

The following statutes are commonly used to prosecute fraud in federal jurisdictions. Many state and local jurisdictions enforce laws based on the federal code.

- Mail Fraud (Title 18, U.S. Code, Section 1341). Any fraud or swindle that uses or involves the mails in an integral fashion.
- Wire Fraud (Title 18, U.S. Code, Section 1343). Using wire, radio or television communication during an interstate commerce fraud.
- Racketeer Influenced and Corrupt Organizations, or RICO (Title 18, U.S. Code, Section 1961, et seq.). Prohibits the investment of ill-gotten gains in another enterprise, using coercive or deceptive acts to acquire an interest in an enterprise, and the conducting of business through such acts.
- False Claims and Statements (Title 18, U.S. Code, Sections 1001-1014). Prohibits false claims or statements to the federal government.
- Major Fraud Against the United States (Title 18, U.S. Code, Section 1031). Prohibits fraud upon the United States involving procurement contracts of $1,000,000 or more.
- Federal Securities Laws (The 1933 and 1934 Acts). Prohibit false statements and malfeasances of duty in securities transactions.
- Conspiracy (Title 18, U.S. Code Section 371). A combination or agreement to accomplish an unlawful purpose, or to use illegal means in accomplishing a lawful purpose. The purpose need not be accomplished in full. Conspirators can be individuals or corporate entities.
- Tax Evasion, False Returns and Failure to File (Title 26, U.S. Code, Sections 7201, 7203, 7206(1), et seq.). Violations of the tax code.
- Bankruptcy Fraud (Title 18, U.S. Code, Section 151, et seq.). Covers misconduct in bankruptcy proceedings, including intentional bankrupting or bust out schemes.
- Federal Corruption Statutes (Title 18, U.S. Code, Section 201, et seq.). Chapter 11 of this portion of the code contains 19 separate provisions, describing a variety of

conflicts of interest and corrupt conduct involving public officials, including bribery, illegal gratuities, and misuse of office.

- Embezzlement and Misapplication of Bank Funds (Title 18, U.S. Code, Section 656, et seq.). Covers the illegal confiscation and misuse of funds in federally regulated institutions.
- Bank Fraud (Title 18, U.S. Code, Section 1344, et seq.). Any scheme or artifice used to defraud a federally chartered or insured bank.
- Obstruction of a Federal Audit (Title 18, U.S. Code, Section 1516). Makes it a felony to obstruct a federal auditor in the performance of his or her duties.
- Identity Theft and Assumption Deterrence Act (Title 18, U.S. Code, Section 1028). Makes identity theft a federal crime.
- Fraud and Related Activity in Connection with Computers (Title 18, U.S. Code, Section 1030). Though most crimes using or involving computers are prosecuted under traditional fraud, theft and embezzlement statutes, this law makes certain criminal activities federal offenses.
- Economic Espionage Act of 1996 (Title 18, U.S. Code, Sections 1831-1839). Makes theft of trade secrets a federal offense.
- Money Laundering (Title 18, U.S. Code, Section 1956). Prohibits transactions used to launder illegal funds.

LEONE, LOUIS AND RAYMOND

In 1964, the Leone brothers convinced their neighbor, Frederick Gruebert, to help them mount an invoicing scam. Gruebert was the comptroller for a Brooklyn department store called J.W. Mays. Using company checks provided by Gruebert, the brothers and a gang of accomplices counterfeited stacks of Mays' checks. The brothers acquired the proper security paper by creating a phony business and ordering security paper that required a large blank area in the middle of the page. The blank area was cut from each form and used to make the bogus Mays' checks.

The gang established 17 phony companies and paid them with the counterfeit checks. Once each check cleared, the funds were withdrawn and deposited into a stock brokerage account, from which they were disbursed to the gang's anonymous leader, who was believed to operate from Buffalo, New York.

The Leone brothers and five accomplices drew almost $1 million from Mays before they were caught. One of the Mays' bank accounts was overdrawn and an internal investigation soon discovered why. Raymond Leone was arrested when he arrived at a bank to withdraw funds. His accomplices were arrested soon after. The mastermind was never found.

Related Entry:

CHECK TAMPERING

LIABILITIES AND EXPENSES, CONCEALED

Concealing liabilities and expenses is a form of financial statement fraud. The act can be difficult to detect because there frequently is not an audit trail. There are three common methods for concealing liabilities and expenses: Liability/Expense Omissions, Capitalized Expenses, and Failure to Disclose Warranty Costs and Liabilities.

Liability/Expense Omissions

The preferred and easiest method of concealing liabilities/expenses is to simply fail to record them. These entries may or may not be recorded at a later time, but a possible future recording does not change the fraudulent nature of the current statements.

Omitted liabilities are probably the most difficult to uncover. A thorough review of all post-financial-statement-date transactions, such as accounts payable increases and decreases, might aid in the discovery of omitted liabilities in financial statements.

Often, perpetrators of liability and expense omissions believe they can conceal their fraud in future periods with other income sources such as price hikes.

Capitalized Expenses

Capital expenditures are costs that provide a benefit to a company over more than one accounting period. The purchase of manufacturing equipment is an example of this type of expenditure, since the equipment will generate product (and thus, profits) for several years. While revenue-based expenses (such as the labor on a project) must be recognized in the period they are incurred, capitalized expenses may be spread out over several periods.

Because generally accepted accounting principles are ambiguous about capitalizing costs, this is a favorite category for committing fraud. On the one hand, expenses might be recognized too gradually—staving off the bulk of the expense into a later time, perhaps years in the future. On the other hand, fraudsters might record revenue-based expenses (such as labor costs, which ought to be recognized immediately) as if they were capitalizable expenses. In the latter case, income in the early periods is overstated. Then, as the assets are depreciated, income in subsequent periods is understated.

Diligent examiners always question capitalization. Some issues to consider: Can a company capitalize the cost of a machine repair because it benefited the company for more than one year? Or is the company trying to manipulate net income? Are there really more than 12 months of service in the new parts? Is the total dollar amount material to the production of sales?

Expensing Capital Expenditures

In some cases, management records costs that should be capitalized as expenses. This allows the company to minimize its net income for tax purposes. Internal budget constraints also pressure accounting personnel into miscoding capital items to expense accounts.

Returns and Allowances and Warranties

Improper returns and allowances occur when a company fails to accrue the proper expense and offsetting liabilities for potential product returns or repairs. It is inevitable that a certain percentage of products sold will, for one reason or another, be returned. It is the job of management to try to accurately estimate what that percentage will be over time and make provision for it. In warranty liability fraud, the liability is usually either omitted altogether or substantially understated. Another similar area is the liability resulting from defective products (product liability).

Related Entries:

FINANCIAL STATEMENT FRAUD
OCCUPATIONAL FRAUD AND ABUSE

LOAN FRAUD

Loan fraud may be committed by borrowers who obtain loans under false pretenses, by lender employees who collude with borrowers, or by those who administer loan services improperly.

Loan Fraud Schemes

- Loan officers knowingly or unknowingly accept *falsified applications,* sometimes for nonexistent borrowers, as the basis for loans. Borrowers may furnish convincing false information or obtain a loan officer's cooperation.
- Loan officers make *sham loans* to accomplices who then share the proceeds. The loans are charged off as bad debts, or the bogus loans are paid off with the proceeds of new fraudulent loans.
- A loan officer unilaterally creates a portfolio of *nonexistent borrowers* and uses the proceeds for him or herself.
- Borrowers *pledge the same collateral* with different lenders before liens are recorded and without telling the lenders.
- Insiders in two or more separate institutions arrange *reciprocal agreements* that provide for each institution to buy the others' loans or to lend funds to one another. Reciprocal agreements allow institutions to hide bad loans from regulators (by temporarily selling the loans and removing them from the company books) or to boost their capital holdings for an audit (by borrowing funds from other institutions). Naturally, reciprocal agreements are informal, oral arrangements. Swapping bad loans is known as a *daisy chain.*
- In *linked financing,* large deposits are offered to the institution (usually through a broker) on the condition that loans are made to particular persons affiliated with the deposit broker. High returns are promised, but the deposits are usually removed

before the loan term ends. Sometimes kickbacks are paid to the broker, loan officer, or institutional management.

Non-Performing Loans

A non-performing loan may become delinquent for legitimate reasons or as the result of fraud.

Fraud schemes resulting in a non-performing loan include:

- *Fraudulent Appraisals*—The cash flow cannot support an inflated loan and, therefore, debt amount.
- *False Statements*—The loan was made on false or fraudulently presented assumptions.
- *Equity Skimming*—There was never any intention to make the underlying loan payments.
- *Construction Over-Budget Items*—The over-budget amount might be a concealment method for other schemes such as embezzlement, misappropriation, or false statements.
- *Bribery*—The loan was made because the lender received a bribe or a kickback from the borrower.
- *Land Flips*—The purpose of the loan was to finance the seller out of a property, which has an artificially inflated value.
- *Disguised Transactions*—Transactions that are sham transactions, without substance, made to conceal other ills.

Construction Loans

Construction lending has different vulnerabilities than other types of lending. Risks are greater with new construction projects than improving existing structures. Most construction fraud schemes are related to estimates of costs, developer overhead, draw requests, and retainage schemes.

Estimates of Costs

When borrowers approach a lending institution for construction financing they typically have a development plan, complete with an engineering report, appraisal, and budget for construction costs. As the project continues, the budget may be revised to reflect actual expenses. If the loan agreement has been properly documented and enforced, no material differentiation from the budget should occur without the lender's knowledge and consent. However, the developer/borrower might misrepresent the true nature of the under-or over-budget amount to mislead the lender. The impact of change orders might result in the loan becoming out of balance (cost to complete exceeds available loan and equity funds).

Generally, developers hide or conceal their over-budget construction costs in contingency items or by removing allocations from tenant improvements and applying them to basic construction. Most budgets contain a contingency line item in the event of actual costs exceeding the budgeted amounts.

Developer Overhead

Developer overhead is a budget item ripe for abuse. Developer overhead supplies the developer with operating capital while the project is under construction. The overhead is added as a construction cost, whose ultimate collateral is the property. The lender disperses two types of funds from the same loan: real-estate funds for improving the property, and developer overhead to supply the developer with working capital. Dishonest developer personnel, sometimes in collusion with lending personnel, claim excessive funds as developer overhead. Historically, some troubled construction loans or foreclosures due to fraud have been totally disbursed in the developer overhead category.

Draw Requests

Construction loan advances are generally supported by draw requests. A draw request is the documentation substantiating that a developer has incurred the appropriate construction expenses and is now seeking reimbursement or direct payment. A typical fraud scheme in this area involves requesting advances on the loan for inappropriate costs, such as personal expenses and/or construction costs for an unrelated project. Draw requests provide the greatest opportunity for a developer to commit fraud against the lender because the lender relies upon the developer's documentation.

Retainage

Retainage is the amount withheld from each draw request until such time as the construction is complete and the lien period has expired. There are at least two reasons why construction loans contain a retainage provision— (1) to keep the contractor's interest in the project until all the work has been completed and accepted by the owner, and (2) to assure that the work of subcontractors is completed and that the general contractor pays the subcontractor.

Red Flags of Construction Loan Fraud

High Turnover in Developer's Personnel

Typically, when a developer experiences a high degree of turnover, something is wrong with the internal operation. This is often a preamble for other problems to come.

High Turnover in Tenant Mix

Major changes in the tenant mix of a commercial project (such as a retail center or an office building) may indicate a management problem or something improper in the allocating of pass-through expenses, such as utilities, maintenance, etc.

Increased Change Orders

If enough change orders are entered, the originally planned project may be altered to such an extent as to render the underwriting inappropriate. Change orders can have the same impact on a project as altering the original documents. As with anything that is contracted for on a bid basis, change orders may indicate collusive bidding. Change orders indicate the original project was not feasible and short cuts are shoring up other problem areas. The architect and engineer on the project, in addition to the lender's inspector, should approve change orders.

Missing Documentation

Missing or altered documentation is a red flag for any type of fraud scheme. Key loan documents include the appraisal, architect and engineers report, assignment documents, utilities documents, budgets, work schedules, leases, easements, letters of credit, land studies, surveys, title policies, and zoning documents. Disbursement documents include all checks issued, lien releases, and loan closing documents. Draw request documents include AIA Form (or its equivalent), bank reconciliation's, and canceled checks for subcontractors, inspector reports, and loan balancing form, receipts, title updates, and wire transfer instructions.

Loan Increases or Extensions, Replacement Loans

A loan being continually extended, coupled with repeated requests for loan increases, might indicate that the real estate project cannot support the debt service. Typically, loan increases pay for the interest and extension fee. Loan increases may indicate that the loan was made to a related party or made as a loan to hasten a sale or other transaction, and thus was not properly underwritten. Perhaps higher appraisals are being obtained on a "made-as-instructed" basis. Loan increases and extensions may be used by the lender to conceal a non-performing loan. Because rewriting a loan may attract loan review, replacement loans—new agreements that retire the former ones—are often used rather than a simple rewrite of a loan.

Cash Flow Deficiencies

An unexplained cash flow deficiency may be caused by an internal fraud, such as embezzling. The project cash flow may also reflect any of the above schemes.

Change in Ownership

A change in ownership, commonly referred to as a business divorce, might indicate fraudulent activity. It is not uncommon to have a working partner and an equity (money) partner. When the two partners become disenchanted with their relationship and seek a "separation," fraud may be the cause or the result.

Disguised Transactions

Transactions disguised to conceal their true nature often involve the lender and either an existing customer or new customer. Banking personnel engage in fraudulent schemes to forego the requirement to record additional loan loss reserves.

- One method "sells" OREO (other real estate owned) property to an existing customer or a new customer in exchange for making a new loan on another unrelated project.
- Another method of concealment conducts the transaction through nominees. For example, a bank might be required to recognize an additional loan loss reserve due to the lack of performance on a particular loan. The bank may request that the project (underlying collateral) be sold to another party, and the financing arranged by the bank. The borrower then forms a new entity (nominee or shell company) to purchase the property; a new (generally higher) appraisal is obtained and the property is sold. Most concealment requires collusion among the lender's personnel, the borrower, and the appraiser.

Related Entries:

DE ANGELIS, TINO
FINANCIAL INSTITUTION FRAUD
MORTGAGE FRAUD
REAL ESTATE FRAUD

LOCATING HIDDEN ASSETS

See, HIDDEN ASSETS

LOCKHEED AIRCRAFT CORPORATION

The conviction of the Lockheed Aircraft Corporation for bribing officials in a number of countries, including Japan, Italy, and the Netherlands, launched a governmental scrutiny of corporate corruption and helped pass legislation against bribery and corruption in international business relations.

An investigation in the late 1970's revealed that the Lockheed Aircraft Corporation had bribed officials in a number of countries for over a decade. Lockheed officials gave $2.6 million in bribes to Japanese officials, including former Prime Minister Kakuei Tanaka, to facilitate the sale of 21 Lockheed jets to a Japanese airline. In Italy, Lockheed provided $1.6 million to the nation's former Defense Minister Mario Tanassi, former air force chief of staff General Luigi Fanali and three others in relation to the sale of 14 aircraft between 1968 and 1970. Fanali was sentenced to 21 months in prison, and Tanassi was removed from Parliament and sentenced to 28 months. Italy's president, Giovanni Leone, resigned in 1978 as part of the fallout from the scandal.

Lockheed itself was fined $647,000. Though no executives were named in the charges, evidence showed that the company's former president Carl Kotchian authorized the payments to Japanese officials.

Related Entry:

CORRUPTION, OCCUPATIONAL

LOPEZ, JOSE IGNACIO DE ARRIORTUA

In 1993, Jose Ignacio Lopez de Arriortua, one of the automotive industry's fiercest efficiency experts, left General Motors to join Volkswagen. According to Lopez's former GM colleagues, Lopez purloined four binders and a set of computer disks containing GM secrets, which detailed plans for a factory GM was preparing to build in Spain. Lopez had been spearheading the project for the world's largest carmaker until joining VW.

Once he arrived at VW, Lopez began a building project in Brazil strikingly similar to GM's. Lopez was also accused of stealing GM's parts-and-price lists, and the design files on forthcoming car lines. While Lopez was winning market share for VW, GM sales slipped into depression.

Lopez resigned from Volkswagen in 1996. Harried by GM attorneys, VW agreed in 1997 to pay GM $100 million to settle the dispute. And VW promised to buy $1 billion in parts from GM over the next seven years.

After resigning from VW, Lopez became a management consultant. He was called Superlopez in Spain. He lectured to businessmen in his Basque homeland concerning

"The Third Industrial Revolution." Superlopez's revolution was based on the "New Value to the Customer Paradigm," which Carlta Vitzthum of the *Journal* summarized as "a sea change in corporate strategy where bosses encourage workers to achieve the fundamental goal of making customers happy above all else."

A grand jury impaneled by the U.S. Department of Justice indicted Lopez in 1999, and formal charges were filed in 2001 for multiple counts of wire fraud, interstate transportation of stolen property and transportation of a victim of a scheme to defraud. However, Spain refused to extradite Lopez, arguing that the charges against Lopez were not sufficient for international extradition.

Source:
The Wall Street Journal, January 10, 1997, January 13, 1997, February 28, 1997, March 3, 1997, March 25, 1997, January 19, 1998, July 27, 1998, May 23, 2000, and June 16, 2001.

Related Entries:

CORPORATE ESPIONAGE
INFORMATION CRIME
INTELLECTUAL PROPERTY FRAUD

LYONS, SOPHIE

One of the most daring fraudsters and criminals of the late nineteenth and early twentieth century, Sophie Lyons' career was all the more remarkable for her gender. In a time when women's options were limited, she commanded teams of men in various criminal gangs. William S. Devery of the New York Police Department called her "The Queen of Crime," a moniker the tabloid press of the day was happy to adopt and improve upon.

Sophie Lyons was born on December 24, 1848 in New York City. Her mother went by the names of Julia Keller and Sophie Elkins at different times in her life, and was an excellent shoplifter; her father was named Sam Levy, and made his career as a professional housebreaker. Lyons learned thievery as a child. She was arrested at 12, and admitted later, "All during my childhood I did little but steal and was never sent to school. I did not learn to read or write until I was 25 years old."

Lyons met her boon companion in Edward "Ned" Lyons, a burglar from England who had made an underworld reputation as part of a gang that stole $786,879 from the Ocean Bank of New York in 1869. With Sophie in attendance, a group of Lyons' people stole $150,000 from a safe in the Philadelphia Navy Yard in 1870. After Sophie and Ned married, she temporarily ended her criminal career to play the homemaker in a Long Island mansion complete with servants and the finest furnishings. Though she occasionally took shoplifting trips into Manhattan, it was Ned Lyons who got the couple in trouble. He served six months in 1871 for stealing diamonds from a jewelry store, and was imprisoned again shortly after his release, this time in Sing Sing.

In a gesture worthy of film noir, Sophie got herself convicted for grand larceny and was also sentenced to Sing Sing. In less than a year she had masterminded her husband's escape. She arranged for a gang member on the outside to pose as a lawyer, and then to conceal his pass in the roof of his mouth. Ned Lyons later used a duplicate pass to walk out through the prison gates, wearing a wig and mustache. Later Sophie acquired some wax through the prison black market and used it to make an impression of the key that opened the cellblock's main door. (These, at least, are the stories told by Sophie and others recounting their lives in crime.)

The Lyonses were again arrested in 1876 and sent back to Sing Sing. On her release in the 1880's, she deliberately learned the art of the con game and blackmail. Lyons sometimes portrayed a wealthy woman who pulled up outside a bank during the lunch hour, when only one clerk was working. Her accomplice, the driver, explained to the clerk that he would need to attend the Madame in the carriage since her health prevented her moving from it. While Sophie shared conversation and used a worthless check to open an account, her confederates were emptying the cash drawer and taking anything else they could find.

In Europe she posed as an heiress and stole from the elite in luxury hotels and villas. She described one $250,000 venture in which "Mrs. Lorillard picked out the particular pieces of jewelry she wanted to wear at the reception and closed up the bags, turning them over to the maid to place in the safe. The maid came out of the apartment with the two bags and I met her in the hall and began to ask her some trivial questions. She stopped to talk with me and laid down the bags. While I kept her engaged in conversation a comrade of mine crept up, substituted another bag for one of the jewelry receptacles and slipped off. I continued to talk a little longer, and then the girl and I parted."

In her last crime, she and a woman named Carrie Mouse opened the New York Women's Investment and Banking Company, which promised 15 to 20% returns. Their clients, or victims, were "widows and other women of means," from whom Lyons and Mouse stole an estimated $200,000.

Lyons reformed after the investment scam and became a lecturer and gossip columnist for the *New York World.* She was treated as a celebrity. Later she married Billy Burke, a confederate from her early days as a con artist. Lyons was murdered in Detroit in 1924, bludgeoned by three burglars who were ransacking her house. She left an estate valued at $750,000.

Sources:
De Grave, K. Swindler, Spy, Rebel: The Confidence Woman in Nineteenth Century America. Minneapolis, MN: University of Minnesota Press, 1995.

Nash, J. *Encyclopedia of World Crime.* Wilmette, IL: Crime Books, 1989-1990.

MANAGED CARE FRAUD

Managed care fraud is a form of health care fraud committed by insurance companies against policyholders. Provider fraud also occurs in managed care settings, part of the approximately $100 billion in fraudulent health care billing each year.

Common acts include the automatic referral of sicker and more costly patients to providers outside the network, offering service at inconvenient locations or hours to suppress patient traffic, kickbacks to providers and suppliers, failure to provide services, deficient treatment, falsifying credentials, and deceptive enrollment practices.

Types of Managed Care

Some managed care only modifies traditional fee-for-service payments. The patient is free to choose a provider and a claim is submitted for reimbursement by either the insured or the provider. The managed care element institutes utilization reviews, prior authorizations, second surgical opinions, and hospital pre-authorizations. In health maintenance organizations (HMO's) the insurer may employ a staff of providers or contract with individual physicians or physician groups. The insured selects a primary care physician through whom all treatment is initiated. The physician receives a flat fee per month from the managed care organization, though some fees still may be paid on a fee-per-service basis at a reduced rate. Physicians within the network perform any specialty care, or the patient is penalized economically. In preferred provider organizations (PPO's), the patient chooses a provider from a list of participating providers in the network. The patient is penalized for treatments outside the network, but not as severely as in HMO's. Preferred providers usually bill the managed-care headquarters.

Fraud Rates in Managed Care

Analysts disagree about whether fraud is less prevalent in managed care than in indemnity settings, but observe that managed care provides unique opportunities for abuse. The National Healthcare Anti-Fraud Association warns that fraud in managed care is "more subtle and difficult to detect" than in other forms of care.

Indemnity coverage may encourage over-utilization, but managed care can increase the temptation for providers to maximize their income by withholding treatment. For example, a Pennsylvania doctor injected children with sterile water to save on the cost of vaccines he was required to provide.

Providers may also abuse managed care through improper billings. In one case, several doctors who owned a fitness center insisted on giving every new member a physical, for which they billed the managed-care. Each physical listed a diagnosis such as shortness of breath.

Managed Care Schemes

Against the Insurance Company

- Inflating reports of patient traffic and treatment costs to induce payers to increase future per-patient fees.
- False claims for services not covered by fixed capitation payments.
- Falsification of quality of care and/or treatment-outcome data.

- Providers misrepresenting their credentials or qualifications for admission to a given payer's network of managed care providers.
- Managed-care employees approving claims from offices no longer doing business with the HMO, but where treatment of members continues due to existing problems.
- Providers giving kickbacks to managed-care employees for placing certain patients in their panel.

Against the Insured

- Inadequate treatment.
- Establishment of inconvenient appointment hours, service locations, etc., to suppress the number of patients.
- Referring patients to providers outside the network in exchange for kickbacks.

By the Insured

- Network members loaning or selling cards.
- Enrolling non-eligible persons.
- Failing to un-enroll ex-spouses.
- Out-of-network falsified emergency treatment in collusion with providers.

Red Flags of Managed Care Fraud

- Providers who regularly waive co-payments or deductibles.
- Unusual referral patterns, too high or too low.
- Unusually high pattern of referrals to pharmacies, laboratories, or
- specialty care physicians.
- High number of emergency room referrals.
- Patient complaints about the treatment.
- A high number of services that fall outside covered services.

Source:

Lippman, H. "New Ways to Fight Fraud Includes Sampler of Scams." *Medical Economics Publishing Business & Health,* August 1995.

Related Entry:
HEALTH CARE FRAUD

MANAGED EARNINGS

Managed earnings literally refer to various accounting strategies that companies use in preparing their reports to investors. Examples include accounting for mergers, restructuring, and one-time write-offs for business divestiture. Amid a series of corporate scandals in which companies were found committing financial statement fraud under the guise of managed earnings, many observers use the term ironically. In some exchanges, managed earnings are synonymous with financial statement fraud.

Managed Earnings, Abuse, and Fraud

Companies can legally manage their earnings with a range of accounting strategies. But many have crossed the line into abuse, and some into outright fraud, by inflating the value of mergers, creating partnerships to hide debts off the main company's balance sheet, and forging dubious or unethical relationships with auditors. For example, though one-time write-offs are legal for certain items or activities, companies have used the strategy for computer-servicing costs, which are properly treated as ongoing expenses.

In the mid-1990's many technology companies took the one-time write-off for "in-process" research and development. Someone acquiring the company would claim immediate charges against earnings, justified because the research might never find a commercial application and the application might have no value as an asset. However, for the company's future earnings, the bigger the immediate write-off, the smaller the amount of "goodwill" that must be carried on the acquirer's books and written off over time, thereby boosting future earnings. (Goodwill is the term for the premium that an acquiring firm pays above the net worth of the target company's hard assets. Accounting rules require goodwill to be periodically tested for impairment, with a resulting deduction taken for any discovered decline in value, which lowers profits.)

Investors have been conditioned to pay attention to "operating" earnings, which is profit before one-time write-offs. Companies encourage that, because "reported" earnings—what's left after write-offs—have grown far more slowly for shareholders in recent years.

A Typology of Managed Earnings

The following is condensed from remarks by the former Securities Exchange Commission Chairman Arthur Levitt, in a speech at New York University in 1998. Levitt describes the abuse of managed earnings and proffers suggestions for reform.

"Earnings reports too often reflect the desires of management rather than the underlying financial performance of the company. This is the pattern earnings management creates: companies try to meet or beat Wall Street earnings projections in order to grow market capitalization and increase the value of stock options. Their ability to do this depends on achieving the earnings expectations of analysts. And analysts seek constant guidance from companies to frame those expectations. Auditors, who want to retain their clients, are under pressure not to stand in the way. . . . .

"Flexibility in accounting allows a company to keep pace with business innovations. Abuses such as earnings management occur when people exploit this pliancy. These practices aren't limited to smaller companies struggling to gain investor interest.

Five of the more popular strategies are 'big bath' restructuring charges, creative acquisition accounting, 'cookie jar reserves,' 'immaterial' misapplications of accounting principles, and the premature recognition of revenue.

"Big Bath" Charges

"Companies remain competitive by regularly assessing the efficiency and profitability of their operations. Problems arise, however, when large charges are associated with companies restructuring. These charges help companies 'clean up' their balance sheet giving them a so-called 'big bath.'

Creative Acquisition Accounting

"During the 1990's whole industries were remade through consolidations, acquisitions and spin-offs. Some acquirers, particularly those using stock as an acquisition currency, saw an opportunity to engage in another form of 'creative' accounting that I call 'merger magic.'

"Companies classify an ever-growing portion of the acquisition price as 'in-process' Research and Development, so the amount can be written off in a 'one-time' charge, removing any future earnings drag. Equally troubling is the creation of large liabilities for future operating expenses to protect future earnings—all under the mask of an acquisition.

Miscellaneous "Cookie Jar Reserves"

"A third illusion played by some companies is using unrealistic assumptions to estimate liabilities for such items as sales returns, loan losses or warranty costs. In doing so, they stash accruals in cookie jars during the good times and reach into them when needed in the bad times.

Materiality

"Materiality is another way we build flexibility into financial reporting. Using the logic of diminishing returns, some items may be so insignificant that they are not worth measuring and reporting with exact precision.

"But some companies misuse the concept of materiality. They intentionally record errors within a defined percentage ceiling. They justify the deception, which often involve clear violations of GAAP by arguing that the effect on the bottom line is too small to matter. However, in today's markets, missing earnings projection by a penny can result in a loss of millions of dollars in market capitalization, so small discrepancies do matter.

Revenue Recognition

"Companies try to boost earnings by manipulating the recognition of revenue. Some companies are recognizing [revenue] before a sale is complete, before the product is delivered to a customer, or at a time when the customer still has options to terminate, void, or delay the sale.

The Need for Reform

"U.S. capital market supremacy is based on the reliability and transparency of financial statements. Therefore, I am calling for immediate and coordinated action: technical rule changes by the regulators and standard setters to improve the transparency of financial statements; enhanced oversight of the financial reporting process by those entrusted as the shareholders' guardians; and nothing less than a fundamental cultural change on the part of corporate management as well as the whole financial community.

"I believe this problem calls for immediate action that includes the following specific steps:

- *Improving the Accounting Framework.* This should include a supplement to the financial statement showing beginning and ending balances as well as activity in between, including any adjustments. This will enable the market to better understand the nature and effects of the restructuring liabilities and other loss accruals.
- *Clarifying the ground rules for auditing of purchased R&D.* We also are requesting that they augment existing guidance on restructurings, large acquisition write-offs, and revenue recognition practices.
- *Strengthen materiality assumptions.* The concept of materiality cannot be used to excuse deliberate misstatements of performance. Materiality is not a bright line cutoff of 3% to 5%. It requires consideration of all relevant factors that could impact an investor's decision.
- *Improve auditor training and independence.* We rely on auditors to put something like the good housekeeping seal of approval on the information investors receive. The integrity of that information must take priority over a desire for cost efficiencies or competitive advantage in the audit process. High quality auditing requires well-trained, well-focused, and well-supervised auditors.
- *Improve audit-committee skills and independence.* Qualified, committed, independent, and tough-minded audit committees represent the most reliable guardians of the public interest. Many audit committees members lack expertise in the basic principles of financial reporting and the mandate to ask probing questions."

Case Study—R&D Write-Offs and Operating Vs. Reported Profits

Jack Ciesielski, publisher of the Analyst's Accounting Observer newsletter, analyzed public records for 1999 and found that U.S. companies took 247 write-offs for in-process research and development (R&D) last year, totaling $19.6 billion. That year the SEC began to challenge these write-offs.

As part of its $37 billion merger with MCI Communications, MCI WorldCom proposed what would have been the largest R&D write-off in history: a one-time charge approaching $7 billion. After a challenge from regulators, the long-distance firm reduced the charge by $3 billion. The case illustrates that while managed earnings may not always be illegal, they may be abusive.

Figures from the Goldman, Sachs newsletter *First Call* show that from 1994 to 1998 reported profits for companies on the Standard and Poor Index did not grow at the same pace as operating profits.

Operating Profit	Reported Profit
1994: $33.00	1994: $30.60
1998: $45.79	1998: $37.71
Change: +39%	Change: +23%

Sources:
Levitt, A. "The 'Numbers Game.'" *NYU Center for Law and Business,* September 28, 1998.

Mulligan, T. "Can You Trust the Numbers?" *Los Angeles Times,* May 23, 1999.

Related Entry:

FINANCIAL STATEMENT FRAUD

MARGOLIES, IRWIN

Irwin Margolies was a New York City jewelry manufacturer with a reputation for bankrupting companies, leaving his partners penniless and himself enriched. In 1980, he ran an invoice fraud against a business factor. A factor purchases a business's accounts receivable for a discount, perhaps 85% of the total, then collects the amount due from debtors. Over fourteen months, Margolies submitted invoices on phony accounts to factors at John P. Maguire & Co. worth more than $10 million. Margolies had turned the invoice fraud into a variant of the Ponzi scheme by having his accountant make monthly payments on the phony accounts. As long as the accounts were kept current, no one at Maguire would suspect; meanwhile, Margolies continued to cash phony invoices for 85% of their face value.

In June 1981, a dealer from a prominent jewelry house informed Maguire that Margolies' invoices were illegitimate. Investigations by local and national authorities continued for months while Margolies attempted to hide his assets in Switzerland and Israel. In January 1982, a man hired by Margolies abducted and killed Margaret Barbera's (Margoiles' accountant) assistant. The same man, an ex-con named Donald Nash, shot Barbera in a parking garage. While trying to dispose of her body, he was surprised by three employees from the CBS studios, which kept offices next to the garage. Nash killed two of them, but did not see the third man.

Margolies and his wife were convicted of fraud and income tax evasion in December 1982; Mrs. Margolies was sentenced to three years in prison, while Mr. Margolies received 28 years, at the time the longest sentence ever given a white-collar offender in New York. Nash was convicted of murdering Barbera, her assistant, and two others, and drew numerous life sentences. Margolies was convicted in 1984 on two counts of murder. He was also sentenced to 25 years to life for each count, to be served after his 28-year sentence for fraud.

MEDICAID/MEDICARE FRAUD

According to a report by the Department of Health and Human Service (HHS), Medicare fraud is a sizeable, but decreasing, problem. In 1996—the first year the HHS conducted a comprehensive fraud audit—Medicare overpaid providers an estimated $23.2 billion, or 14%, of total fee-for-service spending. In 1997, Medicare overpaid something over $20 billion, or 11% of fee-for-service disbursements. In FY 1998, Medicare overpaid about $12.6 billion, or 7.1% of fee-for-service disbursements. Initial figures for 2000 found that overpayments were down to $11.9 billion.

In 2004, the federal government won or negotiated more than $605 million in judgments, settlements, and administrative impositions in health care fraud cases. The Medicare Trust Fund received transfers of more than $1.51 billion during this period as a result of these efforts, as well as those of preceding years, and an additional $99 million in federal Medicaid money was similarly transferred to the Centers for Medicare and Medicaid Services (CMS) as a result of these efforts.

Although it has no firm numbers on the cost of Medicare fraud, the General Accounting Office placed Medicare on its list of high-risk government programs in 1992 because of its vulnerability. Fraud risk increased as the percentage of claims processed electronically doubled from 36% to 72% between 1990 and 1994.

AARP Members Remain Skeptical

Despite significant achievements by government regulators against Medicare/Medicaid frauds, a poll of members taken in 1999 of the American Association of Retired Persons (AARP) found that nearly 90% thought health care fraud was increasing or holding steady. Almost 80% said they were unaware of efforts to reduce the problem.

Criminals Collecting Benefits

A problem attracting attention in recent years involves the collection of government benefits by convicted felons and fugitives. According to published reports, $32 million in Medicare payments were made on behalf of 7,438 incarcerated beneficiaries between 1997 and 1999, and at least 27,700 fugitives were paid some $76 million in Supplemental Security Income since 1996. Federal law prohibits most prisoners from receiving Medicare and Medicaid payments and bars fugitive felons and probation/parole violators from receiving SSI.

Medicaid/Medicare Fraud Schemes

Medicaid/Medicare schemes include:

- Billing for services not rendered.
- Billing for services not medically necessary.
- Double billing for services provided.

- Upcoding (e.g. billing for a more expensive reimbursed service or product than the one provided.)
- Unbundling (e.g. billing separately for groups of laboratory tests performed together in order to get a higher reimbursement.)
- Fraudulent cost reporting by institutional providers.
- Kickbacks for referring patients.
- Providing services by untrained personnel.
- Failing to supervise unlicensed personnel.
- Distributing unapproved devices or drugs.
- Creating phony health insurance companies or employee benefit plans.

Prevention of Medicaid/Medicare Fraud Schemes

Qui tam or whistle-blower lawsuits, in which informants share in the proceeds of any funds recovered, have dramatically increased the success of anti-fraud efforts. Over half of the fraud cases handled by HHS in 1997 developed from allegations in qui tam cases. Enforcement has also been aided by application of the 1986 False Claims Act, which is credited with recovering approximately $148 billion in the ten years following its passage.

Anti-Fraud Efforts are Successful

The U.S. government reports that fraud rates in the Medicare and Medicaid programs have declined due to increased enforcement and the use of technology.

Most Medicare carriers have adopted anti-fraud software for their private claims processing. The largest Part B carrier, Pennsylvania Blue Shield, began using it for Medicare claims in April 1994. In the first year, the software more than doubled savings from payments not made to suspicious providers, from $2 million in 1993 to $5 million in 1994, according to the General Accounting Office (GAO.)

Physicians Comment on Medicare Fraud

According to a report published in 2000 in the *Journal of the American Medical Association*:

- Nearly one of three physicians says it is necessary to "work" the health care system to provide high quality medical care.
- More than one of three physicians says patients have asked physicians to deceive third-party payers to help the patients obtain coverage for medical services in the last year.
- One of ten physicians has reported medical signs or symptoms a patient did not have in order to help the patient secure coverage for needed treatment or services in the last year.

Sources:
Coalition Against Insurance Fraud. www.insurancefraud.org

"Crime Pays." *The Wall Street Journal,* April 24, 2001.

Eisler, P. "Fed's War Against Healthcare Fraud Escalates." *USA TODAY,* February 23, 1999.

Healthcare Fraud Report Fiscal Year 2002. www.usdoj.gov/dag/pubdoc/hcfacreport2002.htm

"Hearing of the Democratic Task Force of Medicare Abuse 2000." *U.S. Department of Justice,* December 3, 1997. www.usdoj.gov/dag/pubdoc/hipaa00ar21.htm

Jackson, W. "GAO Tells HCFA to Fight Medicare Fraud with Software." *Government Computer News,* October 16, 1995.

"Nora Dowd, Director of Health Fraud Education Project, before the Senate on: Attacking Medicare Fraud, Waste and Abuse." *Federal News Service,* December 3, 1997.

Stringer, W. "Government Sets Up Medicare Fraud Hotline." *The Associated Press,* February 24, 1999.

Stringer, W. "The 1986 False Claims Act Amendments: An Assessment of Economic Impact." *Taxpayers Against Fraud,* September 1996.

Related Entries:

COLUMBIA/HCA
HEALTH CARE FRAUD
PROVIDER FRAUD

MERCHANT PROCESSING FRAUD

Merchant processing fraud is a form of financial institution fraud and credit card fraud arising in the relationship between financial institutions and independent sales organizations that settle or clear credit card transactions for retail merchants. Fraud is committed by the clearing business against the financial institution by submitting falsified receipts for payment, and by validating merchants who participate in a plan when the plan is prohibited by financial institution's guidelines.

Red Flags of Merchant Processing Fraud

The following may indicate or encourage fraud in merchant processing:

- Rapid and uncontrolled growth in the number of merchants processed by the bank.
- Inadequate expertise and staffing.
- Known weak financial capacity of an Independent Sales Organization (ISO).
- Inadequate risk control systems relating to the activation of merchant accounts.
- Insufficient monitoring of low-quality merchants.
- No evaluation of ISO conformance to established underwriting standards.

Preventing Merchant Processing Fraud

The following may prevent fraud from occurring:

- Ensure management is sufficiently experienced for the type and level of activity proposed.
- Establish sound selection criteria regarding the reputation, experience, and financial capacity of each ISO.
- Establish adequate controls relating to merchant account activation.
- Implement appropriate risk-monitoring systems, including exception reports that identify undesirable merchant activity.
- Provide for periodic audits, particularly relating to ISO merchant selection and underwriting.
- Review the adequacy of reserves against ISO-related losses.
- Ensure that the bank or the ISO's maintain adequate insurance naming the bank as beneficiary in the event of fraudulent merchant transactions.

Case Study—Small Bank is Hit

A small community bank expanded its merchant processing activities by partnering with a start-up clearing business. Though the bank was happy with the growth in its receipts, officers noted an upward trend in monthly chargebacks, primarily from one merchant. A review determined that the merchant category was prohibited under bank policy, and the oversight committee had denied the particular merchant's application. Investigators examined the bank's portfolio of merchants and discovered four additional prohibited merchants. Applications by two of these had also been denied. Applications for the remaining two had never been submitted.

The bank froze the processing business's funds and settlement accounts, but significant damage was already done. The volume of activity generated in a matter of months resulted in excessive chargeback rates that severely affected liquidity and rapidly depleted the bank's capital. The processing business was contractually obligated to cover the losses, but declared bankruptcy. Though the business was required to carry insurance coverage to cover improper chargebacks, the proprietors had never purchased such a policy.

Source:
Hodson, K., and Hodson, M. "Leasing & ISO's: Two Wallops from Fraud." *The RMA Journal,* July 1, 2001.

Related Entries:

CREDIT CARD AND DEBIT CARD FRAUD
FINANCIAL INSTITUTION FRAUD

MILKEN, MICHAEL

Michael Milken attended the University of California at Berkeley from 1964 to 1968. While in college he managed investments for several clients, earning their confidence by accepting 50% of any losses while his clients kept 100% of any profits. It was also during this time that Milken read *Corporate Bond Quality and Investor Experience,* by W. Braddock Hickman. The author compared the performance of high-risk bonds with the returns generated by the bonds of blue-chip companies, those with favorable credit ratings, as determined by agencies like Moody's and Standard & Poor's. High-risk bonds were not rated by such agencies, or were rated as substandard. Hickman argued that a portfolio of these high-risk bonds outperformed blue-chip investments. Higher risk meant higher interest payments; while the best-rated bonds paid 4 to 6%, a high-risk portfolio could earn 9 or 10%. Not only did Hickman's numbers check out, Milken discovered a follow-up study by T.R. Atkinson that extended Hickman's findings through 1965. He began sprinkling high-risk bonds in the portfolios he managed.

After graduating from Berkeley in June 1968, Milken moved to Philadelphia, where he had been accepted to the prestigious Wharton School of Business. On the side, he took a position with a small financial services firm called Drexel Ripley Harriman, otherwise known as "The Department" among resentful veterans. In 1973, Milken was transferred to Drexel's office in New York City. In 1973 the $2 million in profits that Drexel reported came solely from "The Department."

Traditionally, companies who could not trade on Wall Street borrowed from banks and insurance companies. But this money came with strict covenants about what the borrower could do with the money. A company could issue new shares of stock, but this diluted the value of existing shares. Beginning in 1977, Drexel added to its trading operation by issuing new bonds on behalf of unrated or poorly-rated companies. The company sold $125 million in new issues in 1977, about 25% of that year's junk bond market. In 1978, the Department sold $440 million; the nearest rival posted $150 million. Over the next two years, Drexel dominated the junk-bond market, which rose to $2 billion a year.

Milken led Drexel into several areas of junk bond trading. The company became a "market maker," meaning that Drexel guaranteed that buyers could always sell their bonds. Drexel would either find a buyer for the bonds, or do the buyback itself. Along with others, Milken established several junk-bond mutual funds. First Investors Fund for Income (FIFI) nominally run by David Solomon, controlled between $400 and $500 million by the end of 1978.

Drexel authorized Milken to trade in "secondary offerings" of junk bonds. In these transactions, an institutional bondholder such as an insurance company sold its bonds to Drexel. Milken then sold the paper to his network of investors, profiting on the "spread," i.e. the difference between what he paid the insurance company for the bonds and the selling price. The spread might reach 30 percentage points. Because secondary bond offerings are not registered with the SEC, Milken could set his own price.

In 1978, Milken and a handpicked retinue transferred to Beverly Hills and became known as "The Coast." In 1981, The Coast sold a billion dollars in junk bonds for the first time. Of $1.5 billion in junk issues that year, Drexel sold $1.08 billion. In 1983, sales tripled to $4.9 billion. Drexel issues accounted for 70% of the market, and Milken influenced, directly and indirectly, the other 30%. Thanks to the Milken revolution, Drexel's profits had risen from $2 million in 1973, to $6 million in 1979, and to $150 million in 1983.

In 1982, Milken raised $100 million for Charles Keating, who used half of those funds to buy the Phoenix-based Lincoln Savings and Loan. On the Keating issues, Milken had demanded Drexel's usual 3% underwriting fee, plus a 10% stake in Keating's largest holding company, American Continental Corporation (ACC). After the deal closed, Keating used $12 million of Lincoln deposits to buy out Milken's share of ACC. Federal regulators called this a "prohibited affiliated transaction" that appeared to be a kickback.

Most S&Ls failed because they were too damaged financially by the time deregulation allowed them to compete with their investments. Of those that encountered foul play (about 25%), most failed due to embezzlements; misapplication of funds (speculating with money earmarked for construction, for example); improper investments with related parties; and other financial tricks such as "land flips." A crash in the junk bond market from late 1989 through 1990 decimated the portfolios of many S&Ls, especially Columbia Savings and others that had placed more depositor funds into high-yield bonds than the law allowed, and which had become dependent on their junk-bond holdings for liquidity.

Milken played a role in the scandal by having a network of S&Ls and affiliated companies trade in one another's junk bonds According to published reports, Milken sometimes over-funded a deal; he sold $110 million in bonds for a client who asked for $100 million. The client used the extra $10 million for purchasing other bonds from other Milken-backed businesses. However, Milken's role was relatively minor. Closing federally insured S&Ls cost the taxpayers between $300 and $500 billion. At their highest point, S&Ls held about $14 billion in junk bonds. And once the junk-bond market recovered in 1991, many investors profited on their holdings.

In 1982, Milken led Drexel into the leveraged-buyout market, in which a company mortgages its property and future earnings to acquire another company. In 1985, Drexel conducted 73 leveraged buy-outs (LBOs), issuing some $6.7 billion in junk bonds. The nearest performer was Salomon Brothers, doing nine deals worth $1.4 billion. 1985 profits at Drexel exceeded $600 million. In 1986 Drexel conducted $4 trillion dollars in transactions, yielding about $522.5 million in profit.

When Victor Posner mounted a hostile takeover of the Fischbach Corporation, Milken showed what he was capable of. Posner had settled a dispute with Fischbach's board in 1980 by signing a standstill agreement. Under the terms, Posner was barred from acquiring more than his 25% stake in Fischbach, unless someone else filed a 13(D) form, announcing the purchase of at least 10% of the company's stock. In effect, someone else had to put Fischbach "into play" before Posner could make another offer.

In late 1983, Posner discussed the Fischbach situation with Milken, who agreed to help. Days later, an insurance company named Executive Life filed a 13D, declaring its recent acquisition of 10% of Fischbach stock. Executive Life was owned by Fred Carr, a Milken mercenary who put some $7 billion of the insurance company's cash into Drexel junk bonds. Fischbach's lawyers pointed out that Executive Life had filed a 13D, as the Posner agreement demanded. But under the special rules governing the investments of insurance companies, Executive Life should have filed a 13G.

According to government charges, Milken asked Ivan Boesky (a close friend of Milken's) to buy enough stock to exceed the 13D limit, promising to cover any losses. Boesky began buying the shares and Posner closed the deal. About six months later, Boesky sold his shares on a London exchange for $45 a share to Pennsylvania Engineering, owned by Viktor Posner.

Boesky and Milken worked together in other ways. "Because of his extraordinary control over the junk-bond market," James Stewart writes, "Milken could buy back securities at artificially low prices from Drexel clients who had no way of knowing their actual value; sell them to Boesky at a small profit; have Boesky resell the securities to Drexel at a much higher price; and in turn resell them to Drexel clients at still higher prices." Milken also arranged losing bond trades on behalf of Ivan's Boesky Corporation, generating tax credits.

"The Predators' Ball"

On May 12, 1986, Dennis Levine, a key member of Drexel's M&A team, was arrested for insider trading. A year earlier, officials at Merrill Lynch had received an anonymous letter from a Caracas bank, warning that Merrill Lynch employees were involved in an insider trading scam. Though poorly typed, the message was clear enough:

"Dear Sir: please be informed that two of your executives from the Caracas office are trading with inside information.A copie with description of ther trades so far has been siubmitet to the S.E.C. by separate mail. As is mention on that letter if us customers do not benefit from their knolegd, we wonder who surveils the trades done by account executives.Upon you investigation to the last consequecies we will provide with the names of the insider on their owne hand writing."

When the SEC pressed the bank, officials there pointed to Dennis Levine, who was using the accounts to stash profits he made selling Boesky information on upcoming deals being handled by Drexel. Levine named several accomplices, including Martin Siegel and Ivan Boesky.

Boesky's relationship with Milken was exposed as part of Boesky reorganizing his company. While closing out the old company's books and transferring assets to Boesky, Ltd., attorney Peter Testaverde pressured Boesky's chief accountant about a $10,000 accounts payable entry that lacked proper documentation. The accountant, Setrag Mooradian, had been cited for improper accounting before he came to work for Boesky, and apparently cooperated in Boesky's machinations because his reputation would have made it difficult to find such profitable work elsewhere. Agitated and impatient, Mooradian exclaimed, "Why the [expletive] do you care about a little $10,000 when I've got $5.3 million sitting over here?" Mooradian was speaking of a $5.3 million credit he had slipped into Boesky's books, which was money that Milken owed to Boesky in their underground partnership. To cover his slip, Mooradian obtained an invoice from Drexel, promising to pay $5.3 million "For consulting services, as agreed upon March 21, 1986." When the SEC discovered the document in a search of Drexel materials, the link between

Boesky and Milken was solidified. Boesky admitted to the relationship and pled guilty to insider trading charges. He agreed to testify against Milken and wore a wire microphone in a meeting with Milken, though Milken said nothing incriminating during the recording.

According to his several admissions and a variety of publicly available documents, Milken had conspired with Boesky to manipulate stock prices and to profit from those manipulations; shared in the profits of investment partnerships, run by his brother Lowell and others, when those partnerships traded in stocks of Drexel-backed companies; and created artificial tax losses for favored clients.

The Milken prosecution was led by U.S. Attorney Rudolph Giuliani, who would later become Mayor of New York City. Between March 1989, when Milken was charged with 98 counts of insider trading, and mid-1991, when he pled guilty, Congress held hearings to discuss collapsing S&Ls, corporate raiders, and junk bonds in general. In a plea deal, Milken admitted to six of the insider trading counts, while the SEC prosecution team secured the right to include in the plea summary an overview of 70 "other crimes" in which the government had reason to believe Milken participated. Judge Kimba Wood sentenced Milken to 10 years, later reduced to two years, and he could never again participate in the trading of securities. He was released in 1991, the sentence being reduced to his time served of 18 months.

Drexel Burnham Lambert was served with a six-count indictment for mail, wire and securities fraud; insider trading; and stock parking (hiding the true ownership of stocks). The firm settled out of court for $650 million, with about half the amount going to Drexel stockholders and clients. Drexel filed for bankruptcy in 1992.

In 1996, Milken's activities again gained the SEC's attention. Though he had been barred from the securities industry for life, Milken brokered deals between MCI Telecommunications and Rupert Murdoch's New World Enterprises, and for Ted Turner, who sold his Turner Broadcasting Empire to Time-Warner in 1997 with Milken's help. He earned almost $100 million in consulting fees for these services, added to an estimated net worth of $3 billion. When SEC investigators accused Milken of violating the terms of his probation, he agreed to pay back $49 million he'd earned on several deals. But in public statements delivered by his attorney, Milken emphasized that he had not been charged with anything and had only paid the money to avoid trouble.

Meanwhile Milken engaged in a campaign to rehabilitate his public image. He funded charitable projects run by the Milken Foundation. He created the Milken Institute, a think-tank designed to aid America's troubled cities. He taught classes at Harvard and other universities. He filed a libel and defamation suit against author James Stewart, for allegations Stewart made in *Den of Thieves*, a Pulitzer Prize-winning account of the Drexel affair; after several years, the case was decided in Stewart's favor.

Later Milken founded Knowledge, Inc., providing for-profit education aimed at adults. After he was diagnosed with prostate cancer in 1996, Milken became active in funding and promoting cancer research. At this writing, Milken's cancer was in remission, and he was a popular figure on television talk shows, discussing his charitable activities, for-profit education, and cancer issues.

Source:
Wells, J., CFE, CPA. "Man or Monster? Michael Milken." *Frankensteins of Fraud,* Austin, TX: Obsidian Publishing Co., 2000.

Related Entry:
SECURITIES FRAUD

MINKOW, BARRY

Barry Minkow became one of America's most infamous fraudsters as the CEO of his ZZZZ Best Carpet Cleaning, and defrauding investors of more than $100 million. Minkow formed ZZZZ Best in 1981, when he was just 16 years old. He had worked as a telephone solicitor for his mother's employer, a local carpet service. Inspired to establish his own business by what seemed the easy pickings of the cleaning business, Minkow soon discovered the cash flow issues that plague all businesses, particularly startups.

Unable to meet payroll, Minkow stole cashier's checks and cashed them at a liquor store. Since he was too young to open a checking account, his initial frauds were relatively small. But once he turned 18 and established his own account, he began kiting checks on a regular basis.

On the strength of Minkow's inflated receipts, a local bank loaned him funds to expand his business. Minkow had to use most of the funds to cover his previous losses, so he could not manifest the expansion. He next turned to a loan shark for funds, and began attracting private investors to place money in his enterprise. He added offices constantly, even though none of the operations was successful. Nevertheless, Minkow continued on his mission to convince the world that he was "the most successful entrepreneur that had ever lived."

In 1985, Minkow purchased a defunct public corporation, chartered in Nevada, and prepared for a stock offering. The funds would be used for a new venture, a "restoration business" that refurbished buildings damaged by fire or flood. But Minkow used the funds to cover the debts he had been hiding in his books since his entry into the business market. He convinced his Big-Six accounting firm that his restoration business had millions in accounts receivable; however, these figures were faked and provided by one of Minkow's co-conspirators, who pretended to head a sham firm in debt to Minkow.

Minkow raised over $10 million in the offering, the bulk of which also went to cover past debts. Still, Minkow's power as a salesman continued to win over investors. At its height, ZZZZ Best's outstanding stock exceeded $240 million in value, and was touted as one of the strongest stocks on Wall Street by reputable firms and investors.

As he prepared to make a second public offering, hoping to take over a rival company, Minkow's fraud began to unravel. A housewife in Los Angeles told a reporter that Minkow had defrauded her of several thousand dollars in a credit card scam. The reporter discovered other Minkow customers with similar complaints. The newspaper reports prompted a general investigation of ZZZZ Best, which ended with Minkow's arrest. In 1990 he was sentenced to 25 years in prison for defrauding investors of over $100 million; in 1991 his sentence was reduced to two years in addition to three years of probation.

Following his release, he began lecturing about business fraud on television and radio and in public appearances, and writing anti-fraud materials.

Related Entry:

FINANCIAL STATEMENT FRAUD

MONEY LAUNDERING

Money laundering is a process in which the origin of funds from illegal enterprises—drug smuggling, corruption, fraud, and other acts—is concealed. Perpetrators move the funds through various channels before reclaiming them from what appears to be a legitimate source. The International Monetary Fund estimates that laundered funds comprise 2% to 5% of the world's gross domestic product. These estimates suggest that laundered funds total somewhere between $590 billion and $1.5 trillion each year. Despite stepped-up enforcement efforts during the 1990's, money laundering continues to grow. According to information from the U.S. Congress, transactions have been getting larger in volume and the schemes more complicated, involving multiple shell corporations or the purchase and sales of securities.

Money Laundering Offenses

Acts prohibited by money laundering laws include:

- Assisting someone to retain the proceeds of crime.
- Acquiring, possession, and use of criminal proceeds.
- Concealing or transferring proceeds to avoid prosecution or a confiscation order, also known as "Own Funds" money laundering.
- Failing to disclose knowledge or suspicion of money laundering.
- Alerting targets of a criminal investigation.

U.S. Financial Institutions and Money Laundering

Statutes specifically prohibit institutions from handling funds from drug-trafficking, terrorism, or bank fraud. Reformers want to expand the laws to include funds from corrupt officials.

Major U.S. banks, including Citibank, Chase Manhattan, and the Bank of New York, have been accused of allowing foreign financial institutions to launder drug money and engage in other illegal activities. These and other respected institutions provide correspondent banking services of U.S.-based banks. Correspondent banking allows U.S. banks to offer services to clients of offshore banks in places the smaller banks do not have offices.

A Senate subcommittee has recommended that U.S. banks be completely barred from opening correspondent accounts with shell banks—those without a real physical presence. The subcommittee also recommended that U.S. banks take extra caution before opening accounts with banks with offshore licenses or in jurisdictions identified by the U.S. as "non-cooperative" with international anti-money laundering efforts.

Voluntary guidelines approved by banking associations direct "enhanced scrutiny" to high-value accounts linked to foreign leaders and their business partners. The measures become mandatory for institutions that are known to have kept accounts for money launderers.

Overview of Money Laundering

Money laundering generally takes place in three stages:

- *Placement*. Funds are placed into the financial system or retail economy or are smuggled out of the country. Cash is converted into other forms such as travelers' checks, postal orders, stocks, and other forms.
- *Layering*. Complex layers of financial transactions are executed to disguise the source and ownership of funds. Funds are transferred between offshore bank accounts and shell companies through electronic funds' transfer. Trading in stocks, commodities and futures through brokerage houses also creates layers.
- *Integration*. The funds are integrated into the legitimate economic and financial system. Integration can be accomplished in several ways.
  - The establishment of anonymous companies in countries where the right to secrecy is guaranteed. Individuals then grant themselves loans from the laundered funds.
  - Perpetrators may also claim tax relief on the loan repayments and charge themselves interest on the loan.
  - Sending false export-import invoices in which goods are overvalued allows the launderer to move money from one company and country to another with the invoices serving to verify the origin of the monies placed with financial institutions.

- Funds are transferred to a legitimate bank from a bank owned by the launderers. So-called off-the-shelf banks are easily purchased in many tax havens.

Methods of Laundering Funds

Funds are usually laundered using one of three channels: legitimate businesses, buy/sell transactions, and offshore havens.

Legitimate Businesses

Proceeds from illicit activity can be laundered by a legitimate business through the overstatement of revenue, overstatement of expenses, or deposits of currency. Businesses that collect cash receipts—such as restaurants, retail stores, and rental services—are especially effective for these purposes.

Revenues are overstated by falsifying the amounts of legitimate receipts, generating phony receipts, or by inflating the cost of goods sold. Expenses are overstated by generating phony invoices, overstating or faking consulting fees, creating ghost employees, or by inflating or faking depreciation costs.

Deposits of currency can be used to hide illicit funds because currency is fungible. However, a net worth analysis will still reveal a surplus of unknown funds unless the perpetrator has accounted for those funds in the business's accounts—as revenues, loan proceeds, sale of assets, or investments.

Buy/Sell Transactions

Real estate or other property transactions can be used to launder funds. For example, a person buys a house with a fair market value of $2 million—but the sale is listed as $1 million, with the balance paid off-book with currency.

Offshore Havens

A number of countries maintain strict bank secrecy laws that prevent U.S. investigators from accessing suspects' accounts. These countries include Cayman Islands, Bahamas, Switzerland, Panama, Netherlands Antilles, and elsewhere.

However, many of these countries began loosening their restrictions in the 1990's, under pressure from the U.S. to at least turn over information about accounts held by suspects under indictment. Particularly after terrorist attacks against the United States in 2001, nations around the world agreed to cooperate in tracing funds.

Methods of Moving Funds Into and Out of the United States

Moving Funds Out of the U.S.

Funds may be moved physically, using luggage or some form of concealment, or by flying or shipping the funds on unregistered craft. Wire transfers under $10,000 may be used to circumvent currency-reporting laws. Cashier's checks can be mailed to offshore accounts, usually in amounts under $10,000.

Attorneys, accountants, and money managers may operate trust accounts for clients, supposedly using the funds in business operations for the client. Currency, cashier's checks, and phony business and personal checks can be deposited into brokerage accounts. Wire services allow users to send funds, which can be accessed by the receiving party at any of the services domestic or foreign offices. The sender is not required to show identification and may use passwords and code in the transmission.

Moving Funds Into the U.S.

Launderers use shell corporations incorporated in offshore havens to make "loans" to legitimate businesses in the U.S. funds are disguised as "finder's fees" or consulting payments.

Corporate salaries from offshore companies may be used, providing funds through company checks, wire transfers, or cashier's checks. Some funds may be secreted into the country. In certain cases, currency previously taken out of the country is declared at customs upon re-entry, so that the money does not appear to have come from illicit dealings.

Paperless Laundering

The cutting edge of this crime is paperless money laundering. Transaction cards such as debit, credit, and more recently smartcards, are used to transfer illicit funds and to disguise the source and origin of those funds. Smartcards can make anonymous peer-to-peer or card-to-card transfers. Further, the ability to move money across international borders via chips containing value will also create a challenge for law enforcement. Money launderers using electronic cards can cross the U.S. border with funds, and then transfer the money to other cards.

Sources:
Atlas, Riva D. "Report Says Money Launderers Exploit Banks." *The New York Times*, February 5, 2001.

Bielski, L. "The Money War." *Technology to the Rescue,* January 2002.

"Brian L. Stafford, Director of the U.S. Secret Service." *Federal News Service,* March 30, 2000.

Dancel, R. "Banking Quarterly: A Roadmap to Money Laundering." *The Philippine Daily Inquirer,* August 17, 2001.

Financial Investigations. IRS Publication No.1714.

Related Entries:

BCCI
CASH FLOW ANALYSIS
FINANCIAL PROFILE
HIDDEN ASSETS
NET WORTH ANALYSIS

MORTGAGE FRAUD

Mortgage fraud occurs when an individual purposefully provides inaccurate, fraudulent or incomplete information to a lender in order to secure a mortgage that they otherwise might not be granted. This could range from an individual claiming to have a higher income than they actually have to providing falsified proof of identification or a falsified appraisal of the property. Here are the five main forms of mortgage fraud:

- **Identity fraud** occurs when a fraudster assumes the identity of another homeowner and then uses that false identity to pose as the homeowner. Identity theft can occur when personal information is taken from credit cards, stolen from government and business databases and on unsecured websites. The personal information obtained can then be used to assume the title on a home, sell property or obtain a mortgage on a piece of property or other properties in the homeowner's name. Identity fraud is the fastest growing type of fraud in North America (it accounts for 40% of all reported consumer crime) according to the Federal Trade Commission and Canadian and U.S. law enforcement.

- **Employment fraud** takes place when an individual interested in purchasing a home provides an altered or forged employment letter or pay stub that falsely inflates income and does not disclose additional financial obligations.
- **Property fraud** describes what happens when someone claims a higher value for a property than the one that actually exists, or when the property is misrepresented. Examples would be a commercial property being represented as residential or the age of the home listed as newer than it actually is, air loans (see definition in "Schemes" section below), or title fraud.
- **Intent to Reside** is also considered to be fraudulent. Stating that there is intent to reside on a rental property is a fraud that is committed because an owner-occupied property can qualify for up to 95% financing and a lower premium.
- **Equity fraud** occurs when there are recent large deposits without proof of sources, investment statements without an intention to redeem or financial statements that do not have a name.

Common Fraud Schemes

There are several common mortgage fraud schemes. These are the most popular:

Property Flipping

This scheme occurs when the value of a property being sold is fraudulently inflated. Properties used in these types of schemes often have little value in the marketplace. The seller inflates the value of the property using a phony appraisal to show to buyers who qualify for a substantial mortgage. Once the mortgage is delivered, the home is then sold or "flipped" and the mortgage is taken over by another buyer. At this point, the false appraisal remains with the property through multiple transactions which makes it difficult to determine the true value of the property. The end buyer, who is not part of the fraud, is conned into thinking they are purchasing a reliable investment property. Instead, they find that the value of the property was over-inflated when they try to sell it. This buyer is left to repay a high mortgage on a property whose market value is far less than the mortgage.

"The Bump" or the "Oklahoma Flip"

Variations of "Property Flipping" are called "The Bump" or the "Oklahoma Flip"; the latter being one of the most popular schemes in Edmonton. Like Property Flipping, the scheme involves a fraudster who buys a cheap, sometimes rundown house, who then flips it several times, sells it back and forth to himself or his friends (or in most cases a numbered company he controls). No money changes hands, but it allows the con men to inflate the value of the house and get mortgages for well over the value of the property, and then just disappear.

Real Estate Title Fraud

This scheme ties into identity theft. Using someone else's personal information obtained from credit cards or stolen from unsecured websites is a way for a fraudster to garner the information necessary to illegally assume the title on a home.

Silent Second

In this mortgage scheme, the buyer of a property borrows the down payment from the seller through the issuance of a non-disclosed second mortgage. The primary lender believes the borrower has invested his own money in the down payment, when in fact, it is borrowed. The second mortgage may not be recorded, which further conceals its status from the primary lender.

"Straw-buyers"

Fake loan applicants are known as "straw buyers" in the mortgage world. A straw buyer is usually offered a payment, (often several thousand dollars) for the use of his or her name and credit information. The straw buyers may not know that their names will be used on a mortgage application. It is not excused by law for straw buyers to claim unawareness of their information being used to commit mortgage.

Inflated Appraisals

Inflated appraisals are often involved in criminal mortgage fraud and "flipping" schemes, which defraud financial institutions. Appraisers work with other parties in these cases and in addition to mortgage brokers and developers, to fraudulently inflate values on houses that are then bought and resold several times by the insiders and dumped on unsuspecting buyers. The properties often end up in foreclosure. The banks lose money, and legitimate buyers turn into victims because they overpay and don't have the ability to sell or refinance. Communities deteriorate when the frauds collapse, leaving abandoned homes and depressed property values.

Foreclosure Schemes

In this scheme, the fraudster is on the hunt for homeowners who risk defaulting on loans or whose houses are already in foreclosure. The perpetrators then trick the desperate homeowners into thinking that they can salvage their homes by transferring the deed and paying up-front fees. The perpetrator profits from these schemes by remortgaging the property or keeping the fees paid by the homeowner.

Equity Skimming

Equity skimming involves a scam-buyer offering to alleviate you from financial trouble by promising to pay off your mortgage and give you a portion of the money when the property is sold. The fraudster may suggest that you move out quickly and transfer the deed as soon as possible. The "buyer" then collects rent while never making any mortgage payments, which forces the lender to foreclose. Even though the original owners of the house signed over their deed, they were not necessarily relieved from the obligations of their loan.

Air Loans

Air loans fall under the category of Property Fraud. It's a form of mortgage fraud where the property is misrepresented and either doesn't exist or is not what the loan says it is, such as a storage locker falsely advertised as a condo. An example of an air loan is a broker who fabricates borrowers and properties, creates accounts for payments, and maintains custodial accounts for escrows. The broker may set up an office with a bank of telephones, each one used as the employer, appraiser, credit agency, etc., for verification purposes.

Red Flags of Mortgage Fraud

Some of the common indicators that serve as warning signs for potentially fraudulent activity during a purchase or refinance transaction include:

- The transaction being completed without a face-to-face meeting with the client
- Recent activity on the title to the property (e.g. registration of a transfer or mortgage discharge)
- The client(s) will only provide a cellular number for contact purposes
- Inquiries and established credit are inconsistent with age, income, or profession
- Direction to pay the funds to an unrelated third-party individual
- A counter check is presented for deposit or identification versus a personalized check
- The employment information provided cannot be verified
- The seller or investment advisor discourages the buyer from seeing or inspecting the property

Sources:

"Consumer Protection, Fraud and Security, Real Estate Fraud Q&A." *Canadian Banker's Association.* <www.cba.ca>

"Growing Fraud in the Mortgage Industry." *Fraud, Phishing and Financial Misdeeds (blog),* July 31, 2005. <fraudwar.blogspot.com>

"Housing appraisals." *CTV.ca*

Vandeleer, Kim. "Mortgage Fraud: Protect Yourself." *Calgary Real Estate News,* December 2, 2004.

Related Entries:

LOAN FRAUD

MUSICA, PHILIP

(A/K/A DR. FRANK DONALD COSTER, FRANK COSTA, WILLIAM JOHNSON)

Philip Musica captained a family of bootleggers through the Prohibition era, eventually entering legitimate business under the assumed identity of Dr. Frank Donald Coster. As Coster, Musica was president and CEO of McKesson-Robbins Pharmaceuticals and was building the company into one of the leading distributorships of drugs in the world. He also siphoned millions from the company, concealing his actions with a number of devices, including shell companies and $18 million worth of phony inventory. In December 1938, after authorities had discovered his true identity and his ongoing fraud at McKesson-Robbins, Musica shot himself in the bathroom of his estate in Fairfield, Connecticut.

Musica's first criminal conviction was for a kickback operation in which he bribed corrupt inspectors at the New York City waterfront to underweigh his cheese imports, which reduced his tariffs. He pled guilty to the charge in March 1909 and was sentenced to two years in prison, but President Howard Taft pardoned him in October, at the request of the Italian ambassador.

The following year Musica, along with his parents and his brothers George and Robert, established US Hair, importing human hair from Europe for wigs. Musica traveled to Italy and elsewhere, arranging finances for the company, and opening branch offices in London, Berlin, St. Petersburg, Hong Kong, and Yokohama. In 1912, authorities discovered that much of US Hair's business was a sham. The family had committed a range of acts, including forging bank drafts, letters of credit, invoices, and accounts receivable. A shipment for US Hair was seized by authorities, which found the crates mainly empty, stuffed with paper and topped off by a layer or two of hair.

Musica was the only family member convicted. He served almost four years in The Tombs prison in New York City before his release in 1916. While in prison, Musica worked as an informant for the warden's office, and he continued this role after his release, as part of a U.S. Attorney's special wartime task force designed to root out Fascist sympathizers. During this time he adopted the pseudonym, William Johnson. He was indicted in 1919 for perjuring himself and was the subject of an inquiry by the U.S. Congress, which was investigating abuses by the U.S. Attorney's task force. The charges were dropped and Philip Musica again changed identities, this time as Frank B. Costa, new owner of Adelphi Pharmaceuticals Company. Musica used the company's permit for 5,000 gallons of denatured alcohol to provide bootleggers with product. Prohibition authorities shut the company down in 1922, but made no arrests.

In 1923, Musica adopted the identity of Dr. Frank Donald Coster, a German-born chemist with a Ph.D. from the University of Heidelberg. Along with his brothers George and Robert, Musica established Girard & Co., named after his mother's family. As he had with Adelphi, Musica used government alcohol permits to supply bootleggers. The company kept up a front by distributing certain products, such as a hair tonic called Dandrafuge, and a liniment, Painophobe. Mainly, though, Musica employed chemists to "clean" the products, i.e., to distill the alcohol and prepare it for sale to bootleggers.

Building on his success with Girard & Co., Musica was able to secure financing for a takeover of McKesson-Robbins in 1926. The company had an honorable lineage dating to 1835, but had fallen on hard times since the turn of the century. Musica was to preside over its rejuvenation, which he accomplished partly by supplementing business with illegal liquor sales, but also by consolidating the company's network of independent retailers and distributors into company-owned and directed operations.

When Prohibition was repealed in 1932, McKesson-Robbins began dealing in legitimate alcohol, but Musica had in the meantime established another fraudulent business. He claimed that McKesson-Robbins Canada dealt in "crude drugs," the raw pharmaceutical ingredients from which manufactured drugs are made. Musica's brother Arthur kept up an office representing several shell companies supposedly doing business with the Canadian subsidiary, but the crude-drug business was entirely faked. The subsidiary's books were kept hidden, seen only by Musica and his brothers George and Robert, both of whom were officers of McKesson-Robbins.

An SEC investigation later found that the brothers pretended to buy crude drugs from five Canadian suppliers (later found to be dummy concerns), paying for them with McKesson money. They then pretended to sell this merchandise to foreign dealers. To complete the fraud, they drew up elaborate fake documents and hired secretaries who sat in empty offices in Canada and Brooklyn, New York, rerouting mail in order to have the envelopes stamped with Canadian postmarks. The SEC found that the auditors, who didn't physically check the inventory, were duped. Over a 12-year period Mr. Coster and his brothers had stolen about $3 million from the company.

By 1937 McKesson-Robbins' annual sales were $174 million, with earnings of $3.6 million. Musica, in his guise as Dr. Frank Coster, was asked by the Republican Party to run for president the following year. He wisely declined the invitation, but could not avoid exposure much longer. A shareholder contingency was becoming dissatisfied with Musica's authoritarian style and his secretiveness, and the independent wholesalers and retailers were chafing at the restrictive covenants they'd been forced to sign in harder times. One of Musica's oldest allies at McKesson-Robbins, a respected New England businessman named Julian Thompson, led an investigation of the company's accounts, expecting to clear his friend's name and save the business. Instead, Thompson's audit discovered the crude-drug operation was phony. Subsequent investigations by private and public sources traced Frank Coster's history through various aliases to Philip Musica.

On December 16, 1938, as federal marshals parked in front of his mansion and prepared to arrest him, Musica shot himself in an upstairs bathroom while facing the mirrored lavatory. While the company's auditors had followed the usual rules, the SEC found the standards to be weak because they merely let auditors take the company's word for financial results, without further checking. Partly as a result of the McKesson-Robbins scandal, the SEC introduced new rules requiring auditors to physically examine inventories of a company and its subsidiaries.

PriceWaterhouse voluntarily refunded about $522,000 in audit fees to the company. According to company records, a Price Waterhouse witness later said he found on Mr. Coster's desk a copy of a book called *"What Interests People and Why,"* with the following passage marked: "The truth ... is that no practical system has ever been devised by which the complicated finances of a large institution can be thoroughly checked up so that every transaction is verified, except at prohibitive time and cost."

Source:
Wells, J., CFE, CPA. "Citizen Coster: Philip Musica." *Frankensteins of Fraud.* Austin, TX: Obsidian Publishing Co., 2000.

Related Entry:

FINANCIAL STATEMENT FRAUD

NET WORTH ANALYSIS

The net worth analysis is one of the fundamental methods fraud examiners use to trace a suspect's gathering and use of funds. After a financial profile is completed, examiners perform a net worth analysis, measuring the person's assets, liabilities, income, and expenses. The net worth analysis can reveal changes in the suspect's assets and income with known sources, and then be used to infer the amount of funds coming from unknown, possibly illicit, sources.

The Net Worth Formula

Net worth is determined within a specific time frame, for example, one year before alleged activity began until one year afterward. The formula for analysis proceeds in steps:

- Assets minus Liabilities = Net Worth
- Net Worth minus Prior Year's Net Worth = Increase in Net Worth from previous year
- PY Increase minus Known Expenses = Total Net Worth Increase
- Total Increase minus Funds From Known Sources = Funds from Unknown Sources

Legal Authority of the Net Worth Analysis

According to *U.S. v. Sorrentino*, 726 F.2d876 (1st Cir. 1984), the net worth method is admissible as evidence if the examiner "establishes the defendant's opening net worth (computed as assets at cost basis less liabilities) with reasonable certainty and then shows increase in his net worth for each year in question which, added to his non-deductible expenditures and excluding his known non-taxable receipts for the year, exceeded his reported taxable income by a substantial amount… The jury may … infer willfulness from the fact of underreporting coupled with the evidence of conduct by the defendant tending to mislead or conceal."

Related Entries:

CASH FLOW ANALYSIS
FINANCIAL PROFILE
HIDDEN ASSETS
MONEY LAUNDERING

NIGERIAN 419

Nigerian 419 is one of many terms that identify investment scams emanating or purporting to emanate from Nigeria, a country known for rampant corruption over the past few decades. The number "4-1-9" is the section of the Nigerian penal code that addresses fraud schemes. It is a form of advance fee fraud, demanding funds up front for a payoff that never arrives.

Nigerian 419 fraud grosses hundreds of millions of dollars annually and the losses continued to escalate through the 1990's into the new century. In all likelihood, there are victims who do not report their losses to authorities due to either fear or embarrassment.

The United States Secret Service established "Operation 4-1-9" designed to target Nigerian advance fee fraud on an international basis. In 2000, the Financial Crimes Division of the Secret Service received approximately 100 telephone calls from victims/potential victims of 419 fraud and 300-500 pieces of related correspondence per day. In 2002, U.S. Customs Service reported that the 419 scam cost U.S. residents over $100 million. In 2005, the Federal Trade Commission received more than 55,000 complaints about these schemes; almost six times as many as in 2001.

How the 419 Fraud Works

The typical 419 scheme uses the following tactics:

- An individual or company receives a letter or fax from an alleged "official" representing a foreign government or agency.
- An offer is made to transfer millions of dollars in funds into a personal or corporate bank account.

- Common explanations for the source of funds include money from wills, C.O.D. of goods or services, purchase of real estate, conversion of hard currency, transfer of funds from over-invoiced contracts, sale of crude oil at below market prices, or the writer was the recipient of an award.
- The letter writer uses a third-party account to avoid the corrupt Nigerian government and various Mafiosi.
- The criminals obtain the names of potential victims from a variety of sources including trade journals, professional directories, newspapers, and commercial libraries.
- Criminals do not target a single company, but rather send out mailings en masse.
- The sender may claim he is a senior civil servant in one of the Nigerian Ministries, such as the Nigerian National Petroleum Corporation (NNPC).
- Recipient is offered a commission up to 30% for assisting in the transfer.
- There is a sense of urgency in the wording; the typing may be sloppy, the printing fuzzy, the confidential nature of the transaction is emphasized.
- Recipient is encouraged to travel overseas to complete the transaction.
- Recipient is requested to provide blank company letterhead forms, banking account information, telephone/fax numbers.
- Recipient receives numerous documents with official looking stamps, seals, and logos, testifying to the authenticity of the proposal.
- Eventually recipient must provide up-front or advance fees for various taxes, attorney fees, transaction fees, or bribes.

Constant Manipulation

The pitch letter, while appearing transparent and even ridiculous to most, does eventually find someone desperate or foolish enough to hope it is true. This sets the victim up for a two-layered scheme or scheme within a scheme.

If victims do travel to Nigeria or a border country to complete the transaction, they may be told that a visa will not be necessary to enter the country. The Nigerian insiders bribe airport officials to pass the victims through Immigration and Customs. Because it is a serious offense in Nigeria to enter without a valid visa, the victim's illegal entry may be used by the fraudster as leverage to coerce the victims into releasing funds. Violence and threats of physical harm may be employed to further pressure victims. In June of 1995, an American was murdered in Lagos, Nigeria, while pursuing a 419 scam, and numerous other foreign nationals have been reported as missing.

Victims are often convinced of the authenticity of 419 schemes by the forged or false documents bearing counterfeit official Nigerian government letterhead and seals, as well as false letters of credit, payment schedules, and bank drafts. The fraudster may establish the credibility of his contacts, and thereby his influence, by arranging a meeting between the victim and "government officials" in real or fake government offices.

In the next stage, some alleged problems concerning the "inside man" will suddenly arise. An official will demand an up-front bribe or an unforeseen tax or fee to the Nigerian government to be paid before the money can be transferred. These can include licensing fees, registration fees, and various forms of taxes and attorney fees. Normally each fee paid is described as the very last fee required. Invariably, oversights and errors in the deal are discovered by the Nigerians, which will necessitate additional payments and allow the scheme to be stretched out over many months.

Several reasons have been submitted for why Nigerian advance fee fraud has undergone a dramatic increase in recent years. The explanations are as diverse as the types of schemes. The Nigerian Government blames the growing problem on mass unemployment, extended family systems, a get-rich-quick syndrome, and, especially, the greed of foreigners.

Case Study—419 E-mail

A woman who eventually turned it over to authorities received this e-mail. It is reproduced on the website of the National Fraud Information Center.

Subject: Business Proposal

Date: Tue, 31 Oct 2000 09:19:31

Sir,

REQUEST FOR URGENT BUSINESS RELATIONSHIP

First, I must solicit your confidence in this transaction, which is of mutual benefit. This is by virtue of it's nature of being utterly confidential. I am sure and have confidence of your ability, and reliability to prosecute a transaction of this great magnitude.

We are top Officials of the Federal Government Contract Review Panel, who are interested in importation of goods into our country with funds which are presently trapped in Nigeria. In order to commence this business, we need your assistance to enable us transfer funds into your account.

As members of the Contract Review Panel set up by the Government of Nigeria to review all contracts from 1983 to the present, we have identified a lot of inflated contract funds which are presently floating in the Central Bank of Nigeria ready for payment. By virtue of our position as Civil Servants and members of this Panel, we cannot acquire this money in our names, in this regard I have been delegated by my colleagues of the review Panel to look for an oversea partner into whose account we would transfer the sum of US$21,320,000.00 (Twenty - One Million, Three Hundred and Twenty Thousand United States Dollars) hence we take the liberty to write you.

The money will be shared as follows:-

1. 20% for the account owner
2. 70% for us (The Officials)
3. 10% to be used in settling taxation and all local and foreign expenses.

Please note that this transaction is 100% safe, and risk free, and the whole process will take between 7 to 10 working days from the date of receipt of the following information by /Fax : [number deleted], Your Company's signed and stamped letterhead with a transcribed "Text" which we would send to you upon receipt of your reply with a letter of interest.

The above information will enable us write letter of claim, and Job description by using your Company name to apply for payment for the above stated amount.

Please acknowledge the receipt of this letter using the above Tel/Fax number.

Detailed information of this pending business transaction will be sent to you as soon as I hear from you.

Yours faithfully,

DR. DAVID AKPATA

NOTE: PLEASE QUOTE THIS REFERENCE NUMBER(VE/S/09/99)IN ALL YOUR RESPONSES.....

E-mail example contributed by Mrs. C. Kemner, 31 Oct. 2000:

For more information, please visit the U.S. Secret Service website: www.secretservice.gov.

Sources:

Zuckoff, Mitchell, "The Perfect Mark." May 2006. thenewyorker.com

Related Entries:

CON SCHEMES

CONSUMER FRAUD

NURSING HOME FRAUD

Nursing home fraud is a form of health care provider fraud. Financial fraud is acknowledged to be a major problem in the nursing home industry, particularly those in which Medicaid supports all or most of the residents.

Common offenses include:

- Claims are made for residents who have already been permanently discharged, or who reside at least part of the time with relatives.
- Upgrade frauds are common, in which claims are made for higher categories of dependency than the patient requires.
- Claims are made for ghost employees on staff payroll.

- Nursing homes sometimes conspire with residents to conceal an incoming resident's assets, helping the person to qualify for Medicaid benefits.
- Medical records and other custodial documents are falsified, to conceal quality of care lapses or to obtain funds.

Source:
Tonry, M., and Reiss, A. "*Beyond the Law. Crime in Complex Organizations.*" Chicago: University of Chicago Press, 1993.

Related Entry:

HEALTH CARE FRAUD

OCCUPATIONAL FRAUD AND ABUSE

Occupational fraud and abuse is committed by someone using his or her occupation for personal enrichment through the deliberate misuse or misapplication of the employing organization's resources or assets. Occupational frauds are committed by employees, managers, officers, or owners of an organization.

The three major types of occupational fraud are: ASSET MISAPPROPRIATION; CORRUPTION, OCCUPATIONAL; and FINANCIAL STATEMENT FRAUD, which are covered in separate entries.

The Fraud Tree

The complete classification of Occupational Fraud, drawn from *Corporate Fraud Handbook* by Joseph T. Wells, is shown on the following page.

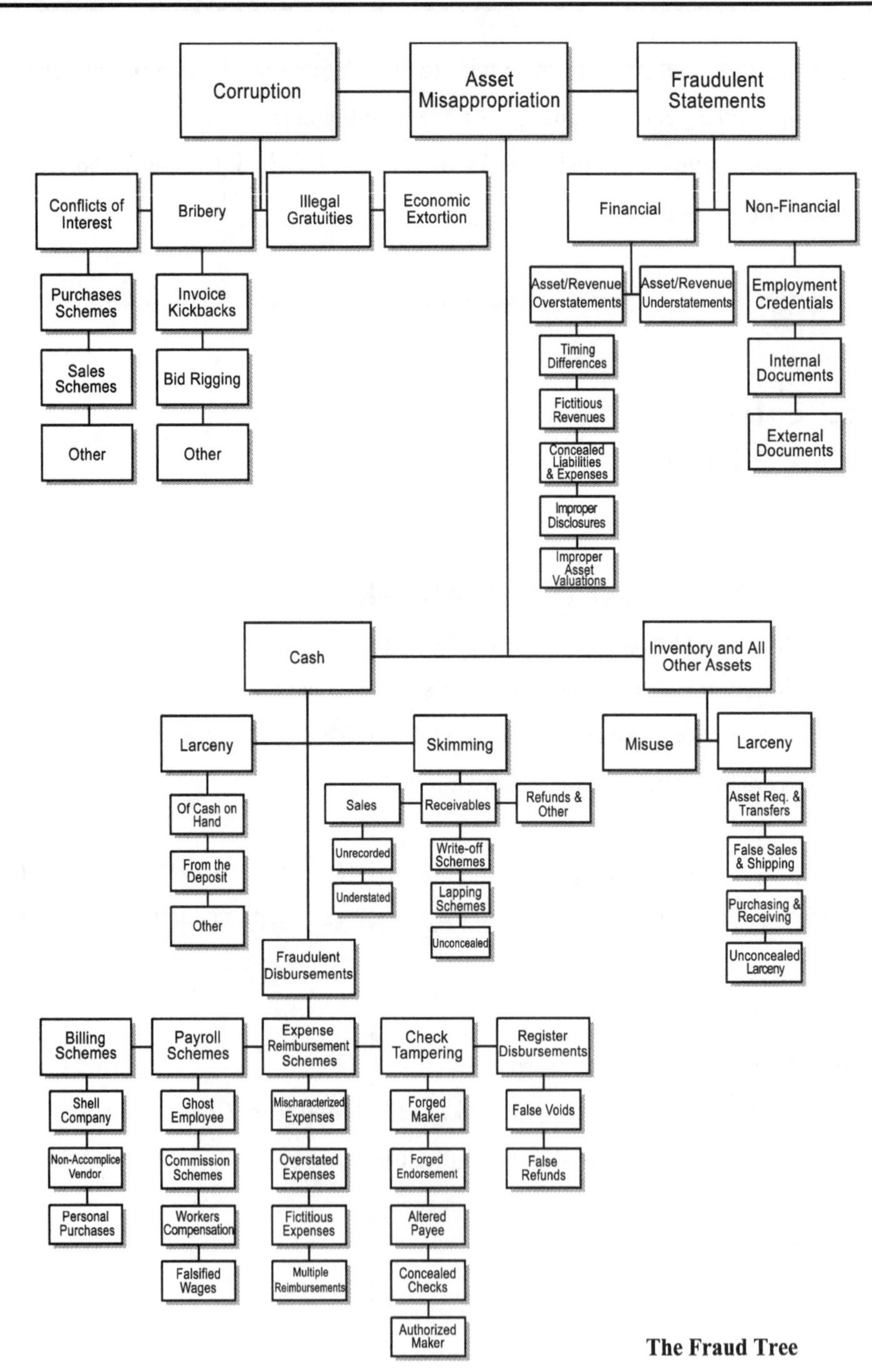

The Fraud Tree

The Report to the Nation

The *Report to the Nation on Occupational Fraud and Abuse*, also known as the *Wells Report*, was first published by the Association of Certified Fraud Examiners in 1996. The stated goals of that report were to:

- Summarize the opinions of experts on the percentage and amount of organizational revenue lost to all forms of occupational fraud and abuse;
- Examine the characteristics of the employees who commit occupational fraud and abuse;
- Determine what kinds of organizations are victims of occupational fraud and abuse; and
- Categorize the ways in which serious fraud and abuse occurs

In 2002 we issued our second *Report to the Nation.* Like the first Report, the 2002 edition was also based on detailed case information supplied by CFEs, but this report expanded on the first. In 2002 we revised our survey instrument to gather more useful information on the specific methods used to commit occupational fraud. We also gathered information on the legal dispositions of the cases, which had not been included in the 1996 *Report*.

In the 2004 edition of the *Report*, we again expanded its scope. Our 2004 survey of CFEs was designed to gather the same key information that was present in the first two editions of the *Report to the Nation*, but in this edition we added key questions on methods of detection and the effectiveness of anti-fraud controls in limiting fraud losses. We also added more demographic questions on the perpetrators and victims of occupational fraud to give us an even better picture of who commits fraud and who suffers from it. The 2006 *Report to the Nation* includes updated statistics, largely focusing on the scope that was covered in 2004.

Among the highlights of the 2006 Report are the following:

- This study covers 1,134 cases of occupational fraud with a median loss of $159,000. All information was provided by the Certified Fraud Examiners (CFEs) who investigated these cases.

- Organizations suffer tremendous costs as a result of occupational fraud and abuse. Participants in this study, anti-fraud specialists with a median 16 years' experience in the fraud examination field, estimate that the typical U.S. organization loses 5% of its annual revenues to fraud, down 1% from 2004. Applied to the US Gross Domestic Product for 2006, this translates to approximately $652 billion in total losses, which is $8 billion less than in the 2004 report.
- Our data strongly supports Sarbanes-Oxley's requirement for audit committees to establish confidential reporting mechanisms. Occupational frauds in our study were much more likely to be detected by a tip than through other means such as internal audits, external audits, and internal controls. According to the report, 44% of the million-dollar frauds were detected by tip.
- Confidential reporting mechanisms reduce fraud losses significantly. The median loss among organizations that offer anonymous reporting mechanisms was $100,000. In organizations that did not have established reporting procedures, the median loss was $200,000.
- While Sarbanes-Oxley only requires publicly traded companies to establish confidential reporting mechanisms for employees, our data suggests that these programs should also embrace third-party sources such as customers and vendors. Among cases that were detected by a tip, 64.1% of the tips came from employees, 10.7% of the tips came from customers, 7.1% came from vendors, and 18.1% came from anonymous sources. Companies that have implemented basic employee hotlines to ensure Sarbanes-Oxley compliance could detect significantly more frauds by making their hotlines available to third parties as well.
- More effective internal controls are needed to detect fraud. Internal Controls ranked fourth – behind "Internal Audit" – in terms of the number of frauds detected in our study.
- Small businesses suffer disproportionately large losses due to occupational fraud and abuse. The median cost experienced by small businesses with less than 100 employees was $190,000 per scheme. This was higher than the median loss experienced by all but the very largest organizations. Small businesses are less likely to be able to survive such losses and should better protect themselves from fraud.

- The loss caused by occupational fraud is directly related to the position of the perpetrator. Frauds committed by owners and executives caused a median loss of $1 million, which is nearly five times higher than the losses caused by managers, and almost thirteen times higher than the losses caused by employees.
- Most occupational fraudsters are first time offenders. Only 8% of the fraudsters in our study had a previous conviction for a fraud-related offense. Criminal background checks can help organizations make informed hiring decisions, but they will not weed out all fraudsters because most frauds are committed by seemingly honest employees.
- The most cost-effective way to deal with fraud is to prevent it. According to our study, once an organization has been defrauded it is unlikely to recover its losses. In approximately one-sixth of the cases the victim made a complete recovery, but those cases tended to be small. Just over 42% of victims recovered nothing at all.

The full *2006 Report to the Nation* can be downloaded at no charge from the ACFE website: www.ACFE.com.

Major Academic Research on Occupational Fraud and Abuse

The first major academic treatment of occupational fraud and abuse was Edwin Sutherland's *White-Collar Crime.* Sutherland defined white-collar crime as illegal acts committed by upper-status individuals in the course of their occupations. He was chiefly interested in corporate acts such as antitrust violations, and believed that an executive culture that tolerated and sometimes encouraged fraud was responsible for the economic damage of the crimes.

Donald Cressey, one of Sutherland's students, focused on embezzlers, who he called "trust violators." In *Other People's Money: A Study in the Social Psychology of Embezzlement*, Cressey asserted, "Trusted persons become trust violators when they conceive of themselves as having a financial problem which is non-sharable, are aware this problem can be secretly resolved by violation of the position of financial trust, and are able to apply to their own conduct in that situation verbalizations which enable them to adjust their conceptions of themselves as trusted persons with their conceptions of themselves as users of the entrusted funds or property."

Cressey's work was the basis for what became known as the Fraud Triangle. One side of the triangle represents a perceived unsharable financial need, the second side a perceived opportunity, and the final a rationalization of the act.

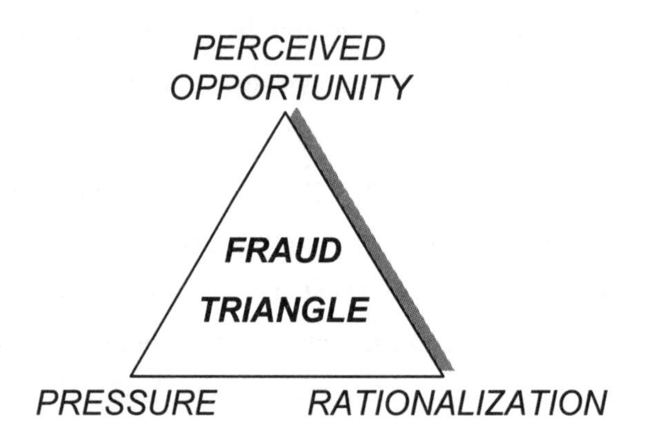

Exploring embezzlers' motivations, Cressey found, "When the trust violators were asked to explain why they refrained from violation of other positions of trust they might have held at previous times, or why they had not violated the subject position at an earlier time, those who had an opinion expressed the equivalent of one or more of the following quotations: (a) 'There was no need for it like there was this time.' (b) 'The idea never entered my head.' (c) 'I thought it was dishonest then, but this time it did not seem dishonest at first.'"

Dr. Steve Albrecht and two colleagues, Keith R. Howe and Marshall B. Romney, analyzed 212 frauds in the early 1980's, publishing their findings in *Deterring Fraud: The Internal Auditor's Perspective*. Like Cressey, Albrecht, et al., explored the motivations of the perpetrators of occupational frauds and abuses. They classified nine motivational factors:

- Living beyond means
- An overwhelming desire for personal gain
- High personal debt
- A close association with customers
- Feeling pay was not commensurate with responsibility
- A wheeler-dealer attitude

- Strong challenge to beat the system
- Excessive gambling habits
- Undue family or peer pressure

In 1983, Richard C. Hollinger of Purdue University and John P. Clark of the University of Minnesota published the results of their survey of nearly 10,000 American workers, titled *Theft by Employees*. Hollinger and Clark concluded that employees steal primarily as a result of workplace conditions. Besides the economic impact of fraud, they considered "the incalculable social costs ... The grand total paid for theft in the workplace is no doubt grossly underestimated by the available financial estimates."

Hollinger and Clark reviewed five hypotheses about employee theft:

- Sutherland's contention that group norms become the standard of conduct
- Cressey's "non-sharable financial problem"
- Contemporary employees, specifically young ones, are not as hardworking and honest as those in past generations
- Every employee can be tempted to steal from his employer
- Job dissatisfaction

Hollinger and Clark favored the fifth hypothesis. However, the researchers did exclude certain external factors in their profile of those employees most likely to commit fraud. They found that people with certain backgrounds or status are more likely than others to commit fraud. These include:

- People with few ties to the organization or local community
- New employees
- Part-time employees
- Unmarried employees
- Employees in low-paying, low-status jobs
- Alcohol and drug abusers
- Reckless individuals who enjoy breaking rules and dangerous activities
- Individuals who associate with others who steal

Other Academic Research

Research on occupational fraud and abuse continues to expand. Some notable findings are summarized below.

- Researchers Kitty Calavita and Henry Pontell found that boardroom-led embezzlement schemes were so common that they coined a term, "collective embezzlement," to describe "the siphoning off of company funds for use by top management."
- Retail associations say employee theft adds 2% to the average purchase. However, Dr. James Coleman pointed out, "Many managers see certain types of employee theft as a 'fringe benefit' that helps make up for low wages or other occupational problems. Some of the alleged cost to the public may therefore be more illusory than real, because an end to employee theft might force employers to pay higher wages or make costly improvements in working conditions."
- The authors of a study at Cambridge University suggested that employee theft acts as a positive economic force, increasing job satisfaction, and boosting production. Employees feel a greater personal attachment to a workplace they can manipulate to their own ends. However, some limits must be placed on thefts—either by employees themselves or through internal controls—or the practice can bankrupt an organization.
- Coleman reports that a study of factory workers found that workers defined some property as off-limits and other items as freely available. Designated "company property" included power tools, heavy machinery, testing equipment, and other expensive items. Personal items belonging to fellow workers were off limits. A number of items were designated of "uncertain ownership" and free for the taking, including scraps, light tools, nails, screws, and electrical tape.
- Kevin Murphy, writing in *Honesty in the Workplace,* compiled six possible reasons that employees steal:
  - Economic pressure—to cover debts or to attain a luxurious lifestyle.
  - Demographic factors—certain types of people, such as those who are unmarried, are socially less stable than others.
  - Opportunity for theft.

- Dissatisfaction with their jobs, supervisors, coworkers, or organization.
- Norms that condone theft.
- Power gained from the money or prestige gained by fraud.

2005 National Business Ethics Survey

The Ethics Resource Center conducted a *National Business Ethics Survey,* published in 2005. Based on interviews involving 10,053 American workers, it analyzes trends in workplace ethics, the implementation of formal programs, the ethical culture within organizations, the impact of programs, and factors that pose risks of misconduct. Results are summarized below.

- 26% of employees observed some form of misconduct in 2005. However, when employees were provided a list of specific behaviors that constituted misconduct, 52% claimed to have observed at least one type of behavior. Similar percentages of employees observed misconduct in public and private for-profits (both 25%), non-profits (26%), and government agencies (29%).
- First-line supervisors are most likely to observe misconduct. However, senior management is 21% more likely to report the misconduct than first-line supervisors.
- If employees work at an organization that has recently undergone restructuring, a merger, or an acquisition, they are 11% more likely to observe misconduct.
- 69% of employees report their organizations implement ethics training, up 14 percentage points from the 2003 NBES. Employees in larger organizations are more likely to report that their organizations provide training; however, growth is evident across all organization sizes. 90% of employees from organizations that provided this service found the ethics training useful.
- 65% of employees indicated their organizations have a place they can seek ethics advice.
- 73% of employees said that their organizations provided a means by which they could report misconduct anonymously.
- 55% of employees who observed misconduct at work reported it to management, down 10 percentage points from the 2003 NBES.

- 59% of employees were satisfied with the organizational response to reports of misconduct, which is a two percent decrease from 2003 and a 2% increase from 2000.
- 67% of employees reported that their supervisors evaluate ethical conduct as a part of performance reviews; a 7% decrease since 2003.
- Five of six elements of a formal ethics and compliance program measured by NBES have increased over time.
- In 2005, 86% of employees indicated that their organizations provide written standards of ethical business conduct; a 19% point increase from 1994.
- The types of conduct most frequently observed in 2005 include: abusive or intimidating behavior towards employees (21%), lying to employees, customers, vendors, or the public (19%), situations that place employee interests over organizational interests (18%), violations of safety regulations (16%), and misreporting of actual time worked (16%).
- Furthermore, 13% of employees observed e-mail or Internet abuse;
- 12% observed discrimination on the basis of race, color, gender, age or similar categories;
- 11% observed stealing or theft;
- 9% observed sexual harassment;
- 8% observed provisions of goods or services that fail to meet specifications;
- 7% observed misuse of confidential information;
- 5% observed falsification or misrepresentation of financial records or reports;
- 6% observed alteration of documents;
- 4% observed improper use of competitors' inside information;
- 3% observed price fixing; and
- 3% observed giving or accepting of bribes, kickbacks, or inappropriate gifts.
- Employee perception that top management talks about ethics, keeps commitments, and models ethical behavior have all risen since 2000. However, the employees who agreed that top management keeps commitments have declined by three points since 2003, from 84% to 81%. Moreover, the perception that the top management provides

information and communicates efforts has not changed since 2003; the latter has remained at 89% and the former at 80%.

Source: www.ethics.org/nbes2005/

2005-2006 KPMG Integrity Survey

KPMG conducted a survey in 2005-2006 in order to examine the presence of corporate fraud and misconduct since Sarbanes-Oxley (SOX) became effective in 2002 – two years after the first integrity study was conducted in 2000. The results of the most recent survey are summarized below, based on interviews with 4,056 employees from a range of organizations and job responsibilities:

- 74% of employees observed misconduct in the 12 months prior to the survey, marking virtually no change since the 2000 integrity survey, when 76% of employees claimed to have observed misconduct.
- Likewise, the survey revealed only a 1% increase in employees who observed misconduct that could cause a "significant loss of public trust if discovered," at 50%.
- Among employees in sales and marketing functions, 33% observed false or deceptive sales practices; 20% observed improper gathering of competitors' confidential information; and 19% observed violation of contract terms with customers.
- Among employees in accounting and finance functions, 27% observed entrance into customer contract relationships without proper terms, contracts or approvals; 24% observed breaching of computer, network, or database controls; and 18% observed stealing or misappropriating assets.
- Among employees in research, development, and engineering functions, 25% observed mishandling of confidential or proprietary information; 21% observed others engaging in activities that pose a conflict of interest; and 15% observed improper gathering of competitors' confidential information.
- Among employees in government and regulatory affairs functions, 41% observed false or misleading claims to the public or media; 28% observed others providing inappropriate information to analysts or investors; and 25% observed others providing regulators with false or misleading information.

- Of the reasons employees may engage in misconduct, 57% cited pressure to "do whatever it takes" to meet company goals, down 8% since 2000; 55% said they believed that employees did not comprehend the standards of their position, up 5% since 2000; and 52% cited that employees may not believe that their code of conduct is taken seriously, down 21% since 2000.
- Upon discovery of misconduct, 81% of employees say they would notify a supervisor or another manager, while 53% would attempt to resolve the matter directly. These numbers represent an 18% and 13% increase since 2000, respectively.
- 78% of employees said that they would feel comfortable reporting misconduct to their supervisor and 62% said they would feel comfortable reporting to local managers, while only 32% felt comfortable reporting to the board of directors or audit committee.
- Of the perceived outcomes of reporting misconduct, 67% of those surveyed felt that appropriate action would be taken and 64% felt that their report would be handled confidentially, while about half felt that they would be protected from retaliation. All three of these perceived outcomes represent approximately a 5% increase since 2000.

Occupational Fraud and Abuse in the United Kingdom, Canada, and Australia

The following material summarizes findings on occupational fraud and abuse in certain parts of the United Kingdom, Canada, and Australia.

England

The British Retail Consortium reported that the cost of theft in the retail sector, including crime prevention, has cost the retail sector £2.13 billion in 2005, up from £1.96 billion in 2003. Offenses ranged from theft of company property to gaining a financial advantage at someone else's expense.

Managers are the biggest perpetrators, making up half of all fraud carried out in the U.K. A report carried out by KPMG Forensic Accounting, which surveyed more than 800 managers in England, found that 50% of firms were aware of fraud at work, but 40% did not report it.

A 2003 survey by KPMG found that 75% of responding companies had suffered fraud that year, and employees were blamed for most of the losses. While employee fraud is the most prevalent type of fraud experienced by organizations, financial reporting fraud and medical/insurance fraud are the most costly. In fact, financial reporting fraud more than doubled its rate of occurrence since the last survey. In 1999, 75% of reported frauds were perpetuated by employees; 48% were by employees in collusion with third parties. Thirty-five percent more companies reported crimes to the police in the last year than five years ago. Forty-two percent suffered inventory theft; 33% check forgery and counterfeiting; and 24% kickbacks, bribes or secret commissions. In 76% of cases, companies claimed that early warning signals had alerted them to the problems but 24% admitted that those signals had been ignored.

Scotland

Reported fraud in Scotland has risen 30% to almost £1billion. According to BDO Stoy Hayward's Fraudtrack survey, fraud rose almost 80% in 2005 from the year before, and over 200% since 2003. When 1,500 employees were surveyed, the majority said they would report a dishonest coworker, but did not know who to alert.

Canada

In 2001, an Ernst & Young survey reported that 25% of the Canadian workforce—3.2 million employees—had either committed fraud against their employers or knew someone who had done so in the past year. Only 34% of employees said they had actually reported a fraud they knew about; 83% said they would be likely to.

The incidence of fraud or personal awareness of it ranged from 27% among employees in government, health care, construction, and service industries to 23% in finance, technology, and other professional sectors.

Respondents were split on the effects of technology on fraud. About 40% said technology made fraud easier to commit while 41% thought it made committing fraud more difficult.

CANADIAN SURVEY ON OCCUPATIONAL FRAUD

Dominic Peltier-Rivest, Ph.D., M.Acc., CFE; Concordia University in Montreal (Quebec); and the ACFE recently completed a survey regarding the impact of occupational fraud in Canada.

Detecting Occupational Fraud in Canada: A Study of its Victims and Perpetrators is based on a nationwide anonymous Web survey of all Canadian members of the Association of Certified Fraud Examiners (ACFE). The purpose of this study is to describe how frauds are committed in Canada, explain how they are detected, describe who perpetrates them, explain the characteristics of the victim entities and document the outcomes of the fraud cases.

Below are some of the highlights of the study:

- The median fraud loss of the 90 occupational fraud cases reported in this study was C$187,500. These occupational frauds had been ongoing for a median 24 months before being detected.
- One quarter (25.6%) of the fraud cases caused losses to the victim organization of at least C$1 million.
- Participants in this study – anti-fraud professionals with a median 15 years of experience in the fraud examination field – estimated that the typical Canadian organization loses 5% of its annual sales to fraud every year.
- 90% of all of the occupational fraud cases involved asset misappropriations with a median loss of C$200,000. 38.9% of the cases had a corruption component with a median loss of C$250,000. 11.1% of the cases involved fraudulent financial statement schemes with a median loss of C$1,075,000.
- The most affected industries in our survey were government & public administration (13.3% of all cases), retail (11.1%), and banking and financial (10%).
- Private companies were more affected than public companies; 38.2% of the fraud cases we reviewed occurred in private companies, compared to 23.6% in public companies.

- Smaller organizations, with less than 100 employees, accounted for 42.2% of the victim organizations represented in this study. Small companies suffer disproportionately large fraud losses, with a median of C$150,000. This is likely caused in large part by small organizations tending to have fewer internal controls than larger entities due to their limited resources.
- Forty-two percent of the occupational frauds reported in this study were detected through tips from employees, vendors, customers, or anonymous sources. By comparison, only 18.9% of the frauds were detected by the organization's internal controls, 13.3% were detected by internal audits, and 6.7% were detected by external audits.
- While only 24.4% of the victim organizations used a formal fraud reporting mechanism or hotline to prevent and detect fraud, those organizations that had such a mechanism in place experienced much lower median fraud losses than organizations lacking an established reporting mechanism (C$90,099 versus C$197,500). Furthermore, the time it took to detect fraud was reduced from 24 to 18 months for those organizations.
- Organizations that conducted surprise audits on a regular basis experienced much lower median fraud losses than other organizations (C$60,000 versus C$195,000) and their time to detection was lower by 6 months.
- Organizations that provided fraud awareness or ethics training to their employees and managers had median fraud losses of C$100,000 as compared to C$222,000 for organizations that did not offer such training. The median number of months until fraud was detected was lower by 6 months for those organizations that conducted fraud training.
- Forty-two percent of occupational frauds were committed by employees, as compared to 38.6% for managers and 19.3% for owners/executives. Owners/executives tended to commit the largest frauds with a median loss of C$1 million. More owners/executives' frauds (52.9%) were detected by tips than by any other detection method.

- The departments that accounted for the highest percentage of occupational fraud cases were, in order, sales (17.4% of all cases), executive/upper management (15.1%), accounting (15.1%), and customer service (12.8%).

The full report will be released in the spring of 2007 and can be downloaded at no charge from the ACFE website, www.ACFE.com.

Australia

According to a 2005 PricewaterhouseCoopers Global Economic Crime Survey, 63% of organizations in Australia experienced economic crime between 2003 and 2005 – a 16% increase in the 2003 survey. Of the perpetrators, 67% were employees of the organization. Fifty-four percent of those held positions of middle management or above. Fifty-nine percent dismissed the perpetrator and 54% pursued criminal charges. Twenty-five percent of those charged were sentenced

Ernst & Young International Survey

Ernst and Young administered surveys about occupational fraud and abuse to international businesses in 1997, 2000, 2003 and 2006.

1997 Results

In October 1997, Ernst & Young surveyed 11,000 senior executives in major organizations in 32 countries, of whom 1205 (11%) replied. Among these results:

- Approximately three-quarters of respondents reported being victimized during the preceding five years.
- Over 50% had been defrauded in the preceding 12 months.
- 88% of United States respondents had experienced fraud in the preceding 12 months.
- More than half of the frauds were committed by employees who had been with the organization for more than five years.

2000 Results

A follow-up to the 1997 survey was conducted in 2000. Some of the findings included:

- More than two-thirds of respondent organizations had experienced fraud in the previous year.
- Nearly 10% of those had suffered more than 50 frauds in the year.
- The single worst fraud suffered by each respondent during the last 12 months cost an estimated loss of $172 million, of which only $49 million (29%) had been recovered.
- The main sources of recovery were from the fraud perpetrators themselves and, to a lesser extent, insurance.
- Of the 43 respondents who had suffered more than 50 significant frauds in the previous year, almost half were from the banking and financial services sector, with three of these frauds exceeding $25 million.
- High value frauds were not restricted to a particular sector or country: organizations in 23 sectors suffered losses of more than $1 million.
- Employees of the organization committed 82% of frauds.
- Of these, management committed almost a third.
- Nearly half of the employees who defrauded their firms had been with the organization for over 5 years; nearly a quarter had been with the organization for over 10 years.
- Of those employees who perpetrated the worst fraud in the last 12 months, 38% were prosecuted; 28% were dismissed.
- 42% of respondents were insured against fraud losses.

2003 Results

Ernst & Young conducted another follow-up survey in 2003. The data revealed the following:

- Fraud does not discriminate by geographic region, industry or size of a company.
- 85% of the "worst frauds" were carried out by insiders.
- 55% of frauds were carried out by persons in management positions; 85% of whom had been in the position for less than a year.
- 63% of respondents believed asset misappropriation to be the worst possible outcome of fraud.
- 21% of respondents were most concerned about financial-statement reporting fraud.

- Most losses resulting from fraud were valued at less than $100,000.
- 13% of the worst losses resulting from fraud were valued at over $1,000,000.
- Companies recovered greater portions of fraud losses than in 2000 (51% recovery in 2003; 29% recovery in 2000).
- Loss recovery appears to be the result of noncomplacency by insurers, banks and suppliers.
- The use of electronic evidence in fraud investigations was only used in 5% of cases.
- 88% of respondents are satisfied with forensic investigation.

2006 Results

In 2006 Ernst & Young conducted its 9th Global Fraud Survey, which focused on fraud risk in emerging markets, whereas the previous ones examined the general causes of economic crime. The results are as follows:

- Almost 20% of respondents had experienced considerable fraud in the past two years.
- Internal controls are considered the best method to prevent and detect fraud. Almost 90% of respondents believed internal controls were adequate within their organization to identify and investigate fraud quickly.
- Globally, 42% of companies lack a formal anti-fraud policy. Compared to 2003, when 53% of respondents had anti-fraud policies, the 2006 figure indicates only a 5% increase at 58%.
- Nearly 50% of respondents identified bribery and corruption as the greatest risks in emerging markets; in developed markets however, the greatest risk cited was internal fraud in collusion with third parties, at 31%. This differs from the 2003 survey, when asset misappropriation was believed to be the greatest risk.
- In businesses in remote locations, managers are said to have the ability to cause considerable financial statement error.
- Half of respondents now investigate fraud in the interest of identifying and improving control weaknesses, marking a dramatic increase from the 2003 survey.
- Approximately 60% of respondents in developed countries suspect that their operations are at a higher risk for fraud in emerging markets.

- 75% of respondents that suffered fraud in the past few years experienced it in their developed country operation. For 32%, it occurred in an emerging market.
- More than a fourth of respondents do not consider anti-fraud measures expressly when they invest in a new market.
- One third of respondents would rather hire an external specialist when fraud occurs.

Employee-Committed Computer Crimes

Besides causing defalcations, employees may commit computer crimes for profit or revenge.

The most prevalent methods of committing computer crime are:

- Altering or falsifying input
- Altering or falsifying output
- Data file manipulation
- Communications systems manipulation
- Operating systems manipulation
- Computer operations manipulation

Sabotage by disgruntled employees is a growing problem. Experts say the level of employee destruction has never been so high since the phenomenon has been tracked. Two of the most common acts of revenge are theft of company property and breaches in the company's computer network, according to an annual survey of Fortune 1000 companies by Pinkerton Inc. The firm estimates that employee retaliation occurs in only 1% of dismissals, but could be as high as 5% at companies that do not handle layoffs well or that have a hostile corporate culture.

Telecommuting and the spread of Internet devices have made it easier for dismissed workers to wreak havoc outside the company premises. Wireless networks in offices and factories can penetrate walls and have a range of 300 feet. Security experts suggest cutting off employees' connections to the corporate networks before letting the employees go.

Even if disgruntled workers cannot access company computers, they can use the Internet to spread false information in chat rooms and send out fake news releases. Blue-collar workers can damage systems by destroying the physical property or by reprogramming computers involved in manufacturing processes.

Fraud Inside Dot-Coms

A study by Kroll Associates, released in 2000, found that the top managers at "dot com" companies were four times more likely than the general population of corporate directors and officers to have had legal trouble in the past. Of 70 Internet executives investigated, 27 (39% of the total) had backgrounds tarnished by such incidents as:

- Securities and Exchange Commission violations
- Insurance fraud
- RICO charges
- Undisclosed bankruptcies
- Frauds committed overseas
- Ties to organized crime

Of the 1,000-1,500 background investigations Kroll conducts each year—in connection with initial public offerings, financings and mergers and acquisitions—about 10% of the individuals have background problems.

Kroll said young people founding dot-com businesses were often duped, especially by older people, because the businesses did not conduct adequate research on candidates. In a typical case, "Young Internet entrepreneurs bring inexperienced business people who promise to lead the founders to business success and IPO riches. They invest a small amount of their own money as a show of commitment. Then, with systems and controls not yet in place, the 'leaders' proceed to milk the start-up for exorbitant 'consulting' fees and live their personal lives at the company's expense."

Organizations Responding to Fraud

In previous years, managers were often reluctant to report fraud to the police or seek official redress. In a 1999 survey, KPMG found that one-third of the organizations failed to report frauds. KPMG's 2003 survey revealed that reports of fraud are increasing, presumably due to passage of the Sarbanes-Oxley Act in 2002. Organizations are not only reacting to fraudulent activity, but establishing measures to prevent fraud from occurring. In the 2005 survey, 77% of respondents confirmed that their company implemented a code of conduct to articulate the values and standards of the organization. Eighty-one percent of employees said that they would report misconduct to a supervisor or manager. These statistics demonstrate willingness within the organization as a whole to fight fraud.

Sources:

"Scottish Business Briefing-March 13th" Scotsman.com, March 13th, 2006. Accessed September 29th, 2006.

"Global Economic Crime Survey 2005; Australia." PriceWaterhouse Coopers, 2005. Accessed October 2, 2006.

Ernst & Young's 9th Global Fraud Survey; Fraud risk in emerging markets. www.ey.com, 2006.

Coleman, A. "Bosses Turn Blind Eye to Work Fraud." *Associated Newspapers,* May 13, 2001.

Dennier, C. "Tax Will Damage Rural Economy." *Aberdeen Press and Journal,* May 7, 2001.

Donaldson, T. "Survey—Mastering Management: Adding Corporate Ethics to the Bottom Line." *Financial Times (London),* November 13, 2000.

"Fighting Fraud." *The Accountant,* January 25, 2001.

Henderson, Bartholomew. *fraudabc.com.* San Jose: iUniversity Press, 2001.

KPMG's U.S. Fraud Survey. *Business Wire,* December 16, 1998.

KPMG's U.S. Fraud Survey 2003, KPMG Forensics, 2003.

Murphy, Kevin. *Honesty in the Workplace.* Pacific Grove: Brooks/Cole Publishing, 1993.

Smith, R. "Organisations As Victims of Fraud, And How They Deal With It." *Australia Institute of Criminology,* September 1999.

Smith, R. "Fraud: What Response?" *Australian CPA,* November 1999.

Related Entries:

ASSET MISAPPROPRIATION

ATTITUDES TOWARD AND PERCEPTIONS OF FRAUD

AVOCATIONAL CRIME

BEHAVIORAL THEORY OF FRAUD
BRIBERY
CAUSES OF FRAUD
COMPUTER CRIME
CORRUPTION, OCCUPATIONAL
COST OF FRAUD
FINANCIAL STATEMENT FRAUD
PREVENTION POLICIES FOR FRAUD

ORGANIZATIONAL CRIME

See, CONTRACT AND PROCUREMENT FRAUD
CORPORATE CRIME

ORGANIZED CRIME AND FRAUD

The Secret Service describes organized crime as a loosely similar number of criminal groups, who sometimes cooperate with each other, and sometimes antagonize one another, but who generally conduct independent operations. Perhaps the most infamous example of fraud and organized crime involves Al Capone, the famous Chicago gangster whom federal authorities could not convict of bootlegging or murder, but who was finally imprisoned for tax evasion.

According to a Secret Service spokesperson, "The organized criminal groups of the past have historically been Italian organized crime families. However, in addition to these traditional groups, which continue to exist, there are emerging organized criminal groups from the Nigerian, Asian, Middle Eastern, and Russian communities, all of which seem to have some direct involvement in various forms of financial crime."

Nigerian groups are known to target financial institutions in the United States and abroad. These groups are involved in all types of fraud, using multiple identities and false documentation throughout the world. In addition to the traditional fraud schemes, the Nigerian and West African criminal element is also known for its abilities to transport currency and heroin transnationally. It is suspected that much of the money obtained through the fraudulent activity conducted by the Nigerians is used to finance their drug trafficking operations.

Organized crime groups have compromised global payment systems through credit card and other access device fraud, fraudulent identification, bank fraud, telecommunications fraud, and financial fraud relating to computer intrusions, often with the use of false identification. Members of an organized group arrested by federal authorities were found at the time of arrest to be in possession of fraudulent identification, counterfeit credit cards, counterfeit payroll checks, counterfeit traveler's checks, and cloned cellular telephones.

Organized Crime and Health Care Fraud

In late 1999, the Government Accounting Office (GAO) released a study of the Medicare, Medicaid, and private health insurance sectors, which confirmed that organized crime is heavily involved in health care fraud. The GAO examined seven cases of health care fraud. The investigation found that in those cases alone, about 160 health related groups—medical clinics, physician groups, labs, or medical suppliers—had submitted fraudulent claims. The perpetrators were not health care workers; they were career criminals with records for securities fraud, forgery, and auto theft. Offenders were extremely mobile, moving from New Jersey to California, for example, before authorities in the first state could arrest them. The criminals illegally obtained beneficiary names and medical provider numbers, which they used to file false claims.

Sources:
"Brian L. Stafford, Director of the U.S. Secret Service before Senate on: Governmental Affairs, False Identification, and the Internet." *Federal News Service,* May 19, 2000.

Edelman, S. "Eljay B. Bowron, Director of the U.S. Secret Service, February 1997 Speech: Med Mob Under Microscope." *The New York Post,* November 19, 2000.

PARK, YUN SOO OH "TOKYO JOE"

"Tokyo Joe" sold stock advice on the Internet. In 2000, the SEC brought civil charges against Yun Soo Oh Park and his company, Tokyo Joe's Societe Anonyme, for defrauding subscribers from at least July 1998 to at least June 1999 through illegal touting and lying about the Societe's performance record.

Park was born in Seoul, South Korea sometime in the late 1940's. He was a lawyer in Tokyo, a real-estate investor in Seattle and owner of Tokyo Joe's Classic Burrito restaurant in New York City. He began posting stock picks in chat rooms in 1997 usually calling himself "TokyoMex." He later developed a subscription-based website called "Tokyo Joe's Societe Anonyme," which amassed as many as 3,800 members around the world, paying as much as $200 a month.

Park illegally bought stock on at least 10 occasions before he recommended them to his members, and then cashed in after his recommendations drove up the stocks' price, a practice known as scalping. For example, Park bought 16,000 shares of Vialink Co. on Dec. 11, 1998, and three days later recommended Societe Anonyme members buy the stock. As prices increased from $7.38 a share to $8.50, he sold, while recommending his subscribers held their shares. Park committed illegal touting when he failed to disclose that DCGR International Holdings Inc. paid him 100,000 shares to promote the company. Park also posted false performance results on his website, indicating his stock picks had gained up to 2,900%.

Park later agreed to return $750,000 of his trading profits. His lawyers argued that his stock picking was protected free speech because his advice wasn't tailored to any particular individual. Park's defense hinged on a case brought before the U.S. Supreme Court in 1985. At that time, the SEC was seeking to prevent Christopher Lowe from providing investment advice through a newsletter he published. Lowe had been convicted of misappropriating a client's funds and covering up a fraud and was forced to give up his registration as an investment advisor.

Lowe's defense largely depended on the court's interpretation of the Investment Advisors Act of 1940, one of the last in a series of measures Congress enacted to eliminate certain abuses in the securities industry, which were found to have contributed to the market crash in 1929 and the Great Depression of the 1930's.

The Investment Advisors Act defines an investment adviser as someone who, for compensation, engages in the business of advising others, either directly or through publications or writings, as to the value of securities or the advisability of investing in, purchasing or selling securities. However, as long as communications between people offering investment advice and their subscribers remain entirely impersonal and do not develop into any kind of fiduciary or person-to-person relationships, the publishers of that information are not considered by the Court to be investment advisers under the law.

The Court eventually concluded that Lowe did not fit the description of a personalized investment adviser. Lacking a personal nexus between the professional providing services and a client, and if the individual who is speaking is not exercising any kind of judgment on behalf of a specific individual, the Supreme Court had said government regulation of the speech was not legitimate. In its opinion, the court held that in creating the law, "Congress, plainly sensitive to First Amendment concerns, wanted to make clear that it did not seek to regulate the press through the licensing of non personalized publishing activities."

However, U.S. District Judge Charles P. Kocoras distinguished *Park* from *Lowe*, and noted that the defendants met the basic definition of investment advisers because they engaged in the business of advising others, either directly or through publications or writings disseminated electronically and in print. Besides, Judge Kocoras pointed out, "Fraudulent speech is simply not entitled to First Amendment protection of any kind."

Related Entry:

SECURITIES FRAUD

PARMALAT

Italy-based dairy industry giant Parmalat imploded almost instantaneously around Christmas of 2003. A series of suspicious financial moves culminated when a €3.95 billion hole was found in the company's accounting records. Parmalat claimed to have an account in a Cayman Islands subsidiary called Bonlat with Bank of America for €3.95 billion that simply did not exist. The fact that Parmalat forged a near €4 billion bank deposit to carry out this fraud – with elementary tools like scissors, paste, and a copy machine – was only the breaking point. After the company filed for bankruptcy protection, investigators found that Parmalat had understated its debt by €10 billion, and overstated total net assets by €15 billion. As the largest bankruptcy in European history, the revelation sent shock waves throughout the corporate world. The scandal was as complex as any of the white-collar American crimes that had surfaced over the previous decade.

In 1961, at age twenty-two, Calisto Tanzi opened a pasteurization plant in Parma, Italy. Fast forward twenty years and Parmalat, a multinational company boasting sales in products ranging from dairy to bakery goods, was booming in the 1980's. In 1990, the corporation, which employs 30,000 people in thirty countries, was first listed on the Milan stock exchange.

Parmalat raised eyebrows in early 2003 when it attempted to sell €500 million bond issues, which never went through. After the company stopped trying to sell the bonds, Italian fund managers planned to meet with Parmalat executives to discuss accounts. Three weeks later, chief financial officer Fausto Tonna resigned and was replaced by Alberto Ferraris. As a new CFO, Ferraris was shocked to find a company debt of €14 billion, more than double the debt recorded on the balance sheet. Concerned, he went straight to Tanzi, who infamously replied, "eight billion, eleven billion, fourteen billion – it's all the same."

In November, Parmalat announced that it would collect a €150 million bond settlement from the liquidation of Epicurum, one of the company's subsidiaries. The money was to be used to satisfy a €150 million interest payment. Two weeks later, however, Parmalat announced that Epicurum was not able to liquidate, and that it was making a "potential plan for the Group's industrial and financial restructuring." The subsequent days sent Parmalat into a financial tailspin. It didn't take long for shareholders to catch wind of the shady business taking place within Parmalat. The company's shares were hammered. Every member of the company's financial backbone resigned, including Ferraris, who was replaced by Luciano Del Soldato. Less than a month later, when the company missed a €150 million bond payment, Del Soldato quit and was replaced by Enrico Bondi, who was called by the government to aid the company. Less than a week after that, Tanzi himself stepped down from his position as chairman and chief executive officer and Bondi was called to cover his position. To make matters worse, the story that Parmalat forged the Bank of America letter of credit for €3.5 billion in liquid assets hit the media.

Following this brazen string of events, PricewaterhouseCoopers was hired to ascertain Parmalat's assets and liabilities. Yet, before the auditors could announce that Parmalat overstated its 2003 Earnings Before Interest, Taxes, and Depreciation by 530% and understated its liabilities, the company declared that about €7 billion in liquid assets, believed to exist in a Bank of America account, did not exist at all. Tanzi was taken into custody and by the end of January 2004, Parmalat filed for bankruptcy, with an audit classifying its debt near €14.5 billion.

As it turns out, Parmalat had been purchasing debt-ridden and loss-making companies for over a decade. Rather than doing anything to help these entities recover, Parmalat hid its liabilities in intercompany transactions, thereby simulating profits and leaving itself in deceptively good financial standing.

It took the Italian judicial system ten months to charge indictments against the company and individuals involved in the scandal. In early October 2004, a judge indicted the first two participating individuals, former Parmalat auditors of Grant Thornton, on charges of false accounting and market rigging. Audit firms Deloitte & Touche and the Italian offices of Bank of America were accused of abetting the fraud by helping to hide Parmalat's true financial state. Tanzi and fifteen others were charged with false accounting, market rigging, and misleading Italy's market regulator.

In June 2005, a Milan judge sentenced ten ex-Parmalat executives and a lawyer to jail for up to two and a half years for crimes including market rigging and obstructing regulators. Tanzi, if convicted, faces up to fifteen years in prison.

Current Status of Parmalat

Parmalat is in increasingly solid financial standing due to the direction of Enrico Bondi's recovery strategy. The company delivered an 18.4% rise in earnings from 2005 as of March 31, 2006.

Sources:
"Parmalat: Timeline to turmoil." Bbc.co.uk. September 12, 2006

"How it All Went Sour." Time.com, September 12, 2006

"The Parmalat Syndrome." sfweekly.com, September 12, 2006

"Italy: Italy Judge sentences 11 to jail in Parmalat case." Corpwatch.org, September 12, 2006

"Parmalat SpA." Wikepedia.org, September 12, 2006

"Parmalat Readies New Share Listing." *Forbes.com*, September 21, 2004.

"Parmalat Founder's Sentence Almost Over." *Forbes.com*, September 25, 2004.

"Update 2: House Arrest Ends for Ex-Parmalat Chief." *Forbes.com*, September 27, 2004.

"Ex-Parmalat CFO Reportedly Blames Tanzi." *Forbes.com*, October 3, 2004.

"First Court Hearing Set in Parmalat Case." *Forbes.com*, October 4, 2004.

"Update 7: Judge Indicts 2 Former Parmalat Auditors." *Forbes.com*, October 5, 2004.

"How Parmalat Went Sour." *Business Week Online*, January 12, 2004.

"Italy's Parmalat, Milking Investors Through Financial Statement Fraud." *Fraud Magazine* (Vol. 18, No. 5, pp. 29-31, 51-53), September/October 2004.

"Milk Gone Bad." *Report on Fraud* (Vol. 6, Issue 5, pp. 4-7), March 2004.

Related Entry:

FINANCIAL STATEMENT FRAUD

PAYROLL SCHEMES

Payroll schemes are a method of fraudulent disbursements, which are a form of asset misappropriation, the most common method of occupational fraud and abuse. Payroll schemes typically involve altering an existing employee's records, or creating a bogus employee. The most common method is falsifying an employee's claim for pay by altering the timecard, type of work performed, or rate of pay.

A ghost employee scheme requires altering payroll records—the beneficiary might be an accomplice, or the perpetrator uses an alias, corroborated by the personal information of a friend or relative. Supervisors may create ghosts in their work reports, or office personnel may enter ghosts directly into the payroll accounts.

There are two ways to falsify commissions based on sales and services: (1) falsify the value of sales or service, and (2) increase the rate of commission. Ghost employees can be used for commission schemes, but doing so is difficult since commission payments are based on recorded sales or services. Commission disbursements are sometimes used to disguise kickbacks and other forms of corruption.

Detection and Prevention of Payroll Schemes

For general payroll schemes and ghost employee schemes:

- Have someone other than the payroll department distribute checks.
- Require positive identification of each payee.
- Look for duplicate names, addresses, or deposit accounts.
- Require supervisors to authorize overtime and to refer timecards directly to payroll.
- Review excessive overtime or overtime worked by a single employee in a department.
- Compare the personnel list and the payroll list. Determine whether any employees have failed to execute the tax withholding forms, or have not elected to receive any health benefits or other optional withdrawals, such as enforced savings plans.
- Verify that each employee's Social Security Number matches the valid combination listed by the Social Security Agency.

For commission schemes:

- Compare commission expenses to sales figures.
- Verify rates and calculation accuracy.
- Establish a mean for earnings and review salespeople with above-average commissions.
- Analyze uncollected sales revenue by salesperson.
- Contact a random sample of customers to confirm sales.

Red Flags of Payroll Fraud

The following audit program will help spot red flags to payroll distribution fraud:

- Are personnel records maintained independently of payroll and timekeeping functions?
- Is the payroll accounting function independent of the general ledger function?
- Are changes to payroll made without approval of the personnel department?

- Are references and backgrounds checked for new hires?
- Are all wage rates authorized in writing by a designated official?
- Are signed authorizations on file for employees whose wages are subject to special deductions?
- Are bonuses, commissions, and overtime approved in advance and reviewed for compliance with company policies?
- Are sick leave, vacations, and holidays reviewed for compliance with company policy?
- Are appropriate forms completed and signed by employees to show authorization for payroll deductions and withholding exemptions?
- Is the payroll periodically checked against the personnel records for terminated employees, fictitious employees, etc.?
- Is a time clock used for office employees as well as factory workers? If a time clock is used, are timecards (1) punched by employees in the presence of a designated supervisor and (2) signed by a supervisor at the end of the payroll period?
- Are timecards and production reports reviewed and compared with payroll distribution reports and production schedules?
- Are payroll registers reviewed and approved before disbursements are made for (1) names of employees, (2) hours worked, (3) wage rates, (4) deductions, (5) agreement with payroll checks, and (6) unusual items?
- Are all employees paid by check out of a separate bank payroll account?
- Are payroll checks prenumbered and issued in numerical sequence?
- Is access restricted to un-issued payroll checks and signature plates?
- Are checks drawn and signed by designated officials who do not (1) prepare payroll, (2) have access to the accounting records, or (3) have custody of cash funds?
- Are payroll checks distributed by someone other than the department head or the person who prepares the payroll?
- Is the distribution of the payroll rotated periodically to different employees without prior notice?

- Is the payroll bank account reconciled by a designated employee who (1) is not involved in the preparing of payroll, (2) does not sign the checks, or (3) does not handle the check distributions?
- Do payroll bank account reconciliations procedures include comparing the paid checks to the payroll and scrutinizing canceled check endorsements?
- Are the payroll registers reconciled to the general ledger control accounts?
- Is a liability account set up for all wages that have remained unclaimed for a certain period of time? If yes, (1) have these wages been deposited in a special bank account, and (2) is identification required to be presented at the time of their subsequent distribution?
- Are distributions of hours (direct and indirect) to activity or departments reviewed and approved by supervisory personnel?
- Are actual payroll amounts reviewed and compared to budgeted amounts, and are variances analyzed regularly?
- Do adequate procedures exist for timely and accurate preparation and filing of payroll tax returns and related taxes?
- Are employee benefit plan contributions reconciled to appropriate employee census data?
- Are adequate, detailed records maintained of the entity's liability for vacation pay and sick pay? Are they reconciled to the general ledger control accounts periodically?

Related Entries:

ASSET MISAPPROPRIATION
FRAUDULENT DISBURSEMENTS
OCCUPATIONAL FRAUD AND ABUSE

PERSONAL INJURY FRAUD

Personal injury fraud is committed by making false representations in claims for medical treatments covered by workers' compensation policies or by the Personal Injury Protection coverage of auto insurance policies. Personal injury fraud is most often the result of a staged or exaggerated loss or accident.

No firm numbers exist for personal injury fraud. Between 1994 and 2000, payments to medical providers for treatment of accident victims grew by 20% from $247 million to $297 million, according to the Automobile Insurers Bureau. If 10% of those funds were disbursed to fraudulent claimants, the cost of personal injury fraud would be close to $30 million yearly.

An investigation in New York by the *New York Post* found:

- Suspicious accidents rose 848% in five years within the state, from 154 in 1993 to 1,306 in 1998, with most of the cases in the metropolitan area.
- Of 1998's 1,306 suspicious accidents, 159 were considered deliberately staged, up 180% from 1993.
- State insurance companies claim "no fault" insurance personal-injury fraud cases jumped 35% in 1998, from 5,214 to 7,042, an increase since 1993 of 516%.
- The state insurance department conducted criminal investigations for 195 accidents in 1998.

Characteristics of Personal Injury Fraud

Personal injury fraud is characterized by:

- A claim filed for an accident that never happened.
- The claimant exaggerates a personal injury.
- An accident reported in a workers' compensation claim is not job-related.
- Doctors who render excessive or unnecessary treatment.
- The occurrence of "Jump-ins," in which several passengers of a car involved in an accident file claims for false injuries over a period of several months. Special Investigation Units have uncovered a number of such insurance fraud rings in urban New Jersey neighborhoods. The rings usually include doctors, lawyers, and insurance brokers.
- Suspicious injuries that occur in the workplace when no one else is around to witness the accident.
- Multiple medical claims filed for "soft tissue" injuries (strains and sprains) that are difficult to diagnose.

Personal Injury Fraud in 19th and 20th Century America

According to Ken Dornstein's history of personal injury fraud in America:

- America's first group of accident stagers made their livings by faking injuries while riding steam trains in the 1800's.
- Arson rings in New York City during the 1890's netted millions, including a tenement-building blaze that killed 100 people while netting a $2,500 insurance payment.
- Auto accident racketeers of the 1920's included gangsters based in New York City's Lower East Side.
- Many people engaged in self-mutilation for profit during the Great Depression.
- Whiplash industries, filing mainly against automobile insurance, proliferated in the 1960's and 1970's.
- Estimates in the 1920's put losses to fraudulent auto claims at $20 million. When Benjamin Laulicht and his brother were arrested in the 1920's for staging accidents between horse carriages and motor taxis in New York, the district attorney said insurance rates could go down by 20%.
- Initially the major corporate defenders of personal injury suits were not insurers, but railroads, inundated with personal injury claims in the last quarter of the 19th century. Many claims were legitimate from horrible train wrecks, but others were faked.

Sources:

Campanile, C. "Crash Scams Driving Up Car Insurance." *The New York Post,* June 14, 1998.

Covaleski, J. "Everything Old Is Fraudulent." *Best's Review,* December 1996.

Kurkjian, S. "Injury Claims Flourish in Loophole Fraud, Investigated While Therapists and Lawyers Profit." *The Boston Globe,* July 16, 2001.

Related Entry:

INSURANCE FRAUD

PHARMACY FRAUD

Pharmacy fraud is committed by misrepresenting products or by violating laws and regulations governing the distribution of prescription drugs. For example, a pharmacist can conspire with a physician and a patient to dispense a generic drug rather than a brand-name drug and profit on the difference in price. A pharmacist might fill an insured prescription, then buy it back at a discount from the patient and sell it again. Some pharmacists distribute drugs with street value to patients, who sell the drugs and kick back to the pharmacist.

Pharmacy Fraud Schemes

Fraud committed through pharmacies will usually take one of the following forms.

- Merchandising—substituting something of value for a prescription drug.
- Billing for brand name drugs but dispensing generic drugs.
- Billing beyond amount prescribed.
- Billing for drugs not prescribed.
- Billing for a high-priced generic drug, but dispensing a lower-priced generic drug
- Package size differential—billing third-party payers for the price of drugs purchased in small package sizes when they were purchased at less cost in larger quantities.
- Black market purchasing—purchasing drugs at significantly reduced rates then dispensing at regular prices.
- Providers or provider staff notes drugs as dispensed to phony patients, then sell or use the drugs themselves.

On-Line Pharmacies

If traditional pharmacies have experienced fraud problems, online pharmacies have experienced those problems exponentially. Two-hundred national websites have been identified by the National Association of Boards of Pharmacy. These sites dispense prescription drugs but do not provide online prescriptions. According to the FDA, it is illegal to provide a prescription drug to a customer without a prescription. Of the over 400 sites that offer prescription drugs and prescriptions, half are located in foreign countries. Medicine sold by online pharmacies range from GHB (the date rape drug) to

Viagra. Providers tout their product as less expensive than U.S. purchased drugs. While this is an attractive offer to customers, it can be dangerous because many of the drugs are not equivalent to the legitimate versions.

- Nine were willing to sell prescription medication with no questions asked, while several others would supply such drugs on the basis of a questionnaire alone.
- In many cases, these were international sites selling such popular medications as Viagra, Propecia, and Xenical.
- Providers touted their product as less expensive than U.S. purchased drugs, but these drugs were subtly different than their domestic equivalents and were provided with no pre-screening or prescription.

Three Types of Online Pharmacy Fraud

According to the Food and Drug Administration, pharmacy fraud through online pharmacies takes one of three forms:

- A website sells medication that is completely useless, such as advertisements promising "miracle cures." In 1996 and 1997, a California company called Lei-Home Access Care sold HIV/AIDS blood tests and then fabricated the results.
- A site sells medication that has not been approved by the FDA, or medication that is contaminated, altered, mislabeled, or expired.
- A site sells legitimate products but avoids the well-regulated procedures governing the dispensation of such materials. For example, organizations that offer prescription drugs without requiring a prescription.

Industry Self-Regulation

In 1999, the National Association of Boards of Pharmacy (NABP) created its listing of the Verified Internet Pharmacy Practice Sites (VIPPS). The listing offers online pharmacies a voluntary certification provided by the NABP. While non-member sites are not necessarily fraudulent, member sites are guaranteed to be safe and fully licensed.

Sources:

"Buying Medicines and Medical Products Online." *U.S. Food and Drug Administration.* www.fda.gov/oc/buyonline/faqs.html

"Regulating Online Pharmacies: Can the Industry Police Itself?" *MDNetguide,* 2001.

U.S. Food and Drug Administration. www.fda.gov; accessed October 3, 2006.

Related Entry:

HEALTH CARE FRAUD

PHARMING

Pharming is an attack in which a user is fooled into entering sensitive data (such as a password or credit card number) into a malicious website that impersonates a legitimate website. It is different from phishing in that the attacker does not have to rely on having the user click on a link in the e-mail to direct him or her to the fake website. Furthermore, a phishing scam can be quickly discovered if the Internet user notices that the web address is different from the one he or she expected to appear after clicking on that link. This is not the case with pharming because the hacker changes the DNS, a more obscure code, rather than the IP address, which is familiar to even a novice Internet user.

Pharming allows many victims to be perpetrated at once, as opposed to phishing, in which the perpetrator has to attack each user individually. Pharming actually exploits a vulnerability in the DNS (Domain Name System, which is a list matching domain names, like www.google.com, to their respective IP addresses) server software that allows a hacker to acquire the domain name for a site and redirect the website traffic from a legitimate site to a false one. So even though the user types in the correct website address, the pharming program sends the user to an illegitimate site that looks like the real thing. There is usually no visible difference between the fake website and the legitimate one except for the IP address. Unknowingly, the user is then providing passwords and information directly to the hacker.

Prevention

Computer users should change the default administrator username and password on their router. Most routers do not automatically take the user to a place where they can set their own password during installation. Further, users should deactivate the HTTP server feature in the router. Changing the password can secure the DNS. Antivirus software and spyware removal software *does not* protect against pharming.

If foul play is suspected, a simple Windows procedure can help determine whether or not the site has been pharmed.

1. *Open a command prompt:* From the Start menu, click on Run…, type *command* (or *cmd*) and press Enter.
2. *Look up the IP address:* Type *nslookup 123.45.67.89* and press Enter, replacing 123.45.67.89 with the suspicious IP address.

If the domain name that appears looks familiar, it is probably safe to continue.

Risk

On September 20th, 2007, Cisco released a warning that 77 of its Small Office/Home Office (SOHO), Remote Office/Branch Office (ROBO), and Teleworker business routers could be at risk. Though pharming is not known to have caused any financial losses at this point, the scam has potential to do substantial damage and is a serious security threat.

Sources:
"Drive-By Pharming Attack Could Hit Home Networks." Copyright: 2007 Computer Business Review and CBRonline.com; accessed March 6th, 2007. www.cbronline.com/article_news.asp?guid=B2D823D1-D77D-471F-96B2-0DED432A0CA2

Wikipedia entry. "Pharming" Copyright: 2007 Wikipedia; accessed March 6th 2007. en.wikipedia.org/wiki/Pharming

"Cisco Lists 77 Routers at Risk of 'Drive-by Pharming" Copyright SPAMfighter 2003-2007; accessed March 6th, 2007. www.spamfighter.com/News-7828-Cisco-Lists-77-Routers-at-Risk-of-Drive-by-Pharming.htm

Related Entries:

COMPUTER CRIME

COMPUTER FRAUD

INTERNET FRAUD

PHISHING

PHISHING

"Phishing" is a popular new scheme that involves tricking businesses or individuals into providing passwords, account numbers, or other sensitive data by claiming to be from an actual company the victim does business with. A solicitation for information appears to come from a legitimate business and can occur over the phone (e.g., a call from the victim's "bank" saying their account has been compromised and requesting PIN numbers, account numbers, or passwords), or via e-mail (which is the most common technique). An individual receives an e-mail that appears to come from eBay, PayPal, a financial institution. The e-mail states that the customer must immediately log into his account in order to update his information. The link directs the individual to a fake site which captures his identifying information such as Social Security and PIN numbers, mothers' maiden name, and financial account numbers.

The average loss from phishing is $2,320, which is much less than other forms of identity theft schemes such as family or friends stealing $15,607 on average from the victim, or the theft of paper mail which has an average loss of $9,243. Still, it is crucial for people to recognize this fraud so they don't fall victim to it:

- Phishing occurs mostly by e-mail. As described above, the sender of the e-mail pretends to be a legitimate bank, government agency, or retailer and asks the recipient to "confirm" his or her personal information for any of these or other made-up reasons: your account will be closed if you don't give the information, an order has been placed in your name, or your information has been lost because of a computer glitch. Don't ever respond to these e-mails. Legitimate banks, government agencies, and retailers do not e-mail you for your password of other identifying information.
- Do not click on any link in an e-mail that asks for your personal information. The links included in the e-mails sent by phishers will take you to a phony website that looks just like the website of the real company or agency. If you followed the instructions, you would enter your personal information on the website which would go straight into the hands of identity thieves.
- Ironically, phishers may even say that they are from the fraud departments of popular companies and ask you to verify your information because they suspect you may be a

victim of identity theft. Other tactics include the phisher claiming to be from a state lottery commission who requests people's banking information to deposit their "winnings" in their accounts. Again, never give any personal information via e-mail.

- Phishing can also happen by phone. Verify caller's identity and contact their company for legitimacy. Instead of fraudsters sending spam, they might call you and pretend to be from a company or government agency, making the same kinds of false claims and asking for your personal information. If someone contacts you and says that you have been a victim of fraud, verify the person's identity before you provide any personal information. Legitimate credit card issuers and other companies may contact you if there is an unusual pattern indicating that someone else might be using one of your accounts. However, they only ask if you made particular transactions; they don't request your account number or other personal information. Law enforcement agencies might also contact you if you've been the victim of fraud. To be on the safe side, ask for the person's name, the name of the agency or company, the telephone number, and the address. Then get the main number and call to find out if the person is legitimate.
- Phishers also target people who list themselves on job search sites. They pretend to be potential employers and ask for your social security number and other personal information. Before giving anyone your personal information, follow the above advice and make sure to verify the person's identity.
- Be suspicious if contacted unexpectedly and asked for your personal information. It is difficult to determine a company's legitimacy by reading an e-mail, going to a website, or talking to someone on the phone. If you're contacted unexpectedly and asked to give out your personal information, a red flag should go up that something is "phishy." Legitimate companies and agencies do not operate this way.
- Act immediately if you've been hooked by a phisher. If you provided account numbers, PINs, or passwords to a phisher, notify the companies with whom you have the accounts right away. For information about how to put a "fraud alert" on your files at the credit reporting bureaus and other advice for ID theft victims, contact the Federal Trade Commission's ID Theft Clearinghouse, www.consumer.gov/idtheft or toll-free, 877-438-4338.

Related Entries:

COMPUTER CRIME
COMPUTER FRAUD
INTERNET FRAUD
PHARMING

PLAGIARISM

Plagiarism is the intentional representation of another person's work as one's own. Plagiarism can take place in every media—print, audio, and images of every sort. The act may be committed for profit, academic gain, or as a hoax.

Case Study—Term Papers on the Internet

Seth Stevenson, writing for *Slate* magazine online, surveyed the range of college term papers for sale on the Internet. Selecting papers on topics in history, psychology, and biology, Stevenson had each paper graded by judges.

There were dozens of free sites. Some required a donation of a paper to receive a paper, but most did not. The sites from which Stevenson acquired free papers included EssaysFree.com, BigNerds.com, and OPPapers.com. Stevenson's judges rated the first two papers as failures, while the third paper received a C+/B-.

Among sites selling pre-written papers, Stevenson chose AcademicTermPapers.com, which charged $7 per page; PaperStore.net, $10 per page; and A1Termpaper.com, $50 to $75 per paper. Judges rated the AcademicTermPapers.com material in the C- to B+ range; the PaperStore.net material in the B range; and the most expensive material, from A1Termpaper.com, a C-.

Finally, Stevenson bought a custom paper written at his request from PaperMasters.com. Like most services, PaperMasters charges between $7 and $20 per page. Stevenson requested "A 4-page term paper on David Foster Wallace's Infinite Jest. Investigate the semiotics of the 'addicted gaze' as represented by the mysterious film of the book's title. Possible topics to address include nihilism, figurative transgender, the culture of entertainment, and the concept of 'infinite gestation.'" The result—4 pages on a 1,100-page novel from a nonsense assignment—was rated a C+.

Case Study—Stephen Ambrose

The most celebrated case of plagiarism in recent memory was committed by historian Stephen Ambrose, who was discovered to have copied entire passages and specific language for his book on WWII fighter pilots, *The Wild Blue*, from a book by a fellow historian. Thomas Childers' book, *Wings of Morning*, was acknowledged in a footnote as a source, but several passages in Ambrose came directly from Childers, and were not marked with quotation marks.

The following are excerpts from each book, with Childers appearing first and Ambrose next.

> *"Up, up, up, groping through the clouds for what seemed like an eternity. No amount of practice could have prepared them for what they encountered. B-24s, glittering like mica, were popping up out of the clouds all over the sky."* Thomas Childers, *Wings of Morning*

> *"Up, up, up he went, until he got above the clouds. No amount of practice could have prepared the pilot and crew for what they encountered. B-24s, glittering like mica, were popping up out of the clouds over here, over there, everywhere."* Stephen Ambrose, *The Wild Blue*

> *"The bombardier, navigator, and nose-turret gunner were forced to squat down, almost on hands and knees, and sidle up to their stations through the nose wheel well of the ship. Once inside, the three men, fully dressed in their bulky flying gear, would be squeezed into a cramped compartment.... The remaining members of the crew entered the plane by crawling up through the open bomb-bay doors, no more than three feet off the ground."* Thomas Childers, *Wings of Morning*

> *"The bombardier, navigator, and nose turret gunner were forced to squat down, almost on hands and knees, and sidle up to their stations through the nose wheel well of the ship. Inside, the three men had to squeeze themselves into a cramped compartment. ... The other crew members entered the plane by crawling up through the open bomb bay doors, about three feet off the ground."* Stephen Ambrose, *The Wild Blue*

At least two other Ambrose books, *Citizen Soldiers* and *Nixon: Ruin and Recovery 1973-1990*, also borrow freely from source books without using quotation marks.

Sources:
Lewis, M. "More Controversy for Stephen Ambrose." *Forbes.com,* January 9, 2002.

Noah, T. "Ambrose Comes Clean, But His Publisher Fibs." *Whopper of the Week: Simon & Schuster,* January 10, 2002.

Stevenson, S. "Adventures in Cheating, A Guide to Buying Term Papers Online." *Slate Magazine,* December 11, 2001.

PONZI, CHARLES

Known as the Father of the Ponzi scheme, Charles Ponzi, or Carlo Ponzi, was born in 1882 in Parma, Italy. He came from a family of hoteliers and was sent to Rome for a university education. But a string of gambling debts and criminal charges for theft and forgery cut short his schooling and prompted his family to send him to America. At the age of 19 he arrived at Boston Harbor. In his self-published autobiography, *The Rise of Mr. Ponzi*, he claimed that he had only $2.50 with which to begin his new life. He had left with $200 in cash from his family but lost the greater part by gambling with some of his shipmates.

Ponzi worked at odd jobs and clerked for several years before leaving Boston for Montreal, Canada. There he found employment as a bank clerk in the Banco Zarossi, a small operation that served the Italian populace. Ponzi and Zarossi began handling international wire transfers, but they rigged the process so they could hold the funds for an extended period. They lost most of the money they held in bad investments, and the Banco Zarossi was eventually closed due to bankruptcy. Zarossi was arrested soon after.

Ponzi, who was using the alias Carlo Bianchi, was apprehended in a train station, having cashed a forged check a few days before. He served twenty months in a Canadian jail. A few weeks following his release in 1910, he was arrested in Plattsburg, New York for helping a group of Italian immigrants cross illegally into the United States. He was sentenced to two years at a penitentiary in Atlanta.

Ponzi drifted along the Gulf Coast for a couple of years before returning to Boston in 1916, where he secured a job clerking for an import-export firm. In 1918, he married Rose Gnecco and joined her father in his wholesale grocery business. The company went bankrupt in a year and Ponzi returned to the import-export firm.

Ponzi hatched what would become known as the Ponzi scheme in December 1919. A coalition of international postal services had begun selling postal reply coupons after World War I ended. Each coupon was good for one stamp in any of the affiliated countries; this allowed the mail services to continue operations smoothly despite the instability of most European currencies at the time. Ponzi reasoned that he could persuade investors to capitalize on the fluctuating currency prices by using the postal reply coupons in a series of exchanges. Ponzi claimed the process worked as follows:

- He converted one dollar to the Italian lira—a depressed currency—and had an associate use the proceeds to buy postal coupons in Italy. The dollar's high exchange rate allowed him to buy several times as many coupons with the dollar than he could in America.
- He redeemed the coupons in America for American stamps. Now he had, for example, three times more stamps than he could have bought with the dollar.
- He sold the stamps in bulk at a discount to large firms, who were happy to save on mailing costs.
- He paid his investors their generous dividends (50% every 90 days) and pocketed a substantial profit.

However, Ponzi never performed any of those steps. Instead he used money from his latest round of investors to pay those who'd purchased his "securities" earlier. By convincing people to reinvest their funds he was able to postpone his financial obligations even longer.

Reporters at the Boston Post, who discovered his conviction in Montreal as Carlo Bianchi, exposed Ponzi's scheme in early August 1920. Ponzi proclaimed his innocence, but by the end of the month a federal audit confirmed his operation was bankrupt, owing perhaps $4 million or more to investors.

After his arraignment, Ponzi jumped bail and fled to Florida, where he sold swampland as investment property. He and his wife Rose were both arrested in Jacksonville in 1924 and charged with fraud. The charges against his wife were dismissed but Ponzi was ordered to stand trial. However, an errant judge, not realizing he had one of the country's most infamous swindlers before him, allowed Ponzi to post bail. He fled on a ship bound for Genoa, Italy. Authorities later apprehended him when the ship docked in Houston, Texas. Ponzi was convicted in federal court in 1925 and sentenced to 5 years imprisonment. After serving 3 years he was turned over to the Massachusetts judicial system, which sentenced him to seven more years.

Though he fought the deportation charges against him, Ponzi was forced to return to Italy in 1934. Frederico Mussolini, who was eager to hear how his countryman had wreaked such havoc in the American financial system, received him warmly. His family connections eventually won him an appointment as the business manager to an Italian airline headquartered in Rio de Janeiro. He lost the position when it was discovered that the airline was being used to smuggle diamonds, strategic materials, and spy communications to the Fascist regime. Ponzi was apparently innocent, later expressing his consternation that he had not been recruited into the effort.

Sometime in the 1940's he paid a small press in Brooklyn, New York to print his autobiography, *The Rise of Mr. Ponzi.* Extant copies are available at the University of Texas and the Library of Congress, but the book was never reprinted. Charles Ponzi died penniless in a charity ward outside of Rio in 1949.

Source:
Wells, J., CFE, CPA. "Meet Mr. Ponzi: Charles Ponzi." *Frankensteins of Fraud,* Austin, TX: Obsidian Publishing Co., 2000.

Related Entry:

PONZI SCHEME

PONZI SCHEME

A Ponzi scheme is an illegal business practice in which new investors' money is used to make payments to earlier investors. In accounting terms, money paid to Ponzi investors, described as income, is actually a distribution of capital. Instead of returning profits, the Ponzi schemer is spending cash reserves, all for the purposes of raising more funds. Where a basic investment scam raises money and disappears, the Ponzi scheme stays in business by circulating investor funds. There are usually little or no legitimate investments taking place. Most of the funds are used by promoters for expensive lifestyles and transferred into property or offshore accounts. Schemes typically run for at least a year, although some Ponzis have flourished for a decade or more.

The Better Business Bureau has labeled Ponzi-style financial rings "the biggest single fraud threat confronting American investors." Highly publicized nationwide booms in real estate (1980's) and the stock market (1990's) gave rise to an epidemic of investment fraud. Every one of the top frauds cited by the North American Securities Administrators (including Internet and other high-tech scams, telemarketing, and abusive sales practices) has been run as a Ponzi scheme. According to the Securities Exchange Commission (SEC) and the North American Securities Administrators Association (NASAA), scammers pitching phony securities cost U.S. investors between $10 and $15 billion a year—more than a million dollars an hour. Many of these scams use the Ponzi method—paying off a few early investors with other investors' money—to stir up business. Telemarketing boiler rooms, whose frauds cost an estimated $40 billion a year, often run Ponzi schemes.

Ponzi Enforcement

The Federal Trade Commission (FTC) and the Securities Exchange Commission (SEC) are the nation's two major enforcement organizations that target Ponzi schemes. Federal jurisdiction privileges allow FTC and SEC agents to pursue scams across state borders. For example, an operation may be incorporated in Delaware, sell most of its products in Los Angeles, and bank its profits in Missouri. Prosecuting has to encompass each venue and relate local activities to the larger scheme.

The SEC files about 500 complaints a year against unscrupulous investment promoters, and 25% of those are Ponzi schemes. However, the largest number of Ponzi scheme complaints are filed on the state level by state authorities, including attorney generals and state-level regulatory agencies. The FTC shuts down about 10 pyramid schemes every year and takes action of one form or another against dozens of bogus investment opportunities. While the SEC can pursue civil and criminal complaints, the FTC's powers are limited to civil remedies, usually an injunction and a financial judgment for investor losses.

The Difference between a Ponzi Scheme and an Illegal Pyramid Scheme

A Ponzi scheme and an illegal pyramid scheme both use new investors' money to pay earlier investors. The difference between the two lies in the way each scheme is promoted. Illegal pyramids generate revenue by continually recruiting new members. The promoters may offer merchandise or services for sale—or may not—but the only significant revenues come from recruitment. Though a pyramid-style compensation plan is not illegal, it is illegal to run a business in which recruiting new people generates all of the funds.

In a case before the California Appeals Court, the Omnitrition Company argued that, like Amway and other well-known companies that sell distributorships, Omnitrition had established specific protocols for moving their nutritional products. The court rejoindered, "Omnitrition cannot save itself simply by pointing to the fact that it makes some retail sales. There must be evidence that the program's safeguards are enforced and actually serve to deter inventory loading and to encourage retail sales… Omnitrition's focus was in promoting the program rather than selling the products." The only way to make the $10,000 a month income promoters quoted was to sign on more members. "The promise of lucrative rewards for recruiting others tends to induce participants to focus on the recruitment side of the business at the expense of their retail marketing efforts, making it unlikely that meaningful opportunities for retail sales will occur."

Amway and Mary Kay, perhaps the best known of legal companies with pyramid style compensation plans, have survived several court challenges by pointing to their extensive product lines and their insistence that distributors make sales outside the company and don't overload their inventories. Amway has also lost several cases. As a rule of thumb, most courts apply the *70-Percent Rule*, which requires at least 70% of a distributor's profits come from retail sales. Of course this figure can be hard to verify. Distributors routinely sign falsified compliance statements because if they do not, promoters warn, the authorities will shut the whole thing down and everyone loses. So an illegal pyramid scheme is promoted as a pyramid—investors know they will only make big money if they keep recruiting people. In a Ponzi scheme, investors believe they are putting money into a legitimate business opportunity.

The differences become significant during prosecution. An illegal pyramid is prosecuted by showing that the offenders generated revenue mainly through recruitment; the company's pyramidal structure is an element of the charge. Pyramid schemes are sometimes charged as illegal lotteries because, prosecutors have successfully argued, the participants are totally dependent on the actions of others for any compensation. In another prosecution strategy, operators are charged with falsely representing potential earnings, since the mathematical limits of the pyramid make the promised $10,000 a month impossible or extremely against the odds. Again, the pyramidal structure itself is an issue in the case.

With Ponzi schemes, prosecutors approach the case as a deceptive business practice. The prosecution focuses on how the promoter simulated legitimate business, and on a cash flow analysis showing how promoters spent the funds entrusted to them.

Prime Bank Ponzi Schemes

A variation of the Ponzi scheme that proliferated through the 1990's and into the new century purports to offer the investor a chance to invest in the top-secret exchange of financial instruments by the world's top financial institutions. The notes supposedly exchanged by these institutions are sold as "prime bank" instruments, because they are guaranteed by the prime organizations in the field.

There is no such thing as a prime bank instrument. The premise is false. However, the sales pitch may use a variety of terms. Following are some common ways this Ponzi scheme is presented to investors:

- Project invests in prime bank notes or prime bank instruments, standby letters of credit or bank guarantees, medium term notes, bank debentures, bankers' acceptances, or discounted cashiers' checks.

- Investment opportunity is part of a secret market or secondary market, high-yield investment program, or roll program.
- Program is endorsed by the Federal Reserve Bank, Federal Reserve System, Federal Deposit and Insurance Corporation (FDIC), the United Nations (UN), International Chamber of Commerce (ICC), the Federal Bureau of Investigation (FBI), the Securities and Exchange Commission (SEC), World Bank, Bank of England, and the Commission for Under Developed Nations—all legitimate organizations, none of which endorse investment opportunities.
- References to certain trusts that carry part of the name of a very well known or famous bank, such as Credit Swiss Foundation for the Poor, Bank America's Trust Foundation for the Under Privileged, Swiss Bank's Trust Management Fund, various pension funds, or other well-known organizations.

Sources:

Association of Certified Fraud Examiners. *Recognizing Ponzi Schemes,* 1999.

Bocagna, D. "The Many Faces Of Ponzi." *FDN Fraud Report,* May 2001.

Related Entries:

BENNETT, JOHN G., JR.
BENNETT, PATRICK, AND GWEN
CONSUMER FRAUD
GOULDD, BILL
PONZI, CHARLES
TRIPPET, ROBERT

PREDATORY LENDING

Federal regulators define predatory lending as lending involving one or more of these elements: unaffordable loans based on the borrower's assets rather than his or her ability to repay; inducing a borrower to repeatedly refinance his mortgage so that the lender can charge high fees or points; and engaging in fraud or deception to hide the full costs of a loan.

Predatory loans are often packed with excessive fees, costly credit insurance, and balloon payments. These loans are made by companies with a well-marked public presence as well as by individuals and criminal organizations (traditionally known as "loan sharks"). While most states cap interest rates between 25 and 30% per year, many lenders charge from 250% to more than 1,000%.

Potential Victims

An estimated 22 million Americans, nearly 85% of whom make less than $25,000 a year, do not have bank accounts and turn to check-cashing firms, liquor stores, loan sharks, and other predatory lenders to carry out their financial transactions. Among minority populations, nearly 25% of families have no bank account, making these communities prime targets of predator lenders. About 10% of all American families lack basic banking services.

Subprime Lending

Though a legitimate market for so-called "subprime lending" exists, many companies that specialize in making loans to borrowers whose credit histories prevent them from obtaining credit at a favorable interest rate practice predatory lending. The Federal Trade Commission reports, "As a percentage of all mortgage originations, the subprime market share increased from less than 5% in 1994 to almost 13% in 1999. In 1999 alone, subprime lenders originated over $160 billion in home equity loans, a $35 billion increase from 1997." In 1994, so-called "subprime loans"—those with interest rates 10 points over the prime rate—accounted for 5% of all mortgage loans. In 1999, they accounted for 13%. The value of such loans totaled $15 billion in 1997 and $140 billion in 1999. Undoubtedly, opportunities for predatory lending are up. In 2004, this lending accounted for 12.2% of total loans, marking a minute decrease, but more than doubled in 2005 to account for 28.2% of all loans.

Wall Street investment banks have indirectly subsidized predatory lenders by raising funds for subprime loans. In 1995, $18.5 billion in subprime loans was securitized, a figure that reached $56 billion in 2000. From 1989 to 2000, these banks sold more than $316.2 billion in bonds for subprime lenders.

According to a study by the National Community Reinvestment Coalition, disparities in lending practices are largely based on race. In 2005, 54% of loans made to blacks were subprime, while only 23% of loans made to whites were subprime. This marks a 3% increase for blacks and a 14% increase for whites since 1998. Subprime loans for Hispanics and Native Americans also make up a large percentage of all loans, at 40.7% and 35% respectively. The elderly are frequent targets of predatory home equity lenders, as well because they often have substantial equity but live on fixed or declining incomes. Attorneys for the FTC have suggested, "If a lender targets borrowers for predatory practices based on age, race, and/or sex, such targeting, depending on the facts, also could violate the ECOA [Equal Credit Opportunity Act]."

Methods of Predatory Lenders

Banks establish few branches in low-income neighborhoods, and most do not make small loans, the kind of credit that low-income citizens need. These people turn to predatory lenders who operate by utilizing extortionate interest rates, high fees, refinancing and home equity scams, balloon payments, and other deceptive practices. High-priced loans are pushed on unsuspecting borrowers who do not have the income to meet the mounting payments; usually these cases end with foreclosures, bankruptcy, and deterioration of neighborhoods.

Payday Loans and Rent-to-Own

To obtain payday loans, consumers borrow against their next paycheck, at annual percentage rates ranging up to 500% or more. A two-week loan of $200 costs an average of $36. These loans are offered by check-cashing establishments, which charge a fee for each transaction. U.S. Treasury research indicates that a minimum wage worker can pay an average of $18 per month for cashing paychecks.

Low-income families obtain appliances, television sets, and other products from rent-to-own stores where charges usually amount to two and three times the value of the item. On a $200 television set, a consumer may pay $500 to $600 over the life of a rent-to-own contract.

Check-cashing companies, independent payday lenders, and pawnshops make most payday loans, though some banks have begun moving into the business. The loan amounts range from $200 to $500 each. Borrowers, who usually hold low-paying jobs and have no other borrowing options, hand over a post-dated check or agree to a bank-account debit on their next payday.

Mail Solicitations

Lenders mail checks for specific amounts, such as $1,500.02, particularly to elderly recipients or sweepstakes participants. All the victim has to do is cash the check, which requires signing a legal obligation to repay the loan in monthly installments. A $1,500 loan might require payments of $55.72 for 48 months, for a total repayment of $2,674.56, which translates to an annual interest rate of 31.945%, more than four times the prime rate. Pitch letters often mention the recipient's excellent credit history, and offer up to $100,000 of credit. In a Las Vegas case, the victim had no personal credit history besides a home she had owned with a former husband in the 1960's, and no assets other than her pension and Social Security, but was still pre-approved due to her "excellent credit history."

Home Equity Loans, Title Loans, and Other Asset-Based Loans

Manipulative lenders pressure homeowners into high-interest home equity loans, along with expensive credit insurance and fees that provide little benefit to customers. The terms of these agreements are often obscured or falsified. Older homeowners are often ensnared in predatory loans because they are persuaded to borrow money in home-equity loans for home repairs, health costs, or debt consolidation, according to the American Association of Retired Persons (AARP). With so-called "title loans," the lender takes claim to the borrower's vehicle, boat, or other property in the case of a default. These loans typically charge usurious interest rates and contain strict repayment terms, with steep cash penalties for extending the due date.

Other Practices

- Equity stripping: A relatively large loan is made based on the equity in a property instead of the borrower's ability to repay. When the borrower cannot make the payments, the lender acquires the equity and often acquires the property through foreclosure.
- Flipping: A lender persuades a borrower to refinance a loan repeatedly. Each transaction earns the lender fees while driving the borrower further into debt.
- Home improvement loans: A contractor gains a borrower's consent for a home improvement loan with exorbitant interest rates and fees. A variant: At the end of the demolition phase, the contractor demands that the borrower sign a loan at an even higher interest rate.
- Mandatory arbitration clauses: These agreements, popular with loan makers, waive the borrowers right to a jury trial. An arbitrator of the lenders choosing usually must settle loan disputes.
- Packing: The borrower loads a loan agreement with costly and unnecessary insurance policies. Their cost is added to the loan's principal.

Businesses as Victims

Predatory lenders do not only prey on individuals. In poor neighborhoods, particularly those settled by minorities, predatory lenders finance businesses that are turned away by legitimate institutions. Bodegas, discos, and retail stores borrow tens of thousands of dollars, often at interest rates of 10% per week, though some "preferred customers" negotiate for more favorable rates. According to the *New York Times* the average interest rate in Latino neighborhoods—where the lenders are known as "prestamistas"—is 2% to 5% per week, or 104% to 260% per year.

Predatory Lending by Banks

Some state banks have entered the short-term or payday loan business. Though bound by state-issued usury laws, these institutions skirt regulations by partnering with federally chartered banks, which are exempt from state laws. There is no federal usury law. A state bank initiates the loan, but the federal bank issues the loan and then quickly sells it to the state bank. In 2000, about $14 billion of these loans were issued to about eight million people; the practice was virtually unheard of until the late 1990's. Between 5% and 10% of payday loans in 2000 were made through national banks, according to industry estimates.

The state bank usually buys the loan from the federal bank within a day, and is responsible for collections and 95% of the risk of non-repayment; the state bank also keeps 95% of the loan profits. The federal institution is nothing more than a front for avoiding usury laws.

State banks also avoid laws by invoking a bit of federal law allowing banks to offer interest rates from their home states to other states where they do business. For example, Delaware has no usury laws, so a bank there can sell payday loans to customers in other states using the Internet. As long as the issuing bank stays in compliance with its home state laws, there is no offense, regardless of the laws in the borrower's state.

Responses to Predatory Lending

Many states, including California, Georgia, New Jersey, New Mexico, Arkansas, North Carolina, Connecticut, Illinois, Massachusetts, and New York and a number of cities including Philadelphia have adopted anti-predatory lending laws. Unfortunately, these laws do not necessarily have an effect on the amount of predatory lending. In the majority of states that implemented anti-predatory lending laws, the number of loans remained the same. Some states even experienced an increase in these loans after the laws were passed.

Case Study 1

A man known only as "Tony" told the *New York Times* that his "bank" was worth about $20 million. He claimed to average 8 deals per week, cash only, usually charging 5% a week. His largest loan was $2.5 million to build a supermarket in Washington Heights. Tony and his partners used a legitimate mortgage brokering business as a front. The loans are usually secured by property. In the case of default, loan sharks have no legal claim to the property, but the borrowers usually cooperate for fear of reprisal.

Case Study 2

Associates First Capital, owned by Citigroup, was charged by the Federal Trade Commission in April 2000 with deceiving customers about terms, and tricking them into costly loan refinancing and purchases of expensive "credit insurance" that provided little benefit. The insurance is known as single-premium insurance because the cost is financed as part of the loan instead of month-to-month. Associates' targets were primarily poor and unsophisticated borrowers. A joint report in 1999 by the Treasury Department and Department of Housing and Urban Development called single-premium credit insurance "unfair, abusive, and deceptive."

Over five years, Associates earned over $800 million in premiums from single-premium credit insurance while paying out less than $300 million in benefits, leaving more than $500 million as profit. Employees sold the policy as "total payment protection" and were trained to quote the monthly payment with the insurance included automatically. According to the FTC complaint "the Associates employees told the customer that changing the amount of the loan to eliminate these products would require rescheduling the closing, knowing this posed a great hardship for the customer."

Associates sold loans with high fees and other charges, telling customers that they would save money with the package. The company was also cited for harassing customers and disclosing customers' debts to others without permission. Many customers were homeowners who lost equity in their houses, or lost the houses, due to the high fees, points, and credit insurance packed into their loans.

Proposed laws against the practice have been opposed by the banking industry as being too vague and invasive. Most legislation is based on a Philadelphia law, passed in 2001, that calls for fines on lenders who use deception to charge inflated interest rates and fees to low-income borrowers, requires counseling for people obtaining sub-prime home loans, and bars high-cost loans with monthly payments exceeding half of the borrower's income.

Sworn Confession of a Predatory Lender

Critics this spring seized on a smoking gun: the sworn affidavit of Gail Kubiniec, a former assistant branch manager for CitiFinancial Credit Co., a unit of Citigroup Inc. of

Manhattan, the largest U.S. financial institution. Kubiniec, 35, said her Buffalo, N.Y., unit of CitiFinancial routinely pressed unsophisticated high-risk borrowers to refinance into costly new loans, dunned them at home if their payments were late, and saddled them with unnecessary life, loan, and disability insurance.

"If someone appeared uneducated, inarticulate, was a minority or was particularly old or young, I would try to include all the [insurance] coverage's offered," wrote Kubiniec. "The more gullible the consumer appeared, the more coverage's I would try to include."

Citigroup Inc. denied Kubiniec's allegations, contained in a pending federal suit charging CitiFinancial with abusive and unethical lending practices. CitiFinancial announced in late June, however, that it would stop selling the costly and unnecessary loan insurance Kubiniec described.

Sources:
Beckett, P. "Exploiting a Loophole, Banks Skirt State Laws on High Interest Rates." *The Wall Street Journal,* May 25, 2001.

Filkins, D. "In Some Immigrant Enclaves, Loan Shark is the Local Bank." *The New York Times,* April 23, 2001.

"Gary Gensler, Undersecretary Treasury Department on House Banking." *Federal News Service,* June 27, 2000.

Henriques, D., and Bergman, L. "Mortgaged Lives." *The New York Times,* March 15, 2000.

Nader, R. "Payday Loans, Rent-to-Own, and Other Schemes Target the Poor." *San Francisco Bay Guardian,* December 18, 2000.

Oppel, R. "U.S. Suit Cites Citigroup Unit On Loan Deceit." *The New York Times,* March 7, 2001.

"Predatory Lending Practices in the Home-Equity Lending Market." *Federal Trade Commission before the Federal Reserve,* September 7, 2000. www.ftc.gov/os/2000/09/predatorylending.htm.

Pugh, T. "Predatory Lending—The Hunter Becomes the Hunted." *The Orlando Sentinel,* July 15, 2001.

Twohig, P. "Curbing Predatory Home Mortgage Lending." *Housing and Urban Development,* June 2000.

Wisenberg, D. "Predatory Loan Bill Now Philly Law." *Wall Street Journal,* April 23, 2001.

Related Entries:

CONSUMER FRAUD

FINANCIAL INSTITUTION FRAUD

LOAN FRAUD

PREDATORY PRICING

A firm engaging in predatory pricing lowers its price below the average cost of its competitors. The competitors must then lower their prices below average cost, losing money on each unit sold. If they fail to cut their prices, they will lose market share; if they do cut their prices, they will eventually go bankrupt. After the competition has been forced out of the market, the predatory firm raises its price, compensating itself for the money it lost to predatory pricing.

Corporations sometimes use predatory pricing to describe unethical pricing strategies. In one report, the consumer watchdog organization, Citizen Action, charged that a telecommunications company had engaged in predatory economics by the following actions:

- Deregulating prices/raising local rates
- Blocking interconnection agreements
- Slowing or blocking network access
- Opposing regulatory guidelines
- Maintaining high access charges
- Omitting yellow pages revenues from rate calculations

Source:
Krebs, J. "U.S. West's Monopoly Game: A Consumer Report." *Washington Citizen Action,* May 28, 1997.

Related Entries:

ANTITRUST
CORPORATE CRIME

PRETEXTING

According to the Federal Trade Commission (FTC), pretexting is the practice of obtaining personal information under false pretenses. It is the act of creating a scenario wherein the actor pretends to be another to solicit private information about someone from the holder of such information. The actor essentially establishes a rapport with the holder of information by inferring that he/she is the person whose information is being sought.

Hewlett-Packard

Media drives legislation. At least this appears to be the case with federal antifraud statutes, as seen from the fall of Enron and the subsequent passage of the Sarbanes-Oxley Act, as well as the pandemonium within Hewlett-Packard (HP) and the related passage of the Telephone Records and Privacy Protection Act. In light of the current scandalous environment brought to light by HP's board of directors, this article will focus on what pretexting is, review legislation and a case-in-point, as well as discuss whether it is permissible to use the ominous method to obtain information in fraud investigations.

On September 5, 2006, Newsweek unleashed the fall-from-grace story that seemingly started out as an ordinary attempt by former HP Board Chair, Patricia Dunn, to seek further information about an insider leak of confidential information about the company's long-term strategy. In January of the same year, without informing the rest of the board, Dunn authorized a group of electronic-security investigators to secretly look for records of private phone communications of the other directors (private phone communications being personal cell phone and home phone calls). Five months after Dunn organized and authorized this activity, she surprised the rest of the board with the methods used as well as the director who leaked the information. Soon after the Newsweek article was published, the United States House Committee on Energy and Commerce requested a laundry-list of information regarding the leak investigation, referred to by Dunn and HP as the "Kona 2 investigation" (Kona 2).

In October 2006, California Attorney General Locklear filed charges against five individuals involved in Kona 2, including Patricia Dunn; former HP senior counsel, Kevin Hunsker; and private investigators Ronald DeLia, Matthew Depante, and Bryan Wagner. The five are charged with (1) conspiracy; (2) fraudulent use of wire, radio, or television transmissions; (3) taking, copying, and using computer data; and (4) using personal identifying information without authorization. On December 7, 2006, HP settled state civil charges brought against the company for more than $13.5 million.

At the time of publication, only one individual involved in Kona 2 has been federally charged.

On January 11, 2007, Bryan Wagner pleaded guilty to identity theft and conspiracy in federal court, after admitting that he engaged in pretexting and illegally acquired social security numbers and phone records of two former HP board members and a couple of journalists. However, the federal investigation into Kona 2 is ongoing. It is not implausible that federal prosecutors will use Wagner's plea and assistance in the case to gather additional evidence before charging other persons involved in Kona 2.

Legislation

On January 12, 2007, President Bush signed into law the Telephone Records and Privacy Protection Act (Act), which makes it an offense to obtain confidential phone records information by pretending to be someone else, or by otherwise employing fraudulent tactics from a telecommunications carrier or IP-enabled voice service provider via interstate or foreign commerce. Specifically, the Act imposes a fine and/or imprisonment of up to 10 years upon individuals for "(1) making false or fraudulent statements to an employee of a covered entity or to a customer of a covered entity; (2) providing false or fraudulent documents to a covered entity; or (3) accessing customer accounts of a covered entity through the Internet or by fraudulent computer-related activities without prior authorization."

The following pieces of legislation have traditionally shaped the rules concerning pretexting, the Gramm-Leach-Bliley Act (GLB), the Fair Credit Reporting Act (FCRA) the Fair Debt Collection Practices Act (FDCPA), and the Computer Fraud and Abuse Act (CFAA). It is important to note that this list is not all-inclusive, but rather merely an example of the prominent pieces of legislation affecting pretexting.

- **Fair Credit Reporting Act.** Enacted in 1968, the FCRA sets forth guidelines to protect the privacy of consumers' private financial information. Generally, the FCRA regulates the acquisition, distribution, and use of consumer credit information. However, Section 619 of the FCRA specifically prohibits individuals from knowingly and willfully obtaining information of a consumer from a consumer-reporting agency under false pretenses.

- **Fair Debt Collection Practices Act.** Also enacted in 1968 was the FDCPA, which attempts to further alleviate fraudulent activity in collecting consumer debts. The FDCPA prohibits debt collectors from using false or deceptive methods in obtaining consumer debt information, and collecting, or attempting to collect any debt. Although further removed from the scheme of pretexting, it may conjoin with the FCRA in suits involving pretexting.
- **Computer Fraud and Abuse Act.** Enacted in 1984, the CFAA was designed to lessen the frequency of computer hacking. Particularly, the CFAA prohibits one from knowingly accessing a computer without authorization, or by exceeding his/her authorization, and subsequently gaining access to: (1) information in a financial institution's financial record; (2) a consumer reporting agency's file on a consumer; and (3) information from any "protected computer."
- **Gramm-Leach-Bliley Act.** Enacted in 1999, the GLB strictly prohibits the use of false or fraudulent statements or documents, as well as lost or stolen documents, to gather customer information from a financial institution or directly from the customer. The prohibition is upon individuals who directly contact the financial institution or customer, as well as individuals whom direct another to undertake such activity.

The FTC has traditionally focused on enforcing actions against individuals who falsely represent themselves as customers to gain access to financial information about the customers. Since impersonators are now prohibited from obtaining more than just financial information (i.e., obtaining phone records of individuals by false pretenses is also now illegal), it is important to distinguish the new Act enacted in 2007, from the GLB and other notable statutes. It is also important to keep in mind that most states have adopted state laws to protect individuals from becoming victims of pretexting, among other illegal practices. For example, in September 2006, California passed a law prohibiting individuals from procuring, obtaining, or attempting to procure or obtain, telephone calling pattern records or lists, via fraud or deceit. Therefore, fraud examiners must make sure they understand applicable federal and state laws pertaining to pretexting before beginning an investigation.

Obtaining Information

Sought-after information is often owned by, and in the control of, the individual or entity requesting an investigation. For example, an employer believes an employee has been stealing money from the employer via a lapping scheme. The employer received information that the employee has recently purchased extravagant items that would be unusually expensive for an individual with her salary. The employer believes that the employee might have critical documentation regarding her recent purchases as well as financial documentation relating to the scheme in her desk drawer at the office.

In this case, the fraud examiner is probably able to obtain the documents without running into an invasion of privacy problem. However, where information or documents are in the control of other parties or in uncontrolled locations, legal action is almost certainly required before the fraud examiner can attempt to obtain the evidence. Under no circumstances should the fraud examiner attempt to gain access by alternative means, be it pretexting, theft, or trespass.

Undoubtedly, financial records are the most valuable source of information available to fraud examiners. However, as statutes show, financial records are usually the most difficult type of records to obtain. Often, subpoenas and search warrants are required to access such information. Fraud examiners should understand that bank officials and employees can be questioned and deposed just as potential witnesses can. Legal advice in obtaining financial records should always be sought.

Fraud examiners must be very cognizant of the new federal Telephone Records and Privacy Protection Act as well. It is illegal to obtain confidential phone records information from a telephone carrier under false pretenses. To reiterate, this means one may not obtain telephone records by making false or fraudulent statements or representations of any kind.

Obtaining information contained in public records without revealing your identity as a fraud examiner is generally permissible. Public record information refers to information developed about the public or information open to the public. In seeking public information, the fraud examiner must be aware of, and understand the guidelines of the Freedom of Information Act (FOIA). Most states have adopted similar versions of the FOIA to cover state and local jurisdictions.

Specifically, the FOIA regulates the: (1) type of records that a governmental agency may maintain about a person; (2) conditions under which such information may be disclosed to another government agency; and (3) the circumstances and methods under which an individual may obtain copies of agency records that pertain to that individual. Government records about individuals are generally prohibited from release to another without consent of the individual. Obtaining such information without consent constitutes a claim of invasion of privacy. The FOIA provides for public access to the following information: (1) tax rolls; (2) voter registration; (3) assumed names; (4) real property records; and (5) divorce and probate suits. The following records not deemed public: (1) bank records; (2) trust records; (3) telephone records; (4) passenger lists; and (5) stock ownership.

PREVENTION POLICIES FOR FRAUD

Fraud prevention efforts not only save an organization money, they can prevent the organization from being sanctioned if fraud is discovered. An effective general fraud prevention policy should include the following:

- Analytical review of suspicious increases in expenses, cost of sales, receivables/decreasing cash, inventories, sales/decreasing cash, returns and allowances, and sales discounts.
- Fraud assessment questioning, a non-accusatory interview technique used as a part of a normal audit. The strategy assumes that employees' attitudes are a good indicator of potential problems, and that one of the most effective ways to deal with fraud is to ask about it.
- Enforcement of mandatory vacations.
- Job rotation. Some frauds are detected during sickness or unexpected absences of the perpetrator because they require continuous, manual intervention.
- Surprise audits where possible.
- Management oversight.
- Increasing the perception of detection by educating managers, executives, and employees about fraud, minimizing employee pressures, and monitoring systems.

- Ethics programs that educate employees about ethical principles and their value, and that emphasize the cost of fraud and abuse to the company.
- Reporting Programs. Each employee in the company should know where to report suspicious, unethical, or illegal behavior. Methods include anonymous surveys, drop-off boxes, hotlines, and rewards.
- Disciplinary Action, which may range from a reprimand and probation to a demotion or criminal charges.

PROVIDER FRAUD

Provider fraud is perpetrated by a medical practitioner, medical supplier, or medical facility on patients or customers in order to increase their income by illicit means. The National Health Care Anti-Fraud Association reported that in 2005, at least 3% to 10%, or $51 billion to $170 billion, was lost to fraud nationwide in the health care industry. Providers commit most health care fraud, about 80% by most estimates. This does not mean that providers are more venal than others. But they have access to sophisticated equipment and possess greater knowledge of medical techniques, procedures, and terminology, than others.

Though patients are sometimes aware of fraud and abuse by providers, they are often reluctant to accuse caretakers of wrongdoing since they rely on continued services. In some cases, patients receive discounts from fraudulent providers, usually by an improper waiving of the patient's insurance deductible.

Any health care provider—including anesthesiologists, dentists, podiatrists, ophthalmologists, and allergists—can commit fraud. Typically these providers waive co-payments, bill for unnecessary services, overstate services, or bill for services not performed. Other violations include altering dates of service or some other aspect of the patient's eligibility. Certain types of providers tend to commit fraud more often, and are treated in their own entries.

General provider frauds include:

- Billing for services not provided

- Billing of "free" services
- Incorrect reporting of diagnoses or procedures to maximize payments
- Waiver of deductible and/or co-payment (unbundling, up-coding)
- Overutilization of services
- Kickbacks and bribery
- Misrepresentation of dates or descriptions of services
- Billing non-covered services as covered items
- Eligible provider billing for services provided by ineligible provider

The Range of Providers

The following chart illustrates the range of medical providers, all of whom have opportunity to commit fraud.

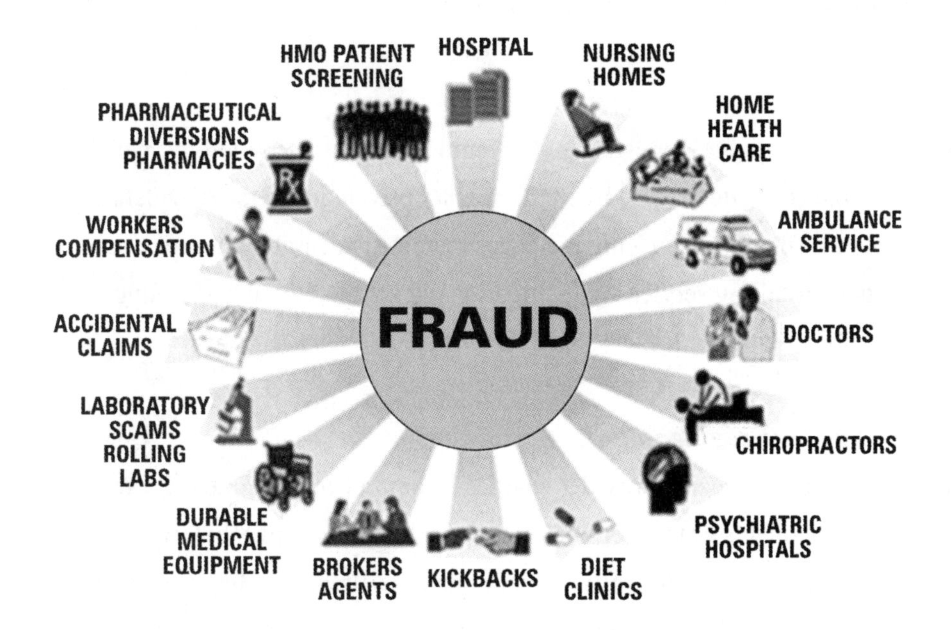

Source: Blue Cross Blue Shield

Provider Fraud Schemes

False Diagnoses

To obtain payment for uncovered services, physicians disguise the treatment. Common services not covered are:

- Annual physical examination
- School physicals
- Weight loss programs
- Stop smoking programs
- Investigational or experimental procedures
- Cosmetic surgery

Adding Services

Adding services never rendered to dates of actual services.

Code Gaming

Services are identified using the Physicians' Current Procedural Terminology, which is supplemented by the codes developed by Medicare and private insurers. Providers and insurers often have difficulty identifying the codes that most accurately describe services provided. Providers or billing services may intentionally submit claims containing inappropriate combinations of codes.

Unbundling Charges/Fragmentation

Simple unbundling occurs when a provider charges a comprehensive code for a service, but also charges components of that service separately. In the examples below, the provider is overpaid because the fee for the total procedure already includes the value of its component parts. Unbundling can be detected through the use of a computer program that determines whether each code submitted is a component of one or more comprehensive codes.

Procedure Code	Service Billed	Correctly Billed Procedure
58150 58720 49000 44955 58740	Total Hysterectomy ($1300) Removal of ovaries & tubes ($950) Exploration of abdomen ($671) Appendectomy ($250) Lysis of Adhesions ($5500) **Total Charge $3721**	Total Hysterectomy 58150 **Total Payment $1300**
29877 29870	Knee arthroscopy with debridement ($1650) Diagnostic knee arthroscopy ($1625) **Total Charge $3275**	Knee arthroscopy with debridement 29877 **Total Payment $1650**
47610 47600	Cholecystectomy with common bile duct exploration ($1997) Cholecystectomy ($705) **Total Charge $2702**	Cholecystectomy with common bile duct exploration 47610 **Total Payment $1997**

Global Service Period Violations

Billing for a major procedure such as surgery as well as related procedures, when the fee for the major procedure already includes the fee for related procedures during the predefined time period (the global service period). This type of fraud is possible because most surgery includes all related services for a set number of days before and after the surgery. Detection is made more difficult by the fact that services may be rendered by more than one provider.

Upcoding

Billing for a higher level of service than was rendered. A common form of upcoding occurs in pharmacy fraud when the pharmacist fills a prescription with a generic drug, but bills for the more expensive branded version.

Misuse of "New Patient" Codes

Billing established patients with new patient codes.

Provider-Perpetrated Pharmacy Fraud

Providers or provider staff causes drugs to be dispensed to phony patients, then sell or use the drugs themselves.

Red Flags of Provider Fraud

- Pressure for rapid adjudication of claims, such as same-day claim payment and special handling.
- Threats of legal action for delay in making payments.
- Frequent telephone inquiries on claim status.
- Charges submitted for payment with no supporting documentation available (X-rays, lab results).
- Individual provider using P.O. Box as return addresses.
- Insured's address on claim form is the same as provider.
- Routine (not specialized) treatment for patients living more than 150 miles from the provider.
- Referring physician and provider of service in the same professional corporation.
- Medical records have been altered.
- Medical records have additional information attached that can make an apparent non-covered service now covered.
- Missing pages of medical records during the period of time under review.

Detecting and Investigating Provider Fraud

- Most tips come from "external sources," mainly subscribers.
- Most insurers send out an "Explanation of Benefits" form to all subscribers and expressly invite inquiries about fraud. Subscribers are sent brochures that describe anti-fraud activities and provide contact information.
- Computer analysis of records can be used to examine physician practice patterns and to review utilization. Two different providers may claim to have treated the same patient on the same day, for example—which can be detected by an automated review that flags any patient account with more than two providers for the same condition.

- Excessive billings report may show that a provider is submitting large amounts of expenses.
- The membership/enrollment file should be compared periodically to the Social Security file to determine payments made on behalf of insured individuals who are deceased. The membership file also may be compared to the file from the vital statistics department to search for divorced policyholders who improperly continue coverage.

Investigation Tips

If a company is suspected of dealing with a fabricated provider:

- Call the telephone number on the bill to determine if the provider exists. (A fictitious provider may actually have rented a location and established a telephone number.)
- Contact the licensing board or province to determine if the alleged provider is licensed to practice in the area at the time the service was allegedly provided.
- Check the Social Security Number or tax identification number listed on the provider bill with the licensing board.
- Visit the alleged provider's address to determine if it is a valid address. (Speak to the superintendent to determine who lives at that address.)
- Contact a postal inspector to verify what mail is being dropped at that address.

Related Entries:

CHIROPRACTIC FRAUD
HEALTH CARE FRAUD
HOME HEALTH FRAUD
HOSPITALS, INSURANCE FRAUD BY
LABORATORY FRAUD,
NURSING HOME FRAUD
PHARMACY FRAUD
PSYCHIATRISTS AND PSYCHIATRIC FACILITIES, FRAUD BY
SUPPLIER FRAUD,
WORKERS' COMPENSATION FRAUD

PSYCHIATRISTS AND PSYCHIATRIC FACILITIES, FRAUD BY

Financial fraud in psychiatry is committed by providers and facilities that falsify diagnoses or treatments. No firm numbers exist for losses to fraud in psychiatry.

Congressional Hearings on Fraud in Psychiatry, 1992

A large number of reports of fraud in the psychiatric field during the late 1980's prompted Congressional hearings in 1992. In a report to the House Select Committee, David Baine of the U.S. General Accounting Office listed the following difficulties in evaluating government spending on mental health care:

- The subjective and variable nature of mental-health disorders.
- Differences in the intensity and duration of treatments, and the overall level of care, dispensed by various doctors and facilities.
- The lack of generally accepted mental-health standards.
- The lack of statistical information about the results produced by particular treatments.

Chairing those hearings, Representative Patricia Schroeder of Colorado summarized the committee's findings: "Our investigation has found that thousands of adolescents, children, and adults have been hospitalized for psychiatric treatment they didn't need; that hospitals hire bounty hunters to kidnap patients with mental health insurance; that patients are kept against their will until their insurance benefits run out; that psychiatrists are being pressured by the hospitals to increase profit; that hospitals 'infiltrate' schools by paying kickbacks to school counselors who deliver students; that bonuses are paid to hospital employees, including psychiatrists, for keeping the hospital beds filled; and that military dependents are being targeted for their generous mental health benefits."

Reform and Managed Care Decrease Fraud

Reforms in regulation and the emergence of managed care helped stem the fraud in this area. From 1990 to 1997, the average private hospital stay for psychiatric treatment dropped from 26 days nationwide to less than 10 days. A study by the National Hospital Discharge Survey in 2004 concluded that the average hospital stay was 7.1 days. A third of the for-profit psychiatric hospitals in the nation and half of the ones in Texas closed during this period. Managed care proponents assert that the drop reflects a concomitant decrease in fraud. Critics of managed care say these numbers do reflect a decrease in fraud, but also indicate managed care administrators are overzealously reducing treatment.

The issue has not gone away. In 2000, Dr. Edward Drummond, author of *The Complete Guide to Psychiatric Drugs*, wrote, "Many adolescents are irritable, aggressive, and impulsive because they are upset about their life circumstances. In recent years some of these teenagers have found their way into psychiatric hospitals, labeled with the diagnosis of bipolar disorder and placed on medications. Some psychiatric hospitals made a practice of admitting adolescents in distress, using the diagnosis of bipolar disorder inappropriately in order to increase their billing to insurance companies. This practice was so widespread that the federal government finally intervened, charging the hospitals with fraud and assessing fines of millions of dollars. Many of these children did not have bipolar disorder at all, but were acting inappropriately because of stresses in their families, with their friends, and at school."

Psychiatrists and Psychiatric Facilities

Abuses include:

- Billing for services never rendered and non-covered services such as weight loss services and biofeedback.
- Billing for services under psychiatrists name when service actually performed by a non-covered but licensed provider, e.g., drug counselor, or minister.
- Billing for services performed by an unlicensed employee.
- Admitting patients with false diagnoses.

Psychiatric Hospital Fraud

During the past decades, health care benefits have expanded to cover treatments for substance abuse, alcoholism, and mental depression. Generally, health insurance allows for coverage of inpatient treatment up to 28 days, enabling hospitals to collect up to $40,000 per patient.

Abuses include inpatient hospitalization when outpatient treatment would be more appropriate. Forcible admission of people who pose no threat to the community or themselves, batteries of blood tests, X-rays, shock treatment, and other services. One such treatment is known as "wave" therapy. The doctor "waves" his or her hand during routine rounds, then submits bills to the government program or insurance companies for $125 in individual therapy.

Abuse in the Admissions Process

Some psychiatric treatment facilities have developed programs for patients who exhibit symptoms of both psychiatric illness and substance abuse problems. Fraud occurs when a patient is admitted on the basis of a diagnosis which reflects the patient's insurance coverage rather than the patient's illness. Psychiatric hospitals have been accused of finding something wrong with a patient when it is discovered that he or she has insurance coverage. A physician or psychiatrist may often admit these patients without an examination.

Fraud in the Treatment Process

The following types of abuses can occur with regard to psychiatric treatment:

- Extending the length of treatment programs or delaying discharges because patients have additional insurance benefits remaining.
- Illegitimate treatment programs and forms of therapy: "fat farms," biorhythm, art therapy, music therapy, and group therapy at ballparks or shopping malls.
- Engaging in excessive treatment of psychiatric patients such as thyroid testing, drug tests, or psychiatric evaluation tests.

Abusive Marketing Practices

Many hospitals rely on marketing as a means of encouraging treatment and generating referrals. Overly aggressive marketing methods include paying bonuses to employees to persuade or pressure prospective patients to undergo a psychiatric evaluation and to admit themselves for treatment; encouraging patients to admit themselves by offering financial incentives such as payment of plane fare, child care, COBRA payments, and waivers of patient co-payments or deductibles.

Financial Rewards for Referrals

Many facilities are dependent on outside sources of patient referrals such as physicians or other clinicians. This dependence has led some hospitals to develop economic relationships in order to obtain referrals:

- Rewarding clinicians who refer patients by referring patients who need outpatient treatment to those clinicians.
- Allowing allied health professionals who refer patients to provide therapy for their own patients at the hospital, while non-referring allied professionals are not allowed to use the hospital.
- Paying medical directors or other physicians an incentive bonus linked to the overall profitability of the hospital.
- Paying a physician who is under contract to the hospital but who provides no services.

Red Flags for Psychiatric and Substance Abuse Claims

- Treatment takes place far from patient's home.
- Diagnosis becomes alcoholism when state mandate reimburses alcoholism like any other illness.
- Patient is on disability.
- Provider's credentials are questionable.
- Documentation of treatment is lacking.
- Ancillary services are not treatment oriented.

Sources:
Drummond, M.D., E. *The Complete Guide to Psychiatric Drugs.* New York: John Wiley & Sons, Inc., 2000.

Oliver, M. "Industry Seems to Invite Fraud." *The Orlando Sentinel,* November 21, 1994.

Payer, L. Disease-Mongers: Doctors, Drug Companies, and Insurers Are Making You Feel Sick. New York: John Wiley & Sons, Inc., 1992

Smith, M. "Mental Health Managed Care Brings Concerns; Financial Limits Blamed for Shorter In-Patient Stays." *The Houston Chronicle,* March 23, 1997.

Related Entries:

HEALTH CARE FRAUD

PROVIDER FRAUD

PYRAMID SCHEME

See, PONZI SCHEME

QUACK

A quack is someone who practices medicine without a license, uses unconventional methods and treatments, and whose treatment is not effective.

The quack is mentioned in texts from ancient Babylon—the type's shifty practices were specifically prohibited in the Hammurabi Code. Since then, countless sham doctors and fake healers have exploited sick people, hypochondriacs, and those merely trying to buy back lost youth or elusive beauty, with all manner of dubious theories, worthless devices, and dangerous practices. No civilization has been immune to the charlatan's appeal; even the French enlightenment, the great 18th century burst of rationalism and agnosticism, served as a playground for "Count" Cagliostro and the Comte de St. Germain, gloriously phony "doctors" who fooled the educated upper classes with their miracle cures and absurd practices.

America has been particularly susceptible to medical tricksters of all sorts. Every so often, when Americans think they have seen the last phony cancer cure or the final Electro-Magnetic miracle gadget, along comes a brand-new variation on the ancient games, peddled by another glib-tongued swindler looking to turn human misery, fear, and gullibility into a personal fortune.

Related Entries:

CONSUMER FRAUD

HEALTH CARE FRAUD

QUESTIONED DOCUMENTS

See, COUNTERFEIT DOCUMENTS

QWEST COMMUNICATIONS INTERNATIONAL INC.

One of the largest telecommunications company in the US, Qwest Communication was charged by the SEC in October 2004 with securities fraud and other violations of federal securities laws. According to an SEC report, the Commission's complaint alleges that, between 1999 and 2002, Qwest fraudulently recognized over $3.8 billion in revenue and excluded $231 million in expenses as part of a multi-faceted fraudulent scheme to meet optimistic and unsupportable revenue and earnings projections. Without admitting or denying the allegations in the complaint, Qwest consented to entry of a judgment enjoining it from violating the antifraud, reporting, books and records, internal control, proxy, and securities registration provisions of the federal securities laws.

In December 2005, former Qwest CEO Joseph Nacchio was indicted on 42 federal charges of insider trading. He was accused of illegally selling $101 million in stock. Former CEO, Robin Szeliga, pled guilty to insider trading and agreed to cooperate with federal investigators in order to reach a plea bargain. Executive Marc B. Weisberg pled guilty to charges of wire fraud and was sentenced to 60 days of home detention on top of being fined $250,000 for his role in the Qwest fraud. Qwest has agreed to pay $250 million to settle SEC charges of fraud in a deal that did not include individuals.

Source:
www.sec.gov/news/press/2004-148.htm

REAL ESTATE FRAUD

Real estate fraud is committed by making false representations in the course of trading real estate. Fraudulent appraisals, bogus mortgage-backed securities, equity skimming, land flips, nominee loans, and mortgage pulling are some of the methods. As reported by the Internal Revenue Service (IRS) in 2003, the booming real estate industry has led to an increase in the number of real estate fraud investigations. The number of investigations initiated by IRS doubled from 107 in 2001 to 215 by September 2003. In 2004, the statistics reflected a three year high of the number of cases recommended for prosecution as well as indicted, convicted and incarcerated.

In addition, the IRS has more than 4,000 returns under audit involving individuals and entities associated with the real-estate business.

Source: www.irs.gov/newsroom/article/0,,id=118224,00.html

Real Estate Fraud Schemes

Appraisal Fraud

Appraisers, licensed by the federal government, perform independent property valuation. Professional associations for appraisers include the Appraisal Institute, which issues the MAI designation, the American Society of Appraisers, and the National Association of Real Estate Appraisers.

Appraisers use several different kinds of reports. The *letterform* report is used when a client is familiar with the area and supporting data, therefore, is not necessary. The report consists of a brief description of the property, the type of value sought, the purpose served by the appraisal, the date of value, the value conclusion, and the signature of the appraiser. Financial institutions generally do not use this form for credit decisions.

Financial institutions use the short form usually for residential real estate loans. The report varies from one to four pages and consists of check sheets or spaces to be filled in by the appraiser about pertinent property data.

The *narrative form* includes all pertinent information about the area and the subject property as well as the rationale for the estimated value. It includes maps, photographs, charts, and plot plans. Financial institutions use narrative reports to support real estate lending and investment decisions on large commercial real estate transactions. Any other type of appraisal report (i.e., letter form or short form) on these complex transactions would likely be considered inadequate.

Determining "Value"

Value is comprised of four elements: utility, scarcity, demand, and transferability. Real estate appraisals assign three types of values to property. *Fair market value* is an estimate of the price the property would bring if freely offered on the open market with both a willing seller and a willing buyer. The *sales price* is the price actually paid for the property. *Loan value* is the percentage of a property's value (fair market value or sales price) a lender can or might loan a borrower.

Fraudulent Appraisals

Fraudulent appraisals may result from:

- Intentional use of an incompetent appraiser.
- "Stacking the deck" by giving the appraiser improper or false assumptions to use in arriving at the value such as:
  - Assume zoning will be changed for a higher and better use when in fact zoning will not be changed.
  - Assume unrealistically high vacancy and low expense rates.
  - Assume unrealistically high income, selling prices, or absorption—the rate at which vacant space will become rented.
  - Otherwise influencing the appraiser, e.g., paying above-market fee or promising future business.
  - Direct collusion with the appraiser to commit fraud.

USES FOR FRAUDULENT APPRAISALS

- To obtain approval on marginal or substandard loans to attain or exceed goals in order to be promoted or receive commission, bonus, or raises.
- To justify extending or renewing a "bad" loan to avoid recognition of a loss that might defer commission, promotion, bonus, or raises.
- To avoid adverse publicity and regulatory, management, and shareholder disapproval because of excessive losses.
- To avoid recognition of a loss on real estate owned, and to permit additional capital infusions.
- To gain funds for other uses.

OREO and Fraudulent Appraisals

National banks are subject to federal regulation regarding real estate holdings (OREO, or "other real estate owned") not being held as collateral. Real estate acquired as the result of foreclosure or the taking of a deed in lieu of foreclosure on defaulted loans is subject to OREO regulations. Among other things, the regulations require that the carrying value of OREO must be the lower of the loan balance or the current appraised value. In addition, monies spent to complete an OREO project cannot be capitalized and must be expensed if such expenditures are not supported by appraised value. A fraudulent appraisal may be used to avoid writing down the value of OREO or to support capitalizing additional expenditures.

Mortgage-Backed Securities

A mortgage-backed security is issued by a financial intermediary, usually a mortgage banker, commercial bank, or savings and loan association, and collateralized by mortgage pools. Collateral pools are typically composed of government-guaranteed mortgages or mortgages guaranteed by the issuing intermediary.

The issuer is responsible for acquiring and servicing the mortgages and marketing the securities. Security holders receive a "pass-through" of the principal and interest payments on the entire pool, less the amount to cover the cost of servicing and fees. The most common fraud schemes involve fraudulent representations or disbursement of mortgage pools.

Equity Skimming

An individual, entity, or group purchases single-family homes. Typically, the financing is for a percentage of the purchase price (e.g., 80% – 90%) and the owner puts up the balance. The home is then rented. The owners collect rent from tenants but do not make the mortgage payment. The owner may later resume payments or allow the mortgage to be foreclosed.

Although the mortgage eventually might be foreclosed, the owners have recouped their original investment plus any rental payments not applied to the mortgage. In addition, the owners received state and federal tax benefits during the holding period.

This scheme is most successful with non-recourse mortgages. Although equity skimming eventually collapses and the purchasers risk being sued for deficiencies (if the loans were recourse), the scheme continues to be practiced. It has become an increasing problem as many residential homes are auctioned and bulk purchases are encouraged.

Land Flips

Land flips occur by buying and selling real estate quickly, often several times a day or within a few months of purchase, increasing the sale price each time. The sales are often transacted between related parties or among several shell corporations. Land flips may be used to generate fraudulent earnings, fraudulent assets, or to support higher comparable prices for other appraisals. Almost every land flip involves collusion between the customer and the appraiser, with the lender or investor the victim. This scheme also has been perpetrated between lending institutions to avoid loan loss reserve increases, in which case the succession of deals is sometimes called a "Daisy Chain."

Nominee or Strawman Loans

Loans made in the name of a straw borrower or agent having no substance, while the identity of the real borrower is left undisclosed to the lender.

Mortgage Pulling

For the purpose of disguising loans exceeding a bank's legal loan limits, loans are made to a partnership's members who by prearrangement then invest in a single risky venture in a total amount exceeding the lending limit. In reality, the single borrower is the partnership, and the collateral is the partnership's property. Mortgage pulling might involve fraudulent loan applications and payoffs to the individual partners for participating.

Red Flags of "Made-as-Instructed" Appraisals

- The appraiser used has never been used before, is not on an approved list, and has no professional credentials or those offered are of questionable credibility.
- Appraisal fee is unusually high.
- Invalid comparables are used.
- Supporting information is missing, insufficient, or contradictory.
- Market data does not support the price and absorption figures used to arrive at value.

Detecting Fraudulent Appraisals

The following may indicate unrealistic or bogus appraisals:

- The appraisal does not match documents on file, such as leases, comparables, absorption rates, residual values, capitalization rate, or legal description.
- Signs of insufficient demand for the project to assure absorption of the property into the marketplace.
- The absence of competitive advantage over other projects.
- Indications the project may not be sensitive to changes in local economic conditions.

Related Entries:

LOAN FRAUD

MORTGAGE FRAUD

REGISTER DISBURSEMENTS

Register disbursements are methods of causing fraudulent disbursements, which is a form of asset misappropriation. Like cash larceny, these schemes target a company's cash flow—but instead of taking incoming cash from receipts or deposits, the perpetrator takes outgoing funds. These acts can be committed by anyone who exchanges funds with customers. Some disbursements are made directly to the employee or the employee's account, while others require an accomplice, who splits the proceeds with the dishonest employee.

There are two basic fraudulent disbursement schemes which take place at the cash register: false refunds and false voids.

False Refunds

Refund monies can be obtained by creating a fictitious refund (e.g., a $50 return for a video game that was never sold), or by overstating the amount of a legitimate refund (e.g., a $100 refund for a $50 video game). Credit cards make good tools for refund schemes because no cash exchanges hands—the funds are disbursed electronically to a credit card account in either the employee's or an accomplice's name.

False Voids

In another strategy, the perpetrator rings up a sale correctly, then voids the sale as if it never took place, pocketing the funds. This method is successful only if employees make their voids without approval, forge a manager's approval, or if a manager conspires with the employee.

Fraudulent register disbursements cause shrinkage in inventory, since the item in question is not returned to inventory, or is returned at an amount greater than its true value. Inventory shrinkage is common, but high numbers or spikes in numbers suggest fraud.

Perpetrators conceal shrinkage by falsifying the physical counts of inventory, or by disbursing small amounts that do not exceed control levels set by management for closer review. Most perpetrators destroy all records of the transaction.

Detection and Prevention of Register Schemes

Fictitious Refunds or Voided Sales

The refunds or discounts given by each cashier or salesperson—a single employee or group of employees may disburse refunds more often or in greater amounts than normal.

Store owners should post signs in the register area asking customers to request and examine their receipts. This requires a proper accounting for each sale and prevents employees from using discarded customer receipts for fraudulent purposes.

Make random service calls to customers who have returned merchandise or voided sales, verifying the legitimacy of transactions.

Analysis of Decreases in Gross Sales and/or Increases in Returns and Allowances

Analyzing the relationship between sales, cost of sales, and returns and allowances can detect inappropriate refunds and discounts. An analysis of refunds, returns, and allowances with the actual flow of inventory reveals some fraud schemes. The refund should cause an entry to inventory, even if it is damaged inventory. Likewise, a return will cause a corresponding entry to an inventory account. There should be a linear relationship between sales, returns, and allowances over a relevant range. Any change in this relationship should require a verifiable explanation, such as a change in the manufacturing process, change in product line, or change in price.

Register Scheme Red Flags

- Inappropriate employee segregation of duties. For example, the cashier should not perform register counting and reconciling.
- Cashiers, rather than supervisors, have access to the control keys that are necessary for refunds and voids.
- Register employee has authority to void own transactions.
- Register refunds are not methodically reviewed.
- Multiple cashiers operate from a single cash drawer without separate access codes.
- Personal checks from cashier found in register.
- Voided transactions are not properly documented or not approved by a supervisor.
- Voided cash receipt forms (manual systems) or supporting documents for voided transactions (cash register systems) are not retained on file.
- Missing or obviously altered register tapes.
- Gaps in the sequence of transactions on register tape.
- An unusual number of refunds, voids, or no sales on register tape.
- Inventory totals appear to be forced.
- Multiple refunds or voids for amounts just below the review limit.

Source:
Wells, J. CFE, CPA. Corporate Fraud Handbook. Hoboken, NJ: John Wiley & Sons, 2004.

Related Entries:

ASSET MISAPPROPRIATION
FRAUDULENT DISBURSEMENTS
OCCUPATIONAL FRAUD AND ABUSE

RENTAL CAR FRAUD

Rental car frauds involve staged accidents with rental vehicles and other insurance scams, theft of rental vehicles, and the use of rental vehicles to commit other crimes.

- *Bodily Injury Claims.* These are usually committed via staged accidents. An individual rents a car and opts for the company's insurance package. The renter drives the vehicle into a "beater" car driven by an accomplice. The beater car may have several occupants, all of who complain of soft tissue injuries. These scams may also involve attorneys and medical personnel as accomplices.
- *Double-Bind Insurance Scams.* The renter buys insurance from the rental company that includes a loss damage waiver that provides coverage if the vehicle is stolen or damaged. With an accomplice the renter stages an accident in which the beater car is at fault. The renter files a claim with the beater car's insurance company as if the car was his own and receives payment for the damage. The renter returns the car to the company, claiming it was damaged in a parking lot. The loss damage waiver relieves the renter of responsibility for the damage.
- *Theft of Vehicles.* The renter buys a loss damages waiver, then strips or sells the car, reporting it to the rental company as stolen. Many vehicles are sold in Mexico. The identification and credit card used by the renter may be stolen. In some cases, foreign nationals rent a car, which they then ship overseas, usually to a developing nation.
- *Committing Other Crimes Using a Rental Vehicle.* Rental vehicles may be used to transport drugs or contraband. If the perpetrator is apprehended, his own vehicle cannot be impounded. The vehicles may be abandoned, stripped, or sold afterward.

Source:
Howell, D. "What Everyone Should Know About Rental Car Fraud." *The White Paper,* August/September 1995.

Related Entries:

INSURANCE FRAUD—PROPERTY AND CASUALTY
PERSONAL INJURY FRAUD

REPORT TO THE NATION ON OCCUPATIONAL FRAUD AND ABUSE

See, COST OF FRAUD; OCCUPATIONAL FRAUD AND ABUSE

RESEARCH GUIDE

The Internet is one of the best methods for obtaining information about all types of fraud. It can also be useful in gathering information to assist you during a fraud examination.

The APPENDIX contains tips for using the Internet to conduct research and a list of useful websites.

RÉSUMÉ FRAUD

A report from the U.S. House of Representatives in 1988 estimated that one in three applicants falsifies his or her education, work history, job description, salary, or criminal history. According to an article from Reuters news service, the background search firm ADP Screening and Selection Services conducted a study in 2003 and discovered that more than 50% of the people on whom it conducted employment and education checks had submitted false information. That number increased from 40% in 2002. A private study found that 44% of organizations had experienced at least one incident of résumé fraud.

Common acts of résumé fraud include:

- Exaggerated or wholly falsified educational background.
- Omitted or incorrect employment dates.
- Exaggerated expertise.
- Exaggerated experience.
- Phony self-employment.
- Phony consulting.

REVENUE RECOGNITION, IMPROPER

Recording revenue and/or expenses in improper periods is a form of financial statement fraud. Generally, revenue should be recognized when a sale is complete, and expenses should be recognized in the same period as the revenues produced by the expense.

Recognizing Revenues Early

Generally, revenue should be recognized when a sale is complete, that is, when title is passed from the seller to the buyer. The completed contract method does not record revenue until the project or sale is 100% complete. In certain cases—long-term construction contracts, for example—companies may use the percentage of completion method(s), recognizing revenues as each phase of the project is completed and accepted by the customer.

The following example depicts a sales transaction in which the revenue is recognized early. In December 2006, the sales revenue ($17,000) is recorded. The company has signed a contract for the sale, but the goods and services have not been delivered; the project is not even scheduled to start until January 2007. But the company recognizes the sale anyway.

Date	Description	Ref.	Debit	Credit
12/31/06	Accounts Receivable	120	17,000	
	Sales - Project C	401		17,000
	To record sale of product and services - Project C			
	Fiscal Year End - 2006			

Matching Revenues with Expenses

Another way to falsify revenues is to record the sale and the costs associated with that sale in different periods. If recorded correctly, the revenue and its associated costs would be recorded in the accounting period in which they actually occurred. In the last example, the sale was recorded in December 2006. If the project is completed in January 2007, then, and only then, will the company record the costs associated with the sale.

01/31/07	Cost of Sales-Project C	702	13,500	
	Inventory	140		13,500
	To record relief of inventory for Project C			

01/31/07	Labor Costs - Project C	550	2,000	
	Cash	101		2,000
	To record payroll expense for Project C			

INCOME STATEMENTS	Incorrectly Stated		Correctly Stated	
	Year 06	**Year 07**	**Year 06**	**Year 07**
Sales Revenue				
Project B	$25,000		$25,000	
Project C	$17,000			$17,000
Project D		$26,500		$26,500
Total Sales	$42,000	$26,500	$25,000	$43,500
Cost of Sales				
Project B	$22,500		$22,500	
Project C		$15,500		$15,500
Project D		$21,400		$21,400
Total Cost of Sales	$22,500	$36,900	$22,500	$36,900
Gross Margin	$19,500	($10,400)	$2,500	$6,600
G&A Expenses	$2,500	$3,000	$2,500	$3,000
Net Income	$17,000	($13,400)	--------	$3,600

Recognizing the revenue early, and the costs later, affects the company's income statement. The year 2006 yielded a net income of $17,000+, while year 2007 produced a loss ($13,400).

If done properly, the sale, cost of sales, and labor costs would all be recorded in the same accounting period. In this case, the revenues and expenses are recorded together in January 2007, yielding net incomes of $0 and $3,600.

Channel Stuffing

In a practice known as channel stuffing, a company ships large amounts of products, and then pressures distributors to accept the large shipments of products, even though the distributor cannot sell the product. Unofficially, the distributors are allowed to return any unsold product, but the company recognizes the revenue as if the sales are final.

Related Entries:

FINANCIAL STATEMENT FRAUD
FINANCIAL STATEMENT FRAUD, ANALYSIS OF STATEMENTS

RITE AID PHARMACY

By the late 1990s, Rite Aid was the third largest pharmacy chain in the US. It operates 3,400 stories in 28 states and the District of Columbia and has 72,500 employees. Between the period of May 1997 to May 1999, Rite Aid was accused of overstating its income to show positive revenue growth each quarter. When the fraud came to light, Rite Aid was ordered to restate its pre-tax income by $2.3 billion and net income by $1.6 billion. This was the largest restatement recorded to date. According to the SEC, former CEO, Martin L. Grass, son of Rite-Aid's founder Alex Grass, caused Rite Aid to fail to disclose several related-party transactions. These transactions, according to the SEC, benefited Martin Grass at the expense of Rite Aid's shareholders. The SEC also alleged that Grass fabricated Finance Committee minutes for a meeting that never occurred, in connection with a corporate loan transaction.

In May 2004 Grass was sentenced to eight years in prison for his role in falsely inflating the value of the company, the deliberate falsification of financial statements, and intentionally falsifying SEC filings. He was also fined $500,000 and given a sentence of three years of probation for the multi-billion dollar accounting fraud. Grass confessed to backdating contracts and severance letters. He also admitted to misleading the company and federal investigators about a $2.6 million real estate deal. He met with employees who were requested to testify in front of the grand jury and encourage them to lie in order to protect him.

Grass received the heftiest sentence of those involved in the Rite Aid fraud. Former CFO, Franklyn M. Bergonzi, received a 28 month prison sentence, while former VP, Eric S. Sorkin, was sentenced to five months in prison and five months house arrest. Former VP, Philip Markovitz, received a one month jail sentence followed by five months house arrest. Vice chairman and chief counsel, Franklin C. Brown, was found guilty in October 2004 of 10 criminal counts. He was the only defendant who went to trial to be found guilty by the jury. He was given a 10 year prison sentence for conspiracy, obstruction, lying to federal regulators and witness tampering. In October 2006, after serving a year and a half in prison, he filed a motion that prosecutors did not properly disclose all the audiotapes and videotapes they possessed and that his experts have found evidence on the tapes that can help prove his innocence. He is expected to stay in jail until November 2013.

After Grass was let go from Rite Aid, Timothy Noonan served as an interim CEO. He was charged with one count of withholding information from company investigators.

Sources:
www.cbsnews.com/stories/2003/06/18/national/main559152.shtml

Related Entries:

FINANCIAL STATEMENT FRAUD
SECURITIES FRAUD

SARBANES-OXLEY ACT

On July 30, 2002, President Bush signed into law the Sarbanes-Oxley Act (Public Law 107-204). This law significantly changes the laws of corporate governance and the rules and regulations under which accounting firms must operate. The Sarbanes-Oxley Act is designed to: (1) restore investor confidence in capital markets; (2) help eliminate financial statement fraud in publicly traded companies; and (3) significantly increase the penalties for corporate accounting fraud. The Sarbanes-Oxley Act is very complex, and as such, a broad overview of the most pertinent sections of the Act will be discussed herein. For a more detailed look at the legislation, refer to the Act itself (thomas.loc.gov). The most significant changes brought on by the Act include:

- The creation of the Public Company Accounting Oversight Board
- Requirements for senior financial officers to certify SEC filings
- Management assessment of internal controls
- New standards for audit committee independence
- New standards for auditor independence
- Enhanced financial disclosure requirements
- New protections for corporate whistleblowers
- Enhanced penalties for white-collar crime

Public Company Accounting Oversight Board

Section 101 of the Act establishes a Public Company Accounting Oversight Board (PCAOB), whose duties include overseeing public company audits, setting auditing standards, and investigating acts of noncompliance by auditors or audit firms. The PCAOB, which is composed of two CPAs and three non-CPAs, is administered by the Securities and Exchange Commission.

All public accounting firms must be registered with the PCAOB in order to legally prepare or issue an audit report on a publicly traded company. All such firms must disclose, in part, the names of all public companies they audited in the previous year, all public companies they plan to audit in the upcoming year, and the annual fees received from each public client for auditing, accounting, and non-auditing services.

The PCAOB must implement standards for auditing, quality control, ethics, independence, and other issues relating to audits of publicly traded companies. In addition, the PCAOB must follow strict reporting guidelines as set forth in Section 103 of the Act.

The authority to conduct regular inspections and investigations of public accounting firms allows the PCAOB to assess firms' legal, regulatory, professional, and ethical compliance with the Act.

For more information on the PCAOB, including the full text of all professional standards issued by the Board, please refer to the PCAOB website (www.pcaobus.org).

Corporate Governance

One of the most significant changes by the Sarbanes-Oxley Act is the requirement that Chief Executive Officers and Chief Financial Officers of public companies personally certify annual and quarterly SEC filings. Essentially, these certifications require CEOs and CFOs to take responsibility for corporate financial statements, as well as prevent officers from delegating this responsibility to subordinates. Sarbanes-Oxley mandates two types of officer certifications, criminal certifications (Section 906; codified at 18 U.S.C. § 1350), and civil certifications (Section 302).

Criminal Certifications

Periodic filings with the SEC must now be accompanied by a statement, signed by the CEO and CFO. The statement certifies that the report fully complies with the SEC's periodic reporting requirements, and that the information contained therein fairly and materially presents the financial condition and results of the company's operations.

Corporate officers who *knowingly* violate the certification requirements are subject to fines of up to $1,000,000 and/or imprisonment of up to 10 years. Corporate officers who *willfully* violate the certification requirements are subject to fines of up to $5,000,000 and/or imprisonment of up to 20 years.

Civil Certifications

Additionally, the CEO and CFO must each certify the following in their reports:

- He/she has personally reviewed the report;
- Based on his/her knowledge, the report does not contain any material misstatement that would render the financials misleading;
- Based on his/her knowledge, the financial information in the report fairly represents all material aspects of the company's (1) financial condition, (2) corporate operations, and (3) cash flow;

- He/she is responsible for designing, maintaining, and evaluating the company's internal controls;
- He/she has evaluated the controls within 90 days prior to the report;
- He/she has presented his/her conclusions about the effectiveness of those controls in the report;
- He/she has disclosed to the auditors and the audit committee any material weaknesses in the controls and any fraud, whether material or not, that involves management or other employees who have a significant role in the company's internal controls; and
- He/she has indicated in his/her report whether there have been significant changes in the company's internal controls since the filing of the last report.

Officer/Director Duties & Restrictions

Section 403 of the Act establishes new disclosure requirements for stock transactions by directors and officers of public companies, and individuals who own more than 10% of a publicly traded company's stock. The Act further specifies content and timing requirements of blackout period notices that must be provided to directors and officers. Reports of changes in beneficial ownership by these individuals must be filed with the SEC by the end of the second business day following the transaction.

The SEC must further establish rules requiring public companies to disclose whether they have adopted a code of ethics for senior financial officers. Should a company neglect to implement a code of ethics, it must explain the reasons therefore. Furthermore, should a company change a code of ethics it must give immediate public disclosure of such change. Where there are material changes in a company's financial conditions or operations, the company must publicly disclose the changes in "plain English… on a rapid and current basis."

Public companies may not, directly or indirectly, make personal loans or extend credit to officers or directors *unless* a consumer lender gives a consumer loan, which is of the type the company normally makes to the public.

Management Assessment of Internal Controls

Under Section 404 of the Sarbanes-Oxley Act, the SEC is to promulgate rules requiring all annual reports to contain internal control reports, which, (1) state managerial responsibilities for establishing and maintaining internal control procedures, as well as (2) provide assessments of the effectiveness of internal control structures and financial reporting procedures.

Examples of internal controls covered by this section include, but are not limited to:

- Controls over initiating, authorizing, recording, processing, reconciling, and reporting significant account balances, transactions, and disclosures included in the financial statements;
- Controls related to the prevention, identification, and detection of fraud;
- Controls related to initiating and processing of non-routing and non-systematic transactions; and
- Controls related to the selection and application of appropriate accounting policies.

Examples of disclosures that must be included within the internal control report:

- A statement of management's responsibility for establishing and maintaining adequate internal control structures;
- A statement identifying the framework that management used in conducting the assessment of the effectiveness of the company's internal control structure;
- Management's assessment of the effectiveness of the company's internal control structure as of the end of the company's most recent fiscal year, including disclosure of any material weaknesses identified in the company's internal control structure, and an explicit statement as to whether the or not the internal control structure is effective; and
- A statement that the company's independent auditor has issued an attestation report covering management's assessment of the company's internal control structure. The auditor's attestation report must also be filed with the annual report.

In performing the internal control assessment, management must choose a suitable internal control framework against which to evaluate the design and effectiveness of the company's internal control structure. The most commonly used model in the United States is the Internal Control — Integrated Framework established by the Committee of Sponsoring Organizations ("COSO") of the Treadway Commission, which provides five components of effective internal controls:

- Control Environment
- Control Activities
- Risk Assessment
- Information and Communication
- Monitoring
- Additional management duties include:
- Determining which internal controls to test when (1) performing the assessment, and (2) considering the significance of each control, individually and in the aggregate;
- Evaluating the likelihood of a misstatement to the financial statements as a result of a control failure;
- Evaluating whether additional controls are in place to mitigate the aforementioned occurrence;
- Determining which locations or business units to include in the assessment, if applicable;
- Evaluating the design and operating effectiveness of internal controls using a guided framework;
- Evaluating the probability of the occurrence and magnitude of potential misstatements resulting from internal control deficiencies;
- Determining whether potential misstatements could constitute material weaknesses (any deficiency where the likelihood of potential misstatement is more than remote) or significant deficiencies (any deficiency where the likelihood of potential misstatement is more than remote and the magnitude is more than inconsequential;
- Providing sufficient documentation to support internal control assessments (including documenting the design of the internal controls, as well as the results of management's testing and evaluation); and

- Communicating the assessment findings to the independent auditor and any other applicable parties.

Recognizing that companies have differing internal control structures, the rules state that the nature of the testing performed by management will depend on the specific circumstances of the company and the significance of the control being tested. However, inquiries alone are generally not a sufficient basis for a managerial assessment.

New Standards for Audit Committee Independence

The audit committee for each publicly traded company is responsible for hiring and overseeing the company's outside auditors. Each committee member must also be a member of the board of directors, and no committee member may receive compensation for any work other than his/her services on the Board or any Board committee. If at least one member of the committee is not a "financial expert," the company must explain the reasons therefore to the SEC. In addition, the committee must establish procedures for receiving and dealing with complaints and anonymous employee tips regarding irregularities in the company's accounting methods, internal controls, and auditing measures.

New Standards for Auditors

Sarbanes-Oxley requires auditors to report directly to audit committees. Reports must follow strict standards to ensure that audit committees are aware of questionable accounting policies or treatments used in the preparation of the corporate financial statements. Pursuant to the Act, all auditors must report the following to the audit committee in a timely manner:

- All critical accounting policies and practices used;
- Alternative GAAP methods discussed with management;
- Ramifications of the use of alternative treatments;
- Treatment preferred by the auditors; and
- Any other material written communications between the auditors and management.

Enhanced Review of Periodic Filings

Sarbanes-Oxley requires the SEC to make regular and systematic reviews of disclosures made by public companies in their periodic reports to the SEC. Reviews of a company's disclosures, including its financial statements, must be made at least once every three years.

Restrictions on Non-Audit Activity

Sarbanes-Oxley precludes public accounting firms from performing the following acts on behalf of their audit clients:

- Bookkeeping services;
- Financial information systems design and implementation;
- Appraisal or valuation services, fairness opinions, or contribution-in-kind reports;
- Actuarial services;
- Internal audit outsource services;
- Management functions or human resources;
- Broker or dealer, investment adviser, or investment banking services;
- Legal services and expert services unrelated to the audit; and
- Any other service that the Public Company Accounting Oversight Board proscribes.

There are certain other non-audit services – most notably tax services – that are not expressly prohibited by Sarbanes-Oxley. However, in order for a public accounting firm to perform these services on behalf of an audit client, that service must be approved in advance by the client's audit committee, which must also be disclosed in the client's periodic SEC reports.

Enhanced Financial Disclosure Requirements

Pursuant to the Act, the SEC requires publicly traded companies to disclose "all material off-balance sheet transactions, arrangements, obligations, and other relationships the company may have with unconsolidated entries or persons that may have a material current or future effect on the company's financial condition, changes in financial condition, liquidity, capital expenditures, capital resources, or significant components of revenues or expenses." Furthermore, pro forma financial statements that are filed with the SEC, or included in any public disclosure or press release, may not contain any untrue statements or omissions that could make them misleading.

Protections for Corporate Whistleblowers

The Sarbanes-Oxley Act establishes broad new protections for corporate whistleblowers by setting forth civil protections (Section 806) and criminal liability (Section 1107). In January 2004, the Court in *Welch v. Cardinal Bankshares, Corp.* was the first to apply the Act's equitable remedy for wrongful termination. The Court ordered employment reinstatement of the Plaintiff after finding that the Plaintiff's employer fired him in retaliation for reporting potential accounting misconduct within his company [*Welsh v. Cardinal Bankshares, Corp.*, No. 2003-SOX-15 (Dep't Labor, Jan. 28, 2004)].

Civil Protections

Sarbanes-Oxley § 806 makes it unlawful to fire, demote, suspend, threaten, harass, or in any other manner discriminate against an employee for providing information or aiding in an investigation of securities fraud. In order to trigger Sarbanes-Oxley § 806 protections, the employee must report the suspected misconduct to a federal regulatory or law enforcement agency, a member of Congress or a committee of Congress, or a supervisor.

Employees are also protected against retaliation for filing, testifying in, participating in, or otherwise assisting in a proceeding that has been filed or is about to be filed. As long as the employee reasonably believes she is reporting conduct that constitutes a violation of various federal securities laws, then she is protected.

The protections cover retaliatory acts by the company, any officer, employee, contractor, subcontractor, or agent of the company. If a public company is found to have violated Sarbanes-Oxley § 806, the Act provides for an award of compensatory damages sufficient to "make the employee whole." Penalties include reinstatement, back pay with interest, and compensation for special damages, including litigation costs, expert witness fees, and attorneys' fees.

Criminal Liability

Sarbanes-Oxley Section 1107 —codified at 18 U.S.C. § 1513—makes it a crime to knowingly, with the intent to retaliate, take any harmful action against a person for providing truthful information relating to the commission or possible commission of any Federal offense. This protection is only triggered when information is provided to a law enforcement officer; it does not apply to reports made to supervisors or to members of Congress, as is the case under Sarbanes-Oxley § 806.

In general, the coverage of Sarbanes-Oxley § 1107 is much broader than the civil liability whistleblower protections of Sarbanes-Oxley § 806. While the Sarbanes-Oxley § 806 protections apply only to employees of publicly traded companies, Sarbanes-Oxley § 1107's criminal whistleblower protections cover all individuals (and organizations) regardless of where they work. Also, Sarbanes-Oxley § 806 only applies to violations of securities laws or SEC rules and regulations. Sarbanes-Oxley § 1107, on the other hand, protects individuals who provide truthful information about the commission or possible commission of *any Federal offense.*

Violations of Sarbanes-Oxley § 1107 are punishable by fines of up to $250,000 and up to 10 years in prison for individuals. Corporations that violate the act can be fined up to $500,000.

Enhanced Penalties for White-Collar Crime

- Finally, as part of Congress' general effort to deter corporate accounting fraud and other forms of white-collar crime, the Sarbanes-Oxley Act also enhances the criminal penalties for a number of white-collar offenses. Such offenses include:
- ***Attempt and Conspiracy***. The Act amends the fraud provisions of the United States Code (Chapter 63) to make "attempt" and "conspiracy to commit" offenses subject to the same penalties as the offense itself. This applies to mail fraud, wire fraud, securities fraud, bank fraud, and health care fraud.
- ***Mail and Wire Fraud***. Sarbanes-Oxley amends the mail fraud and wire fraud statutes (18 U.S.C §§ 1341, 1343), increasing the maximum jail term from five to 20 years.
- ***Securities Fraud***. Section 807 of the Act makes securities fraud a crime, providing for fines up to $250,000 and up to 25 years in prison.

- ***Document Destruction***. Sarbanes-Oxley Section 802 makes destroying evidence to obstruct an investigation or any other matter within the jurisdiction of any U.S. department illegal and punishable by a fine of up to $250,000 and up to 20 years in prison. Sarbanes-Oxley Section 802 also specifically requires that accountants who perform audits on publicly traded companies must maintain all audit or review work papers for a period of seven years. Violations of this rule may be punished by fines up to $250,000 and up to 10 years in jail for individuals, or fines up to $500,000 for corporations.
- ***Asset Freezing***. During an investigation of possible securities violations by a publicly traded company or any of its officers, directors, partners, agents, controlling persons, or employees, the SEC can petition a federal court to issue a 45-day freeze on "extraordinary payments" to any of the foregoing persons. If granted, the payments will be placed in an interest-bearing escrow account while the investigation commences. This provision was enacted to prevent corporate assets from being improperly distributed while an investigation is underway
- ***Creating/Using Bankruptcy Loopholes***. Sarbanes-Oxley Section 803 amends the bankruptcy code so that judgments, settlements, damages, fines, penalties, restitution payments, disgorgement payments, etc., resulting from violations of Federal securities laws are non-dischargeable. This was intended to prevent corporate wrongdoers from sheltering their assets under bankruptcy protection.
- ***Bonus Disgorgement***. One of the most unique aspects of the Sarbanes-Oxley Act is § 304, which states that if a publicly traded company is required to prepare an accounting restatement due to the company's material noncompliance, as a result of "misconduct," with any financial reporting requirement under securities laws, then the CEO and CFO must reimburse the company for (1) any bonus or other incentive-based or equity-based compensation received during the 12 months after the initial filing of the report that requires restating, and (2) any profits realized from the sale of the company's securities during the same 12-month period.

SAS 85: MANAGEMENT REPRESENTATIONS

See, AUDITING FOR FRAUD

SAS 99: CONSIDERATION OF FRAUD IN A FINANCIAL STATEMENT AUDIT

See, AUDITING FOR FRAUD

SAVINGS AND LOAN FRAUD

Individuals who hold a fiduciary trust in a savings and loan institution and violate that trust commit savings and loan fraud. The Federal Home Loan Bank Board (FHLBB), in the midst of investigating widespread failures of savings and loans during the early 1990's, defined the ways in which individuals with a fiduciary trust commit fraud:

- Trading on inside information.
- Usurping the institution's opportunities for profit by insiders.
- Self-dealing, or otherwise using the institution for personal advantage.
- Specific acts discovered and forbidden by the FHLBB were:
- Loans to insiders in excess of that allowed by regulating.
- High risk speculative ventures.
- Payment of exorbitant dividends at times when the institution is at or near insolvency.
- Payment for institution funds for personal vacations, automobiles, clothing, and art.
- Payment of unwarranted commissions and fees to companies owned by the shareholder.
- Payment of consulting fees to insiders or their companies.
- Use insiders' companies for association business.
- Putting friends and relatives on the institution payroll.

Source:
Fricker, M., Muolo, P., and Pizzo, S. "Inside Job: The Looting of America's Savings and Loans." *Playboy,* November 1989.

Related Entries:

FINANCIAL INSTITUTION FRAUD

LOAN FRAUD

SCIENCE FRAUD

Science fraud involves falsifying information in experiments or published reports. Though science fraud may be committed for profit, other motivations may also be present. Marcel LaFollette, in *Stealing Into Print*, declares that science fraud "occurs when an author, editor, or referee makes a false representation to obtain some unfair advantage or to injure deliberately the rights or interests of another person or group."

The scientific community follows a peer-review process that prevents fraudulent material from being implemented or becoming public. Colleagues informally review each others' works in progress, results in seminars, papers presented at conferences, and scientific journals. To be judged legitimate by the scientific community, researchers must be able to duplicate the results of an experiment.

TYPES OF UNETHICAL CONDUCT OR MISREPRESENTATION IN SCIENTIFIC AND TECHNICAL PUBLICATIONS

BY AUTHORS	BY EDITORS, ADVISORS, OR STAFF	BY REFEREES
Describing data or artifacts that do not exist	Forging or fabricating a referee's report	Misrepresenting facts or lying in a review
Describing documents or objects that have been forged	Misrepresenting the review process	Intentionally delaying review for personal gain
Misrepresenting or distorting real data	Stealing ideas of text from a manuscript under review	Stealing ideas or text from a manuscript under review
Plagiarism, including deliberate violation of copyright		
Misrepresenting authorship by omission, by listing a non-contributing writer as author		
Misrepresenting publication status		

Source: LaFollette, M. Stealing *Into Print*. Berkeley: University of California Press, 1998.

Science and the Law

There may be no laws that directly address scientific misconduct. There are, however, four types of misconduct that have legal implications.

- Intentionally publishing falsified or fabricated data.
- Deceptive authorship.
- Forgery of signatures.
- Copyright violations.

Case Study—Star Professor Faked Data

Some observers claimed that scientific misconduct is a growing and significant problem for universities. These critics say universities do not adequately oversee researchers' projects, and are eager to sweep offenses under the rug when exposed, for fear of losing funds in the future.

Professor Karen Ruggiero was one of the star researchers in the Psychology department of the University of Texas at Austin. But less than two years into her work there, she resigned her teaching post and confessed that she created two studies with fictional data.

Ruggiero began her career at McGill University in Montreal, where she earned her Ph.D. in 1996, and published several well-regarded studies in collaboration with her mentor, Donald M. Taylor. Ruggiero began to study the psychological effects of discrimination at a time when affirmative action and other racial issues were being debated, a choice that gained her media attention and research funding.

A paper that Taylor and Ruggiero published in 1995, "Coping With Discrimination — How Disadvantaged Group Members Perceive the Discrimination that Confronts Them," has since been cited in more than 50 other psychology studies, according to the Social Studies Citation Index. Another of the author's studies, "Why Minority Group Members Perceive or Do Not Perceive the Discrimination That Confronts Them," was cited 38 times.

After a stint at Cambridge University and Harvard, Ruggiero accepted an offer from the University of Texas to establish her own laboratory and become a tenured professor. Continuing work she began at Harvard, Ruggiero published a study in 1999, along with a post-doctoral assistant, that concluded that individuals from higher social classes were more likely than those from lower classes to blame failure on discrimination rather than on personal faults. The *Journal of Personality and Social Psychology* published the study, "Less Pain and More to Gain." Ruggiero and a team of graduate students later produced a study looking at when women would claim discrimination as a reason for failing an exam. "Why Did I Get a D?" was published in 2000 in the *Personality and Social Psychology Bulletin*.

In the summer of 2001, one of Ruggiero's co-authors asked to review her notes. She refused, and continued to refuse repeated requests. In June, Ruggiero admitted using "invalid data" in the two latest studies. Writing letters asking that the articles be withdrawn, Ruggiero cleared her assistants of any involvement, but did not reveal her method or her reason for falsifying data.

Sources:
LaFollette, M. *Stealing Into Print*. Berkeley: University of California Press, 1998.

Lisheron, M. "Fraud Shakes the Walls of Academia's Ivory Tower. UT Professor Showed Great Promise." *The Austin American-Statesman,* November 18, 2001.

Park, R. *Voodoo Science.* New York: Oxford UP, 2000.

SECURITIES FRAUD

The number of shareholder lawsuits alleging securities fraud declined slightly in 2000, according to a study by PricewaterhouseCoopers. However, that number increased greatly in 2003 with a 37.5% surge in shareholder lawsuits over the previous year. According to the Institutional Shareholder Services (ISS), due to the settlements paid out over WorldCom, Lucent, and other high profile shareholder suits, payouts reached $2.6 billion for 2003 compared to $1.63 billion the previous year.

A seven year low in shareholder suits was marked in 2005, decreasing by over 17% since 2004. The amount of the average settlement, however, grew from $27.8 million in 2004 to $71.1 million in 2005, a 156% increase.

Accounting Fraud Allegations Rise

The percentage of suits alleging accounting fraud rose steadily for a number of years after 1995 when Congress passed the Private Securities Litigation Reform Act. In 2000, 53% of all shareholders' suits contained allegations of accounting fraud, compared to about 40% in 1995.

Reviewing all suits filed since 1998, a PricewaterhouseCoopers study found that 35% of accounting fraud complaints were filed after a company announced a restatement of its financial statements. And once a suit is filed, almost half of all companies sued for accounting fraud are eventually forced to restate their earnings.

About two-thirds of accounting fraud cases in 2000 alleged revenue-recognition violations, such as "channel stuffing," in which sales are recognized on products in the distribution channel, though no sales have actually been conducted.

In 2005, accounting fraud allegations plunged to only 46% of new lawsuits; a ten year low. Compare this to 2002 when 81% of new cases contained such claims. Likewise, only 22% of new cases in 2005 involved a company that filed a restatement of earnings.

Securities Fraud by Brokers

Acts of fraud or abuse committed by securities brokers include extending excessive margin debt to novice investors, failing to disclose or misrepresenting trading risks, liquidating customer accounts without warning, covertly pushing stocks in which the broker or firm has an interest, and trading a customer's stocks excessively in order to generate transaction fees, known as "churning."

All of these crimes, with the exception of churning, are committed by brokers online and in traditional settings. Churning is not an online issue, since customers decide for themselves how often to trade.

The Securities Exchange Commission (SEC) reported an increase in complaints about brokerages' sales practices throughout the last years of the century. Most alleged that brokers pushed stocks and other investments that were not appropriate for customers' needs. Complaints about misrepresentation of investments and their risks are also common. Many investors do not understand margin requirements, according to the SEC.

Spoofing

In 1997, when the SEC required NASDAQ dealers to display the best available quotes from any source, rogue brokers began manipulating stock prices by "spoofing." In spoofing, or posting "phantom quotes," traders try to manipulate stock prices by entering bogus quotes at inflated prices and then canceling them.

NASD Regulations for Online Brokers

Since the first Internet-based trading systems were introduced in 1995, online trading has increased to about 7.8 million individuals trading online, making 807,000 trades per day. Over 200 broker-dealers offer retail investors the ability to trade online. The growth in online trading has been accompanied by a surge in investor complaints related to online trading.

The National Association of Securities Dealers (NASD) issued new regulations in 2000 that address how brokerage firms operate online. Critics have charged that many firms disguise stock recommendations as objective "research" information. The regulations define suitable and unsuitable methods of distributing information online:

- If a firm includes on its website electronic libraries that contain research reports, news clips, quotes, or charts, that action does not constitute a recommendation. A firm may provide a search engine on its site, so long as search results are "not limited ... to securities in which the member makes a market or has made a Buy recommendation."
- Listing all NASDAQ stocks, or subsets such as companies with 25% annual earnings growth, would not constitute a recommendation so long as the list was not based on "subjective factors that the broker has created or developed."
- A broker could freely allow an online customer to access news affecting securities in his portfolios or "watch" list so long as the customer selected the scope of the information.
- Targeting a client or group of customers to encourage purchase of a stock would be unsuitable. An online broker may not send e-mails "stating" that customers should invest in a particular sector, or "urging" the purchase of stocks from a recommended Buy list.
- NASD firms cannot dodge regulations with a disclaimer that reasonably would be viewed as a recommendation.
- In general, any communication that could be reasonably viewed as a "call to action" is inappropriate.

- Brokerages must describe to customers the operation of margin accounts and the risks associated with trading on margin "in a separate document prior to the opening of a margin account."

Analysts Are Not Objective

Critics charge that the research analysts who recommend stocks for Wall Street brokerages often make their recommendations with their own best interest in mind, not the investors who will actually buy the stock. While only 1% of analyst recommendations are to "Sell," nearly half are to "Buy."

Analysts are often paid based upon the investment banking fees generated when their firms raise money for the stock offerings of client companies. Analysts sometimes own shares in the companies they follow or receive discounted shares in a company before the shares go public, making it in their personal interest to push sales of the shares and raise the price. Brokerage firms acquire a stake in a start-up company in exchange for helping it raise money from the public, then issue a positive report to boost the stock price so that the firm can sell its shares at a maximum profit.

Analysts Are Objective

Not all observers agree that analysts are undependable. Mark Hulbert has argued that analysts practice a hyperbole similar to grade inflation by academics, or by companies that label almost all chicken eggs as "large." Hulbert cites a review of more than half a million recommendations made between 1986 and 2000. The analysts' top picks outperformed the overall market and their lowest rated stocks underperformed. These findings suggest that analyst bias is not as common as perceived, though individual analysts and firms do engage in improper promotions. Hulbert advises investors to demand full disclosures of an analyst's affiliation, and to seek out a consensus opinion among several analysts.

SEC Investigation

Testifying before Congress in August 2001, Laura Unger of the SEC said that the agency had found conflicts of interest among analysts at almost all of the nation's largest brokerage firms. SEC staff studied research departments at nine major, but unidentified, brokerage firms. Results showed that analysts helped their investment banking departments win stock underwriting deals by participating in road shows to drum up investor interest and by initiating research coverage in prospective banking clients.

The examinations also determined that many analysts had significant involvement in start-up companies before those companies' shares were offered to the public, and had acquired shares in private companies at prices far below those charged to public investors.

- More than one-quarter of the 57 analysts reviewed had made pre-initial public offering investments in companies they later followed, initiating their coverage with a "Buy" recommendation.
- Three of these analysts executed trades for their own accounts that were contrary to recommendations they made to the public.
- One analyst sold a security short while advising the firm's clients that the company was a buy.
- Six of the firms reported that their analysts had provided bankers with advance notice of a pending change in recommendations.
- Though analysts are required to acknowledge their ownership in companies they follow, the SEC examination found that this information was sometimes omitted from research reports. More than a quarter of the analysts who owned shares in a new company they followed, or whose firm did, issued "Buy" recommendations within a week of the expiration of the lock-up period that limited the ability of insiders to sell shares. This type of recommendation is called a "booster shot" because it helps keep the stock price high while insiders cash out.
- Compliance departments at most firms were inadequate. Only one firm could accurately identify the investments made by its employees in companies underwritten by the firm.

Voluntary Guidelines for Analysts

In 2000, research directors at 14 Wall Street firms endorsed guidelines for defining analysts' compensation, personal ownership of stocks by analysts, and the objectivity of stock reports.

- No research employee should report to a member of a firm's investment banking department.
- Research analysts should not submit their reports to investment bankers at their firms or to corporate management for approval. Drafts of research reports may be shared only to verify facts and only when the research recommendation has been removed.
- Analysts' pay should not be directly linked to specific investment banking transactions.
- Sales and trading desks cannot direct pay to a certain analyst.
- Recommendations should be transparent and consistent. "An analyst's best judgments and should never be bound solely by company input."
- Ratings system for stocks should be clearly defined.
- Valuations and risks of all securities should be explicitly described. Price objectives should be made "with a reasonable basis."
- Disclosure of potential conflicts such as when an analyst's firm also acts as an investment-banking adviser to the company he or she follows must be legible and written "in plain English." Disclaimers should appear in larger-sized type or on the first page of a report rather than the last.
- Analysts should disclose whether they or family members own shares in companies they cover, including private investments made before a company is brought public. Personal trading should be consistent with investment recommendations.

Fraud in Initial Public Offerings (IPOs)

An industry-wide scandal and a slew of lawsuits in 2001 charged that underwriters extracted promises from investment firms to buy shares of new stocks at higher prices than the offering in exchange for larger allocations of IPO's. Investment firms are strictly prohibited from taking orders for follow-up purchases of a stock before the initial pricing is completed because it could give investors a false impression of demand for a stock on the open market.

Some fund managers said they were asked what their interest was in buying more stock after trading began and why they placed buy orders ahead of time. Some said that they were interested in buying shares and asked about the price. That price was always higher than the offering price. Generally, the fund managers said they made commitments to buy at least two to three times the number of shares that they were allocated at the offering. "It's never that you have to," Andrew J. Kessler of Velocity Capital Management told the *New York Times*. "It's the wink and the nudge."

Some participants admitted the practice, but denied they had done anything wrong. While underwriters are permitted to try to prevent a new stock from sinking as soon as it starts trading, an accepted practice known as stabilization, they can do so only by buying shares at the offering price or lower. And they cannot pass this responsibility on to their clients without discussing it.

The fund managers generally placed limit orders which are filled at or below a set price. If the new stock rose, they did not have to buy at a super-inflated price. If a fund manager did not want to be a long-term investor, he would sell the stock after a few days, sometimes trading through a different firm. The practice is sometimes called "puking" a stock back to the market.

Sources:
"Examinations of Broker-Dealers Offering Online Trading: Summary of Findings and Recommendations Office of Compliance Inspections and Examinations." *U.S. Securities and Exchange Commission,* June 11, 2001.

Hakim, D. "Worthy or Wobbly? Complaints Challenge Fairness of Late 1990's Boom in I.P.O.'s." *The New York Times,* May 2, 2001.

Hulbert, M. "Strategies." *The New York Times,* July 1, 2001.

Institutional Shareholder Services: scas.issproxy.com/Newsletter/issscasjanuary2004.html

Karp, R. "New Dog, Old Tricks: Online Trading Abuses Mirror Those in the Bricks-and-Mortar World." *Barron's,* July 2, 2001.

Morgenson, G. "Wall Street Firms Endorse Ethics Standards for Analysts." *The New York Times,* June 13, 2001.

Simon, R. "Complaints about Broker Practices Are Climbing, According to the SEC." *The Wall Street Journal,* April 21, 2001.

Weil, J. "Number of Shareholder Lawsuits Charging Firms with Securities Fraud Fell." *The Wall Street Journal,* May 29, 2001.

Related Entries:

ADELPHIA
BENNETT, JOHN G., JR.
BENNETT, PATRICK AND GWEN
BRE-X
CENDANT CORPORATION
FINANCIAL STATEMENT FRAUD
GLOBAL CROSSING
INSIDER TRADING
LEBED, JONATHAN
LEESON, NICK
MILKEN, MICHAEL
PARK, YUN SOO OH "TOKYO JOE"
SARBANES-OXLEY ACT
TRIPPET, ROBERT
TYCO
VESCO, ROBERT
WORLDCOM

SHELL COMPANY

Shell companies are fictitious entities created for the sole purpose of committing fraud. They may be nothing more than a fabricated name and a post office box that an employee uses to collect disbursements from false billings. However, since the checks received will be made out in the name of the shell company, the perpetrator will normally also set up a bank account in his new company's name, listing himself as an authorized signer on the shell company's account.

A person will probably have to present a bank with a certificate of incorporation or an assumed-name certificate in order to open a bank account for a shell company. These are documents that a company must obtain through a state or local government. The documents can be forged, but it is more likely that the perpetrator will simply file the requisite paperwork and obtain legitimate documents from his state or county. This can usually be accomplished for a small fee, the cost of which will be more than offset by a successful fraud scheme.

If it is discovered that a vendor is falsely billing a company, investigators for the victim company may try to trace the ownership of the vendor. The documents that were used to open a bank account in a shell company's name can sometimes help determine who is behind the fraudulent billings. If the corrupt employee formed his shell company under his own name, a search of public records at the local courthouse may reveal his identity.

To avoid being detected through a records search, some perpetrators form their shell companies under another name. It is common, for instance, for employees to set up shell companies in the name of a spouse or other close relative. Male fraudsters often establish shell companies under their wives' maiden names. An employee might also form the company under a completely fictitious name.

Another issue involved in forming a shell company is the entity's address—the place where fraudulent checks will be collected. Often, an employee rents a post office box and lists it as the mailing address of his shell company. Some employees list their home address instead. A comparison of employee addresses to vendor addresses might reveal shell companies in an accounts payable system.

Employees often use their home addresses to collect fraudulent disbursements because many businesses are wary of sending checks to vendors that have a post office box for a mailing address. Other common collection sites for shell company schemes are the addresses of relatives, friends, or accomplices.

Related Entries:

BILLING SCHEMES
EQUITY FUNDING
KREUGER, IVAR

SKIMMING

See, CASH THEFT SCHEMES

SOCIAL SECURITY FRAUD

Social Security fraud perpetrators obtain funds or identification through misrepresentation. Common acts include falsified applications, unreported supplemental income, using another person's number, and obtaining a number under false pretenses. Social Security Administration (SSA) employees may steal numbers or issue numbers for nonexistent people, using the numbers for personal gain or selling them to others.

The role of the Social Security number in American life is large. Several other government agencies are permitted by law to use Social Security numbers, but there is no law either authorizing or prohibiting their use. Banks and other financial institutions use the numbers to report interest earned on accounts to the Internal Revenue Service (IRS).

Other government agencies use Social Security numbers in computer matching operations to stop fraud and abuse. For example, using Social Security numbers, some state death records are matched to Medicare records to uncover Medicare and Social Security fraud. Colleges and other institutions use the numbers as a de facto identification card.

Inspector General on SSA

Due to ever increasing concern about fraud, Congress created the Office of the Inspector General for the Social Security Administration in 1995. In 2001, IG James Huse spoke before a Congressional committee about his office's anti-fraud efforts. Though the SSA continued to struggle with fraud, the Inspector Generals (IG's) office had made significant progress.

In 1996, an audit report estimated that the annual cost to SSA in erroneous payments to prisoners was $48.8 million. Legislation directly prohibiting these payments was passed in 1999, removing the need for computer matching agreements between SSA and prison authorities to be renewed every 18 months. According to the IG, eliminating the time-consuming process of matching allowed the SSA to identify and cease payments to more than 69,000 prisoners in FY 2000. Many of the identifications were based on more than 260,000 prisoner alerts that were received in large part because of the legislation.

Examining abuse in the area of death benefits, the SSA matched all 11.7 million auxiliary beneficiaries against SSA's Death Master File and found that SSA had paid an estimated 881 deceased auxiliary beneficiaries $31 million in Old Age Survivor and Disability Insurance (OASDI) benefits after their dates of death. On average, these deceased individuals continued to be paid for some 63 months after death. The study also revealed significant error rates in SSA's death matching process and the system SSA used to keep its death records up-to-date.

From October 1999 to March 2000, the Office of Inspector General (OIG) audits, investigations, and evaluations resulted in $29.7 million in questioned costs, $4.3 million in recommendations that funds be put to better use, 173 indictments, and 126 convictions representing nearly $39 million in investigative recoveries, restitutions, fines, or penalties.

In the Inspector General's 2005 Report to the President, there were over $19 billion in questioned costs between FY 2001 and FY 2005. In that same time span, 36,565 successful criminal prosecutions took place as a result of OIG investigations, totaling nearly $17 billion in recoveries.

Sources:
"James G. Huse, Jr., Inspector General of the Social Security Administration Before the House Committee on Ways and Means." *Federal News Service,* May 10, 2001.

"A Progress Report to the Nation; Fiscal Year 2005." www.ignet.gov, August 2006. Accessed October 12, 2006.

Related Entry:
COUNTERFEIT DOCUMENTS

SOUTH SEA BUBBLE

The South Sea Bubble was the name given to an investment program that went awry, and eventually became criminal, in England during the early 18th century. Robert Hartley,

Chancellor of the Exchequer, arranged for the government's debt to its short-term creditors to be incorporated as "The Governor and Company of Merchants of Great Britain Trading to the South Seas and other parts of America and for encouraging the Fishery." Effectively, the incorporation bestowed on the creditors exclusive rights to trade with South America along most of the continent's east coast, and along the entirety of the west coast.

The South Sea Company, as the operation came to be known, successfully kept up the government's cash flow, but in June 1715 a new crisis developed. The government owed millions of pounds in interest on the South Sea funds. Robert Walpole, First Lord of the Treasury, convinced creditors to convert much of their claim to stock in the South Sea Company, or to receive an annuity from the government at the standard rate of 5% annual interest for a span of years. However, since most creditors had claims paying 7% to 9% interest, converting to South Sea stock was the only sensible option. The government thus owed the South Sea Company a debt equal to the government securities which were converted to stock, but the interest rates were adjustable, and the government could pay the debt back when and if it had the means to do so. Nearly all of the government's debt was converted into South Sea shares.

The conversion was potentially good for everyone involved, but only if the South Sea shares kept a healthy value and growth. Skeptics proclaimed publicly that the shares were nowhere near the quoted price of 200 shillings each; they were worth perhaps 140 shillings each, according to the skeptics' estimate. To help move the price upward, government representatives gave shares to prominent people, giving the impression that these notables supported the Company. In fact these people never bought or received shares. Many received cash payments—the representative gave the person a document that quoted the shares' current value and a projection for what the shares would be worth some time in the future; the new shareholder then "sold" the shares back to the government at the boosted future price. For example, Lord Green might be given title to 100 shares at 200 shillings, which were expected to sell for 300 shillings in a year; the Lord signed the shares back over to the government at 300 shillings each, and was given 100 shillings per share in cash as the "profit" on the sale.

Additionally, the company puffed its share price by recruiting foreign investors from Europe, where many nations, including France, were having currency and national debt problems of their own. In 1720, the company sponsored a special midsummer dividend of 10%, though this was mainly a paper transaction since investors mostly converted the unexpected windfall to more South Sea stock. The company began making loans to its stockholders, knowing full well that much of these funds were eventually used to purchase more South Sea stock. Finally, company representatives bought South Sea stock anonymously, to simulate brisk trading. The scheme was enormously successful. In a period of 3 months during the year 1719, South Sea shares rose from 370 shillings to 900 shillings, and continued to rise thereafter.

The company helped precipitate its own end by pressuring its government supporters for monopoly protection. Under South Sea pressure, Parliament passed what would later become known as "The Bubble Act," which forbade businesses to incorporate without a Royal Charter. The Act also prohibited those currently holding Royal Charters from performing any activities not specifically authorized by the original charter. The legislation was intended to help South Sea outperform the myriad of smaller rivals that had sprung up in its wake. Supposedly as South Sea expanded its monopoly into various corners, its shares would become even more valuable. Instead, South Sea shares fell—from its peak of over 1,000 shillings, the stock price had decreased to 520 by September 1720, and to 290 in October. By Christmas the price was 191 shillings, a 600-point fall in four months' time.

Parliamentary supporters rushed to mount an exchange of South Sea stock for stock in the Bank of England and the East India Company. Meanwhile, opponents opened an investigation. By spring 1721, reports showed that almost 600,000 pounds of South Sea stock sold was bogus. Company accounting records had obviously been erased or altered. Government representatives and private citizens were exposed for improper dealings that enriched them at the Treasury's expense.

Robert Walpole, who as Lord of Treasury had been instrumental in creating the Company, became Prime Minister in 1721. Always aboveboard in his personal dealings, Walpole set about saving the company, deferring payments owed to the government, and having the Bank of England pay the company cash for annuities owed to South Sea by the government. Walpole's arrangement worked. South Sea stock ceased trading in 1750, but the company continued to deal in government securities until 1854.

Though some prominent citizens were tried for fraud, and a few spent time imprisoned in the Tower of London, most survived with their reputations and most of their wealth intact. Walpole eventually restored the economic health of the English crown and became known as one of the nation's great leaders.

SUPPLIER FRAUD, HEALTH CARE

Supplier fraud is a form of health care provider fraud. The chief offense in this area is improper billing. The following are examples of supplier fraud.

Ambulance Transportation

Ambulance transportation providers may fraudulently bill for more mileage than incurred, for trips never taken, or for non-covered trips.

Infusion Care

Fraudulent schemes perpetrated by infusion care centers include billing for services at abnormally high fees in comparison to cost, billing for non-covered patients, billing in excess of physician's prescription, billing for unnecessary treatment, and paying kickbacks to the prescribing physician.

Durable Medical Equipment Suppliers

Durable medical equipment suppliers may engage in schemes involving:

- Falsified prescriptions;
- Excessive supplies;
- Equipment not delivered or billed before delivery;
- Billing for equipment rental after equipment was returned;
- Non-covered supplies, i.e. incontinent care kits; and
- Lymphedema pumps.

Related Entry:

HEALTH CARE FRAUD

TAX FRAUD

Tax fraud is the willful evasion of tax obligations, through simple prevarication or through formal methods such as illegal shelters and money laundering. The Internal Revenue Service (IRS) estimates yearly tax fraud losses at $300 billion, approximately one-third of the nearly $1 trillion collected each year.

It is not a crime to attempt to lower one's tax bill, provided IRS regulations are followed. Tax avoidance refers to lowering one's tax bill through legitimate deductions, credits, and shelters. Tax evasion refers to illegal methods of tax reduction.

Each year the IRS prosecutes about 3,000 taxpayers for tax evasion. Offenders include individuals and businesses that commit evasion, and promoters of illegal evasion techniques such as phony trusts, fancy charities, and offshore accounts. The IRS estimates that certain professions have particularly high evasion rates:

Evasion Rates by Profession	
Auto Dealers, Restaurateurs, and Clothing Stores	40%
Traveling Salespeople	30%
Doctors, Lawyers, and Accountants	20%
Farmers	18%

Source: Coleman, J. "The Criminal Elite: Understanding White-Collar Crime." New York: St. Martin's Press, 1998.

A study by McGraw and Scholz in 1991 tested whether subjects were more likely to respond to different appeals to comply with the tax code: an appeal to civic virtue, an appeal to self-interest, and no appeal at all. Though conventional wisdom had suggested the ethical, community-based appeal would be the strongest, the study found no significant difference in the effects of the three approaches.

Criminal investigators in the 1990's said they were uncovering more cases of preparers who inflated clients' expenses, fabricated deductions, or claimed unallowable credits and excessive exemptions.

The IRS "Dirty Dozen"

Not all tax fraud scams are committed against the government. The IRS lists the following as the 12 most common scams aimed at taxpayers, each promising to exploit a loophole in the tax code. None of these claims are true.

African-Americans Receive a Special Tax Refund

Thousands of African-Americans have been misled by people offering to file for tax credits or refunds related to reparations for slavery. There is no such provision in the tax law. Promoters have charged clients to prepare a special claim for this refund. Besides the losses paid to promoters, taxpayers can be fined $500 for filing reparations claims if they do not immediately withdraw them when notified by the agency.

Employers Do Not Have to Withhold Taxes from Wages

Promoters instruct employers not to withhold federal income tax or employment taxes from wages paid to their employees. These schemes are based on an incorrect interpretation of tax law and have been refuted in court.

Individuals Do Not Have to File Tax Returns

Promoters claim they do not have to file or pay taxes and charge a fee for their "secret." Some promoters do file and pay taxes, but will not publicly admit it. Anyone who fails to file or pay taxes is subject to civil and/or criminal tax penalties.

Paying Taxes Is Voluntary

Though this is one of the oldest scams around and has been argued in legal venues, U. S. courts have continuously rejected the argument. Promoters sell "un-taxed packages," dispensing advice that can cause participants to incur civil and/or criminal tax penalties.

Pay Income Taxes on an Item and Receive the Item Free

In a common telemarketing scheme, promoters tell people if they pay the income tax due on an award, they will receive the item or its cash equivalent free. After paying the money, participants may receive nothing at all or an item of little value. In fact, the IRS tracks legitimate awards through a 1099 form presented to the recipient by the promoter. Any payments on legitimate awards are made to the IRS directly, not to third parties.

Social Security Tax Refunds

Participants are offered refunds of the Social Security taxes they have paid during their lifetimes. For a "paperwork" fee of $100, plus a percentage of any refund received, promoters promise to file a refund claim with the IRS. This hoax fleeces the victims for the up-front fee. The law does not allow such a refund of Social Security taxes paid.

Refunds are Available for a Fee

Refund scheme operators offer to "borrow" a participant's Social Security Number or give them a phony W-2 so it appears they qualify for a big refund. Many of these false refund claims are detected by the IRS before disbursement. Others are detected later, and the participant must repay the refund and may incur penalties and interest.

EITC Credits Can Be Borrowed

Promoters claim they can "share" one client's qualifying children with another client in order to allow both clients to claim the Earned Income Tax Credit. For example, if one client has four children they only need to list two for EITC purposes to get the maximum credit. The preparer will list two children on the first client's return and list the other two on another client's tax return. The preparer and the client "selling" the dependents split a fee. Both are subject to civil and criminal actions.

IRS Agents Collect Payments Door-to-Door

Promoters pose as IRS agents who have supposedly been assigned to collect payments. In fact, special agents, field auditors, and collection officers of the IRS may visit taxpayers, but they carry picture IDs and usually contact taxpayers beforehand.

Trust Funds Are Tax-Free

Promoters of abusive trust schemes may charge $5,000 to $70,000 for "trust" packages. The fee enables taxpayers to have trust documents prepared, to utilize foreign and domestic trustees as offered by promoters, and to use foreign bank accounts and corporations. Although these schemes give the appearance of the separation of responsibility and control from the benefits of ownership, these schemes are in fact controlled and directed by the taxpayer. A legitimate trust is a form of ownership that completely separates responsibility and control of assets from all of the benefits of ownership.

Home-Based Business Fronts Offer Tax Relief

Promoters offer tax "relief" by having individual taxpayers deduct most, or all, of their personal expenses as business expenses by setting up a bogus home-based business. However the tax code firmly establishes that a clear business purpose and profit motive must exist in order to generate and claim allowable business expenses.

Pay Phones with Volume Controls Provide Tax Relief

Promoters sell expensive coin-operated pay telephones to individuals, contending they can claim a $5,000 Disabled Access Credit on their tax return because the telephones have volume controls. In reality, the Disabled Access Credit is limited to bona fide businesses that are coming into compliance with the Americans with Disabilities Act.

Employment Tax Fraud: A Pivotal Court Ruling

A privately held air-conditioning company agreed to pay three workers in cash for specific jobs. The company's owner agreed on the condition that the workers would receive the necessary 1099 forms to report the cash income to the IRS. Six years after the fact, the IRS sent a notice to the company, saying that the three workers were not independent contractors and that the company owed back employment taxes as well as a fraud penalty for nonpayment of the taxes. The company asked the U.S. Tax Court for a review of the case, arguing that the IRS had no case because the three-year statute of limitations had long passed.

Though the IRS also argued that the fraud negated the statute of limitations, the Tax Court disagreed. The court said that fraud exists only if there is intentional wrongdoing to avoid taxes. Since the owner of the company thought he was complying with the tax laws when he hired the three workers, the IRS could not prove fraud. The three-year statute of limitations on the legal status of the workers therefore remained intact. No taxes or penalties were owed. (*See:* U.R. Neely v. Commission of Internal Revenue, 116 T.C. No. 8, No. 14936-98.)

Crackdown on Business Consultants

According to the Internal Revenue Service, as many as 8.5 million people work as consultants, two-thirds of them in construction, the service industry, and retail or wholesale trade. In response to widespread abuses in the 1990's, the IRS began teaching its auditors how to uncover tax cheating by many self-styled business consultants and by corporations that use former employees as consultants to avoid withholding income, Social Security, and Medicare taxes.

The audit technique guide, posted at the IRS website, instructs auditors to check the business records of consultants to determine whether they are improperly deducting vacations and family travel on their tax return. Auditors are urged to look closely at consultants who do not report a profit, those who work in resort areas, and those who deduct large expenses but report little revenue, especially in health-related fields. These people may be improperly writing off vacations or the cost of a second home.

The guide also covers former employees who return to their old jobs as consultants, an issue that grows as companies increase the outsourcing of many functions. Treating workers as independent contractors relieves employers of the duty to withhold taxes and to match Social Security and Medicare taxes. It also frees them of the costs of health insurance, pensions, and other benefits. Microsoft, IBM, and many other companies have been among those who have fought with the agency over the issue.

The most extreme form of tax resistance from businesses has come from a few thousand small business owners who assert that no law requires them to withhold taxes and who have taunted the IRS. For a while these groups were encouraged by the failure of the agency to act decisively. But the IRS did move against some of the top leaders in

2001, an action discussed below under "Business Protest Income Taxes and Withholding Requirements."

Another area rife with abuse is travel deductions. The law states that the primary purpose of travel must be business and must be documented. But tax evasion seminars instruct people that they can write off family travel if they just contact a few potential clients, which is false.

Enforcement Lagging

In recent years, IRS enforcement efforts have been curtailed by budget reductions, a lack of qualified personnel, and by public pressure from citizens groups and the U.S. Congress. Since 2001, the IRS has been focusing its efforts and resources on reorganizing and recruiting new agents in order to track down tax cheats.

During 2005, the Justice Department's Tax Division authorized prosecutions against 1,256 defendants for tax crimes, an increase of more than 43 percent over the 877 defendants authorized for prosecution in 2001.

Critics charge that the agency does not pursue non-filers, focusing instead on reviewing returns with suspicious deductions. Wealthy individuals and businesses often pay only a portion of their indebtedness, even after an audit. The percentage of federal taxes paid by large corporations has declined from about 25% in 1950 to 7% in the 1990s. Despite the low number of non-filers being punished by the IRS, the rate of enforcement is increasing. In FY 2001, 464 investigations were initiated by the IRS; in 2003, that number increased to 536. There were 269 prosecution recommendations in 2001; 302 in 2003. There were 257 indictments in 2001 and 234 in 2003.

In 2003, when Mark Everson took over the IRS, he made a gallant effort to eliminate tax cheats by focusing in on the largest corporate taxpayers. The results of this stance are as follows: One in five of the largest corporate taxpayers were audited with the IRS's faster and more targeted procedure. Enforcement revenue from these audits totaled $17.7 billion in 2005 – up $7 billion since 2003. In addition, 20% more income-tax returns were audited in 2005 than in 2004.

Earned Income Credit

The earned income tax credit (EITC) has been a part of the American federal income tax system since 1976. Designed originally as a mechanism to remove the extreme regressivity of the taxes imposed by the Federal Insurance Contribution Act (FICA), from which revenues fund the Social Security retirement and disability programs, the EITC has now grown into a major wealth redistribution device benefiting the working poor having one or two children. The EITC is a negative income tax that has had bipartisan political support in the United States. For the 2006 tax year, the maximum amount of the EITC increased from $4,204 in 2005 to $4,536 (for taxpayers with two or more children and adjusted gross income of $34,962 in 2005 to $36,348). The current EITC is indexed for inflation and will continue growing each year that there is inflation.

Critics of the EITC have pointed out that the nature of the credit rewards those individuals who are willing to lie about earning income that they have not actually earned. During the 1995 filing season for the 1994 tax year, the General Accounting Office estimated that the Internal Revenue Service (IRS) made erroneous EITC payments in the amount of $4 billion to $5 billion. Since 1995, after receiving additional enforcement appropriations and after Congress amended the law to require the use of Social Security numbers for children, the amount of erroneous refunds has declined. In FY 2002, the IRS protected approximately $435 million in erroneous EITC claims. The IRS estimates that a substantial percentage of the erroneous refunds are due to fraud.

During the 1995 filing season, the IRS promoted electronic filing of returns and also supported a program where those taxpayers entitled to refunds could secure loans from banks in anticipation of the tax refund. Under the electronic filing program, refunds were typically authorized within one or two days. When a taxpayer secures a refund anticipation loan from a bank, the IRS makes an electronic fund transfer directly to the bank. The rate of electronic filing and the use of refund anticipation loans were very high for those returns claiming the EITC, much higher than other returns. The popular press reported that unscrupulous commercial return preparers combed through poor neighborhoods inducing taxpayers to file fraudulent returns. Of course, the return preparers charged very high fees for these returns and often had very low costs because they used computers, computer software, and electronic filing.

The IRS has discontinued the refund anticipation loan program for returns since the 1995 filing season. In addition, the IRS has delayed issuing refunds on those returns where the EITC exceeds the amount of tax due on the return. Finally, the IRS has started questioning a higher percentage of returns that have suspicious characteristics. In the meantime, Congress has changed the law to require that all taxpayers claiming the EITC based on one or two children provide the Social Security number of each child. The additional requirement of providing a Social Security number for children has improved enforcement, but only in cases where more than one individual is claiming the same child. The IRS computers now compare and crosscheck Social Security numbers. In this way, the IRS computer identifies cases where more than one taxpayer has claimed the same child as the basis for the credit.

Under the existing system, however, there is no way to make any further checks to determine the child's age or relationship to the taxpayer. As a result, it remains a common practice for unscrupulous return preparers to go through poor neighborhoods and pay individuals for the Social Security numbers of children who are not currently being claimed by anyone. This practice is very difficult for the IRS to detect when the children are children of parents who are not working or who are members of the underground economy and not filing returns.

The current level of fraud remains high but unknown. Estimates are in the $500 million to $4 billion per year range. Because the maximum amount of the EITC has increased, the dollars lost to fraud may actually be increasing while the number of fraudulent returns decreases. The level of EITC fraud detected on electronically filed returns rose from 6,220 in 2000 to 16,908 in 2002. In 2005, the Department of the Treasury claimed that more than one in four EITC dollars are issued in error due to fraud. Since 2003, the IRS has worked to implement new technology and procedures for stronger surveillance of high-risk applicants to reduce fraud and mistakes.

Offshore Tax Havens

Banks incorporated in areas outside of the U.S. have long offered "secret" accounts for U.S. citizens, which could be used to hide income from the IRS. The banks, which might not even have a physical address, offered offshore credit or debit cards allowing U.S.

citizens to access their accounts from anywhere in the world, and use the cards to purchase goods without leaving a record. These companies were not violating the laws of the countries in which they operated. They were not required to cooperate with tax authorities or to inform them whose accounts offshore credit cards were linked to.

New laws passed in 2000, promoted by the Organization for Economic Cooperation and Development and the Financial Action Task Force, targeted a blacklist of these so-called offshore tax havens. Nations hosting the banks were warned that if they did not cooperate with tax authorities in the U.S. and Europe, they would suffer severe retaliatory measures, including trade embargoes. The IRS required U.S. banks to file a Suspicious Activity Report whenever money was transferred to one of the tax havens on the blacklists. The Bahamas, Caymans, and Antigua quickly capitulated.

Using Offshore Business to Evade Taxes

Several cases in 1999 and 2000 focused on companies that established offshore operations for the purpose of evading taxes. United Parcel Service (UPS) and Alliant Energy are only two examples of the several cases that were investigated.

UNITED PARCEL SERVICE

UPS created a separate company to act as an insurer for its packages. The company rarely loses or damages packages and is rarely liable to customers, but the insurance operation was funded at exorbitant levels. In the UPS case, the United States Court of Appeals for the 11th Circuit, in a 2-to-1 decision, rejected the United States Tax Court's finding that UPS used a sham insurance policy to move profits to an untaxed insurance affiliate in Bermuda.

The company had endowed the offshore insurance company with $1 million a year, a lower court had found. The purpose was to act as a front so it could funnel offshore its profits from insuring parcels against damage or loss. Judge Robert P. Ruwe of the Tax Court had rejected the arrangement as purely a tax-avoidance scheme, prompting UPS to set aside a $1.4 billion reserve in the event it lost the case on appeal. But Appeals judges overturned the ruling.

"Even if the odds of losing money on the policy were slim," the appeals court majority wrote, the insurer with which UPS made the deal assumed "a genuine obligation." The judges wrote, "A history of not losing money on a policy is no guarantee of such a future."

In a dissenting opinion, Judge Kenneth L. Ryskamp said the trial had revealed "overwhelming evidence" from UPS's own documents, actions, and testimony by its executives that the insurance scheme was purely a tax avoidance shelter. "In an arm's length transaction," he wrote, "UPS would have had to cut in half the prices it charged customers to insure their packages against loss or damage, which would have reduced profits."

ALLIANT ENERGY

Around the same time of the UPS decision, a Court of Appeals in St. Louis overturned a federal district court ruling that Alliant Energy, which operated a large Iowa electric utility, had engaged in sham stock trading to eliminate nearly $100 million of taxes. In that case also the appellate judges held that the appearance of a business purpose, with at least some prospect of profit or risk of loss, was sufficient to render a corporate tax shelter legitimate.

The St. Louis Appeals Court ruled that Alliant's hiring of a third-party to engage in extensive instantaneous trading of stocks back and forth in foreign companies was not a sham. The ruling made no mention of expert testimony that all of the trades were done at pre-arranged prices that guaranteed the creation of tax losses. That technique, testimony showed, insulated Alliant from price swings that would have exposed it to investment losses that could have swamped the tax savings.

In Alliant's case, the third-party was usually Foote, Cone & Belding, an advertising agency. However, the court reasoned, had Alliant fabricated the trading partner instead of using an existing company, the conduct of the trades would have been illegal. Nevertheless, even though the company's risk of loss in the trades "may have been minimal," the court ruled that was partly because it "did its homework before engaging in the transactions."

Taxpayers Defrauding Preparers

A former H&R Block tax preparer that posted a message on the Internet telling the company's customers how to cheat on their income taxes was sued by the firm for "encouraging and aiding customers to defraud Block." The message, which was posted on a bulletin board operated by Yahoo, told taxpayers how to doctor information in their employee wage and tax statements, or W-2 forms, and have Block consultants prepare returns that would result in inflated tax refunds.

The message read: "Take your original W-2 and make a nice new one using a laser printer. Change a number so it looks like an input error. Say, subtract a digit from income, add one to withholding or transpose a number. Don't be a pig about it. Just go for a few thousands dollars." It advised people to visit a Block office during "peak" hours "so you are sure to get a new preparer." It urged taxpayers to refuse electronic filing because, Block alleged, that would make it harder to detect the false W-2. "Get your co-workers, friends and family to join the fun."

The Kansas City, Mo., company prepares tax returns for millions of people each year. Block makes loans to clients based on their anticipated refunds and recovers its money from those refunds. If the IRS rejects a fraudulent return that the company used as the basis for a loan, then Block has to absorb the loss.

The person responsible for the posted messages, who left Block in July 1997 to start a tax-consulting business, said the posting was a joke intended to show how easily Block clients can commit fraud. In a counter suit, he accused the company of trying to silence criticism. The message was posted in March 2000 using the alias "jack_straw_67201" (a reference to a Grateful Dead song). The company discovered the identity of the poster by serving a subpoena on Yahoo.

Businesses Protest Income Taxes and Withholding Requirements

Al Thompson is a business owner who in the 1990's became the best-known advocate of the position that American companies and their workers do not have to pay income taxes. Thompson and others claim that "the federal government has no jurisdiction to collect income taxes"—only income from foreign sources or employers based abroad is subject to American income taxes.

Calling themselves the "tax honesty movement," supporters claim that "most Americans have been tricked into paying taxes in a conspiracy involving Congress and federal judges, aided by every major news organization." The movement is promoted through websites, seminars, and correspondence from Thompson and others, like Thurston P. Bell and Larken Rose of Pennsylvania, neither of whom has formal legal training, and who each offer slightly different theories about Section 861 of the tax code.

After a lengthy deliberation of several years, in which the scofflaw movement gained momentum, the IRS countered that the protesters' position "is refuted by the express and unambiguous terms" of the tax code and a 1955 Supreme Court ruling holding that "Congress applied no limitations as to the source of taxable receipts" subject to income taxes. Besides legal disputes, there were ethical quandaries in the movement. Workers at some companies complained that their employers kept the withholding taxes for themselves instead of giving them back to workers.

Sources:
Chevreau, J. "There's No Place to Hide: Offshore Banking Isn't Illegal, But Keeping It Secret from the Taxman Is." *National Post,* May 5, 2001.

Elstein, A. "Aiding Tax Fraud: H&R Block Finds No Humor in Ex-Worker's Online Advice." *Wall Street Journal Online.*

Johnston, D. "IRS Warns Small Business about Taxes." *The New York Times,* June 7, 2001.

Johnston, D. "Chief Admits IRS Is Lax on Tax Fraud." *The New York Times,* April 6, 2001.

Johnston, D. "A Smaller IRS Gives Up Billions in Back Taxes." *The New York Times,* April 6, 2001.

Johnston, D. "Courts Rejects IRS Efforts to Limit Tax Shelters." *The New York Times*, June 22, 2001.

Johnston, D. "IRS Guide Focuses On Consultants." *The New York Times,* June 21, 2001.

Taxpayers Against Fraud, The False Claims Act Legal Center (TAF). www.taf.org

Department of the Treasury, www.whitehouse.gov/omb/budget/fy2005/treasury.html

Related Entry:

ATKINS, CHARLES AND WILLIAM HACK

TELECOMMUNICATIONS FRAUD

Telecommunications fraud is committed by any act of misrepresentation or theft of service within the telecommunications system. The number one telecom fraud in America is cell phone fraud. The theft of service in both wired and wireless systems is illegal.

Consumer Fraud Telecommunications Scams

Consumer fraud in telecommunications costs consumers and businesses an estimated $12 billion a year. Schemes include:

- Prepaid phone cards. Some cards are only valid within a narrow range. Other cards charge higher rates than advertised.
- Websites with adult entertainment ads that say, "Click here to see more." The click reroutes a local phone call and turns it into an international one, to places such as Chad and Caribbean countries. Offshore companies that profit by long-distance billings usually operate the companies that run these websites. A large U.S.-based carrier like AT&T pays these companies a share of any phone charges the company connects. Having the local phone company install an international block on the computer line can prevent this scheme.
- Big businesses often depend on telephone switching equipment, called private branch exchanges, to handle calls. Manipulating this, a perpetrator will call the company pretending to be an AT&T service technician "repairing" the phone lines. The person taking the call is told that a test is being conducted. The person is asked to complete the test by touching 9, 0, and the pound sign and hanging up. By pushing 9, 0, and pound, the person transfers the perpetrator to an outside line from which he can make long-distance calls on the company's bill. Sometimes perpetrators asked for Extension 900, which accomplishes the transfer also. This scheme can be avoided by instructing employees that phone companies do not request help from their customers in checking phone lines.

Source:
Sanchez, E. "Beware of Phone Fraud." *Sacramento Bee,* May 15, 2001.

Related Entries:

CELL PHONE FRAUD, OR CLONING
CONSUMER FRAUD
TELEMARKETING FRAUD

TELEMARKETING FRAUD

Telemarketing fraud is committed by misrepresenting the cost or nature of merchandise, sweepstakes, or awards. Victims of telemarketing fraud are swindled out of an estimated $40 billion a year. The National Consumers League reports that in 2005, telemarketing victims averaged a loss of $2,892, up from $1,974 in 2004. The total loss in 2005 was $4,921,932, compared to $2,561,835 in 2004. According to one survey, 92% of American adults say they have received postcards or letters promising they had "definitely" been awarded a "guaranteed" prize. Of those responding, 69% never received the promised prizes.

Salespeople are trained in obfuscation, reading lists of prizes quickly into the phone, emphasizing big-ticket items like jewelry and cars, not mentioning that the odds of actually winning anything besides a trinket are astronomical. In one operation, victims were told they had won a "Winnebago." They were asked to pay a handling fee of $2,900, a fraction of the cost of a new RV. About two months later, victims found a UPS driver at their door delivering a "Winnebago tent."

Telemarketers deliberately target the elderly, the unemployed, and those who have previously purchased telemarketed items. In a Louis Harris poll, some 5.5 million Americans said they had bought items by telephone in the past two years and were exploited in the process.

The hit-and-run nature of phone rooms, the geographical distances between the crooks and their victims, and the resources and priorities of law enforcement agencies all make enforcement efforts difficult. Only about one in 100 victims ever files a complaint.

In recent years, the Internet has become increasingly popular method of telemarketing fraud. The number one scam currently found on the Internet, according to the National Fraud Information Center, is fraudulent credit card offers making false promises of credit cards, regardless of bad credit, for a fee paid upfront. Among the top ten schemes on the World Wide Web are business opportunities and work-at-home scams.

Alliance Against Fraud in Telemarketing

The National Consumer's League (NCL) umbrella of operations is designed to monitor telemarketers with several tools, including the Alliance Against Fraud in Telemarketing and the National Fraud Information Center (NFIC). These projects are funded by businesses and run by the League in order to gather and disseminate information about scams, ultimately to lobby enforcement agencies with this information. Companies such as Citibank, MasterCard, Visa, MCI Communications, AT&T, and Federal Express (all of whom would stand to gain if fraudulent telemarketing were eliminated) consider it cost effective to invest in the prevention of fraud.

In its first year-and-a-half, the Alliance answered over 145,000 calls from bilked customers. About 35,000 complaints were filed with the FTC, and 25 investigations (with multiple complainants) were opened. The NFIC also tracks the incidence of telemarketing and other frauds and ranks the scams by their frequency. The top ten telemarketing frauds of 2005 as compiled by the NFIC were as follows:

2005 Top Ten Telemarketing Frauds

1. Prizes/Sweepstakes	31%
2. Scholarships/Grants	11%
3. Magazine Sales	9%
4. Credit Card Offers	9%
5. Fake Check Scams	7%
6. Advance Fee Loans	6%
7. Lotteries/Lottery Clubs	5%
8. Work-at-Home Plans	3%
9. Phishing	3%
10. Travel/Vacations	2%

Centers of Telemarketing Fraud

Fraudsters in the telemarketing circuit have their own contacts, networking groups, and methods. A hot spot for setting up scam centers is in Florida, where a strip of warehouses and storefronts running from Miami to Fort Lauderdale is known as the Maggot Mile. Nevada, mainly Las Vegas, and Southern California, where Los Angeles is the preferred home of the office toner con, are also centers of telemarketing fraud. Cities with a high rate of violence and drug-related crime are ideal for the telescammer. Police and public attention are more focused on incidents which are taking people's lives rather than financial crimes. On the other hand, small towns in outlying areas may welcome telemarketers with little or no questions in order to bring more jobs into the community.

Telemarketers targeting U.S. consumers from offices located in Canada cost consumers approximately $70 million a year. Canadian courts levy lighter penalties, usually a fine or a short prison term, compared to the United States, where offenders can be sentenced to five years in prison for each defrauded victim. The perpetrators, mostly Canadians and some Americans, operate boiler rooms with hundreds of people calling 16 hours a day, seven days a week.

In a typical Canada-based scheme, victims are told they have won a lottery jackpot or other big prize. For the prize money to be released they are told, they must pay a duty, tax, or fee of several thousand dollars. They are asked to send a check or wire the money to a bank account or a postal box, quickly, so they do not forfeit the prize money. To make it look official, victims often are given phony award numbers and telephone numbers for contacting lottery officials. In reality, customs service officials say, no duties are ever levied for claiming a foreign lottery prize or on money or checks moved across U.S. borders.

Staff Exploitation

The customers of fraudulent telemarketing operations are not the only victims. Fronters (those placing the telemarketing calls) are often poorly educated and easily taken advantage of by the career criminals who run the operations. Salespeople may face hidden costs in the work agreement similar to the ones involved in the items they push on unsuspecting customers. For example, boiler room operators hold back parts of their phone lists and sell them to crewmembers as "hot leads."

Telescam veterans know how to operate a gift sting that bilks both the customer and the salesperson. Operators overstate the retail value of the gifts, so the customers get less than they paid for; then, by giving agents an inflated wholesale cost, the operators can pay these workers less commission, which is figured on the "profit margin" between wholesale and retail.

The salespeople in boiler rooms are sometimes as desperate as their victims. Most are unemployed, with little education or marketable skills. Telemarketing promises easy work and big pay without any experience. Many people who start out as fronters, however, are serving an apprenticeship in their criminal careers. They are wooed with cars, cellular phones, and other perks. Former workers have reported that supervisors sprinkled lines of cocaine along the phone bank table, and threw handfuls of money into the air, promising the proceeds to whoever made the next sale.

Employees are also exploited when no Social Security or payroll taxes are deducted from paychecks, so they owe big tax bills at the end of the year. Fronters' commission payments are often shorted or withheld. Paychecks frequently fail to clear the bank. Owners promise big profit shares for a month or two, then shut down the business. They tell the workers that creditors or regulators have frozen their assets. Workers lose their jobs and usually their last weeks' commissions. For the last few months, however, the owners have been taking in $25,000 to $30,000 a week.

Better Business Bureau Deceptions

Some operations actually encourage their marks to call and check with the Better Business Bureau (BBB) and with former customers, giving out the numbers for the person to call. These numbers ring at phony lines set up by the scammers, which give out a glowing recommendation. Phone rooms have been known to set up reference arms with titles like "The Better Business Bureau of America" or "International Better Business Bureau" to recommend their ventures. If a potential victim does reach the legitimate Better Business Bureau, chances are the report will contain little or nothing of use. The information in these files is usually ambiguous and out of date.

Telemarketing Suppliers

The telemarketing industry relies on a number of sources to supply its phone scripts, mailing lists, merchandise, phone banks, and auto dialers. Mailing lists and phone lists are sold for a few cents per name. Lists of people who have been stung before or who have bad credit records fetch between ten and fifteen cents per name. By supplying telemarketers with the tools of their trade, these companies make telescamming possible. Many of the suppliers are aware of telemarketers' criminal intentions and choose to ignore them.

Turnkeys

Turnkeys comprise an industry of their own by providing the collateral a telemarketing scam needs—turnkeys launder credit card receipts and checks, sell auto-dialers and phone lists, and provide the merchandise portrayed as valuable prizes.

Legitimate businesses, however, are routinely implicated in this scurrilous industry. The U.S. Postal Service, for instance, carries tons of telemarketing ads. In the early days of the industry, telemarketers used the Postal Service to deliver merchandise C.O.D., but when the postal service mounted an aggressive campaign against fraud, companies turned to credit card billings to avoid the scrutiny.

Independent Service Organizations

Telemarketers often have difficulty securing credit card services from reputable institutions. Many banks will not open credit-processing accounts for businesses that do a substantial amount of their business in phone sales because these accounts typically incur a high rate of "chargebacks." Federal law gives consumers 60 days to protest charges to their cards, and if successful, the issuer has to absorb the loss. MasterCard and Visa estimate their losses from phone fraud at $300 million a year. In January of 2006, the Better Business Bureau conducted a survey of Americans regarding identity theft. The number of victims reduced from 9.3 million in 2005 to 8.9 million in 2006. However, the total fraud amount rose from $54.4 billion in 2005 to $56.6 billion in 2006.

Telemarketing operations have learned the difficulties they face when dealing directly with banks. To circumvent this obstacle, phone sales companies hire "independent service organizations," which approach banks on the telemarketer's behalf. The service company agrees with the bank to cover any chargebacks from the operation. The telemarketer is required to post a large bond to cover potential losses, so the service organization is also protected from loss. However, even with a half-million dollar bond, the reserve funds can be quickly depleted when customers start to realize they have been swindled, leaving the service company and/or the bank with enormous losses.

Factoring Companies

Telemarketing operations also commonly engage "factoring" companies. These groups buy credit card receipts from telemarketing concerns at a discount, and then use their merchant bank accounts to convert the receipts into cash. Some factors charge as much as 30% of the receipts' gross value to launder the slips. Factoring is illegal in some states, though crooks find ways to slip through loopholes or disguise their alliances.

International Factoring Companies

Factoring through Asian and European merchants has increased because foreign concerns tend to charge a lower price for their services than American factors do: between 9% and 10% of the gross. Factors have the opportunity to make a great profit, regardless of their locale. They also, however, face the risk that banks will freeze their accounts or sue them for excessive chargebacks. In response to the losses suffered at the hands of dishonest telemarketers, banks and credit card companies have started reviewing their accounts to locate those businesses with inordinate numbers of chargebacks. The financial institution closes these accounts, and may file suit if the account holder can be located.

Check-Cashing Establishments

Another convenient tool at the telemarketer's disposal is the check-cashing store. If a boiler room operation wishes to avoid the risks of setting up a bank account, which might be traced or seized, customers' personal checks are taken to a company that cashes them for a small fee. These establishments rarely require any identification to cash the checks. Customers may complain and try to stop payment on their checks, but they are ordinarily too late.

Telemarketing Terminology

The argot of fraudulent telemarketers is interesting and reveals the attitudes of perpetrators:

- *Banging or nailing the customer.* This refers to closing the deal.
- *Puffing.* A salesperson's most effective skill is *puffing*, the ability to sound convincing while exaggerating the value of a business opportunity or gift.
- *Singing/Crying.* To make the puffing more persuasive, marketers hire *singers* or *criers* to tell potential victims what a great deal they are getting.
- *Heat Calls.* Calls from angry customers who realize they have been swindled are known as *heat calls*, which are handled by someone claiming to be the company's manager or vice-president.
- *Fronter, Closer & Verifier Calls.* Fronters, closers, and verifiers conduct work in a boiler room, typically a rented office space furnished with folding tables and chairs and filled with phones.
  - The *fronter* calls victims and makes the initial pitch. This low-level worker is usually breaking into the business and reads from a script to the prospective customer. Fronters seldom see the merchandise or know the full extent of the operation. Keeping fronters in the dark, at least in theory, limits what they can tell investigators and protects them in the event of prosecution.
  - The *closer* is a veteran. Fronters pass an interested caller to their closer, identified as the firm's "manager," who convinces the person to buy.
  - Next, the caller is passed to a *verifier*, who reads some vague words about the deal and records the person's agreement. These recordings are intentionally vague, leaving out the pitch and key details, essentially recording only the customer's consent. Verifiers also stall customers who call back to complain (*heat calls*), finding reasons why a little more patience will solve the problem and, in some cases, convincing the person to send more money.

Common Telemarketing Strategies and Scams

Senior Scams

Older people are the favorite prey of telescammers. They make up 11% of the population but constitute 33% of the victims of consumer fraud and 63% of all magazine sale scam victims. Forty-five percent of senior citizens have been offered investments by a person unknown to them. Seniors own more than half of all financial assets in the U.S.

Telemarketers usually call in the evening. Nighttime calls find people of every age in more impulsive moods. Seniors may be more vulnerable to pitches promising them extra money and luxury goods because many live on fixed incomes. These lottery-style gambits can seem like an easy way for the elderly to improve their financial status.

The AARP has been active in recent years to promote awareness among seniors that telemarketing swindlers purposely target them. Legislators and law enforcement officials are also realizing action must be taken to combat this type of fraud. Increased awareness is being promoted with specialized training for prosecutors.

Targeting the Unemployed

The unemployed are another favorite target for sweepstakes pitches and job search services. Whereas "the system" has left the jobless without hope, the telemarketer offers a way around official channels. People with bad credit pay telemarketers to "repair" their credit record or get a major card. Instead, they get a list of banks which offer credit cards, commonly published in newspapers, or an application for a card which requires a security deposit for activation, usually several hundred or a thousand dollars. These people are also targeted by advance-fee loan scams, which promise loans in exchange for a fee.

Affinity Fraud

Affinity fraud targets groups of people who have some social connection. Neighborhoods chiefly populated by racial minorities, especially immigrant groups, are often the site of affinity frauds. Religious and professional ties are often exploited. Marketing technology has made it possible for a company to buy targeted lists, not just by location, but also according to buying habits, leisure time activities, and club memberships. The most expensive lists carry the names of people who have already fallen for a telemarketing scam. This is called reloading.

Consolation

When irate customers call telemarketers back to complain, their calls are routed to professionals who placate the caller with more promises and obfuscations. Some boiler rooms have a prearranged communication route for leading complaints through four or five different "departments." This tactic causes many callers to eventually hang up without having spoken to anyone. In some instances, telemarketers confronted with furious callers threatening legal action do award something of value to the customer. Normally the item is worth far less than the person has paid out, however.

If obfuscation and consolation prizes fail to appease the caller, the con turns to threats and intimidation. This is a favorite method for dealing with senior citizens, especially elderly women. Threats are used not just to keep customers from filing complaints, but also to cajole more money out of them. Some telemarketers have actually threatened callers' personal safety if they refused to pay.

The odds in favor of catching a boiler room operation in progress are usually poor. Operations can select a town, set up a room, make their haul, and leave again in a matter of weeks or months. When authorities raid a boiler room, the operation has typically already moved on. If the company owners registered with state regulators, they probably did so under an alias. By the time police arrive, the perpetrators have relocated (often just down the block or across the county line) but the chances of finding them are slim.

Toll-Free Numbers

Toll-free numbers offered by phone service companies are used by some operations. The scam is a toll-free line, advertised in mailers, fliers, and newspaper ads, to lure victims into making the call themselves. The toll-free number usually carries a recording which directs customers to a 900 number that charges the caller between $3 and $10 a minute to hear recorded messages. A favorite device of sellers is to insist that the offer being made is good for less than 48 hours. To secure the opportunity, the customer hands over a cashier's check to an overnight-delivery service. Even if the victim does have second thoughts, he will be unable to stop payment on a cashier's check.

Electronic Debits

Electronic debits allow telemarketers to obtain payment before victims can change their minds about their purchases. Worse, telemarketers can simply use the information to drain the victim's account. This information is usually obtained by telling the victim that the account numbers are needed to "verify eligibility" for a giveaway or "biz op."

Work-at-Home Schemes

Besides franchise offers and other miscellaneous business scams, some of the most prevalent frauds involve work-at-home schemes and FCC related investments. Victims of these phony offerings do not see themselves as part of the telemarketer's prey. They believe they are making a legitimate business investment.

Telemarketers use business-related terms such as exclusive territory, annual gross revenues, and emerging markets in these calls. This helps convince the mark that the biz op is legitimate. A Louis Harris poll found that 1 in 33 cold calls for investments were successful.

Some business-pitch operations are complete fabrications. They offer envelope stuffing or book-review enterprises that do not really exist. Scammers mail out postcards or buy cheap ads in magazines and newspapers. Some may not even take any phone calls. The ads convince the victims to send money to a mailbox. Unlike the U.S. Postal Service, which requires identification from renters, private companies will rent mail drops to anyone for a few dollars a month and can refuse to say who paid for the box.

Business Opportunities (Biz Ops)

Three of the top ten-telemarketing frauds in the NFIC's rating are aimed at people starting their own business. Regulators put losses in fraudulent business opportunities at over $100 million a year, and most observers think the number is far higher. The NFIC points out that in just three recent cases, victims were taken for almost $64 million.

Fly and Buy

Business opportunity scams often gain credibility by setting up a front operation and inviting investors for tours. This part of the ruse is known as the "fly and buy." For example, the Securities Division of the State of Washington prosecuted a case on behalf of a woman who traveled to Colorado and met with a promoter. The promoter offered to let her in on a deal for video pool and video bowling games. Thrilled with the demonstration and her tour guide's promises of quick profits, she paid $13,000 for machines, which broke down in less than three months. When the woman complained to the promoter about the shoddiness of the machines, she was sent two new ones along with a bill.

Shoddy merchandise is a familiar element of the biz op scam. A Maryland ring ran advertisements in *Income Plus* magazine and other investor-oriented publications for a solar-powered car battery recharger. "In seconds, you're off and running," the ad claimed. But the machines were worthless. One investor took the recharger to an electrician and was told it could recharge a battery but that it would take a few weeks.

Other Business Opportunity Scams

Vending Machine and Payphone Scams

Buyers are promised exclusive territories, but find the same area has been sold to many people. Often, the machines do not work or they simply do not make any money.

900 Telephone Number Service

Investors are convinced they can make a fortune charging between $3 and $10 a minute for recorded messages providing entertainment, psychic readings, or information available for free from other sources.

Assembling Jewelry

Unique Gems convinced 15,000 people, mainly recent immigrants, to pay $3,000 each for necklace-making kits. Enrique Pirela, the company's top officer, contributed $85,000 to the Democratic National Committee for seats at a fundraising dinner. While there, Pirela had his picture taken with President Bill Clinton then used the photo in his promotions. By the time a Miami circuit judge shut down the operation, Unique Gems had taken in $15 million.

Employment Services

The phony employment service is similar in nature to the biz op. Preying on the unemployed, these scams promise good jobs, many of them overseas with the added enticement of "tax free" wages. Victims pay between $250 and $1,000 for the service. Some get lists of government jobs, which are available free, or listings from classified ads. Most get nothing.

The FTC won a judgment in the 1990's against Regency Services, Inc. and Omega Promotions, Inc., two Florida companies that advertised openings for cruise ship tour guides, electronic specialists, and chemical engineers. Regency and Omega promised to arrange interviews, and convinced callers answering their ads to turn over their checking account numbers.

Once the interview was arranged, an automatic debit would be made to the customer's account. But the FTC charged, "The defendants invariably debited consumers' checking accounts for as much as $399 without their authorization, and provided consumers with no services at all." Often, these operations disguise themselves as "résumé services" to avoid the licensing requirements of employment agencies.

Inventions Schemes

Using ads, these operations solicit inventors to submit their product ideas to promotions firms, which supposedly specialize in bringing new products to the market. Inventions are supposedly evaluated and appraised, and nearly always endorsed. The firm offers to submit the product to manufacturers for a fee. The FTC maintains that "practically or in reality" these companies guarantee that if the client pays for the promotions package, the invention will make money. These promotions are "very expensive, but almost always fruitless."

In a landmark case, the FTC charged the American Institute for Research and Development, Inc. (AIRD) and its predecessor, American Inventors Corporation (AIC), with running a deceptive inventions-promotion scheme that bilked consumers nationwide out of thousands of dollars each over a 20-year time span.

Promoters used print ads, in-person, and telephone sales presentations to offer two basic services: (1) a "feasibility report," priced from $250 to $495, to evaluate the patent ability and marketability of the inventor's product, and (2) a "representation agreement" that promised to prepare, file, and prosecute a patent application, and to promote the product to industry representatives. The representation agreement cost rose from $5,490 to $11,990.

The complaint alleged that the firms obtained design patents, which have little or no commercial value, instead of the utility patents they promised. Furthermore, people were told that only a select few inventions were accepted, when virtually every person who applied was brought into the program. AIRD and AIC also encouraged their customers to expect huge financial gains when, the Federal Trade Commission charged, "in 20 years of business, perhaps no more than 13 customers have realized any financial gain at all" as a result of the companies' services.

Victims received a useless recommendation for their product and a coding from the U.S. Bureau of Standard Industrial Code (SIC). The code generates a list of manufacturers who make products similar to the inventors', but regulators say the "lists of manufacturers that come from classifying your idea with the SIC usually are of limited value." Some victims thought they were securing a patent in their promotions deal, but instead received only a Disclosure Document from the U.S. Patent Office, available to the general public for $10. The document is not a patent but a statement of "evidence of the date of conception of the invention" and does not guarantee rights to any future products.

Credit Services

Advance-fee loan, credit rating, and credit card scams are among the most common telemarketing frauds. The simplest credit scam promises that the company will secure a loan for the applicant, regardless of credit history and references, if the person pays an upfront fee, usually between $35 and $75. Checking account debits are a favorite payment method, as are 900 numbers, which charge by the minute (up to $40 or $50 per call) to hear information widely available that provides no help in obtaining a loan for the listener. Occasionally, loan information and applications may be mailed out to the victim, but usually, after the fee has been paid, the operators are not heard from again.

South Florida was overrun with advance-fee operations until the state passed a law against them in 1992. Before the prosecutions, the West Palm Beach Better Business Bureau was reporting about ten thousand complaints about phone loans a year.

Credit repair scams promise to "wipe away" or "doctor" or "cosmeticize" blotches on credit, insinuating they have ways of changing or disguising a person's credit history. Though there is no way to erase bad credit, people are charged hundreds of dollars.

Prime-rate credit card scams assure customers they can get a major card for a small fee even if their credit rating is poor. Victims receive an application for a MasterCard, which they could obtain in any department store.

Telemarketers also push "secured" cards, requiring a cash deposit (usually a $250–$300 minimum) in the issuer's bank to activate the card. Perpetrators may provide an invalid card, a card with less value than promised, or one with exorbitant, previously undisclosed interest rates.

Real Estate

In real estate scams buyers are pressured to act quickly on a "once-in-a-lifetime, now-or-never" deal. The investors are led to believe there is no time to investigate the venture and that if they hesitate they will miss the opportunity. Promises of big profits for little or no involvement are the norm in real estate scams. The investor is misled into assuming the promoter is letting them in on a special offer or an exclusive deal.

A variation dispenses with the actual land and sells information about real estate. Companies tout the riches available in real estate through seminars and books, which claim to offer "secret" ways to cash in, usually a collection of tips available cheaper or free elsewhere.

OTHER REAL ESTATE SCAMS

- Timeshares in condominiums for vacationers or reserved space in campgrounds—the property is nonexistent or misrepresented.

- Options—Newspaper ads coax investors into buying “options” on property. Supposedly, the option locks in a present-day price on behalf of the purchaser, who can exercise the option later if he wishes to buy the land or to sell it at a profit. Sometimes the investor has bought nothing but a piece of paper—the “agent” has no authority to make deals on the property. Occasionally, the option is only valid for a few months, or is too vaguely worded to be enforceable. Usually there is an actual plot of land, but in most instances it is undevelopable due to location or zoning restrictions, and is therefore worthless.
- Developed Property—Many buyers are shown the same property. If any property does change hands, it is not the one the buyer was shown.

Art/Rare Items

Paintings worth little more than their canvas and oil are tagged as “masterpieces” sure to grow in value. Lithographic prints, mass-produced by the thousands, are sold as “limited editions.” According to the FTC, the most popular artists to counterfeit are Salvador Dali, Pablo Picasso, Marc Chagall, and Joan Miro.

Collectibles and Memorabilia

Telemarketers also commonly hawk collectibles and household decorative items such as vases, bric-a-brac, and figurines. Again, these supposedly valuable objects are nothing more than cheap, shoddy merchandise. War memorabilia is especially popular, particularly items related to the Civil War and World War II. Documents and keepsakes from any bygone era are on the fraudulent telemarketer’s best-seller list. Stamps are sold as rare when they are in fact worthless.

Coins are another prime moneymaker for telemarketers. “Certificates of authenticity” and “appraisals” are included with the merchandise to reassure customers, but these documents are usually produced by the sales company or doctored from a legitimate original.

Precious Stones

"High-quality" gems are offered for wholesale prices. Customers are told they are being offered a special deal due to fluctuations in the market or because their names are on an industry list. The FTC warns that "most consumers lose a large percentage of the money they invest" in gemstones. Gemstone scams are often run from Canada, targeting American customers.

Companies offer "brokerage" services, which can liquidate the stones at a moment's notice should the investor need the cash back quickly. The stones not only have a grading certificate and appraisal documents; they are sealed in a plastic wrap to guarantee flawless condition. The real purpose of the seal—which victims are told must not be broken if the gems are ever to be offered for sale—is to keep buyers from making a genuine inspection of the article.

Once a victim makes a buy, a company spokesperson calls a second time, saying that if the person buys more stones his "gemstone portfolio" will be more attractive to prospective buyers and at auctions advertised in company literature. If the victim buys additional items, a company broker will inevitably call with "good news." The brokerage will have found a buyer for the victim's holdings, but before the transaction can go through, the customer must pay some "minor fees." These may be passed off as finders' fees, brokers' commissions, examination fees, international duties, or taxes. There may be a provision requiring the victim to buy more stones before making the sale.

A variation on the scheme targets those who have already bought gems from telemarketers and whose names are taken from insider lists. The caller claims to be a broker representing an "overseas buyer" ready to purchase the listener's portfolio. But, invariably, the buyer must have a few more stones in the portfolio—which the caller offers to supply—in order to make the sale, and there are fees and commissions to be paid.

According to the FTC, "Whatever the approach, consumers inevitably end up with gemstones worth only a small fraction of what they paid. In addition, the promises of easy resale, outside buyers, and upcoming auctions have all proven false. Consumers who believe these promises can expect to lose all their investment money."

Precious Metals

Telemarketing operations play on a fluctuating market by offering gold, silver, and platinum. Sometimes the metals are bogus. Otherwise, victims lose money due to undisclosed fees, commissions, and hidden charges.

Selling Free Information

Companies involved in free information schemes take out ads in newspapers and magazines, or buy spots on talk radio, promising they can locate government jobs, get deals on liquidated equipment, or find student loans. All this information is available cheaply or free to the public, through government offices, on the Internet, and from other sources. One need only know where to look.

The NFIC warns, "Federal agencies and the USPS never charge application fees, sell study guides for job tests, or guarantee that an applicant will be hired." For jobs that require competency exams, the agencies usually offer free sample questions to help the applicant prepare.

Study courses that claim to prepare the buyer for passing government aptitude tests, and in some cases promise high scores and a guaranteed job, are also part of the free-info racket. Other bogus offerings promise to make the buyer rich by linking into a network of government auctions selling vehicles and equipment at discount prices.

Maybe the most widely broadcast offering in the info racket is the college scholarship locator service. Student Aid Inc., a New York City firm, provides an example. SAI guaranteed students and their parents that for a $97 fee they would receive at least $1,000 in scholarships or grants. "In reality," government prosecutors showed, "the defendants almost never obtained scholarship money for consumers."

SAI used a common clause in its contracts to keep from paying refunds "requiring students [to] produce letters of rejection from every scholarship on their search list even though the list included scholarships whose deadlines had passed or for which the students did not qualify."

Whatever information scholarship services do provide is available for little or nothing (at most, a $5 or $10 fee) from legitimate institutions. The perpetrators imply that they have insider connections, or that they actually administer the dispersal of monies, when in reality they merely provide lists of scholarships offered by foundations and universities.

Charity Fronts

For an increasing number of groups calling themselves nonprofit, charitable concerns are not what they appear. Very little or no money goes to the advertised cause. Police and firemen's associations have in some cases lent their names to telemarketing fund drives which only give about 35% of their collections to the group. Some boiler room operators claim they are representing various charities when they place a call—for inner-city children, or for the Lions Club or the Jaycees—when they are in no way affiliated with the charity.

An enormous amount of money is donated to social relief. Donations average $120 billion a year for American charities, mostly coming from individuals. By blending in with the vast number of charitable organizations, telemarketers convince victims they are contributing to a worthwhile cause. They often say donations will be given to disease victims or suffering children to convince victims to contribute.

A new twist to this scam is the impersonation of handicapped workers by boiler room operators. Phone pros call victims, claiming to be handicapped or disabled, and attempt to sell light bulbs and other household products. The merchandise is priced at three times its actual value. The operators pocket the money.

Door-to-Door Promotions

Sweepstakes promoters using a charity front offer the possibility of new cars and cash prizes to contributors. The raffle approach—tying the number of "chances" to a set amount—helps drive up how much the victim is willing to give. A favored device of phony charities is to send school-age children door-to-door, saying they are raising money for anti-drug programs or for a group that takes underprivileged kids on trips. Some of the children repeat what they are told in exchange for a few dollars. Others believe they will receive rewards and free trips when in fact they, too, are being scammed. A number of watchdog groups, including the National Charities Information

Bureau, keep files on charitable organizations and publish standards for legitimate organizations to meet.

Prizes, Sweepstakes, and Discount Services

The most common give-away is known as the "1-in-5." A postcard arrives in the mail telling the receiver they have already won a prize. A new Lincoln Continental tops the list, along with $5,000 in cash, a diamond necklace, a living room set, and $500 in gift certificates for clothing and household furnishings. The odds of winning any of the prizes are astronomical. Victims are given trinkets or coupons redeemable only for the company's own shoddy merchandise.

Winners who call back are often asked to stipulate how they intend to spend their winnings for the company's "records," or for "publicity materials." Then they will be asked to pay a processing fee or to prepay the taxes on their winnings. Sometimes winners pay immediately by dialing a 900 number, which charges them for a 10-minute call even if they hang up right away. This practice is a further violation of telemarketing laws, which require a toll number to disconnect no less than 30 seconds after the caller hangs up.

Magazine Subscriptions

A productive front for prize hawkers is the magazine subscription service. Prepaid subscription offers extract money from customers through credit cards and bank debits then never deliver the publication. In other instances, the processing fees far exceed the actual value of the subscriptions. Usually, sweepstakes companies give themselves inventive names such as "Next World Enterprises," or "MagTopia." Others adopt the name of recognizable business such as Publisher's Clearinghouse. To raise the confidence factor, the victims are given a number to call to verify their winnings, which reaches a dummy recording.

Office and Marketing Services Scams

Telemarketing offenses are classified as consumer fraud, yet many businesses are affected by office supply and marketing services scams.

In the now infamous toner scam, an invoice for toner is sent to a company. The cons have usually called beforehand, gotten the name of the employee in charge of supplies, and addressed the invoice to that person. Although the office never ordered or received any toner, the con men are relying on poor communication to cover their ruse. The invoice will most likely be sent to the accounting department and paid, even though the toner will never be shipped. If the proper controls are in place at every level of business operations, this scheme should be detected.

The caller may get a company representative to accept a trial or promotional shipping of the product. He may claim to be a supplier for the company or a new salesman from a regular supplier. The product arrives and an invoice follows a couple of weeks later. If the company tries to send the product back, it is returned to them. To avoid further complications, the company will often settle the bill.

Any sort of office supply, from paper to shelving to cleaning products, can be part of a scam. Medical supplies shipped to doctor's offices and clinics are pushed in a similar fashion. Individual households can be the targets of these ploys as well. Water purifiers are often used in tandem with giveaway offers; the victim buys a filtering device at an inflated cost in order to qualify for the giveaway. Pyramid-style operations often use household products and health-related merchandise, such as vitamins or skin-care cream, as part of their machinations.

In cases where the telemarketing fraudsters do deliver product it is often of low quality resulting in poor output, and can also cause damage to the machines since the products do not have the system matched materials that the original products use. This results in technical support hotline calls, service calls, and dissatisfied customers. Counterfeiters utilize these channels to get their illegally trademarked product to the end user. In trade violations, customers look to the manufacturer to solve these problems and the manufacturers do address them at considerable expense since they want to ensure customer satisfaction and continued brand loyalty.

Recovery Rooms

Recovery room operations target those who have already lost money to a telemarketing scam in a practice known as *reloading.* Posing as a consumer advocacy group or a law firm, telemarketers offer victims a chance to recover any funds they may have lost and bring the perpetrators to justice. Once the victim agrees, legal, investigative, and other fees will begin to emerge. The NFIC finds that recovery rooms are falling off, however. These deceptions have not been in the top ten list of scams since 1995.

TELEMARKETING FRAUD SCAM BY SCAM

Business Opportunities/ Employment	Business Opportunities Fly & Buy Franchising Exotic Animal Ranching Vending Machines, Video Games, etc... Telecommunications Technology Invention Promotions Work-At-Home Overseas Employment Guaranteed Jobs
Credit Services	Advance Fee Loans Secured Credit Cards Credit Applications Credit Repair
Real Estate	Campground/Condo Timeshares Property Options Mineral Rights
Art/Rare Items	Paintings Limited Editions Furnishings Rare Coins Keepsakes War Memorabilia
Precious Stones/ Precious Metals	Gemstones Silver/Gold Market
900 Numbers/ 800 Numbers/ Internat'l Calls	Entertainment Lines Business Opportunities Offshore Calls Credit & Loan Deals Employment Services Prize Giveaways

Selling Free Information	College Scholarships Government Publications College diplomas
Charity Fronts	Fire/Police Groups Handicapped Salespeople Light Bulbs/Household Products Candy/Magazine Sales Youth Volunteers Medical Charities Social Causes Underprivileged Children
Prize/Give-Aways/ Sweepstakes	Free Film Household Products Travel Magazine Subscriptions Imposter Publishers Clearinghouse
Office & Household Supplies	Toner Paper Medical Supplies Water Purifiers Cleaning Products
Recovery Rooms	Phony Law Firms Imposter Enforcement Agencies "Consumer Protection" Groups
Internet	Work-At-Home Prize/Sweepstakes Credit Card Issuing Advance Fee Loans Magazines Telephone Slamming Buyers Club Credit Card Loss Prevention Nigerian Money Offers Business Opportunities

Case Study – 50 State Distributing

According to an investigation by the U.S. Postal Service, a Las Vegas operation called 50 State Distributing, Inc. trained many telemarketers in the 1980's. The company pushed advertising specialties to small businesses, items such as ink pens with *ABC Motors* printed on the casing, for business reps to give out to clients. In 1974, when 50 State opened, the advertising specialties business was booming.

The operation took telemarketing to a new level when it started offering "gifts" with purchases. Operators at 50 State promised business owners that, in addition to their purchase, they would receive a valuable prize. Owners, expecting to write off the purchase on their taxes and keep the "gift" as a bonus, jumped at the deal. However, the merchandise was shoddy, and the prizes, if they ever arrived, were worthless.

Postal inspectors raided 50 State in 1981. The Postal Service is especially vigilant against telescams because operators use the mail as an instrument to distribute their materials. In 1990, the post office delivered 63.7 billion pieces of third class mail, such as the postcards and circulars which telemarketers send to potential victims. Third class paper made up almost 40% of the Postal Service's total mailings, representing $40.4 billion in revenue. The achievements of the raid were less than grand: the corporation known as 50 State paid a small fine and no one was convicted.

Hundreds of operators began fraudulent telemarketing careers through 50 State. Postal authorities estimate that people who learned the trade at 50 State ran four-fifths of the telefrauds they encountered in the 1980's. More than a decade later investigators were still encountering people trained in the 50 State boiler room.

Case Study – Elderly Victims

By the time Betty Malburg's family discovered she had been repeatedly swindled by fraudulent telemarketers, she had less than $100 in her bank account. The 76-year-old widow from Ottawa, Kansas, demonstrated just how much money she lost by pulling a 4-foot register tape from her pocket. The grand total for 1995: $5,327.05.

Malburg said she had been called so many times by so many people, it all ran together. But one scam artist who gained her confidence stands out in her mind. "He was a very nice man. I thought he was my friend," she said. "He was always calling." He told her she had won a Bahamas vacation if she would pay for the hotel. She was promised a new Cadillac, which was hard to refuse because her car was 12 years old. "I was going to get a new car. I was going to prove to my family that I won something," she said. "I was dumb enough … to give him my credit card number."

Case Study – Tim O'Neil

In another case, Fred Schulte, author of *Fleeced!* relates the pitch delivered to an elderly woman in Philadelphia by Tim O'Neil. The woman told detectives about the more than $10,000 for which O'Neil and his lieutenants swindled her. O'Neil's call to mollify the woman's protests was recorded by the FBI. On the line, he insists the "collectibles" the woman bought, including "actual bullets excavated from the Civil War," are genuine and valuable.

> *Do you wear pendants? This is a beautiful, is a diamond. . . I'm not gonna ask you to spend a penny. . .*
>
> *How old are you? God bless you. . . 89 . . .*
>
> *We're gonna get that out to you. . . Look for it in the middle of next week, and then give us a call and then let us know how you like it. . . .*
>
> *Well I hope I put a little sunshine in your day. OK, honey and God bless you. Oh don't cry now, we're here to take care of you. . . . We'll be here and if you need to talk to anybody at any time you give us a call okay? Bye, bye, and God bless you.*

Case Study – Consolidated Payphones

Fred Schulte also describes how a California man flew to Fort Lauderdale to meet with Jim Brown of Consolidated Payphones. Consolidated had an office staff, salespeople enthusiastically discussing placement arrangements with customers, a manufacturing area where technicians assembled the phones and tested the dialing pads with an electric pencil, and a warehouse with boxes of phones ready to be shipped.

The victim was impressed with what he saw and left a $14,000 check with Brown. He mailed Brown a check for an additional $11,000 when he got home. The victim would lose a total of $29,000, including the $3,000 he paid to a Consolidated "consultant" who scouted locations for the pay phones.

Consolidated Payphones was a highly detailed sham. The phones shown to the victim were bought from a supplier and set up for investor tours. The testing devices were linked to a computer, which played out a dummy pattern on the screen whenever someone touched the electric pencil to the dialing pad. The boxed phones in the warehouse were not real, either. A Consolidated executive told prosecutors that Dalton "bought empty boxes and hired two people from the labor pool...and he drove over to pick up cinder blocks...He had them put the cinder blocks in these cartons and seal them up and put them on the floor like there were phones in them."

Biz Op Red Flags

Whatever the nature of the opportunity, there are signs that indicate that it is not legitimate. Among the most common are:

- Classified ads urging the prospect to call an 800 number.
- Wild, unsubstantiated claims about potential earnings.
- Promises about exclusive territories, assurances about good locations, or the assistance of a professional locator.
- References specified by the company.
- The lack of a complete disclosure document containing information about the promoter's experience, lawsuit history, audited financial statements, and substantiation for earnings assertions.

Sources:
Gordon, M. "Phone Fraud, Canadian-Style, Becoming a Problem In the U.S." *The Association Press,* May 7, 2001.

"William R. Duffy President and C.E.O. International Intellectual Property Protection Inc. Before Senate on Small Business Office Supply Scams." *Federal News Service,* March 28, 2000.

Related Entries:

CON SCHEMES
CONSUMER FRAUD
INTERNET FRAUD

TONE AT THE TOP

In January of 2001, Walt Pavlo received a 41-month federal prison sentence for money laundering, wire fraud, and obstruction of justice. Pavlo claimed that he was pressured by his bosses to commit financial statement fraud at MCI WorldCom. As a senior manager in billing collections, he dealt with customer payments, credits, and reconciliations of accounts. Upper management described revenue projections and, according to Pavlo, pressured employees to meet or exceed these projections. As Pavlo watched his bosses manipulate the organization's financial records, he and his colleagues soon began to do the same. Pavlo and his supervisors then began meeting to devise ideas on cooking the organization's books. His supervisors taught him how to conceal uncollectible debt, which boosted the company's assets and profits. Pavlo's employees then followed his fraudulent example. Auditors eventually found Pavlo's unusual journal entries, confronted him, and he confessed.

Similar to others who commit white-collar crime, Pavlo at first didn't believe he was doing anything wrong. He felt that he was just doing his job and making his employers happy by altering the company's financial data. He convinced himself that the problem ultimately would remedy itself – a highly unlikely scenario in which he believed that the company's revenues would grow enough to cover his transgressions.

Even highly educated and well-experienced employees can become white-collar criminals if their bosses pressure them enough. Pavlo held an industrial engineering degree and an MBA and had worked for five years at WorldCom but that didn't stop him from succumbing to the wishes of his supervisors and then corrupting his employees.

After his conviction, Pavlo left behind his wife and two young sons to serve his prison sentence.

What can employers do to prevent the creation of wayward employees? Setting a good tone at the top is a start.

'TONE AT THE TOP' DEFINED

An organization's leadership creates the tone at the top – an ethical (or unethical) atmosphere in the workplace. Management's tone has a trickle-down effect on employees. If top managers uphold ethics and integrity so will employees. But if upper management appears unconcerned with ethics and focuses solely on the bottom line, employees will be more prone to commit fraud and feel that ethical conduct isn't a priority. In short, employees will follow the examples of their bosses.

The National Commission on Fraudulent Reporting (the Treadway Commission) released a groundbreaking study in 1987 that reported the causal factors that lead to fraudulent behavior and financial statement fraud. According to the commission, the tone at the top plays a crucial and influential role in creating a ripe environment for fraudulent financial reporting.

Corporate greed at the executive level has destroyed hundreds of companies, drained stockholders of their investments, and left innocent employees without work. Ken Lay, Jeffrey Skilling, and Andrew Fastow from Enron; Bernie Ebbers from MCI/WorldCom; and Dennis Kozlowski at Tyco have become household names, and are synonymous with what's wrong with our corporate system. Furthermore, these individuals represent only a small percentage of the executives who have abused their posts of power to commit corporate fraud. According to the SEC, over 100 public company CEOs have been sued over the last five years for committing white-collar crimes. These CEO criminals were sending a clear (though perhaps unintentional) message to their employees that *committing fraud is acceptable as long as it makes the company seem profitable.* Obviously, they weren't setting an ethical tone at the top for their employees.

Major Fraud Factors

Three major factors common in many large organizational frauds contributed to Walt Pavlo's downfall:

- **Meeting analysts' expectations** – Upper management and employees who feel pressure to perform to the expectations of analysts can lead to occupational fraud.
- **Compensation and incentives** – Pavlo was eligible for thousands of dollars in stock options each year, beyond his salary, if he was able to meet his financial targets.
- **Pressure to reach goals** – Obviously, the greater the pressure and fear employees feel to meet revenue goals, the more likely they are to turn to fraud to meet those goals. With the help of Pavlo's supervisors, he delayed write-offs and dressed-up the revenue to make it appear that they were collectible.

Common Ethical Violations

According to the 2005 National Business Ethics Study (NBES), from the Ethics Resource Center (www.ethics.org), the falsification and misrepresentation of financial records constituted 5% of the ethical violations reported in its survey. Following are the other common types of ethical violations observed by employees (as well as their corresponding percentages) in the workplace.

- Abusive or intimidating behavior of superiors toward employees (21%)
- Lying to employees, customers, vendors, or the public (19%)
- A situation that places employee interests over organizational interests (18%)
- Violations of safety regulations (16%)
- Misreporting actual time or hours worked (16%)
- E-mail and Internet abuse (13%)
- Discrimination on the basis of race, color, gender, age, or similar categories (12%)
- Stealing, theft, or related fraud (11%)
- Sexual harassment (9%)
- Provision of goods or services that fail to meet specifications (8%)
- Misuse of confidential information (7%)
- Price fixing (3%)
- Giving or accepting bribes, kickbacks, or inappropriate gifts (3%)

The NBES points out that every organization needs to be able to answer this question: How much misconduct is considered acceptable/inevitable within the organization? This question will help prepare upper management to focus on the ways it can deal with employee behavior problems.

Why Employees Don't Report Unethical Conduct

According to the NBES, only 55% of employees in 2005 said they reported misconduct that they observed in the workplace, a 10% decrease from the previous survey in 2003.

In the 2003 NBES survey, employees under age 30 with little tenure with an organization (less than three years) were the least likely of any group to report ethical misconduct because of their fear of retaliation from management and coworkers. They also felt that managers would consider them "trouble makers" if they reported unethical conduct. Middle managers and senior managers were most likely to report misconduct. However, in 2005, there was no significant statistical relationship between age/tenure and reporting. The top reasons for not reporting unethical conduct, according to the 45% of employees who *didn't* report misconduct, were the following:

No Corrective Action

Employees who were cynical of their organizations felt that nothing would be done if they came forward and reported misconduct. In 2005, 59% of those who didn't report misconduct felt as though no corrective action would be taken if they *had* reported unethical conduct. However, the NBES states that these employees might have had unrealistic expectations for how organizations should handle misconduct reports. Privacy restrictions might prevent the companies from telling whistle-blowers how the report was handled and what punishments were assessed to the suspicious perpetrator. The organization should stress the privacy factor to convince these employees that their reporting will be handled appropriately even if the whistle-blower might not find out about it.

No Confidentiality of Reports

Those who see but don't report misconduct, fear that if they were to come forward with a report, their identities would be revealed.

Retaliation by Superiors

Not surprisingly, this same group of employees also felt that if their identities were exposed, they would have to suffer retaliation from their superiors.

Retaliation by Coworkers

Similar to retaliation by superiors, employees who withheld reporting unethical behavior in the workplace feared that their coworkers would find out who blew the whistle and retaliate against them.

Unsure Whom to Contact

A small number of the employees who didn't report misconduct (18% in 2005) said they were unclear whom to contact to raise their suspicions of unethical conduct.

Employees who witnessed their companies actively following their code of ethics were the *most* likely to report misconduct in the workplace, according to the 2005 NBES. They were also more likely to be satisfied with their organization's response to reported misconduct. Those who work for organizations that implement formal ethics programs were considerably more prone to reporting the misconduct that they observed. Those who don't report misconduct might have had a poor experience trying to do so. Executives must reach out to those disenfranchised employees and reiterate that the identity of all whistle-blowers will remain confidential.

Conveying Responsibility, Accountability

Organizational leaders can take several steps to convey the message of individual and corporate responsibility and accountability to its employees, contractors, and investors.

Set an Ethical Tone at the Top

Upper management has to lead by example and actions. These actions should include rewarding ethical behavior while punishing unethical actions. An organization should have sanctions for engaging in, tolerating, or condoning improper conduct.

Establish a Code of Ethics

An organization should produce a clear statement of management philosophy. It should include concise compliance standards that are consistent with management's ethics policy relevant to organizational operations. This code of ethics should be given to all employees (and contractors) who'll be required to read and sign it.

Carefully Screen Job Applicants

According to the ACFE's *Fraud Examiners Manual*, one of the easiest (and obvious) ways to establish a strong moral tone for an organization is to hire morally sound employees. Too often, the hiring process is hastily conducted. Organizations should conduct thorough background checks on all new employees especially managers and those who will be handling cash. These background checks should include a thorough examination of the candidate's educational credentials, criminal record, history of employment, and references. Speaking with former employers or supervisors can provide valuable information about a person's reputation for trustworthiness, moral conduct, and loyalty.

Assign Proper Authority and Responsibility

Place ethical employees where they're able to thrive without resorting to unethical conduct. Organizations should provide employees with well-defined job descriptions and performance goals. The employees' managers should routinely review these goals to ensure that they don't set unrealistic standards. They should also provide training so that employees maintain the skills to perform effectively. Regular ethics training will also help employees identify potential trouble spots and avoid getting caught in compromising situations. Finally, management should quickly determine deficiencies in an employee's conduct and work with him or her to fix the problem.

Mandate Anti-Fraud and Ethics Training for Staff

Use training sessions for all staff (including upper-level personnel) as tools to communicate and reinforce the organization's values, expectations, and stance on corporate compliance including its code of ethical conduct, continuing procedures and standards, and employees' roles and responsibilities to report misconduct. The training sessions should also inform employees about acts and omissions prohibited by law and by the organization to help them avoid situations that could lead to criminal conduct. Common training techniques include lectures, training films, and interactive workshops. Regularly emphasize compliance standards.

Implement Effective Disciplinary Measures

No control environment will be effective unless there's consistent discipline for ethical violations. Consistent discipline requires a well-defined set of sanctions for violations and strict adherence to them. If one employee is punished for an act and another employee isn't punished for a similar act, the moral force of the organization's ethics policy will be diminished. The levels of discipline must be sufficient to deter violations. The organization could also reward ethical conduct to reinforce the importance of organizational ethics.

Implement a Confidential Hotline

According to the ACFE's *2006 Report to the Nation on Occupational Fraud and Abuse*, occupational frauds were more likely to be detected by a tip than any other means such as internal audits, external audits, or internal controls. Additionally, organizations with hotlines had a median loss of $100,000 per scheme and detected their frauds within 15 months of inception. By contrast, organizations without hotlines suffered twice the median loss and took 24 months to detect their frauds. The mere mention of an anti-fraud, confidential hotline can deter fraud. When employees are aware of workplace ethics, their likelihood of engaging in misconduct decreases, according to the 2005 National Business Ethics Study. An organization can place an advertisement in the staff break room with a hotline number that employees can call to confidentially report suspicious fraudulent activity in the workplace.

Establish a Whistle-Blower Policy

A whistle-blower policy should allow employees to report or seek guidance about actual or potential criminal conduct by others within the organization while retaining anonymity or confidentiality and without fear of retaliation. Additionally, in many organizations, whistle-blowers could be protected by state and federal law. Consult with your legal counsel to train and educate employees about whistle-blower protections.

Follow-Through with Reports of Misconduct and Promote Effective Internal Controls

Organizations must have a standard procedure for dealing with fraud allegations. The management team must conduct a full-fledged investigation when misconduct is reported. After an offense has been detected, the organization must take all reasonable steps to respond appropriately to prevent further similar offenses including any necessary modifications to its program to prevent and detect violations of the law. Those at the top of the organization are responsible for clearly stating and upholding the message that all employees are required to act within the organization's ethical code of conduct. This message *must* be enforced to prevent and deter fraud in the organization.

Create a Culture of Doing the Right Thing

When an organization implements all of the above steps and assures that everyone in the organization (especially those at the top) are actively maintaining corporate standards it will create a culture of "doing the right thing." Organizations should *always* strive for this ultimate goal.

Sources:
ACFE, AICPA. *Fraud and the Tone at the Top.* www.acfe.com/fraud/tools.asp

Related Entries:

PREVENTION POLICIES FOR FRAUD

TRAVEL AND ENTERTAINMENT EXPENSE REPORT FRAUD

Travel and entertainment expense report fraud is a form of occupational fraud and abuse, committed by employees while traveling on company business. Methods include mischaracterizing expenses, overstating expenses, creating fictitious expenses, and multiple reimbursements. According to a statement in the 2006 Sarbanes-Oxley Compliance Journal, these types of fraud ranked second as the greatest controllable cost in most organizations.

- *Mischaracterized Expenses.* Items or services purchased for personal use are reported as business expenses. Examples include purchasing fuel for personal trips with a company credit card, reporting personal gifts as gifts for business contacts, and reporting golf or other recreation as business expense when it was not. Certain purchases that may appear as fraud at first glance may be legitimate. For example, a sales agent may purchase a children's video for a client because the client's children continually interrupt meetings.

- *Overstating Expenses.* Expenses may be inflated by altering or adding numbers to receipts and reports, by claiming non-existent cash tips, or by inflating mileage reports. Specific examples include claiming per diem for five days when the travel lasted three days, falsifying the amount of taxi receipts, or altering hotel invoices.
- *Creating Fictitious Expenses.* Examples of expense items commonly faked include university tuition, office supplies, and meals.
- *Multiple Reimbursements.* Invoices are submitted to more than one department for reimbursement, or are modified for repeated submission. Examples include copied airline tickets, and applying for reimbursement for a hotel bill when the bill was paid for with a company credit card.

Who Commits TER Fraud?

The most likely perpetrators are:

- Valued, hard-working employees above suspicion
- Married
- Members of religious organizations
- College-educated
- Without arrest records
- Social conformists
- Acting alone

Investigating TER Fraud

Using an electronic spreadsheet of an individual's transactions, TER fraud may be discovered by sorting and matching. The spreadsheet generally contains:

- Date and day of the week of each transaction and its posting
- Type of expenditure
- MCC Code, identifying vendor types
- Vendor name
- Location of purchase

- Amount of purchase

Sorting by day of the week may be revealing, particularly for transactions on weekend days or holidays. Sorting by vendors may reveal repeated purchases or vendor accomplices. Sorting by the type of purchase may reveal multiple purchases or unreasonable purchases, such as six meals charged on one day.

Red flags include:

- Invoices from European vendors with American style dating
- Invoices from foreign countries with a currency other than the host country's
- Sequential numbering of invoices
- Invoice alterations
- Illegitimate descriptions in invoices
- Illegitimate or non-existent vendors

Paper trails, the use of Excel, or other "do-it-yourself" tracking techniques are no longer reliable. The Sarbanes-Oxley Act (SOX) of 2002, which requires strict documentation for efficiency and control, has boosted the market for automated Travel and Entertainment Expense systems which can detect red flags faster, reducing this form of occupational fraud.

Related Entries:

EXPENSE REIMBURSEMENT SCHEMES
OCCUPATIONAL FRAUD AND ABUSE

TREADWAY COMMISSION

See, COSO

TRIPPET, ROBERT

Robert Trippet was born in 1927 in Bartlesville, Oklahoma, where his father ran the Savings and Loan Association. He attended the University of Oklahoma and later the university's School of Law. As a lawyer in Tulsa, he began handling oil revenue contracts. He expanded his business when he married Helen Grey Simpson, daughter of J.R. Simpson, one of Tulsa's prominent oilmen.

In 1953, Mr. Simpson turned over the family's main holdings—the Home-Stake Oil & Gas Company and the Home-Stake Royalty Corporation—to his eldest son, O. Strother Simpson. Trippet convinced his brother-in-law to expand Home-Stake into tax-shelter drilling operations. Trippet touted his clients' "actual out-of-pocket costs," as opposed to the actual amount of money they put in. On a single unit of participation, an investor in the highest tax bracket who bought a $20,000 unit incurred "actual out-of-pocket costs" of $5,000. (The other $15,000 would have gone to taxes, so it's already counted as a gain in value.) Any gain in the total real value of the investment, and any money withdrawn during the life of the drilling operation, was taxed as capital gains (around 30%) instead of income. Over a 12-year program, investors could earn 350% or more on their money.

In 1958, Strother Simpson accused Trippet of embezzlement and resigned from the company. Trippet then began selling to investors in New York City and the East Coast. William Murray, whose flair as "an imaginative tax and estate-planning specialist" had attracted clients from the corporate world, assisted him. Through Murray, Bob picked up participants from General Electric, Warner-Lambert, Pepsi-Cola, and Colgate, among others.

Also in 1959, Home-Stake entered the market for "secondary recovery," which refers to the synthetic extraction of oil or gas. In these operations, analysts confirmed that an ample pool of oil existed on a property. But no one could bring the oil to the surface using conventional methods. Secondary recovery operations were using new drilling techniques such as steamflooding, in which hot water injections forced the oil into the pumping apparatus. "We have been able to eliminate entirely from this program any wildcats or semi-proven prospects," Trippet promised clients, though the government had made steamflooding investments totally tax free because the odds of actually recovering a significant amount of oil remained solidly *against* the investor. By 1963, Bob was selling $10 million a year, and he expanded his clientele into the world of show business, with the help of an investment counselor named Martin Bregman, who would later produce the films *Serpico* and *Dog Day Afternoon.*

Trippet needed a constant source of new money because the poor performance of his drilling operations had turned Home-Stake into a Ponzi scheme. He had used a large portion of the 1959 receipts to pay off participants who had bought into Home-Stake's very first offerings in 1955. (Each investment "program" matured in 4 years.) Using those funds for payments meant that the 1959 drilling operations weren't fully funded. Over time, the combination of under funding and underproduction forced Trippet to use new investors' money to pay off earlier programs, with the debt mounting constantly.

Because he couldn't hide all his losses, Trippet began recommending that clients donate their shares to charity, taking a tax deduction at a highly inflated, Trippet-provided price. Trippet valued a $19,000 unit for $40,000 to $80,000 by counting future receipts, which never materialized. In the 1960's Trippet began illegally circulating what he called the Black Book in lieu of the company's SEC prospectus. The Black Book was a leather-bound collection of documents and photos, stamped in gold letters with each investor's name, promising new profits in California properties. "Steamflooding is without doubt the most important development in the secondary recovery industry in many years. Success ratios are good, and outstanding results are being achieved. We calculate that we will be able to recover 18,863,100 barrels of oil allocable to the interests of our participants at an excellent profit for them."

In fact, Home-Stake's steamflooding programs weren't making any money. A buried disclosure in the 1966 prospectus showed that the programs in 1963, '64 and '65 had failed: the '63 program had returned less than 20% of its investors' cash; the '64 program, less than 10%; the '65, none. But thanks to Trippet's manipulations, sales for 1967 exceeded $11 million, followed by $17 million in 1968, nearly $20 million for 1969, and $25 million in 1970.

In March 1971 the SEC filed a complaint attacking Trippet's use of the Black Book in 1970, demanding that Trippet return all investors' money for that year. Trippet settled by giving back $5 million of the $23 million he raised.

As Home-Stake's financial condition worsened and its wells continued to fail, Trippet stalled and raged. On July 16, 1973 the Home-Stake board fired him, but allowed him to stay on as chairman. In 1972 the SEC announced criminal charges forthcoming against Trippet associates Harry Fitzgerald, Frank Sims, Conrad Greer, auditor Norman Cross, and the board of directors along with Trippet himself. The IRS challenged the donation of Home-Stake units to charities, finding them grossly overvalued, and demanded payment of $10 million in delinquent taxes.

Trippet was tried in Tulsa in 1973 for 38 criminal violations, including 22 counts of securities fraud, 23 counts of filing false tax documents, and three counts of mail fraud. Forensic accountant Sammy Hughes filed an affidavit demonstrating that Trippet had used investor monies to pay dividends. Hughes said Home-Stake had legitimately turned a profit, a tiny one, in 1964 and had lost money every other year of its 19-year lifespan.

Judge Allen Barrow made no secret of his disdain for the prosecutors, calling the affair "a showplace of U.S. Government indecision in the area of prosecutory discretion." After Trippet and his co-defendants struck a plea bargain, Barrow haughtily announced:

"Now, at the conclusion of long manipulations, pleas of guilty, nolo pleas and three acquittals, transfer and retransfer, three pages of transcript in daily copy, certain aspects of the so-called Home-Stake trial have become clear to me as the trial judge. The whole thing is not what was pictured by some eastern newspapers and magazines in their colorful or sensational reports of, however you want to call it, 'the century's greatest swindle.' I have seen evidence that there was a grandiose promotional scheme that went sour. I know that the men concerned in the matter confessed by their pleas a degree of wrongdoing in that pleas of guilty and nolo contendere have been entered to various charged offenses. These men admit having done wrong, having violated the trust that the individual reposed in them. One must accept these confessions of fault and abide by the judgments upon themselves hereby pronounced."

Barrow sentenced Bob Trippet to three years' probation and a $19,000 fine, plus a $100,000 payment to the Home-Stake bankruptcy trustee.

Investor suits and amended complaints from the IRS and SEC dragged on for another 20 years. In 1983, Trippet and other company officials settled investor suits worth some $20 million. In 1988, a civil jury convicted Trippet, Vice President Frank Sims, Treasurer Elmer Kunkel, and Auditor Norman Cross. Later the 10th Circuit Court of Appeals overturned the verdict because the trial judge had instructed the jury to consider whether the defendants "aided and abetted" the scheme as well as whether each man played a direct role. A U.S. Supreme Court decision had recently found that a private plaintiff had no right to press an aiding-and-abetting charge. In October 1996, the last class-action suits were settled, with the terms sealed by the court. Tulsa news sources estimated that Trippet was found liable for about $75 million, plus over $6 million in attorney's fees.

Source:
Wells, J., CFE, CPA. *"Frankensteins of Fraud."* Austin, TX: Obsidian Publishing Co., 2000.

Related Entries:
FINANCIAL STATEMENT FRAUD
PONZI SCHEME
SECURITIES FRAUD

TURNER, GLENN

Glenn Turner ran a pyramid scheme during the 1970's and 1980's under the banner *Dare to Be Great!* Turner came from South Carolina, "the son of a $500 a year tobacco farmer," a lineage which, he claimed, proved his motivational system worked. He was a nobody with an eighth-grade education and a cleft lip—"poor harelipped Glenn," as Turner described himself. If he could make it, anyone could. Beginning in 1967, Turner promoted his simplistic, clichéd self-esteem publications and tapes as a "business opportunity." By 1969, "poor Glenn" was signing a thousand new distributors a month. Within three years his flock numbered 75,000 in eight countries.

Turner logged over 500,000 miles a year leading seminars he billed as "Adventures" in self-realization. His approach was unabashedly circus-like. He was accompanied by two midgets wearing matching costumes. Events began with the little people leading the crowd in chants for an hour or more—"Go-Go-Go-Go! Mmmmmmoney!!"—which was known as "money-humming." Inspired participants leaped onto chairs, shouted, hugged one another, and spun in a circle with clenched hands, often waving handfuls of money and throwing it into the air.

In Turner's system, participants paid $300 for Adventure I, a set of cassette tapes and printed materials involving self-esteem and getting rich. Adventure II offered a similar package for $700. After purchasing the $900 Adventure III, participants were authorized to sell Adventure products to others. Adventure IV cost $5,000 and admitted participants fully into the organization then charged them more money to attend seminars, sales meetings, and conventions. A fast-track package offered to move participants immediately into Adventures III for $1,000.

Besides motivational materials, Turner's catalogs featured merchandise lines with names like "Fashcot" (wigs), "Emcot" (fur coats), and "Transcot" (a trucking firm). Distributors got a 10% discount on purchases from any of the 70 subsidiary companies. But distributors got rich—or expected to—by convincing other people to become distributors. For $5,000 worth of *Dare* products sold, participants kept $2,000 to $3,000. Koscot distributorships sold for $5,000, though Turner did not produce the product.

The FTC, SEC, and Postal Department all took action against Turner in 1971. Turner eventually drew fraud charges in all 50 states as well, with 1,500 distributors among the plaintiffs. In one New York town of 7,000 people, 1,000 residents had joined the Turner scam. The New York attorney general found that of 1,604 participants in Turner's Koskot subsidiary, only 79 made more than $5,000 a year. The FTC estimated that 70,000 investors lost $44 million.

Turner's defense attorney, F. Lee Bailey, was himself indicted for helping promote the Turner plan, though he was acquitted in 1975. The various Turner trials produced legal precedents for taking down future pyramid operators, and inspired states across the nation to write laws against pyramiding. Turner was convicted of misdemeanor charges in Pinellas County, Florida in 1973, fined $2,500 and placed on probation for 5 years.

Turner ran for state senator in Florida in 1974, but lost. He was said to have liabilities approaching $200 million. Despite later convictions in the 1980's and 1990's, Turner continued to sell self-improvement products on the Internet and elsewhere.

Source:
Norman, B. "Thursday A Most-Wanted Attorney." *New Times Broward-Palm Beach,* September 28, 2000.

Related Entry:

CONSUMER FRAUD

TYCO

Tyco International is a conglomerate headquartered in Bermuda with U.S. headquarters in New Jersey. Largely known for manufacturing a range of products from electronics to medical supplies, the company became the subject of controversy in 2002 when the Securities and Exchange Commission (SEC) began investigating ex-CEO Dennis Kozlowski, former CFO Mark H. Swartz, and ex-general council Mark Belnick. Examination of Tyco's bookkeeping led to the executives' September 2003 indictment for grand larceny, corruption, conspiracy, and falsifying records. The SEC found that Kozlowski and Swartz had managed to swindle over $170 million in corporate loans without proper disclosures, approvals, and notifications, and had pocketed approximately $430 million by misstating Tyco's finances and manipulating the company's stock price. Belnick was indicted for falsifying business records to hide nearly $17 million in loans given to him by Tyco.

Charges of corporate abuse were bolstered by Kozlowski's ostentatious lifestyle; yachts and Harley Davidsons, property on 5th avenue in New York City, a waterfront mansion in Boca Raton, Florida, and real estate in Nantucket, Massachusetts. The homes were filled with equally lavish decorations: extravagant artwork, a $6,000 shower curtain, a $15,000 umbrella stand. Kozlowski is perhaps most infamous for the $2 million party he hosted on Sardinia in honor of his wife's birthday, during which he showcased his stolen riches in the form of an ice sculpture of Michelangelo's "David," whose male part emitted a fountain of vodka. Swartz and Belnick also dipped into the Tyco account and purchased a swanky upper-east-side NYC apartment and a Central Park flat, respectively, along with other expensive property. Essentially, the defendants blurred the lines between Tyco International's bank account and their own to support executive excess.

First Trial

In July 2004, following a six month trial against Kozlowski and Swartz, a mistrial was declared after juror Ruth Jordan received improper contact via letter and telephone from a defendant. She also allegedly signaled "o.k." to Kozlowski – a gesture that did not go unnoticed in the courtroom. In a separate trial, however, a grand jury acquitted Belnick of all corporate wrongdoing.

Second Trial and Criminal Charges

In the second trial in July 2005, prosecutors abandoned the charge of enterprise corruption. On June 17th, 2005, the Manhattan Supreme Court found Kozlowski and Swartz guilty on twenty-two counts, including grand larceny, conspiracy, falsifying business records, and securities fraud against company shareholders for over $400 million. Kozlowski and Swartz were sentenced to between eight and one third to twenty-five years in prison on September 19, 2005. Kozlowski has been ordered to pay nearly $170 million in fines and restitution and Swartz has been ordered $72 million in fines and restitution.

SEC Charges

The SEC had delayed separate but related civil cases against the duo. Tyco International must pay the SEC a civil penalty of $50 million to resolve allegations for the violation of securities laws which were violated under Kozlowski's watch. The SEC will then distribute the money to harmed investors.

Sources:
"Tyco Paying SEC $50M on Accounting Charges." Forbes.com, August 30, 2006

"Tyco Trial II: Verdict First, Law Second." Forbes.com, August 30, 2006

"Three Tyco Execs Indicted for Fraud." CNN.com, August 30, 2006

"Tyco Fraud." SecuritiesFraudFYI.com, August 30, 2006

"Tyco International." Wikepedia.org, August 30, 2006

"How Did Tyco Defraud Shareholders?" *SecuritiesFraudFYI.com*. October 7, 2004. www.securitiesfraudfyi.com/tyco.html.

Masters, B. and Johnson, C. "Former Tyco Executive Acquitted." *Washingtonpost.com*, July 16, 2004.

Maull, S. "Top Count is Withdrawn in Tyco Retrial." *Lancaster Online*, September 29, 2004.

"Securities and Exchange Commission v. L. Dennis Kozlowski, Mark H. Swartz, and Mark A. Belnick." Complaint filed in the United States District Court, Southern District of New York, September 11, 2002. www.sec.gov/litigation/complaints/complr17722.htm.

"SEC Sues Former Tyco CEO Kozlowski, Two Others for Loans." U.S. Securities and Exchange Commission, September 12, 2002. www.sec.gov/news/press/2002-135.htm.

"Tyco Fraud." Edgar Snyder & Associates, May 2003. www.edgarsnyder.com.

Related Entry:

SECURITIES FRAUD

VESCO, ROBERT

Robert Vesco was born in Detroit in 1935. Vesco, a high school dropout spent a few years working in body shops and machine shops, Vesco then landed a job as a blueprint operator and trainee draftsman at the Packard Motor Company. Later he worked for Reynolds Aluminum, which transferred him to the Reynolds headquarters in New York City in 1959.

Vesco eventually became a freelance salesman for Eagle Aluminum Products, which helped him make the business contacts necessary to acquire a company called Captive Seal, a struggling operation that held a patent on a specialized gasket used in aerospace equipment. He managed to list the company on the American Stock Exchange without registering or auditing its books for the SEC by purchasing a shell corporation called Cryogenics Ltd. and merging Captive Seal as a subsidiary. Both companies were later subsumed into the International Controls Corporation (ICC) in the summer of 1965. By 1968, ICC held more than a dozen companies, and Vesco had built a reputation as a rising star in the world of manufacturing conglomerates.

Vesco committed his first major fraud during his takeover of Electronic Specialty, a California based operation, founded and chaired by William H. Burgess, that was founded to produce electric razors, which later shifted into aircraft manufacture. After unsuccessful negotiations with management, Vesco sold his stock holdings and leaked a rumor he was backing out of the deal, even though he was assembling a new bid. Judge Ed McLean reviewed the case and declared:

- The initial tender offer by ICC was misleading;
- Burgess's charges met the standards for proceeding to trial;
- Burgess would probably win at trial.

But Judge McLean would not prevent Vesco's taking over Electronic Specialty. "A preliminary injunction here might do the stockholders more harm than good," he wrote. On appeal, Judge Morris Lasker found, "Vesco made misleading statements on several key occasions, in private discussions with Electronic Specialty and in public releases, claiming he had no intention of proceeding to a tender offer, when he in fact did." However, Lasker added, "The requested relief is impractical, inappropriate and punitive in nature," and refused to impose any sanctions against Vesco.

In the move that made his reputation, and eventually made him a fugitive, Vesco approached Bernard Cornfeld about taking a stake in Cornfeld's International Overseas Services (IOS). Cornfeld had become well known and rich by promoting mutual funds, an investment vehicle that had been around since the 1920's, but was not widely used until Cornfeld began selling them in the late 1940's. By the late 1950's, Americans were holding $17 billion in mutual funds. The concept was simple enough: instead of investing directly in the market, mutual fund investors bought shares in the fund. The managers of the fund invested the cash in a diversified portfolio, and returned the profits to investors.

In 1962, Cornfeld created a "Fund of Funds" (FOF) that invested in other mutual funds. Fees and what the industry calls "front-end load charges" were Cornfeld's favored tools for knocking off his customers. IOS salesmen cut 8-1/2% from every dollar invested; commission and fees together pushed the damage to 9 or 10%. That meant if the investor "paid" $1,000 to their IOS account, they only "invested" $900. Since the average mutual fund was returning 8 or 9% a year, the investor's first year earnings went to Cornfeld and his salesmen. When Cornfeld added another layer with the Fund of Funds, he charged customers to transfer their money from FOF into the individual funds and a management fee; the front-end load might reach 15%. That whittled a $1,000 investment down to $850. The Fund of Funds held about $1 million in October of 1962; a year later, it held $17 million. By 1965, FOF was booming with $200 million. Besides funneling money to other IOS funds, FOF bought stakes in all of America's premier mutual funds.

In May 1970, Henry Buhl, Chairman of the Board of Directors of FOF, suggested that Vesco take over Investors Overseas Services. The company had just mounted a successful IPO on the London Exchange in late 1969. But IOS was bust. There were still millions in the various funds, nearly $500 million in the Fund of Funds alone. But the IOS umbrella corporation was bankrupt. Vesco's ICC was hurting financially as well. Vesco promised the IOS board he would extend them a $20-million line of credit, with $5 million up front. "It is not our intent to assume control of IOS," he said, reading from a prepared statement, "but simply to benefit by what may be an attractive investment opportunity." Unless a full reorganization was effected by July 1971, Vesco would receive cash payments worth $3.5 million, plus stock warrants representing one-third of the company. Vesco was already making preparations behind the scenes to loot the company. Between November 1970 and March of 1971, he caused IOS to place some $10 million in a bank in which he held interest.

In a showdown at a stockholders' meeting in Ontario, Vesco voted shares from the company's stock option plan, violating a direct order from a Canadian judge. He won by a 100,000-vote margin out of 34,000,000 shares voted. Judge Stanley Sporkin reviewed Vesco's activities and noted that a 1967 order declared that any company acquiring more than 1% of IOS stock became "a legal subsidiary" of IOS, and thus was in violation of a ban that prevented IOS from trading its shares in American markets, or holding a direct interest in American companies.

Prosecutors in Canada, Switzerland, and the United States all moved to file charges against Vesco. The SEC accused Vesco of draining $224 million from various funds under the IOS umbrella, using the money "to further personal interests and pursuits."

As he was battling the SEC charges, Vesco also became a subject of the investigation in the Watergate scandal that would topple the Nixon administration. Vesco had made at least two payments to Maurice Stans, head of the Committee to Re-Elect the President, or CREEP: $200,000 in cash, which was omitted from the campaign's legal disclosure forms; and a check for $50,000 that made it on record. The cash was ultimately delivered to G. Gordon Liddy, who used the monies to fund the break-in at the Watergate building and other covert programs on behalf of CREEP. After Maurice Stans was indicted, Vesco and Don-Don Nixon, the president's nephew and an employee of Vesco's, left the country. Vesco hid his money in various shell corporations protected by the secrecy laws of the Bahamas, Panama, Switzerland, and other money-laundering havens. He continued to do business even while in supposed exile.

Vesco received asylum in Costa Rica from José Figueres Ferrer, the beloved Costa Rican president. "I admire the regulatory work of the American government," said Figueres, who was affectionately known throughout the country as Don Pepe, "But with Vesco they overdid it. I think he offended their vanity because he was able to stay out of jail." He also was supported and for a time sheltered by Lyndon Pindling, Prime Minister of the Bahamas, and kept an elaborate headquarters there. During these years, Vesco allegedly conducted business with the Caribbean's most powerful drug smugglers, including Carlos "The Jackal" Lehder. In 1989, when Lehder was captured and sentenced to life in prison, he agreed to testify against his former associates, including Vesco. A U.S. grand jury indicted Vesco on charges of aiding and abetting.

Vesco was arrested and tried in the Bahamas several years after he fled the United States, facing charges of wire fraud, for transferring money from IOS into shell corporations by wire service; obstruction of justice, for his role in illegally donating fund to CREEP; and mail fraud, for a $50,000 payment he mailed to Henry Buhl for helping him take over IOS. However Judge Emmanuel Osadebay found all 3 charges lay outside the Bahamian government's jurisdiction. The wire fraud statute required crossing state lines and the Bahamas had none; bribing an American official violated American laws; and mail fraud wasn't a crime mentioned in the Bahamian books.

Vesco was forced to leave Costa Rica in 1978, as the government there changed hands and the American authorities placed more pressure on leaders to turn over the fugitive. Having lost much of his support in the Bahamas as well, Vesco was able to secure asylum from Fidel Castro in Cuba, promising to arrange black-market deals on behalf of the government there. Though he brokered a few market deals for the Cubans, Vesco never brought anything major to fruition. He owed Cuban authorities a million dollars for the losses on a single deal, some food-processing equipment that was nabbed by U.S. customs.

Castro had already become tired of Vesco in 1995 when he got wind of an operation that Vesco was planning along with Don-Don Nixon. Nixon claimed he had discovered a wonder drug that would "wipe out 90% of the pharmaceutical companies, leave 50% of the hospitals empty and change the political, social and economic structure of the world." Don-Don's wife, Helene, had been diagnosed with breast cancer in 1985, and was given an experimental drug the doctor called Trioxidal. Dubbed "TX" for short, the drug is obtained by cooking down the citronella plant, whose extract has become a popular insect repellent used in outdoor candles. The Castro government, which had built state-of-the-art biotechnology operations, demanded to have first option on the drug. When tests showed the compound did not provide the relief that Nixon, Vesco, and others were claiming, Castro ordered Vesco arrested.

During the summer of 1996, Vesco appeared before a tribunal of three judges. Vesco was sentenced to 13 years in prison.

Source:
Wells, J., CFE, CPA. "The Outlaw: Robert Vesco." *Frankensteins of Fraud.* Austin, TX: Obsidian Publishing Co., 2000.

Related Entry:
SECURITIES FRAUD

VIATICAL INSURANCE FRAUD

Viaticals are settlement companies that broker life insurance policies to investors who buy these policies for cash, usually from the terminally ill. Frauds include applicants who falsify health statements and immediately sell the policy to a viatical, and viaticals who misrepresent life expectancy and other information to investors.

In a typical and legal exchange, the investor receives payments from the insurer when the policyholder dies. About $1 billion in viatical settlements were sold each year in 1998 and 1999, up from just $50 million in 1991. Viaticals have branched into brokering policies for healthy seniors, in what is called "life settlements," a vast market potentially worth $108 billion.

A policyholder sells his or her policy for a fraction of its face value, depending on the person's estimated life expectancy. Normally the policyholder receives about 65% of the policy's value. The viatical solicits investors to buy the policy and receive the death benefit when the viator dies. Out of its portion of the investment, the viatical company pays premiums on the policy to keep it in force until the viator dies. In some cases, the company may require that investors pay the premiums.

Any type of insurance can be used in a viatical settlement—whole life, universal, term, or group life provided by an employer. But the policy must allow the viator to assign or transfer it to an unrelated beneficiary. And the viator must have owned the policy for a minimum of two years before he sells it.

The North American Securities Administrators Association, a group of state investment cops, named viaticals one of the top ten investment scams of 1999. Thirty-three of the 73 viatical companies *Consumer Reports* found operating in 2000 had been in trouble with regulators in the past two years. Among the violations were:

- Failure to register with securities or insurance authorities.
- Misuse of investor funds.
- Misstatements about the medical condition of patients.
- "Cleansheeting," in which viaticals solicit patients with life-threatening chronic or terminal conditions to lie about their health and apply for life insurance policies, which are then resold to investors.

Laws against Viatical Fraud

All states require policies to include a two-year period in which fraud must be discovered by the insurer in order to cancel a policy, but unscrupulous viatical brokers have become adept at hiding fraudulent activities for the two years.

In the last few years, states have been progressively passing laws involving viaticals. For example, Arizona legalized the classification of viaticals as securities; Kentucky introduced a licensing exam for viatical brokers; and Mississippi requires licensure for viatical settlement providers.

Case Study—Hoyt Steven Wauhob and Michael Lee Davis

In the first case of cleansheeting ever prosecuted, Wauhob and Davis were participants in Southwest Viatical, a viatical brokerage service in Texas, during the mid-1990s. A tip to the Fraud Unit of the Texas Insurance Department revealed that the two were cleansheeting policies with recruits from the Dallas AIDS Resource Center.

An investigation found that both men were felons, Wauhob for drug charges and Davis for homicide. A screen of insurance company records found that Southwest was acquiring policies with an accomplice, a First American agent named Sammy Squyres II, who was peddling rigged policies for other companies as well.

An informant with AIDS revealed that Hoyt Wauhob had recruited him to apply for four insurance policies with different companies and convinced him not to reveal his condition. The informant received $5,000.

Prosecutors charged several accomplice viators with fraud, and then granted them plea bargains in exchange for their testimony against Wauhob and Davis. Squyres cooperated with the investigation. Wauhob later gained immunity to testify against Davis.

Aggregated testimony showed that viators were paid between $4,000 and $7,000 to file false applications, plus a finder's fee of $1,000 for any new viators they brought to Southwest. Davis and Wauhob kept the policies current by paying the monthly premiums. Squyres received commissions from the insurance companies he sold for, plus fees from Davis and Wauhob. Michael Davis was found guilty in June 2000 and sentenced to six concurrent 60-year prison sentences.

Source:

Barron, D. "Investigating and Prosecuting Viatical Fraud." *White-Collar Crime Fighter,* May 2001.
www.insurancefraud.org/

Related Entries:

INSURANCE FRAUD

INSURANCE FRAUD—LIFE INSURANCE

WEIL, JOSEPH

Joseph Weil claimed he was born in 1875, though official records show 1877, the son of German-American grocers in Chicago. A high-school dropout, young Weil was working at an accounting firm when he discovered the employees were embezzling, so he blackmailed them for his silence. Weil established himself as a con by selling phony tonics and cures, wares of the "snake-oil salesman."

Weil achieved wealth and infamy running scams around the horse races. Bookmaking was legal in most American cities, with results communicated to each shop via Western Union. Weil set up phony Western Union offices and convinced marks he had inside contacts that would delay the race results until they could place a bet and end up a sure winner. Usually the first bet would not work out—the mark would be somehow prevented from making the bet, or the tip would turn out to be wrong. Weil and his associates pretended they too had lost money, but used this shared sense of loss to draw the mark into even larger games. For particularly long and lucrative cons, Weil rented a banquet hall or lodge, outfitted realistically, and might use 100 actors to simulate a betting parlor. A telegraph wire stretched to another room in the building where accomplices monitored and simulated the legitimate race results. In a variation, the mark was convinced to purchase thousands of dollars worth of electronic equipment that Weil promised would provide millions in payoffs from tapping Western Union wires.

Weil later said his favorite scam involved real horses he owned and raced, known as the "ringer deal." As a member of the American Turf Association circulated a rumor that he was about to replace an all-but-useless horse named Black Fonso—whose string of failures produced even higher odds—with a super fast horse Weil was training in secret, the ringer would collect on the huge odds and make everyone rich. There was no switch, and Black Fonso lost as usual. Weil claimed that he had lost as well, though he had never placed a bet on anyone's behalf, pocketing the money he'd collected from his would-be conspirators.

Weil several times dodged legal trouble by successfully arguing that Chicago law defined a "confidence game" as the taking "advantage of an unwary stranger," whereas his victims were all Chicago businessmen, fully aware of the illicit nature of Weil's propositions.

He also ran a land scheme that tricked recipients into believing he'd given them free vacation land in northern Michigan, for which they need only pay a processing fee. Weil supposedly collected over $16,000 and split an equal amount with a co-conspirator who filed the phony papers on the worthless lots. Enlisting Chicago heir Romeo Simpson to provide references for an investment scam, they garnered a small fortune convincing investors he could return $1,000 on a $100 investment. Weil claimed he had a system for the horses, and would place bets on others' behalf. After a short time, he returned the $100 with a $25 profit and claim he was henceforth only accepting $500 bets. This version of the Ponzi scheme rose until a few high-rollers were providing large payoffs, which were arranged to be lost, due to unfair circumstances of some sort. Simpson and Weil reportedly made $480,000 a year.

Through banking scams and phony letters-of-credit, Weil continued to prey on the rich and greedy. He later rationalized, "The men I swindled were also motivated by a desire to gain money, and they did not care at whose expense they got it...I took money only from those who could afford it and were willing to go in with me in schemes they fancied would fleece others."

Weil failed at several attempts conducting legitimate business. He claimed that he had invented purchase premiums when he tried to sell coffee beans under an assumed name with the promise of a free (cheap) piano after the purchase of a lifetime's supply, but when his identity was discovered, the operation failed. He also failed a vending machine operation, a small circus, selling the Catholic Encyclopedia door-to-door, and running the Hotel Martinique in Chicago. Supposedly a resident of the hotel left Weil in possession of stolen bonds, for which he drew a term at Leavenworth Federal Penitentiary.

Despite his bad luck, he was able to continue his criminal career into his seventh decade, mounting oil and mining scams, among others. After his wife died, Weil remained in Chicago, greeted by many, but harassed by the police. "They refuse to believe I have reformed," he told Saul Bellow in a 1956 interview. He complained, "There are no good confidence men anymore because they do not have the necessary knowledge of foreign affairs, domestic problems, and human nature." He lived until 1975.

Source:
Marinacci, M. *"The Yellow Kid."* 1997. Retrieved from pw1.netcom.com/~mikalm/weil.htm

Related Entry:

CON SCHEMES

WHISTLEBLOWER

Whistleblower is the popular term for people who alert authorities to wrongdoing by their employer. Whistleblowers can file suit against their company and request that the government join the lawsuit as a co-plaintiff. If the government agrees to join the suit, portions of any proceeds recovered are paid to the whistleblower.

The Whistleblower Law

The False Claims Act is sometimes called the Whistleblower Law because it lays the legal framework for employees to file suit against their companies and receive a share of the damages. The U.S. Congress first enacted the Claims Act in 1863 as a weapon against profiteers and gunrunners.

The False Claims Act contains so-called *qui tam* provisions, which allow whistleblowers to file False Claims Act lawsuits against companies and individuals that defraud the government. (*Qui tam* is short for a longer Latin phrase, meaning, "he who brings an action for the king as well as for himself.") From the beginning the law contained provisions for sharing recovered proceeds with the whistleblower. Congress drastically weakened these provisions in 1943.

In the mid-1980's, as a defense procurement fraud scandal was exposed, Congress amended the False Claims Act to encourage employees to come forward. Whistleblowers who brought successful cases were entitled to 15% to 30% of the government's recovery, and the defendant guaranteed the whistleblowers' attorney's payment of their regular hourly fees. Companies and other entities that defraud the government are liable for treble damages and a $5,000 to $10,000 penalty for each false claim. The amendments were passed in 1986.

Since the False Claims Act was amended, the government has participated in over 5,000 *qui tam* prosecutions and recovered over $8 billion. Twelve states—California, Delaware, Florida, Hawaii, Illinois, Louisiana, Massachusetts, Nevada, New Mexico, Tennessee, Texas, and Virginia—and the District of Columbia passed local False Claims Acts for whistleblowers who expose fraud against state and local governments.

The whistleblower does not need to have personal knowledge of the fraud to file a False Claims Act case. The lawsuit can be based on information the relator learned from a friend, relative, competitor, etc. As long as the information is not publicly disclosed and the government has not already sued the individual or company for the fraud, the relator may bring a qui tam lawsuit. (Tax fraud, however, cannot be the basis of a False Claims Act case.)

The timing of a lawsuit can be critical. The first person to file a case under the False Claims Act for a particular fraud preempts all other cases. So if a whistleblower plans to bring a case, it is important to do so before another whistleblower beats them to the courthouse. Potential whistleblowers also should keep in mind that the False Claims Act has a statute of limitations that may be as short as six years.

Industries and Programs Where *Qui Tam* Suits are Likely

By 1997, more than half of *qui tam* suits were filed against health care companies (see figures below). Defense procurement fraud is the other major area in which these suits are filed. Other types of businesses or programs, which have been subject to *qui tam* suits are public works and federal construction projects, research programs, customs, environmental programs, loan guarantees, underpayment of royalties on leased lands, agricultural subsidies, and municipal bonds.

Qui Tam Statistics

Since the False Claims Act was amended in 1986, the government has joined more than 5,000 *qui tam* lawsuits and recovered approximately over $8 billion. Records show that the number of suits was relatively low—around 200 or less annually—until 1994. The number of suits filed per year peaked in 1997 with 533. Health care fraud gradually rose during the 1990's to become the most targeted area for *qui tam* suits.

Recoveries also continued to rise in the mid-1990s before increasing almost threefold in 2000 to $1.2 billion, chiefly driven by a large number of recoveries against defense contractors (www.ffhsj.com/quitam/fcastats.htm).

Case Study—James Alderson and Columbia-HCA

James F. Alderson was a financial officer with Quorum Health Resources, a Montana hospital. After he learned that the hospital's management routinely filed fraudulent cost reports with Medicare, he refused to file "aggressive" claims that the company knew were not reimbursable. He was asked to create a secret set of accounts that tracked the actual workings of the business, in contrast to the false reports being filed with the government.

Alderson alerted authorities in 1996. He later filed a False Claims Act lawsuit against Quorum Health Resources Inc. and Columbia/HCA Health care Corporation. The Justice Department joined the qui tam lawsuit in October 1998. The action resulted in the largest government investigation of Medicare fraud ever and produced a record civil settlement in 2000 of $745 million.

Source:

Eichenwald, K. "He Blew the Whistle, and Health Giants Quaked." *The New York Times,* October 18, 1998.

Ekstrand, Laurie E. "Information on False Claims Act Litigation." The United States Government Accountability Office, January 31, 2006

Related Entry:

SARBANES-OXLEY

WHITACRE, MARK

Mark Whitacre ran the Biotechnology division of Archer Daniels Midland from 1989 to 1995, when it was revealed that Whitacre had been acting as a government informant in a price-fixing investigation. Whitacre himself was later convicted for his role in the price-fixing and for embezzlement.

Whitacre joined ADM in 1989. By 1992, he was regarded as the heir apparent to President James Randall. But Whitacre's career took a strange turn in 1992, when he told

Michael Andreas (son of ADM's CEO Dwayne Andreas) that a Japanese engineer whom he knew as Fujiwara had called him. Fujiwara discussed ADM's difficulties with the Biotechnology operation, on which they'd spent $1.5 billion dollars and which was not producing. Whitacre told his superiors that Fujiwara was offering to help ADM for $10 million.

When Michael Andreas told his father that Whitacre had spoken with Fujiwara, who seemed to know a great deal about ADM's lysine operation, Dwayne Andreas called in the FBI, claiming that the company was being spied on by foreign competitors. Away from his superiors at ADM, Whitacre admitted to FBI Agent Brian Sheperd that there was no Fujiwara. Additionally, Whitacre revealed that he and several others were meeting with Japanese lysine producers, discussing how much of the market each company ought to get, how much each company would agree to produce annually, and other issues—ADM was pushing its competitors to form a secret council that adjusted production and prices in consort, keeping the price of lysine higher than it normally would be if the companies competed.

From 1992 to 1995, Whitacre wore hidden microphones and arranged meetings for the FBI's hidden video cameras. In May 1995, FBI agents raided ADM headquarters in Decatur, Illinois, and left summonses for ADM's highest officials, including Whitacre, so as not to blow his cover. But when Whitacre himself confessed to an ADM lawyer, "I'm the mole," the lawyer promptly withdrew as Whitacre's counsel and informed his superiors of the revelation.

ADM fired Whitacre and pressed charges against him for embezzling $2.5 million. The announcement did not surprise authorities. Just a day before the company announced the charges, Whitacre told the Department of Justice he'd been inflating capital improvement costs on the lysine factory. The proceeds were stashed in several offshore accounts. Whitacre protested that ADM well knew about the inflations — he was told these were "undocumented compensation" payments to an elite circle of insiders. The Department of Justice withdrew Whitacre's immunity agreement and charged him with the embezzlement of some $9 million. He was also charged in the price-fixing conspiracy with Michael Andreas and Terry Wilson.

In 1997, Whitacre was convicted of embezzlement. Three other ADM executives pled to similar charges and received prison sentences and/or fines. Whitacre was sentenced to nine years in prison. ADM paid $100 million for its role as the instigator in the price-fixing conspiracy, at the time the highest antitrust fine ever paid. Whitacre, Michael Andreas and Terry Wilson were found guilty of criminal conspiracy in 1998. Andreas and Wilson were each sentenced to two years in prison and fines. In a final ironic twist to a bizarre case, the judge deemed Whitacre the leader of the conspiracy and gave him a more severe punishment, a three-year prison sentence.

Source:
Wells, J., CFE, CPA. "It's a Wonderful Life: Mark Whitacre." *Frankensteins of Fraud.* Austin, TX: Obsidian Publishing Co., 2000.

WHITE-COLLAR CRIME

"White-collar" crimes are often defined as ones with predominantly pecuniary motives: the white-collar criminal offender is able to gain monetarily by exploiting through deceit either some feature of how money is loaned, stored, or transferred, or by conducting a false business transaction. These acts are perpetrated by a broad criminal element, from single individuals to loosely knit groups, and highly sophisticated, transnational criminal enterprises.

The FBI and White-Collar Issues

The FBI defines white-collar crime as illegal acts characterized by fraud, concealment, or violation of trust that are not dependent upon the application or threat of physical force or violence. Individuals and organizations commit these acts to obtain money, property, or services; to avoid the payment or loss of money or services; or to secure a personal, political, or business advantage.

The FBI's White-Collar Crime Program is the largest and most diverse of all FBI criminal programs. During fiscal year 1998 (10/1/97 - 9/30/98), the White-Collar Crime Program used approximately 25% of FBI agent resources and achieved 36% of the FBI's total convictions. As of 2006, White Collar Crimes are down 28% from 2001. The

Bureau tracks four categories of white-collar crimes: economic crimes, financial institution fraud, government fraud, and public corruption.

Economic Crimes

Investigations primarily involve mail and wire frauds, counterfeit negotiable securities, bankruptcy, insurance, computer frauds, telemarketing and investment frauds, and other business-related frauds directed against individuals and businesses.

Financial Institution Fraud

Investigations primarily involve check frauds, loan frauds, embezzlements, misapplications, and bribery matters occurring within or against national and international financial institutions, such as banks, savings and loans, and credit unions.

Government Fraud

Investigations focus on fraud, corruption, and conflict of interest in all federal agencies and programs. Government fraud also includes environmental crimes, healthcare fraud, and antitrust violations.

Public Corruption

Initiatives are aimed at combating breaches of public trust by federal, state, and local officials and their private sector accomplices. Among these categories, certain acts have been identified as priority crime problems. These include healthcare fraud, telemarketing fraud, environmental crimes, financial institution fraud, public corruption, insurance fraud, bankruptcy fraud, securities fraud, computer crimes, fraud against the government, and money laundering.

White-Collar Crimes and Violence

Though usually considered non-violent and victimless crime, financial crimes are often conducted in conjunction with, or for the purpose of funding, inherently violent crimes such as drug trafficking, weapons trafficking, extortion, or, in some cases, terrorism. Acts of environmental damage and product liability cause injury, disease, birth defects, and death. Collectively these acts claim more lives than the 18 to 20 thousand lost to murder each year.

Including labor offenses in the term, white-collar crime looks even more deadly. In an average week, more than 4 million 12-17 year olds are employed in the U.S. Of these, 683,000 are only 12 or 13 years old. Children as young as 8 and 10 years old work on American farms. About 290,000 children work unlawfully in U.S. farms, factories, and businesses, where many are subjected to such dangers as pesticides, construction site accidents, sharp implements, and more.

According to the National Institute for Occupational Safety, about 200,000 children are injured on the job annually in the U.S., with about one third of the injuries being serious enough to require emergency room treatments.

Statistics

White-collar crimes are not tracked in either of the federal government's crime reports—the *Uniform Crime Report* and the *National Crime Victimization Survey*—due to a rift in what constitutes this type of crime. What is known from tracking individual crimes is that white-collar acts cause dramatically more financial damage than street crimes, which cost an estimated $13.3 billion a year. The estimates of major white-collar crime all exceed this figure: $400 billion a year in occupational fraud, $250 billion a year in antitrust violations, and as much as $300 billion a year in tax fraud. According to a survey conducted by the National White-Collar Crime Center (NW3C), 46.5% of Americans suffered white collar crime victimization in 2005.

Statistics on particular acts or types of acts are available by searching newspapers and journals, websites, government publications, government and law enforcement agency reports, annual reports of companies, and from professional groups like the Association of Certified Fraud Examiners. The National White-Collar Crime Center (NW3C) collects and publishes statistical data regularly via its newsletter and website.

Development of the Term

Criminologist Edwin Sutherland, who first used it publicly in a 1939 speech to the American Sociological Society, coined the term "white-collar crime." He defined it as "a crime committed by a person of respectability and high social status in the course of his occupation." Though the actions and perpetrators might vary, these crimes all involved "the violation of delegated or implied trust." The cooperative, if clueless, victim was necessary for the predication of the crime.

Sutherland's work focused on business crime. In *White-Collar Crime*, published in 1949, Sutherland examined crimes committed by members of 70 of the largest U.S. corporations. All had at least one criminal or civil decision against them, and most of the corporations had committed multiple offenses. Sutherland charged that 97% of the corporations were recidivist offenders. Though referring explicitly to criminal acts, the term also included offenses charged in civil court and is still used in this fashion today.

The term's definition has broadened over the years. Herbert Edelhertz, a former prosecutor with the Department of Justice, defined white-collar crime as "an illegal act or series of illegal acts committed by nonphysical means and by concealment or guile to obtain money or property, to avoid the payment or loss of money and property, or to obtain business or personal advantage." The major revision to Sutherland's usage is that the offender need not be in the upper tiers of society. Con games and other acts of financial impropriety are covered by the term. The Bureau of Justice Statistics uses this definition in its publications.

Marshal Clinard and Richard Quinney distinguished between *occupational crime*—"offenses committed by individuals for themselves in the course of their occupations" —and *corporate crime*—"offenses committed by corporate officials for their corporation and the offenses of the corporation itself."

A conference of the National White-Collar Crime Center (NW3C) in June 1996 yielded a definition that again emphasized the status of the offender: "White-collar crimes are illegal or unethical acts that violate fiduciary responsibility of public trust committed by an individual or organization, usually during the course of legitimate occupational activity, by persons of high or respectable social status for personal or organizational gain."

Dr. James Coleman, author of *The Criminal Elite: Understanding White-Collar Crime*, has argued that the term includes not only fiduciary violations, but also acts against the general public such as false advertising and environmental damage. Coleman divides the field into "property crimes, which cause only economic damage; and violent crimes, which cause injury, sickness or death."

David Friedrichs, author of *Trusted Criminals*, asserts that the multitudinous acts and effects of white-collar crimes "force us to confront the harsh realization that the distinctions between crime and order are not as great as we like to imagine, and that those who benefit most from a stable social system often do the most to threaten its well-being. Few areas of human activity reveal more starkly the complex relationship between the creative and the destructive aspect of human nature."

Writing about the work of criminologist Gil Geis for a collection of his essays, Robert Meier asserted, "Geis largely has eschewed allegiance to the lure of a grand theory of crime, including white-collar crime, and his approach may more aptly be considered an example of theoretical agnosticism. His approach to white-collar crime is not a theoretical, but it does not show the commitment to a particular theoretical perspective like that of Sutherland. Geis's writing is probably more accurately descriptive rather than theoretical, although his work does show awareness of various theoretical perspectives."

In fact, Geis has expressed impatience with the debate over the term. "The task of defining white-collar crime is in many ways wearisome, perhaps best left to those with a predilection for medieval theological debates," he writes. While acknowledging Sutherland's pioneering efforts in fraud studies, Geis has found the elder scholar's work obstructionist in the matter of definitions. "The semantic waters have been so muddied by Sutherland that today it seems wisest to move upstream rather than to attempt a purification project." Nevertheless, Geis finds, "However metaphorical and imprecise, the term *white-collar crime* conjures up a real set of ills and is particularly satisfactory in solidifying an emotional and intellectual concern about such ills."

While the term serves a general use, further work in the field should develop taxonomies based on the content of law, the degree of harm, characteristics of offenders, modus operandi, and types and nature of victims. These factors were the guide for *Occupational Fraud and Abuse*, an analysis of fraud crimes committed in the workplace.

White-Collar Crime and Fraud

The terms *white-collar crime* and *fraud* are intertwined in meaning, but not synonymous. Low-level employees in industrial jobs commit some frauds, but these employees would not qualify as white-collar. And white-collar crime encompasses a range of abuse outside of fraud, such as environmental damages and unsafe-product liability issues.

Sources:

Coleman, J. *The Criminal Elite: Understanding White-Collar Crime.* New York: St. Martin's Press, 1998.

"Brian L. Stafford, Director of the U.S. Secret Service." *Federal News Service,* March 30, 2000.

Khera, I. "Business Ethics, East Vs. West; Myths and Realities." *Journal of Business Ethics*, March 2001.

Tresslar, T. "Business and White-collar Crime." *Dayton Daily News,* February 18, 2001.

Related Entries:

CORPORATE CRIME
OCCUPATIONAL FRAUD AND ABUSE

WIRE TRANSFER FRAUD

Wire transfer fraud is the improper and/or illegal use of wire transfers. Common acts include transferring money to accounts controlled by wire-company insiders or their accomplices, and selling account information to outsiders.

Wire transfers of funds began in the United States in the 1940's. The number of transfers rises every year, and the incidence of wire transfer fraud does also.

Wire Systems

The most common methods for transmitting funds include Fedwire, book-entry securities service, and the Clearing House Interbank Payment System (CHIPS). Fedwire, a transfer system established by the U.S. Federal Reserve System, enables bank accounts in about 7,800 depository institutions to be debited and credited virtually instantaneously through Federal Reserve Banks.

Wire transactions primarily complete interbank purchases and sales of federal funds; purchase, sell, and finance securities transactions; disburse loan proceeds or repay loans;

or conduct real estate business. The book-entry securities service, also operated through Federal Reserve Banks, facilitates the custody and transfer of federally guaranteed mortgage-backed securities, all U.S. Treasury securities, many federal agency securities, and certain international agency securities. CHIPs are used primarily for international electronic money transfers.

Typically, wire fraud perpetrators are knowledgeable about wire transfer activity, have at least one contact within a target institution, and are aggressive in carrying out the theft. Institutions known as banking points handle transfers; a banking point is any institution or business capable of receiving electronic transactions, such as banks, savings and loans, credit unions, brokerage firms, and insurance companies. On any day, $1 trillion to $2 trillion moves among financial institutions.

Wire Fraud Schemes

- Bank employees who have access to correct account identification information can transfer money improperly—insiders wire funds to themselves and/or related parties.
- Outside parties may pose as customers, having used pretext calls to obtain correct account information from the bank.
- People posing as wire room employees in another bank or a branch office order transfers to dummy accounts in another bank.
- People having legitimate access to sensitive account and daily code information for a limited time (for example, computer consultants) conduct improper transfers or sell the information to outsiders.
- Bank officers' and customers' authorization, oral or written, is improperly obtained or forged. People forge orders to transfer money to their own accounts when the recipient account is actually in the name of someone else.
- Unauthorized personnel gain access to the wire room and its equipment, or the actual transmission is intercepted and altered.

Preventing and Detecting Wire Transfer Fraud

- Written policies and procedures for wire transactions should be circulated.
- Unannounced audits and random transaction verifications should be conducted.

- The person authorizing wire transfers should not be the same person who orders the wire transfer.
- Those ordering transfers should have secure passwords.
- A current list of those ordering wire transfers and a log of all transfers should be maintained.
- Persons who handle wire transfers should be required to take a vacation occasionally.
- Persons not involved with the wire transfer process should perform reconciliations of accounts affected by wire transfers.
- All confidential information about accounts and wire transfers should be kept in safe rooms secured with locks.
- All paper trash should be shredded.

Audit tests include:

- Reviewing call logs for randomly picked transactions made back to the banking points to verify their authenticity.
- Reviewing documentation of past wire transfers activity from bank statements or bank online transaction history for a daily debit and credit match of each transaction.
- Obtaining written confirmations of transactions from the wire transfer provider to determine the timeliness of their receipt.
- Reconciling problems promptly caused by the usual custom of ending all wire transfers for a day in the mid-afternoon. Though some customers contend they should receive credit and interest on funds received at the end of a day, wire transfers made past afternoon closing time are credited the next business day.

Bank Audits

Financial institutions should ensure the following safeguards when transferring funds:

- Provide customers with unique codes that are required to authorize or order wire transfers.
- Maintain and update lists of employees authorized to perform wire transfer transactions.

- Compile audit trails of incoming and outgoing wire transactions, as well as the employee responsible for each portion of the transaction.
- Review all wire transfer transactions at the end of each day to ensure that the original transfer instructions were executed correctly.
- Contact recipient businesses and ensure authenticity of fund transfer requests.
- Do not accept faxed instructions.
- Require that bank employees not involved with the wire process reconcile all accounts affected by wire transfers.
- Ensure the in-house wire operations manual is available only to authorized personnel and secured when not in use.
- Tape-record all incoming and outgoing calls for wire transfer instructions.
- Carefully screen wire transfer personnel applicants.
- Reassign wire transfer employees to other departments when they give notice that they are resigning.
- Require all employees to take at least five consecutive days of vacation each year.
- Never disclose sensitive information over the telephone until the customer information file has verified the caller's identity and authorization.
- Separate duties among wire employees who transmit or receive requests for funds so they do not also verify the accuracy of the transactions.
- Train employees on proper internal controls, fraud awareness, and the importance of protecting information. Share alerts issued by the Federal Reserve on fraudulent schemes.

Related Entry:

FINANCIAL INSTITUTION FRAUD

WORKERS' COMPENSATION FRAUD

In 2005, the National Insurance Crime Bureau confirmed that workers' compensation fraud costs Americans over $5 billion annually. Moreover, fraud and abuse account for an estimated 10% of the cost of workers' compensation premiums.

Workers' compensation laws require employers or their insurance plan to reimburse an employee (or on his behalf) for injuries that occurred on the job regardless of who is at fault and without delay of legal proceedings to determine fault. The injury may be physical, such as a broken limb, or mental, such as stress.

Common Schemes*:* Schemes are generally broken down into four categories: premium fraud, agent fraud, claimant fraud, and organized fraud schemes.

- *Premium Fraud*: Employers misrepresent the nature of the work their employees perform in order to reduce risk-based premiums, and underreport the number of employees and the rate of salaries.
- *Agent Fraud*: Agents issue certificates of coverage indicating the customer is insured, but never forward the premium to the insurance company.
- *Claimant Fraud*: Misrepresenting the circumstances of any injury or fabricating that an injury occurred.
- *Organized Fraud Schemes*: Organized fraud schemes are composed of the united efforts of a lawyer, a capper, a doctor, and the claimant. This scheme is used not only in workers compensation cases, but also in other medical frauds such as in automobile injuries.

Claimant Profile

Workers' Compensation claimants who commit fraud tend to have one or more of the following characteristics:

- Under age 40
- Not receiving Social Security disability benefits
- Out longer than the particular disability seems to warrant
- Excessively demanding of a quick claim determination
- Has unstable work history; changes jobs often
- Develop a disability when a plant shutdown or massive layoff is imminent
- Moves out of state after sustaining injury
- Use a post office box as a mailing address
- Is in line for early retirement

Sources:
Fraud Examiner's Manual
www.FairIssac.com; accessed September 6, 2006

Related Entries:
HEALTH CARE FRAUD
INSURANCE FRAUD
PERSONAL INJURY FRAUD

WORLDCOM

WorldCom emerged gradually into the telecommunications field, first appearing in 1988 under the name Long Distance Discount Services (LDDS). Two years later, a CEO by the name of Bernard Ebbers was appointed, who would lift the company to its peak before watching it plummet into a world of fraud. In August of 1989, it merged with Advantage Companies, Inc. Six years later, in 1995 LDDS became known as LDDS WorldCom.

Under this name, the company experienced an accelerated growth spurt in the 1990's, charged largely by the number of companies merging with it – Compuserve (bought from H&R Block), Metromedia Communications Corp., and MCI Communications, to name a few.

On October 5, 1999, MCI WorldCom and its rival, Sprint Corporation, publicized a $120 million union between the two companies, which would have been the largest merger in history, at that time. The new company, called WorldCom, would have beat out AT&T for the number one spot as the largest communications company in the United States. Plans for the merger were halted, however, when the U.S. Department of Justice and the European Union raised objections, citing that the merger would create a monopoly. This lead MCI WorldCom and Sprint to terminate the merger on July 13, 2000. That same year, however, MCI WorldCom decided to stick with the name WorldCom, regardless of the merger cessation.

The Scandal

Because WorldCom abandoned the merger, it experienced a drastic stock decline in 2000. Several years before the slump, CEO Bernard Ebbers began amassing considerable wealth as a result of his investment in the rising stock of WorldCom. His extravagant lifestyle, supported by an estimated $1.4 billion included ownership of a minor league hockey team, Canada's biggest ranch, a trucking company, and yacht company. WorldCom's decline would have a severe impact on his personal bank account; his stock in the company financed his other businesses. When banks began asking Ebbers to cover margin calls on his WorldCom stock, he became desperate. In 2001, he convinced the WorldCom board of directors to grant him over $400 million in corporate loans and guarantees. When this method failed, Ebbers resigned without repaying the loans. He was replaced by John Sidgmore in April 2002.

Two months later, an internal auditor for WorldCom discovered approximately $3.8 billion in fraud. From 1999 to May of 2002, the company used fraudulent accounting strategies in an effort to inflate its finances, delaying the decline in WorldCom stock. The fraud was carried out by first reducing reserve accounts held to cover liabilities of obtained companies from 1998 to 2000. Furthermore, the company hid expenses between 2000 and 2002. While WorldCom secretly struggled, executives misrepresented and delayed expense reports in order to feign growth for investors. Essentially, the company inflated revenue by almost $4 billion. Later, it was found to have been inflated by an outstanding $11 billion.

It did not take long for WorldCom's board of directors and audit committee to be notified. Scott Sullivan (CFO) was fired and David Myers (Controller) resigned. The 2001 external auditor, Arthur Andersen, withdrew the opinion for that year, and the SEC began an investigation, ultimately filing a civil suit in a New York federal court. WorldCom publicly announced that it had cooked its books by overstating its income over a five-quarter period.

In July, less than one month after the fraud was detected and after firing some 20,000 employees over the course of a few years, WorldCom filed for Chapter 11 bankruptcy protection for $107 billion in corporate liabilities – the largest in United States history – emerging with around $5.7 billion in debt and $6 billion in cash, along with a slew of lawsuits. WorldCom stock became valueless. Bondholders were compensated 35.7 cents per dollar. Reimbursement is still pending for other creditors.

The Charges

Because Bernard Ebbers was the CEO while the fraud occurred, he was held largely accountable, but took no responsibility, claiming ignorance. On March 15, 2005, he was found guilty of nine felonies: one count conspiracy, one count securities fraud, and seven counts of filing false statements with securities regulators. Ebbers was sentenced to twenty-five years in prison. At the time of the sentence, he was sixty-three years old. Contingent upon behavior, he may be eligible for release at age eighty-three.

Former executives including CFO Scott Sullivan, controller David Meyers, accounting director Buford "Buddy" Yates, and accounting managers Betty Vinson, and Troy Normand also faced criminal charges for conspiracy to commit securities fraud, among others.

As of October 7, 2005, Verizon bought out MCI, formerly WorldCom, for a reported $7.6 billion. MCI is now known as Verizon Business.

Sources:

"WorldCom." Thecheatingculture.com, September 7, 2006

"The Rise and Fall of Bernard Ebbers." Forbes.com, September 7, 2006

Olavsrd, T. "Judge OKs WorldCom Settlement." *InternetNews.com*, July 7, 2003.

"Securities and Exchange Commission v. WorldCom, Inc." Final Judgment in the United States District Court, Southern District of New York (Civ No. 02-CV4963 (JSR)), May 2003.

"WorldCom: Why it matters." *BBC News*, June 26, 2002.

"World-Class Scandal at WorldCom." *CBSNews.com*, June 26, 2002.

Related Entries:

FINANCIAL STATEMENT FRAUD

SECURITIES FRAUD

APPENDIX

A GUIDE TO SUCCESSFUL SEARCHING

Running Searches

The Internet is not so much a service as a tool. To tap its abilities, you have to learn how to construct proper queries—how to ask for what you want. The most serious impediment to locating good information is the user's lack of search skills.

Key Words

Most searching uses keywords. For instance, to find the latest statistics on check fraud, the logical keywords are *check fraud*. But if you typed in those words, the search engine would return numerous sites that have nothing to do with check fraud. By placing both words inside quotation marks ("check fraud") you will get better results. Still, the list of hits will be in the thousands, so you may want to narrow the search using the techniques below.

BOOLEAN OPERATORS

The best way to utilize a search engine is to use two, or possibly three, keywords that best describe the topic. If the words succeed one another, as in the case of "check fraud," then it may be beneficial to use *Boolean operators* to aid one's search.

Boolean operators are symbols that help the search engine to better understand exactly what it is searching for. Putting the "+" symbol between "check+fraud," for example, will indicate to the search engine that it is to search only for pages which have the word "fraud" immediately following "check." If you insert the word "and," so that the search reads "check and fraud," the search engine will understand to search for websites and pages that contain both the words "check" and "fraud," but not necessarily right next to each other.

Some of the more common Boolean operator symbols, or connectors, are shown below.

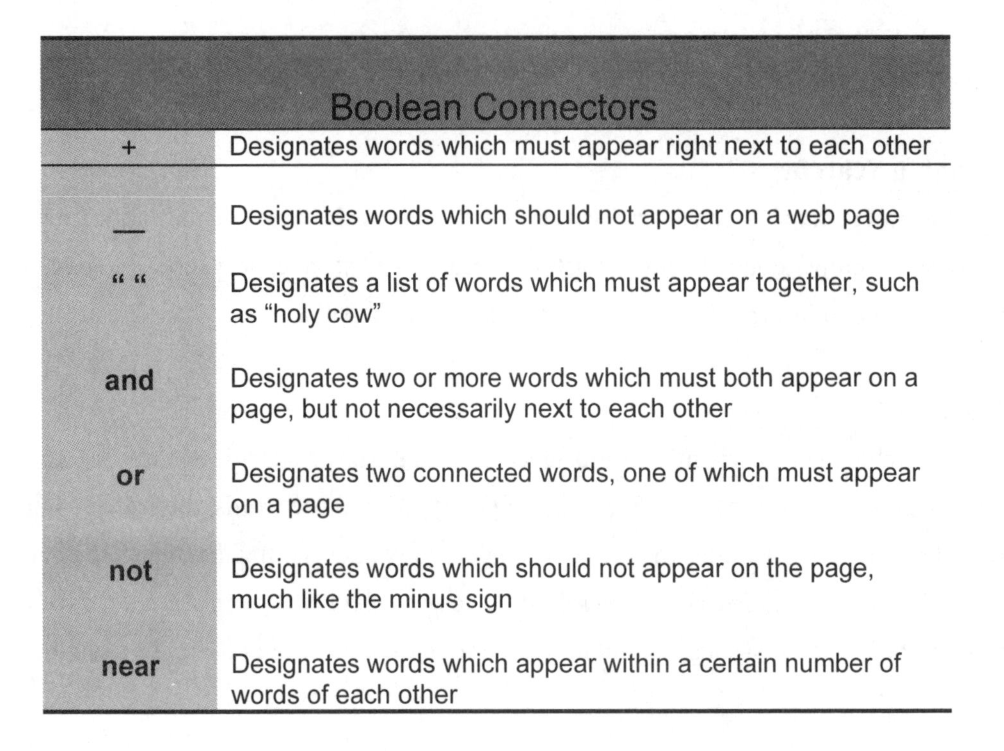

Boolean Connectors	
+	Designates words which must appear right next to each other
—	Designates words which should not appear on a web page
" "	Designates a list of words which must appear together, such as "holy cow"
and	Designates two or more words which must both appear on a page, but not necessarily next to each other
or	Designates two connected words, one of which must appear on a page
not	Designates words which should not appear on the page, much like the minus sign
near	Designates words which appear within a certain number of words of each other

RESERVED WORDS AND NOISE WORDS

Because the connector words *and, or, not,* and *near* are reserved for searches, these words are ignored when they appear in a phrase. Other common words that perform connecting functions in phrases—such as *in*, *of*, and *the*—are also ignored, unless the user puts the entire phrase in parentheses. (See *Searching with Phrases*, below, for more direction on reserved and noise words.)

Below are some of the common noise words ignored by most search engines. *And* and *or* are marked with an asterisk because they are also reserved words.

The	and *	of
His	my	there

When	is	are
So	or *	it

Advanced Search Techniques

Many search engines allow users to construct complex queries that target information in specific terms. The following techniques are supported by the LEXIS-NEXIS® services. Not every search engine will respond to these queries. To determine a search engines or database's abilities, consult the service's FAQ or search help page.

Searching with Phrases

To search for compound terms or concepts, enclose phrases in quotation marks. For example, to search for the phrase "first class."

Enter: **"first class"**

Adjacent words (tax free, dog bite, automobile accident, first class, etc.) are searched as individual words appearing in the specific order entered. You do not need to enclose them in quotation marks. For example, to search for documents with the phrase "first class."

Enter: **first class**

If the phrase you are searching contains a word used in Boolean searches, such as AND or OR, you should replace the reserved word with a space when entering your search. For example, to search for articles with the phrase "black and white."

Enter: **black white**

When searching phrases that contain a noise word, such as **of** or **the**, replace the noise word with a space when you enter your search. For example, to search for articles with the phrase "Terms of Endearment."

Enter: **Terms endearment**

Connectors and Priority Searching

When you use multiple connectors in a search, the LEXIS-NEXIS® services process the search according to a priority order that works much like an algebraic equation. The following table lists the connectors along with an explanation of each connector's function.

Connector	Function	Example	Order of Priority
OR	Links synonyms, alternative forms of expression, acronyms, etc.	**doctor or physician**—finds either doctor or physician.	1
PRE/n	Requires both words to appear in the document, the first word must precede the second word by n words. Use this connector when a different word order would change the meaning.	**southwest pre/2 air or airline**—finds Southwest Air or Southwest Airlines.	2
W/n	Links search words and phrases to create concepts. The letter n stands for a number from 1 to 255. W/n does not specify a word order.	**doctor w/5 malpractice**—finds doctor within five or fewer words of malpractice, regardless of which word appears first.	3
W/s	Looks for documents with search words in the same sentence.	**doctor w/s malpractice**—finds doctor in the same sentence as malpractice.	4
W/p	Looks for documents with search words in the same paragraph.	**doctor w/p malpractice**—finds doctor in the same paragraph as malpractice	5
AND	Links words or phrases that **both** appear anywhere in the same document, no matter how close or far apart.	**doctor and malpractice**—finds both doctor and malpractice anywhere in the same document.	6

AND NOT	Excludes documents that contain the word or phrase following it. Use this connector with **caution** because it can exclude relevant documents. Always use this connector at the end of your search.	**doctor and not malpractice**—finds the word doctor anywhere in the document, but the word malpractice cannot appear anywhere in the same document.	

USING PARENTHESES

Sometimes the priority in which connectors operate has an unintended effect on your search request. To get the desired results, use parentheses to group your concepts. For example, you might think the following search will find documents about Bill Clinton or George Bush:

bill w/3 clinton or george w/3 bush

But, the *www.nexis.com* service interprets this search in the following manner:

- clinton or george
- bill within three words or fewer of clinton or george
- bush within three words or fewer of clinton or george, that is also within three words or fewer of bill

Use parentheses to force the names to stay together in two separate search concepts. For this example, you would enter:

(bill w/3 clinton) or (george w/3 bush)

The parentheses override the normal priority of the connectors, allowing each concept to be interpreted separately. This search will find articles about Bill Clinton or George Bush.

Number-Related Commands and Capitalization

ATLEAST Command	Use this command when you want your search terms to appear a defined number of times in a document. For example, use the following search to find documents that contain an in-depth discussion of the Comprehensive Environmental Response, Compensation and Liability Act (CERCLA): **atleast10 (cercla)** This search command requires CERCLA to appear in every document at least 10 times. You can use any number 1 to 255 with the ATLEAST command.
Plural	Use this command when you want to find only the plural form of a term. For example, use the following search to find only the plural form of the word Williams: **plural (williams)**
Singular	Use this command when you want to find only the singular form of a term. For example, use the following search to find only the singular form of the word Williams: **singular (william)**
CAPS, **NOCAPS**, and **ALLCAPS**	Use these commands when you want to specify upper and lower case characters for your search terms: CAPS - word(s) must have one or more capital letters NOCAPS - word(s) must have no capital letters ALLCAPS - word(s) must have all capital letters For example, use the following search to require that the word AIDS appears in all capital letters: **allcaps (aids)** Use the following search to require that the phrase, "law of the land, appears with one or more capital letters: **caps (law of the land)** Use the following search to require that the word law appears without any capital letters: **nocaps (law)**

Special Characters / Wildcards

More advanced search engines will respond to certain special characters. The asterisk (*) and the exclamation mark (!) are referred to as special characters, or "wildcards." Use them as substitutes for letters in words. Each has a different function.

ASTERISK (*)

Use the asterisk (*) to replace a letter or letters in a word. You can use more than one asterisk (*) in a word and you can use it anywhere in a word except as the first letter.

bernstn**	finds the **ei** or **ie** spelling of the name
wom*n	finds woman and women
bank* **	finds any word beginning with bank and which has no more than three letters after the **k**; will pick up banker and banking, but will not pick up bankrupt or bankruptcy

EXCLAMATION MARK (!)

Use the exclamation mark (!) to replace an infinite number of letters following a word root. You can use only one exclamation mark (!) in a word and it must be at the end of the word *root*.

litigat!	Finds variations of the word litigate (litigator, litigated, litigation, litigating)
acqui!	Finds variations of the word acquire (acquired, acquiring, acquisition)
book!	finds book or bookkeeper, but will not find book-keeper or book keeper, because these are read as two separate words
NOTE:	Words that work best with the exclamation mark are those that are unique in their truncated form. For example, if you search for **fir!** (thinking that you want to find "fired," "firing," or "fires"), your results will also include "first," "firm," and so on.

VETTING INFORMATION SOURCES

The following information is adapted from "Evaluating Internet Research Sources," by Robert Harris. A full and updated discussion is available in *WebQuester: A Guidebook to the Web* (Dushkin McGraw-Hill) containing chapters on search tools (engines, directories), search techniques and strategies, critical thinking about information, Web ethics, and citing Web sources.

The principles outlined here apply to information sources generally, not just to those available through the Internet. Harris suggests the key factors in information quality are *credibility, accuracy, reasonableness,* and *supporting evidence.*

The signs of deficiency in each category are cited below.

Signs of Weak Credibility

- Anonymity.
- Lack of Quality Control—scholarly and organizational sources use peer review to evaluate information; the type and frequency of control ought to be indicated.
- Negative Metainformation—e.g., excessive use of glowing reviews and endorsements.
- Bad grammar or misspelled words. Most educated people use grammar fairly well and check their work for spelling errors. An occasional split infinitive or comma in the wrong place is not unusual, but more than two or three spelling or grammar errors is cause for caution, at least.

Signs of Inaccuracy

- Inappropriate tone or style for factual information.
- No date on the document.
- Vague or sweeping generalizations.
- Old date on information known to change rapidly.
- Very one-sided view that does not acknowledge opposing views or responds to them.

Signs of Unreasonableness

- Intemperate tone or language ("stupid jerks," "shrill cries of my extremist opponents.")
- Overclaims ("Thousands of children are murdered every day in the United States.")

- Sweeping statements of excessive significance ("This is the most important idea ever conceived!")
- Conflict of Interest ("Welcome to the Old Stogie Tobacco Company Home Page. To read our report, "Cigarettes Make You Live Longer," click here." or "The products our competitors make are dangerous and bad for your health.")

Signs of Weak or No Support

- Lack of supporting evidence and citation of sources.
- Numbers or statistics without an identified source.
- No corroborating sources present the same information or acknowledge that the same information exists.

List of Useful Websites

Search Engines

About.com	http://www.about.com
All Search Engines	http://www.allsearchengines.com
AltaVista	http://www.altavista.com
Complete Planet	http://aip.completeplanet.com
Dogpile	http://www.dogpile.com
Excite	http://www.excite.com
GO.com	http://www.go.com
Google	http://www.google.com
HotBot	http://www.hotbot.com
I Won	http://home.iwon.com/
Infomine	http://infomine.ucr.edu/
Internet 101	http://www.internet101.org
Law Crawler — Legal Issues	http://lawcrawler.findlaw.com/
Legal Engine	http://www.legalengine.com
LEO Directory — Directory of Law Enforcement Related Sites	http://www.terrymartin.us/Peace.htm
LookSmart	http://search.looksmart.com
Lycos	http://www.lycos.com
Mamma.com	http://www.mamma.com
Meta 360	http://www.meta360.com
Metacrawler	http://www.metacrawler.com
Monster Crawler	http://www.monstercrawler.com
MSN	http://www.msn.com
Multicrawl	http://www.multicrawl.com
My Way	http://goto.myway.com
Net Ferret	http://www.ferretsoft.com/download.htm
Netscape Search	http://www.netscape.com/
Northern Light	http://nlsearch.com
Overture	http://www.content.overture.com/
ProFusion	http://www.profusion.com
Search Engine Watch	http://searchenginewatch.com/
Search Monger	http://www.searchmonger.com/
Search.com	http://www.search.com
Search Site	http://www.searchsite.com
Snap	http://www.snap.com
Surf Wax	http://www.surfwax.com/
The Big Hub	http://www.thebighub.com/
WebCrawler	http://www.webcrawler.com
Web Search	http://www.websearch.com
Yahoo!	http://www.yahoo.com

News Sources

ABCNews.com	http://abcnews.go.com
APB On-line — Crime, Justice, Safety	http://www.apbon-line.com/
CBS	http://www.cbsnews.com

CNN Interactive	http://www.cnn.com
CRAYON	http://www.crayon.net
Dialog	http://www.dialogweb.com
Factiva	http://www.factiva.com
Find Articles	http://www.findarticles.com
FOX	http://www.foxnews.com
Highbeam	http://www.highbeam.com
Investigative Reporters and Editors	http://www.ire.org
LexisNexis	http://www.lexisnexis.com
Market Watch	http://www.marketwatch.com
MSNBC	http://www.msnbc.msn.com
MSN Money	http://moneycentral.msn.com/home.asp
NBC	http://www.nbc.com
News Central	http://www.All-links.com/newscentral/
News.com	http://news.com.com/
Newslink	http://newslink.org
Refdesk	http://www.refdesk.com
Reuters	http://www.reuters.com/home
Salon	http://www.salon.com/
Slate	http://www.slate.com
The Council of State Governments	http://www.csg.org
Wired News	http://www.wired.com/news

Newspapers

Annapolis Capital-Gazette	http://www.capitalonline.com/
Augusta Chronicle	http://chronicle.augusta.com
Baltimore Sun	http://www.baltimoresun.com
Boston Globe	http://www.boston.com/news/globe/
Casper Star-Tribune (WY)	http://www.trib.com
Chattanooga Times Free Press	http://www.timesfreepress.com
Chicago Sun Times	http://www.suntimes.com/index
Chicago Tribune	http://www.chicagotribune.com/
Christian Science Monitor	http://www.csmonitor.com/
Colorado Springs Gazette	http://www.gazette.com
Daily Gazette (NY)	http://www.dailygazette.com
Dallas Morning News	http://www.dallasnews.com
Desert News (UT)	http://www.deseretnews.com
Detroit Free Press	http://www.freep.com
Evansville Courier & Press (IN)	http://www.courierpress.com
Florida Times-Union	http://www.jacksonville.com/
Fort Worth Star-Telegram	http://www.dfw.com
Gainesville Sun	http://www.gainesville.com
Houston Chronicle	http://www.chron.com
Knoxville News-Sentinel	http://www.knoxnews.com
Los Angeles Times	http://www.latimes.com
Miami Herald	http://www.miamiherald.com
Missoulian (MT)	http://www.missoulian.com
New York Daily News	http://www.nydailynews.com

New York Post	http://www.nypost.com
Newsday	http://www.newsday.com
Norfolk Virginian-Pilot	http://www.hamptonroads/pilotonline.com
Orange County Register	http://www.ocregister.com
Orlando Sentinel	http://www.orlandosentinel.com
Raleigh News and Observer	http://www.newsobserver.com
Roanoke Times	http://www.roanoke.com
Salt Lake Tribune	http://www.sltrib.com
San Diego Union-Tribune	http://www.signonsandiego.com
San Francisco Chronicle/Examiner	http://www.sfgate.com
San Jose Mercury News	http://www.mercurynews.com
Seattle Times	http://seattletimes.nwsource.com
Sioux City Journal	http://www.siouxcityjournal.com
St. Paul Pioneer Press	http://www.twincities.com/mld/twincities/
St. Petersburg Times	http://www.sptimes.com
The New York Times on the Web	http://www.nytimes.com
USA Today	http://www.usatoday.com
Wall Street Journal	http://online.wsj.com
Washington Post	http://www.washingtonpost.com/

University Library Sites

Brigham Young University	http://www.lib.byu.edu
Cal State Long Beach University	http://www.csulb.edu/library
Carnegie-Mellon University	http://www.library.cmu.edu
Claremont Colleges	http://voxlibris.claremont.edu
Cornell University	http://www.cornell.edu/libraries/
Drexel University	http://www.library.drexel.edu
Duke University	http://library.duke.edu/
Eastern Michigan University	http://www.emich.edu/halle/
Georgetown University	http://www.georgetown.edu/home/libraries
Harvard University (HOLLIS—Harvard On-line Library Information System)	http://lib.harvard.edu/
Indiana Univ./Purdue Univ.	http://www.ulib.iupui.edu
Iowa State University	http://www.lib.iastate.edu
Johns Hopkins University	http://www.welch.jhu.edu
Kansas State University	http://www.lib.ksu.edu
Louisiana State University	http://www.lib.lsu.edu
Mansfield University	http://lib.mansfield.edu/index.html
Miami (OH) University	http://www.lib.muohio.edu
Middle Tennessee State University	http://library.mtsu.edu/
MIT University	http://libraries.mit.edu/
New Mexico State University	http://lib.nmsu.edu
North Carolina State University	http://www.lib.ncsu.edu
Princeton University	http://libweb.princeton.edu
Tulane University	http://library.tulane.edu/
University of Arizona	http://www.arizona.edu/home/libraries.php
University of Cal-Berkeley	http://www.lib.berkeley.edu

University of Cal-Los Angeles	http://www2.library.ucla.edu
University of Cal-Riverside	http://library.ucr.edu
University of Florida	http://web.uflib.ufl.edu
University of Houston	http://info.lib.uh.edu
University of Idaho	http://drseuss.lib.uidaho.edu
University of Iowa	http://www.lib.uiowa.edu/
University of Maine	http://www.library.umaine.edu
University System of Maryland and Affiliated Institutions	http://www.itd.umd.edu/
University of Michigan	http://www.lib.umich.edu
University of Minnesota	http://www1.umn.edu
University of New Orleans	http://www.uno.edu/
University of North Carolina	http://www.ils.unc.edu/index.html
University of North Carolina-Charlotte	http://www.uncc.edu/
University of Virginia	http://www.virginia.edu/libraries
Vanderbilt University	http://www.library.vanderbilt.edu
Washington University	http://www.lib.washington.edu

State Government Listings

Alabama	http://www.alabama.gov
Alaska	http://www.state.ak.us/
Arizona	http://az.gov
Arkansas	http://www.state.ar.us/
California	http://www.state.ca.us/
Colorado	http://colorado.gov
Connecticut	http://www.ct.gov
Delaware	http://delaware.gov
Florida	http://www.myflorida.com
Georgia	http://www.georgia.gov/
Hawaii	http://www.hawaii.gov/
Idaho	http://www.state.id.us/
Illinois	http://www.illinois.gov/
Indiana	http://www.state.in.us/
Iowa	http://www.iowa.gov/
Kansas	http://www.accesskansas.org/
Kentucky	http://kentucky.gov/
Louisiana	http://www.louisiana.gov/
Maine	http://www.maine.gov/
Maryland	http://www.maryland.gov/
Massachusetts	http://www.mass.gov/
Michigan	http://www.michigan.gov.
Minnesota	http://www.state.mn.us/
Mississippi	http://www.state.ms.us
Missouri	http://www.state.mo.us/
Montana	http://mt.gov
Nebraska	http://www.nebraska.gov
Nevada	http://www.nv.gov.
New Hampshire	http://www.nh.gov/

New Jersey	http://www.state.nj.us/
New Mexico	http://www.newmexico.gov
New York	http://www.state.ny.us/
North Carolina	http://www.state.nc.us/
North Dakota	http://www.nd.gov
Ohio	http://www.ohio.gov/
Oklahoma	http://www.OK.gov
Oregon	http://www.oregon.gov/
Pennsylvania	http://www.state.pa.us/
Rhode Island	http://www3.sec.state.ri.us/
South Carolina	http://www.sc.gov
South Dakota	http://www.state.sd.us/
Tennessee	http://www.tennessee.gov/
Texas	http://www.state.tx.us/
Utah	http://www.utah.gov/
Vermont	http://vermont.gov/
Virginia	http://www.virginia.gov/
Washington	http://www.state.wa.us
West Virginia	http://www.wv.gov/
Wisconsin	http://www.wisconsin.gov/
Wyoming	http://wyoming.gov/

Telephone Numbers & Addresses

AT&T AnyWho	http://www.anywho.com
555-1212	http://www.555-1212.com
Big Yellow	http://www.bigyellow.com
Bigbook	http://www.bigbook.com
Bigfoot	http://www.bigfoot.com
Database America People Finder	http://adp.infousa.com
E-mail addresses	http://www.iaf.net
GTE Superpages	http://www.superpages.com/
Homepage Finder	http://www.help4web.net
InfoSpace	http://www.infospaceinc.com
InfoUSA	http://www.infousa.com
Military Locator Service	http://http://www.militarytimes.com/
Military Personnel Records	http://www.archives.gov
Naked in Cyberspace	http://www.technosearch.com/naked/directory.htm
PayPhone	http://www.payphone.com
People Search	http://www.peoplesearch.net
Phone Numbers (Infobel)	http://www.infobel.com/teldir
Register.com	http://www.register.com
Semaphore Corp	http://www.semaphorecorp.com
Switchboard	http://www.switchboard.com
The PI Mall	http://www.pimall.com/
U.S Web Finder	http://uswebfinder.com
WhoWhere?	http://www.whowhere.com
Worldpages	http://www.worldpages.com

Yahoo! People Search	http://people.yahoo.com
Yellowbook	http://www.yellowbook.com/

Maps

4Anything Network	http://www.4maps.4anything.com
Excite Travel	http://www.excite.com/
MapBlast	http://www.mapblast.com
MapQuest	http://www.mapquest.com
Maps On Us	http://www.mapsonus.com
Mileage Calculator	http://www.indo.com/distance/

Databases — Public Record Searches

BRB Publications, Inc.	http://www.brbpub.com
ChoicePoint	http://www.choicepoint.net
ChoicePoint: AutotrackXP	http://atxp.choicepoint.com/
DCS Information Systems	http://www.dnis.com
Thomson Dialog	http://www.dialog.com
Diligenz	http://www.diligenz.com
Dun & Bradstreet	http://www.dnb.com
Experian	http://www.experian.com
Fedworld	Http://www.fedworld.gov
G.S. Public Record Services	http://www.gaprs.com
InfoUSA	http://www.infousa.com
KnowX	http://www.knowx.com
LexisNexis	http://www.lexisnexis.com
Loc8fast	http://www.loc8fast.com
Merlin Information Systems	http://www.merlindata.com
Noncommercial Organizations	http://www.pir.org
Public Data	http://www.publicdata.com
Searchsystems.net	http://www.searchsystems.net
Security Software Solutions	http://www.veris-ssn.com/
US Datalink	http://www.usdatalink.com

Legal Resources

Docusearch	http://www.docusearch.com
Administrative Office of the U.S. Courts	http://www.uscourts.gov
Attorney search	http://lawyers.findlaw.com
California Laws	http://www.leginfo.ca.gov/calaw.html
Courthouse News	http://www.courthousenews.com/
Cyber Securities Laws	http://www.cybersecuritieslaw.com
Divorce Central	http://www.divorcecentral.com
Federal Legislative Information on the Internet	http://thomas.loc.gov/
FindLaw	http://www.findlaw.com/
FindLaw California Codes and	http://california.findlaw.com/CA01_codes/in

Statutes	dex.html
Florida Statutes	http://www.fdle.state.fl.us/statutes/
Law on the Web	http://www.law.com/
Lawyers	http://www.lawyers.com/
Legal Ethics	http://www.legalethics.com/index.law
Legal Info Institute of Cornell	http://www.law.cornell.edu/
Legal Research on the Web	http://gsulaw.gsu.edu/metaindex/
Martindale-Hubble	http://www.martindale.com
Money Laundering and Terrorist Financing	http://www.occ.treas.gov/BSA/BSAmain.htm
National Center for State Courts	http://ncsonline.org/
Nolo	http://www.nolo.com
Online Sunshine - Florida Legislature	http://www.leg.state.fl.us/
Practical Law	http://www.\practicallaw.com/
Reporters Committee — Freedom of Press	http://www.rcfp.org
Reporters Committee — Taping Conversations	http://www.rcfp.org/taping/index.html
U.S. Supreme Court Decisions	http://www.fedworld.gov/supcourt/index.ht m
U.S. Supreme Court Internet Sites	http://llrx.com/features/scourtsites.htm
University of Chicago Law School	http://www.lib.uchicago.edu
University of Mass. Law	http://www.umass.edu/legal/
Virtual Law Library	http://www.law.indiana.edu/v-lib
Washington Document Services	http://www.wdsdocs.com
West Legal Directory	http://www.lawyers.findlaw.com

Government Sites and Criminal Justice Resources

Bureau of Alcohol, Tobacco, Firearms, and Explosives (ATF)	http://www.atf.treas.gov/
Bureau of Export Administration's List of Denied Persons	http://www.bis.doc.gov/dpl.Default.shtm
Central Intelligence Agency	http://www.cia.gov
Class Actions	http://www.classaction.com/
Class Action Clearinghouse	http://securities.stanford.edu/
County Sheriff's Offices — By State	http://www.corrections.com/links/
Court Websites	http://uscourts.gov/
Courtlink	http://www.lexisnexis.com/courtlink/online/
Database of Government Websites	http://www.usa.gov/
Federal Citizen Information Center	http://www.pueblo.gsa.gov
FBI Law Enforcement Bulletin	http://www.fbi.gov/publications/leb/leb.htm
U.S. Department of Homeland Security	http://www.dhs.gov
Fed World	http://www.fedworld.gov
Federal Bureau of Investigation Home Page	http://www.fbi.gov/
Federal Bureau of Prisons	http://www.bop.gov/

Federal Election Commission	http://www.fec.gov
Federal Election Commission information	http://fec.gov/ans/answers.shtml
Federal Inspector General Community	http://www.ignet.gov/
Federal Judicial Center	http://www.fjc.gov/
Florida Department of Corrections	http://www.dc.state.fl.us/
Florida Department of Law Enforcement	http://www.fdle.state.fl.us/
Florida Department of State	http://www.dos.state.fl.us/
Florida Government Website	http://myflorida.com/portal/Government
GovSpot	http://www.govspot.com
Internal Revenue Service	http://www.irs.gov
Investigator's Guide to the Sources of Information (GAO/OSI-97-2)	http://www.gao.gov/special.pubs/soi.htm
Library of Congress	http://www.loc.gov/
National Address Server	http://www.cedar.buffalo.edu/adserv.html
National Archives	http://www.archives.gov
National Center for State Courts	http://www.ncsconline.org
National Criminal Justice Reference Service	http://www.ncjrs.org
Noblis	http://www.noblis.org
Nonprofit Gateway	http://www.usa.gov/Business/Nonprofit.shtml
Directorate of Defense Trade Controls	http:/pmddtc.state.gov/
Police Officers Internet Directory	http://www.officer.com/
Public Access to Electronic Records — PACER	http://pacer.psc.uscourts.gov/
Published List of Recalls – National Highway Traffic Safety Administration	http://www.nhtsa.dot.gov/
Royal Canadian Mounted Police	http://www.rcmp-grc.gc.ca/
SEC Enforcement Regulatory Actions	http://www.sec.gov/rules.shtml
SEC Enforcement Division of Enforcement	http://www.sec.gov/divisions/enforce.shtml
Securities & Exchange Commission EDGAR	http://www.sec.gov/edgar.shtml
Selective Service System	http://www.sss.gov
Sex Offenders Registry	http://www.fbi.gov/hq/cid/cac/states.htm
Social Security Death Index Search	http://www.ancestry.com/search/
SSN Validation Database	http://usinfosearch.com/ssn_validation_database.htm
State and Federal Prisons	http://www.bop.gov
State and Local Government on the Internet	http://www.statelocalgov.net
State Legislatures	http://www.ncsl.org/
Superior Information Services	http://www.superiorinfo.com

Texas Department of Public Safety — Convictions	http://records.txdps.state.tx.us/
USA.gov	http://www.usa.gov
U.S. Commodity Futures Trading Commission	http://www.cftc.gov
U.S. Department of Justice	http://www.usdoj.gov/
U.S. Department of Justice — Computer Crime and Intellectual Property	http://www.cybercrime.gov/
U.S. Federal Inspectors General	http://www.ignet.gov/
U.S. Federal Communications Commission	http://www.fcc.gov
U.S. Federal Deposit Insurance Corporation	http://www.fdic.gov
U.S. Federal Food & Drug Administration	http://www.fda.gov
U.S. General Services Information	http://www.gsa.gov
U.S. Government Printing Office	http://www.access.gpo.gov/
U.S. Federal Trade Commission	http://www.ftc.gov
U.S. Government Accountability Office	http://www.gao.gov
U.S. Patent and Trademark Office	http://www.uspto.gov
U.S. Postal Service	http://www.usps.gov/ncsc/
U.S. Supreme Court	http://www.supremecourtus.gov
United Nations Crime & Justice Information Network (UNCJIN)	http://www.uncjin.org
Vital Records Database	http://www.vitalrec.com
Voter's Registration	http://www.governmentrecords.com/
White House	http://www.whitehouse.gov

Other Fraud-Related and Websites of Interest

ACFE Albany Chapter	http://www.albanyacfe.org
ACL—Data Analysis Software	http://www.acl.com
Active Most Wanted and Criminal Investigations	http://www.activemostwanted.com
Association of College and University Auditors	http://www.acua.org
AFU and Urban Legends Archive	http://www.snopes.com
Any Birthday	http://wwwanybirthday.com
Association of Certified Fraud Examiners	http://www.ACFE.com
Better Business Bureau Web Server Home Page	http://www.bbb.org
Broward County Sheriff's Office	http://www.sheriff.org
CBA: Consumer Tips for Visa and MasterCard	http://www.cba.ca
Check Fraud Tips	http://www.ckfraud.org/
Company Site Locator	http://www.switchboard.com
Company Sleuth	http://www.companysleuth.com

Computer Security Institute	http://www.gocsi.com
Consumer Education — Fraud	http://www.ftc.gov/ftc/consumer.htm
Cop Net	http://www.copnet.org/
Corrections Industry	http://www.corrections.com/
CPA Directory	http://www.cpadirectory.com/index.cfm
Check Fraud	http://www.ckfraud.org
Black Book Company	http://www.blackbookonline.info/
Cyber Space Law Center	http://www.findlaw.com/01topics/10cyberspace/index.html
Cyberensics	http://www.cyberensics.net/
Dan Moldea	http://www.moldea.com
Deadbeat Parents (Federal Registry)	http://www.acf.dhhs.gov/
Employment Schemes	http://www.usps.com/websites/depart/inspect/fraud/emplmenu.htm
EndFraud.com	http://www.endfraud.com
Financial Scandals	http://www.ex.ac.uk/~RDavies/arian/scandals/
Forensic Accounting Information	http://www.forensic-accounting-information.com
Forum on Fraud, Scams & Abuse Perpetrated on Senior Citizens	http://seniors-site.com/fraudm/forum.html
Fraud Bureau	http://www.fraudbureau.com
Fraud Index	http://www.scambusters.org
Fuld & Company's Internet Intelligence Index	http://www.fuld.com
High Technology Crime Investigation Association	http://htcia.org/
Hoover's	http://www.hoovers.com
Identity Theft – Privacy Rights Clearinghouse	http://www.privacyrights.org
Identity Theft – Federal Trade Commission	http://www.ftc.gov/bcp/edu/microsites/idtheft/
Identity Theft Assumption and Deterrence Act	http://www.identitytheft.org
Inspection Service Consumer Fraud	http://www.usps.com/postalinspectors/
Internet Anti-Scam	http://www.nerdworld.com/nw1319.html
Internet Center for Corruption Research	http://www.icgg.org
Internet Chain Letters	http://hoaxbusters.ciac.org
Internet Fraud Complaint Center	http://www.ic3.gov/
Inventor Fraud Center, National	http://www.inventorfraud.com
Investor Protection Trust	http://www.investorprotection.org
Justice Reference Service, National	http://www.ncjrs.org/
Loss Prevention Concepts	http://www.lpconline.com/
Missing Money	http://www.missingmoney.com
Municipal Bond Scandals	http://www.lissack.com
BBB Wise Giving Alliance	http://give.org
National Fraud Information Center	http://www.fraud.org

National White Collar Crime Center	http://www.nw3c.org/
Network Solutions — Website operator information	http://www.networksolutions.com/
Nigeria-The 419 Coalition Website	http://home.rica.net/alphae/419coal/
Noble Ventures - Asset Searches	http://www.nobleventures.com
Offshore Business News & Research	http://offshorebusiness.com
On-line Fraud Info Center	http://www.fraud.org
On-line Scams	http://www.ftc.gov/ftc/consumer.htm
Other Consumer Frauds	http://www.usps.com/postalinspectors/fraud/othrmenu.htm
Ponzi Schemes	http://www.crimes-of-persuasion.com
Compliance Headquarters	http://www.complianceheadquarters.com
Privacy Tools	http://www.privacytools.com/
Privacy Rights Clearinghouse	http://www.privacyrights.org/links.htm
Scambusters	http://www.scambusters.org/index.html
Scams and Swindles	http://www.swindles.com/
ScamWatch	http://www.scamwatch.gov.au/
Security Management Online	http://www.securitymanagement.com/
Software & Information Industry Association Anti-Piracy Division	http://www.siia.net/piracy/
SSA Fraud Reporting	http://www.socialsecurity.gov/
Taxpayers Against Fraud	http://www.taf.org
TD Bank Fraud Prevention	http://www.tdbanknorth.com/bank/fraud_prevention.html
Cybertrust	http://www.cybertrust.com
Urban Legends Reference Pages	http://www.snopes.com
Virus Bulletin	http://www.virusbtn.com/resources/prevalence
Website hoax - F-Secure	http://www.f-secure.com/virus-info/hoax/
Website hoax - Kumite	http://www.vmyths.com
Website hoax — Symantec	http://www.symantec.com/avcenter/hoax.html
Whistleblower's Website: Phillips and Cohen	http://www.phillipsandcohen.com
World Bank	http://www.worldbank.org

Health Care/Insurance Fraud

(4)Medical Ethics	http://4medicalethics.4anything.com/
AMA Select	http://www.ama-assn.org/aps/amahg.htm
America's Health Insurance Plans	http://www.ahip.org
American Bar Association — Medicine & Law Committee	http://www.abanet.org/tips/medicine/links.html#fraud
American Medical Association	http://www.ama-assn.org/
Coalition Against Insurance Fraud	http://www.insurancefraud.org
Corrections Links — Health Care	http://www.corrections.com/healthnetwork/
Department of Health and Human Services OIG	http://www.hhs.gov
Departments of Insurance - State	http://www.bsg.com/resources/relatedSites/stateDept.asp

Ed Hayes — Indexes to medical sites	http://www.edhayes.com/
Excluded Parties List	http://www.epls.gov/
Health Information Technology – U.S. Dept. of Health and Human Services	http://www.hhs.gov/healthit/federalprojectlist.html
Health Law Resource	http://www.netreach.net/~wmanning/
HIPAA	http://www.cms.hhs.gov/HIPAAGenInfo/
Insurance Fraud Research Register	http://www.ifb.org/IFRR/ifrr.asp
International Association of Special Investigation Units	http://www.iasiu.org
Medical Economics Magazine	http://www.memag.com
Medical Information Bureau	http://www.mib.com
Medicaid Fraud Alerts – Center for Medicare and Medicaid Services	http://www.cms.hhs.gov/MCAIDFraudAbuseGenInfo/
Medicare Fraud and Abuse Training — On-line	http://www.phppo.cdc.gov/
National Association of Insurance Commissioners	http://www.naic.org
National Coalition on Health Care	http://www.nchc.org
National Council against Health Fraud	http://www.ncahf.org/
National Fraud Information Center	http://www.fraud.org
National Health Care Anti-Fraud Association	http://www.nhcaa.org
National Insurance Crime Bureau	http://www.nicb.org
National Medical Reporter — Health Care links	http://medicalreporter.health.org/links.html
National Practitioner Data Bank	http://www.npdb-hipdb.com
Net-Trace Insurance Links	http://www.nettrace.com.au/resource/investigation/insurance.htm
Office of Inspector General	http://oig.hhs.gov/
Office of Investigations	http://www.ssa.gov/oig/guidelin.htm
PDR — Physician Desk Reference	http://www.pdr.net/
Property Casualty Insurer's Association of America	http://www.pciaa.net/sitehome.nsf/main/
Quackwatch Consumer Health Fraud	http://www.quackwatch.org/
Research America — medical links	http://www.researchamerica.org/links/index.html
Seattle University Law Library	http://www.law.seattleu.edu/library/
The Health Law Resource	http://www.netreach.net/~wmanning
The HMO Page	http://www.hmopage.org
Ultimate Insurance Links	http://www.ultimateinsurancelinks.com/
University of Florida – College of Medicine – Compliance	http://www.med.ufl.edu/research/rac/compliance/
Insurance Quotes	http://www.insurancequotes.com/
Workers Compensation Information	http://www.comp.state.nc.us/ncic/pages/all50.htm

State Insurance Fraud Divisions (not all Divisions have websites)

Alabama	http://www.aldoi.gov
Alaska	http://www.commerce.state.ak.us/insurance
Arizona	http://www.id.state.az.us/fraud.html
Arkansas	http://insurance.arkansas.gov/
California	http://www.insurance.ca.gov/0300-fraud/index.cfm
Colorado	http://www.dora.state.co.us/Insurance
Connecticut	http://www.ct.gov/cid/
Delaware	http://www.state.de.us/inscom
Florida	http://www.fldfs.com/fraud/
Georgia	http://www.inscomm.state.ga.us/
Hawaii	http://dccakaku1.hawaii.gov/dcca/areas/ins
Idaho	http://www.doi.state.id.us/
Illinois	http://www.ins.state.il.us/
Indiana	http://www.in.gov/idoi/
Iowa	http://www.iid.state.ia.us/
Kansas	http://www.ksinsurance.org
Kentucky	http://www.doi.state.ky.us/kentucky/
Louisiana	http://www.ldi.state.la.us/
Maine	http://www.maine.gov/pfr/insurance/
Maryland	http://www.mdinsurance.state.md.us
Massachusetts	http://www.mass.gov/doi/
Michigan	http://www.michigan.gov/
Minnesota	http://www.state.mn.us/portal/mn/jsp/home.do?agency=Commerce
Mississippi	http://www.doi.state.ms.us/
Missouri	http://insurance.mo.gov/
Montana	http://sao.mt.gov
Nebraska	http://www.doi.ne.gov//
Nevada	http://www.doi.state.nv.us
New Hampshire	http://www.nh.gov/insurance/
New Jersey	http://www.njdobi.org
New York	http://www.ins.state.ny.us/nyins.htm
North Carolina	http://www.ncdoi.com/
North Dakota	http://www.nd.gov/ndins/
Ohio	http://www.ohioinsurance.gov/
Oklahoma	http://www.oid.state.ok.us
Oregon	http://www.cbs.state.or.us/external/ins/
Pennsylvania	http://www.ins.state.pa.us/ins/site/default.asp
Puerto Rico	http://www.ocs.gobierno.pr/
Rhode Island	http://www.dbr.state.ri.us
South Carolina	http://www.doi.state.sc.us/
South Dakota	http://www.state.sd.us/drr2/reg/insurance/
Tennessee	http://www.state.tn.us/commerce/insurance/
Texas	http://www.tdi.state.tx.us/

Utah	http://www.insurance.utah.gov/
Vermont	http://www.bishca.state.vt.us/
Virginia	http://www.scc.virginia.gov/division/boi/
Washington	http://www.insurance.wa.gov
West Virginia	http://www.wvinsurance.gov/
Wisconsin	http://oci.wi.gov/
Wyoming	http://insurance.state.wy.us/

Telecom Fraud/Security

AT&T Fraud Education	http://www.consumer.att.com/global/english/consumer_information/fraud.html/fraud/att.html
Federal Communications Commission	http://www.fcc.gov/
Help Net Security	http://www.net-security.org
International Engineering Consortium	http://www.iec.org
National Association of Securities Dealers (NASD)	http://www.nasd.com/
Neural Technologies	http://www.neuralt.com/
Travelassist Magazine — Phone Card Fraud	http://www.travelassist.com/mag/a27.html

Auditing

American Institute of Certified Public Accountants	http://www.aicpa.org
COSO	http://www.coso.org
Government Auditing Standards	http://www.gao.gov/govaud/ybk01.htm
Institute of Internal Auditors	http://www.theiia.org
Internal Auditing World Wide Web	http://www.bitwise.net/iawww
International Auditing and Assurance Standards Board	http://www.ifac.org/IAASB/
UNC Business Manual	http://www.unc.edu/finance/busman/

Investment Resources

Corporate Information	http://www.corporateinformation.com
FreeEDGAR	http://www.freeedgar.com
Kiplinger	http://www.kiplinger.com
Thestreet.com	http://www.thestreet.com/
Wall Street Net	http://www.wallstreetnet.com/

International Sites

Global Search Engines

Bubl link	http://bubl.ac.uk/
Euroseek	http://www.euroseek.com/
Matilda — Mega Search Engine Australia	http://www.aussieseek.com
Search New Zealand	http://www.searchnz.co.nz/
Voila	http://www.voila.com/
WebWombat	http://webwombat.com.au/

Newspapers

BBC News	http://news.bbc.co.uk
Evening Standard	http://www.thisislondon.co.uk
Financial Times	http://news.ft.com/home/
International Herald Tribune	http://www.asahi.com
Le Monde	http://www.lemonde.fr
Newspaper Society	http://www.newspapersoc.org.uk
The Daily Telegraph	http://www.telegraph.co.uk
The Guardian Unlimited	http://www.guardian.co.uk
The Independent	http://www.independent.co.uk
The Irish Times	http://www.ireland.com
The Newspaper Society Database	http://www.nsdatabase.co.uk/index.html
The Scotsman	http://www.Scotsman.com
The Times On-line	http://www.timesonline.co.uk
Times Higher Education Supplement	http://www.thes.co.uk
Times of India	http://timesofindia.indiatimes.com

News and Information Services

BBC News	http://www.bbc.co.uk
Canada.com	http://www.canada.com/national
Euronews	http://www.euronews.net/
Future Events News Service	http://www.fens.com/
Global Investigative Journalism	http://www.globalinvestigativejournalism.org/
Hansard (House of Commons Debates	http://www.publications.parliament.uk/pa/cm/cmhansrd.htm
Irish Times	http://www.ireland.com/
ITN On-line	http://www.itn.co.uk
Microsoft Network News	http://uk.msn.com/
NewsNow	http://www.newsnow.co.uk
NineMSN	http://ninemsn.com.au/
Sky News	http://news.sky.com/skynews/home
The Economist	http://www.economist.com
The PA Group	http://www.thepagroup.com/

UK Business Park — Media News	http://www.ukbusinesspark.co.uk
Yahoo UK News	http://uk.news.yahoo.com

Libraries

Aberdeen University	http://www.abdn.ac.uk/diss/library
British Library	http://www.bl.uk
Cambridge University	http://www.lib.cam.ac.uk
Edinburgh University	http://www.lib.ed.ac.uk/lib
Exeter University	http://www.library.ex.ac.uk/
Glasgow University	http://www.lib.gla.ac.uk/
King's College, London	http://www.kcl.ac.uk/iss
Oxford University	http://www.ox.ac.uk/libraries/
Public Libraries (UK)	http://dspace.dial.pipex.com/town/square/ac940/weblibs.html
University, London's Global	http://www.ucl.ac.uk/
University of Bath	http://www.bath.ac.uk/library
University of East Anglia	http://www.lib.uea.ac.uk

Telephone Numbers

AOL International Directories	http://site.aol.com/netfind/international.html
Infobel World	http://www.infobel.com/teldir/
The Global Yellow Pages	http://www.globalyp.com/world.htm
UK Tracker	http://www.angelfire.com/on/touchtone99/tracker.html
Yellow Pages	http://www.yell.com/ucs/HomePageAction.do

Maps

Maporama	http://world.maporama.com/idl/maporama/default.aspx
MapQuest	http://www.mapquest.com
MultiMap	http://www.multimap.com/map/places.cgi
Ordnance Survey	http://www.ordnancesurvey.co.uk/oswebsite/
Street Map	http://www.streetmap.co.uk
The RAC	http://www.rac.co.uk
UK On-line	http://www.ukonline.com/contents/ukmaps.html

Legal Resources

Access to Law	http://www.Accesstolaw.com/
Centre for Commercial Law Studies — University of London	http://www.ccls.edu/
Consumer Law Center	http://www.hg.org/consume.html

Dundee University Legal Websites Directory	http://www.Dundee.ac.uk/law/
FindLaw International Resources	http://www.findlaw.com/12international/
Her Majesty's Court Service	http://www.hmcourts-service.gov.uk/
InfoLaw Gateway	http://www.infolaw.co.uk
Lawlink	http://www.lawlink.ie
The International Centre for Commercial Law	http://www.legal 500.com/index.php
The Law Commission	http://www.lawcom.gov.uk
The Law Society of England and Wales	http://www.lawsociety.org.uk/home.law

Government Sites and Law Enforcement Sites

Australia — Attorney General's Department	http://www.ag.gov.au/
Australia's Ministerial Council on Consumer Affairs	http://www.consumer.gov.au/
Australia/New Zealand's Ministry of Consumer Affairs	http://www.consumeraffairs.govt.nz/index.html
Australian Courts and Legislation	http://www.nla.gov.au/oz/law.html
Australian Department of Foreign Affairs and Trade	http://www.dfat.gov.au/
Australian Privacy Commissioner	http://www.privacy.gov.au/
Government Information Centre	http://www.direct.gov.uk/en/index.htm
Information Commissioner Office	http://www.ico.gov.uk/
Department of Trade and Industry	http://www.dti.gov.uk
Financial Services Authority	http://www.fsa.gov.uk
Foreign and Commonwealth Office	http://www.fco.gov.uk
HM Treasury	http://www.hm-treasury.gov.uk
IK Police Forces	http://www.police.uk
International Centre for Criminal Law Reform and Criminal Justice Policy	http://www.icclr.law.ubc.ca/
Investment Management Regulatory Organisation	http://www.fsa.gov.uk
National Criminal Intelligence Service	http://www.direct.gov.uk/en/index.htm
New Zealand Ministry of Consumer Affairs	http://www.consumeraffairs.govt.nz/
New Zealand Government On-line	http://www.govt.nz/
New Zealand Police Links	http://www.policeassn.org.nz/links.htm
Organized Crime - Nathanson Centre	http://www.yorku.ca/nathanson
Patent Office	http://www.patent.gov.uk
Royal Canadian Mounted Police	http://www.rcmp-grc.gc.ca/
Serious Organised Crime Agency	http://www.soca.gov.uk/
The European Commission	http://ec.europa.eu/

The Home Office	http://www.homeoffice.gov.uk
The National Archives	http://www.nationalarchives.gov.uk/default.htm
The Financial Services Authority	http://www.fsa.gov.uk
United Kingdom Parliament	http://www.parliament.the-stationery-office.co.uk
Worldwide Embassies and Consulates	http://www.embassyworld.com/

Specialized Fraud-Related and Websites of Interest

Association of British Insurers	http://www.abi.org.uk/
Australian Institute of Criminology	http://www.aic.gov.au/
Department for Work and Pensions	http://www.dwp.gov.uk/
Fraud Web	http://www.fraudweb.co.uk
HM Treasury Fraud Reports	http://www.hm-treasury.gov.uk/
New Zealand – Scam Watch	http://www.consumeraffairs.govt.nz/scamwatch/index.html
Serious Fraud Office	http://www.sfo.gov.uk
The Insolvency Service	http://www.insolvency.gov.uk/

Auditing

UK National Audit Office	http://www.nao.org.uk
HM Revenue and Customs	http://www.hmrc.gov.uk/
Insolvency Procedures and Corporate Rescue	http://www.insolvency.gov.uk/
Association of Business Recovery Professionals	http://www.r3.org.uk/
Institute of Chartered Accountants in England and Wales	http://www.icaew.co.uk
Association of Charted Certified Accountants	http://www.acca.co.uk
Charted Institute of Management Accountants	http://www.cimaglobal.com
Institute of Chartered Accountants of Scotland	http://www.icas.org.uk
Institute of Chartered Accountants in Ireland	http://www.icai.ie
London Society of Chartered Accountants	http://www.lsca.co.uk/
London International Financial Futures and Options Exchange - Euronext	http://www.euronext.com

About the Author

Joseph T. Wells is founder and Chairman of the Board of the Association of Certified Fraud Examiners, the world's largest anti-fraud organization. After graduating with honors from the University of Oklahoma, Mr. Wells spent two years on the audit staff of Coopers and Lybrand.

He then was appointed a Special Agent of the FBI. Over the next ten years, Mr. Wells investigated thousands of fraud cases, ranging from nickel-and-dime con artists to former Attorney John Mitchell for his role in the Watergate case. In 1982, he left the government to form Wells & Associates, a firm of criminologists specializing in fraud detection and deterrence.

Since becoming Chairman of the ACFE in 1988, Mr. Wells has lectured to tens of thousands of business professionals, written eleven books, and authored scores of articles and research projects. His writing has won numerous awards, including the top articles of the year for both *Internal Auditor Magazine* and the *Journal of Accountancy*.

In addition to his duties as ACFE chairman, Mr. Wells is a professor of fraud examination at the University of Texas where his pioneering work has been recognized by the American Accounting Association, which named him Accounting Education Innovator of the Year in 2002.

Mr. Wells has served on various senior committees of the American Institute of CPAs and he is a member of the AICPA's Business and Industry Hall of Fame. He has been named to *Accounting Today* magazine's annual list of the "Top 100 Most Influential People" in accounting for the last nine years in a row.